The Second Coming of

COMMON SENSE

ADDRESSED TO MY

Fellow American Citizens

Regarding

Our Second and Final American Revolution

We the People

Must Now Decide Our Nation's Future

by
A. J. Wildman

The Second Coming of

COMMON SENSE

by
A. J. Wildman

© 2008 A. J. Wildman

ISBN 1-881399-31-1

First Printing February 2008
VirtualBookWorm.com

Companion book by A.J.Wildman:

Common Interest printed 2004

Published by
Beaver Pond Publishing
P.O. Box 224
Greenville, PA 16125

Printed in the U.S.A.

Contents

Appendix

Dedication

This book is dedicated to you,
an American.

Yes, to you the individual American Citizen.

o   o   o   o

The Second Coming of Common Sense

Purpose

T his offering presents to my fellow Americans a current day rendition of Thomas Paine's American Revolutionary classic *Common Sense*.

Today's *Common Sense* presents this concerned citizen's analysis of current problems within our American "National System" — the way America really works on a day-to-day basis. And most importantly, *how* We as a united American people could prudently and practically decide to address and begin resolving those problems for the Common Good. And do it now.

The purpose is to say what needs to be said in the interest of the Common Good of our citizens — the absolute goal being to initiate a Great American Discussion and Debate, that will coincide and collide with the 2008 U.S. Presidential and Congressional Campaign that began ramping up too early in 2007.

Simply put this is an analysis of what is wrong in various public policy areas within our National System and how we could realistically confront and resolve such issues starting as early as 2007, but for certain as 2008 progresses. It is intended to present perspectives on critical issues, to promote the common understanding of acceptable social concepts, and present solutions to long-standing public problems. This is not an attempt to convince or dictate, but rather to share objective perspectives and review aggressive solutions to key public issues for your consideration.

This is a direct challenge to the American public – our fellow American citizens in particular — to consider and to potentially embrace the bold yet socially prudent, solution-oriented proposals contained herein.

The *Second Coming of Common Sense (CS2)* is published with the intent of making your life and the lives of those you know and love, better.

Further, it is offered with the hope and prayer that after private consideration of these contents, that you would decide to take action to demonstrate your approval and support thereof,

to in some way assist in making these
social and economic solutions part of your daily life
and the lives of the other 300 million of
Our Fellow American Citizens.

— AJW

My Personal Thanks

To a few thousand people!

Those kind people that I talked with over the last 25 years,
most of whom were complete strangers.

To those that spontaneously and graciously gave of their time,
and listened to the concepts and proposals
in all of those one-on–one conversations.

It is their personal feedback — freely commenting
for and against what they were hearing
that more than anything else has determined the final content
of the proposals that are the heart and soul of this book.

It is my firm belief that
the nation we all love,

Shall be forever in their debt…

o   o   o   o

Also to Thank

CS2 and my first book *Common Interest*
were both written over a number of years.

And one of my favorite things was the
hours spent having breakfast at local restaurants.

So many quiet moments to think, write, edit,
and all the talks with the staff and other local folks.

My thanks to the owners of Johnson's Restaurant,
and Violet and Shelby; Leesburg, VA

My thanks to the owners of Leesburg Restaurant,
and Loretta; Leesburg, VA

My thanks to the owners of Georgetown Cafe,
and Greg; Leesburg, VA

And since March of 2007 in Yorktown, VA,
thanks to the owner of Pop's Restaurant
Joe Allen and his son Randy
that makes great omelets,
and the staff
Ale (Allie),
Ashley,
Katie,
Kristin,
Mary,
Tiffany.

My thanks so for many good times and meals!

Part 1
Introduction

From the Author

"With Absolute Intent"

Allow me to be very clear on a few points from the very start of this unfortunately one-sided conversation. First, the concepts, proposals, and challenges presented for your consideration, are entirely this American citizen's personal creation and responsibility.

Also, that you are reading one American citizen's critique of our National System.

Further, that these contents were written with all due sincerity and with the professional objectivity of a career systems analyst and business problem solver — seeking to define a practical vision of America's future, as well as discussing how we as a Democratic nation can initiate deliberate actions toward that future in the months leading up to the 2008 National Election.

Finally and most importantly, please consider that these contents are intended to be taken by you the reader as seriously as a heart attack...

o   o   o   o

This is a National Reality Check — Consider Yourself Fairly Warned

Herein you will find practical analysis and what will in several cases 'initially' sound like radical approaches — aggressive solutions to difficult national problems.

Viable social and economic reform legislative leadership is offered because our currently declining National System requires nothing less if the American voyage is to be re-directed in favor of the Common Good of our citizens!

<u>A Conversation About America</u>

Imagine that you and I are talking with each other. It could be anywhere — at home, work, lunch, on a break, on a bus or an airplane, on vacation, at youth soccer or little league. I have just told you I am writing a book on *what is wrong with America and how to fix it* and asked if you would listen to some of my proposal ideas and give me your feedback. You have graciously accepted and we begin our conversation. Consider it as though we are sitting together having a *very* long cup of coffee. These are always interactive talks. Some people talked more than others, but everyone had comments and/or questions.

Please note that I am not a professional writer. My writing style somewhat mirrors my spoken delivery and is generally conversational and informal. I will inject a certain amount of humor and sarcastic comments at times. Some may think it inappropriate since these are such serious topics, but I feel it releases some of the tension that may arise, and it is just my style. You will feel that some passages are a bit repetitive, and for the most part it is intentional. Also, note the 4-circle notation used throughout – it is the way I like to accent a given point or to form a logical break.

o   o   o   o

CS2 is a review of serious public topics and objective subject matter analysis thereof. The public problems addressed and the direct solutions offered to resolve them are at times very sobering subject matter, and we will need to keep our national sense of humor about us as we consider what is ahead.

In the coming months and years,

- We will deliberately call our faltering, elected national leadership to task,
- We will dictate the hard, but necessary restructuring of certain base-line national industries,
- We will challenge every American to Civil Responsibility, and
- We will define a "citizen acceptable" Vision of our national future for the Common Good.

If the day-to-day problems of regular Americans and the implementation of real solutions to those same national issues are not what you are personally interested in — or — if you are among the "shrinking well-off" minority that <u>like</u> the way things are today <u>and</u> how "those things" are likely to evolve let's say for the next two (2) generations of <u>your</u> family — then I would suggest you go and find some mindless fiction to pass the time.

You may then observe from the sidelines as the rest of us go about our nation's business and bring our national house to good order.

And to all I say, be assured that this is not business — this is as personal as it could possibly get — times 300 million American citizens!

<u>One Acting for the Many</u>

At key times in our nation's and world's history, it has been a solitary man or woman that has come forward freely taking the personal risks to do, to say, to write what was needed in order to focus the general public's attention and so to spark the National Change process. However, for any such change to have taken root and grown into something truly beneficial for society, it had to have the support <u>and</u> personal involvement of other concerned individuals. People just like you and those you know and love.

It is only logical therefore that the greater the vision and the greater the magnitude of the Change being proposed, the more people like you that are not only needed, but absolutely required to make it happen. You count!

Without any doubt whatsoever, I know — and I know that you know – that this is rapidly becoming one of those critical moments in time and in human history for that matter. Therefore, like it or not that makes this is <u>our</u> moment in time and We the People must determine to stand together and take action — for there is just too much at stake.

o o o o

In 1776, a regular American *colonist* Thomas Paine took the challenge upon himself and wrote *Common Sense* to provide the rationale for his anxious fellow American colonists to unite and finally confront an <u>external</u> force in their American Revolution, and to create <u>their</u> nation.

Today, a regular American *citizen* could stand idly by and watch while the fabric of our society and our desired national way of life is slowly being destroyed. Therefore, this writing has been dutifully prepared for consideration by my anxious fellow American citizens.

My very personal and patriotic desire with this writing is to provide the practical rationale for my fellow American citizens to unite and confront primarily <u>internal</u> forces with a Common Vision, and by Constitutional Right attend to our Second and Final American Revolution, and to preserve <u>our</u> nation.

What I ask and challenge you for in return is your objective consideration of these contents, which are offered for the Common Good and future sake of our families and our nation.

Therefore, I humbly and with absolute intent,
present these findings for our common understanding
which are only,

Common Sense

— A. J. Wildman

My Inspiration and Our Example

"In the Spirit of Common Sense"

Do you know or remember the name Thomas Paine from American history? Are you familiar with the revolutionary writer's efforts on our nation's behalf? *The Second Coming of Common Sense* will either refresh or newly bring some of his writing to your attention and appreciation. His national vision, logical reasoning for the Common Good, personal bravery, and accomplishments for America, later for France, and undoubtedly for the world in general — serve as my inspiration and are at the heart of this effort for my fellow American citizens and our great country.

Thomas Pain was born in Thetford, England, on January 29, 1737. Just thirty-seven years later in 1774, the newly re-named Paine found himself in the New World, in the city of Philadelphia in the England's American colony of Pennsylvania. Thomas Paine came to the American colonies with letters of introduction from Benjamin Franklin, to whom he had been introduced while both were doing business in London.

The England born Thomas Paine was an experienced stay-maker (a maker of women's corsets) by trade having been trained by his father. Paine had also been a tax collector in England and had only limited writing experience. At personal risk and of his own free will, this regular colonist made himself into a revolutionary writer. He had only been in the American colonies for eighteen months when his radical pamphlet entitled *Common Sense* was first published in mid-January of 1776.

Only a few weeks after its first release, George Washington wrote on the message of *Common Sense*, to Joseph Reed of Pennsylvania on January 31, 1776:

> *"A few more of such flaming arguments,*
> *as were exhibited at Falmouth and Norfolk,*
> *added to the sound of doctrine and*
> *unanswerable reasoning contained in the pamphlet Common Sense,*
> *will not leave numbers at a loss to decide upon the propriety of a*
> *separation."*

It was Benjamin Rush, one of the eventual signers of the Declaration of Independence representing the Pennsylvania colony that had the idea for Paine to write about the colonies breaking away from English rule. However, the writing contained in *Common Sense* was purely Paine's creation — his practical analysis of the day-to-day state of affairs that faced the American colonists.

In *Common Sense* he stated in the plain, everyday language of colonial America, the rationale for a complete break with England. Paine focused the consideration of the American colonial population on the pure, practical logic for separation from the Mother country.

A Revolution — by the People...

It was Paine's vision of the colonies' epic struggle against the "old order of things" and the regrettable, but necessary taking up of arms against their own countrymen in order to realize their dreams. Paine wrote that the growing colonial conflict with the English monarchy of King George III required,

"a declaration of independence"

He wrote on the Vision that became our Democracy and made the Challenge that led the colonists, our national ancestors to the war that created our nation...

Background, Terms, and Common Perspectives

"Common Perspective Does Not Imply Acceptance"

In order to set an overall frame of reference and provide a glimpse of subject matter to be covered herein the following items are presented:

1. This Project for America
2. The National System
3. A Partial List of Public Grievances with "Our" U.S. Congress
4. The Screamers
5. Illegal Occupant (IO)
6. American Industry Restructuring
7. A Historical Political Challenge for Consideration

o   o   o   o

1. This Project for America (PFA)

This first piece is not intended to be self-promotional, but give you some background on the effort that eventually produced what you are now reading.

Acting as an individual I took it upon myself to use the analytical and problem-solving skills developed over a 34-year Information Technology (IT) career combined with my absolute love for our country — to research, to develop, and then bring these findings to my fellow American citizens.

What may surprise you is that the proposed solutions to the social and economic issues presented herein do not represent my personal opinions, in all cases. To offer only my opinions would defeat the objectivity, spirit, and proper function of systems analysis. I will submit that the solutions overall do represent the reconciled opinions of the Silent Majority and the true Spirit of America. These contents are the results of literally thousands of conversations with everyday Americans.

The sub-title of *Our Second and Final American Revolution* is absolutely serious and it is a reality that will need to be embraced by the American public and electorate if we desire to maintain our nation.

All projects have a starting point – a reason to begin. This one simply started with a concerned American trying to figure out how to solve our nation's War on Drugs. That was the origin of this entire experience.

My working background in the IT business was first as a computer operator, then a programmer, systems analysts, system designer, project manager, and manager. More than anything else my professional skills are in problem analysis, solution development, and project coordination. I have had viable experience in both corporate and federal government sectors.

o   o   o   o

The Initial Assignment – End the War on Drugs

"To Solve the National Hard Drug Problem"

I originally conceived of and gave myself this assignment around 1980! Yes, a <u>long</u> time ago. Even then many of us were getting frustrated with government's inability to deal with the growing hard drug (primarily cocaine) problem – via the so-called "War on Drugs." That was the name given to the newly re-organized national drug fighting effort in 1972 by President Richard M. Nixon, some 35 years ago — a period two and a half times longer than the 14 years (1919 to 1933) that the national Prohibition of Alcohol was in force. Neither Prohibition yielded the intended results.

In 1980, I was a systems analyst and had completed my first ten years in the IT industry. The way I looked at it, my profession was solving business problems. My experience taught me that business problems could be solved either by designing and implementing a new computer-based system and/or by improvements to related policies and operational procedures. A new computer system is not always the right or best solution.

I left the IT business in December 2002 in order to devote full-time effort to completing the book *Common Interest* and to bring the National Drug Reform (NDR) to the attention of my fellow Americans. Over my career I often took on assignments that required tedious coordination and/or the resolution of difficult project situations. It was often a difficult process, but the results were rewarding and the varying projects were challenging. I truly enjoy the process of bringing order to chaotic situations, and those challenges prepared me for what I am doing now.

o   o   o   o

One day, as a curious citizen I had a conversation with myself about the nation's "hard" drug problem. I thought to myself, what if Congress came to me and gave me the task of researching and developing a solution to the national drug problem? I am systems analyst. I solve business problems. Just how would I approach it? From that point, *'the assignment'* developed into a hobby of sorts. I developed an initial approach to tackling the problem based on my own perspectives and convictions. Then began the perpetual series of informative one-on-one presentations, asking people for their feedback and opinions.

The Initial Audience and Opinion Poll

Over the years I developed what is referenced many times herein as the National Drug Reform (NDR) proposal. The NDR proposal's design, policies, and operational approaches were refined based on the direct feedback of people of all ages, backgrounds, and attitudes. I believe those folks represented a real cross-section of the American public's view on ending the drug war and many other issues. Among the men and women I spoke with were those from the following groups and others:

Accountants
All classes – representing the lower, upper, and the masses in the middle.
All races
Automobile Mechanics
Authors
Bicycle Repair Specialists
Blue-collar workers
Carpenters
Chiropractors
Church leadership of various faiths
Computer (IT) industry people of all job types
Conservatives, Liberals, and Moderates
Corporate Executives
Co-workers (many of them)
County Assembly Members
Daycare Workers
Democrats, Independents, Libertarians, Republicans, Greens, and the
	Undecided
Dentists
Doctors of many disciplines
Drug counselors
Drug testing technicians
Electricians
Farmers
Firemen
Foreign workers from many countries
Foreign visitors
Former cocaine addicts
Grandparents and Great-Grandparents
Hair salon specialists
Heterosexuals – Straight!
Homosexuals – Gay, Lesbian
House-parents – women/men work at home
HVAC technicians

Illegal Occupants
International travelers here on business and/or vacation
Lawyers of various specialties
Librarians
Little league parents
Massage Specialists
Medical Doctors and Nurses
Non-citizens
Orthodontists
Other Legal Occupants
Parents and Step-Parents
People born in other countries
People representing all the world's major faiths
People that have been my boss and client
People that have worked for me
People without religious faith
Physical Therapists
Plumbers
Police Officers – state, county, and local
Poor people, rich people, and the masses in the middle
Professional workers
Recovered alcoholics
Rescue Squad personnel
Restaurant owners
Retail sales staff
Roofers
Secret Service
School counselors
Schoolteachers – pre-K thru 12, public and private
Single parents
"Soccer" Moms and Dads — and Little League, too
Small business owners
Taxi cab drivers
Teenagers
The faithful and faithless
U.S. Marshals
Waiters and waitresses
White-collar workers
Voters and non-voters
and others....

A diverse and interesting cross-section of the people that yielded many great conversations! Did you notice how few politicians there are on the list? We can always obtain their collective legislative opinion by watching the evening news and reading newspapers and magazines.

The NDR One-on-Ones – A Real Public Survey

Have you ever been asked your opinion or polled like that? Most people have not. Those that talked with me enjoyed the opportunity to share their opinion on that type of real issue, and to be sincerely asked for their questions and comments.

At the very start of the opinion gathering process I often spoke with people in small groups of two to four people in casual conversation. However, I quickly observed that more often than not, people would not feel free to provide their real opinions in front of others. They were inhibited by other people knowing what they really felt about the drug issue and did not bring up other public issues that were of concern to them. Therefore, I changed my approach, the one-on-ones began, and there have been a few thousand of them over the years.

The rate of activity on the project went up and down over the years as *life* has a way of getting in the way of these self-assigned projects. How many of us have known or even been a person trying to write a book on something? There just never seems to be the spare time and the solitude required to complete or even to work on it. Family, work, and things in general so easily get in the way of such personal endeavors.

Over the years, it probably averaged over two presentations per week. I do not mind introducing myself to people I have never met. I am generally easy to talk with and encourage people's comments. Basically, if I saw the opportunity to get somebody's time for 10 or 15 minutes, I was on it! No mercy! I would simply state, "I am writing a book on national drug reform and I would appreciate it if you had the time to hear it and give me your opinion," in a totally non-threatening manner.

To the absolute credit to the nature of our people, I rarely got a 'no' in reply – and again most were complete strangers – one-time encounters. In our conversation they would at least hear the short version of the NDR program. And very often these impromptu conversations went well beyond 15 minutes.

My Sense of the Public's Attitude

These real, 'person-in-the-street' opinion sessions were most informative and have made all the difference. In the talks, people told me what they liked and did not like, and they spoke about their frustrations with various other problems within the National System, not just the drug issue. Weighing their comments, I continually refined the NDR design thereby increasing the probability of acceptance by the general public and the program's likelihood of success when implemented. Therefore, it is with extreme confidence I believe that the "net" of all their — the general public's concerns and comments are accounted for in the NDR Proposal.

That belief most importantly means to me that the NDR proposal, as well as the 25-plus proposals that make up the America Agenda to be presented, will be found socially acceptable by the vast majority of the American electorate. This objective sense of the public's interest in the Common Good – in doing what is right for our citizens is extremely important to me and is at the heart of the CS2 message to you.

I must note that I have had an interest in news, politics, and world events since I was a child. Therefore, this self-assignment was not totally out of left field considering my personal interests and my lifelong curiosity in things political.

I am a native born Washingtonian, and proud of it! Having worked in and around both Baltimore City and Washington, DC all of my adult life I have had the opportunity to have good conversations with people from many states across our nation and a good many countries, as well. Frankly most of the people in the DC metropolitan area are from somewhere else. I moved back there from the Baltimore area myself in the early 1970's.

I firmly believe that all my direct conversations with so many different people over the years on the NDR proposal, on many other domestic and foreign policy issues, and discussing the various world events as they have occurred over the last 25 years — has taught me many things about the general public's heart and their mutual desire for a better world for us all to live in.

Those real insights, along with my background in problem solving, my desire to be of good service to my country, and my faith — have provided me with the strength and confidence required to continue with this challenge that can be so overwhelming at times — and the inner peace I have as it unfolds.

All that said, I believe that I write for the Silent Majority of Americans. It is purely the challenge of my lifetime. And I am so thankful for the opportunity.

o   o   o   o

2. The National System

The **"National System"** is the title I use when referring to America's social and economic structure — the way in which America *really works* on a day-to-day basis – or to put it another way the *Status Quo*.

Status Quo is defined in the *Merriam Webster's Collegiate Dictionary 10th Edition*, as follows:

> "state in which; the existing state of affairs;
> **seeks to preserve the *status quo*"**

The National System includes the good, the bad, and the ugly aspects of the American experience today.

o   o   o   o

Some years ago a major American corporation used the following as the key phrase in a national advertising campaign,

"The System is the Solution"

As a career systems analyst and computer system designer, I always enjoyed that line. What they did not so obviously state in their advertisement was the underlying reality that speaks directly to our current national situation, that being,

"The Current System therefore is the Problem"

And that in a nutshell, ladies and gentlemen is our Common Problem. And how we agree to fix "it" or not — is our challenge. "It" in this case is our *American National System.*

o   o   o   o

You are reading a 2007/ very early 2008 literary critique, if not an assault upon the way some things are currently being done and run in our country. To be crystal clear, the message of *The Second Coming of Common Sense* is written and presented with the same confrontational intent as Thomas Paine's writing in *Common Sense*. Only time and your response will tell if this sincere call and challenge to my fellow American citizens could ring as true today. I believe it can and that it will.

The basic condition of our American National System could be framed as follows:

- Many negative social and economic conditions in the National System have slowly grown to feel customary just because they been allowed to exist for so long, e.g., various forms of crime, poverty, hunger, unemployment, out-sourcing, and homelessness.

- Various public conditions appearing to be normal, even though they are an increasing burden to society and/or have become a functionally counter-productive if not a <u>destructive</u> factor in the National System, e.g., the failed War on Drugs, illegal immigration, and the increasingly dysfunctional Criminal Justice System allowing murder, rape, and pedophile crimes to continue.

- Certain day-to-day parts of the National System we are <u>forced</u> to tolerate, but if they had to be explained objectively to an outsider, would be difficult to justify, e.g., the lack of medical insurance for all Americans, the pro-industry National Energy Policy, the uncontrolled industries such as Oil, Banking, and Pharmaceuticals to name a few, .

Not a "comfortable" condition for *We the People* in many ways.

The 'direction' of our National System over the last couple of decades and in the last six years <u>in particular,</u> has increasingly been determined by a 'shrinking minority' of self-interested entities. These entities are various socially and economically irresponsible, self-interested people along with organizations and entire industries that are slowly destroying the fabric and future of America one person, one family, one business, and one community at a time.

We the People cannot and will not allow this to continue!

o   o   o   o

3. A Partial List of Public Grievances with "Our" U.S. Congress

The following is just a partial list of significant public issues that the U.S. Congress, in particular and the White House are failing to address. No great secrets here. Our initial *Grievance List* will be referred to many times in CS2:

- Automobile/Truck Theft
- Commodity Market Abuses
- Contaminated Food Supply
- Crimes of Physical Assault
- Crimes of Financial Assault
- Drug War in our Streets
- Employment/Income (viable and legal)

- Ending the Iraq War
- Gangs in Our Communities
- Global Warming
- Homelessness
- Housing Costs
- Hunger
- Illegal Immigration – ending it
- Interest Rates on Primary Family Residence
- Katrina Clean-up
- Judicial Legal Complex (JLC)
- Medical Insurance for all American citizens – cradle to grave
- Military Industrial Complex (MIC)
- Oil Industry Windfall Profits and Other Abuses
- Over-weight children, teenagers, and adults
- Poverty Among Our Citizens
- Public Education
- Pre-meditated Murder
- Pre-meditated Pedophile Crimes Against our Youth
- Pre-meditated Rape
- Prescription Medicine Costs
- Stem Cell Research
- Social Security Solvency
- War on Terror

Many of our common public problems will be positively addressed if not resolved to the public's satisfaction with the timely and appropriate implementation of the proposals to be presented in Part 3 — An American Agenda for 2008 and Beyond. The continued existence of these and other long-standing public problems shall no longer be tolerated by the American electorate. And neither will the U.S. Congress that by their wrong actions and inactions <u>allows</u> it all to continue.

Remember — that the initial Grievance List *only* contains thirty (30) of the issues that help define and explain the public's disapproval with the Status Quo of our National System, <u>and</u> with the U.S. Congress whose job responsibility it is to resolve such economic and social issues – for the Common Good.

They need to remember that Election Day 11-1-2008 is coming. We are coming!

<u>But What About Abortion and Gay Rights</u>

Funny – how those two issues are not on the Grievance List, even though they were such burning issues in the days leading up to the 2006 election. I realized those two topics were not there well after preparing the list. But why not, since they are the hot issues (with an occasional stem cell or two thrown in) that the political parties, mainly the Republicans, run around the country screaming about as most recent elections approach.

Just as in 2004 — those two "issues" were blatantly used by the Republican Party to whip up funding support and "target" the type of voters easily driven by such personal hot buttons to turn-out and help keep a failed presidency in office for *four more years*. Along with those Terror Alerts right out of the Bush Administration that increased weekly right up to Election Day and then mysteriously stopped! That is what happened folks.

Once again, the lead Republican Party campaign strategist and domestic propagandist – the Ayatollah Rove (I did not coin that title for him, but I did think of it before hearing it in the news). Once again, he played the religious types *like a cheap violin* — using them to achieve yet another un-deserved victory – and maintain POWER. Any questions?

I spoke with more than one such voter (usually Republican) a few months after the 2004 election and they realized they were had and were disgusted about it. To their credit, some of them and others turned-out in 2006 and got partial revenge on the Congress and on the Republican Party in particular. And those Congressional incumbent upsets in both parties were only a taste of what should be in store for the whole Congress in 2008.

o   o   o   o

I will not go into these issues in CS2 beyond what is noted here, because they are not public problems to be "solved". They cannot be prevented just because somebody gets legislation passed – at least as long as we still have a Democracy!

Again, those two social issues are not on the list because they are not public problems. Being for or against them is strictly a personal point-of-view. And to be clear, neither is a religion-based mindset! I have spoken with confirmed atheists that were totally opposed to or fully accepted both of them.

Objectively Speaking

Issue One

Whether or not to have an abortion is a most difficult, free-will, life decision

— that primarily of course involves the woman, and at times the man as well. If a given pregnancy is one that causes the serious consideration of such a painful decision it cannot help but leave permanent psychological marks.

If the personal decision is to have an abortion or a child is born and immediately given up for adoption or a child is born into terrible life conditions and/or an unappreciated even abusive environment – the woman unfortunately carries that knowledge with her for the rest of her life! And bluntly the fact is that there are far more people walking around 'the world' today than there would be if abortion was more socially acceptable – hard truth, but the truth all the same.

Preventing Late Term (as early as month five and beyond) abortions when the Mother's life is not at risk, and mandating that having the "tubes tied" of those that would use abortion as birth-control (for they can be un-tied later) — represent "reasonable" civil control on the part of the American public — and *Nothing* more than that!

Abortion is a terrible decision for anyone to have to consider let alone decide to do. However, in our Democratic society where separation of Church and State were written into our Founding National Rules and for reasons just like this – it is a necessary civil Right.

The *screamers* on this issue need to spend their time and energy addressing the social and economic conditions that places *some* people in these situations. That way they might actually do something to reduce such occurrences, because unfortunately they will never stop occurring – it is simply a hard part of life.

Issue Two

The natural Gay or Lesbian orientation of a person as opposed to them being a natural Heterosexual male or female *is not a freewill decision*. The people that will not accept the real science and/or cannot think of anything more important to worry about and get involved in someone else's personal business REALLY need to review that Grievance List for a moment.

And if their particular Holy book and/or type of 'clergy-person' tell them it is a sin — that is just wonderful – for them! It is their freewill decision to have the opinion.

The lamest rhetoric I have ever heard come out of a televangelist mouth is the when someone is 12 or 13 years old, he or she freely decide whether or not to be heterosexual or not! And when they are preaching that to the choir, little do they know that many in the choir know they are a fool for saying it! And I so would dearly love to hear them ask — on national television — the daughter of the current Vice President of the United States whether she was 12 or 13 when she decided.

Enough said.

o   o   o   o

Frankly, these are two very unique issues. The Founders knew too well about religious persecution, which is why we have the law in the first place. They forcefully wrote the basic Right To religious freedom, as well as the Freedom From religious persecution into the Constitution to protect the People from other people's views on religion.

I am a Christian and very proud of it. And when some conversations turn on these issues I flatly point out that when Christ was on earth and practicing His ministry — He <u>did</u> <u>not</u> <u>get</u> <u>into</u> <u>politics</u>! He was only concerned with helping people, not controlling them. Some people and those in religious leadership would do well to pray on that!

Further, it might do some people well to seriously consider – to realize — that both religious leaders <u>and</u> politicians, too often have less than holy reasons for pontificating on such issues.

Besides if you cannot convert a devout Yankee fan into a Red Sox fan, or vice versa, what possible hope is there in issues such as these?

I hope you can somehow appreciate how difficult it is attempting to write on such sensitive subject matter.

Amen.

o   o   o   o

4. <u>The Screamers</u>

You already have and will be reading many references to this very real, yet rarely recognized political entity and force that I have labeled and refer to repeatedly as the ***Screamers***. This is a good place to formally introduce them to the American public in concept and example. They help to perpetuate the *Status Quo*.

In general, they are the people and/or groups that can be relied upon to overtly cry out when potential solutions are offered to various public problems. In truth, most of them are <u>absolutely</u> well-intended. However, in reality they only contribute to the killing of viable public reform based upon their own, often narrowly focused perspective on a given issue or on the real world for that matter. Issues, such as real drug reform, national medical insurance for all citizens, a national citizen id card, the repatriation of illegal immigrants, strict immigration controls by country of origin, and of society's prudent use of the death penalty — to name just a few — always brings out the *Screamers!*

What these individuals and groups do not realize or refuse to acknowledge is that they <u>are</u> at times <u>un</u>intentionally helping those with far less then publicly responsible motives and sometimes the real bad guys, as well. Certain industries (and other entities) do covertly promote the public protesting of the well-intentioned for their own self-serving purposes, more or less using good people/groups to sustain bad, counter-productive policy and blocking positive change.

<u>A Classic Example</u>

While there will be details on this topic later, for a moment let's glance at the decades old, pathetic example of marijuana legalization. In this case, it is the Pharmaceutical (primarily) and Alcohol industries, as well as the real bad guys being the drug barons, traffickers, and distributors – <u>that are all on the side of leaving the National Drug Policy just the way it is</u>! The Plain Truth is that they <u>all</u> want the status quo to remain unchanged. They could be odd-bedfellows, but have been bed-fellows a very long time. And there are other parts of the National System that also profit from our counter-productive National Drug Policy.

Did you ever think about our failed War on Drugs in that context before? Most people I spoke with had not. Maybe take another look at the Grievance List and consider what *entities* directly benefit from the *status quo* regarding the various line items. Give it some thought because we must go <u>through</u> those same entities as we act to correct problems in the National System.

Those Screamers that always cry-out against realistic reform of our National Drug Policy – that is the full legalization and decriminalization of marijuana — may not like that guilt by association, but that's the true net result of their actions to-date against such practical drug policy reform. And some 9 out of 10 Americans that I have spoken with disagree with them. It could be a difficult reality, but it is a real factor in how America works on a day-to-day basis. The net result in this example is that the alleged War on

Drugs continues with all the crime, death, addiction, un-necessary criminal records, imprisonment, and all the other negative impacts it perpetuates within the National System and inflicts upon our fellow Americans. And all drugs are readily available <u>everywhere</u>!

o   o   o   o

More examples will be noted later, but for now it would serve for good people in those groups to reflect on the following:

When well-intentioned good guys find themselves,
on the same side of a public issue <u>with</u> the bad guys,
the good guys need to <u>wake-up</u> and review on their position.

To evaluate the "real" benefits and public success of their efforts,
for they are indeed although unintentionally
<u>helping</u> the bad guys succeed.

A harsh reality.

The Screamers work to prevent positive social <u>and</u> economic change, due often to their narrow view of the world on a single issue. Not the Big Picture.

For example, briefly consider the "avoidable" negative impacts of the uncontrolled drug business places on the lives of so many of our people in the past, today, as well as tomorrow unless we move beyond these useless types of bottlenecks and implement the practical changes required to correct such dysfunctional aspects of America's National System.

We the People, have the power to move beyond the marijuana legalization *type of impasse* – to prudently alter the Status Quo and correct such past mistakes in public policy, thus preventing further societal decline and the human suffering that such policies guarantee.

It is just common sense…

5. <u>Illegal Occupants (IO)</u>

Speaking of Screamers…, I determined to initiate the discussion on the *illegal immigration crisis* now although it will be touched on in various areas herein and in particular under the American Population Management (APM) proposal.

<u>What's in a Name</u>

First, "what to call" the foreign born individuals that acting upon their own *freewill* decided to enter our nation via a route they knew to be <u>absolutely</u> illegal, being against Federal law and the will of the American people. We the People *never* invited them in!

Also, most of them enter with the intention of staying permanently if they can get away with it? This is a *pre-meditated* violation of our national boundaries. Technically this is a variation of "breaking and entering" at the national level instead of the usual home or business invasion – instant felony.

There is an on-going, boring debate about what to call the border violators that make up this group. The usual terms like illegal immigrants or illegal aliens are said to be offensive or demeaning by those (the screamers) supportive of this free-will driven, "illegal" flow of people into our nation. However, they cannot come up with a name that they like either – you know one that can get around that nasty "illegal" thing!

The facts are that there are multiple federal laws against them being here, they were born outside the U.S., they are citizens of <u>another</u> country, they are now occupying space and housing in our nation as un-invited entrants, and most have some form(s) of false, i.e., forged identification.

In business I enjoyed developing names for things over the years, but it took a while to come up with something appropriate for this group. I offer the name of **IO** for "**Illegal Occupants**" as the on-going, public title for anyone that is physically in our country and came here some way other than through the legal process. I will use **"IO"** throughout CS2 when referencing such individuals or the group as a whole.

I hope you like it!

<u>The Truth of the Matter</u>

In all sincerity, you should be detecting a generally negative attitude regarding the IO crisis in these words. Absolutely correct! That is simply because CS2 boldly and without apology represents the overriding attitudes and frustrations of the American citizens and taxpayers.

As a clarification to the world - that the sign at the base of the Statue of Liberty reads,

"Give me your poor, your huddled masses yearning to be free."

It does <u>not</u> say,

"Give me your excess population that you do not want or care to deal with."

Is that clear enough? The IO issue is by my observations and frequent talks with other Americans, a real and present aggravation to the American electorate. And it is often a sore point with those that immigrated here <u>legally</u> and <u>properly</u> became naturalized citizens!

<u>There is No Leadership like *No Leadership*</u>

Over the last 21 years since then President Reagan and the Congress passed the 'band-aid' 1986 Immigration Act, our politicians and various self-interested lobbies have both ignored and encouraged the flow of IOs. Our elected national level 'leadership' have totally failed to enforce our existing Immigration Control Policy to protect American society, although they have liked talking the IO issue when fund-raising and during re-election campaigns.

It is obvious that the greatest percentage of IOs arrive by land from the Central and South American (CSA) countries and Mexico in particular. At the same time, millions of the IOs have arrived from all around the world. They come via airplane or ship, under the cover of business, vacation or for education, but then failed to leave the country on the date they agreed. Others are those that originally came here legally through the Visa program, <u>but</u> also failed to leave the country as they declared in their paperwork.

The U.S. Census Bureau recently estimated that there are 11 to 15 million IOs currently in the country, but it is could easily be 20 million — who really knows? It is a situation that is totally out of control, everyone knows it, and the U.S. Congress bears the responsibility.

The U.S. Congress is not acting to help the states fight the influx of IOs and facilitate their deportation — which is their responsibility. The budgets of states like Arizona, New Mexico, and California for example, are absolutely being hammered by this IO overhead. Towns <u>all</u> across the country are being required to pass laws to punish employers that hire them and against landlords that rent to them. All of which could be avoided if the Congress would simply do their job — as you will read more than once herein – per their basic job description **it is the responsibility of Congress to solve the problems that cannot be resolved at the local or state level.**

In my conversations with people on political issues, quite often they will bring up the topic of IOs and express their frustration with what it is doing to our nation. The VAST majority of the American public is totally disgusted with this invasion and the no guts, no action Congress. That is to say nothing about the current resident of the White House that blatantly encourages the IO flow strictly for political reasons (helping business obtain cheap labor) and keeps trying to find an acceptable way to say *'path to amnesty'*. But, there just ain't no acceptable way to be saying that!

They Prefer Option Number One

Congress is consistently taking the *classical first option* when it comes to problem-solving and considering Change options – that is *to do absolutely nothing!* To let things just continue as they will – the status quo is therefore protected due to inaction! Regrettably, that is Congress' first choice when it comes to numerous public problems. And that will all be coming to an end!

The Hard Economic Reality to be Reconciled

For too many years and increasingly since the band-aid Immigration Act of 1986, our economy has grown un-naturally with the uncontrolled infusion of population and the related buying of goods and services they generate. Say what? This means that our economy has grown in ways it would and should not have if we had controlled borders and these IOs were not here acting as consumers and workers.

> Strictly by comparison it would have grown slower and that would not have been a bad thing for the Common Good of Main Street, although Wall Street will gag on those words. It is called natural economic growth. What a concept!

Correspondingly the incidents of murder, robbery, gangs violence, rape, as well as the unnecessary educational, medical, housing, federal and state prison space, and other social service costs at all levels of tax-payer funded spending – would never have happened. Remember those points and all of that avoidable human suffering during the next election when your man or woman is seeking re-election.

The practical economic adjustments that will necessarily need to be made are what concerns some businesses and investors, as well as the politicians that can actually grasp of Big Picture — not all of them do.

The multi-year adjustments during the eventual repatriation of most of the IOs and many of their *citizenship-born* children will be perceived as pending loss by an anxious business community – and there will be losers as well as winners. These will be hard, but manageable economic and human changes. No one said this was going to be easy, but the national bleeding must be stopped and the healing begun or the patient shall be forever damaged.

Just as with the un-doing of our failed National Drug Policy – We the People are now forced to correct the legislative in-action of the past in order to preserve the Common Good of citizens and our country for the future. And the future is now – history starts today!

Some Thoughts on the IO Invasion

- Over the years the IO situation has been covertly and overtly promoted by large and small business. American business (hospitality, agriculture, and cleaning services in particular) has always had a love affair with the cheap labor that crosses our borders illegally. This is one of those unspoken truths that everyone knows about. And even though the business community will claim no responsibility for it, they have lobbied (often covertly) against any legislation that would put anything more than a worn band-aid on this open and bleeding National wound.

- Not wanting to control IOs is one of the unspoken reasons why Congress always runs away from the public need for a National Identification Card System for all citizens and visitors. Think about that for a while.

- IOs come from countries on every continent. I remember hearing several years ago the about an unfortunate woman from Poland that drowned in the Rio Grand river trying to cross from Mexico into the U.S.

- The flow of more IOs is also directly encouraged and sponsored by family, friends, and businesses within our own borders, as well as other IOs already in the country. And the governments of CSA countries aggressively encourage the flow.

- IOs are uninvited visitors, not guests. This national border violation most commonly occur when someone illegally crosses our wide-open land borders with Mexico (mostly) or Canada.

- Yes, there is Mexico – that has not been willing to work with our government to enforce any system to reduce and/or control the flow. And why should they? They have it all right now. They functionally have the Congress of the United States of America and the Bush II White House in particular in their back pocket!

- Mexico and the other CSAs, are dumping their unwanted population – sending their most illiterate and too often criminal citizens here. And at the same time they are receiving remittances in the amount of billions of dollars annually as all those little revenue centers send dollars back home, transferred with the *gleeful* help of 'our' fee collecting, Latino-friendly banks.

- The Mexican government openly promotes the constant, daily stream of IOs across our Southern border. Many have traveled from Mexico's southern border with Guatemala and Belize from other CSA countries — with the required pay-offs to various gangs, and Mexican police, military, and officials along the way.

- Mexico was given NAFTA on a silver platter. We neglected the need to send them and the other CSA countries **Planned Parenthood** as part of the package! And that is not intended as a comic remark.

- Mexico also grows the base crops, manufactures, and traffics in all types of 'hard' drugs across our wide-open, non-fenced border all the way to our neighborhoods. The next time someone references the Mexican government as our partner in the Drug War ask them what planet they are visiting from.

Overall these conditions will be coming to an end and the controlled world-wide repatriation will begin.

The Growing Political Storm

The entire IO issue will be a critical and politically unavoidable issue in the up-coming 2008 Presidential and Congressional campaigns. However, it is the Congress of the United States of America that could address this national problem (and many others) at any time. Presidents have come and gone since 1986, but with a normal 90-plus percent incumbent re-election rate, the members of both houses of Congress are around for decades. They are responsible…

Question — can you name one (1) single member of Congress or any president in the last 21 years that has stood up in public and loudly demanded that the IOs from South of the Border and around the world must quit coming? No you cannot — because it has never happened!! And that includes your state's favorite sons and daughters in Congress.

Grimly, it is fair to say that the IOs and their domestic support groups (the screamers for this issue) are enjoying better representation within the halls of Congress than does the Common Good of the American public. This totally unacceptable condition within the status quo of our National System will now come to a practical conclusion.

o   o   o   o

Again the Common Interest of all citizens – us – is to be addressed and be our first priority.

One of the most difficult things to do in a society is to correct past mistakes and/or inaction, in economic and social policy – I said **difficult**, but **not impossible** to correct. We can, we must, we will address our Population Management issues and the lack of federal law enforcement.

We Americans are a compassionate people, slow to anger. We cannot help but cheer the underdog because that is what <u>all</u> of our ancestors once were. However, we must deal with this and other issues <u>now</u> so that our children and those that follow them will be able to enjoy their own country.

And as a direct by-product of our prudent actions, other nations of the world will be forced to deal with their internal population and social problems, and that in time could make living conditions within their home countries worthy of their own people remaining there!

o   o   o   o

What comes next is guaranteed to produce a series of political chain reactions – Industry Restructuring. Revolutions, even a legislative type such as this one — are not easy – they are only necessary.

6. American Industry Re-Structuring

"We the People — do not owe any company, corporation or industry
a profit or even its continued existence,
if it would come at the expense of our People and our Society"
"So let the battle lines be drawn"

The American Industry Re-Structuring (AIR) Program

Concept – *New Rules*

Have no illusions regarding what is before us, my fellow Americans — this is where the rubber meets the road – and the bullet meets the bone!

For the Common Good to prevail over the naturally occurring evolution of Corporate Greed, the People shall now debate and commonly agree as to how business will be *permitted* to operate within the American National System. An interesting statement, don't you think?

The Common Good and the National System

Logically, we will acknowledge that certain 'essential components' of the National System to have become operationally dysfunctional with regard to the Common Good of the people and the economy we all must depend upon. The un-elected leadership of such business entities are more and more helping themselves without concern for the Common Good and all under the cover of "my job is making money for the stockholders." And our elected national leadership either willingly promotes the growing abuse or stands by with a mystified look on his or her face.

That increasingly counter-productive national condition not only hits families, but most businesses small and large as we find ourselves being forced to tolerate avoidable economic conditions (need I say Oil). Forced to tolerate the Economic Oppression by the unspoken, unwritten, and non-legislated "RIGHT" – that is silently claimed by various commercial and bureaucratic entities.

This un-Democratic, quietly dictatorial Consolidation of Power will not be allowed to continue. *Reason* shall call this regressive economic oppression for what it is – the greed and self-serving domination of the Few at the literal expense in dollars and actual lives among the Many. Priceless American lives are lost every day due to a broken medical system, the worthless National Drug Policy, and the optional and now failed Iraq war to name just a few sources.

As I will ask more than once, when in the last 50 years my fellow Americans did the lives of our people become so cheap, that they are thrown away on such *preventable* things? An undeclared Legislative Kill Factor (LKF) against We the People, that benefits certain self-serving, civilly irresponsible businesses and special interests has been written into our national laws and policies.

> There is no common sense in any this — it is profits and influence, over people and peace. "Beware ye, also of false profits".

This national Status Quo that has increasingly been servicing the Special

Interests will be thoughtfully and deliberately confronted and restructured by the absolute intent of the Many to preserve, protect, and defend the Common Good. Thomas Paine framed changing the status quo and confronting the obvious flaws of colonial America,

> "..., a long habit of not thinking a thing *wrong*, gives it the superficial appearance of being *right*, and raises at first the formidable outcry in the defense of custom. But the tumult soon subsides. Time makes more converts than reason."

Certain business entities on the domestic front and those with increasingly foreign entanglements (need I say Oil, again) have had their day and frankly their way with us! The People and the Common Good will now be served.

Key operational components of the National System that impact the successful operation of business large and small in America – will no longer be directed by faceless corporate executives and Boards of Directors, a powerful minority, and un-American foreign policy. The tail shall not wag the dog!

The industries and business "Entities" addressed under the AIR program will be re-directed from purely self-serving priorities and the lobbying it promotes, to motivations that only promote the Common Good of our people, other businesses in the National System, and the society as a whole. The long held public perception of, and the actual utilization of these Entities within our National System, will be made-over to serve the Common Good of America's economy and society. And these changes will <u>not</u> be voluntary or optional.

Not Privately or Government Run – A Practical Compromise

This will <u>not</u> be a re-structuring where the government would assume day-to-day control over these Entities. At the same time the dysfunctional private industry management of them can no longer be afforded or tolerated..

There is a practical management facility to be created that lies somewhere between the purely privately-run and the often screamed about and dreaded government-run model. The form and function of that operational facility will vary from industry-to-industry and business-to-business depending on what will best accommodate the Common Good of America Citizens and provide a National System re-designed to insure a viable future for our <u>people</u>. And it will all be done with the "informed consent" of our citizens — and <u>no one else</u>.

So now let us talk about Business...

o   o   o   o

"Our" Dysfunctional National Infrastructure Industries

This is a preview of the types of publicly beneficial, yet corporately radical AIR programs to be employed in the deliberate restructuring of certain currently *dysfunctional* industries within our National System.

The initial set of AIR program proposals will be presented in Part 3 – An American Agenda, under the heading of Industry Restructuring and the particular sub-heading of Existing Industries. To provide a working example, the industry that was used to initially develop this economic model will be previewed below – that being the Medical Insurance Industry.

The AIR program proposals presented focus on a group of industries that are in some unavoidable manner woven into our economic system and impact the lives of virtually every American, each family, and other businesses on a monthly if not daily basis. Therefore, this somewhat odd set of bed-fellows has been generally categorized as National Infrastructure Industries (NII). There are of course other entities (e.g., Coal, Natural Gas, the Automobile industry or what is left of it and the Commodities Market) that could easily be added to this list. But for now, those at the head of the list and that most deserve to be there are — in somewhat random order:

1   The Medical Insurance Industry
2   The Pharmaceutical Industry
3   National Drug Reform (Controlling the Hard Drug Industry)
4   The Oil Industry
5   The Banking and Credit Card Industry
6   The Tobacco (Nailing the Most Deadly Drug) Industry
7   The Defense (Military Industrial Complex) Industry

Consider this for a few moments:

I submit that the two (2) greatest "problem causing and perpetuating entities" that face the world today are driven by the Oil Industry and the Illegal Drug Industry – our numbers 4 and 3, above. And they will both be dealt with!

o   o   o   o

Applying the AIR Program within Our National System

As I know you can imagine after considering that list, the industries in this vital grouping along with their entrenched Congressional lobbying machines (talk about screaming) could be viewed as doing the American economy and our people far more harm than the practical good they <u>could</u> and <u>should</u> be providing, and all in the name of stockholder dividends, executive compensation, and maintaining their piece of the pie at any cost – the status quo, again.

The AIR program will provide "levels of operational restructuring" that will be applied to given industry or business dependent upon what is required to reach a functional reconciliation within the National System that is acceptable to the American public — what will be of best service *our* nation's short <u>and</u> long-term economic health and our society in general.

Another era of "greed" in the American national voyage is over, just as the "Robber Baron type" scenarios of the past were eventually "dealt with" by legislation or Crash — it is time for these entities to be put in their place for the Common Good of the nation.

o   o   o   o

The De-Profitization of Infrastructure Industries

"De-Profitization" is a core concept of the American Industry Re-Structuring — AIR Program.

The concept of the "De-Profitization" of Infrastructure Industries firmly declares – that certain of our national industries and large individual businesses when found appropriate, will necessarily be restructured from their current charter of operation and their for-profit or non-profit organizational status. This is a civilly responsible 'reckoning' of their current power and influence within day-to-day America.

Remember that real Change within any country's National System creates both winners and losers – always has and always will. It can be accomplished peacefully as we will do it or by sharp contrast the way it is unfolding in Iraq!

In these scenarios American society, American workers, and other businesses will be the winners. At the same time we will need to reasonably facilitate the transition of the losers — businesses and especially the workers/employees to the newly structured National System. Loss cannot mean destruction, because we are talking about our own people. However there will also be prudent limits to the considerations granted.

Remember, I said everything is on the table. And the table is set! We can get to there from here…

o   o   o   o

Being selected for implementation of the AIR program guidelines will result in the short-term to permanent restructuring of certain publicly held (stockholder involved) corporations. Some points for consideration in this process include:

- Freezing of share price on the stock market.
- Future trading will be strictly controlled and could be halted.
- The eventual removal from the stock market in some cases.
- Having the existing share prices fixed for buy-back.
- Existing stockholders would be bought out over a number of years, e.g., about seven (7).
- Corporate assets could be sold off (to American buyers) to help expedite the buy-out process.
- Stock buy-back will make all that investment capital available for other purposes in the economy. A very good thing.

These publicly acceptable Changes will be plain and simple, and will not be negotiable. No back-room deals will be permitted. New and publicly practical laws will be enacted, foolish laws and loop-holes will be *rapidly* revised or eliminated, legislative corrections made where possible, and routine patterns of corporate greed will be reconciled to the Common Good.

It is just common sense.

o   o   o   o

At Their Beginning

In years past, the founding entrepreneurs of today's large publicly held corporations, initially sought simply to build a business and provide income for their family and for their employees.

I call such basic forms of non-stock encumbered businesses, an Income Generating Entity or IGE. IGEs produce goods and/or services in the economy and provide employment, income, and some level of benefits to the owner/operator and their employees. These are the types of businesses that built America and are required to sustain it.

Over the years many of those companies evolved into stock-held corporate entities. In time those founding men and women were succeeded by a series of executives and Board of Directors that in recent decades are increasingly driven by spreadsheets and are primarily interested in stockholder dividends and their increasingly excessive compensation. Further, most have a corporate field of vision that is generally being less than twelve (12) months into the future. That is the basic reason why it took Detroit twenty (20) years to a least figure out they were getting their corporate butts kicked by foreign imports! And they are still dragging one foot.

> Technically, and the only justifiable rationale (excuse) for the actions of the un-elected leadership of these corporate entities, is to acknowledge that however their business may negatively impact the average American, another business or the overall economy is simply not part of their job description. It is not what they were hired to worry about or to do! Some of them have even acknowledged that publicly!

The Plain Truth is that a given executive's (freewill) ability to ignore of the Common Good of the people and of the nation if necessary, in favor of the corporate bottom line — and their own paychecks — is the very reason why *they get paid the big bucks!* If they did not do it, they would be fired, and someone willing to do that job would replace them.

Are there any questions?

Our Example of Dramatic Public Driven Change

When the American colonists boldly took on England's King George III, his ministers, and the National System of the British Empire — they put it all on the line. On July 4, 1776 when the selected representatives of the common people (all of whom the King viewed as peasants) stood together and made their *Declaration of Independence* — the war that had been simmering since 1774 truly began.

In that war, the brave Few took up arms acting for the Many — went to war for themselves, their families, and their neighbors. In the end, approximately 25,000 of them or roughly one (1) percent of the colonial population lost their lives in that struggle — which against America's population today would be about 3,000,000 of our people or nearly 1,000 lost from <u>every</u> county in the country.

For a moment consider that level of human sacrifice that represented on the part of the colonial population. They were not professional soldiers — they were farmers, tradesman, merchants, and doctors one day – and some were dead in battle shortly thereafter. They represented the nation's first National Guard setting the standard for the troops that are fighting this <u>very day</u>.

Just as during the revolution, there are true citizen soldiers that have paid the ultimate price in battle or will carry the scars of battle for the rest of their lives, and they come from communities in every state and DC. And it is bad enough for our regular military to lose a single life or suffer such wounds. God bless all those that serve in our military.

o   o   o   o

Our Challenge

CS2 is calling upon Americans to join in <u>the</u> final battle for control over America's National System. To confront the negative ways that our country *really works today* – and insure that *our Common Will dictates* the positive ways it shall *really work tomorrow!*

Our national ancestors stood and fought against centuries of governmental tyranny and established a form of government designed to serve the Common Good of the Masses instead of the pleasure of the Few. However, the other side of the Sword of Tyranny still remains to be dulled.

We the People are now challenged to bring about a Democratic Economic System designed to benefit the Common Good of us all. A fair and balanced system that is designed under the Rights granted to us by our U.S. Constitution. It will be an economic reconciliation and revolution that will directly confront the natural evolution of a Have/Have-Not society that is the cruel norm in too many countries, and is aggressively working to control all aspects of American society.

We cannot – We will not allow this to continue. It is nothing less than an Economic Reformation that is the Democratic heart and soul of our Second and Final American Revolution.

Yes, We the People are now challenged to confront the excessive power gained by the Kings and Queens of Industry, along with their campaign funded ministers now serving in the United States Congress, and the all too cooperative current inhabitant of the White House and his side-kick.

And thanks to the U.S. Constitution that our national ancestors provided for us, We the People of today will not be required to fire a single shot to be successful in our historical revolution! To be crystal clear, while there many public problem areas addressed and workable solutions clearly set forth in CS2, *none of them* are as volatile nor as required to secure the nation's future than those that will initiate and bring to a successful conclusion the binding reconciliation between Industry, the un-elected politically powerful, and the Common Good. And the Common Good of our citizens and society shall prevail!

The Plain Truth

The Plain Truth answer is to that question and too many other agonizing public problems is that the dynamic duo of self-serving special interest lobbies *plus* national politicians desiring to maintain their positions of public power unfortunately *equals* the intentional promotion and die-hard preservation of *the dysfunctional status quo* within our National System — at any cost.

The Truth only requires a relatively few words to be spoken or written. Fortunately for us the same brevity of words also applies when defining practical, publicly acceptable solutions to our national problems. *The Second Coming of Common Sense* presents over twenty (25) such solutions designed to promote and preserve the Common Good of our fellow American citizens.

It has been said that *money is the root of all evil*. I say to you now that the unchecked *lust* for power and wealth, and its retention at any price — *is the cause of all evil.* That lust now runs too freely through the halls of our Congress and far too much of corporate America.

To be sure, We the People must now conduct and aggressively bring to satisfactory resolution a final reconciliation between the National System and the Common Good of our fellow Americans citizens and society. Therefore, everything is on the table.

o　　o　　o　　o

Their American Revolution gave the world a living model of Democracy in Government Order designed for the Common Good of the Masses.

Our American Revolution will provide the world with a living model of Democracy in Economic Order also designed for the Common Good of the Masses.

We shall accomplish all of this for ourselves, for our children, and for theirs.

That is our Challenge…

The AIR Model's First Challenge

"If We Do Not Have Our Health"

I have reviewed this concept with numerous people and it has been very well received.

It was the process of researching the proposal on health care for ALL Americans that caused me to initially develop the AIR concepts and model, including what is termed the de-Profitization of publicly held corporations. Therefore, the first corporate entity to be presented for review under the AIR program will be the Health Care "Insurance" Industry.

The full version of this proposal is contained in An American Agenda. However, key portions are included next with some changes to provide you with a viable frame of reference and practical example. The Health Insurance Industry is a prime example because it will experience the full impact of the AIR re-Structuring and de-Profitization process.

Other industries and businesses will do well to observe what could be their eventual fate and make appropriate voluntary changes to avoid it — rather than working behind the scenes to prevent it!

Health Care for All Americans

Insurance versus Providers

There are two (2) basic functions that comprise Health Care in ours or any other country. One is the Insurance or administrative function and the other is the Provider function.

The Health Care Insurance (HCI) function generally covers various cradle-to-grave routine medical treatment, hospitalization, rehabilitation, and long-term care needs, as well as dental, and vision care needs. HCI is an **administrative** function and has to do with enrollment, claims processing, coverage options, cost of services, making payments for services rendered, and preventing fraud.

The Health Care Provider (HCP) function is comprised of doctors, nurses, hospitals, laboratories, rehabilitation facilities, etc., those trained and charged with the proper **delivery** of health care services to the patient.

The HCI administers the dollars, while the HCP performs the work. The former is *not rocket science* while the latter is philosophically *intended* to provide a better quality of physical and mental life through *preventive* medicine, appropriately timed treatment, emergency care, and the effective and minimal use of medication. Does that sound about right?

The vast majority of people that I have spoken with over the years believe that national health care is a forgone conclusion. Their primary concerns are how much more or less will it cost me, what level of coverage would I have, what organizational form will it take, and when (how soon) will it finally happen?

Not that a national health care system is an exciting prospect to the American public, but they feel that 47-plus million of our people with little to no medical coverage is wrong and that it needs to be dealt with. And with insurance costs climbing every year and more people un-insured or less insured all the time, it is seen as a practical necessity. At least by the public!

And people want to know why isn't it done, yet?

Now let We the People take a look at resolving the National Health Care problem.

The People's Challenge is Hereby Issued to the U.S. Congress

On the behalf of my fellow Americans, I do bluntly challenge the entire 535 members of the U.S. Congress to answer the following question:

> Will the Congress once and for all provide ALL American (citizen) men, women, and children with basic cradle to grave health coverage – with the target date for said universal coverage to take effect on 1-1-2009?

Yes or No, are the only permitted answers. Even though it will most likely be done retroactively by the new congress.

It is time come clean with the American public. After all, working out this type of common public problem is exactly what the U.S. Congress was originally created and chartered to do. They are responsible for solving our common problems — issues that cannot be resolved at the local, county, city or state levels. It is their job!

And Their Final Answer Is…

If their answer is **NO**, we can all simply quit wasting public resources perpetually studying and discussing it, and move on other topics. The growing number of unfortunate Americans without health insurance coverage can just accept living without it and **stop their constant whining and complaining!**

Because obviously for a few decades now the Congress of the United States of America and whoever the president happened to be (not counting the Clintons that at least tried, but got crushed) – were and are under the absolute control of various medical and pharmaceutical industry lobbyists – obviously **do not care** about them. The lobbyists have won the war! We the People have lost.…

Face it *my fellow Americans* that **is** where we are today! The truth is still the truth even if it is being blatantly ignored. And that grim reality applies in more than one issue we will be dealing with.

However, if their answer is **YES**, and how could there be any other response if an irate American electorate really presses the issue on all the candidates during the primaries and all the way to 11-4-2008.

If so, then just what practical form could the new national HCI entity take? Let's take a look!

Health Care Insurance First

This AIR Program proposal will directly address the HCI function, only. Addressing the HCI function first is the operationally practical approach to take, and it will cause publicly beneficial changes regarding the HCP function as well – along with strong "side effects" for our old buddies in the Pharmaceutical Industry.

The HCP function could be addressed as a separate issue at some later time. For now, urgently needed operational improvements must be deliberately applied to the grossly redundant, expensive, and counter-productive administrative function that is today's HCI Industry.

As a frame of reference, a primary argument over the years has been driven by the issue of government versus privately run health care. Both are wrong. Our answer was found between the two. The fireworks begin here.

U.S. Health Insurance Group (HIG)

Finally, I offer the **fourth option** that will not only be something new in the national health care debate, but what I believe will become our "final answer".

In summary, the American business community – working in conjunction with but not directed by federal and state governments — will assume control and management of the nation's HCI system.

The existing Medical Insurance Industry (MII) corporate entities will be required to rapidly consolidate operations into a single, non-profit entity that will be administered outside of the government by a consortium made up of American business representatives.

This viable, public approach would involve the following:

- Creation of a fully, non-profit entity called the U.S. Health Insurance Group (HIG) to be operated and administered by the American business community. The HIG would not be a government agency or a stock held corporation.

- This new insurance entity's mission will be to provide the American public with a centralized and efficient HCI system.

- All existing for-profit and nonprofit health insurance companies, including divisions and/or subsidiaries of multi-insurance corporations, will be legislatively mandated to restructure and fully transfer their operations into the HIG entity.

- Since the HIG will not be a government entity, it will not involve civil service jobs. Employment in this entity would follow a private industry model.

- The creation of this entity would be a joint venture between the federal government (we the taxpayers) and American business community, including Wendy's, Ford, Starbucks, Sears, Hallmark, Wal-Mart, Home Depot, every grocery store, every other small and large business in the country, and so on – right down to you and us!

- The Provider portion (e.g., doctors, nurses, etc,) of the Medical Industry will not be legislatively addressed by this public policy.

- Existing stockholders will be bought out over a multi-year period at the stock price as of January 2008 or some prudent, not inflated share price. Selected corporate assets could be sold off (to Americans, only) to expedite the buy-out.

- Existing executives will be retired and their excess compensation packages will pass into U.S. economic history. Keeping the Congress from doing the right thing for decades has been their mission. The new management will have a new and improved publicly oriented mission.

- The new management of the HIG could be compensated with reasonable high six-figure incomes and benefits, not the multi-million dollar compensation packages executives now receive. And I assure you that there will be no shortage of qualified people seeking those positions. I'm sorry, but running an HCI company is simply not rocket science!

- The HIG will see to it that Americans will have basic cradle to grave medical coverage to be effective by January 1, 2009.

- In time all existing government operated health insurance functions, would also be systematically merged into this entity, as well.

- There would be HIG operating units in every state, major city, etc., as required to support the enrollment, claims processing, and fraud prevention. All jobs will be domestic-based and all out-sourcing will be recalled.

As a very positive "side-effect" the ever-loving Pharmaceutical industry will have only one (1) entity to deal with (just like our Canadian cousins) when negotiating the cost of prescription drugs – the HIG that works for us! That industry's long run of greed is about to end.

o   o   o   o

That's it in a nutshell folks — our long waited solution to the National Health Insurance for All Americans problem.

Granted that it might sound a bit odd at first, but it will grow on you. I will not spend anymore words explaining the overall issue here, see Part 3 for that. However, I have a comment for those that are thinking "they will never let that happen."

They have kept this and many other things a problem for us because *We* have not said, "enough already."

The Congress will begin doing what We say only IF it is said loudly and clearly enough. We do have the Right, the opportunity, and the obligation to say just that between now and 11-4-2008.

It will be our way or the highway for Congress!

o   o   o   o

7. A Historical Political Challenge for "Your" Consideration

And now for the *final answer* to our on-going problems with the dysfunctional U.S. Congress.

On Presidential Election Day 11-4-2008 – *we American citizens* will again have the Constitutional opportunity to go to polls to elect a new President and Vice President. Too bad it is not sooner!

Please consider that if we choose to, we will make this Election Day the truly historical national event it so desperately *needs* to be. We will focus on the fact that every two (2) years We the People have the opportunity to re-elect, or not, the entire 435 members of the House of Representatives, as well as 33 or 34 members of the Senate. Yes, every two (2) years. An we could forget worrying about term limits!

All 535 members of our dysfunctional Congress continue to have their jobs only because we keep voting them back into office. We the People can come together and throw some 468 of them all out of office on 11-4-2008. And, I objectively believe the country will be better off if we "just do it".

The nation, the Congress as a body, and both Parties got a minor taste of what that could feel like on 11-7-2006 when the part of the disgusted American electorate went to the polls and bounced enough long-term incumbents in both houses to give the Democrats a majority in the House and the Senate. And many of the incumbents that were re-elected had much tighter races than they were used to. Miracles can happen and that was just our warm-up!

I submit that, that Election Day was We the People, the real owners of America firing a Democratic warning shot across the figurative bow of Congress and signaling the start of the Second American Revolution. The power shift it initiated was truly a shot heard across the country and around the world. We did not even get out the big guns yet, but we'll be back!

On Congressional Probation

I say to you that We must look at the 435 members of the House and the 33 members of the Senate that will be up for re-election on 11-4-2008 as being on Congressional Probation for their jobs until that day arrives. This is a pass/fail situation for Congress, and they are currently failing.

In the interim, Congress will need to demonstrate to an even more disgusted electorate that they are legislatively worthy of retaining their cherished jobs. Many of the proposals in An American Agenda presented herein can be easily be implemented or be well on their way by that critical date. We must direct our focus and questions on the 468 members up for election in 2008, just as much as the candidates for President and Vice President.

If the Congress sees the light, decides to lead, and begins actually passing prudent legislation (despite the lobbyists) over that time period they might get to keep their jobs. It will be a hard sell. It would serve Bush II very well not to start vetoing such legislation — for it will be over-ridden. And put him on notice not to use his terribly abused legislative Signing Statement Authority to gut that legislation. Because We will be watching everything. The Congress may need to suspend the Signing Statement Authority for the remainder of his term. And the Supreme Court would need to insure the action stuck.

Further, from what I have learned it could take Congress less than 90 days to remove him (and the VP) from office – just something to be considered. All of that is of course not intended to be at all threatening — it is just the

People's Right.

o   o   o   o

That simply summarizes the technically logical sequence of political events we <u>could</u> see played out before our very eyes! This is all very serious folks. The useless games must end for the sake of our Common Good.

Please give it all some thought. Review the Grievance List again and consider how little Congress does to functionally address those serious national issues and others not listed. There will be more on this in Part 5.

o   o   o   o

Part 2
Our American Condition

Time and Reason

With the opening words of *Common Sense,* Thomas Paine addressed the American colonists acknowledging that what they were about to read was 'not in accordance' with the existing order of things. He stated that what followed was different and would not necessarily find initial favor with many of them.

Paine was writing to his fellow colonists about the National System of their day — the way that England's American colonies really worked socially, economically, and of governmentally on a day-to-day basis. He wrote with particular emphasis on the hereditary nature of the English monarchy and the aristocracy's absolute power over the masses.

After all, they were about to read about historically radical governmental and societal changes. Thomas Paine wrote to his fellow colonists regarding the acceptance of Change:

> "PERHAPS the sentiments contained in the following pages, are not yet sufficiently fashionable to procure them general favor; a long habit of not thinking a thing *wrong*, gives it the superficial appearance of being *right*, and raises at first the formidable outcry in the defense of custom. But the tumult soon subsides. Time makes more converts than reason."

Reason and the Common Good

Yes, **Time** often does make converts more than *reason* – as people often need a period of time to ponder a topic no matter how logically it is presented. **But, Reason must first be presented for consideration!**

What is critical in a true problem-solving process is that the reasoning must be developed as objectively as possible. To leave no doubt, it must be acknowledged that objectivity *always* has a frame of reference it is based upon. And in CS2 that frame of reference is the Common Good of some 300 million American citizens – no one and nothing else! That public-minded objectivity focused squarely upon the Common Good of our citizens and society *as a whole body*, has been my over-riding concern and goal in the development of what you will read herein.

o o o o

I will define the basic philosophy and primary public interest requirements that are the foundation upon which the social and economic concepts and solution-oriented proposals presented are based. We Americans have long expected that our elected leaders <u>could</u> present us with publicly-oriented approaches and clear legislation that would actually solve our common problems. That our so-called national leadership <u>could</u> finally demonstrate the personal creativity, public leadership, and their political "guts" by resolving the hard issues that confront day-to-day America. *However*, We the People are still waiting — and we have waited long enough!

The *Second Coming of Common Sense* (CS2) aggressively confronts the fact that the needs and interests of the Americans — our fellow citizens — and even those of many American businesses are being functionally ignored by that <u>elected</u> national leadership. To be crystal clear — they are ignored in favor of individuals, groups, and industries with narrow and self-serving agendas. Those being the politically and financially influential Few that acknowledge <u>no</u> responsibility for nor have a real concern about the Common Good of the people — only <u>their</u> own wants, desires, and financial benefit.

Therefore, *We the People* must once again stand together and determine to face and conquer the issues that our current national leadership, of their own free will, has decided to ignore or are collectively incapable of resolving.

o o o o

For some perspective on the words that helped the colonists to come to terms with Paine's overall challenge — that they should declare their war of independence from the British Empire, I have placed the closing words of *Common Sense* here for your review. It spoke to the colonists about finally facing and resolving their hard challenges – just as we will soon be coming to face ours.

> "These proceedings may at first appear strange and difficult; but, like all other steps which we have already passed over, will in a little time become familiar and agreeable; and, until an independance is declared, the Continent will feel itself like a man who continues putting off some unpleasant business from day to day, yet knows it must be done, hates to set about it, wishes it over, **and is continually haunted with the thoughts of its necessity.**"

> *— Thomas Paine, January 1776*

Truly, the written word at it's very finest.

o   o   o   o

You will see these words again, after we have reviewed our hard challenges laid down in CS2 and the proposals that *We the People* can decide to act upon to preserve the Common Good.

American Themes

"No apologies are owed or will be offered to any person, any group, or any nation"

Basic National Themes

To overview the basic philosophy and primary public interest requirements upon which the concepts and solution-oriented proposals that comprise the initial American Agenda were developed, four (4) underlying national themes are presented:

- America and Americans First
- Common Interest
- Civil Responsibility
- Free Will Accountability

These are important themes that speak to the common beliefs of our people and the national spirit of America. To provide for mutual understanding some background on each is presented.

o   o   o   o

America and Americans First

This is the *primary theme*. Straightforward and to the point! Again, no apologies will be offered as this core requirement is presented and driven home. It strictly means we will take any action in domestic and foreign policy to care for our country and our *citizens'* needs first and foremost.

Secondary to our citizen population, we will consider the *needs* of legal, non-citizen occupants. Going forward those individuals will be held to higher standard of conduct and civil behavior than is currently being practiced in too many cases. Or their privilege to remain in our country will be revoked and they will return to their country of origin.

Beyond those — the *wants and desires* of all other countries and their respective citizens that are currently IOs (Illegal Occupants) in our country will be of the least concern in the framing of future policy. They will be commonly viewed as a negative and preventable factor in areas such as immigration control policy, employment opportunities, and social services of all types!

To be very clear — as We the People sit down together to resolve our nation's common problems, it is a discussion and debate for and by citizens, only — any and all other party's, simply back away.

America First

This simply means that the needs of America come before the needs of any other country, whether we are addressing domestic or foreign policy matters. Our nation supported by the good will of the American public works for good purposes all over the world. However, we are all too often taken for granted and are increasingly harassed by various other parties with narrow-minded and negative views of the world. These types of situations must be "prudently and decisively dealt with" both to improve the quality of life for our nation and that of the world in general.

It must be acknowledged, not that it could be ignored, that our foreign policy in many areas has been an increasing national embarrassment and somewhat of a disaster since 2002. The American public realizes that we have been headed in the wrong direction and that we must decisively act to turn the wheel of our national voyage in a positive direction.

An America that is performing *good-works* is still the best hope for a better world.

Americans First

The needs and interests of American citizens — with absolute emphasis on the group that are citizens — will come before the needs of any other group, again whether we are talking about domestic or foreign policy matters.

As a real example of the policy corrections to be made under An American Agenda — for many years we have had various job hiring preferences such as for veterans and those with various physical and mental challenges. Those are only proper in our society and those will continue with some prudent revisions.

An Example of Near-Term (2008) Legislative Action – Citizen Hiring Preference Policy

Going forward, there will be an over-riding preference given to American citizens to be hired before **any non-citizen**. This revised national employment policy directive specifically applies to all **taxpayer funded jobs, public sector,** e.g., local, state, federal, and military positions. Foreign-born, non-citizens will find it very difficult if not impossible to obtain these jobs any longer.

The Screamers for various non-citizen groups will be out in force over this one, but enough is enough.

This prudent approach may be called whatever someone likes — We do not care! For one thing it is the only practical policy to follow in a shrinking *quality* job pool. Also, it unashamedly is taking care of our own people in filling taxpayer funded public sector jobs (with their associated job security and good benefits) just as other countries so regulate. Remember — Americans First!

Those non-citizens that have already secured such positions will continue in them. However, such public employment opportunities (privileges) will no longer be an option. And any existing laws to the contrary will be dealt with swiftly!

There will be more on this policy under the proposal entitled the U.S. Re-Employment System.

International Population Containment Responsibility

That is mouthful isn't it?

It is time for every country to adjust their domestic policy and social structures such that they will be held responsible for all of their own citizens. Bluntly this means controlling and managing their population growth! You know the concept of "planned" parenthood and responsible family sizing that is historically ignored for religious *reasons*.

To those in various religions that reject family size responsibility and/or prescribe ten (10) children per faithful family and will stand to "scream" at those statements – hear this.

> With regard to the seldom talked about concerns that the world will some day in the future become *functionally* over-populated – well, *welcome to the future*! The world has been in that not so delicate condition for some years now!

Too many countries with too many people are covertly and overtly sending their population elsewhere — often times resulting in problems in those other countries whether they were invited (as in France) or not (as in America). I am not suggesting that immigration between countries be stopped altogether, <u>BUT</u> simply common sense must finally be applied.

New international rules of civil conduct must be acknowledged and all people held accountable. In situations where cultural and religious differences are involved – the visitor will be "expected to respect" the society that they have been <u>allowed</u> to enter or they will <u>expect</u> to be deported.

> If the Masses of world desire Peace — which we do — then the Few in the world that freely disturb it must be called to Civil Responsibility. Such people and groups must be confronted and told that if they really want to live in a society which they or their parents lived in before coming to their new host country – then they will be required to pack-up and return to that place. Just go! And they will often not like what they find there.

France finds itself in that situation today. The growing Moslem population that "was invited in" years ago by the French government in oil related deals, has become a disturbance and some unruly percentage of them do not want to blend into French society. Periodic riots and the almost <u>daily</u> burning of cars cannot be considered blending in! A straightforward, no-nonsense international Civil Conduct Agreement signed by <u>all</u> nations would put such people on notice for their freewill behavior.

England is also struggling with people and groups that do not want to honor traditional English culture. And they are finally beginning to tell such people to adjust or leave!

The IOs that American society is struggling with today do in fact come from all over the world with the majority of course from Central and South America and greatest percentage from Mexico. These are blatant examples of nations dumping their excess population on other countries – Mexico on America in particular.

If a given country in 2008 has more people than it can humanely support (food, shelter, medicine, clothing, employment), but refuses for the usual political reasons to address that imbalance with their own people – *they will required to deal with it.* The catch phrase will be **"If you make them — you can keep them."** And in particular, families with large numbers of children will be required to remain in their home countries and not burden them on another.

America's useless Immigration Control Policy must take some hard turns and all the games will come to an end. The "legal" immigration rules will be publicly presented, reconciled, revised, and enforced for a change. All immigration will probably need to be frozen for several years while we conduct our upcoming national housekeeping exercise, achieve control over our own borders and a minor little thing called Homeland Security.

The U.S. Southern Fence – A Very Necessary Evil

In 2008 the U.S. Congress will act to put in place a full 2,000 mile U.S. Southern Border Fence consisting of parallel chain link fences to be complimented with razor-wire and motion sensors. It will be rapidly put in place and guarded. A no-brainer of a public works program. And the easy flow of IOs – and drugs — will be permanently interrupted.

If the Congress does not take such action in 2008 <u>and</u> immediately override potential Bush II veto, it will serve as just another justification for the electorate. And as mentioned before, the 435 members of the U.S. House of Representatives and 33 of 100 members of the U.S. Senate should not bother running for re-election in 2008! Continued Congressional in-action will produce decisive public re-action.

So how is all this sounding to you thus far? Pretty intense at times.

Common Interest

Those two words imply that the fundamental interests and needs of the American public as a united group are of the greatest importance, and will not be neglected in favor of the few among us with selfish and shortsighted agendas.

The Common Interest of **all** must be important in American Democracy, but it must have a realistic and practical balance. The Majority interests must acknowledge and consider the needs of the Minority interests whatever they may be, **while not permitting** those minority-centered interests to negatively impact the Common Good. And this balance applies to individuals and entire industries.

This is all about the real challenges of true public leadership! And we are not talking about race, gender or any of the usual suspects here!

Helping Those to Help Themselves

Our common goal will be to constantly act to help our fellow Americans at an economic and social disadvantage to progress to a higher level of living status. That means helping individuals to (and insisting they will) earn it. Our good will assistance *must* be met with their commitment to work and better themselves, because American taxpayers will no longer pay for free rides or national pity parties! Yes, I said pity parties!

It is in our national, Christian-based character to be forgiving and to help those in need. However, those with need must be willing to step up and work with the system (not work the system) to better their lives and anyone else they are responsible for!

A **stern part** of our national challenge is how We — not They — will determine to deal with the *have/have-not realities* that are fast reaching critical mass in our society. We must determine to move forward together as a maturing Democratic society and nation. Every country in the world struggles with these imbalances and most do a terrible job of it.

In case you are wondering, these points are not being written as a Liberal, they are purely American.

> We must and will commonly agree to raise the **bottom** levels of the economic food chain in America. We will practically confront the reality that a growing numbers of individuals (30-plus million) and families at the lower end of the economic system are our fellow Americans and they are struggling to simply survive. We will act to **fix** the problems.

> And at the same time we will act to reverse the destruction of the Middle Class.

The growing negative effects of a "survival of the fittest" mentality in the pursuit of false profits, and the blatant retention of wealth and political power to benefit the Few in America will be neutralized.

In the 1920's, the Few were running the country and ran it right into the ground on that dark day in 1929. It can happen again. Remember, "Those that do not learn the lessons of history are doomed to repeat it." That economic collapse required nothing less than World War II to recover the world economy.

Today, among other national and international "items" — the un-checked greed of the Oil Industry, the world Banking System on the edge of disaster, and the worldwide, self-perpetuating Military Industrial Complex that President Dwight D. Eisenhower warned the nation about 45 years ago must all be confronted, restructured, and never again allowed to use people and countries like a casual game of Risk.

And we cannot afford wait until the November 2008 election to begin the required national consciousness adjustments.

<u>Our Leadership?</u>

During the final weeks of the 2006 Congressional Election campaign both political parties "obscenely" demonstrated in front of the American public (and the world) that their *first priority* was the retention and/or attainment of **Power – for the sake of power!**

Congressional incumbents were <u>not</u> seeking re-election for the opportunity to better *serve* the Common Good of the People. Their common goal was to <u>retain</u> the Power of their position <u>and</u> party in order to preserve, protect, and defend the *dysfunctional status quo* of the National System.

Truth is Truth!

o　　o　　o　　o

The Few have been gathering wealth and political power at an accelerated rate over the past decade and during the last six years in particular. In the meantime, the Many are experiencing a decreasing quality-of-life, fewer viable employment opportunities, even less political influence, and being forced in continue living with a host of avoidable public problems.

The *First American Revolution* forever disturbed an un-interrupted evolution of dictatorial forms of government. It gave the people of all other countries a living example of people-driven government – the Many not the Few could direct a nation's voyage.

The *Second American Revolution* will renew and preserve that model of people-driven government – the Many not the Few in control. The U.S. Constitution provides us the Right to re-take that control that has been slipping away in recent times.

> Furthermore and most importantly this revolution will act to reconcile the age-old struggle between the Have and the Have-nots – the economic tyranny that <u>always</u> evolves as the financially and politically powerful Few, overtly and covertly act to make the economy of a given country serve their wants and desires before the needs of the struggling Masses.
>
> We the People will now confront the tedious and volatile issues of the day, conquer them as a united people, and once again set an

example for the world.

We will begin making national course corrections for the Common Good as soon as possible – which means starting in 2008.

Common Interest calls for each of us to actually be concerned with the Common Good of **all other** American citizens and the nation overall — and to be personally ready and willing to do what is needed to insure it.

Something as simple, yet absolutely critical to your future as making certain that you and yours are registered to vote on 11-4-2008. We the People, each by Right have that one (1) shot to fire each Election Day. Be Prepared – be *loaded to vote* for our nation's future on that day.

Civil Responsibility

An increased public awareness and acceptance of the concepts and obligations of Civil Responsibility at all levels of American society and business, is required to insure America's short and long term prospects.

Since the beginning of my research into the various social and economic issues that impact the American way of life, I have become absolutely convinced of the necessity for our society to embrace and promote the requirement for Civil Responsibility on the part of all Americans, as well as business and industry.

Further, our nation just as any other has the Sovereign Right to demand at least that same level of conduct on the part of **all non-citizens and visitors** to our shores, or they will be gone – and the criminals first.

The simple fact of the life is this – that the negative 'free will' behavior of a fractional minority among us – the people that freely decide not to act civilly responsible, does in turn cause the majority of the population – physical harm, useless expense, and other avoidable problems that directly decrease in our local and national quality-of-life.

We must promote Civil Responsibility and the prudent concern for the Common Good of our fellow Americans.

The public expectation of *Civil Responsibility* applied throughout the American National System is at the heart of the message of CS2.

That is all, short and sweet.

Free Will Accountability

Individual, free-will — what a concept!

Without intending to get biblical on you, it is accepted by most people that every person has free-will with regard to what they choose to do, or <u>not</u> do, in various situations throughout their life. Each of us has deliberate control over our personal actions.

That personal control and decision making authority applies whether someone is deciding to take a long over-due day off, or which of five (5) random people standing on a street corner to shoot — just because they feel like doing it! All of us make our choices everyday.

The free-will issue primarily comes into play with regard to proposals aimed at dealing with and <u>severely</u> decreasing criminal activity in our society. To begin with, free-will crimes such as murder, pre-mediated rape, the physical assault of minors, the smuggling of people into the country, gang activity, and hard drug trafficking and sales — **will no longer be tolerated** by the law-abiding, tax-paying American public! Are you OK with that? Those and other <u>optional</u> criminal acts will be systematically and <u>sharply</u> reduced over the next seven (7) years starting in 2008.

This is to be an American Reformation!

o   o   o   o

What is accepted as *civil* **conduct and behavior** in American society will be openly debated, publicly clarified, confirmed, and accepted by the electorate. From that point of Common Agreement everyone will know the new rules and absolute punishment in advance! Is that too much to ask? I and at least 90% of those I talk with think not!

Specifically, and with few exceptions free-will crimes involving violent physical or predatory financial assault on another person or persons will be met with extreme punishment. The Death Penalty (administered by lethal injection) with no option of a lengthy imprisonment will be fairly and effectively utilized to *reduce and deter* the vast majority of such **free will** crimes. This approach will <u>really</u> cut down on repeat offender cases, don't you think?

Anyone that is now sitting there, murmuring that the Death Penalty (DP) is not a true deterrent to free will crime, please explain why it works so well in countries where it is the rule. Is the human DNA different there?

But we are talking about our country and what is civilly acceptable and required to make life here safe for our people. Because what we have been doing for years is definitely not getting the job done!

The classic screaming Liberal against even civily prudent use of the DP, as well as those that simply make their living off the self-perpetuating, revolving door Judicial Legal Complex (my term for the Justice System), have had their way with society for decades and collectively they have failed American society.

Now it is We the People's turn.

o   o   o   o

A Look into the Our Controllable Future

I have literally had few thousand conversations with people over the last 25-plus years about public policy issues. Those two-way conversations have provided me with what I believe to be a real insight regarding the public's over-riding attitude on many issues. Everything in my political writing has been refined by the feedback varying issues received from those conversations and the passion with which people often spoke on them. The American public wants, needs, and deserves positive Change – and we are very tired of waiting for it.

Here is a stern example of what I firmly believe the American public (as well as the people of many other countries) will accept regarding how a civilized, Democratic society shall deal with certain free will criminals:

The Death Penalty Act (DPA) of 2008 – Effective on 03-01-2009

The U.S. Congress by October 1, 2008 will pass legislation to cover the following scenario:

Effective March 1, 2009 — a person walks into the store with the intent to rob it. That person has a gun or another potentially lethal weapon, and whether it was their intent to do it or not, they wind up killing one or more persons in the store.

> To be crystal clear — It will be understood that when a person possesses a weapon in the commission of a crime and a murder occurs, the murder will be considered pre-meditated.

Due to security cameras, DNA, eyewitnesses, etc., the person is identified and is <u>obviously</u> guilty – beyond a doubt. Once apprehended the person will go directly to jail with no bail opportunity. They will then will receive **"a"** single fair trial in a standard Court of Law, and will then be so convicted with no appeal process allowed because <u>again we are only talking about the obviously guilty</u> — there is <u>no</u> question of quilt – the reality in <u>well-over</u> 50% of cases.

Beyond that formal conviction a separate Grand Jury may provide prudent oversight and quick, final review in order to certify the conviction.

Subsequently the person will be sentenced to a fixed three (3) months in prison on Death Row, at the end of which they will receive the Death Penalty (DP) by lethal injection.

> Incidentally, when first discussing this option with people I used a 6-month prison term before the DP was administered. However, both men and women said why wait for six months, so I cut it to three! The public is sick of death, crime, and 'sicker' of paying for prisons.

You would be absolutely amazed if not stunned at how many people of all types and beliefs will vote for the DPA when given the opportunity. In this and other programs you would also be surprised to know that Liberals approve of it as well, proving that even Liberals have their limits!

<u>And Two More For Now</u>

The DPA will also be applied to <u>pre-meditated</u> rape. Every woman I asked about that option simply nodded or said "yes". This will be reviewed more later, but "date rape" situations would not be included here since there are too may gray areas. However, the pre-meditated, predatory acts of this kind will be met with extreme and expedient justice.

Further, in the discussions on the application of the DPA on perpetrators of free will murder and pre-meditated rape, people and not just parents, began *telling me* to add "pedophile crimes" to the list. And so it is there.

Therefore, pre-meditated murder, rape, and pedophile crimes will initiate the DPA implementation by 2009. If we demand it!

We the People are fed-up! Those that challenge these rules shall lose..

Financial Assault

Under the heading of Financial Assault we could soon be adding the free will predatory crimes of *identity theft* and schemes aimed at swindling innocent people out of their wealth to the list. We will have order.

o o o o

More on these matters under An American Agenda, but for a few moments please consider the Plain Truth fact that we have excessive, redundant crimes in this country because the existing Criminal Justice System allows it to continue! Someone once described the Criminal Justice System as an unproductive industry.

This portion of the *status quo* within our National System shall be changed for the sake of the Common Good. It will absolutely result in people being saved from death and assault everyday.

"I" — Could Just Scream!

The ever-growing Criminal Justice industry, again that I have labeled the Judicial Legal Complex (JLC) – consisting of all levels of the courts, the lawyers, various Liberal groups, and the "almighty law" have not succeeded in making our neighborhoods safe — did you notice I do not include police officers in that grouping.

The statistically verifiable, grim result of the JLC's efforts is just the opposite and the resulting public condition will no longer be tolerated or paid for by our tax dollars.

We the People, by Common Agreement will determine to effectively crush such criminal behavior in America. We will no longer continue to allow such acts by our own citizens, and will be extremely less tolerant of any such behavior on the part of non-citizens, and IOs in particular.

Frankly, every time I hear or read about career opportunities for people in the "growing field" of criminal justice — or — advertisements referring to professional criminals (e.g., car thieves), it makes **me** want to *scream*!

We the People will act to reel in the JLC over the next seven (7) years to truly clean-up our streets and decrease the demand for law schools. Again, what a concept!

Our people will see this coming and quickly realize they need to find other more positive fields such as math, energy, science, environment, and engineering to make their way. Our nation requires that domestic brain trust to be grown to insure America's future as a world leader.

And Consider This

The DPA legislation in conjunction with other American Agenda programs such as the U.S. Re-Employment System, and a restarted Selective Service (Draft) System will facilitate our nation's absolutely attainable goal to virtually eliminate criminal gang activities no later than 12-31-2014, the unofficial end date of our 7-year Second and Final American Revolution.

We can and we will make these things happen.

And we will never need to build another prison!

o   o   o   o

Our National Themes are Just More Common Sense

If you generally agree with the hard, but practical rationale behind those National Themes and the civil codes they speak to, then it is easy to appreciate that the overwhelming number of your fellow Americans are of the same mind.

Thus for the sake of our nation and its positive destiny we must acknowledge the existence of such Common Agreements among the vast majority of our 300 million fellow citizens. In essence, those four (4) basic Themes form the very foundation of America's "publicly acceptable" future — the cornerstones of our much needed National Vision. And frankly, they represent the real manner in which the vast majority of We the People already live our lives.

A real National Vision of our country's "potential" future runs through the remainder of this book and is for you to ponder in your private moments.

Be encouraged, my fellow Americans. We the People have the collective Power and the Constitutional Right to demand and have any such civilly responsible changes implemented. We only need to Stand United!

o   o   o   o

**"Some people see things as they are and say why.
I dream things that never were and say why not?"**

— Robert F. Kennedy

<u>We the People Are in This Together</u>

"Like it or Not"

It has been said that you should always aim to identify with your audience whether speaking or writing, in order to deliver a message of interest and value to them. Know your audience!

In this case, I not only needed to have a good sense of what is important to my audience, but the audience truly needs to have some sense of each other as well. Thus, the reason for this piece is to provide you with some mutual awareness of each other. They are — you are – the 209-plus million or so Americans of voting age 18 and older, and all with their own interests and points-of-view. It is therefore common sense that,

> ***the only way to address and hopefully to connect
> with such a diverse group,
> is to address their "common interests…"***

Of Common Interest

To intentionally be repetitive, it simply must be <u>America</u> <u>first</u> — all other nations and their problems being at the very most secondary. To me this defines bone-marrow level American patriotism, and absolute concern for our great country. I am not talking about isolationist or protectionist policies at all, so if you are going down that distracting thought path I say – STOP right there!

In simple reality, America <u>in</u> <u>conjunction</u> <u>with</u> other peace loving countries will be required to lead if this planet is going to be fit place to live in the near and distant future. And it must be acknowledged that we will need to lead far better than we have in these recent years — and in areas both foreign and domestic.

Common Interest also implies that the concepts and proposals presented are focused upon the needs of American "citizens" be they native born or naturalized, which means taking care of our national family. It is the concern for the Common Good of Americans, first and foremost — the natural and sovereign right of every country of earth.

The interests of any "legal occupants and visitors" are important, but are considered as secondary in all aspects. All IOs are a far distant third, and they will be dealt with herein. While America is "the" classic melting pot society of world history, there are practical limits to immigration flow and those limits have been grossly exceeded by an unchecked flow (by our elected officials) of IOs from all over the world.

Again, we need to remind the world and Mexico in particular, that the sign at the base of the Statue of Liberty does not read,

> **"Send me your excess population that you do not wish to support or do not care to deal with"**
> **— or —**
> **"Please send everyone!"**

That is not at all intended to be funny. It is just the Plain Truth. We are a very compassionate people and nation, but we do have our limits and they have long since been violated! Most likely freezing all U.S. immigration for a few years starting in 2008 will be part of the necessary course of action — more on that later.

o   o   o   o

The U.S. Census — The American Population

"Two is the minimum definition of We the People"

An American Profile

The following will provide some common perspectives on the American population and the electorate using statistics from the somewhat aged U.S. Year 2000 Census. These are the population numbers that most of us hear about, but rarely have the occasion to review. Two (2) population tables are presented next that provide some practical frame of reference on where you are in the Big Picture.

The first chart recaps the U.S. Year 2000 Census. It lists yearly totals for "Resident" males and females that were living when the 2000 census was taken. According to the census, the American population had reached 281,421,906 people in that year.

Of that total, some 209,279,149 were age eighteen (18) and above in 2000, meaning that would be the maximum count of potential voters in national, state, county, and various local elections. However, I said, that is maximum "potential" number of voters which today is greater than the number of citizens that are currently "permitted by law" to vote in federal elections!

More on that nasty little issue a bit later when we review the Federal Reform proposals.

After reviewing the U.S. Census Bureau's official qualifiers on the 2000 Census numbers my conclusion is that the totals are "mainly" comprised of citizens, but cannot be considered an absolute count of them.
Within the Census, undoubtedly some citizens were missed and some non-citizens were counted. Whatever the case, it is the set of numbers I determined to use to represent the count of American citizens.

That qualification may seem a little excessive, but I am very concerned about the objectivity and reliability of any numbers that I quote to you, never wanting anyone to feel that the data is slanted in any manner. You are probably familiar with the expression,

"There are lies, damn lies, and then there are statistics"

— *Mark Twain*

The American Population Management (APM) proposal presented herein will in time provide us with the first up-to-the-minute statistics on all the inhabitants of our country – ever!

A key component of APM is a complete national registration of all persons (legal and not) within the 50 states and DC. This program will become an on-going and key component of life in America. We will each have a National Identification Number (NIN). It will be displayed on our National Identification Card (NIC) that will contain among other things our photograph — and fingerprints which cannot be forged.

For the minority among us that are now freaking out about the implementation of a true biometric National Id Card simply realize that you are just that – the minority. And your past *screams* and those covertly, negative forces that do not want such a practical tool of a civil society to be implemented will now be silent – the People's work must be done.

o   o   o   o

Imagine that if we already had this practical national facility (as most developed and many under-developed countries already do) in place when Katrina hit the Gulf Coast, by comparison how simple it could have been for people to find each other! They could for example, go to a local police station anywhere in the country and have their NIC scanned or if they had lost it while fleeing the storm, just have their fingerprints scanned, and easily been re-united with family. Not rocket science.

The nation would have had a very reliable way to identify those that had perished and those still missing, which we factually will never know about that natural disaster. It would have helped us to efficiently deliver urgent services to those in need, reduced confusion, and helped to prevent the massive fraud that occurred.

The NIC facility needs to be in place to help our people in such future events and for many other practical reasons. This new and unique Citizen Id will allow us to straighten out many other social programs by giving us a central control point to manage our nation's population inventory (and tax dollars). Again, many other nations have effectively utilized a similar facility for decades.

> Seriously consider the Plain Truth that we have been attempting to manage our nation's inhabitant inventory — citizen and not without a part number! It is no wonder that our national people inventory is out of control.

> Also accept the harsh reality that there are various groups of good and bad intent that very much want it to remain that way. This dysfunctional condition has mostly been perpetuated by those that directly benefit from the confusion — and they will continue to work hard behind the scenes to keep it *that way*! So when someone stands up and starts *screaming Big Brother*, just politely ignore them! It will soon pass.

U.S. Year 2000 Census by Birth Year

A note regarding the birth counts for years 2001 thru 2008:

I did a simple projection of male and female birth rates for years 2001 through 2008, meaning the numbers are not exact, but do provide a viable perspective. As you can see, I rolled the numbers forward using the same counts from the year 2000.

Technically, the 2000 census accounted for **281,421,906** people, and with the charted projections through 2008 the grand total would be some **311,866,946** citizens. However, I did not reduce the yearly counts based upon mortality rates or increase them by the number of new naturalized U.S. citizens sworn in over those years. That explained, herein I determined to reference the total number of U.S. citizens to be **300,000,000** – a good round number.

Coincidentally, in late October 2006 it was announced that the U.S. population had officially passed the 300 million citizen mark!

You can scan the yearly chart and locate yourself and family members. It is OK to write in the book!

U.S. Year 2000 Census by Birth Year

Age as of Year 2008	Birth Year	Number of Males	Number of Females	Total Population
2000 Census		138,053,563	143,368,343	281,421,906
Under 1 yr	2008*	1,949,000	1,856,630	3,805,630
1	2007*	1,949,000	1,856,630	3,805,630
2	2006*	1,949,000	1,856,630	3,805,630
3	2005*	1,949,000	1,856,630	3,805,630
4	2004*	1,949,000	1,856,630	3,805,630
5	2003*	1,949,000	1,856,630	3,805,630
6	2002*	1,949,000	1,856,630	3,805,630
7	2001*	1,949,000	1,856,630	3,805,630
8	2000	1,949,017	1,856,631	3,805,648
9	1999	1,953,105	1,867,477	3,820,582
10	1998	1,938,990	1,851,456	3,790,446
11	1997	1,958,963	1,873,836	3,832,799
12	1996	2,010,658	1,915,665	3,926,323
13	1995	2,031,072	1,934,031	3,965,103
14	1994	2,058,217	1,961,488	4,019,705
15	1993	2,109,868	2,008,279	4,118,147
16	1992	2,137,829	2,041,401	4,179,230
17	1991	2,186,291	2,081,029	4,267,320
18	1990	2,191,244	2,082,812	4,274,056
19	1989	2,108,157	2,006,936	4,115,093
20	1988	2,087,228	1,988,614	4,075,842
21	1987	2,054,008	1,956,842	4,010,850
22	1986	2,079,560	1,972,671	4,052,231
23	1985	2,065,127	1,954,277	4,019,404
24	1984	2,048,582	1,926,439	3,975,021
25	1983	2,091,280	1,954,732	4,046,012
26	1982	2,078,853	1,972,745	4,051,598
27	1981	2,107,162	2,020,693	4,127,855

Age as of Year 2008	Birth Year	Number of Males	Number of Females	Total Population
28	1980	2,071,220	1,978,228	4,049,448
29	1979	1,965,673	1,875,409	3,841,082
30	1978	1,921,549	1,837,099	3,758,648
31	1977	1,875,400	1,798,182	3,673,582
32	1976	1,853,972	1,787,269	3,641,241
33	1975	1,905,899	1,838,640	3,744,539
34	1974	1,832,383	1,787,277	3,619,660
35	1973	1,914,947	1,874,853	3,789,800
36	1972	2,010,807	1,974,005	3,984,812
37	1971	2,134,724	2,107,801	4,242,525
38	1970	2,174,238	2,115,732	4,289,970
39	1969	2,019,782	1,991,793	4,011,575
40	1968	2,008,877	1,985,244	3,994,121
41	1967	2,018,017	2,008,556	4,026,573
42	1966	2,100,855	2,087,294	4,188,149
43	1965	2,265,621	2,250,497	4,516,118
44	1964	2,247,529	2,263,639	4,511,168
45	1963	2,250,122	2,266,938	4,517,060
46	1962	2,268,083	2,285,731	4,553,814
47	1961	2,287,341	2,321,163	4,608,504
48	1960	2,352,606	2,358,828	4,711,434
49	1959	2,213,034	2,253,642	4,466,676
50	1958	2,256,543	2,290,677	4,547,220
51	1957	2,178,451	2,229,419	4,407,870
52	1956	2,128,468	2,180,195	4,308,663
53	1955	2,151,115	2,190,345	4,341,460
54	1954	2,009,570	2,077,993	4,087,563
55	1953	1,976,128	2,043,564	4,019,692
56	1952	1,909,672	1,975,473	3,885,145
57	1951	1,843,021	1,915,523	3,758,544
58	1950	1,871,638	1,936,877	3,808,515
59	1949	1,769,463	1,847,534	3,616,997
60	1948	1,815,785	1,891,651	3,707,436
61	1947	1,778,423	1,856,617	3,635,040
62	1946	1,372,415	1,445,145	2,817,560
63	1945	1,386,859	1,463,741	2,850,600
64	1944	1,375,187	1,462,265	2,837,452
65	1943	1,384,196	1,479,824	2,864,020
66	1942	1,222,709	1,317,443	2,540,152

Age as of Year 2008	Birth Year	Number of Males	Number of Females	Total Population
67	1941	1,139,778	1,237,235	2,377,013
68	1940	1,111,560	1,208,384	2,319,944
69	1939	1,061,679	1,159,548	2,221,227
70	1938	1,033,865	1,137,207	2,171,072
71	1937	971,203	1,081,948	2,053,151
72	1936	958,320	1,081,733	2,040,053
73	1935	950,651	1,079,260	2,029,911
74	1934	864,156	996,164	1,860,320
75	1933	874,079	1,022,372	1,896,451
76	1932	856,145	1,008,370	1,864,515
77	1931	855,331	1,027,017	1,882,348
78	1930	844,517	1,030,658	1,875,175
79	1929	798,517	989,752	1,788,269
80	1928	791,164	1,000,532	1,791,696
81	1927	751,433	973,735	1,725,168
82	1926	717,281	959,852	1,677,133
83	1925	695,865	955,776	1,651,641
84	1924	647,773	908,794	1,556,567
85	1923	599,742	861,039	1,460,781
86	1922	579,368	852,548	1,431,916
87	1921	521,708	793,200	1,314,908
88	1920	467,013	740,352	1,207,365
89	1919	406,546	665,502	1,072,048
90	1918	364,815	616,747	981,562
91	1917	317,289	565,774	883,063
92	1916	279,234	522,095	801,329
93	1915	244,874	485,320	730,194
94	1914	204,981	430,173	635,154
95	1913	173,520	383,810	557,330
96	1912	139,395	326,086	465,481
97	1911	113,731	287,928	401,659
98	1910	89,678	238,226	327,904
99	1909	68,980	197,406	266,386
100	1908	54,437	163,780	218,217
101	1907	39,693	129,373	169,066
102	1906	29,537	101,421	130,958
103	1905	21,097	76,998	98,095
104	1904	14,704	57,976	72,680

Age as of Year 2008	Birth Year	Number of Males	Number of Females	Total Population
105	1903	10,308	42,536	52,844
106	1902	6,804	29,199	36,003
107	1901	5,202	21,960	27,162
108 & over	1900	10,057	40,397	50,454
Totals		**153,645,563**	**158,221,383**	**311,866,946**

Some interesting numbers to look at. Personally I used to think that the Baby Boom was a population bubble that was moving through the US economy. As you can see the birth rate went up after 1946 and pretty much stayed in that range. It is functionally like a tsunami!

U.S. Year 2000 Census by Generational Group (GG)

A Practical Generational View

This second chart summarizes and categorizes the yearly counts above. It groups the citizen population into sixteen (16) year increments. The sixteen (16) year block is based on a common definition of the famous post-World War II, American Baby Boomer Generation from 1947 through 1962.

You and I, and every other U.S. citizen are in there someplace. My birth year is 1948 making me a second year, leading edge Baby Boomer and proud of it! According to the Generational Groupings, the Boomers are designated as GG4.

Generational Group					
Birth Year Range	**Age in the Year 2008**	**Number of Years**	**Number of Males**	**Number of Females**	**Total Population**
Group GG7					
1995 to 2008	0 to 13	14	27,433,805	26,152,136	53,585,941
Group GG6					
1979 to 1994	14 to 29	16	33,440,299	31,782,595	65,222,894

Generational Group Birth Year Range	Age in the Year 2008	Number of Years	Number of Males	Number of Females	Total Population
Group GG5 1963 to 1978	30 to 45	16	32,534,722	31,974,819	64,509,541
Group GG4 1947 to 1962	46 to 61	16	32,809,341	33,655,232	66,464,573
Group GG3 1931 to 1946	62 to 77	16	17,418,133	19,207,656	36,625,789
Group GG2 1915 to 1930	78 to 93	16	9,027,139	12,921,676	21,948,815
Group GG1 188x to 1914	94 & over*	25+	982,124	2,527,269	3,509,393
Totals			**153,645,563**	**158,221,383**	**311,866,946**

* Note: Ages 94 and over were combined into one group. That was due to the far lower number of people at the highest ages.

I believe the Generational Group breakouts will provide readers with a useful frame of reference, especially when considering the unique interests and issues of the citizens in each age range.

Further, the more recent a person's Generational Group, the greater the interest they *should have* in these contents and the solutions proposed — only because they will be living the longest with the results of this crucial national problem solving process. Whatever problems are or are not properly resolved.

o   o   o   o

The Most Concerned – Will you be 18 to 29 Years Old This Year?

To restate, although Americans of all ages will have something to gain and lose in the actual response to the proposals under discussion, the most recent two groups representing the youngest of our people should find them of particular concern and common interest!

Generational Group 6 – ages 14 to 29

This group contains the year 2008 age range of 18 to 29, or about 48 million voting age young Americans – representing the youth of the Silent Majority.

They have within their **potential** voting power-base the ability, if not the definite necessity to demonstrate their displeasure with today's status quo. They can Demand that prudent changes be made and help Drive the process to improve conditions in America for both the short and long-term. To be clear, long-term means well *beyond* the 30 day, 90 day, and one-year budget cycle mentality of bureaucratic and corporate America.

Consider that with GG4 (18 to 29) on one end, GG6 (46 to 61) on the other, and GG5 (30 to 45) working in the middle — Change could not be prevented if we all decided to work together and make it happen!

Generational Group 7 – ages 0 to 13

This innocent group of our youngest Americans is solely dependent upon their now living parents, grandparents, and great grandparents to take care of this national business for their sake. This is the Group that has the absolute most to gain by our actions and of course the most to lose by our inaction. They are young and not aware of how messed up things are right now. We are Responsible for them.

And A Challenge to the Political Science Community

I do hereby make a personal and professional challenge to Political Science professionals, applicable academicians and institutions of higher learning, including community colleges, state universities, and the wide range of public and private — colleges and universities.

Do you have the latitude to consider altering your prepared course material to discuss the concepts and proposals presented herein? You and those who work with or instruct, need to actively participate in this most significant public debate.

To state it very plainly, your students and their generation have the most to gain or lose in "future America" and that is why it is beyond critical that they are objectively informed on today's issues and encouraged to help identify, validate, and implement solutions to society's issues and problems starting now! Therefore, please strive to get your students interested and involved in their future — today!

In so doing, <u>you</u> will not be studying political history — you will be helping to <u>write</u> it…

Reconciling Our Minority and Majority Interests

"To the Greatest Extent Possible"

We the People – must determine to realistically acknowledge and then prudently address our most sensitive public issues — those that require common understanding, compromise, and constructive Change in order for us to move ahead as a Democratic society — a long overdue national group therapy exercise.

Some of those that reviewed parts of the draft were concerned that these topics were too sensitive to discuss, suggesting that it should either be softly delivered or not included it all. However, my intent here is not to deliver a feel good message and/or ignore addressing major problems – the 535 members of the U.S. Congress have obviously written that into their job description!

We the People need to read these contents, consider them privately, and then begin to <u>discuss</u> the issues <u>with</u> <u>each</u> <u>other</u>. Not argue! Those informal discussions will produce a shared <u>community</u> understanding <u>and</u> perspective on real issues – I did not say acceptance — that is needed to promote an atmosphere of compassion and cooperation, as well as individual and national maturity.

o   o   o   o

In *Common Sense*, Paine wrote on the Origin and Design of government. The first paragraphs are presented here – I **bolded** part of it, but the capitalizations are <u>all</u> Mr. Paine's. Consider their situation and then ours. Then ponder the rude examples of tyrannical governments around the globe that are causing trouble *today* within their country and in others using religious differences (sometimes within their own religion) to excuse or cover their true agendas and public failures. From *Common Sense*,

> Some writers have so confounded society with government, as to leave little or no distinction between them; whereas they are not only different, but have different origins. **Society** is produced by our wants, and **government** by our wickedness; the former promotes our POSITIVELY by uniting our affections, the latter NEGATIVELY by restraining our vices. **The one encourages intercourse, the other creates distinctions. The first a patron, the last a punisher.**

> Society in every state is a blessing, but government even in its best

state is but a necessary evil; in its worst state an intolerable one; for when we suffer, or are exposed to the same miseries BY A GOVERNMENT, which we might expect in a country WITHOUT GOVERNMENT, our calamity is heightened by reflecting that we furnish the means by which we suffer. Government, like dress, is the badge of lost innocence; the palaces of kings are built on the ruins of the bowers of paradise. For were the impulses of conscience clear, uniform, and irresistibly obeyed, man would need no other lawgiver; but that not being the case, he finds it necessary to surrender up a part of his property to furnish means for the protection of the rest; and this he is induced to do by the same prudence which in every other case advises him out of two evils to choose the least. WHEREFORE, security being the true design and end of government, it unanswerably follows, that whatever FORM thereof appears most likely to ensure it to us, with the least expense and greatest benefit, is preferable to all others.

Imagine what Thomas Paine could have written and communicated to the world with MS/Word, Adobe Acrobat, and the Internet!

o   o   o   o

All for One While We Consider

As we the citizens of the United States of America come together to deal with what is *our moment in time*, the Change process will be best served if we approach the national reconciliation only as Americans, and not as one or more of the following:

Baptist
Buddhist
Catholic
Charismatic
Christian
Conservative
Democrat
Evangelical
Fundamentalist
Green
Hindu
Independent
Jew
Liberal

Lutheran
Methodist
Moderate
Mormon
Moslem – Shiite and Sunni
Native American
Native-born American
Naturalized American
Non-Believer
Non-Voter (until next time)
Presbyterian
Protestant
Republican
Zealots of Any Kind!

Prejudice is not something anyone is born with. It is learned perception and behavior.

In advance I must clarify with all sincerity, if you find yourself thinking what follows is sounding at all prejudicial, PLEASE, **just let it go.** Because you would be reading it wrong, for that is absolutely not my intent or that of the message presented in CS2. At the same time I will bluntly acknowledge that the words attempting to properly frame and summarize such *worldwide realities* cannot please everyone, and will be very 'biting' on some ears — and it needs to be! Again, I do not write about Fantasyland.

Because remember, just like love, sometimes the truth really hurts…

And, frankly be a bit thankful you are not trying to write this piece yourself …

o   o   o   o

The Public Policy Challenge

If a new or proposed change to an existing public program is of sufficient benefit to the "majority" of Americans, it must properly *consider* the "minority" of us, as well. However, the opposite must also apply. Any policies and programs designed for the Few among us must also consider the Common Good of the Many. It is a matter of practical and humane balance in public policy.

For some decades social and economic programs have sought to provide greater access and opportunity for various minority groups within our country. Regardless of where you stand on those social programs, they <u>have</u> succeeded in giving more of <u>our</u> citizens "opportunities" in education, employment, and material wealth than they would have had if the *National System* had not been realistically Changed over the years to address such social and economic imbalances. Key areas include:

- The American-Black minority
- The Female majority
- The Physically Challenged

Not that many other countries have done (or even tried to do) what we as an open, Democratic society have accomplished in the last 50 years – since 1958. Think about it.

There are those among us that believe too much has been done in those and other areas and those that believe that too little has done. Neither of those fortunately small groups of citizens will ever be satisfied, and we simply will not waste anymore of our precious time and resources trying to respond to their whining.

This book is all about restructuring the National System to the benefit of the Common Good of <u>all</u> American citizens.

<u>Speaking of Ethnic Politics</u>

For some perspective, here is a high-level ethnic profile of American citizens. The numbers are somewhat aged numbers, but are informative:

American-Asians	10,000,000
American-Blacks	36,000,000
American-Caucasians	196,000,000
American-Latinos	37,000,000
American-Natives	3,000,000
American-Others	<u>3,000,000</u>
	285,000,000

Source: U.S. Census Bureau, Statistical Abstract of the United States 2002

Socially responsible legislation at the federal and state levels resulted in the deliberate mixing or integration of not just American-Blacks, but other American minorities as well with the American-White majority — a bold, yet socially appropriate adjustment for a maturing nation.

I intentionally keep repeating American this or that, because that is what We are. Whether native born or a naturalized citizen, we are all members of the best national club that there is – we are Americans!

I challenge the various _____-American groups to start either calling themselves American-_____ or just simply Americans – what a concept!

We can no longer *tolerate or $upport* such self-serving and too often negative labels. In recent years some of these groups have fostered more separatism than unity and for strictly self-serving reasons. They are missing the point. The IRS non-profit/tax-exempt status of some public groups needs to be reviewed and in some cases be revoked.

There is a very, fine line between censorship and Freedom of Speech and we must be first protective of our citizen's Rights. I said our <u>citizen's</u> Rights <u>not</u> those of visitors.

Further, We the People will no longer be concerned about the Political Correctness (PC) of calling such entities to task for the counter-productive disturbance some have become. They represent other forms of national pity parties that We the People *in order to maintain a more perfect union,* shall no longer condone.

Again, while there can be a fine line between defending the Common Good and suppressing valid decent, the difference can be easily distinguished. Public dissent is our Civil Right and Civil Responsibility, however, individuals and organizations that promote anger, hatred, and separatism will not be tolerated.

<u>In Warning</u>

Further, and specifically those visitors that are here from other countries and use our open society to breed and/or promote agendas that are contrary to the political and religious freedoms that are the core values of the American ideal will find themselves deported along with their families!

Anyone that was not born here is only (legally) standing on our soil because we have permitted it. That permission can and will be revoked, including Permanent Resident Alien status, naturalized citizenship, and border-baby (also called anchor) citizenship status! They will leave their generational hatreds and social problems of their home society behind them and not attempt to perpetuate them on our shores.

Our common American ancestors left the traditionally, degenerate social conditions of the Old World Order behind to escape the political and religion-based abuses it heaped upon the masses for thousands of years. We will not allow it come here and breed even though in recent years it is certainly trying to do just that.

Is that clear enough?

Only the mandated public exposure to other groups of people in the school and work environments over these past decades has "facilitated" various groups within our society to slowly become more comfortable with each other, and thankfully more tolerant, as well. The Baby Boomer generation was the first to begin shedding the racism (White toward Black, and Black toward White) that our parent's and prior generations grew up observing as normal social conduct.

Again, it must be acknowledged that while the day-to-day relations between American-Whites and American-Blacks has greatly improved over the 40-plus years there are and will always be individuals in both groups that continue to have issues! *Prejudice* in its various frames of reference is unfortunately present all over the world — all nations face this issue in some form. They just come in different flavors.

> I will share a scenario that I personally know to have taken place only a few years ago. An American-Black teacher once commented to two American-White high school students in a casual non-confrontational conversation that 'African-Americans were not capable of being prejudiced – only Whites could be prejudiced against African-Americans.'

> They were floored, but did argue the point with her. How does her narrow and simply prejudiced view of the world strike you? That from an educated person and teacher — and we wonder why there are problems? And I have been shocked to hear comments come out of American-Whites that I would have expected better of. Fortunately, the numbers of people still clinging to such attitudes is itself a shrinking minority.

One of my personal little sayings is that, "people will always be the greatest form of entertainment that there is. The problem is that it is not always good entertainment."

ALL 300 Million

Yes, all 300 million of us possess some personal awareness of prejudices even if they are small and <u>never</u> touch another person. It is simply a part of being <u>human</u>. That's you, me, and <u>everybody</u> else, do not kid yourself otherwise, but that does not make it right! Sometimes it is an instinctive reaction that comes to your mind, but each person can learn not to allow those negative impulses to be part of their personality or daily consciousness. It is for each person to develop the civil and human habit of treating all people with the same respect and decency that they desire to be shown.

That is what my Mother and Sunday school taught me to do.

It is the simple concept that is common in all religions and decent communities – the practice of *doing unto others as you would have them do unto you.*

o   o   o   o

The point is that along with the Liberties we expect as citizens, we also have an unwritten individual obligation to be socially responsible and understanding toward our fellow citizens no matter what they look like or what they believe. This is after all what America is all about!

A Reality Check

Let us realistically and honestly acknowledge than unlike many of the other issues that the proposals in the American Agenda will be able to resolve, the complete reconciliation of ethnic, social class, and political influence can never be fully realized.

Perfect ethnic and financial balance cannot be attained (it is even hard to define what that would look like). Not in an open Democracy such as ours, under Chinese capitalism, and certainly not under military dictatorships, pseudo-Democracies or in the various religious monarchies (e.g., Iran) that are causing so many problems in the world today.

The good news is that the Second American Revolution has the real potential to transform the often talked about Old World Order into a real New World Order that is actually worthy of such a grand title. We Americans over the next seven (7) years have it within our power and in our Common Interest to demand such Changes and see them happen before our very eyes.

We only need to decide that today's Status Quo will not be "allowed" to be tomorrow's. Remember it is our destiny we are determining.

o   o   o   o

Again, prejudice of one group toward another group based upon race, national origin, religion, tribe, wealth – **whatever** — is a reality in **every** country on the face of the earth whether they want to admit or not. And most do not. Over the years America has voluntarily done more to accomplish national maturity in those areas than any other nation. And that is a big reason why the "true" leadership of other countries acts in opposition to us. We make them and their national social policies look bad – because they are. They live to serve the Few at the expense of the Many.

o   o   o   o

These are certainly very sensitive areas and difficult points to address, but they must be openly and objectively reviewed. Over the last number of decades various public groups in America have wanted, if not demanded special treatment due to some abuse they and/or their predecessors had to endure.

In the minds of many Americans — including those within the very same ethnic groups, there is a growing sentiment that these "pity parties" have gotten old, dysfunctional, and are somewhat embarrassing. Some well-known and very-respected people such as Bill Cosby have been moved in years passed to speak out against the conduct and attitudes of members of their respective group and have come under attack for just speaking the Plain Truth. The Screamers will go after anybody, even their own people.

And I mean "getting old" and downright <u>boring</u> to continually hear members of our various groups continually asking for special treatment, especially when it is due to injustices that occurred to those that left this earth many years in the past.

Where We All Came From

Factually, if you go back far enough in history, you will see that <u>all</u> of our pre-America ancestors were severely oppressed by someone, at some point. And many were oppressed more than once by those inside, not just outside of their own country!

Many of those groups were treated very poorly when they first immigrated to this country (the Irish for example, and God love them). But they worked and learned and like the other groups, <u>blended into</u> American society thus enriching themselves, their families, and the country. They did not come here to be a _____-American. They desired to be an American – period! And that is what we will <u>demand</u> of people going forward, or they are missing the point and do <u>not</u> need to be here. Is that plain enough?

Most ethnic and religious group members came to colonial America fleeing terrible conditions and/or following the hope that it offered. My father's family left England for the colonies in the late 1600's; my mother's family (the Neely's) left Ireland to come here in the early 1700's – which was well before America became America. And you can bet they did not leave the Old World behind, as did so many others that came here in those primitive years, and sail across that dangerous ocean because their lives were a Tea Party back home. It was not.

The ancestors of today's American-Blacks were taken (with the direct involvement of <u>and</u> benefit to people in <u>power</u> in their native countries) by force from their lands and brought to these shores. Even that community that by far has had the most difficult struggle for social and economic equality in America has attained the opportunity for common status within American society. That practical observation will make some people of both sides of that issue groan.

That is exactly what I'm talking about. We all need to acknowledge our differences of opinion on issues such as this – about social and economic equality, in particular. This is precisely what our Second American Revolution is all about. We must finally start to see all Americans simply as Americans. The men, women, and children that comprise the 300 million American citizens, must accept that we are all on this national voyage together. We must encourage each other, help each other when <u>needed</u>, and expect if not demand the same level of civil consideration on the part of every citizen.

The bottom-line is that **going forward,** American society should not care about how someone's ancestors were treated, how their parents treated them, how the community treated them, etc., because that is called **life**! For every person that blames their bad circumstances, inappropriate or even criminal behavior on such factors, there are <u>far</u> more people of an identical or worse backgrounds that are good and responsible citizens. Again, the *pity parties* are very old, boring, and frankly we do not care to hear about nor can we afford then anymore.

The practical point is this — <u>All</u> original members of the groups that today comprise American society, those that preceded us faced hard conditions, but *persisted*. Their struggles and eventual success in overcoming their challenges created a place for their descendants at the table in the greatest country in the world. And how many of us would want to go through what our ancestors did or even to live in the countries they left behind? Think about that. Obviously, we see people still trying to get out of some of those countries, today!

It is time for all groups in this country, and each of us individually, to take responsibility for where we are in the great circle of life in America — even though we may not want to take that responsibility. It is always easier to blame things on society or somebody else, rather than our own lack of personal motivation.

We will best honor their hard struggles and sacrifices by working together to build a better America for all of our people to live and prosper in.

To Preserve, Protect, and Defend the Common Good of All of our Citizens.

o   o   o   o

It is Who They Distrust

Taking on a Global Perspective

The People of a given country do not fear and/or distrust the People of other nations.

However, they can feel that way about the Political Leadership of other nations, and too often with good cause.

This realistic perspective simply declares that the Few are not representing the Common Dreams and Desires of the Many.

The fruitless actions of the Few that causes intrigue, distrust, and too often war, versus an attainable world condition of trust, cooperation, and Peace.

That is the world's regrettable situation today,
And it is being made worse as opposed to better
Because the Few maintain the Power over the Masses,
by the perpetuation of needless hatreds and fears!

And that Old World Order tradition could be Replaced...

We Make Them Look Bad

The reason why the living example of America's open Democracy attracts such distain from certain governments and certain influential people in the world's troubled countries with their failed societies, is that we make them look bad! They especially do not like that some of their young desire to leave for America or another "freer" society.

At times such dysfunctional, foreign leadership acts to blame the poor and often oppressive conditions in their countries on us. This is a bad joke on their people! It is pure domestic propaganda to distract their people away from those really in power that are responsible for the continued hard conditions that exist there — the *real* political, religious, and economic leadership of their own country. The devious, negative, self-serving power brokers that are the dictators, monarchs, and the real religious "leadership" behind pseudo-elected national leaders such as exist today in Iran and Iraq. Internal chaos is preferred over order.

At the same time you can look around the world and find places where there is a <u>peaceful</u> blending of ethnic groups, as well as differences within a given religion.

For example, Shiite and Sunni Moslems live and worship in peace in our country. They work together and can even socialize if they so desire. This is because here they are <u>not</u> under the watchful eye and control of authority hungry, dominating, and civilly irresponsible religious "leaders" (clerics) telling them to hate and/or to blow each other up! That *in a nutshell* is what is going on in Iraq right now! Again, this is not rocket science — just the freewill, calculated manipulation of the masses by way of religion to sustain political power and control — nothing more.

And it has nothing to do with God.

o   o   o   o

Forget about full-blown Democracy. Just a simple *outbreak of Peace* would stun the Middle East populations and transform those Old World Order societies. However, this is not permitted to happen by the true political leadership! And it is all very transparent. For a moment look at the sad status quo in Iraq, Iran, Israel with her nasty playmates, and others – as if you knew nothing of their history. Freely analyzed all of those political situations have the same roots.

It always comes down to influence, ownership, power, and control – *over* — people, business, and property. That is the heart and soul — the Dark Side of the *Old World Order*.

My perspective on Iran's current leader with a name that is too long, is that he is a classic example of a presidential puppet. The real powers in Iran, are often seen standing behind him in cleric robes. Simply put, if they had not approved of him he would not be in power in the first place, and if he did not serve the clerics every dictate, he would simply be removed (*dead or alive*). And he knows it.

That pretty-well sums up the governing mentalities of the Old World Order societies – again the Few that the rest of the world is struggling to deal with today. And is a current day example of why our ancestors got the h__ out of there when they could!

America's Social Progress

Over the last 50 years, America has taken tremendous steps in social maturity. Again, just think of what it was like in 1957. Think of the laws and social conditions that did and did not exist at that time — the economic and social prejudices on the parts of **all** groups – racial, ethnic, gender, physically challenged, etc. Yes, <u>all</u> groups have prejudices — there are no exceptions or exemptions. It would be prudent to consider how many countries (e.g., in the Middle East and Africa) that have made <u>zero</u> or negative progress over those same 50 years! And how many of those same countries are a problem for the world <u>and</u> their own people today?

However, to America's credit and as an undeniable example to the people of the world, of the power of Democracy, we <u>have</u> struggled through some of our national problems, matured as a free society, and are the better nation for it. And there are two basic factors that made it all possible.

The first is the underlying character of the nation that is rooted in the non-denominational, Christian-based core beliefs and values of our fore-bearers. It was the basic American compassion for the struggles of others, which motivated some regular citizens to lead the fights to secure equal Rights, treatment, and opportunities for them. They worked diligently to make civilly responsible Changes to the National System — they succeeded and our nation was improved.

The second, being our beloved national charter — the U.S. Constitution, providing the vehicle by which the National System could legislatively be Changed to correct bad policy and open doors to more of our fellow Americans. And, usually, without firing a shot!

o   o   o   o

The Interests of Citizens and Other Legal Occupants (OLOs)

The proposal on American Population Management that addresses Immigration Control follows shortly, but I fell it worth emphasizing a few points here. In CS2 the interests of the 37-plus million American-Latino <u>citizens</u> (2002 Census numbers above) are considered and protected the same as any citizen group, since they indeed <u>are</u> our fellow American citizens – plain and simple.

Some thoughts from my conversations with American-Latinos include:

- They are both irritated and embarrassed over the whole illegal flow of Latino IOs into America giving them a bad image with other Americans. And the situation has only worsened considerably in the Bush II years.

- They are rightfully concerned that people may think of them as being an IO just because they appear to be Latino.
- They know that IOs from (non-Latino) countries all over the world are also here, but are unfairly flying low, under the pubic radar because they just blend in easier and frankly there are fewer of them.
- They know that not all Latinos can move to America and they do not want them to!
- The hard reality is that many Latinos came to this country partly to escape the less than desirable fellow citizens of their native country. And frankly as more of the *lower forms* of humanity from those countries enter our country illegally and insert themselves in American-Latino communities the quality of life in those neighborhoods (and the nation) is degraded.
- The increasing numbers of IOs with their lesser values, paranoid attitudes, and criminal habits help to re-enforce the very culture the legal immigrants came here to get away from.

Therefore, it must not be assumed that all American-Latinos, as well as the OLOs from many other countries around the world, are supportive of the constant illegal immigration by their former countrymen.

The unchecked (by our Congress) invasion America has been enduring from all parts of the world must be stopped and reversed until we have our national house in order. It will take us several years to accomplish that national housekeeping, but then it took much longer to get it in this condition.

Logically speaking, we cannot complete that required housekeeping until sometime after it finally begins?

The hard bottom line is that the political advantage the IO invasion "has enjoyed" with both Republicans and Democrats in the halls of the U.S. Congress must come to an abrupt end in 2008. **The "Bush Open Door to All Illegal Immigrants" policy — must be cancelled by Congress, and ASAP.**

Congress knew well enough the last week in June 2007 to drop the amnesty-type Immigration Bill, even when Bush II tried one more half-hearted run at it. They are smart enough to know that passing such a bill would end their time in office! And it probably will not see the light of day until 2009!!!!!

Cynically, and for the Silent and Disgusted Majority I must observe that all of the rhetoric that has been spit-out on the Immigration Bill in 2007 has accomplished nothing. Face it sports fans, this is exactly what the Status Quo lovers wanted — to have Congress <u>do</u> <u>nothing</u>. They have won yet another victory. Mexico happily keeps shoving people and drugs right up and across the border. The IOs keep coming and American society continues to degrade.

o   o   o   o

<u>Not a Great Wall – A Practical Fence</u>

The well-lobbied U.S. Congress and Bush administration have studied and worked so very, very hard to conceive of and approve building a highway sound-barrier type wall "in sections" that are a combined 700 miles in length (the sum of all its parts <u>IF</u> it gets built) across a 2,000 mile border. They have literally delivered us a <u>less</u> than half-as___, <u>non</u>-solution!

We will demand that they begin building a real Southern Border Fence in 2008 and it will be <u>2,000</u> <u>miles</u> <u>long</u>. It will be constructed of parallel chain link fences topped with razor wire.

The entire IO problem that has slowly worsened since Congress' last "amnesty" legislation in 1986 — is a classic example of what is wrong in the relationship between the American public, business interests, and the Common Good. The U.S. Congress must be harshly reminded that it is supposed to be the defender of the *We the People* – NOT — They the Illegal!

And they expect to keep their jobs...

Those points cannot be re-enforced enough. The historic fabric of American society is at direct risk. These are bone-marrow issues we are reviewing.

o   o   o   o

Our National Challenges

As Thomas Paine started the fourth paragraph of Common Sense,

> *"The cause of America is in great measure the cause of all mankind."*

A true statement then, and with regard to America's role to the world it is even more so today. Therefore, considering some of the deteriorating conditions in our nation and parts of the world today, whatever We the People determine to do (or not to do) over the next seven (7) years is just as critical as at the time of our nation's birth.

And considering that our destiny is currently <u>not</u> under our control it is fair to say it is even more important...

For Them Only One – For Us So Many

It was not simple. It was simply magnificent. The American colonists struggle against the oppressive, powerful, and self-serving British Empire to secure their new nation's independence and to control their own destiny.

And it was not easy.

In January of 1776, Thomas Paine published the radical revolutionary pamphlet, *Common Sense*. In that magnificent, radical document that was so critical to igniting their revolution, Paine challenged the English colonists of the thirteen American colonies to come together and make a "declaration of independence" as a *united people* -- to boldly and historically take control in determining the form and substance of their common future.

The American colonists our national ancestors mainly comprised of farmers and craftsmen bravely stood up and answered the challenge of their time! To repeat, there were less than 3 million colonists at the time of the Revolution and some 25,000 of them <u>died</u> in that multi-year armed struggle.

We cannot complain about the comparatively minor personal sacrifices that we <u>will</u> be facing as the status quo of today is confronted and constructive national Change is made to happen. And I do not refer to our people dying and wounded in Iraq, Afghanistan, and the other places they are serving around the world <u>right now</u>.

Each of us will be required to assume some amount of short-term, non-physical sacrifice(s) in our coming legislative struggle that will Change the National System and in the end determine the nation's future — for the Common Good.

> Indeed, *We the People*, are already enduring such individual and common discomforts or this entire presentation is complete nonsense – purely, foolish rambling. But, it is not and we all know it!

> I don't know about you, but I am beyond being tired of *We the People* being treated by our elected and the non-elected national leadership like ***powerless peasants***. Are you?

The Plain Truth is that we are being viewed and so considered — and under the current National System's Power structure we functionally are just that! Haven't you had enough of that status quo?

Our national ancestors took the bold and sometimes physically sacrificial actions required to benefit their families, their neighbors, and their fellow colonists, and **after years** of actual warfare they became the first Americans. Those *Chosen Few* were the very first people to feel the Freedom, the Liberty, and the absolute Blessings of being an American.

Today, you and I – We the People of all 50 states, and DC, are challenged to take action for the Common Good of all those that are now American citizens. While we will not need to resort to physical warfare to resolve the national issues presented herein, it will prove to be an absolutely historical test of our desire for a Common Vision — the united resolve to force positive Change to actually happen. And happen rapidly!

It will be a policy and legislative war presided over by our U.S. Constitution. The contest will directly determine who will really be in control of America now and for "as long as we all shall live." We already live in the greatest nation the world has ever known. Our blunt challenge is to *do whatever it takes* to keep it that way!

We have our Democracy and our beloved Constitution that allows America to mature and self-correct our society's course as we sail on our national voyage. Once again it is time for us to come together, to unite in Common Purpose, and put steadier hands upon our ship's wheel, because we have been led off our desirable and prudent course.

We only need to get back to some of the basic values, common responsibilities, and shared principles that made America a great nation to start with. We the People need to clarify the basic set of civil responsibilities and expectations of our citizens and our society. We must be absolutely firm in calling those to task that do not honor those Common Responsibilities, and in so doing, we will declare our resolve to make America's destiny one that will serve the Common Good of us all.

Should, after open public debate the proposals presented are found to be commonly acceptable to the vast majority of the People – and I do solemnly believe that acceptance will be the end result — We have it within our Power and our Rights to Demand that our elected officials implement them.

And to do it now!

It is our time to take action, to lead our leaders, and as a result reaffirm American Democracy as the model for the world, of the ultimate system of government — a free and open society built upon the basic principle that every man, woman, and child **matters**. That we are all indeed created equal in the eyes of God and each other.

As 230 years of U.S. history demonstrate, once We the People come together to confront <u>any</u> situation foreign or domestic that threatens our national well-being, and <u>agree</u> that the approach declared to resolve it is fair and prudent for the Common Good — We can do and accomplish <u>anything</u>.

The Challenge

Our national challenge and the binding, national reconciliation we are about to engage in today is far more complicated a struggle than they faced in 1776.

We are now challenged to take American Democracy to the next level of maturity.

We are now challenged to fairly and <u>forcefully</u> resolve our internal issues to make America all it needs to be for itself and the world.

We are now challenged to acknowledge the ongoing, avoidable, international foolishness that has caused the world to become *a far worse place* over the last several decades rather than the better place it should be — and that we will now determine to make it.

America needs to honestly admit our role in some of that international foolishness — to call other nations and their <u>real</u> leadership to task for their irresponsibility toward the Common Good of <u>their</u> own people and others as well.

WE THE PEOPLE, will begin to do these Right things because WE have the power, the ability, the Privilege, and the National Obligation to do whatever needs to be done. The people of so many other nations do not have our U.S. Constitution and a national history of actually correcting wrongs in our National System that are in the Common Interest of the Masses.

o o o o

It has been said that, *"Those to whom much is has been given, much is expected."*

It has also been said that, *"We do these things not because they are Easy, but because they are Hard."*

We the People can and will do these hard things because we are Americans!

And while I am challenging all Americans to answer this call, I am speaking to my fellow Baby-Boomers in particular — for it is now our watch.

Therefore, just as our national ancestors did when they stood and struggled together, won their war, and created our nation,

**We Americans must now stand together,
to take the actions that will Define and Insure
our nation's proper Destiny,
and make our children proud of us...**

o o o o

Part 3
An American Agenda
for 2008 and Beyond

A "Purely" American Citizen Based Agenda

*"No apologies are owed or will be offered to any person,
any group, or any nation"*

Introduction

Simply stated, what is required at this juncture in our nation's history is a National Agenda that is devoid of biased party politics freed from self-serving special interest influences.And that is a revolutionary concept!

My sincere goal and patriotic intent is for these contents to be read by my fellow Americans and then to be seriously debated by individuals and groups in every town in our nation. Further, to present a publicly acceptable National Vision with a straightforward strategy designed to get the nation moving aggressively in that direction. A Common Vision and a strategy that we Americans can agree to, embrace, and begin to see enacted – and that means starting in 2008!

The analytical challenge is to make such a practical and logical case that the majority of the electorate will be personally motivated to endorse most if not all of the concepts and proposals presented. To earn the public's acceptance of *An American Agenda* that will aggressively address and correct many existing national problems and will bring into focus an attainable Vision of our nation's future.

Bold statements, but frankly — do you see anyone else especially our elected leadership with all the resources and expertise at their disposal, even attempting to do something constructive about the Big Picture? Including the 18 announced Presidential candidates (as of 7-4-07). Serious, long-standing problems will now be confronted and resolved — rather than being ignored or studied and re-studied forever – and never being resolved.

The initial set of solution-oriented approaches and proposals presented in CS2 are more than adequate to define and begin the deliberate restructuring of our National System for the Common Good of our citizens and to declare our Second and Final American Revolution (2AR).

o   o   o   o

Proposals for the Common Good

"For We the People to prevail, everything must be on the table"

"Often Times the Hardest Things to Do – Are the Right Things to Do"

Our Aggressive and Nationally Practical Baseline Agenda

I have been researching and considering various social and economic reform issues for many years and will not burden you with many of the details of that history herein. I will repeat that the actual public problem that first caught my curiosity and initiated this entire experience some 25 years ago was the national War on Drugs. Everything that is found in this book has evolved from that personal decision to research, analyze, and attempt to develop a viable and publicly acceptable solution to that complex national problem.

Many of the CS2 proposals really began to come together in 2003. I believe they combine to offer a group of workable approaches that pro-actively address key public issues with the Common Good of American citizens and therefore the day-to-day quality of life in America as the driving requirements.

The American Agenda proposals vary in purpose and complexity. Several are only a few pages of public policy concept, but will make the necessary points on the purpose to be served by that proposal area. Most offer concept and working detail on what is being proposed. There will be no questions about the intent of each.

Some of the kind folks that reviewed drafts said they had to re-read some parts in order to really understand what was presented. Not that it was hard, but these are issues that most of us do not normally take the time to consider. I know I did not before beginning the process years ago. Proposal topics range from:

- putting the highly effective, non-aerobic exercise program – Pilates — in all public schools (K-12) for the health and physical conditioning of our children,

- explaining why so many kids and adults cannot learn, presenting how to <u>correct</u> the problems, and also putting that solution in all public schools and other places as well,
- re-establishing the Selective Service Draft to save our younger adults and other viable public purposes,
- making pre-meditated murder, and rape, and pedophile offenses subject to immediate Death Penalty punishment,
- creating a unique National Citizen Identification system and registering all American citizens and Other Legal Occupants (OLOs) – the 2010 US Census started early and made far more productive,
- rapid construction of the 2000 mile Southern Border fence to deter both IO and drug flow,
- the repatriation of the majority of IOs from <u>all</u> over the world,
- the full legalization, decriminalization, and medical availability of marijuana,
- winning the War on Drugs and the public control of hard drugs,
- and the admittedly radical, yet absolutely required restructuring of certain industries, such as:
  - o Medical Insurance
  - o Pharmaceuticals
  - o Tobacco
  - o Oil
  - o Banking
  - o Defense – the Military Industrial Complex

The objective is that the shared public understanding and general acceptance of this set of problem-solving proposals will cause the start of our virtual Second and Final American Revolution.

Further, that the public's overwhelming reaction to CS2 (for and against) would actually *save us all* from experiencing the dreaded, predictable, boring, irritating, insulting, and un-productive coming performance in the 2008 Presidential and Congressional campaigns — which have began too early. *To turn those campaigns upside-down*, because nothing less is required between now and 11-4-2008.

We would then observe Real political campaigns made up of hard problem-solving debates and where some of the fixes actually begin implementation <u>during</u> the 2008 campaign. Not another year-plus of mindless, fruitless, political propaganda and BS — with a final 60 days of talking about how "lousy" the other candidate is and nothing of substance being addressed at all.

The Congressional and White House candidates will not be allowed to dance around real problems this time or ever again. We the People, have had enough of that and our nation cannot afford it anymore. Nevermore!

Our Agenda Proposal Groupings

I have grouped the initial set of 27 proposals into four (4) functional categories starting at the Federal level, which are:

- Federal Reform Programs
- National Programs
- Local Community Programs
- Industry Restructuring

A few proposals are light in delivery and content, while others are very thought-provoking, contain multiple programs, and are upsetting to the status quo! The purpose of these is to facilitate the sharing of <u>real</u> background and perspective in order to promote <u>common</u> <u>understanding</u> (I did not say nor could anyone expect total acceptance) on issues of importance to American <u>citizens</u>. You will be the judge. You are who I am writing to.

Federal Reform Programs

1   Presidential and U.S. Representative Term Amendments
2   Voting Day Reform – Access to the Polls
3   Eligible Voter Reform
4   Real Campaign Finance Reform

National Programs

5   American Population Management (APM)
6   English as First and Only Language
7   The U.S. Re-Employment System
8   National Drug Reform (Controlling the Hard Drug Industry)
9   Re-Considering the Military Draft – Saving Our Youth
10   Zero Tolerance for Free-Will Crime by All People
11   The Family Support Administration
12   Family Basic Asset Protection
13   American Owned Business Preference Policy

Local Community Programs

14   Local Pride and Accountability
15   Education – The "Final Answer" for Many Students <u>and</u> Adults
16   Physical Fitness for Our Children

Not what could be called a light or a complete listing, but we had to start somewhere and if this set does not do the trick — We are in Big Trouble!

An American Agenda is offered presented as nothing less than a top-down American Citizen Platform for the 2008 Presidential and US Congressional campaign.

o o o o

In Our Beginning

Our national ancestors, the American colonists came to a radical conclusion regarding their desired national vision and on a viable strategy to take them there. Although, the changes that we must face today are considerable and will touch each one of us, they actually pale in comparison to the historic challenge they boldly took on and were victorious over. Their revolution was fought with muskets, bayonets, cannon, and blood. Our revolution will be won by way of *individuals voting*, domestic legislation, strict enforcement of new and existing laws, and rational international treaties.

It will be the Pen rather than the Sword, but not necessarily without the threat of the sword in some specific cases. And do not doubt for an instant the absolute intensity of the struggle that will be engaged when these proposals are openly and seriously considered by the American electorate for implementation.

To borrow a phrase (currently being used in a religious context), the first American Revolution was the common people – the American colonists exercising *"Intelligent Design"* against the status quo – the tyranny of the Old World Order. In doing so our American Democracy was created and America was born as a free nation. They acted together to remove an oppressive form of government that had always been the natural order of things and in doing so created the first government designed to serve the Common Good of the People – the Masses and not the self-serving Few.

We are now challenged, to execute an *"Intelligent Re-design"* operation – to dictate a series of prudent adjustments to our National System designed to preserve the Common Good of today's Masses – our citizens and the nation. The self-serving Few will lose the power and control over that National System (and us) that they are increasingly abusing — and as a result the often talked about New World Order – designed to serve the Common Good of the Masses will finally begin to materialize and start its relentless spread across this struggling planet.

Have no doubt. We the People hold the future in our united hands!

o   o   o   o

This time instead of less than 3 million colonists, we have Common Interest of some 300 million citizens to join in the contest.

This time We will not be changing our form of government for it is still finest in the world. Rather, We will be calling our elected leadership to task for their consistent failure to serve the Will and Common Good of the people. For not doing the job the Congress and every White House administration are elected by the People to do.

We will make known our common demands and the specific issues to be addressed by Congress and to be acted upon before the 2008 election. We will not allow anymore "do nothing" Congresses (and Administrations) regardless of which party is in control of the House, Senate, and White House.

Currently the two parties only seek retention of Power and Control to maintain the dysfunctional status quo of today's American National System. It is hard to argue with that observation.

We <u>will</u> demand real Solutions and observable Progress, as well as deliberate and steady movement toward a little mentioned state of affairs called, *Peace* — on both the domestic and foreign fronts. What a concept...

o   o   o   o

We the People, are now being tested in an increasingly uncomfortable struggle between the Masses and "they" the politically influential Few and certain industries — over the Common Good of the American society. The colonist's war was a physical war. Our war is a philosophical and intellectual confrontation that will be settled legislatively under the umbrella of the American people's ultimate protector – the ***U.S. Constitution***.

In the Constitution's revolutionary predecessor, the ***Declaration of Independence***, the Thomas Jefferson laid down these words regarding the <u>people's</u> <u>responsibility</u> to <u>watch-over</u> their government and to take action when needed to maintain proper <u>control</u> <u>over</u> their <u>society</u>:

> *That to secure these rights, Governments are instituted among Men, deriving their just powers from the consent of the governed.*
>
> *That whenever any Form of Government becomes destructive of these ends, **it is the Right of the People to alter** or to abolish it, and to institute new Government, laying its foundation on such principles and organizing its powers in such form, as to them shall seem most likely to effect their Safety and Happiness.*
>
> *Prudence, indeed, will dictate that Governments long established should not be changed for light and transient causes; and accordingly all experience hath shown, that mankind are more disposed to suffer, while evils are sufferable, than to right themselves by abolishing the forms to which they are accustomed.*
>
> *But when a long train of abuses and usurpations, pursuing invariably the same Object, evinces a design to reduce them under absolute Despotism, it is their right, it is their duty, to throw off such Government, and to provide new Guards for their future security.*

(Amen)

Herein we will <u>not</u> be talking about the "throwing off" of our government, but will be bluntly calling the <u>current</u> U.S. Congress and White House to task for their growing disregard for the fate of the Masses.

We the People, will be causing a publicly viable shift *to alter* the true Balance of Power in day-to-day America – where all of us really live.

One versus Many

I would point out that in 1776 Thomas Paine presented the entire argument for a "declaration of independence" and his narrative on the Origin and Design of Representative Government to the American colonists in a 46-page paperback size pamphlet. While I would never minimize his monumental task it is fair to point out that Paine in his writing to his fellow American colonists "only" had one overall problem to deal with in order to straighten out their National System problems. His *Common Sense* proposal to solve their common problem was "just" a revolutionary war of independence against the British Empire!

Some 230 years later I am writing to my fellow American citizens about an 'incomplete collection' of public problems and their prudent solutions that will allow us to conquer major issues we have within our National System. This national struggle will require *more common sense* on our parts to conduct prudent legislative combat operations against "ourselves" to achieve victory! We will be facing a national reconciliation that could be as difficult and uncomfortable as when our national ancestors struggled for their national independence.

Many of the American Agenda proposals could not be fully detailed in 46 pages each. However, my goal in each is to provide sufficient data and crystal-clear direction to *begin* the national debate.

The American Press – those that the Founders appointed as watchdogs of our freedom — along with the Internet will provide all the details needed and much more.

o   o   o   o

My analytical intent with CS2 is to provide you with objective perspectives on serious issues and common sense approaches to actually address them. With the shared awareness of the perspectives presented in An American Agenda, my prayer is that it will cause of us all to start moving toward an agreeable National Vision.

Realistically, most of us do not like to deal with politics let alone dig into it, and if our elected leadership were *actually doing* the job (for us!) we would not need to bother with this! However, they are not — so we must in order to first control and then to preserve the Common Good of the nation for <u>our</u> people.

So please take of your time to read and consider these Agenda contents that have been sincerely prepared for your information and encouragement, and our mutual, national understanding.

Again, please pardon the varying detail in these proposals, but my baseline goals and intent are achieved to have each of these meaningful issues raised and considered by you and us! There will undoubtedly be vast amounts of information on these and other topics (pro and con) over the months leading up to the historic 11-4-08 US Presidential and Congressional Election Day.

On the Bar of Civil Responsibility

"First it will be Stabilized and then it will be Raised"

Regarding Social Programs and Change

It took the American Civil War, another hundred years, and the U.S. Constitution for us to come to terms with one of our major national imbalances. The People addressed a problem created by those in power in prior generations.

The time has come when various special interest leaders must acknowledge that true progress that has been made in recent decades driven by new laws and changing individual and public attitudes. Practical progress made by *individuals* within each of these groups that have stood up, worked with the system, and moved ahead.

We must all acknowledge that there are those in every group, American-Whites included, that will sit and wait for whatever special treatment or handout they can get. And, after receiving it they may well sit and wait for more. The Clinton administration to their credit made it harder for people to keep playing the system. There are successful and unsuccessful people within all groups that make up America today. And the successful of these groups are found at all levels of society and business, as well.

America was not founded or originally populated by people who could not or would not pull their own weight. They worked or they died. Some worked very hard, but still perished. We have a segment in our society which again crosses all groups, that expects for one reason or another that the System, our tax dollars, owes them something. They say and/or feel that, "I have had a hard life, and the System owes it to me." I have had people look me in the eye and say that!

Well, enough is enough, and as I like to say, "When you finally reach the point where you want to yell that you have had enough of something — you really mean you have had **too much** of it!"

o   o   o   o

Therefore, instead of continuing to lower the bar as we have been in the habit of doing in recent decades in too many areas within the National System, we must raise the bar of Civil Responsibility and to increase Civil Expectation – for every person and every business! We must be prepared and willing to help those that need help in working to improve their personal and family situation – and to build "domestic" businesses, as well.

However, at the same time *We the People* will be prepared and very determined to publicly <u>kick</u> those that need it! No more free rides and no more pity parties! No more self-serving, publicly irresponsible lobbying that in the end is destroying the Common Good.

The concept of increased Civil Responsibility in public policy development is extremely important if we are to <u>not</u> <u>only</u> continue to progress as a nation and mature positively as an open society, but even to exist as the America that we desire and expect to live in.

The stakes have never been higher and that is the Plain Truth.

o   o   o   o

<u>The ACLU is Hereby Challenged for the Common Good</u>

The American Civil Liberties Union (ACLU) — if ever there was an institution that Americans have a love/hate relationship with – this is the one.

The ACLU is hereby challenged to <u>assist</u> in the prudent review and implementation of many parts of the American Agenda, including items such as the critical National Citizen Registration process — <u>rather</u> than trying to <u>fight</u> them with legalistic, academic, and philosophical rationales.

Understand that we are <u>not</u> asking for their approval, because it is not their country to define — it is <u>ours</u>! We want, if not expect their national network to be **pro-active** in support of that grand, national housekeeping exercise, and other proposals as well. It would be to their organization's great credit to support such efforts.

Need I point out to the ACLU that the "A" does not stand for American – it does not stand for illegal and/or irresponsible!

You never know, but in due time their public interest organization could come to be known as,

> The American Civil Liberties and Responsibilities Union – the ACLRU!

It is a question of prudent balance and the challenge is made. Peace…

o   o   o   o

We the People, in order to maintain a more perfect union,

must reach a common, national agreement on what it is that America truly stands for. Americans are a strong and caring people blessed by God with free will, as well as having been provided with our US Constitution by the Founders. Therefore, once We as a united people resolve how the National System should be changed to serve the Common Good, we can and will attend to making it so!

The current national election cycle leading up to 11-4-08 **must be approached** as a major decision point in our nation's history, because like it or not — that is precisely what it is!

Some hard and sensitive public issues that have been functionally ignored for years, if not decades cannot be allowed to drift any longer. Herein we will review viable solutions to several of these hard problem areas. More issues and their practical resolutions will be developed in the future.

These solution-oriented proposals aggressively attack the hard issues and will raise many eyebrows, and I pray will begin the very loud public debate that the American electorate desires, deserves, and has too long been waiting to have. CS2 is not a feel good book – even to those that will embrace what it presents for review. Serious change at this level cannot be easy. *The agony* often requires a bit more agony to be experienced in order to finally realize *the ecstasy*. That summarizes what the American colonists experienced leading up to and through their Revolution. However, in the end they had free a nation, a people-driven Democracy, and became the first American citizens.

America today must have a realistic framework for our Social and Economic systems – the National System — which We the People will commonly understand, embrace, support, realize in the <u>near</u> term, and accept as the viable path to our desired national destiny.

I am what you would call a realistic optimist, but an optimist for certain otherwise I would not have kept pursuing this personal project when the negative thoughts, magnitude of the issues, and as life's events came to discourage the effort. You just have to suck it up, keep pressing forward, and <u>never quit</u>! Again, there is just too much at stake.

I without question believe that we Americans can and shall re-take control of our nation's ship of state. We will begin in 2008 to make the necessary changes — the right changes for the Common Good of us all.

o   o   o   o

Think of an 11-year old Child that You Know

As you read and are considering the Agenda proposals I ask that you occasionally think of an 11-year-old child that you know. It could your child or grandchild, a niece or nephew, or the child of a friend.

Then consider our Second American Revolution as a seven (7) year struggle that will begin to yield real results starting in 2008 — if We take action now.

To quietly ponder how the proposed social and economic changes (or lack thereof) could play out and re-shape the world by the year 2014, when that child is 18 years old, graduating from high school, and heading out into the world to further their education and/or to enter the workforce — because right now that is not a pleasant picture. And it is far worse for today's inner-city 11-year olds!

In too many cases an 11-year old child living in the inner cities of America must contend with far harsher day-to-day conditions and must confront hard situations and choices. The proposed social and economic changes presented will be true life-saver for many today's inner city children and spare the parents much grief. To be clear, we must solemnly acknowledge as a nation that every American child counts. Because they do!

Our American Challenge Circa 2008

Future Americans will look back at this time — our moment in time — and grade us on our response to this challenge. And the children are watching us today.

The National Vision will become clear — a vision purely *Of Common Interest* of all American citizens. So let the lively and sure to be intense debate over that desirable National Vision for the Common Good of *all* Americans — begin. The rest will be the history that We the People will write over the next seven years — for better or for worse — in what could be our Second and Final American Revolution!

As We the People sit down together
to resolve America's common problems,
it is a discussion and debate for citizens, only.
Any and all others simply back away.

Our over-riding national policy priority
that must define all of these proposals is simply,

America and Americans First

o   o   o   o

Fortunately for us The Founders, and all those that have struggled, and fought, and died (and those that are unfortunately dying this very day) — created our government, provided us our Constitution, and have preserved it over all these years.

And so, it is now time for *Us the People* to stand together and against the forces that are not honoring all those sacrifices, the spirit of America, and the Intent of the Founders.

The existing Status Quo of our National System is not what our society now requires in order to Preserve the Common Good of *all* of our citizens or to finally resolve our long-standing national issues.

Therefore, We the People, have a lot of work to do!

o   o   o   o

And now for An American Agenda

1. Federal Reform Programs

Introduction

The Federal Reform Proposal grouping within An American Agenda addresses legislation and policies having to do with what could be considered to be administrative and management issues within our Democratic system of government. The proposals included for your consideration are:

1   Presidential and U.S. Representative Term Amendments
2   Voting Day Reform – Access to the Polls
3   Eligible Voter Reform
4   Real Campaign Finance Reform

o   o   o   o

1   Presidential and U.S. Representative Term Amendments

Issue/Problem

This Federal proposal addresses two changes regarding terms of office of the President and Vice President of the United States and the 435 members of the US House of Representatives. This proposal does not seek to alter the existing term of office of the 100 members of the US Senate.

These changes will require two (2) amendments to the US Constitution. However, they are very straightforward and should move through Congress and the required ratification by individual state legislatures swiftly. The new terms of office that the 27th and 28th Amendments to the U.S. Constitution shall authorize, will require the term changes to be enacted retroactively in 2009, for those elected to office in the November 2008 National Election.

Why are such changes required? Simply stated all election campaigns have steadily starting earlier and thus are longer in duration, are outrageously expensive, and have resulted in decreasing productivity at the highest legislative level of our government – the US Congress. It is no surprise that as of July 2006, the Congress greater disapproval rating than Bush II. It is like worse and worser!

We will no longer permit nor can we afford this irresponsible and counterproductive cycle to continue. Therefore, We the People will direct the Congress to make the appropriate Constitutional changes to address the problems.

The People's Sense

The President of the United States' Term of Office – Effective January 2009

The President (and VP implied) is currently allowed to serve up to two (2) consecutive terms in office of four (4) years each. Under the 27th Amendment to the US Constitution the President's term of office would be changed to a single six (6) year term. This change has received nearly unanimous support in my talks with people.

This prudent Constitutional change, will not only slow the unproductive flow of presidential campaign politics it will also make the American national political process more efficient, in general. The President would know that he or she did not have to worry about re-election and could concentrate on doing the nation's business for the vast majority of the 6 year term. The single term approach works very well at the state Governor level.

The nation would no longer need to suffer through the year-plus Presidential re-election campaigns. Not to mention the November 2008 campaign for President with a total of 18 declared candidates a full 18 months ahead of the election. So much wasted time. The 2008 presidential election is the best time to implement such a change since a new President will be elected.

The 27th Amendment is so simple and straightforward that the Congress will have an extremely difficult time confusing the issue or attempting to justify delaying its implementation. And we will be watching!

The U.S. House of Representatives' Term of Office – Effective January 2009

The US House members currently serve an "unlimited" number of two (2) year terms, as long as they can continue being reelected. The Founders did not intend for "national politician" to become a career, but that is the least of our worries.

Under the 28th Amendment to the Constitution the US House of Representatives' term of office will be changed to four (4) year terms and would remain unlimited in number, as long as they may keep being re-elected.

We will continue the practice of having all 435 members being up for re-election at once. The Senate is structured such that one third of the 100 members are up for re-election every two (2) years (i.e., 33 in 2008, 34 in

2010, 33 in 2012, and so on. There is no <u>viable</u> reason to bother staggering the House election in such a manner.

If *and probably* the Congress suggests "studying" that option, WE will tell the Congress not to go there. Since it would only offered as a politically motivated <u>delaying</u> tactic and would conveniently take them <u>years</u> of study to figure out. Sort of like how "term limits" has been studied and dropped! No games will be tolerated with this.

This more efficient House term change will yield positive results for the legislative process in Congress. Currently the US House members spend entirely too much of their short 2year term fund-raising millions of dollars to run for re-election and not nearly enough time taking care of the people's business. The fundraising distraction will be reduced allowing them more time under the Capital Dome – where they belong.

The 28th Amendment is also straight-forward and we will not tolerate legislative delay in its passage by Congress or the required state-level ratifications.

o   o   o   o

Both of these amendments to our U.S. Constitution will be highly effective. The exact wording will not need to be much more complicated than what you have just read. This legislation will move quickly through the US Congress, as well as the required ratification by the states to be effective for the terms starting in 2009. The people of every state can let their state legislators know of their approval and to just get it done!

It will be very interesting to observe how Congress plays with these two prudent and practical changes. To guard against legislative gamesmanship these Amendments will be so written as to take effect retro-actively with the 2009 terms even if proper ratification by the states is not completed until after the 2008 election, which it most likely will not.

That's it, short and sweet, and very beneficial to the proper functioning of <u>our</u> Democracy.

o   o   o   o

Think of these as We the People's <u>first</u> public *problem solutions*. These are two common sense proposals that <u>every</u> potential candidate for national office in 2008 would be required to clearly state their position upon. These are our first steps in changing the Status Quo of the today's dysfunctional

National System. It will be two for our side – the first legislative battles and victories in our Second and Final American Revolution.

2   Voting Day Reform – Access to the Polls

"Making it far easier for the We the People to Vote"

Issue/Problem

This Federal proposal addresses long-standing and quite avoidable proce-dural issues regarding our national level elections. These Democratically practical changes could rapidly "trickle down" to state, county, and local level elections, as well. The issues here boil down to date and time!

The first issue is the date-scheduling of the Presidential elections (e.g., 2008, 2014!), as well as the off-year Congressional elections (e.g., 2010, 2012). In particular, this reform will alter the day of the week in the month of November that voting occurs. The second issue addresses the hours that Polling places will be open and most importantly when they will all be required to close.

This will get hot! In general, both political parties and the lobbyists in particular will not like these publicly oriented pro-voter-access changes. The Republican Party will be more opposed than the Democratic Party, but both will most likely try to stall these reforms until the public speaks. Our revolution picks up some steam.

The People's Sense

First, the traditional first Tuesday voting date in November will be imme-diately and permanently moved to the first Saturday in November. This will make it far simpler for more Americans to vote. As opposed to Tues-day, Saturday is a 'non' or partial workday for many of the electorate. Sched-uling a trip to the polls would be far easier for many. Parents could take older kids along for the civic experience. Voters would not be rushed be-fore or after their work commute which too often ends up in many not reaching the polls at all.

It will also make finding volunteer workers for the polls very easy.

This change will move the 2008 Presidential Election Day from Tuesday November 4th to Saturday November 1st or 11-1-08. As an added bonus for the electorate, the 2008 campaign would be shortened by three (3) whole days! What a gift.

> As a note — the hotel and restaurant industries will not be happy with this change because they will lose those three (3) days of busi-

ness. Hotels are already booked for those dates. All things are connected.

Second, the range of hours the polls are open will be standardized to approximately 10 to 14 hours. Due to the **6-hour** time zone difference between the Atlantic Coast and Hawaii, the opening times could be staggered. However, the poll closing times will be **simultaneous** across all time zones from Maine and Florida, to California, as well as to Alaska and Hawaii. More Common Sense!

The number of hours the Polling places would be open could be equal across the country. Or Alaska and Hawaii could have a slightly shorter window of hours to vote. It is once every two (2) years and it will be Saturday! So the Screamers can please just hold their breath until they pass out!

Proposed Polling Schedule

A proposed schedule for the 11-1-08 Election Day with "equal" voting hours across all time zones would have polling places opening and closing as follows:

Time Zone		Opening Time	Closing Time	#Hours Open
EST	Eastern	10:00 am	10:00 pm	12
CST	Central	9:00 am	9:00 pm	12
MST	Mountain	8:00 am	8:00 pm	12
PST	Pacific	7:00 am	7:00 pm	12
AKST	Alaska	6:00 am	6:00 pm	12
HAST	Hawaii -Aleutian	5:00 am	5:00 pm	12
HST	Hawaii	4:00 am	4:00 pm	12

This is not rocket science, folks! This incredibly simple and publicly balanced change in poll closing times will totally eliminate the potential for news services reporting East-of-the-Mississippi voting results before people out West have finished voting or have even gone to the polls. There is overwhelming support for these changes on the part of the public.

On the other hand, the political parties (and again the lobbyists that work to control both parties) will not be excited about making it much easier for a greater percentage of the electorate – the Masses to vote. That is the under-lying reason why such common sense changes have not been made before or even discussed. Both parties are now accustomed to "profiling the elec-torate" and banking on certain percentages and types of potential voters not showing up on Election Day. They will not be happy.

These simple changes will decisively shift the Status Quo of voting in America to We the People's favor.

No Amendment Required!

Guess what? As most people are not aware (I know I was not) that Con-gress has the ability to make such a change any time they want to! Go figure. Further, these changes do not require an amendment to the Consti-tution and only apply to Federal elections.

The states, counties, etc., make the laws regarding their respective election dates and times, but cannot interfere with Federal election administration. Now we all know. And the Plain Truth will set us free!

These realistic changes will make it dramatically easier for all Americans to get out and vote. This will result in an increased voter turnout of at least 10 to 15% which in turn will dramatically alter the Political Power struc-ture in America. It will make politicians — starting with the 2008 cam-paign — far more accountable to the real concerns We the People – We citizens — that is if they want to keep their jobs!

Both of these legislative changes will need to be made and in place in time for the November 2008 Presidential/Congressional election. There can be no justifiable "excuse" why Congress cannot do this in a single afternoon.

This will be very public test of the real intent of the **"535"** to serve the American people and our Common Good.

Remember to ask the Presidential candidates where they stand on this is-sue. And in particular ask your state's US Congressional **and state level candidates** running for re-election how soon he or she will get the changes put into law before 11-4-08!

More victories in our revolution!

3   Eligible Voter Reform

Issue/Problem

This proposal is short, but the topic is not very sweet. It speaks to the true spirit of voting rights under our Democracy.

This issue concerns what people are somewhat surprised to learn – why some American <u>citizens</u> are not allowed to vote in Federal and lower level elections.

Today, by law if an American citizen has been convicted of certain types of more serious crimes e.g., a felony of some sort — then <u>fully</u> serves their court prescribed penalty, and are then returned to society — they are too often <u>not</u> allowed to vote again in Federal and lower level elections.

Here is a summary of the overall situation from the website, **voternewsnetwork.com**,

> The legal authority of a State to revoke an inmate's voting rights is based upon the **Fourteenth Amendment**. State laws on allowing convicted felons to participate in elections vary widely. Forty-eight states deny the vote to at least some felons; only Vermont and Maine let felons vote. Thirty-three states withhold the right to vote from those on parole. Eight deny felons the vote for life, unless they petition to have their rights restored, such as Alabama and Florida. New Jersey and Connecticut allow former felons to vote once they have completed parole. Nationally, about 4.2 million convicted felons cannot vote.

Thanks to them for that concise write-up.

A bothersome statistic is that of those 4.2 million citizens that approximately 1.4 are American-Black males.

o   o   o   o

For those of you that are wondering about it, here is the 14th Amendment to the Constitution. Review Section 2 and see what you think.

AMENDMENT XIV   Passed by Congress June 13, 1866. Ratified July 9, 1868

Section 1.
All persons born or naturalized in the United States, and subject to the jurisdiction thereof, are citizens of the United States and of the State wherein they reside. No State shall make or enforce any law which shall abridge the privileges or immunities of citizens of the United States; nor shall any State deprive any person of life, liberty, or property, without due process of law; nor to deny to any person within its jurisdiction the equal protection of the laws.

Section 2.
Representatives shall be apportioned among the several States according to their respective numbers, counting the whole number of persons in each State, excluding Indians not taxed. But when the right to vote at any election for the choice of Electors for President and Vice-President of the United States, Representatives in Congress, the executive and judicial officers of a State, or the members of the Legislature thereof, is denied to any of the male inhabitants of such State, being twenty-one years of age, and citizens of the United States, **or in any way abridged, except for participation in rebellion, or other crime,** the basis of representation therein shall be reduced in the proportion which the number of such male citizens shall bear to the whole number of male citizens twenty-one years of age in such State.

Section 3.
No person shall be a Senator or Representative in Congress, or Elector of President and Vice-President, or hold any office, civil or military, under the United States, or under any State, who, having previously taken an oath, as a member of Congress, or as an officer of the United States, or as a member of any State Legislature, or as an executive or judicial officer of any State, to support the Constitution of the United States, shall have engaged in insurrection or rebellion against the same, or given aid or comfort to the enemies thereof. But Congress may by a vote of two-thirds of each House, remove such disability.

Section 4.
The validity of the public debt of the United States, authorized by law, including debts incurred for payment of pensions and bounties for services in suppressing insurrection or rebellion, shall not be questioned. But neither the United States nor any State shall assume or pay any debt or obligation incurred in aid of insurrection or rebellion against the United States, or any claim for the loss or emancipation of any slave; but all such debts, obligations and claims shall be held illegal and void.

Section 5.
The Congress shall have the power to enforce, by appropriate legislation, the provisions of this article.

o   o   o   o

Currently there are activist groups across the country working state-by-state to overturn such archaic and oppressive laws and secure voting rights for these citizens in all 50 states and DC.

This un-American condition is not right and must be corrected as a matter of prudent national policy.

It was a former US Marshal that first alerted me to what he believes to be a dirty, old political game. His position and that of most people I have spoken with on the issue is that if someone does a crime and performs their court prescribed time — then they must be considered square was society and have the Right to vote in Federal elections, as well as all other levels of voting.

This situation is nothing less than a state-level "Big Brother" stepping on some of our own people, fully intending to keep them down and removed from involvement in the political system. America is better than that!

Points of Contention

There are only a few perspectives that perpetuate this type of legislated oppression:

- The narrow-minded somewhat "churchy" viewpoint is that voting should only allowed to those of good character and not those that have broken society's laws. That is not even worth a comment.

- Another viewpoint would offer that anyone that has committed a particularly heinous crime of physical assault and/or murder and been released after serving their sentence, should never again be permitted to vote.

   To that very sincere and far more publicly viable perspective I will offer that if today's Criminal Justice System (which will be radically changed by other proposals herein) "finally" assigns a sentence to such an individual — that penalty is then fully served, and the person returned to open society – it is then proper for that individual to have the right to vote. And that is not a Liberal rationale. Like it or not they

— 126 —

have literally paid society's price for their crime.

That is strictly because American society represented by our currently dysfunctional the Criminal Justice System has legally passed judgment over and carried out its considered penalty on that individual. They did the prescribed time for their crime and must again be permitted voting rights as a regular citizen.

Going forward however, it will be for us deal to "finally" deal with the perpetrators of specific freewill criminal actions involving physical and financial assault against other people and society as a whole. That publicly acceptable proposal will be reviewed shortly.

- Finally, the third viewpoint is one that deliberately supports utilizing felony level crimes to restrict the future voting rights of people in general and in some instances particular groups from voting for purely political reasons.

It is this old viewpoint that I fear and believe to be the primary reason for such laws to exist at all and continue to linger. They are a holdover from generally darker days in our political history and obviously that darkness still needs to be *illuminated*. This is a clear example of what I mean by correcting the legislative errors and sins of the past.

The People's Sense

Not allowing someone to vote after paying their legal debt to society makes him or her feel at best a second-class citizen which does not tend to build much faith or fondness for the legal system or the government. It would tend to make them feel and speak un-favorably to others regarding the law, government, and the act of voting in general. This will all be corrected and avoided in the future.

This is an abusive situation where "States Rights" has a negative impact on the Common Good. And it must be confronted and resolved. The legislative battle to end this Voting Rights atrocity that is being waged on a state-by-state basis needs to be resolved by the U.S. Congress in one simple act!

The Congress, 50 State Governors, and the DC Mayor will confer together to rapidly develop and enact the simple and required legislation. It must be in effect for the 2008 election to insure Voting Rights at the Federal level – at least — for all persons that have served their court prescribed penalty and returned to open society. This will include those that are released and serving out their probation period, if any. If someone is out of prison –

they can vote even if they are liable for many years of follow-up probation.

It is a simple matter of treating our citizens correctly. States Rights can no longer be used to suppress the Voting Rights of our citizens. It is the proper action of a maturing Democracy, as well as being the civil and decent thing to do.

That is all that should need to be said of this. Let us get it fixed!

o   o   o   o

4   Real Campaign Finance Reform

Issue/Problem

The public's need to prudently reform election campaign fund-raising is nothing new. Real campaign finance reform is about the struggle to control the excessive and imbalanced influence of the Special Interest money that is pouring into national elections. The same can be said for the state election process, as well.

The end result of this well-funded influence on American politics over the last several decades is that the same men and women keep getting re-elected to high, public offices. The same predictable, Congressional members that the Special Interest lobbyists are so used to 'dealing' with to get what they want. The lobbyists help them keep getting re-elected and in turn the members of Congress either keep certain legislation from reaching a vote or know how to vote when the right Bill is sent to the Floor. It is part of today's "Old Boy and Old Girl System" of the U.S. Congress.

Point of Reference

In a version of the *Merriam-Webster* International Dictionary the word 'bribe' is defined as follows:

> **1** : a price, reward, gift, or favor bestowed or promised with a view to pervert the judgment or corrupt the conduct esp. of a person in a position of trust (as a public official)

Right out of the book!

o   o   o   o

It is the Plain Truth of "purchased" political influence and how it is used to not only influence, but direct and control national policy and legislative decisions. Obvious examples of this real influence are:

- The Bush II first term National Energy Policy that was developed behind closed doors with the Energy Industry lobbyists – with the Big Oil leading the way, assisted by the Natural Gas and Coal industries.
- The Medicare Reform legislation that the Medical and Pharmaceutical industries helped Congress write, that did not favor the Masses. See the movie, *Sicko*.
- The Pharmaceutical industry successfully lobbying to make it illegal for Americans to buy the same medications in Canada and Mexico at a

far cheaper price.

- The Banking industry successfully pushing through the Bankruptcy Reform Act late one night.
- The continued lack of enforcement of existing Immigration Control Policy and the Congressional refusal to strengthen it for at least critical, national security reasons. Remember that seven (7) more years of no action under Bush II is a daily victory for more millions of Illegal Occupants over the Majority will of the American Public — and for those businesses that want cheap labor to keep right on coming.
- The continued delay in building a Southern Border Fence. The creative Congress 'succeeded' in approving funds for a 700 mile fence to cover a 2000 land border. That is not even a half-a____ solution. And where is that partial fence?
- The continued existence of a failed and publicly, destructive 'joke' of a National Drug Policy. That for instance keeps the non-addictive, medically proven, and God-given cannabis (marijuana) plant illegal to please the Pharmaceutical industry. And at the same time Congress has never tried to make *nicotine* the *most addictive* and regularly used drug in the nation illegal, to keep the Tobacco and Medical industries happy. Over the last forty (40) years, Tobacco has only killed some 18,000,000 Americans — and pot a total of zero.
- The absolutely out-of-control Defense industry, i.e., the Military Industrial Complex. See the movie, *Why We Fight*.

o   o   o   o

It is our reasonable Right and Expectation under American Democracy for the Legislative Branch of government to serve the People and our Common Good. This is not happening in a growing number of critical areas. Rather the U.S. Congress is being influenced and directed by persons representing only certain industries and their stockholders – and in some cases other entities such as the Oil producing countries of the world.

And the High Court

Speaking of Judicial Branch, the U.S. Supreme Court recently ruled in opposition to such funding controls. It could be observed as a ruling that honored "The Law" and completely ignored the Democratic Reason and *common sense*. I say the control and prevention of the abuse of political Power by the Few over the Many is exactly what the US Constitution is all about.

The Court needs to re-consider the People's Rights and move to require practical, Democratic reforms in campaign finance laws that are designed to control, if not eliminate such obvious abuse of power and influence over the Common Good of the Masses.

The People's Sense

Since Congress is unwilling and/or unable to control itself and stop serving those not so interested in the Common Good, We the People must now act to correct the obvious abuses of Power. Any such reforms will of course wait until after the 2008 election season. However, that does not mean We will not bring it up as candidates for President and Congress seek our votes during the 2008 campaign. Yes, We will!

A Few Thoughts

As a public over-sight authority the Federal Elections Commission (FEC) strictly monitors and maintains very detailed accounting on the source of contributions to political campaigns at the Federal level for Congress and for the Office of the President. The FEC sourced data is open for public information inquiries and a good deal of these figures are to be found today on the Internet (www.FEC.gov) during the campaigns.

We could simply review the total contributions donated by industries, associations, and other non-individual citizen entities, from highest to lowest. We could then determine how far down those list to go and either limit or totally restrict future donations from that source to political candidates and parties for some period of years — if not permanently.

o   o   o   o

We could develop a list of "special interest" entities, mainly industries that would be generally prohibited from contributing to Federal level campaigns — entities that have proven by their deliberate, free will actions to place their interests over the Common Good of the People, society, and the National System. Things could get pretty intense as those entities fight to stay off of that list. An example of a few entities that would easily head that list today are:

- Medical Insurance Industry
- Pharmaceutical Industry
- Tobacco Industry
- Energy Industry — Oil, in particular, as well as Coal and Natural Gas
- Banking Industry
- Credit Card Industry
- Investment House Industry

- Defense Industry, i.e., the Military Industrial Complex

CS2 will be addressing most of those critical industries in Part 3 – An American Agenda. Therein, We will review the proposed re-structuring of six (6) of existing industries that are currently doing the National System, the American People (us), and our society far more harm than good. As a practical by-product of those non-optional, restructurings the predatory lobbying practices of those industries will be neutralized, if not fully eliminated!

In the final analysis, since We cannot stop certain profit seeking corporations from having their self-serving way with our lives and the nation's economic health — We will simply have our way <u>with</u> <u>them</u>, to Preserve and Serve the Common Good. It is our Democratic Right, because it is our country!

o   o   o   o

In spite of the half-hearted attempts by Congress to implement Campaign Finance reform, the money spent on national campaigns only increases as already evidenced in 2007 and early 2008. For example, over forty (40) millions dollars spent in Iowa before the January 3rd Caucus. Iowa only has a population of about 3 million!

Without question and regrettably, this publicly prudent and practical legislation is absolutely necessary when such a *damaging and dangerous* imbalance exists between the Common Good of the Masses, and the self-interested Few that are imposing a disproportionate amount of influence and control over the political system and our lives!

Real Campaign Finance Reform line laws and spending limits must be imposed. The simple details of which will be aired out in public, with *hard target deadlines* for viable legislation to be enacted and then enforced. That way the public may be provided the details of the legislation, embrace them, and see them put into law for the 2010 campaign, and beyond.

o   o   o   o

2. National Reform Proposals

Introduction

The National Reform group of proposals addresses issues relating to the overall quality and the structure of civil society for the American people – *We the People*. These are concepts, programs, and policies that apply at the state and local levels where we all live and will serve us best when established as national standards with the public's *review and consent*. Commonly accepted standards and expectations will promote the Common Good for our citizens.

These proposals address the types of on-going public issues that *cannot be practically resolved* at the state and local levels. Therefore, it is the baseline job responsibility of the 535 members of the US Congress representing their states' people <u>and</u> the nation as a whole — 'to legislate and resolve' such problems for the Common Good of all American citizens. It is their basic job responsibility and they are consistently <u>not</u> <u>honoring it</u>.

As you review this key group and the remaining proposals in An American Agenda you will begin to see and understand how they work together with overlapping rules and benefits to confront and resolve some of the problems on that Grievance List and others.

5	American Population Management
6	English as First and Only Language
7	U. S. Re-Employment System – The Key to Domestic Peace
8	National Drug Reform
9	Re-Considering the Military Draft – Saving Our Youth
10	Zero Tolerance for Free-Will Crime by All People
11	The Family Support Administration
12	Family Basic Asset Protection
13	American Owned Business Preference Policy

o   o   o   o

About the Big Picture

Three Over-Riding Issues

The American Agenda presentation is built around and upon three (3) over-riding social and economic issues:

- Population Management and Control
- A Common Language – English, only
- Viable Employment for American Citizens First

While these national, bone-marrow issues are addressed in separate proposals, the ramifications of how these critical components are "really" dealt with by our nation are felt throughout every portion of America's National System. And in Plain Truth that same reality applies to every other nation in the world.

Considering the fact that since the time of the Pilgrims circa 1620, and prior to that in Jamestown circa 1607, our nation was partly populated and built by immigrants — it is truly ironic that resolving an out-of-control illegal and legal immigration crisis would wind up being one of the central issues that starts us down the road to solving many of our other national problems, both large and small.

English, or as I would prefer to call it the *American language*, will be declared our single and only language. The use of no other languages will be supported by taxpayer funds. Anyone that desires to come and/or be allowed to stay in our country beyond a short visit must be able to at least speak, if not read and write our national language. No exceptions and no tax breaks will be allowed.

Speaking of employment, since America is no longer a country made up family farms where people can make their living and be more self-sustaining, there must be "viable" employment for our citizens in various other industries and occupations. We will determine how to provide living wage jobs for our citizens first — and only after that will we attend to concerns Other Legal Occupants (OLOs).

It is just *common sense* for the Common Good.

If we **do not** realistically address these three (3) fundamental, national issues to the satisfaction of our own citizens and a naturally growing American economy — there will continue to be an endless cycle of related and avoidable problems, and public pain. *They*, the protectors of the dysfunctional Status Quo will continue win and gain power over our future. *We* will continue to lose and watch as our society degrades.

If we **do make** the hard <u>and</u> nationally appropriate decisions the day-to-day environment for <u>our</u> citizens in <u>our</u> country will improve right before our eyes and simply put, America will become a better place for our people. The dysfunctional Status Quo will have been prudently restructured and made truly "functional" for the Common Good. *They* will be required adjust to a more equitable National System and will survive as they always do.

We will have embraced a viable National Vision. *We* and our descendants will win.

Overall, Population and Employment are like the two weights on a scale — they <u>always</u> determine, based upon how they are balanced in a given nation, the general quality of life in that society.

We the People will now begin the process of re-balancing that scale within the American National System for the Common Good of our society.

o   o   o   o

5. American Population Management (APM)

The Population Issue –
The Practical Place to Start this Grand National Fix

"We the People will decide who is allowed to play in our sandbox"

Issue/Problem

We do not know how many people are in our country illegally, let alone legally!

This National proposal addresses what is viewed as critical priority number one (#1). It will functionally address the effective of management of the US population – citizens and others. Utilizing the programs and procedures implemented under American Population Management (APM) we will be able to identify and serve our own citizens and other legal long-term occupants.

APM introduces the National Citizen Identification (NCI) System that will provide a **Unique Citizen ID** for every American citizen. We will overview the National Population Registration (NPR) program for all American citizens — both native born and naturalized, as well as all other types of OLOs (other legal occupants), such as Permanent Resident Aliens.

A secondary component of APM will be the Immigration Control Program (ICP) that will be used to identify and register **all persons in the country illegally** and will be utilized to control the repatriation of the majority of those individuals over the next several years. Realistically, it took many years (since the Immigrant amnesty legislation of 1986) for them to come here so logically it will take some time for them to return to their country of birth. Remember our Second American Revolution (2AR) is viewed as a seven (7) year effort, but the appropriate repatriation effort will not be allowed to take that long.

The initial implementation of the APM program will be a *grand national housekeeping* exercise with a one-time, total population registration (everyone standing on our soil) to be followed by the on-going maintenance of that critical national management facility. With the implementation of an American NCI, we will merely be accomplishing a long overdue and very necessary catch-up exercise with many other (and less developed) countries!

The public benefits to be realized from an effective APM program are absolutely essential, they are long overdue, and since the 9-11 incidents are even more critical in providing **real** Homeland Security for America. The concepts behind APM grew out of my research and were refined and hardened by public feedback on the problems IOs create for our country.

> Anyone in our government that continues six years after 9-11 to talk about effective Homeland Security and at the same time allows a constant, un-checked daily flow of hundreds of IOs across our Southern border, as well as via ship and airplane – is an idiot! They are not working for the American people and need to be removed from their elected or appointed position, ASAP!

The simple fact is that too many nations (including ours up until now) are not dealing realistically and responsibly with their own population 'control' and management issues — that in turn can cause problems in other countries. The "pushing" of population from one country to another(s) is often a convenient method for a government to use in hiding and/or ignoring various problems in their own country. And one (1) of the main problems being the lack of responsible birth control practices! It is the Plain Truth.

Remember it is our country! America has a set of very correctable social and economic problems that only exist due to the presence of IOs that are here from all around the world. This one-time clean-up and correction process **must begin in 2008**, but it will only happen if **We demand it** of our politicians.

The IOs need to be ordered to stop coming (a fence built) and many of those that are here need to start heading back out the door before the 2008 election or, We the People — *the irritated electorate* will be sending 468 incumbent members of the U.S. Congress out the door on 11-1-2008. Any questions?

That *of course* is not intended to be threatening – it is a promise and just *more common sense*. If the elected members of Congress will not work for us, We as their employers have the legal authority and responsibility for the Common Good to fire them all. This is not intended to be funny. The IO problem is just one of many reasons for us to seriously consider taking such prudent action in November 2008.

APM Relocation for Employment

APM and Employment are logically and strategically linked. The overall

APM program will among other things facilitate as required, the geographic relocation of American workers and their families around the country in order to promote employment opportunities ranging from full time positions to seasonal needs. This will be best coordinated at the county and city levels, from state to state.

For example, the APM program will help facilitate local and regional programs to support businesses and industries such as agriculture requiring seasonal workforces, but without perpetuating the illegal labor flow and controlling (thus minimizing) the use of foreign-born temporary guest-workers. We do not need a Guest Worker program that some people keep talking about putting in place, because we already have a Guest Worker program in place! It needs to be used not abused or ignored.

The concept of coordinated geographic relocation of people was initially developed under the National Drug Reform (NDR) Proposal regarding the effective out-placement of rehabilitated hard drug addicts. Go figure! At times it would be best for some people to live in a new setting or community to help them get a fresh start in life, away from the old neighborhood.

For another viable example, in the future APM would be used to find starter employment for people leaving prison in order to facilitate their entry into the world, but not into the same area they were living when they entered the system. This would support their getting a fresh start, as well. Former prisoners are just that, 'former prisoners' — they are our fellow Americans and we need help them to get on the **right** track. That way everybody wins.

More than once when I was reviewing the educational, social skills training, vocational training, and relocation process developed under the NDR program, people have commented, "why don't we offer that practical kind of help for anyone that needs it?" Their comments were well-taken.

Of course not everyone will need or want to use such relocation services. In many cases if someone were to lose their job and in order to find new employment had to move several hundred miles away, they would just do it. Not that they would want to leave the area they are familiar with and possibly grew up in, but they would do whatever was needed to find new employment. However, not everyone has that personal drive, confidence or the resources to move, but they do have the practical <u>need</u> <u>to</u> <u>go</u>!

As will be reviewed under the U.S. Re-employment System proposal, we will need to facilitate some people in finding employment and possibly help them move to where it is. This coordinated citizen relocation process is <u>already</u> in use in some areas of the country (formally between cities in different states) and with good results. It just needs to become a national standard. No more sitting around waiting for the next un-employment check if viable employment is attainable elsewhere. We will <u>insistent</u> that people help them selves!

Going forward the taxpayer-funded financial support of our citizens *capable of working* will only be provided <u>if</u> the person is in re-training and/or performing whatever viable part or full time work can be identified for them. What a concept! The "alleged" need for immigrant labor will be addressed by getting some Americans to work at whatever needs to be done. No free rides anymore.

> Over the years I have worked along side of many people with some very serious physical conditions. They got up everyday, went to work in spite of their challenges, did a good job, and are respected for it. If they could voluntarily do that, then <u>no one</u> else has a viable excuse – period.

Our economy must continue to evolve against the global economy. We are and will face the challenges of keeping <u>our</u> citizens <u>viably</u> (living wage) employed. The concept of APM is a practical concept that needs to be openly discussed and *rapidly* implemented as a national standard to help us effectively and efficiently deal with the changing economy, re-employment of our people, and **our natural** "citizen-based" population growth.

The NPR process to take will take the place of the 2010 US Census. From that point on we will be have a continuous Census, provided by the information maintained in the related national databases.

APM will be an essential, highly functional system utilized to manage our population and absolutely control any future immigration that We shall determine to permit.

No Amnesty or Path to Citizenship for IOs

<u>Never Again</u>

Obviously, we currently do not have a **functioning** Immigration Control Program (ICP). The out of control IO problem has been allowed to grow for two (2) decades since 1986 when under President Ronald Reagan's administration the last "half-baked" false-attempt was made to resolve and finally control the IO problems of the 1980's. It included a provision for "only" a projected half-million IOs to obtain citizenship. In the end however, anywhere from 3 to 5 <u>million</u> IOs snuck in the door with the illegal documentation they could buy for $50 to $100 per set.

The Congress' and Reagan's pitch at that time was amnesty first, that would be followed-up by sanctions against employers that hired illegal workers. *Does that sound too familiar?* Some 20 years later we are still waiting for those promised sanctions – what a joke.

I was watching Lou Dobbs/CNN one evening in mid-June (2006) when a Border Patrol advocate was a guest and commented that the courts (our taxes) are still processing thousands of cases from that "one-time" amnesty legislation. It is OK to scream about that!

We cannot afford nor can we allow that to happen again. And both parties in Congress and the White House must be on notice not to go way, or else. Bush II will be gone at the end of this term, if he and Cheney are not impeached before that — and Congress realizes they will not get re-elected if such a bill is again passed.

> Bush II has been a legislative lame duck since the summer of 2005 and really does not have anything to lose by pushing such legislation to make certain business sectors happy at the expense of the greater good — and trying to cover it as though he really cared about the Latino community!

Due to the Congress' and the current White House administration's enforcement inaction at the national level — all 50 states and DC are stuck dealing with people that the Feds will not come and take away. It is a pathetic situation that just goes on. The illicit flow is unnecessarily a political hot potato, and as one candidate running in the 2006 election cycle said it is "threatening the very fabric of America society" – which it definitely is! And 9 of 10 people I talk with could not agree more.

The Political Bottom Line

Unfortunately, it appears that IOs, especially the "illegal portion" of the Latino community has been enjoying better representation by the Congress and the White House in recent years than the American people! This pathetic situation will need to be stopped and the illegal immigrant flow from everywhere fully reversed starting in 2008.

The overall IO issue provides another grim example why the current Change process within our National System is broken. The impact of the overt (screamers) and covert lobbying (American businesses and foreign governments in too many cases) that goes into high gear whenever proposals such as a multi-year immigration freeze, the repatriation of IOs, the full legalization of marijuana, and national health care insurance for all Americans are raised – must be neutralized.

The preservation of the Status Quo basically works like this — the lobbyists and special interests Scream, the politicians' run and hide, real action is differed, and the Common Good continues to suffer. It is a publicly vicious and socially unproductive cycle, and it unfortunately repeats itself throughout that Grievance List and many other correctable national issues.

We will join together and begin correcting the Change process within our National System in 2008.

Addressing the National Priority

"America and Americans First"

As mentioned earlier, this is the primary theme and requirement for An American Agenda. It holds particular importance with regard to the Population Management and Employment proposals. Those proposals are practical, straightforward, and to the point! No apologies will be offered for putting our nation's interests and our people first. No other country does!

America First

This means that needs of America come before the needs of any other country whether we are talking about a domestic or foreign policy. Our nation supported by the good will of the American public works for good purposes all over the world. We are too often taken for granted and are increasingly harassed by various external parties with narrow-minded and negative views of the world. This unwarranted treatment must end, and the sooner the better.

The real leadership of other countries (whether political, social, or religious) tries to export their own population management problems to other countries rather than confronting internally failed policies. Some countries, and Mexico in particular, overtly do whatever they can (the Mexico government issues 'how-to' brochures) to encourage their own citizens to leave for America or any other country for that matter — which only shifts one nation's population problems somewhere else, causing other problems in those societies. And so, the sending country still takes no practical steps to correct or control their social and economic problems – or – to control their *excess* population production!

The underlying public condition and politically incorrect social problem that too many countries in Central and South America (CSA) have and try to ignore is over-population and the un-checked birth rates that they irresponsibly perpetuate.

Bluntly stated — when we *gave* them NAFTA we should have insisted that Planned Parenthood had to be included in the deal! And it isn't too late to start. I think that was clear enough?

Americans First

The needs and interests of American citizens, with absolute emphasis on the group that are "citizens" will come before the needs of any other group, whether we are talking about a domestic or foreign policy.

I am absolutely confident that this political philosophy will generate a most positive reaction from the American electorate — the People. So let's get right to the point and discuss this topic realistically and practically from the point-of-view of American citizens, only.

There are currently three (3) distinct groupings of people inhabiting our nation's borders when there should only be two (2), those are:

1.   American Citizens

This group of 300 million citizens (as of October 2006) includes both native born and naturalized Americans. Meaning they were either born here or "legally" came here from their country of birth through the Immigration and Naturalization agencies of our federal government and subsequently went through the multi-year naturalization process in obtaining their American citizenship. They did it the old fashion way, they earned it – and honestly.

I have lived and worked in the Washington, DC metropolitan area for some 35 years. For several of those years I worked as a software consultant to the U.S. Immigration Service, an agency formerly under the Department of Justice, now under Homeland Security. During that time I participated in the complete software upgrade to the computer system used to check travelers into the U.S. at all airport and land ports of entry. Many of you have seen that system in operation. As a side note, at that time the system was called the National Automated Immigration Lookout System or NAILS. Since it was a second version of that system, it was referred to as — NAILS II. Good name!

Over the years I have known and worked with many people that were going through the naturalization process and that had completed what is not always a pleasant experience. Some years ago I was invited to attend the citizenship ceremony of one of the people that worked for me. She was a native of Iran. It is a wonderful and patriotic experience. Those people have gone through the process, earned the right of citizenship, and are justifiably proud of the accomplishment and becoming a new American. And they as a group have very little sympathy for IOs

2.   Other Legal Occupants (OLO)

This group is comprised of those that are in the country **legally** by virtue of having followed the State Department visa process designed to control and monitor the flow of all foreign-born persons entering our nation. Those people are generally coming here for work or to attend school. This group includes those that have been permitted to become Permanent Resident Aliens.

Some percentage of OLOs will be permitted to file for the naturalization process. Others come here to work and live long-term may have no interest or intention of becoming American citizens. The future ability of this latter group to remain in our country is dependent upon their conduct, U.S. employment levels, and to-date various foreign policy considerations. This means that their ability to continue living here could be revoked at any time based on our changing national priorities and/or their conduct, and they would then need to return to their own country.

All persons in this group will be included in and accounted for in the National Population Registration (NPR) process.

3.   Illegal Occupants (IOs)

All of those in this third group under existing Federal laws should not be standing on our soil!

No matter how you put, this group is comprised of those that of their own free-will entered our country **illegally**. They are uninvited entrants and certainly not guests. This trespass most commonly occurs when someone has illegally crossed our land borders with Mexico or Canada.

However, one estimate is that well over 3.5 million have arrived via airplane or ship under the cover of business, vacation or for education, but then failed to leave the country by the date they declared. Still others are here that arrived here legally through the Visa program, but also failed to leave as expected and just disappeared into the country. And they <u>all</u> did these things of their own freewill!

**The bottom line is that they are all here illegally
and their time is just about up!**

o   o   o   o

There is No Leadership like No Leadership

No great secret that the greatest percentage of IOs originate from the CSA countries and the greatest portion of them from good old Mexico. Since the weak Immigration Act of 1986 our politicians and various shortsighted and self-interested businesses along with social lobbies have only continued to encourage this illegal flow – resulting in the growing mess we are being forced to live with today.

Our elected national politicians — the U.S. Congress, has totally failed to protect American society by simply enforcing the Immigration Control laws that are already on the books. And frankly, if they are not stopping it — they are supporting it!

> Without going into <u>any</u> of the viable statistics on what this collective Congressional failure has caused the American public I will point out that there are *graves* to be found today in our country that would <u>not exist</u> if we had a 2000 mile southern border fence and an enforced Immigration Control system. This reality declares that, *the lives of our people have obviously become cheap to Congress.*
>
> This is an example of what I term to be the Acceptable Legislative Kill Factor (ALKF) – that clearly exists when legislated domestic and foreign policy allows for the death of our people.
>
> That is not harsh, it is the Plain Truth. Think about it.
>
> It is profits and campaign fundraising over the people in the US Congress. Do we really want to reward that with re-election?

The U.S. Census Bureau estimated in 2006 that there were 11 to 15 million IOs currently in the country, with over 6 million from Mexico alone. Absolutely, out of <u>our</u> control!

The budgets of states like Arizona, New Mexico, and California for example, are being hammered by this IO overhead. In addition, towns <u>all</u>

over the country (like Herndon, Virginia) are struggling with IO day-worker issues, as well as facing budgetary problems taking care of their own people due to the social service, educational, and criminal justice costs of the IOs invasion. And our Congress will not act to help the states fight the illegal flow and facilitate their deportation, which is their literal responsibility.

Our Bottom Line

The VAST majority of the American public is sick of and disgusted by this un-checked invasion of our country, that is after all is said and done being "promoted" by the no political guts, no action Congress — to say nothing about the publicly dysfunctional occupant of the White House and his side-kick.

o   o   o   o

Thoughts and Perspective on the IO Invasion

Here are a few points to consider regarding the IO invasion over the 'last' 20 years and the 7-plus years in particular.

- American business has always had a love affair with the cheap labor that comes in illegally. This is one of those unspoken truths that every-one knows about. And even though the business community publicly denies it, they have lobbied (often covertly) against any legislation that would put anything more than a Band-Aid on this open, bleeding National wound.

- IOs originate from countries all over the world. I remember hearing several years ago about an unfortunate woman from Poland that drowned in the river trying to cross into the U.S. from Mexico.

- The flow of more IOs is also directly encouraged and sponsored by family, friends, and businesses within our own borders.

- The governments of CSA countries promote the flow north to America and greedily wait for funds to be transferred back. Transfers made oh so easy by our very cooperative, well-lobbied, fee-charging banks. More on them later.

- And then there is Mexico... that more than any other country needs to be reminded that the sign at the base of the Statue of Liberty does not read,

"Send me your excess population that you do not care to deal with"

Mexico, in particular has <u>not</u> been willing to work with our government to establish a viable border control system. And why should they since they have at all right now. The Mexican government *aggressively promotes* this outright "population transfer" – the dumping of their own citizens across the US border — <u>everyday</u>.

Mexican officials permit (or it could not happen inside 'their' borders) <u>and</u> facilitate the passage of IOs from other CSA countries in traveling the entire route northward from their southern borders with Guatemala and Belize, with all the required payoffs, as well as fear of robbery and physical assault along the way. Some would call that facilitation of human trafficking. What would you call it?

Mexico already has NAFTA and the other CSAs are *very quietly* ratifying and implementing as many more NAFTA-type agreements as they can with an all too willing Bush Administration.

Mexico now grows the base crops for cocaine and heroin. They produce crystal-meth and grow marijuana. And then they ship, fly, walk or simply <u>drive</u> it across our currently fenceless, open, 'duty-free' border – <u>everyday</u> direct to our neighborhoods and into our people.

Again, Mexico does not need to establish to viable border control system with the U.S. government, because they already have one that works very, very well for <u>them</u>. The next time someone references the Mexican government as our partner in the Drug War ask them what planet they are visiting from.

And always remember my fellow Americans, that America has not owed the Mexican <u>government</u> a damn thing since the Alamo!

o o o o

An *Inconvenient* Correction – IOBs

People that seek across the border with their kids and drop them in our schools need to be sent back home. That national abuse is bad enough, but the worst offenders are those that come over the border already pregnant and "drop" a baby only for the purpose of falsely claiming citizenship for that *functional baby* that some call "anchor babies" or what I would term and IO Baby or IOB! They could be viewed as really establishing *their* personal foothold and the child is merely a means to an end!

In some percentage of that scenario, after having the IOB they then send for the rest of their family to join them. And they all go right into our schools and social services pocketbook.

Others women come across the border and get pregnant while here to have their IOB. A statistic that would be interesting to know is how many 'un-married' IO women are having those babies. How does the church feel about that *responsible* choice?

These abuses will all end when We get the right leadership.

Law and Spirit

CSA IOs in particular bring their Third World lack of civilly responsible birth control practices into America and intentionally "drop" at least one child.

> The IOs of their own free will *technically* break our federal laws by entering our country and then turn around and violate the *sprit* of applicable law by having their *citizenship* baby.

The 14th Amendment of the US Constitution addresses the citizenship of babies born to non-citizens. Again, for your convenience:

AMENDMENT XIV — Passed by Congress June 13, 1866. Ratified July 9, 1868

> Section 1.

> All persons born or naturalized in the United States, and subject to the jurisdiction thereof, are citizens of the United States and of the State wherein they reside. No State shall make or enforce any law which shall abridge the privileges or immunities of citizens of the United States; nor shall any State deprive any person of life, liberty, or property, without due process of law; nor to deny to any person within its jurisdiction the equal protection of the laws.

o   o   o   o

That is the 140 year old law. What do you think?

This unintended, and from the public's perspective non-existent loop hole needs to be clarified out of existence in 2008. Under revised legislation, fraudulently obtained citizenships will be at least suspended and some will be revoked. Then many will be repatriated – the baby(s), parent(s), and any other kids — with the bath water! It is truly unfortunate, but some children will be required to pay for the sins of their fathers and mothers — forced to grow up in their real country of citizenship!

To repeat — if "our" politicians cannot quit being "their" politicians, they too will be thrown out of their jobs and replaced with those that will — on 11-4-08.

Under the legislation the needs to be enacted in 2008 there will be no citizenship for babies born to IOs. One of the congressmen from Colorado has presented such legislation, but while that may sound good on television, thus far it is just cheap rhetoric. Action is required – where is the beef?

Believe me the world-wide announcement of that single legislative action will automatically slow the inward flow from all directions. Not as many IOs will be traveling here to have IOBs if they do not come with a "get-into-America-free" card! It goes to intent.

Point made. The Congress will act or We will!

o   o   o   o

The Bottom Line

The social and economic problems are caused in the greatest part by the CSA flow across our fenceless southern border. The flow has only increased over the last six years under the **Bush Open-door Illegal Entry Program**. Specifically, it has accelerated because many of the IOs believe that Bush and the special interests will succeed in declaring some sort of an amnesty for them and provide a path to citizenship for all those here illegally.

Fortunately however, thus far that potential national disaster has been avoided. The primary reason it has not been pushed through the well-lobbied Congress is that they know what the voting public will do if they pass such legislation.

And more than anything any lobbying group (or Bush II) can try to offer to persuade Congress to pass such anti-American public legislation – the 535 know the America public's real stance on the IOs. Forget the questionable public opinion polls — the Congress wants more than anything else to keep their jobs – and such legislation would cut them off at the real polls!

The worn-out, typical hype from the pro-IO Screamers is that these illegal visitors are helping our economy. However, that benefit has now been far surpassed by the massive and growing costs of social and medical services they are taking, to say nothing the gangs, the killings, the rapes, and federal (25%), state, and local prison space some of them are occupying!

It is time to stop the IO flow and begin sending **them back home** no matter what country in the world the came from. This is not personal, this is not business — this is American society standing up and saying that this unchecked human invasion cannot continue! Our society and our very way of life will in due time be destroyed, if it is not first stopped and then reversed, as soon as possible.

Only Necessary

We will commonly acknowledge that this is a publicly necessary, but difficult action to consider — even for many of those totally in favor of such aggressive resolutions. Especially when we are sending women and children back to their home countries that often provide lesser living conditions. However, we did not authorize or make the problem – it is the IO adults that came here under their own free will that did.

Our national alternative is to allow them to stay and rapidly increase in number, and perpetuate their growing negatives on the economic and social welfare of America.

The IO issue is a very negative force within today's Status Quo and it will not be allowed to continue. It must be citizens, legal occupants, and authorized visitors, only....

The People's Sense

The following are deemed to be the foundation upon which realistic American Population Management (APM) and Immigration Control Policy (ICP), and supporting legislation will be built. The American electorate will anticipate such legislation to be clearly defined and communicated, passed into law by Congress, and signed by Bush II or over his expected veto (and without any Presidential Signing Statement altering that legislation!) and before 11-4-08.

I acknowledge that is a tall order for the "do nothing" Congress and that they probably will not get all this done before 11-1-08, BUT, those that are elected to the White House and Congress on that historic day will know after hearing it from the electorate during the campaign what the mandate is from the voters and to be immediately about the People's business when they are sworn in January 2009. Clean up the mess and get it done.

Parts of what 'could' get done before 11-4-08:

- As **Job Number One** — the Congress of the United States <u>will</u> issue a unanimous and very "public declaration" to all foreign governments and their people, that all illegal movement of persons into this country will cease immediately. All future violators and their families will be briefly detained, no court process required, and immediately deported back to their home country. And those within this country that were providing them refuse and/or assistance in that illegal entry would be subject to criminal prosecution, including the same immediate deportation if such person(s) not a US citizen and that will include Permanent Resident Aliens.

  As a side-benefit — this legislation will begin to decrease the need for Immigration Lawyers! They will be one of the first occupational groups required to begin looking for other and hopefully more socially productive employment.

- We will initiate the National Population Registration (NPR) of all U.S. citizens for purpose of implementing a unique National Citizen Identification (NCI) Biometric card. It will contain at least photo and fingerprint data and be linked into the secure national database. And for those who are screaming "Big Brother" all I can say is, "Bush II".

- To be clear, all persons desiring to stand on US soil from this point on will be registered – photo and fingerprints, plus! No exceptions or exemptions will be granted, including diplomats and their parties.

- The resulting National APM System database with the viable US population identification data would prove to be a tremendous asset to Homeland Security and our law enforcement at all levels. It will greatly assist local law enforcement to know who they are dealing with in any situation, as well as identifying victims of crime.

  All this is an unfortunate, but absolutely necessary evil considering the current state of the world. I share some of the concerns about the Patriot Act provisions and the way that the Bush II administration has systematically been destroying the Bill of Rights! Those violations will be stopped and corrected.

- As is offered in another proposal, by July 4, 2008 English will be designated as the official language of the United States of America. What a concept!

Additionally, people will need to know English when they arrive here with the intention of living and working. We the taxpayers will no longer be subsidizing the usage of any second language. We Americans do not need another one language in <u>our</u> <u>own</u> <u>country</u>.

- The issue of a "path to amnesty/citizenship" is taken permanently off the table. Stated very plainly,

If a person is here illegally –
they will <u>never</u> be granted U.S. Citizenship.

As stated in writing for
the Silent Majority

- The Congress will authorize and fully fund the rapid construction of a double/parallel chain-linked fence topped with razor wire across the entire 2,000 Southern border with Mexico. It will of course be equipped with motion-sensing technology to automatically notify Border Agents of any activity.

This project will <u>not</u> be let to the highest bidder and it will not be allowed to take forever to build. Congress will modify any existing construction projects as required. For instance, we do not need highway grade sound-barrier walls to keep people out. We could easily electrify the metal fences with solar power!

Further, it would be an excellent public works program for Border States. It could be staffed with a few thousand minor drug offenders now sitting in prisons as part of their final rehabilitation and a ticket back to society when the job is done. Most of them should not be in prison in the first place.

Some Americans would immediately volunteer to help build that fence if provided food and shelter along the way. The patriotic group of American volunteers – the Minute Man Project will enjoy observing the fence's construction. Absolutely!

- Congress will rapidly amend laws that are currently abused to claim US citizenship for babies born of IOs. This cannot be the intent of the existing law and it is absolutely against the will of the American public.

People come across the border to "drop their baby" or get pregnant while they are here, so that they may obtain a foothold with that "functional" child – and obtain a get-into-America-free-card to receive get medical and other public services extracted from our tax dollars. This will end.

- As critical follow-up to that legislation:

    o All IO Babies (IOBs) born illegally in the U.S. since December 31, 2004 or earlier will have their illegally obtained citizenship status **Revoked**. They along with any family members will be immediately repatriated to their home country and without needless court processing.

    o All IOBs born illegally in the U.S. since December 31, 1999 will have their illegally obtained citizenship status **Suspended** and that date will probably moved back into the nineties.

From those dates backward, we will begin to work out any other details.

One option is for those children and their families in the second group to also be repatriated. The child could then be considered for return to the U.S. after they reached the age of 18 or 21 and can speak, read, and write English and satisfy any other immigration requirements at that time. No guarantees.

Further, as we conduct this grand, national housekeeping exercise, it will probably be advisable to suspend citizenship status for children born to "legal" visitors, as well. This would include anyone not a US citizen and could be the rule for several years. This is another backdoor way of gaining citizenship for the children of those that are here and have no intent of becoming citizens themselves. It is another abused way of playing the system and the statistics on this could be very sobering.

Yes, that is very hard policy. But it is fair, prudent policy and to the direct benefit of the Common Good of our citizens and society. We the People did not ask for or create this mess, but We will have to direct the national clean-up.

o   o   o   o

Considerations on the Overall Immigration Policy

Our own people are dealing with reduced employment opportunities caused in part by programs such as NAFTA, and the unchecked corporate

Outsourcing of manufacturing and other jobs such as those in the Information Technology industry to other countries (India) around the world. Therefore the ground rules must change for the sake of the American job opportunities, our economy, and to cut the costly overhead that the un-natural IO population forces upon us.

One of my personal sayings on this issue is that just as every other country has the right to say,

> *"we do not owe anyone that was not born here, and legally, a job or anything else"*

Except maybe a ticket back home. That especially applies to anyone not invited here in the first place.

- All <u>legal</u> non-citizens, desiring to remain in the U.S. will be required go thru proper Immigration and/or State Department procedures to obtain a **new** Alien Worker Id Card is part of the NPR process mentioned above.

  That re-registration will provide us with an updated photo and require fingerprints, as well. We are already beginning to collect such personal data from visitors at international airports. This practical requirement will support our Homeland Security Department in controlling and tracking non-citizens inside our country, and will greatly assist <u>and</u> <u>protect</u> our state and local law enforcement, as well.

<u>Multi-year Freeze Required</u>

As we continue to develop APM policy regarding the non-citizen population, we should very well determine to completely **freeze all** immigration for at least a few years starting in early 2009. America has done this before when it was deemed nationally prudent and it is more than reasonable to do it now.

Further, if we want to put pressure on IOs and the countries that send them here, we must put the squeeze on Legal immigration because their lobbies will in turn put pressure on the Congress. It may sound a bit juvenile, but it will be very effective! Also, we will freeze the issuance of Green Cards and the awarding Permanent Resident Alien status for a few years as well – until things are under practical control. That way people can quit complaining about the application backlogs and just leave!

Actually, there are situations when practical can have the appearance of being cruel.

The existing annual immigration quotas as they exist and do not exist by country will be publicly published on the Internet by the US Congress in 2008 along with all the current exceptions and exemptions allowed by country and any other category of entrant group. This too will be grim reading at times and explain other avoidable issues within our borders.

The annual quotas by country, as well as any exceptions and exemptions by group will be overhauled with the American public's *consent* before Legal Immigration is restarted.

<u>Who Makes the Rules?</u>

I am sure that some of what you are reading is a bit hard to imagine. Or it seems unrealistic to expect such Change to ever happen, even though many are reading CS2 and thinking this all sounds about right to me!

Be assured my fellow Americans that these and so many other positive Changes to be presented, absolutely can and will become part of our daily experience if *We the People* boldly decide to run our own nation. Therefore, please be encouraged!

There is more.

<u>No Non-Citizen Crime Allowed</u>

To assist state and local law enforcement — non-citizen and especially IO crime of any kind against our citizens will no longer be tolerated. This hard-edged legislation will be phased-in with adequate advanced public notice beginning in late-2008 and will be in full force in 2009. There will be more on this topic later.

Serious violators of crime and their families will be subject to <u>immediate</u> repatriation and the loss of any citizenship status. And the person(s) had better not return to the US as so many have done in the past and still do. Going forward we will politely disregard whether or not we have a Reciprocity Agreement with a given country. This will not be handled as returning a criminal, but simply *returning some of their citizens that have wandered off and just needed to be returned*!

And the State and/or Homeland Security Departments will be sent the bill! The states will greatly appreciate that.

Finally, no persons illegally in the country will be employed and no public services will be provided. We are talking about that necessary national housekeeping exercise. Written like a true taxpaying American!

Below the Bottom Line

Granted those do sound like tough policy positions considering what we are putting up with in recent years, but such controls are accepted as standard policy in most other countries. Further, long-standing problems often demand hard actions to <u>correct</u> — and We do intend to correct them. Again, with these types of rational, national policies America is only catching up with what most other nations consider to be normal.

To state the Plain Truth — which is blatantly ignored by the Congress, the White House, and those self-serving lobbyists — is to say that while IOs were a problem prior to the 9-11 tragedy the continued un-checked flow of them instantly became a National Security issue on that tragic day. IOs, drug traffickers, and anyone else can literally drive across our border.

<u>When There is No Leadership</u>

The current situation with the Congress and the White House grimly presents today's Americans with a collective incompetence in National leadership of a magnitude <u>unmatched</u> in 230–plus years of American history. Was that clear enough?

We the People must vigorously pursue and demand the implementation and <u>aggressive</u> <u>enforcement</u> of a viable National Immigration and Border Control Policy.

And in the End

This is the beginning of our Third American Civil War! A domestic revolution — and we will not need to fire a shot.

And again, the Common Good of all our citizens – us – is to be addressed and be our first priority.

One of the most difficult things for any society to do is to correct past mistakes and/or inaction, in economic and social policy – I said **difficult**, but **not impossible** to correct. We can, we must, we will address our Population Management issues and learn to control our nation's borders.

We, Americans are a compassionate people, slow to anger. We cannot help but cheer the underdog because that is what all of our ancestors were. However, we must deal with this and other issues now so that our children and those that follow them will be able to enjoy this country.

There will be other requirements added to the overall APM legislation as the debate plays out over the next number of months leading up to the 11-4-08 election and well beyond it.

And as a by-product of our prudent, internal actions other nations of the world will be indirectly pressured to deal with their internal population and social problems, and that in time could make living conditions within their home countries worthy of their own people wanting living there!

Consider that the leadership of other countries does not hate America, as much as they fear American Democracy. And the fact is that they (Iraq and Iran for example) are afraid to write a Constitution for their country and their people that is half as good as ours.

To close on what I acknowledge is a most difficult, yet critically important APM proposal, I would say that taking care of these population issues is our nation's absolute baseline — and therefore must be pursued and implemented to Preserve the Common Good of our people.

The rest of the proposals presented in CS2 and the others that will be developed in the future only serve to compliment and strengthen this national foundation – the effective and protective management of our own people and society.

The APM proposal you just read is extremely hard policy and honestly I did not like having to write it all down! But nobody else was. As far as I am concerned APM is the toughest thing we must do because it directly impacts individuals and families.

Granted, some of the rest of these proposals do get real tough, if not ugly at times. However, We must take charge of our national well-being for after-all it is our nation. Therefore, these are our problems to be resolved and We the People obviously are required to tell our elected leadership how to do their job.

o   o   o   o

6. English as First and Only Language

"We have one language here and that is the English language."

Theodore Roosevelt

If there were any questions, that is our only answer summarized in eleven simple words.

Issue/Problem

This National proposal declares that English will be the only officially recognized and tax-payer supported language in the United States of America.

This is the second of the three (3) overriding social and economic issues that the American Agenda presentation is built around and upon. The other two (2) are the American Population Management and U.S. Re-Employment proposals that form the functional cornerstones of the overall American Agenda. All three (3) are critical to the restructuring of the National System for the Common Good of our citizens.

At first look my impression was that the proposal clarifying the national language controversy seemed minor in comparison to the other two complex issues, however that turned out not to be the case. As I struggled over the content of the draft, I began to understand just how clearly the language issue demonstrates what is wrong with Special Interest politics and the Congress, and what that irresponsible combination is doing to our National System. These became some of the hardest pages to write in all of CS2.

o   o   o   o

More Common Sense

Logically, a common national language may be seen as both glue and grease within any country's National System. It is *glue* in that it facilitates a common bond of intelligence that allows the people of any nation to easily communicate in speech and writing — whether they are in their native land or upon meeting each other in another country that has some other native language. It is a human comfort to easily communicate with other people.

It is *grease* in that it allows individuals and businesses large and small to easily interact, naturally facilitating effective and efficient communication within their own country, thereby promoting the flow of commerce and industry. It supports open and transparent communication which in turn promotes trust.

English has naturally and functionally served as America's <u>only national language</u> since that historic day in July 1776, over 230 years ago when our national ancestors declared their independence. There can be no prudent or practical rationale presented that could justify why a second language should now be legislatively <u>forced</u> upon American society, the tax-payers, and in particular, *We the People...*

o   o   o   o

This proposal was deemed necessary for inclusion in CS2 to confront yet another negative side-effect of the unchecked Illegal Occupant (IO) invasion of America that is mainly coming from the Central and South American (CSA), predominantly Spanish-speaking nations.

Certain businesses, industries, and some pro-Latino Special Interest entities are lobbying to make Spanish a publicly supported language, funded by our tax dollars and forcing additional burdens on many businesses and a multitude of public services – and all of that only to make it easier for English-illiterate IOs to <u>seek</u> in and exist within our sovereign borders. That's the facts.

At last check 30 of the states had seen the unfortunate, yet public necessity to legislate and make English their state's official language. This includes the <u>southern border state</u> of Arizona that passed "English only" legislation under their Proposition 103 in the November 2006 election – and with a 3 to 1 voter approval margin. Consider that Arizona's citizens live on the border with Mexico and do <u>not</u> want Spanish supported in their state, by their taxes – to say nothing about the IOs that constantly wash through their state.

A somewhat interesting fact is that over 60 other countries around the world, including Belize located on Mexico's southern border, have declared English to be their official national language.

See the website <u>ProEnglish.org</u> for more details on the issue.

The primary and logical reason that English was never designated as America's official language is that it has always been <u>assumed</u> that it was – why legislate the obvious. And you might reasonably ask why we should now be required to pass laws to certify our own language?

The answer to the question "Why" in this case is the same response as for many of the other on-going issues facing the American public – it is the *dysfunctional* Congress of the United States of America.

Dysfunctional, with regard to the Common Good of our citizens, that is. It is both Houses and both political Parties in the Congress that refuse to act responsibly and to Protect the Common Good of American society.

In too many cases, the Congress as a united body works in a "coordinated" manner to Provide legislative action or *pre-meditated inaction* clearly for the benefit of Special Interest entities. Congress' Common Agenda is rapidly becoming retention and use of legislative political power that serves the Few, at the expense of the Many. And the situation has only gotten worse since 2001. Can any objective person argue with that observation?

That "Few over the Many" political reality is what drove the common people to leave the Old World and come to the New World. It later caused our national ancestors, the American colonists to declare their independence from the Old World Order and establish a government designed to be ruled by and for the Common Good of the Masses.

Take a few moments and consider — that oppressive Old World political reality is what We the People are finding ourselves living with today. And even though we do not like to consider that to be America's reality – I know and you know — that statement is far closer to the Plain Truth than any of us want to admit.

o   o   o   o

For now, it would serve us to acknowledge that the US Congress that has pretty well refined their ability to screw-up and/or to ignore even the most practical things. And with regard to the topic of this proposal, they are currently dancing around making English the official and only tax-payer supported language of America.

Let us continue with this heart warming example of Special Interest politics.

You Want the Truth — We Will Share the *Truth*

What the various Special Interest lobbyists are *really* pushing the Congress to do in this case is to enact national legislation certifying Spanish as the *second* tax-payer supported language in America. They do not give a good dam about certifying English — their only concern is for Spanish to be added to the tax-payer's tab! Give that angle some thought if you haven't already.

Further, the Congress and the all too willing Bush II White House are not working on this Spanish-on-Demand legislation because they are worried about a small 'screaming' portion of America's Latino community or that they are interested in Latino campaign donations or to help secure Latino votes down the road — or because they really care about Latino's. The American Latino community legal and IO should not kid itself!

Their Special Interest "mission" is only to make it as easy as possible for non-English speaking, cheap, IO, Latino labor pool to exist and grow within America's sovereign borders. They want cheap labor no matter what language 'it' might speak.

Further, the Special Interest does not care about any of the negative civil behavior of any IOs that seek into America from all over the world, or what conditions they may be required live in after they arrive. They do not care or consider any of that *their* problem! And on top of all that, they definitely do not want their taxes raised to pay for the costs generated. It is commonly known as, "They want their cake and to eat it, too." And so for they are doing just that!

And they are not alone. Today (which just happens to be Saturday August 11, 2007 at about 6:25am, and I am refining the draft a bit before I go to work), in too many cases the Special Interest entities on various issues are clearly winning the struggle for Power and Control over our National System – the way America really works on a day-to-day.

We the People are paying a growing price in actual lives and dollars, and at the same time observing as our nation's quality of life slowly erodes. This is not the way things are supposed to be.

o   o   o   o

With this example of just how little 'that' Special Interest entity really cares for the welfare of the IOs, let us bring our focus back to the Congress and "their" true level of interest in the People's Common Good.

If, we step back at look at the Big Picture for a sobering moment, I believe it is easy to observe that US Congress is also exhibiting less and less concern for the conditions that average Americans are required live in.

The next you hear them referred to as the "do nothing Congress" – consider that they are doing something for Them, but are doing nothing for Us! That is the net result of their work. It is only the Plain Truth, folks.

This would be a good time to refer back to that Grievance List and see how often and well that statement can be applied there. Ponder that for a few moments my fellow Americans. The good news is that We the Power have the absolute Constitutional power to correct this dysfunctional national condition and that approcah will be addressed in Part 5.

o o o o

Our *Crisis*

The overall and growing national Crisis is that IOs are not only being allowed, but are encouraged to trespass and violate our borders by land, sea, and air from all over the world.

That steady IO flow is the intended net result of various Special Interest driven legislation and domestic propaganda campaigns.

This *correctable*, national condition is intentionally being promoted by Special Interest, non-Democratic and overtly *dictatorial* population management policies orchestrated primarily to benefit corporate profits and very short-term thinking — and all at the total expense of the taxpayers and with complete disregard (if not contempt) for American society.

We must declare such dictatorial policies and the increasing social negatives they generate will not be allowed to continue.

o o o o

As a result of Congress' national irresponsibility on such a bone-marrow, national issue — it is now necessary for Americans to demand that English be legislated as our only national language.

This is yet another case where narrow-focused, Special Interest and irresponsible business lobbies with far too much political influence are imposing something on American society that is not in the best interest of the nation or the Common Good of the citizenry.

Again, the Special Interest agenda operating here is the socially inappropriate push to have Spanish in both voice and written applications to become a *mandatory* requirement for private enterprise and countless public service programs.

Looking at the Bigger Picture — Special Interest politics, supported by various screamer groups have thus far succeeded in the total suppression of an absolute Immigration Control Policy and creation of a totally practical National Id System. Now they would force the government (our taxes wasted) and business large and small (the cost of goods and services avoidably increased) to accommodate non-English speaking (or reading or writing) IOs within our National System for long periods of time, if not for the rest of their lives – and without ever being required to learn our language.

Calmly and rationally observed, this is part of a coordinated Special Interest campaign intended to wrestle control of American society away from We the People. This is not conspiracy theory — this is what is happening right before our eyes! To make our country as comfortable as possible for an endless flow of IOs to move in, live, and multiply.

In over 230 years America has never seen the practical need to so accommodate <u>any</u> <u>other</u> <u>group</u> and we are ***not*** going to start now! I call this type of situation Beyond Sense (BS).

This has all the makings of an American nightmare, not a Dream. *We the People* <u>must</u> <u>now</u> <u>awaken</u> and bring an end to this bad dream.

o   o   o   o

A Question of Hemispheric Balance and Nation-to-Nation Responsibility

During the 2006 Congressional campaign a congressman from a middle-America state was on the evening news and was asked about the problem illegal immigration. In his response which was anti-IO, he commented that if the flow of IOs was not stopped it would "ruin the fabric of American society."

I had not heard it put that way before, but thought that it was a good way to frame the situation. Having thought about the meaning of that comment and how it might be presented in CS2, brings me to the following remarks which were a bit difficult to develop, and will be difficult for some to read, but such concepts must be considered as we work together to define <u>and</u> control <u>our</u> nation's future.

Blending into the Melting Pot

Whatever happened to the idea of groups blending into American society?

Using a harsh, yet appropriate analogy — instead of a blending into American society that a legal and fully controlled entry of foreign-born Latinos (and others) could accommodate – there continues to be a deliberate, premeditated, and orchestrated "dumping" of CSA population, northward across the US/Mexican border.

Bluntly put, it has created a virtual social and economic "oil-slick" across our entire country and throughout our National System. The CSA people are arriving in such numbers that they are trying to install their national customs and habits within our borders rather than learning how to adapt to our culture as other ethnic groups have been required to do and have done in the past. So much for blending in!

Going forward, the sources of that growing oil slick must be stopped (a 2,000 mile fence will be a good start) and then cleaned–up in order to Preserve the "traditional fabric" our society, or we can just kiss it good-bye. Is that clear enough?

Note to reader: Again, I can completely understand why this piece in general could be seen as 'somewhat' prejudiced in its tone and content. I will assure you that it is not. It is written from the absolute point-of-view of the average, disgusted American citizen. You know, the Silent Majority. Being absolutely pro-American does not make a person anti-immigrant or a racist of any kind. After all it is our country, so hang in there.

o   o   o   o

That said allow me to explain the "hemispheric" reference. It will be expanded upon later, but this is an appropriate application of a foreign policy concept whose time has probably come. Hold on tight and let's go back about 500 years in our hemisphere's political history.

So there it was, the Western Hemisphere circa 1508. You know about the time that the Native Americans were beginning to introduce the tobacco plant to the world. Talk about paybacks!

Over the next few centuries the New World would be colonized (a nice way to put it) mainly by the England and Spain, with a little bit of the French and some others. However, the main players were England and Spain. In the end things pretty much wound up with England taking control and colonizing what is now America and Canada, with Spain doing the same with what became Central and South America.

Since England and Spain never did get along very well and after it all was sorted out including right through to the "Alamo" — the hemisphere was virtually split in two (2) at what is now the good old US/Mexico border. Go figure! Each "half" was initially conquered, then settled and developed under totally different yet *equally oppressive* dictatorial-style governments, with different 'primary' languages, and different primary religious authorities.

This is where the concepts and reality of Hemispheric Balance, and nation-to-nation responsibility comes into play. To the North it was English and the Protestant Church of England. To the South it was Spanish and the Roman Catholic Church. There were of course some sprinklings here and there, but overall that is how it shaped-up and it stayed that way through today.

o   o   o   o

Bear with me on the following scenario. Sometimes it is beneficial in the problem solving process to observe other similar, but not rally identical situations for a better perspective on the situation you are dealing with. It is perspective that will take some time for us all to think about.

Our buddy *Webster*, defines *ethnic* as,

> a member of an ethnic group; a member of a minority group
> who **retains** customs, language, or social views of the group

We have all heard about the *ethnic cleansing* that took place in Eastern Europe after the fall of the Soviet Union. The Soviets had literally been sitting on top of the ethnic Servs and Croats hatred for each other for seventy (70) years – 7 decades — not allowing them to go after each other again and again as was their "tradition".

But then, as I like to describe it, as soon as the Soviets left those "people" dug up the floors in their homes, pull out the old grenades, and tossed them over the fence at their *neighbors*. After 70 years!

o   o   o   o

We have been watching a similar yet exceedingly worse display taking place in Iraq. Worse because it is a lethal combination of:

— 164 —

- Shiite Moslem vs Sunni Moslem
- Moslem vs Kurds
- Tribal, yes 'tribal' warfare Sunni Moslem tribes
- Tribal warfare Shiite Moslem tribes
- *Eye for an Eye*, payback killings by Shiite's for 20-years of the Sunni minority that under SH's rule had military power over the Shiite majority (60%). And abused that power.
- Shiite and Sunni intruders sent from neighboring countries in the region.
- And, let us not forget, the original reason for the Iraq War, who gets the bigger share of Iraq's oil rights and revenues. But I digress!

Appropriately, there will be more on that grim reality when we review the Military Industrial Complex.

o   o   o   o

You are asking how this applies to our primarily Latino IO problem. Our IO problem would never become that violent. And of course it would not.

However, we are approaching a forced and un-natural, cultural imbalance that is unprecedented in history. I believe it is fair to say that there has never been a "peace time" migration of one culture's people, in this case represented by the CSA countries into another culture – America.

We have watched a few million Iraqi's flee into somewhat accepting neighboring countries, with permission. However, that is wartime and the neighboring countries have complimentary cultures. Those receiving countries are struggling to support what they intend to be only a temporary influx, to be returned when the war ends.

You may ask what this has to do with ending the current Latino invasion of North America. With the 1986 Immigration Act and citizenship amnesty granted what termed out to be several million IOs, our government under the Reagan Administration told the American public that was it. That we had an official Guest Worker Program and that business would then be penalized and prosecuted for employing IOs from then on — just like they are paying lip-service to now.

Some 22 years later, bad history is trying to repeat itself. And if it does, just like the Eagles once sang,

"You call some place paradise, then you can kiss it good-bye"

o   o   o   o

I will somewhat abruptly end this piece now. These are the hard issues for each of us to seriously ponder. And our nation's Destiny is the only thing at risk.

And I must challenge the reader to consider how they would attempt to frame such issues. We are hereby challenged to have this national discussion because America does not have:

- An official national language
- A viable Immigration Control Policy
- A controlled National Id System
- A controlled Visitor Tracking System

We will either have an America they we can recognize or we should declare the United Nations building in New York City the new nation's capital and start living under their jurisdiction.

The People's Sense

As stated, the unfortunate need for us to even address this issue easily ties into American Population Management and the Immigration Control Policy about reversing the Latino invasion (and from around the world) and the growing negative impacts it is forcing upon American society and the taxpayers. This language "side-issue" in that broader IO Crisis needs to be brought to a rapid close and the "US" Congress needs to have English declared and certified as our <u>only</u> language, by let's say July 4, 2008.

Businesses may and government <u>will</u> then quit producing any public materials in Spanish or any other language and wasting our good tax dollars. For example, the growing practice of printing federal, state, and various local public service information in anything but English will stopped. Further, Spanish-only speaking people will be held responsible for bringing their own interpreter with them to public offices, e.g., traffic court.

This is clearly another "or else" type of an issue for any politicians that plan to run in 2008 for the Presidency or the Congress. Challenge them on it when they are campaigning – find out who they are really intending to work for if elected or re-elected.

<u>Some Considerations</u>

- Just as any other group that has come to America, and is expected to

blend into the great melting-pot, the Spanish-speaking will not have the on-going use of their native language supported in this country and certainly not by our taxes.

• The one-language issue will also be inserted into the Naturalization process. Going forward people will be **required** to not only speak English but to read it as well, or their **initial** application for American citizenship will not be granted. Other countries do this and we will make no apologies for finally tightening our *non-citizen rules*.

The same restrictions will be applied to requests for Green Cards and Permanent Resident Alien status, as well. The line will be drawn.

• Large numbers of the IOs flowing into the country from the CSAs do not know any English and may not naturally possess the ability (let alone the desire) to learn it or any other language beyond their own. This does not imply they are un-intelligent, but simple fact is that not everyone has that natural ability to learn another language.

During the National Population Registration (NPR) process, IOs that cannot speak English will be among the first to be repatriated because they are simply the easiest to identify. And no one had better mention the word 'profiling'. Go sit in your local traffic court some day and observe — it is appalling.

• I spoke with a first grade teacher in early 2006 in Loudoun County, Virginia (just outside of DC). She had been teaching in a local elementary school for six-plus years and had changed schools at the start of the school year. She told me that the conditions were the same in both schools and it was getting worse each year – stating that she was in practice having to teach English as a Second Language (ESL) in her regular class since so many kids did not have English language skills. Repeat that in thousands of classrooms across the country.

Do I even need to say how much this degrades our children's education?

What Personally Disturbed Me

On the lighter side, I will share my personal irritation by relating an experience I had with what I consider language related government waste. For many years I have traveled the I-64 inter-state that runs the 60 miles between Richmond and Newport News, Virginia where my father lived and beyond that to the Outer Banks of North Carolina (I love it there). For what seemed years there was not a public rest area on the eastbound side –

it was perpetually under construction. But, it finally opened and is a large colonial style brick building – you know the classic Williamsburg image. So I stopped to check it out one day and see how my Virginia tax dollars were being spent.

I walked up to the men's room and the signage next to the door had the usual little international symbol a man that *is intended* to cover all the bases and below that the word, "Men." No problem. But, below that it had another word, "Hombres." When I saw that ridiculous waste of good taxes — I was disgusted! Virginia is over 1500 miles from the Southern border.

Sorry, but I just had to share that one with you. Have you had a similar experience?

o   o   o   o

They Are to Work for Us

The Congress must be made to remember that they are to work to promote the Life, Liberty, and the Pursuit of Happiness of American citizens. That is their purpose and reason for being as declared by The Founders.

If Congress would only grow some political guts, these types of no-brainer issues could be practically resolved. Such matters would rapidly become a fading memory for Americans and we could stop wasting our tax dollars continuously re-studying or discussing such issues. The People might even begin to appreciate and respect the Congress again. Their job "disapproval" rating in 2007 was higher than that of Bush IIs — which is hard to top!

It would be highly beneficial, IF, the Democratic Party in particular would finally wake up and remember that they, as opposed to the Republicans that willingly bow to Business, are supposed to be the Party of the Ameri-can people and that means American **citizens**.

Democrats were not elected (by the majority of) their Party's voters to serve every foreign-based group that comes here and wants to claim citizen-level Rights and Liberties. Those non-American born people are "screaming" for privileges that they do not deserve and often could not begin to get in their own country.

For years it seemed to me that we functionally have Republican and a semi-Republican Party operating under that beautiful Capitol Dome. And that is functionally not good, for the Common Good !

Yes, the Democratic Party does need to wake-up and realize that while there is certainly a place for Liberal policy considerations in our Democratic system – that there are prudent and practical limits when the Common Good of *We the Citizens* is clearly at stake. Can there any question of that being the case today?

If all the members of US Congress, regardless of Party affiliation, would set about doing the People's work, would declare and aggressively promote a true National Vision for America, then they would not be required to raise millions of dollars to get re-elected. They would be doing it the old fashion way – they would earn it!

Currently, though both Houses of Congress are not demonstrating a patriotic, citizen-oriented stance on this basic national issue and too many others, as well.

Challenge every candidate about this as they come around looking for your donation and vote.

Enough said.

o   o   o   o

7. The U.S. Re-Employment System

"Employment is a Key to Domestic Peace in Any Country"

Introduction

This National program introduces what I call the U.S. Re-Employment System. As stated earlier, the Population Management and Employment proposals are the cornerstones of the overall American Agenda and are critical to the restructuring of the National System for the Common Good.

> I will acknowledge that this is my favorite American Agenda proposal. It presents us with 'the critical societal tool' required to help us to facilitate the resolution of many of our national challenges.

The Re-Employment System will be a straightforward restructuring of existing national and state unemployment and social service systems into a far more efficient and publicly beneficial network. It introduces the concept of Three Employment Sectors, those being the familiar Private and Public sectors along with the newly defined "National Resource" sector.

This proposal will streamline the re-training for re-employment of American citizens as our economy changes, as well as placing efficient controls on Unemployment and Welfare benefits and other social service programs. The improved controls and simplified rules will better serve those *citizens* receiving the benefits, as well as insuring the best use of taxpayer funds.

The Three-Sector Employment System

"A Self-Cleansing National System"

Needless to say that employment is a critical component in our National System just as in every country. Employment pays the bills and Americans must have viable and legal jobs.

The Re-Employment System (RES) concepts were also by-products from the development of the National Drug Reform (NDR) Proposal solution to our nation's hard drug problems – the alleged War on Drugs. It was developed when researching how to structure and facilitate the vocational training of recovering addicts and former drug providers to become legally employable.

Basically, the same Civil Rehabilitation procedures that would be utilized in upgrading a person's educational level, vocational abilities, and social skills to help recovering addicts and former drug providers, will be available to both unemployed and under-employed Americans. Now if someone does not need any or all of those public services – fantastic! However, if they do, active and committed participation will not be optional.

Purpose

The purpose of this piece is to introduce a highly practical system regarding employment in America, and more specifically it addresses the issue of "un-employment" in our country. It will also have positive impacts upon social programs such as unemployment compensation, welfare, housing, etc. Addressing the public's expectation of delivering the most beneficial services to individuals and families for the least amount of taxes expended will be the baseline requirement.

A general nationwide system for assisting the unemployed exists today, since each state (and DC always implied) operates its own unemployment and welfare systems. We will act to refine and standardize these necessary functions into a national network that is still managed and coordinated by the respective states – not by the federal government.

You may already see some connection between addressing drug reform issues via the NDR, and the existing unemployment and welfare systems. Legal employment or lack there of, helps perpetuate *part* of the underlying causes of the drug problem. A person's employability plays a critical role in their near term job opportunities and the long-term success of their overall "civil rehabilitation."

A Matter of Balancing Perspectives

By now some of you are thinking, "Oh good grief, here comes another government program." Not so! We already have these programs at the Federal, state, county, and city levels. They already work to coordinate the unemployed and the rules by which people move unto and off unemployment roles and receive various benefits. And frankly some states do it better than others.

The monthly Labor Department statistics on Unemployment Claims, like the total number of new claims and how this month's compared to last month's total are closely watched and are reported nationally, along with the "estimated" percentage of US Unemployment. The number of new jobs created each month is also reported. The stock markets can and do react to unexpected movement in these numbers, up or down.

Speaking of *"there are lies, dam lies, and then there are statistics"* (Mark Twain) the percentage of the un-employed is what you might call a "soft" number. It does not include counts of those that have quit looking for work or for instance, those taking Automobile Industry buy-outs (lay-offs). Therefore, it could be viewed as politically adjusted (propaganda) in some ways.

There has always been a debate over the concept of very low or 'zero' unemployment. There are two (2) primary perspectives or camps in that debate – the **People** (or Labor) and **Business** (or Management). They both lobby to shape and control national policies on the issue, but lately the People are getting beat up!

The People's Perspective

This camp generally believes that everyone should be employed — a job for everyone, great! This is the right idea since IF everyone had a job then people would be more self-sufficient, lower unemployment costs to society, and less welfare support required. Taxes could be lower or funds could be re-directed to more productive programs. Conceptually, people would be happier working and better able to pull their own weight in society. Their self-esteem is increased and their future would be brighter – addressing basic human needs.

Realistically, unemployed and under-employed (income level) people are more likely to turn to crime to support their economic needs. These groups are also more likely to turn to *products* such as cigarettes, alcohol, prescription and/or illegal drugs to help cope with the stress and anxiety of their day-to-day circumstances. And in some percent of cases, their recreational drug use of those *products* can turn into addiction, which can in turn lead to crime or other socially deviant behavior.

Finally, the uncontrolled IOs are absolutely taking jobs from American citizens — which "in the course of human events" does produce social friction between various groups and between those within the same group, as well.

The Business Perspective

This camp watches the monthly statistics and gets worried when employment gets too low, say 4% or less. They are concerned that if the available pool of unemployed workers gets too small, employers will have to compete for workers and wages will be driven up by the competition. That is how it works!

> This is the defining mindset of those that work to sustain the IO flow.

Therefore, this camp desires a certain level of unemployment with a heavy dash of IOs on top! At the same time they do not like the costs of payroll taxes, medical benefits, unemployment taxes, and welfare programs. IOs are not a problem for too many in this camp and one way or another they "encourage" the flow of them. They publicly ignore the issue and covertly lobby hard against laws that would reduce the availability of this cheap labor pool. This is a key issue in reference to the Civil Responsibility of business and industry within the National System.

The National Requirement

A balance must be struck that most effectively deals with the practical needs of both camps, BUT, must consider the Common Good of the National System that we all live and must work in above all else. An approach that would balance the desires and prudent needs of all parties would need to address these types of issues:

- Providing a viable income and legal employment for all Americans.
- American citizens, native born and naturalized, must be employed before any legal visitor/occupant (i.e., Permanent Resident Aliens).
- Controlling legal immigration and the legal employment of any non-citizens, including what jobs they cannot have.
- Minimizing the costs of unemployment and related programs against our taxes.
- Minimizing the costs of public welfare and related programs against our taxes.
- Re-locating people as needed across the country to respond to seasonal demands, as well as worker resource shortfalls in various areas of the country as the economy evolves over the years.
- Stopping illegal immigration and the future employment of IOs.

And finally, We in America just as every other nation has the Sovereign Right to say,

"America does not owe anyone born outside this country
a job or any social services,

let alone entry into
nor the right to remain inside our borders."

That statement may upset some, but not the vast majority of the American electorate! It is simply, Americans <u>first</u> in America.

Our Traditional Employment Sectors

In America we normally think of two (2) sectors of employment, those being the Public and Public sectors. You are most than likely in there someplace.

The Public Sector of Employment

A philosophical national goal is to <u>minimize</u> the number of people "employed" in the taxpayer funded Public sector. To provide the greatest benefits from these services, while striving to minimize the cost to society in the form of taxes we pay (say amen please).

The efficient operation of any government run function, regardless of its size and complexity, are the People's "expectation." However, we always hear and read stories in the news about gross waste in various programs. This inefficiency is far from a secret, it does exist, and we love to complain about it. The good news is that greater operational efficiency is possible and there are ways to help (if not force) that restructuring process along.

The Public sector is the general heading for what is considered government employment, at all levels. It is funded by personal and business taxes, as well as various fees and tariffs collected by the IRS and other agencies of government. The typical Employment groups included in this sector are the following:

<u>Government Employees:</u>
- Federal
- State
- County
- City
- Towns, etc.

<u>Military Staffing:</u>
- Army
- Navy
- Air Force
- Marine Corps
- Coast Guard
- The National Guard of each state

<u>Contractors:</u>
- Civilian staffing both full and part-time of people working for Private sector companies that provide support to the entities above.

<u>Also, included under the Public Sector:</u>

The following programs are broken out since they provide various direct income and/or benefits funded by our taxes:
- Unemployment Benefits
- Welfare Benefits
- Social Security Benefits
- Medicare Benefits
- Medicaid Benefits
- Others

That pretty well overviews the Public Sector — next.

The Private Sector of Employment

The philosophical national goal here is to maximize the number of people "employed" in the Private sector, by virtue of our ever-loving Capitalistic economic system creating jobs, driven by people buying goods and services, and paying their taxes (yes another amen)!

> Note: "Small business" accounts for about 80% of all jobs in America.

This sector is the general heading for employment in our free enterprise system. It is fairly well driven by the laws of Supply and Demand, under the concept that if a given business provides its customers with desirable goods and/or services, at a competitive price, it will survive in the market place. If a given business does not do those fundamental things well, it will and should fail, whether it has been in business for 6 months or 60 years.

Americans are employed by companies in all lines of business, from hourly workers at Wendy's, your local grocery store, Waste Management Inc., and the Home Depot to the senior management of the NYSE and NASDAQ listed companies, and so many people in the multitude of job types in between — blue collar, white collar, and no collar.

As a note, the Private sector also includes people that could be considered "independently wealthy" – many of whom still get up and go to work everyday — like The Donald, Oprah, Martha, Regis, Warren B., and a guy named Gates! Fine examples of that good work ethic thing!

Why Do You Work?

In the middle of most of the NDR proposal one-on-one's when discussing the vocational rehabilitation component, I ask the person that loaded question. I am now asking you the same question. *Why do you work?* Usually, people would think for a moment sensing I am throwing them a curve and typically respond with one or more of the following:

- I need money.
- I like to pay my bills.
- I like to buy things.
- My kids need shoes.
- I don't like robbing banks!

And then they waited for the punch line. I then presented the following points:

Point #1

The vast majority of the people I spoke with were employed at least part-time and some had 2 jobs. I shared this perspective:

> "You get up and go to work because that is what your roles model(s) did. Your Father and/or Mother or guardian <u>worked</u>. Regardless of what they did for employment, they set the normal behavior pattern that you without much thought began to follow as a teenager or young adult. It helped form what is called a basic work ethic. <u>No one</u> is born with a work ethic, it is learned behavior — and it is learned or not learned."

For a real case in point, the week before Christmas (2006) I was watching Jay Leno and the well-respected actor Samuel L. Jackson was on. Leno asked him why he was known for always working so hard – sometimes doing multiple movies a year and other projects. Jackson fired back it was because both of his parents were always working hard when he was a kid – they were his role model and he had embraced it! There it is.

The majority of the time people follow the role model(s) they observed when growing up, although siblings within the same family (even twins) can reject those models and do the opposite. That is the way people are the world over. Also, in homes where two (2) extremely different models are demonstrated, the children may not all wind up following the better example.

The point to be made here is that not all young people have "good" role models. This basic fact-of-life cuts across all races <u>and</u> all social classes. Some had role models that did as little as possible to get by, playing games with the system for anything and everything they could get, and I mean both technically legal <u>and</u> illegal games.

Point #2

I would then add that we also know how to take care of ourselves because of our role models. Which includes knowing how to clean, taking regular baths, brushing our teeth, using a checkbook, paying bills, speaking civilly to others, having decent manners, etc. Most of us of course take these things for granted, as normal, but in reality not everyone had those models.

Today, there are programs all over this country that teach people these basics. Many of those I spoke with had never considered that circumstance and appreciated the perspective. These are the "life" or social skills talked about in the NDR Proposal as part of the comprehensive civil rehabilitation of recovering drug addicts.

Point #3

I asked what they would do if they suddenly lost their own job for whatever reason?

I usually answered it for them saying, the majority of us would get up and do whatever we needed to get ourselves another job, ASAP! "Most" would aggressively pursue training in new skills if needed. And, although we would prefer not to would even re-locate self and our families to other city, if required. This pro-active response again goes to work ethic, self-motivation, self-esteem, and personal responsibility for self and/or family.

Of course there are those lacking a viable work ethic, self-confidence, feelings of personal responsibility, and some with a perpetual feeling of being a victim (although it is often self-inflicted) that will just sit and do as little as possible to find new work, especially if it meant learning a new job skills and could not begin to conceive of relocating to someplace else.

Please keep these points and people in mind as we continue. You may have an idea where this is going.

Note: By the way, going forward free-will crime (what other type is there?) will become a "decreasing vocational option" as opposed to what it is now. This will be due in great part to the improved functioning of various parts of our National System that will have been restructured by the publicly demanded implementation and enforcement of the solution-oriented proposals in this American Agenda.

o   o   o   o

What About Those Not Employed?

And what about our unemployed fellow American citizens and the non-citizen OLOs (as a reminder, Other Legal Occupants) in our country that require employment to support themselves and/or their family? Let's overview the two (2) groups of people that are not currently employed in the Public or Private sectors.

Group 1 — The Good:

• People that are not eligible for unemployment benefits and are looking for work.

- People that are currently receiving unemployment benefits and are looking for work.
- People that have expended their unemployment benefits and should definitely be looking for work.
- People that may already have some income, but are <u>under</u>-employed due to the types and/or number of jobs available in their local area.
- People that may already have some income, but desire/need more income to live better, but they lack the confidence and/or skills to find that work. This would include part of the valuable and under-utilized resource pool of senior citizens.
- People new to the country that are seeking their first <u>legal</u> employment opportunity. We could ask why they are here at all.

Group 2 — The Not So Good:

- Criminals* living off the fruits of there illicit efforts – car theft, carjacking, identity theft, home break-ins, general thief, robbery, etc.
- Drug barons (although most are outside our country), traffickers, distributors, and the local "hard" drug dealers and their network.
- Independent <u>domestic</u> growers and sellers of marijuana! This group is held out as separately from those that obtain their 'hard drug' products from the external and illegal, international distribution system. Also note that marijuana/cannabis has <u>long been</u> America's number one (1) cash crop at over $87 billion (with a B) dollar a year – an illegal business. More on ending that stupidity later.
- IOs working 'off the table' employment. This would include unfortunate souls from around the world that have bought their way into the U.S. through smugglers and are "working off" the debt owed those people often in crime, prostitution, custodial services, and working in sweat shops.

    * — Please note that 'criminals' very often hold regular, legal, full-time or part-time jobs in addition to their illegal activities. Realize that being a criminal does <u>not</u> mean someone is lazy or lacking intelligence — far from it.

Summary of the Un-Employed

On one hand, **The Good** may be looked at as an under-utilized national resource pool to the nation that due to circumstance, motivation, public coordination or geographic location are not currently able to contribute more into our economic system, gain greater income, a greater sense of self-worth, and a higher standard of living.

On the other hand, **The Not So Good** mainly represent a negative force in America and generate what is termed "negative budget expense items" at all levels of government. They are the exact opposite of what the People desire and expect of a civilly responsible member of American society, whether the person is a citizen or a legal visitor. Therefore, they do not contribute positively to the country — in many ways they decrease the quality of the Common Good and directly increase the negative costs of government.

To repeat, there are programs at all levels of government that are administered to deal with the range of serious public problems caused by that latter group – taking funds and human resources that we could be putting to far better use.

Not that we will ever be able to <u>fully</u> eliminate this group or the government programs required to deal with them. For me state that we could do that, would immediately decrease any credibility I might be gaining with you!

However, it is <u>absolutely possible</u> to make dramatic, and what many will call unbelievable progress in that direction. That I will state and with full confidence!

And that is exactly what We the People shall do.

o   o   o   o

Introducing the Third Employment Sector – The Resource Sector

We have **just reviewed** the variety of un-employed and under-employed people that comprise what will come to be known as the nation's third employment sector – **The Resource Sector.** The three (3) standard U.S. Employment Sectors would then be:
- Private
- Public
- Resource

The **Three Employment Sector System (TESS)** is built upon straightforward and simple concepts. It will be extremely efficient when in operation within our National System. And simple, yet highly efficient system solutions are absolutely the best.

This viable and publicly acknowledged entity within the National System could be thought of as the 'National' Resource sector, because all of the people that comprise the 3rd sector are technically available employees to employers across the nation.

The purpose of the Resource Sector is to act as a national clearinghouse for anyone and everyone that needs help obtaining gainful (and legal) employment – full, part-time, and seasonal. The formal establishment of the Three Employment Sector approach will provide the American economic system with an efficient "Closed Circle System" for re-employment that will offer targeted support to American citizens and legal immigrants. TESS will quickly evolve into that highly efficient and productive methodology that will:

- Allow us to identify and help those seeking employment to find work and/or be trained for a new line of work.
- Allow us to identify those that have trouble with the concept of "honest" work so that they will be properly counseled, trained, and helped to find good work. Former criminals will make up the majority of this group. And as a result of the TESS process, the active number in this group will go down as each year passes. Fewer (bad) criminals = more (good) workers. Believe it!
- To facilitate the development of a single, comprehensive program that will efficiently streamline the existing unemployment and welfare systems – to better serve the public and the taxpayers. The hits just keep on coming!

The clear public goal being first to maximize the percentage of people working in the Private Sector, and secondarily in the Public sector — with some natural level of on-going unemployment expected as people transition between jobs and careers as industries are re-tooled and new small businesses are created.

This approach is not intended to produce zero unemployment.

We deliberately will work to raise the bar of Civil Responsibility with regard to gainful and legal employment for our people, which in turn will result in their having a better life and will promote the Common Good of us all.

o   o   o   o

How TESS Will Work for Us

The following scenario overviews how of the American un-employment and other issues will be addressed by the TESS approach:

- When a person falls out of employment in either the Private or Public sectors they would eventually be expected to seek legal "re-employment" back in one of those sectors.

- Re-employment may be delayed based upon the individual's financial status and need for regular income. Our government has no right or business determining this for a given person, as long as the person is not breaking any laws or seeking tax-payer funded assistance.

  And our government must not seek or be granted the authority to pry into a citizen's living situation. This philosophy will help reverse the violations of the Bill of Rights committed under Bush II and company.

  However, non-citizens may very well be approached in a more aggressive manner.

- A person will continue to apply for Unemployment, Welfare, and the other Social Services offered to help themselves and their family, as appropriate. Those services will continue to be administered as they are today. That process will not change for the time being, which implies the control and delivery of these services will begin to evolve as the nation's new Employment Sector process matures. However, we are not talking about years to observe real public benefits.

- Our existing Social Service entities – local and county to federal levels — will continue to coordinate existing functions. The intent is to bring about practical, procedural improvements that will cause governmental agencies with overlapping services to work together and increase their operational efficiency. That is not intended as a joke.

The TESS will serve as a clearinghouse for needs of individuals and families that require support and services from various publicly-funded agencies. These refinements will allow different agencies to better serve their respective clients, and use our tax dollars more efficiently. This will in turn free-up some public funds for other and more beneficial purposes.

Access to Public Services

In the near future, if a person cannot find new employment on their own and desires any public services, they will be expected to do the following:

- Actively seek new employment, not deliberately play the system as too many still do.

- They will make themselves available for life/social skills and vocational evaluations and counseling, as applicable.
- They will make themselves available for basic educational development, as applicable (e.g., gaining at least a GED – High School diploma).
- They will make themselves available for life/social skills training, as applicable.
- They will make themselves available for vocational training, as applicable.
- They will make themselves available for any short-term employment opportunities, including part/full time community service tasks or with local businesses arranged by their local unemployment office or job placement services. This job placement will be focused at the town, city, and county levels.
- And it will be made very, very clear that they will absolutely not engage in illegal or criminal activities of any kind!

I ask you. Is this basic set of Social Service guidelines too much to ask of someone that society is trying to help and are expending our hard-earned tax dollars on? The taxpayers do not think so!

o   o   o   o

That was a brief introduction to the groups of un-employed and under-employed people that comprise the greater portion of the Resource Sector.

In addition to those, there are Americans of all ages, from teens and college students to senior citizens that need or would benefit from full or part-time employment, but for whatever reason have difficulty in connecting with.

For example, I spoke with a 77 year man the other day that would like to work part-time rather than sitting at home, but is having difficulty being accepted by employers. The TESS employment network would help folks like him.

Again, the good part is that the vast majority of the functions and services mentioned, already exist today and are administered by agencies at all levels of government, which means that we are **already paying** for them. As with the restructuring of the Drug and Alcohol Rehabilitation Center system into the Community Center system under the NDR proposal, we will be implementing operational improvements within the existing social service agencies and making them more operationally efficient.

Overall this is a practical plan we can work with. These operational improvements in turn will provide a higher quality service to both individuals and families – our citizens — that need support finding viable employment and in obtaining access to available social services to improve their living conditions.

All of this along with the benefits to be derived from the other practical proposals of the American Agenda proposals will work together to raise social and civil Expectations in neighborhoods all across the country.

The bar of Civil Responsibility in America will be rising.

o   o   o   o

The People's Sense

As blanket statement, the American people just as the people of every other nation need viable employment and will expect to have hiring preference over any and all non-citizen residents and visitors. This *absolute preference* will apply in the public and private sectors of employment and be written into law, as soon as possible.

Public Employment Legislation

This item was previously mentioned in Part 2. As a working example, for many years America has legislated various job hiring preferences such as for veterans and those with various physical and mental challenges, which is only proper in our society and will continue with some prudent enhancements.

An Example of Near-Term Legislative Action – Citizen Hiring Preference Policy

Going forward, there will be an over-riding preference given to American citizens to be hired before **any non-citizen**. This **National Employment Policy** directive particularly applies to **all public sector** jobs, e.g., local, state, federal, and military positions that are funded by our tax dollars. Foreign-born, non-citizens will find it very difficult if not impossible to obtain these jobs any longer.

Someone may call that whatever they like, *I do not care*, and neither do 90-plus percent of those I have talked with! Further, it is the only practical policy in a shrinking quality job pool. It is unashamedly taking care of our own people to fill **tax-payer-funded** public sector jobs with their associated job security and good benefits, just as other countries so regulate. Foreign-born people come here all the time and go straight after those choice jobs. This will be cut-off!

It will be Americans First and only in such taxpayer funded jobs opportunities. Any questions?

Those non-citizens that have already secured such positions may continue in them. However, such public employment opportunities (privileges) will no longer be an option. And any existing laws to the contrary will be dealt with swiftly! That pretty well sums that up.

o   o   o   o

<u>International Population Accountability Required</u>

To shift the frame of reference just a moment – it is now time for a bit of the Big Picture.

With regard to the long talked about concerns that the world will become over-populated some day in the future – well, welcome to the future! The world has been in that delicate condition for some years now!

Too many countries with too many people already are irresponsibly producing even more of them, and are overtly and covertly working to send their population elsewhere! That 'un-natural' movement in turn often results in problems in the other countries especially where there are cultural and mainly religious differences that make it difficult for the new-comers to *peacefully* be accepted and absorbed into the host nation. And sometimes the new-comers do not want to blend in.

I am not suggesting that immigration between countries be stopped altogether, <u>but</u> prudence must finally be applied worldwide. International public awareness must be raised and accountability must be honored. You know *common sense*.

It is time for <u>every</u> country to adjust their domestic and social structures such that they will be held responsible for <u>all</u> of their <u>own</u> citizens. This frankly means controlling their population growth! You know the touchy concepts of "planned" parenthood, birth control, and responsible family sizing.

The international understanding must be "You make them, you keep them, unless properly invited our to live elsewhere. Otherwise, only short-term visiting is allowed". Is that unreasonable?

Harsh Fact – *Plain Truth*

To those in various religions that reject birth control and/or prescribe ten (10) or more children per faithful family and will "scream" at those statements – **hear this:**

If you go back far enough in time (many centuries) to when those particular rules/doctrine were written into the doctrine of those religions, those were the times when many children either died at birth or did not live to be five (5) years old; when people worked farms and needed extra hands.

And at the brutal bottom line – those were the times when the tyrannical monarchs all over the world simply needed more peasants to work their lands and to be sent off to die in wars. The willing clergy of the day just added it to the "religious doctrine" — the list of things that the "faithful" were expected to do to honor God. Let's face the fact that it had nothing to do with God — it was just the powerful Few selfishly using religion to produce cheap, replaceable labor. And it continues today ....

While I acknowledge the cutting nature of those words and realize that it will definitely burn some ears, the Plain Truth of it must be acknowledged. I know some regular everyday Christians that will have the hair come up on the backs of their neck on those words. Most other Christians do not even think about the issue. And in the end, in everyday society and looking at that Grievance List what real difference does it make.

And other religions have the same archaic doctrine that most of their more responsible followers ignore because it would result in those extra children being born to live in _____ conditions (think about it and you fill in the blank). And the new Pope that has an incredibly hard act to follow falls back to doctrine and declares to the faithful to get out there and have babies. It is sad to see such continued unrealistic and socially irresponsible international leadership in 2007 in that unique and influential religious office.

A civilized and responsible world cannot continue to suffer today due to self-serving "special interest" based dictates and rules that originated hundreds (and hundreds) of years ago. It is a clear example of the difference between religious manipulation and faith in God.

o   o   o   o

To Return to TESS

Sorry, but there is no easy to return from that sermonette.

A few thoughts and legislative possibilities regarding employment in America:

- The Three Sector Employment System will establish a framework for the virtual "recycling" of the American workforce. It will provide the training, as needed relocation and facilitate public and social services to persons and families during employment transition or start-up.

- The epidemic of outsourcing of jobs <u>and industries</u> must be confronted and brought under control if not halted, to help save jobs and careers required for <u>our</u> citizens. This will take aggressive action in legislation and enforcement to gain real control over an issue that does involve both domestic and foreign policy considerations. But America and Americans will be served first!

  The Common Good of our people and our economy must take priority over business interests that are generating 'false profits' at the expense of American jobs — it is a question of responsible balance.

  At some point, it should become difficult for a business to call them selves an American company when they are shipping their production and jobs offshore.

- The existing quotas for foreign workers coming to the U.S. for temporary or multiyear work assignments such as those in Information Technology (IT) related positions must be reviewed, reduced, and probably <u>halted</u> a few years in favor of American citizens being trained via the TESS process for such viable job opportunities. This is a current other source of children being born to non-citizens and claiming US citizenship – that may need to be stopped or at least practically regulated.

  The job category and country-by-country VISA quota (or current lack thereof) needs to be posted on the Internet for public review and adjustment. *We* will determine who is *allowed to play in our sandbox* for the Common Good of citizen employment.

  For example (I am not picking on them, but the facts are the facts), we have a situation where numerous job types are being outsourced to India, but we are still allowing too many Indians to immigrate to the US. We are continuing to allow temporary and full-time IT workers to come to the US from India to take highly desirable domestically based jobs. This is a great deal for India and other countries in that situation, but until at least the outsourcing problem is responsibly dealt with by Congress and American business, this constant stream of people from various countries needs to be cut back if not fully suspended for practical period of years. And I mean starting in 2008.

You can be assured that there will be much more on Employment in America issues as things progress up to the 2008 the election and well beyond...

In Closing

I hope this has provided a reasonable understanding of the U.S. Re-Employment System proposal and how it will work for our people. More details will emerge as time passes and progress is made in the national debate over this proposal and the overall American Agenda.

I believe the Three Employment Sector approach will be seized upon and strongly endorsed by all the state Governors, County Executives, and Mayors across America, regardless of whether they are Democrat, Independent or Republican.

The overall approach to this restructuring has some features that both Conservatives and Liberals can feel good about. The Moderates will be the happiest of all!

o   o   o   o

8 National Drug Reform

"Correcting the Continuing Sins of Our Legislative Fathers, and Mothers"

Issue/Problem

As of 2008, the failed national War on Drugs is 36 or 70-plus years old depending on how you want to look at it.

This CS2 proposal is not the National Drug Reform (NDR) Proposal. That document is over 125 MS/Word pages in length and this book is already too long. Since finding a publicly acceptable solution to the nation's hard drug problem was the issue that started me on this 25 year journey it would have been satisfying to present it here for your review, however, it is now just a side issue within An American Agenda. As you have already read that some of the lessons learned in its development have been applied to proposals such as in the US Re-Employment System, and there are more to come.

The full text of the NDR Proposal can be found on the Internet site, CICRU.org as a "free" download. CICRU (sigh-crew) stands for the Common Interest – Civil Responsibilities Union. It is a grassroots, citizen-based, civil action organization (not another non-profit) that I have established. I see it as the logical follow-on activity to this book. Only time and future events will tell how viable CS2 and CICRU will be with the American public. And while I take nothing for granted, but am optimistic!

o   o   o   o

At first I had this National Drug Reform piece placed under the heading of Industry Restructuring. After all we are talking about a **Domestic Illegal Drug Industry** in the US that has been surpassing the **400 billion-dollar** mark every year without breaking a sweat! Further, Cannabis, more commonly referred to as Marijuana has been the nation's largest cash crop for many years, and in December 2006 it was reported that it alone was an 87 billion dollar industry in the U.S.

In the end, I put this piece that addresses our National Drug Policy here, because it is National level issue that requires absolute, corrective changes being applied to the existing Federal legislation.

Herein we will realistically review National Drug Policy and our future approach to it. We will review how this mess happened and what we will be required to do to fix it!

No more Fantasyland! The "anti-drug" *Screamers* may as well skip to the next proposal on re-starting the Military Draft. Their foolish protests over this issue have helped kill too many people and the nation can no longer afford to listen to their blind stupidity.

The other part of the *"National Fix"* — the prudent creation of the fully "legal" Cannabis industry in America will be reviewed under New and Renewal Industries. It is time for America, as well as the entire developed world to *get real* with the drug business!

Amen.

o o o o

The Old Drug Death Statistics

Presented here as a reference is a classic and commonly referenced 1996 Substance Death Chart and the while it is now over a decade old it demonstrates the point-in-time casualty rate for our most popular national drugs of choice.

Take a look!

1996 Substance Death Chart

Substance(s) Involved	Annual Deaths
Tobacco kills about	430,700
Alcohol and alcohol-related diseases and injuries kill about	110,000
Secondhand tobacco smoke kills about	50,000
Adverse reactions to prescription drugs total	32,000
Aspirin and other anti-inflammatory drugs kill	7,600
Cocaine alone kills about	500
Cocaine in combination with another drug kills	2,500
Heroin alone kills about	400
Heroin in combination with another drug kills	2,500
Marijuana kills	0

I recall the first time I saw the chart and was shocked at the 'surprisingly low' number of heroin and cocaine related deaths. I would have expected the numbers to be much higher considering the billions of taxpayer dollars, the drug-related crime and killings, hundreds of thousands of incarcerations, and the hundreds of thousands of people arrested every year for simple of possession of drugs — with absolutely no involvement in drug sales or trafficking.

Just simple statistical evidence of how absolutely dysfunctional our National Drug Policy is for both our people and our society. And, We the People, will now see to its correction.

Let's see how this tragedy was allowed to happen.

A Brief History of Marijuana (M) and Our Failed National Drug Policy

How Marijuana (M) Became Illegal in America and
How Our National Drug Policy Evolved

"From the very beginning – a grim fairy tale"

Purpose

The purposes here are two-fold. First, to provide the reader with an understanding of the history of the naturally growing, God-given plant Cannabis or Marijuana (herein referred to as M) — from its first known use in ancient China and India — to its 'regular' use by more than 20 million people all across America today. It is the world's most popular substance!

Also, tied into this account is the origin and development of our failed national drug policy. It describes how M became illegal in the 1930's (along with far more dangerous substances) which has resulted in the arrest, conviction, and incarceration of <u>well</u> over 22 million of our fellow Americans. Many of which were only drug users with absolutely <u>no</u> involvement in the trafficking, growth or distribution of this God-given plant.

o · o o o

Over the next pages, you will learn the Plain Truth – such an interesting concept — of how M was originally used in the world, how its use spread across the world and eventually to the America. You will also learn how M, along with the primary hard drugs which are a problem today became illegal in our country.

This drug chronology is primarily built around M, although some references will be made other substances. You will be informed and probably somewhat disgusted by what you read. The legislative history and the special interest politics that drove it were not always pretty. And they still aren't.

In order for us to address the drug problem, it is important for us all to have a common understanding of this history and flawed development our National Drug Policy (NDP). To have a real perspective on how it began and evolved into the public mess it is today – which includes the primary organizations charged with enforcement of policies, as well as, the NDP legislation as currently written and managed.

Also, inter-woven herein are the building blocks of our National Drug Policy (NDP) explaining how it went from non-existent in 1900 to the multi-billion dollar, publicly oppressive government program that it is today. Billions that could, and in our controllable, near-term future will be better spent.

That background and knowledge are of particular importance since our existing NDP and its enforcement at the federal, state, and local levels are contributing to the drug problem and therefore are helping to perpetuate the Illegal Drug Industry! That may sound a bit odd to many people, but it is an accurate assessment.

o   o   o   o

To be clear – Law Enforcement from our local sheriff's office to the FBI and the DEA are absolutely not the problem. These public servants are only charged with trying to enforce the dysfunctional laws passed by legislators at all levels of government. And some of the laws they struggle with are 70 years old. Those that have to fight the Drug War in your locality are at the mercy of failed, ineffective, and unrealistic laws – and equally failed public leadership.

Certainly, some abuses by law enforcement have occurred while enforcing of drug laws against those in the drug business. Frankly, even the finest and well-intentioned of our officers have their limits of tolerance.

Consider that if you were constantly required to deal with vicious, unruly dogs that could take your blood at any time — occasionally you will need to kick some of them. I know I would. It is just another reason why this ridiculous, counter-productive public policy that is killing and locking up far more people than it is saving must be ended. And NOW.

We must now deal with negative interests that are a part the National System – the way America really works on a day-to-day basis —that continue to promote and allow the creation of more users, addicts, and drug dealers, but will not accept responsibility for the situation. Law enforcement is not the problem. The Laws are the problem.

This common base of understanding is critical for us to share as we approach the restructuring of our NDP. The modification of our current legislation to a publicly prudent and practical definition is essential for final victory over our nation's hard drug problems.

o   o   o   o

My original intent for this section in the overall National Drug Reform (NDR) Proposal was provide a brief but informative history on all the primary drugs – M, cocaine, opium (and its derivatives heroin and morphine), and met-amphetamines. How each originated in the world and over the years came to use and at times abuse in our country, and was eventually made illegal.

However, the focus of the Drug Legalization component of the NDR is restricted M. Therefore, I have provided a historical perspective on M, only. I do make references to some of the primary hard drugs in that history when appropriate. M is by far the weak cousin of the other drugs involved.

The history of M is at once interesting, discouraging, and in some ways depressing. You will see in some cases where good, well-intentioned people conceived and implemented what is easily observed in today's light, as narrow-minded, self-serving, shortsighted public laws and programs.

I believe the common understanding of this specific slice of history will help guide us as we rethink the programs implemented by those preceding us. This common knowledge will help guide us as we restructure that failed National Drug Policy for the betterment of our society.

It is absolutely accurate to say <u>all</u> of the drugs that are viewed today as problems, had well-intentioned origins. Most of them actually have some beneficial medical uses when properly used. And today they technically can still provide genuine medical benefit, <u>if</u> administered appropriately (consider today's common hospital use of morphine that is a tremendous pain killer). However, with the exception of M (yes, the exception), all those harder drugs possess incredibly destructive properties when used improperly or abusively.

<u>History Can be Such a Surprising Thing</u>

Interestingly, all the drugs that so torment society today were available, legal, and in <u>common use</u> by the American public as recently as 1930. That's right, legal access to the general public!

These drugs 'began' the transition to illegal status in the United States in the 1930's when the first <u>federal level</u> legislation making M illegal was implemented on October 1, 1937. Herein you will follow the trail M from its origin in ancient China and India, to that date, and up to today.

Here is a reality check! The average person in America in the 1800's and early 1900's could legally obtain opium, morphine, and heroin. A person could order a nice metal-hinged travel style container that provided one syringe, two needles, and two doses for $1.50 in the standard Sears and Roebuck mail order catalog (no slam intended to Sears, that is simply the way things developed; and they were not alone). The person's order was delivered by the U.S. Mail right to their front door in plain paper wrapping. It was commonly used by housewives in mid-America – the Heartland. I am <u>not</u> for a moment saying that common availability was good, just that it was the normal state of affairs in day-to-day America just 70 years ago.

<u>You Should Watch Some Serious Movies</u>

If you would like to get some realistic insights to the U.S. drug world I suggest you checkout the movies *Traffic, Blow,* and *Training Day* (they are a few years old, but the reality is still the same). And in that order, please.

The first film, *Traffic,* follows a group of people through a period of less than a week. It is a dark, reality oriented drama. And it should, but probably would not be allowed to be required viewing in every 7th grade in the country. And it should be <u>parents first</u>, then the kids <u>without</u> the parents, and then group discussion. Some of your kids have already seen it and if you have not it could open your eyes.

The second film, *Blow,* is a romanticized, but true story about the 'enterprising' young American that almost single-handedly started the mass importation of M from Mexico in the Sixties, and in the Seventies did the same for cocaine from Columbia — a real entrepreneur? It is grim viewing, but very educational.

The third film, *Training Day,* is dark, brutal movie providing some hard insights into the realities of the daily drug business in the streets – American streets and neighborhoods. It is probably the next best thing to being somewhere most of us never want to be.

Hollywood did a fine job with these films which are real enough to make an impact. A little viewing homework – and to be certain these are not Disney movies!

History Channel Acknowledgement

For those of you that want a well-documented world history and analysis of drugs and their journey in America, I refer you to an excellent documentary presented by the History Channel; ©2000 A&E Television Networks. All Rights Reserved.

The series entitled, *"Hooked – Illegal Drugs and How They Got That Way,"* is narrated by Roger Mudd and was produced as a two (2) part series, those being:

> Part I   Marijuana – Opium, Morphine and Heroin
> Part II   Cocaine – LSD, Ecstasy, and the Raves

You may find out more than you may want to know about the past. A past filled with good intentions (that did not always go so well), abuse, fear, greed, prejudice, and the bending of laws in every direction. The History Channel should run the full program at least once a month until 11-1-2008!

I strongly recommend that you watch that series, and possibly consider obtaining the set for yourself, a school or any other group to promote better understanding of the path that has taken us to where we are today. I thank the History Channel for presenting such an excellent historical reference.

An Excellent Resource

I want to acknowledge that the History Channel's document history mentioned above served as a primary source on history of M and part of the background on the evolution of our country's drug policy. After watching that presentation I knew there was more history there than I had already put together or cared to spend the time researching. Please forgive me for that indulgence, but re-inventing the wheel and too much historical research are my not favorite things to do. And it saved me a lot of valuable time and gave you quality information.

o   o   o   o

A Brief History of Marijuana (M)

Background

M, is a naturally growing wild plant. It is technically a 'weed' (one of its nicknames). As previously noted, it can grow anywhere in the world, with the exception of the Arctic Circle!

M is used in its natural form meaning it does not require any additives (as we know is commonly done with cigarettes). It is commonly grown to maturity, harvested, dried (just like tobacco), and may be smoked via pipe or in cigarette (joint) forms. It is also used as an active ingredient in food, cookies, and candies. Hence, its affects are experienced from either inhaling or eating the substance.

In human history, M and the more potent product opium, are the world's oldest medicines – yes, medicines! M, is now and has <u>always</u> been the world's most popular drug providing the user with relaxation and euphoric sensations. It also has minor negative side effects. M has <u>never</u> caused a death by overdose, not even in the Netherlands were it became fully legalized in the mid-seventies. The Plain Truth is that hard drugs, alcohol, cigarettes, and numerous prescription drugs cannot make that claim!

The common physical benefits of M are reduced physical pain, simulation of the appetite, and normally creating a feeling of euphoria. In a <u>few</u> cases, dependent upon a given person's attitude toward M or their general mental state, it could create feelings of paranoia, but that is far from the normal reaction. And, the use of M does <u>not</u> cause a person to become aggressive, as domestic propagandists have been telling the public since the 1930's.

<u>In Its Beginning</u>

The historical references of M use originated in ancient China and India. The ancient Chinese utilized its medicinal properties to relieve the effects of stomach pain, menstrual cramps, malaria, and consumption (an old term for cancer).

From the lands of its origin, M began its eventual spread to the rest of the world. It was next seen in use in Greece. In time, Arab traders brought it from India's Ganges Valley to North Africa and Spain. From Spain the conquistadors brought it to the Spanish colonies New World (planting the seeds of a future drug trade).

The colonists made good use of M's truly <u>NON</u>-psychotropic cousin, Hemp. Yes, "non" psychotropic. You will hear details on this later, but for now begin to understand that you could smoke or eat of pound of Hemp and you would not be feeling euphoric! The un-holy joining of Hemp with M was orchestrated by special interest politics and domestic propaganda in the 1930's.

Hemp was a valued raw material for its practical utility in making paper (the U.S. Constitution was written on hemp paper), rope, oil for lamps, heating oil, and one of its oldest uses to make canvas sails for ships of the day. The word 'canvas' was derived from the Latin word cannabis! That well-known colonial drug trafficker Thomas Jefferson secretly smuggled the first Hemp seeds into the American colonies! He and his partner in the business George Washington grew and it and promoted its many uses. And the truth will set us free!

Guess Who Brought M to Europe

In 1804 the French Emperor Napoleon conquered Egypt. While there his soldiers were introduced to an intoxicant unknown in France – it was M. The French were used to drinking their intoxicants, mainly brandy. Instead this new substance was to be smoked. The troops liked the effects of M and that it did not cause hangovers, like their regular brandy would — no pain!

Napoleon took the simple plant back to Paris as a spoil of war where it was enjoyed by artists, authors, students, merchants, and courtesans — yes, all levels of society embraced this new experience. He "innocently" became Europe's first drug trafficker.

From there it moved to London, where it was also used as a smoking substance and as an extract or liquid for medicine. High society ladies used hashish (a much more concentrated, solid form, but still all natural) as an ingredient in confections. They also found Ms medicinal uses for reducing fevers, relieving stomach pains and menstrual cramps, various other body aches, and it helped with insomnia.

Even Queen Victoria used it for relief of menstrual pain (no disrespect intended; it is just history). Additionally, it was used to help Tuberculosis (TB) patients that had lost their appetite. It not only allowed them regain an appetite, but helped them keep down what they ate by keeping their stomach settled. And, of course, it was used recreationally, and was most often smoked.

> Those "natural" remedies are just a few reasons why the Pharmaceutical Industry has lobbied without ceasing overtly and covertly against M legalization for decades — and obviously, very successfully with help from their many pawns – the 'anti-drug' screamers.

To New York City

Next M appeared in the New York City, along with its stronger form, hashish. Both soon became new ingredients in the then thriving, unregulated

"Patent Medicine" industry.

> "Patent" medicine was popular in the 1800's and early 1900's. These were "medicines" (some of which were referred to as snake oils) with secret formulas and were not required to list any ingredients for the consumer to see. This began to change in late 1800's when Congress passed the Pure Food and Drug Act, the first federal legislation over drug production. For the first time producers were required to print the ingredients of their products, the public realized what they were consuming (many containing morphine), and Patent medicines quickly lost much of their appeal.

In America of the 19th century, medicine was primarily consumed rather than smoked as in the Eastern World. Until the latter 1800's, Americans primarily used M for medicinal purposes. Most did not think to use for recreational purposes. It was rarely smoked. However, that would change.

In 1876, the World Exhibition was held in Philadelphia to celebrate the 100th anniversary of Declaration of Independence. The Sultan of Turkey's present to America took the form of Hashish (the concentrated form of M) as a rare and exotic treat to be smoked in the Turkish Pavilion (no disrespect intended here either, just history). Smoking pipes were made available and the curious public smoked Hashish inside the Turkish Pavilion. Many fairgoers enjoyed the experience. Since then that event has been called the largest "pot party" in the US until Wood Stock 93 years later! Isn't history entertaining sometimes?

American entrepreneurs saw this as an opportunity to provide the public with yet another self-indulgence. They quickly opened Turkish smoking parlors in the North. High society matrons, businessmen — all classes, openly or in secret used these parlors to smoke hashish and/or enjoy hashish-laced candies.

The raise of these parlors, coincided in time with the growing American Temperance movement against alcohol. However, the public did not switch its allegiance to hashish parlors. People maintained their preference and love for alcohol. Eventually, the hashish parlors lost their popularity and closed (maybe a point to remember regarding the legalization of M).

The decreased public interest in M continued until the Temperance Movement succeeded with the passage of the 18th Amendment to the U.S. Constitution — the Prohibition on Alcohol that was enacted in 1919. As a result, a "thirsting" nation re-discovered M...

The National Prohibition on Alcohol – A Failed Public Policy Experiment

Alcohol under Prohibition was illegal from 1919 to 1933. However, due to the increasing crime related to bootlegging of alcohol the public demanded action and reality. What a concept! The 21st Amendment to the US Constitution repealed Prohibition after a fourteen (14) year failed national experiment. It is the only Constitutional Amendment ever to be repealed.

Prohibition is a *classic* example of the well-intentioned few, trying to dictate the behavior of the masses, by ignoring the basic demands of the many.

In the 1920s

New Orleans was an international city, the second largest seaport, and the **#1** Party City in the Americas (which it remained until Katrina). So with alcohol now illegal and the need to keep it out of public view, the natural, totally legal intoxicant M came into popular use. The mixing bowl influences of French Cajuns, Blacks, Spanish, Americans, Europeans, and Chinese all blended together to develop the jazz movement. The sounds of jazz and the effects of M formed a natural bond — a bond quite similar to that formed between rock n' roll and M in the late 1950's and 60's.

Into New Orleans, M was shipped from Mexico, the Caribbean, and South America. It was legal, cheap, and popular — sold in jazz clubs, pharmacies, and markets just as cigarettes were.

Public Fears were Exploited by the Press

The American public in the post World War I era was "susceptible" to becoming very worried about and developing fears toward "those among them" that were perceived as unable to use a given substance and remaining in control of their actions. People that were viewed as "not in control of their minds" could frighten the general public.

Irresponsibly, newspapers of that period sometimes intentionally aimed their articles at promoting those fears to help generate sales rather than providing quality, objective journalism — and at times to deceptively promote the political objectives of special interests. Not very pretty then, and it continues to this day in newspapers, on network and cable news, and on the Internet.

New Orleans in the twenties was in the midst of a crime wave, mainly driven by alcohol bootleggers under Prohibition with their territorial battles.

Doesn't that sound familiar?

At that time, the "press" promoted the policy concept that – "if society limited a person's access to a particular substance, in this case M, then the potential for negative public behavior could be controlled or at least be reduced."

Regional groups and politicians used such opportunities to target and scape-goat minorities. State lawmakers sited it as the cause of American Black violence in New Orleans.

The famous and influential newspaper publisher William Randolph Hearst was looking for a big story to stimulate paper sales and he saw an opportunity with the turmoil in New Orleans. Hearst intentionally began publishing "lurid" articles telling his readers that M use was directly contributing to increased public violence, rape, and murder. He thereby helped to establish the initial public connection between M and civil crime. Hearst gets major credit for fanning the flames of public paranoia in his creative writing "just to" stir people's fears and generate newspaper sales. His personal responsibility for such *irresponsible* writing actions is not a secret – although it is little talked about today.

<u>As it was with Cocaine</u>

This domestic propaganda campaign was similar to stories used a decade earlier about American-Blacks and the 'alleged' results of their cocaine use. It was successfully used to force New York lawmakers to initiate the first <u>state</u> <u>level</u> legislation on cocaine to control a drug that was linked to crime, murder, and rape against the American-White population. This nasty piece of history is well-known in the American-Black community.

For some of the American Press of that era, it was not their finest hour.

<u>To Continue the Tale</u>

In 1924 Louisiana joined 14 other states banning the distribution of M for non-medicinal purposes. The ban on 'non-medical' use of M slowly expanded to other states for a variety of reasons. In spite of that movement, even until the early thirties the use M was still fully legal in many states across the country.

And there was still <u>no</u> <u>federal</u> <u>level</u> law.

Then Came the Big One

The Great Depression and Our Evolving National Drug Policy

The political rationale for the original federal legislation on M was actually born out of hard, local economic reality and practical, national necessity.

Starting on September 3rd and running through November 13, 1929 the stock market Crashed and the Great Depression began. As it wore on, all over the country local politicians out of necessity had to be more concerned about Americans in unemployment and bread lines, than non-Americans.

In the Southwest, politicians were worried about the number of Mexicans that were still north of the border. The same group that had been a desirable, cheap work force prior to the Depression. For economic and political purposes the Mexicans were no longer wanted and in some manner they needed to be shown as undesirable. The approach developed was to stigmatize the Mexicans with the use of M and creative stories about uncontrolled violence. True news stories were exaggerated and others were simply made up…

Considering the public crisis national politicians had to respond and it was to be Americans first. Sound familiar?

As a result, in 1931 the Mexican Repatriation Act became law, and was utilized to "encourage" Mexicans to leave the country. Any person from Mexico (or other county below the border) that did not go along peacefully was harassed in various ways. Some are arrested as jobless vagrants, others for violation of the new state laws regarding possession and use of M. New laws were implemented to serve as the vehicle to drive them out of the country.

In an extreme example, in Texas it was "possible" to be caught with a single joint and serve 'life' in prison. There were cases where people served many years, even decades for possession. Some people even campaigned for use of the death penalty, which was fortunately not successful.

Don't Criticize too Quickly

Looking back, it is too easy for us to talk about the prejudicial appearance of those laws and their intention. And the fact is that those motivations did play some part in what happened. However, we must also acknowledge the situation faced by the politicians of the day. Staggering numbers of Americans were unemployed. Our own citizens were out of work and hungry. Growing violence by citizens against non-citizens over the few available jobs was inevitable.

It was a prudent, public necessity. It was then, and still must be a politician's first duty to take care of our own people before worrying about non-citizens whether they are here legally or not! Just as every other country in the world we must to take care of our own people first **and without being required to justify it to anyone!** The reality of a periodic tightening of "legal" immigration flow remains a prudent action and a practical necessity at times.

The Push to Coordinate a Drug Policy

Remember in the early thirties, M was still legal in the US except for several Southwestern states. It would remain so until Harry J. Anslinger (HJA) appointed to be the nation's top drug enforcement agent takes office at the new Federal Bureau of Narcotics (FBN). The new bureau was charged with the role of enforcing the nation's narcotics laws such as they were at the time.

Until his arrival as the head of the new drug fighting bureau, the government had been focusing their attention on heroin and cocaine. However, with the arrival of HJA the political focus would be shifted toward M. It was a new focus born out of the problems in the Southwest with Mexican migrant workers.

In the 1930s the FBN began a program aimed at stopping the use of M and distributed educational material aimed at trying to help keep youth away from it.

How We got from There to Here

I have condensed this history as much as possible. However, that era and what occurred then due to political pressures are directly responsible for setting in motion the mess we are dealing with today. Common knowledge of what has happened 70 years ago will enable us to better determine our approach today in correcting the short-sighted, special interest sins of the past.

Again, it is 1930 and Anslinger is a 38 year old federal bureaucrat with no previous background dealing with the drug issue, let alone M. However, he was a good bureaucrat and so was concerned with protecting his agency and seeing to it that the budget was preserved, if not increased annually. After all that is the game.

HJA did not personally care that much about M as a political issue. He had trouble thinking of a career trying to exterminate a "weed" which at the time, literally grew in the wild all over the country. However, he appreciated the political reality that powerful people, like the publisher William Randolph Hearst, <u>did</u> care about it. So, HJA modified his position and priorities to address the political demands of the day. Political correctness has been around a long time!

Building the Federal Case Against Marijuana

HJA also realized the public had no particular issue with M. It was available and there were generally no problems being experienced by the general population with its use. It grew everywhere and he could not imagine how it could possibly be controlled. It even grew wild along the Potomac River between Virginia, DC, and Maryland.

He preferred that the burden would be left to the states to resolve, instead of making it federal action. However, heavy Congressional pressure from Western and Southwestern states, primarily Texas, Colorado, Arizona, and California forced him to develop a way to make M illegal. They pushed hard for federal legislation and controls.

> HJA did not have adequate funding or people resources to control it. He started with an agency of 300 people and a total budget of 1.5 <u>m</u>illion dollars to address all drug related problems.

The hard reality was that the unemployment problems along the Southwestern border were politically connected to the Mexican immigration issue. And making M illegal was the approach developed to help force the Mexicans out of the country. So HJA, being the good bureaucrat went after the issue with everything he had!

HJA then initiated an over-the-top domestic propaganda campaign against M use working with Hearst and others using the newspapers, as well as the movie media making exaggerated claims about the negative effects of the drug. The use of M by was blamed for violence, insanity, "beastly perversion", immorality, sex crimes, suicide, theft, and murders – and it was just plain domestic propaganda.

o   o   o   o

In defense of Harry Anslinger it should be acknowledged that <u>who</u> <u>ever</u> would have been placed in that office at that moment in history would have done what he did, or else, the Congress would simply have found someone else to do the job. So we should not blame HJA, for overall it was the Congress, lobbyists, and the dark side of that "National System" thing that keeps coming up!

And then Harry got an idea.

How Our Government Made a 'Weed' Illegal

So HJA had to figure out how to make M, a <u>naturally</u> growing plant illegal.

<u>The Model that was Used</u>

What follows equates to legislatively putting a square peg into a round whole! Try following this logic:

- During an earlier high, gang crime period the federal government decided it needed a way to control the possession of machine guns.
- To that end Congress developed and enacted a law called, The National Firearms Act. It required that a person could not give, borrow or transfer a machine gun without a 'Machine Gun Transfer Stamp' in their possession. The catch was that the government would not print any of those stamps.
- The legal fight against the law went right up to the US Supreme Court with the argument that the stamps were not a legitimate taxing vehicle because the government was not collecting any taxes. It was purely to prevent the distribution of machine guns.
- Regardless of the logic of that argument, the Court ruled that the National Firearms Act was legal. And the Machine Gun Transfer Stamp requirement, even though the required stamps were purposely not available, it became the law.

There is <u>no</u> logic in that, but again it was a well-intentioned action on the part of the government to protect the American public. The nation wanted a legal way to keep machine guns away from the bad guys! That type of policy did not worked very well then, and it still dosen't.

<u>And Now HJA had the Means</u>

HJA and the state lobbies now had the legislative model they needed to put controls M distribution. His campaign unfolded as follows:

- A law was proposed that anyone involved in the use, sale, distribution or transfer of M would be required to have a "Marijuana Tax Stamp." Of course government would only print a token number of those stamps.

- HJA next had to convince Congress that M was just a dangerous to society as a machine gun. The Congressional hearings on the first federal law to control M began on April 27, 1937. The objective was to show Congress that M was a horrible and dangerous a drug, worse than even cocaine or heroin! That M caused the user to become insane and capable of performing terrible acts including murder and rape when under its *terrible* influence.

• The newspaper publisher William Randolph Hearst of course covered those hearings in his newspapers and continued to aggressively pile on the negative propaganda about M usage, adding extra newspaper printings with headlines proclaiming its evils.

• Other newspapers and movies of the time were promoting the negative image. The movies included the classic anti-drug propaganda movie, *Reefer Madness*. You should really try to watch this movie. It will give you an interesting look at the times and people. You can find on DVD! Viewed today it is a simple, dark comedy. At that time it served as blatant scare tactics, filled with exaggerations and outright lies to increase public fears. The movie actually portrayed M having worst effects on people than <u>cocaine</u>!

Today, M, heroin, and morphine are all listed on the Schedule I of the DEA's Drug Control Schedules, while cocaine and opium are on the lower Schedule II. The beat goes on.

• HJA also gets credit for telling the U.S. Congress that M was the assassin of youth — a stepping-stone and as he declared a **"Gateway Drug"** to harder drugs like heroin and cocaine. True lies!

Thanks to HJA and Hearst that worked together on the propaganda campaign the *myth* of M being a gateway to hard drugs was born and was set in the minds of the fearful American public. I hope the Screamers are listening. It was simple, self-serving domestic propaganda.

• HJA told Congress that school children were being harmed using M. Just one (1) brave, solitary doctor came forward to dispute that claim in the only positive testimony about M during the hearings. The doctor testified that there was <u>no</u> <u>evidence</u> that M was affecting children in that manner. The members of the Congressional panel verbally attacked the doctor and his testimony was ignored.

• After just five (5) days of the Congressional hearings, the committee approved the Marijuana Tax Law, the first <u>federal</u> <u>level</u> law against M. After several weeks of debate both houses of Congress pass the final version of the bill.

- President Franklin Roosevelt signed the bill into law on August 2 and it went effect on October 1, 1937. HJA had successfully demonized M and proved himself to be an effective bureaucrat and domestic propagandist.

- The group of Western and Southwestern states got the legislation they wanted. The law required that anyone wishing to buy, distribute or sell M must first have a Marijuana Tax Stamp.

- The first penalties established for anyone violating the new law were a $2,000 fine and/or five (5) years in jail. And, again, the stamps were not available for purchase.

To be clear — the Marijuana Tax Law actually stipulated that the person had to have the M physically in their possession <u>when requesting</u> the stamp. **However, if they had the M in their physical possession, without the stamp, they were <u>already</u> in violation of the law!**

o   o   o   o

The First Arrest for Possession of M

Just two (2) days after the law takes effect (October 1, 1937), a man in Colorado is arrested and jailed for possession of M. Four (4) days later, he gets four (4) years in jail and a $1,000 fine. The federal battle against M <u>users</u> not just the providers had its first victim!

And with all that has been done to fight the drug trade, educate the public, and discourage M use since October 1, 1937:

- Some 22-plus million Americans have been arrested, tried, and incarcerated due to federal and state laws – only due to M use – not hard drugs. An incredibly sad and cruel statistic.

- Today M is America's #1 domestic cash crop! So much for control.

After 70 years, it is time to end the Prohibition on Marijuana. Any questions?

The Mayor New York City Tried

In 1938, a year after HJA got the Marijuana Tax Law enacted, he received a strong challenge of a sort from the well-respected and powerful Mayor of New York City, Theorelo J. LaGuardia (the man the named the airport in honor of).   A few years earlier, the Mayor had commissioned a medical study by doctors from the New York Academy of Medicine to review his city's M problem.   This Blue Ribbon group of professionals visited schoolyards, interviewed principles, tested adults.   After a four (4) <u>year</u> study the commission presented the following <u>official</u> findings:

Text taken from the official New York report — the following conclusions are drawn:

1. Marihuana is used extensively in the Borough of Manhattan but the problem is not as acute as it is reported to be in other sections of the United States.
2. The introduction of marihuana into this area is recent as compared to other localities.
3. The cost of marihuana is low and therefore within the purchasing power of most persons.
4. The distribution and use of marihuana is centered in Harlem.
5. The majority of marihuana smokers are Negroes and Latin-Americans.
6. The consensus among marihuana smokers is that the use of the drug creates a definite feeling of adequacy.
7. The practice of smoking marihuana does not lead to addiction in the medical sense of the word.
8. The sale and distribution of marihuana is not under the control of any single organized group.
9. The use of marihuana does not lead to morphine or heroin or cocaine addiction and no effort is made to create a market for these narcotics by stimulating the practice of marihuana smoking.
10. Marihuana is not the determining factor in the commission of major crimes.
11. Marihuana smoking is not widespread among school children.
12. Juvenile delinquency is not associated with the practice of smoking marihuana.
13. The publicity concerning the catastrophic effects of marihuana smoking in New York City is unfounded.

End of report text

The findings offer a sobering insight into the times and lack of truth and prudence in the law even then.

However, in the end regardless of the scientific proof from his study, Mayor

LaGuardia was pressured and subsequently followed the party line on M. The report <u>along with the truth</u> **was buried**...by the power of politics! Are you irritated, yet?

Thus, in spite of the concerned mayor's efforts, M remained illegal in the New York City and everywhere else. And that was 70 years and so many ruined lives ago!

o   o   o   o

<u>1940's and 1950's</u>

From the late 1930"s through World War II, M use and arrests dropped. However, HJA did not stop 'pushing' his programs. He targeted visible music and movie celebrates to get headlines in the press. In some notable examples, the famous drummer Gene Krupa as jailed for nearly three (3) months for possession, and the young actor Robert Mitchum was busted at a pot party and his fine career was almost ruined before it began.

<u>1960's</u>

Despite the potentially harsh penalties, M made a strong comeback in the late Fifties and Sixties with the Baby Boomer Generation. Its affects appealed to intelligent people that wanted to be taken beyond the limits of normal thought and behavior. Some key perspectives at the time were:

- M does not cause **overdose** (OD) deaths.
- M does not produce a physical **dependency,** or to the least extent of all drugs which is still the case.
- M does not lead to **addiction.**

<u>1970's – News Flash!</u>

The U.S. Supreme Court Reverses the 1937 Marijuana Tax Law!

In 1970, the legality of the 1937 Marijuana Tax Law was challenged all the way to the US Supreme Court. The challenge was lead in part by the Timothy Leary, the famous LSD guru. He successfully argued that in order to get the license (tax stamp) you had to first break the law, because in order to request the Marijuana Tax Stamp you had to have the M in-hand, and were technically already breaking the law. Therefore, attempting to get a proper license was self-incrimination.

The US Supreme Court agreed and overturned the federal law. Technically, M was legal once again. The politics of the times had changed, as had the Court's opinion of the law's prudence for the population.

But It Would Not Last Long

However, the actual powers within the Congress — you remember our friends the lobbyists and the screamers — did not agree with the Court on legalized public access to M. The "well-lobbied" Congress still did not view recreational drug consumption as guaranteed by the Constitution. Therefore, the Congress once again acted to criminalize drugs under the Comprehensive Drug Abuse Prevention and Control Act of 1970.

A case where the power of special interest lobbyists even over-ruled the Supreme Court? That does point out however that the Congress can act if it really wants to. Keep that fact in mind for later.

To continue the history lesson

M, or actually the THC substance in it was then placed on the Schedule I of the DEA's Drug Control Schedules where it is still found today along with much harder substances like heroin and morphine.

Schedule I, is the category of drugs that are stated to have no medical benefit "in the United States." And the king has no clothes!

This designation also conveniently prevented M's cousin plant Hemp that contains a non-affecting, less than one-half (.5) percent of THC from being available for agricultural and commercial uses — hurting farmers, manufacturing, and the environment. Certain industry lobbies wanted Hemp production suppressed – they won, we lost, but that too will now be corrected. More on the Hemp issue under New and Renewal Industries.

Possession and use of M after the 1970 Controlled Substance Act continued to be illegal. Of course it did not go away, just moved farther underground and its use peaked during the Seventies in spite of the government's efforts to control the young Baby Boomers.

The failed Prohibition-style approach to stopping the use of M and other drugs was again in full operation. Various special interest industry groups, their cherished screamers, as well as hard drug barons, traffickers, dealers, not to mention the drug hard drug growing countries – all in all an *ex-*

tremely unpatriotic group – really <u>appreciated</u> the U.S. Congress not acting in the Common Good of the American public. Seventy (70) years later they still do! And we keep on electing them?

And the prisons continued to fill up — jailing not just with the providers of these drugs, but the <u>users</u> as well — an absolute disgrace. The government cannot stop the import and distribution of drugs, and so they punish the victims of its availability. This terribly flawed situation will be ended soon by an enlightened and fed-up public.

o   o   o   o

1972 — The National War on Drugs Meets the Vietnam War

In 1972, then President Richard M. Nixon officially started what we then called "The National War on Drugs." He appointed the first Drug Czar to be in charge of coordinating the nation's battle against drugs.
Nixon's primary motivations in taking these actions were both practical and politically prudent:

- A high number of our military people in Vietnam that were using drugs, **mainly M and heroin**, and were coming home addicted to the latter.
- It was a politically good thing to do at home.

Vietnam veterans were required to undergo drug rehabilitation before coming home — with mixed results, but the effort was made.

Closing Out the 20th Century

As the 20th Century drew to an end, M was being used 'somewhat' legally in a few states to help those with Aids and cancer patients in stimulating their appetite. It also helps people cope with nausea after chemotherapy.

However, those needy medicinal users are under random pressure from the federal government, which continues promoting bad federal policy, contributing to less cooperation between state and federal officials, as well as strained relations with the involved public.

And we taxpayers continue to pay for the Domestic propaganda machine and deal with drug related crime in our neighborhoods.

2000 and Beyond

As the new century began, some eleven (11) states have decriminalized possession of small amounts of M. They have determined that legal side effects are more harmful to the population than the drug itself. And they too come under random pressure from the federal government that does not approve of their actions —again, the issue of States Rights.

Today, M remains America's largest domestic cash crop and an estimated 20-plus million Americans smoke pot on a regular basis. Based on a total population of 281 million in 2000, that is about 1 in 14 Americans.

By comparison, in 2000 about eleven (11) million Americans were estimated to be cocaine users! Of those 11 million users it is estimated that 1.5 million were addicts, meaning with the rest were only using the drug *'recreationally.'* Go figure.

<u>This ends the mini-history</u>

Wasn't that a fascinating, yet grim look at a piece of American history?

o   o   o   o

What About Prohibition Today

So let's take look at today and our final answer to the War on Drugs.

I have only selected a few outside references to present in CS2. I have included this piece taken from the website of the National Organization for the Reform of Marijuana Laws or NORML the oldest and longest suffering group working to reverse our failed National Drug Policy. I personally view them as a credible, public interest group. Their concise article speaks volumes and references FBI provided "human" statistics.

Note: As stated this article was copied from NORML's Internet site. NORML had no prior knowledge of my plan to use the article in CS2. I doubt that they will mind it.

o   o   o   o

Marijuana Arrests For Year 2005 — 786,545 Tops Record High... Pot Smokers Arrested In America At A Rate Of One Every 40 Seconds

September 18, 2006 - Washington, DC, USA

Washington, DC: Police arrested an estimated **786,545** persons for marijuana violations in 2005, according to the Federal Bureau of Investigation's annual <u>Uniform Crime Report</u>, released today. The total is the highest ever recorded by the FBI, and comprised 42.6 percent of all drug arrests in the United States.

"These numbers belie the myth that police do not target and arrest minor marijuana offenders," said NORML Executive Director Allen St. Pierre, who noted that at current rates, <u>a marijuana smoker is arrested every 40 seconds in America</u>. "This effort is a tremendous waste of criminal justice resources that diverts law enforcement personnel away from focusing on serious and violent crime, including the war on terrorism."

Of those charged with marijuana violations, approximately 88 percent some **696,074** Americans were charged with possession only. The remaining **90,471** individuals were charged with "sale/manufacture," a category that includes all cultivation offenses even those where the marijuana was being grown for personal or medical use. In past years, roughly 30 percent of those arrested were age 19 or younger.

"Present policies have done little if anything to decrease marijuana's availability or dissuade youth from trying it," St. Pierre said, noting young people in the U.S. now frequently report that they have easier access to pot than alcohol or tobacco.

The total number of marijuana arrests in the U.S. for 2005 far exceeded the total number of arrests in the U.S. for all violent crimes combined, including murder, manslaughter, forcible rape, robbery and aggravated assault.

Annual marijuana arrests have more than doubled since the early 1990s.

"Arresting hundreds of thousands of Americans who smoke marijuana responsibly needlessly destroys the lives of otherwise law abiding citizens," St. Pierre said, adding that over 8 million Americans have been arrested on marijuana charges in the past decade. During this same time, arrests for cocaine and heroin have declined sharply, implying that increased enforcement of marijuana laws is being achieved at the expense of enforcing laws against the possession and trafficking of more dangerous drugs.

St. Pierre concluded: "Enforcing marijuana prohibition costs taxpayers between $10 billion and $12 billion annually and has led to the arrest of nearly 18 million Americans. Nevertheless, some 94 million Americans acknowledge having used marijuana during their lives. It makes no sense to continue to treat nearly half of all Americans as criminals for their use of a substance that poses no greater - and arguably far fewer - health risks than alcohol or tobacco. A better and more sensible solution would be to tax and regulate cannabis in a manner similar to alcohol and tobacco."

YEAR	MARIJUANA ARRESTS
2005	786,545
2004	771,608
2003	755,187
2002	697,082
2001	723,627
2000	734,498
1999	704,812
1998	682,885
1997	695,200
1996	641,642
1995	588,963
1994	499,122
1993	380,689
1992	342,314
1991	287,850
1990	326,850

For more information, please contact Allen St. Pierre, NORML Executive Director, at (202) 483-5500. For a comprehensive breakdown and analysis of US marijuana arrests, please see NORML's report: "Crimes of Indiscretion: Marijuana Arrests in the United States".

o o o o

Just some more sad statistics in the grim fairy tale that is our National Drug Policy, and especially when,

> "The total number of marijuana arrests in the U.S. for 2005 far exceeded the total number of arrests in the U.S. for all violent crimes combined, including murder, manslaughter, forcible rape, robbery and aggravated assault."

To say that our criminal Justice System priorities are misplaced is putting it very nicely.

We will now fix this madness and stop hurting our own people! The U.S. Congress will set about correcting this in 2008 before the November election, or else, We will install a new Congress!

The Bad Lobbies

President Nixon created the office of National Drug Czar in 1972 to lead the fight in the newly declared War on Drugs. Some 35 years later the entity is referred to as the Office of National Drug Control Policy (ONDCP). It is the nation's longest running war — and it has in fact become a domestic war against our own people. This is classic lose-lose domestic policy!

And there is no happy ending in sight under the doomed to failure Prohibition-style battle plan, along with the continued and successful sponsorship of the odd bunch of bed-fellows that are lobbying against any change to it.

o o o o

The overtly and covertly politically influential Pharmaceutical Industry is the most stressed over the possibility of ending the Prohibition on Marijuana and they have vigorously fought it for decades! Just who do you think are the biggest financial supporters of anti-drug use groups?

They are not looking at the collapse of their industry, but will realize a percentage decrease. The "real" medical uses and benefits of this naturally growing, "God given" plant, without any chemical additives whatsoever are numerous and must become available to those in medical need.

By one estimate and who really knows the number, well over 20 million Americans use M regularly.

In a perfect world no drugs would be used, desired or even needed. A brutal accounting shows that tobacco smoking and its second-hand effects are responsible for some 500,000 deaths every year in America alone. In the Netherlands where M (and all drugs) has been fully legalized since the mid-1970s to total number of deaths caused by M use, is ZERO. None have died in the U.S. either.

Therefore, in thirty years, zero deaths from M use versus let's say 15 million slow deaths thanks to the tobacco industry and their lobbyists (one of whom was my Mother at 57 years of age).

Only the Plain Truth about drug legalization and many other public issues will be presented in CS2 and will be discussed in public forums in the future. Such open and honest public debate is a key part of my approach to promoting public awareness and open review of the facts as opposed to the domestic propaganda we are always fed.

> Myth Buster 1 – in the 1930's in order to support the new government public scare campaign Harry J. Anslinger (HJA) the nation's top drug enforcement agent at the new Federal Bureau of Narcotics (FBN) invented the term **"Gateway Drug"** and pinned it on cannabis. Any questions?

> Myth Buster 2 – during that same domestic propaganda campaign, cannabis' cousin the Hemp plant was portrayed to a fearful public as the same physical plant, which it is not. Technically, both of the cousin plants contain THC that is the active substance. Many Americans still identify them as the same plant.

> However, Hemp contains less than one half percent of THC with cannabis at 6-plus percent, which means someone could smoke or eat a pound of hemp and get nothing but a large headache.

> By the way, we could also make cotton type fabric, paper products, canvas for sails, home heating oil, lamp oil, bio-diesel fuel for cars and trucks, and plastic products from much maligned Hemp plant.

> American Farmers have been petitioning for decades to grow this viable crop, but are continually put off by Congress and stronger

lobbies. This foolishness will also end soon.

In other words, for the U.S. Congress, the publicly irresponsible lobbyists, and all of the bad guys in the hard drug business — it is *"Stay the Course".* Does that sound grossly familiar? And anyone that dares to suggest prudent alteration in the approach is screamed at, belittled, but mainly ignored.

That is until now.

o   o   o   o

Action Demanded by the Electorate

The obscene foolishness of the War of Drugs with its Prohibition on Marijuana that has cost us so many American lives, destroyed so many families, and wasted so many taxpayer dollars — must now end. The Prohibition on Alcohol only lasted from 1919 until 1933, and it took two Constitutional Amendments to institute and then repeal. The U.S. Congress could end this *"marijuana madness"* in less than 30 days!

And since it is We the People that will be driving the U.S. Congress on this and other long unresolved issues, we will begin setting legislative deadlines by which our elected officials must act.

They will act or stand up in public and explain their failure to implement legislative changes clearly identified by the People for action. And then they will be voted out of office upon their next re-election bid. We the People will say, "you're fired."

In the case of M legalization the Congressional Legislative Implementation Deadline (CLID) will be set at **July 1, 2009** or before!

There is no practical case that can be made to delay it any farther than that. And we will not wait until the Republicans and Democrats drag us through another presidential election and into 2009 without even mentioning the alleged War on Drugs.

This mandate by the American electorate is one of several legislative fixes, some small and some large, that we will declare for Congress to act upon prior to the November 2008 election. We will improve the conduct, content, and quality of American politics for the Common Good – and do it now!

The bottom line reality is that in order to fix the problems that are so imbedded in the National System — we will <u>expect</u> and in some cases <u>demand</u> that prudent changes or adjustments be made and made over the protests of industry, opposition groups, and the 'screamers' in their various forms.

Like Any Cut Left Unattended

What makes solving the hard drug problem more difficult is that it is both a problem <u>and</u> a symptom of other problems at the same time. I and many other people believe that <u>part</u> of today's drug problem naturally grew as a result other problems in society. Those social and economic problems still exist today and are worse than before. Other parts of An American Agenda will be addressing some of those core issues, as well.

Since those 'other' problems were not properly addressed early on in the 70's or 80's the nation's demand for drugs was allowed to grow into a major problem all its own. Just like a minor cut that goes unattended and becomes severely infected. Again, the difficulty in developing a solution to our nation's drug problem demonstrated to me why more of our complex public issues are not yet resolved. It can be an extremely, hard problem-solving exercise. However, I said they are <u>hard</u> to solve, <u>not</u> impossible to solve!

The bottom line reality is that in order to fix such problems that are so imbedded in the National System, we <u>must</u> expect to make changes or adjustments to that System. These are <u>not</u> changes to our form of government. This and all the other proposals are in <u>no way</u> an assault on our government.

These are changes to how America functions on a day-to-day basis. We will need to agree to change the way we look at some things and the way that some things are currently <u>allowed</u> to work. Not for trivial reasons, but for prudent and practical ones.

o   o   o   o

The implementation of the NDR proposal will be a major step in realizing a better order of things in our day-to-day lives.

It is also critical for us to realize that various Special Interest forces within the National System will as thy always have, discount the potential success of the NDR and attempt in both overt and covert ways to block any potential changes to the way things currently work — protecting the status quo.

<u>As a Partial Explanation</u>

Think of the Special Interest resistance as a means of self-preservation. It is often just a person's, an agency's, or corporation's survival instinct kicking in. Many of us have known that feeling sometime in our lives, particularly if we thought our employment status could be negatively affected. For corporate lobbyists it comes down to maintaining market share, revenue, profits, earnings, bonuses, and the holy grail of stock dividends.

It is Time to End this War

So, critics beware! <u>Do</u> <u>not</u> come to criticize this drug reform proposal on drug legalization or the overall National Drug Reform (NDR) proposal, unless you have equally effective and comprehensive plan in your hand. And, I mean one that the American public will support and see enacted by 2009!

Otherwise stand back out of the way – for the troops are coming with a new, winning plan of attack!

We the People, are coming to the literal rescue of those with the drug problems and those brave souls currently fighting the drug war that is at best a holding action. We are bringing relief to the people on the front lines — our law enforcement, the DEA and ATF officers, and others — to provide added protection for our friends and loved ones threatened by the drug-providing enemy.

o   o   o   o

With this proposal and the overall NDR proposal, the solution to our 35-plus year War on Drugs is displayed for public review and debate, and the end of our national drug problems will finally be within our sight.

<u>Therefore, It is Our Time</u>

So guess what America? We are now, the people, and it is our time. We have the opportunity, if not the responsibility to seriously consider taking this "giant step" as a nation. In doing so, we will also be addressing some associated problems that ripple through the National System. It will be awkward at first, but will soon become part of our improved National System, the new way in which America will work.

We can confidently state that if we continue our current course, approaching the War on Drugs as we have for over three decades, the results are very predictable. A whole lot more bad news.

An analogy I once heard seem to apply to our situation — the one about the frog and the pot of water.

If someone were to throw a poor frog into a pot of boiling water it will jump out immediately, if it can, to save itself. However, if the frog is placed into a pot of cool water and the water that is then slowly heated to boiling, the frog will not jump out, and it will cook! Please do not try this at home!

The War on Drugs is the water and American society is the frog. I don't know about you, but I do like frogs. I just do not want to be one!

o o o o

Yes, America, we are the frogs and the drug business and with its associated problems continue to heat the water we are swimming in. We must stop allowing (yes, I said allowing) our common problems, like that of drugs, to continue heating things up around us! Slowly making our daily lives a little less than they could be, and actually once were.

We, the American public have the intelligence and the power, should we choose to exercise it resolve any of our national problems. In changing the system to fix these problems, there will be winners and losers, just as there has always been when some functioning part of a nation's system has changed.

We, the people, must unite our spirits and creativity as the Founders did when they considered their options – focusing on the Common Good, to do what needs to be done to improve and maintain the Life, Liberty, and the Pursuit of Happiness for all Americans. To accomplish this, the majority needs to continue to act responsibly and must rightfully demand that the minority (all those that would rather not) do the same.

o o o o

Remember, the NDR proposal and this book was developed by me for you. And in this case, you are the decision maker. You are the voter, the phone caller, the letter writer, and the email sender. *You* must weigh the pros and cons of these contents for yourself – to see how they could benefit you and those you care about.

The NDR proposal components have been refined and are presented to you as a true compromise proposal, with a solution-driven approach.

Frankly, I will vote for it, but as written it is not exactly what I would <u>personally</u> prefer to see done in all cases. However, in a pure problem-solving mode, the sole objective is always to solve the problem at hand, to develop an approach without personal opinion affecting the design and absolute functionality of the solution. Also to create a solution that will most effectively address all the client issues and/or problems. In this case, you are the client. We, the people – all 300,000,000 and more of us are the clients. Drug use and its associated public ills are the problems we need to work together to solve. And we need to start solving them now!

We will have a few tough things to do to bring this part of our national house to order. However, it pales when compared to what those brave men and women that preceded us had to face.

Now our national ancestors are watching us, waiting to see if we, *in our time*, will have the vision, the courage, and strength to face this test and overcome one of our complex national challenges.

o   o   o   o

The People's Sense

And the Truth will set them free!

Under the NDR Proposal the naturally growing, God-given plant cannabis or marijuana (M, as I like to write) and <u>only</u> marijuana, **will be <u>fully</u> legalized and decriminalized in the U.S.**, no later than July 1, 2009.

The straightforward legislative changes required will accomplish three (3) primary objectives:

- It will make M legally available for medical use — making it fully available to any Americans suffering with various illnesses and negative reactions to medical treatment — that includes Americans suffering with forms of cancer, Aids, and other medical conditions that have no appetite and/or cannot keep food (or medication) 'down' and are literally starving. And they may have it with or without a doctor's prescription!

- It will be fully legalized and made available for personal use.

- It will decriminalize the possession of M, only. We will <u>cease</u> <u>immediately</u> to arrest <u>ANY</u> drug users regardless of what drug(s) they are using.

  However, we will mandate <u>and</u> enforce the "overall" clean-up of obvious drug addicts for their sake and for the health and safety of the public at large.

o   o   o   o

The Basic Approach

This is described in greater detail in Proposal Number 20 – The Domestic Cannabis Industry.

In general M will be sold under the general guidelines (by locality) governing for hard liquor and with the oversight of the Bureau of Alcohol, Tobacco, and Firearms (ATF), which will be renamed to the Bureau of Alcohol, Tobacco, Firearms, and Cannabis (ATFC). That is not intended to be funny, although it is a bit – and it will need to happen. Cannabis has been the largest cash crop in America for many years.

Further, just as the Canadian government has been on the verge of doing (in spite of continued pressure from our government <u>not</u> to do so) it will become at the most, parking ticket level offense – and no points. Also, as Canada has determined to be realistic, M will be available for sale to those eighteen (18) years of age and older. However, in the U.S. under the NDR provisions an 18-year old must first have graduated from high school. It will be controlled via a simple designation on a person's driver's license.

England has also reluctantly delayed this same practical approach due to political pressure from our government. It must and will end.

The NDR Proposal in Brief

- The required national legislation will be enacted by the US Congress as of **July 1, 2009 or sooner.**

- We will set the National Hard Drug Sale Cutoff Date as of **August 1, 2009.** After that <u>absolute</u> point in time, anyone that decides **of their own freewill** to continue in the trafficking and/or distribution and sale of **hard** drugs (an exact list will be publicized) will be given three (3) chances to be apprehended with an amount of a specific set of drugs that is undeniably intended for trafficking and/or distribution – not just for personal use.

Remember this does threaten <u>not</u> drug <u>users</u>.

- Those individuals will not go to jail, but will be tried and convicted with no plea-bargaining allowed and will then be under standard Criminal Probation.

- They will also be placed under Civil Probation that is described in the NDR proposal. Under Civil Probation, a non-criminal status, they will be evaluated assigned access to drug treatment, social skills training, educational and vocational services as needed, and if needed the services will be <u>mandatory</u>. The same procedures that will be used to rehabilitate drug addicts.

- If, **of their own freewill** they continue in the <u>hard</u> drug business and reach their third apprehension they <u>will</u> <u>go</u> immediately to jail and 3-months after their third conviction they will be given the Death Penalty by lethal injection.

End of problem and taxpayer expense. Any questions.

That's the very short version. And you would be amazed by how many Americans of all types will vote for what you just read. I know I was. And, I mean 80% approval is a low number.

o o o o

Marijuana and its cousin plant Hemp (from which it is **impossible** to get a buzz!) will become legal domestic industries providing jobs and considerable tax revenue.

American farmers have been trying to get the "right" to grow Hemp for years, but have been stuffed by you know who – the screamers and the Congressional lobbyists. The new domestic Hemp industry will be overviewed under the New and Renewal Industries – Proposal Number 19.

<u>Some Random Points</u>

- The overt and covert lobbying against marijuana legalization by the Pharmaceutical, Alcohol, and Petroleum industries to name a few will be stopped or at least ignored by Congress.

- Several hundred thousand men and women (fathers, mothers, sisters, brothers) currently in prison for generally minor drug offenses will be systematically released from jail and their records will be cleaned. Their ability to obtain employment will <u>not</u> be limited by this history.

- Going forward under the revised laws — every month thousands more will <u>not</u> be arrested and/or sent to jail for simple possession. No more beating up of drug users.

Just another reason why we will never need to build another prison! We will soon suspend jail and prison construction projects – maybe diverting those funds to repairing bridges!

- As the prisons are emptied, they will make proper facilities for detoxification of the existing hard drug addict population. Think about the possibilities.

o   o   o   o

The Final Part of Our Answer from Those Who Know Best

Now for the hard part!

The grassroots group Law Enforcement Against Prohibition (LEAP.org) that was created by former law enforcement officers advocates the full legalization **of all drugs** similar to what the Netherlands did in 1976.

While I have long opposed any legalization beyond that already detailed for M, I now believe we need to seriously consider a mid-ground approach short of full drug legalization in the US.

For one thing, the American public would <u>never</u> vote for full drug legalization. Personally, I would not.

If we do not accept a method on controlling the flow of hard drugs, a manner similar to what is now used for controlled (e.g., codeine) prescription drugs, we will not really end the chaos. We must have a transition plan that will wean American society off of hard drugs, with the objective of killing the international drug trade. And this *We* can do.

The Simply Stated Final Answer

Do not be offended at how simply stated this may sound. This is hard public policy.

Logically, it will be prudent policy to allow the possession for <u>personal use only</u> of hard drugs for a controlled multi-year period. It would have a nationally acknowledged start date of mid-2009, or sooner. To be crystal clear, we will <u>stop</u> arresting drug users.

Simply stated, since the U.S. Congress and all other involved parts of our government have proven over the last 35 years to be absolutely incompetent and incapable of stopping the flow of those hard drugs into our country, then We the People will no longer allow them to arrest anyone for possessing those substances for personal use.

> Especially when the government allows the legal Tobacco Industry to kill more American on a single month, than hard drugs kill in an entire year. Any questions?

This realistic national approach will relieve the law enforcement at all levels and the courts of the processing of <u>anyone</u> for <u>drug use</u> as a criminal offense.

Consequently, law enforcement at all levels will freed to attack the trafficking and distribution networks which is what they should have been doing all along.

That newly focused law enforcement capacity combined with the NDR Proposal *"three (3) strikes their dead"* policy for those choosing of their own free will to keep moving hard drugs, will send shock waves through the national and international drug trade. Exactly what is required.

That is not wishful thinking – that is how we will take control of drug use and abuse in America.

It is our choice.

About the NDR Proposal

A Sincere Warning to the Critics of the NDR Proposal

I reasonably expect not only criticism, but also the outright opposition what you have just read and to the NDR proposal, from the usual suspects. To expect anything else would be foolish at best. You cannot please everyone and not everyone can be pleased.

However, I need to make one thing perfectly clear to the critics, including those individuals, agencies, companies, and other professionals currently involved in any segment of the Illegal Drug Industry. To those that will come forward to say, among other things, that I do not have the proper educational background or professional experience to make such recommendations. To those, I simply reply:

> The development of what you have just read and to the NDR proposal was quite necessary.
>
> The simple fact is, that the combination of collective knowledge, intellect, imagination, creativity, legislative power, as well as, the many billions of our tax dollars spent over the last 35 years, have been a colossal failure!
>
> The net results have left us in a situation that would charitably be described as a 'holding action' at the front lines of the conflict, in the very streets of America.
>
> They have failed the American public and our society as a whole. And it can no longer be permitted to continue. The 'professionals' have failed!

o   o   o   o

It is Easier to Study a Problem

Yes, the simple fact is that it is far easier to study a problem, than to solve it! Just do another study on the problem and update the related statistics, rather than developing a concept and approach aimed at resolving it through constructive change. It requires far less creativity and little risk! Unfortunately, this scenario applies to more of our problems than just the War on Drugs.

Consequently, you will not find at the library or on the Internet, is a single comprehensive proposal to end the nation's War on Drugs. If such a proposal had been written and presented to the general public for consideration, you would have heard about it.

That is, not until now.

This writing and the NDR Proposal provide the nation with a real, hardball, but fair solution to the War on Drugs. It has not been an easy solution to develop and a few aspects of the proposal can be difficult at first hearing.

However, after all the tough things we have already faced as a nation and conquered together over the last 230 years, we can do this, too. And we will be an even greater nation by the accomplishment.

It will work, if We take action and make it happen!

That's enough on that for now. The next topic is where things get hot.

9   Re-Considering the Military Draft – Saving Our Youth

Issue/Problem

This National proposal will and should generate much public debate —
which is after all my intent with CS2.

> I was initially considering this piece in early September 2006 about
> time when the Administration, Congress, and the military brass
> agreed they had no plans to re-start the Draft. Whether that was a
> practical military viewpoint or not is a matter of opinion, but it was
> correct pre-election politics for Congress! Since the 2006 election
> few members of Congress have mentioned it.

I fully understand and appreciate that some Americans will be upset about
this proposal, but please give this overview a look. Again, *time makes
more converts than reason.*

The Selective Military Service (SMS) System or the Draft as we used to
call it was closed down in 1973 after the end of the Vietnam War. In general the Draft system required that **all** young man by the age of 19 to register **and** enter the Army for a two (2) period **or** to voluntarily enlist in another branch of the military. There were of course various ways to defer
service such as a being in college or to avoid it all together via some real or
fabricated medical condition — I will not go into that history here.

Background on the American Selective Service System – from Wikepedia.com!

The **Selective Service Act** or **Selective Draft Act** was passed by the Congress of the United States on May 18, 1917 creating the Selective Service
System. The Act gave the President the power to draft soldiers.

World War I

In his war message on April 2, 1917 President Woodrow Wilson pledged
all the nation's "material resources" to the Allied war effort. But what the
Allies most urgently needed were fresh troops. Few Americans, however,
rushed to volunteer for military service. By the end of WWI, some 24
million men had registered, and some 2.8 million had been drafted, meaning that more than half of the almost 4.8 million Americans who served in
WWI were drafted.

The **Selective Training and Service Act of 1940** was passed by the Congress of the United States on September 6, 1940 becoming the first peace-

time *conscription* in United States history. This Selective Service Act required men between the ages 21 and 30 register with local draft boards. The age range was later changed to 18-45.

World War II

In May 1940 Congress appropriated $2.5 billion for Franklin D. Roosevelt's program of rebuilding military infrastructure, but Roosevelt did not feel the country was ready for a peacetime draft. However, on 20 June the Burke-Wadsworth Bill was brought before Congress. That legislation was drafted by Grenville Clark of the *Military Training Camps Association*, a World War I veterans group.

When signed into law by Franklin Roosevelt in 1940, the Burke-Wadsworth Act was the first peace-time draft in United States history. Under the Burke-Wadsworth Act, all American males between twenty-one and thirty-five years of age registered for the draft. The government initially selected men through a lottery system. If drafted, a man served for twelve months. According to the Burke-Wadsworth Act's provisions, drafted soldiers had to remain in the Western Hemisphere or in United States possessions or territories located in other parts of the world. The act provided that not more than 900,000 men were to be in training at any one time, and it limited service to 12 months.

The draft began in October 1940. By the early summer of 1941, President Franklin Roosevelt asked the U.S. Congress to extend the term of duty for the draftees beyond twelve months. The United States House of Representatives approved the extension by a single vote. The Senate approved it by a wider margin, and Roosevelt signed the bill into law.

Following the Japanese attack on Pearl Harbor, Hawaii, on 7 December 1941, thousands of American men and women swelled the United States' military's ranks by volunteering for service.

After the United States entered World War II, a new Selective Service Act made men between 18 and 45 liable for military service and required all men between 18 and 65 to register. The terminal point of service was then extended to six months after the war was over. From 1940 until 1947—when the wartime selective service act expired after extensions by Congress—over 10,000,000 men were inducted.

After World War II

A revised Selective Service Act was passed in 1948 that required all men between 18 and 26 to register and that made men from 19 to 26 liable for induction for 21 months' service, which would be followed by 5 years of reserve duty.

> My thanks to the Internet service at **Wikepedia.com,** the "free encyclopedia", for the informative background on the Selective Service System.

o   o   o   o

To continue

"The Draft" as we knew it ended in 1973, the Selective Service remains as a means to register American <u>males</u> upon reaching the age of 18 as a contingency should the need arise. They still send Uncle Sam's "birthday greeting card" to teenage men.

The SMS registration requirement was suspended in April 1975, but reinstituted in 1980. Therefore, it was available and could have been used in recent years to support the Afghanistan and Iraq war efforts — instead of the politically gutless "backdoor Draft" of our National Guard for foreign deployment that the Bush II Administration decided to utilize.

> Of course if Bush II and Cheney would have tried to start using the Draft, the public may have stopped *Bush's Optional Iraq War* before it started and would have screamed for it to be ended once the justification for it were shown to be, shall we say somewhat "fabricated." And they knew it.

As stated, you did not need to register with the Selective Service, you automatically received that greeting card from your local Draft Board on your 19th birthday — I got mine in July of 1967! And you were <u>expected to report</u> for a pre-induction physical and aptitude test. Again, if you went into the Draft it was a standard two-year commitment to the Army with options to stay permanently if you so decided.

o   o   o   o

How the New SMS Will Help Us Now

The SMS System as it previously existed may not be fully restored <u>however</u>, that is where the national discussion needs to begin. I believe the debate over whether or not it should be restarted should rapidly evolve into exactly what practical form it *will* take and public acknowledgement of the measurable human benefits it would yield for the younger generation and our society as a whole.

Some of the benefits to the individual will be the vocational training, military discipline, and structure for young men (and women) today that proved to be so beneficial for young Americans for decades in the past. It absolutely proved to be a solid and positive starting point in life for many that would not have had it otherwise. Also, those that enter the SMS without a High School diploma will leave with one.

I believe the nation must deliberately move to reinstitute some form of the non-voluntary SMS Draft system and have it ramping up in 2009 at the latest. Even though the Bush II, Iraq War surely muddies the discussion – both concerned parents and seasoned social workers that I have bounced this idea off have been very supportive of bringing the SMS back to help teenagers and younger twenty-something's get a better track on life.

I came to this sobering conclusion after straining my brain for a long time trying to determine what could practically be done with today's High School drop-outs (25-plus percent), as well as other youth both male and female that have been sitting ducks for the drug business, crime, gangs, and now religious zealots.

A better track had to be developed for their good and the nation's. I believe it is far better to build more soldiers than to build and fill more prisons. It all led me eventually to consider this personally surprising, yet nationally viable solution.

The People's Sense

To be crystal clear, the purpose in recommending that we bring back the military Draft induction process is to address various Domestic issues. It is not offered with the intent of building an Army for foreign assignment.

The new SMS is absolutely not for us to build-up troop count in Iraq and a watchful public will not let that happen. Rather we will get the h___ out of Bush IIs optional war, ASAP! That issue will be more bluntly addressed later.

The New Draft – A Viable Means to Desirable Ends

Here are a few thoughts on the why the new Selective Military Service

(SMS) will be of great use to the nation:

- In the first place the military is a very viable option for a lot of young Americans. Further, we will make the American military one that is staffed <u>only</u> with citizens. Although the service of non-citizen volunteers in our military has been outstanding, it is also seen as a backdoor way to citizenship. We will be moving to tighten the current paths of US citizenship and this is one admittedly honorable option that will be withdrawn.

- It would include men and women – equal opportunity ladies!

- Too many of our teens and twenty-something's today have few employment options where they are living and/or are just not that motivated to do something on their own. The truth is the truth.

  A structured life and vocational guidance are what the Draft offered millions of young men for decades and what the volunteer-based military services still offer today. They come out of the standard 2-year tour more mature, more confident, and most were in the best physical condition of their life. They were better prepared for the world often had an improved work ethic, and have learned some basic occupational skill(s). And they had the GI-Bill to help them continue their education.

- With an increasing high school dropout rate now over 25% and with well-over 50% of those in prison not possessing a high school diploma – military service should once again be the next place for young people to go after High School or after having dropped out of it. And it would <u>not</u> be optional.

  That real possibility would undoubtedly keep some of them in high school to graduate. Those that went into the Service would complete their high school education while in there and have the opportunity to get their life going in a more positive direction.

- Again, I have reviewed the idea of bringing back the Draft with social workers and they immediately say, "Yes!"

<u>Over-lapping Problems and Solutions</u>

Are you sitting down? ***The*** over-lapping problem area that really made my brain hurt for a while was — how to go about dismantling the various and violent gangs now operating all over our country! The SMS is the framework to provide us with that answer. The bad will go in and the good will come out!

"Society's most complex problems are made and solved at the unit level — one person at a time"

This is complicated stuff isn't it? But we can fix anything that We the People put our hearts and minds together to fix. Looking back it was probably a national mistake to ever stop the SMS service. With An American Agenda, We are now all about correcting passed errors wherever we can and this is an unexpected issue that needs to be confronted and fixed.

It is just more common sense.

o   o   o   o

The Changing National System

With the proposed ramping down of the failed 35-plus year War on Hard Drugs beginning in 2008 and with major reductions in free-will crime we must determine what to do with those people – our fellow citizens, as well. Idle criminals can <u>really</u> get into trouble!

For starters we will begin rapid *collection and deportation* of any and all IOs known to be involved in gang and other criminal activities – and we will firmly resolve what to do with any family that they have here.

> Because we cannot just go and kill them <u>and</u> their families like Chinese government <u>literally</u> did years ago to stamp-out its drug industry — and users, as well!

And should any of those IOs with criminal history decide of their own free-will to once again violate our national borders (as so many now do over and over again) and are apprehended – they will be <u>toast</u> — not imprisoned or evicted one more time. They will have be warned and know the hard penalty for returning well in advance.

We will have absolute control over our borders and who is allowed to be inside them. We must decide as a nation to quit paying for crime to continue to exist in our neighborhoods! And, especially crimes committed by IOs.

After all that, we will still have some tens of thousands of our citizens with criminal records to "re-tool" for life in civil society. And we can do it.

It is Just Like Baking a Cake

The old saying is,

> "If you want bake a cake, you have got to break a few eggs"

Therefore, it follows that,

> "If we want to have Peace in our streets,
> we will be required to deport and break a few criminals."

Granted this is a lot to take in, but please give it some thought.

o   o   o   o

Coordinated Domestic Victory

The complimentary functioning of the re-instituted Draft system, American Population Management, and the Re-Employment system will work together to facilitate and accomplish the gargantuan civil rehabilitation of 'former' criminals and gang members. Given a choice of prison, 3-strikes you are dead, or the military what do you think their choice would probably be?

Our *common sense* and nationally responsible approach is to deliberately divert at-risk youth and young criminals to a safer and more promising life path, and it will not be optional.

The military would re-write its rules on not accepting people with a criminal record. Let's get real for a change. **Especially** with young first offenders that are at the front edge of a bad life. And whether they are in high school or even in a lower grade, they may be considered for the overall SMS program. There could possibly be a pre-SMS program if they are too young – a program 6 to 12 months in duration and then return to regular school.

This can all be done and it will save thousands of our youth and the heartbreak of their parents, as well.

There are other positive benefits to the National System to be drawn from the re-birth of the SMS program, but this is enough on that for now. This was fairly brief, but it presents the viable concepts that will be easy enough to develop and implement no later than 2009!

Please give this overall proposal some serious thought, because it will be a far better than spending more billion$ of our taxes building and maintaining any more jails and prisons — to say nothing of human loss.

o   o   o   o

Let's Hear It

And this is one of the few instances in CS2 where I will directly challenge people and groups that typically reject such a solution oriented proposal. For, IF they can come up with a better approach that will work at least this well on paper, and I mean get the same real results – then start writing because We the People cannot wait to read it! Or do not complain.

Peace, love, dove!

o   o   o   o

10   Zero Tolerance for Free-Will Crime by All People

Issue/Problem

This National program area aggressively targets what is referred to repeatedly in CS2 as "freewill" crime and how America as a Democratic and Christian-based nation will resolve to finally deal with the people that commit serious criminal acts. This proposal relates directly to our American Themes – the Civil Responsibilities of all American citizens, as well as the Accountability for their Free-Will actions.

Zero Tolerance — does not offer a specific program or system. However, it will implement specific legislative changes within the Judicial System having to do with serious crimes and declaring the pre-determined, <u>no</u> plea-bargaining punishment for anyone committing certain harsh offenses. This proposal addresses how the invisible bar of Freewill Accountability will be raised in our country — and how "reasonable civil rules and strictly enforced laws" will be applied to **all** Americans with simplicity, fairness, and in specific cases with extreme punishment – something called justice!

o   o   o   o

<u>The Point of Control</u>

In American society today, the violent freewill "criminal" activities that a minority of our citizens cause do not fall under the stern control of an absolute monarch and/or a religious dictate — as is the case in other countries that <u>often</u> experience far **less crime** — and also have far **fewer lawyers**. Go figure.

Unfortunately, in American society <u>today</u> the violent criminal activities of a minority of our citizens (and worse non-citizens) falls under the <u>less</u> than stern control of the US Criminal Justice System. Several years ago, I created a working label for the ever-growing Criminal Justice System and the increasingly dysfunctional (there is that word again) results it produces for American society. I call it the **Judicial Legal Complex (JLC).**

A name similar in intent and uncomplimentary tone to the late 1950's term Military Industrial Complex (MIC) used to label the fast growing American Defense Industry. President Dwight David Eisenhower (from 1952 to 1960) warned us about the MIC and referenced it in his farewell address the night before President John F. Kennedy's inauguration. See the movie on DVD, "Why We Fight". He was very right to warn us, because unfortunately all that he predicted has come to pass. More on that later – watch the movie!

Our Criminal Code (crime = punishment) is therefore one *not* driven by a dictator or religious dictate, but by the Common Agreement of *We the People*. And it is that Common Agreement that America will now need to debate, clarify, and toughen because the JLC is failing to provide every person, family, and business with a safe and secure society in which to experience *Life, Liberty, and the Pursuit of Happiness.*

Severe Reductions Required

Further, we will be addressing many of the problems and issues that American society has with the dysfunctional JLC as a simple by-product of eliminating well in excess of 50% of all violent freewill crime!

The day-to-day public results of the refined Criminal Code within the JLC will in a relatively short time free-up valuable dollars and people resources for better uses — say repatriating IOs and Homeland Security for example. Some could be transferred and begin inspecting food shipments from China!

A viable public benefits of this proposal will be the reduced the number of Americans seeking careers in the currently "growing field of Criminal Justice" simply because the JLC will begin shrinking! I cannot stand it when I hear those commercials – it is admitting continual defeat! Our people will logically move toward far more positive careers Information Technology, math, the sciences, nursing, medicine, business ownership, teaching, and the environment — all of which the nation needs for a better future. There will more rewarding careers helping to build a better future for our nation. The right stuff!

To be addressed in particular is the hardening of penalties for certain predatory criminal offenses, with a deliberate targeting of "freewill" crimes involving the **physical or financial assault** of one person on another.

I have often commented when discussing this proposal with people that the reason that we have so much crime in our country, is simply because we allow it. And the time has come for us to stop allowing it.

Simple Rules Make for Civil Societies

Revisions will be enacted to existing legislation that governs our JLC, with the informed and **Common Agreement** — By the People. The resulting positive changes in our day-to-day society and the severe reduction in serious crime will clearly demonstrate to our people and the world — that a free, Democratic, and religiously open society that is rooted in the Christian value of *forgiveness*, is able to declare and enforce strict laws against socially unacceptable behavior. Further, that will all be accomplished with publicly acceptable, stern penalties enforced against freewill offenders.

The JLC revisions will be a binding public reconciliation between:

- a person's Civil Responsibility to society,
- a person's Civil Liberties within our society,
- a basic set values common to all religions,
- and, a person's absolute accountability to civil society for their freewill actions.

Basically, this public reconciliation will result in the creation of an acceptable national *Civil Code of Conduct*. A Common Civil Code by which well over 90% of all American citizens <u>already</u> <u>live</u> our lives by. The Masses will be dealing constructively and decisively with the negative Few. The benefits will be less crime <u>and</u> will decrease <u>any justification</u> for an increasingly oppressive legal authority over the Masses, such as are contained in some provisions of the Patriot Act.

And *We the People* will see to it that the damage done to the *U.S. Bill of Rights* by the Bush II Administration is reversed. Period.

o   o   o   o

If we do <u>not</u> act now to prevent the freewill incidents of crime by both our people and in particular anyone that is not a citizen – then the <u>avoidable</u> death, injury, and imprisonment of our people will continue. We can either decide to have Peace in our streets – and Demand it now – or we will <u>most assuredly</u> be looking at an America right out of one of those movies about a future society (see the movie, *"V for Vendetta"*) that is a virtual police state — and we would <u>not</u> be any the safer for it.

That dismal future is where we are slowly, yet undeniably headed for today — and that grim image of our future is not any part of the acceptable National Vision that we are painting in CS2.

Crime will be reduced — permanently.
Our neighborhoods will once again be safe for children and ourselves.
If we are bold enough to do what must be done!

The People's Sense

Public Perspectives on Crime

This presentation is a prime example what is meant by the term *Intelligent Design in Civil Policy* — when government is truly working to resolve avoidable public problems in the interest of the Common Good. You know, doing their job.

The following are clear examples of solution-oriented, legislative policy and the acceptable public understanding required for them to be implemented into law. These should ignite a most lively public debate! Again, all of these items have been reviewed with regular Americans, have been refined by their direct feedback, and have received majority acceptance. So if you find yourself appreciating what you are reading, you are not alone.

The Death Penalty as Society's Viable Tool

As first identified as a *publicly acceptable* tool under the provisions of the National Drug Reform (NDR) Proposal is the deliberate use the Death Penalty (DP) by lethal injection, as determined to be applicable for certain freewill criminal acts. I did warn you upfront that the message of CS2 is as serious as a heart attack!

Under the NDR, the use of the DP will only be targeted at person's that continue to traffic and/or distribute hard drugs after a nationally publicized and mandated Hard Drug Sale Cut-off Date. To be clear, the DP will never to be used against the drug users, only the hard drug provider network of human predators.

As a side note, we will also be ending the publicly abusive law enforcement practice under the existing National Drug Policy that leads to the arrest of well-over 600,000 drug users a year.

Physical or Financial Assault

As mentioned, in the near future prescribed harsh penalties such as the DP will be deliberately used against those that decide of their own freewill to commit certain types of serious crime upon our people. The initial primary targets of this clarified Criminal Code will be crimes involving *physical or financial assault* on another person or persons.

THEY, like to say "we as a society cannot legislate morality." That is true if laws are only written on paper.

The public's **_Sword_** must be used at times in order to insure the individual compliance with laws written with society's **_Pen_**. The critical point being that it must be *the Public* that first determines the laws that everyone will be held accountable for honoring – not an oppressive monarch or religious entity.

We are with absolute certainty going to start punishing an individual's rejection of society's civil law to the extent required to first attain Peace in our streets — and then to maintain it permanently. The JLC is not currently maintaining that peace, so some things are going to change.

However, this type of policy could be a very slippery slope so the *Liberal's* will need to keep a watchful eye on this, but they must also accept that going forward people will be held accountable for deliberately inflicting harm on other citizens. Be encouraged non-Liberals, in discussions with many hard-core Liberals I learned that they too have limits with regard to how much should be tolerated from those that society is actively trying to help, but that help is unappreciated and disrespected. Yes, Liberals do have limits, too. Believe it!

The Assault Prevention List

The following are the initial pieces of legislation to be passed by the U.S. Congress and to be applied as law in all 50 states and DC — with a target effective date March 1, 2009 — if not sooner.

- **Pre-Meditated Murder** – if a person in the performance of a crime of robbery, car theft, gang activity, etc., unfortunately kills a person(s) **and** it is proven beyond a shadow doubt in a standard court of law that they are guilty of the murder(s), there will be no appeal and no plea-bargaining available to them.

    A special Grand Jury process could be implemented for a final and swift review of the case and final validation of the jury's verdict, but that is all.

    It may be argued that when they walked into that business with a gun they had no intention of killing somebody, but things took an unexpected turn and that "somebody" died. So whether or not it was their "intent" to kill someone in the process of their freewill criminal action does not matter to the public – someone died and now so shall they!

    The person will remain in custody for three (3) months from the day of the Grand Jury's final validation of the court's verdict and then the

Death Penalty (DP) by lethal injection will be administered – period, end of story.

Let's all agree that guns, knives, and bombs do not kill people. People exercising their own freewill <u>on</u> <u>other</u> <u>people</u> <u>do</u>!

And I can guarantee you that at <u>least</u> 8 of 10 Americans will vote for what you just read *and* are about to read.

• **Pre-Meditated Rape** – this is the second crime which will earn those who choose of their own freewill commit it — the DP.

A person that <u>premeditatedly</u> attacks and rapes a person (a woman, a minor or a man) and their obvious guilt is proven a standard court of law with certifiable evidence and all the forensics currently at our disposal – they too will remain in custody for three (3) months from the day of the Grand Jury's final validation of the court's verdict and then have the DP by lethal injection administered to end their life…

They will never have the opportunity to do it again. We will not pay for multiple trails or to try and figure out why they decided to do it in the first place. *We do not care why.* And we will not warehouse them for decades on the taxpayers tab and possibly be paroled. We the People will declare never more!

To be clear, we will differentiate "premeditated" from "date" rape situations. The latter can be the subject of questionable charges and so will not be included under this law. It would be fair to say that such cases may be reduced in occurrence with the implementation of the former.

<u>One Big Reality Check</u>

The other side of this Sword is that we will be required to open legal, public brothels. Yes America, we will acknowledge basic human need and oldest profession in the world rather than trying to suppress or ignore it, and locking people for doing it. Reality must finally rule in America.

And I am <u>not</u> for a moment saying or inferring such human demand could be the primary cause of such predatory attacks. And I will not engage in that worn-out debate. As you will hear a few times in CS2, America is not Fantasyland. Therefore, we will quit living under unrealistic and oppressive laws that were <u>made</u> <u>there</u> in our nation's past.

We will in the process also put some nasty pimps out of business! This realistic social approach will surely initiate high-pitched reactions with those that will be in favor of the first, but will be shocked by the latter. Their screams will be drowned-out in time and/or be over-taken by the applause of former victims. It would theoretically be great if such policies were not necessary, but day-to-day life is not theory.

- **Pedophilia — Crimes Against Children** – this third crime was added due to direct feedback "volunteered" by people (mothers, fathers, and others) that I asked for their opinion on the first two. People told me to add it. I had thought about including it in the initial set, but was uncertain until receiving such direct feedback from the public. An clear example of how public feedback shaped this Agenda.

A former 20-plus year U.S. Marshall that then turned lawyer for many years summed it up pretty well. His long held personal attitude was that pedophiles could be rehabilitated — cured. However, as he spent more time in the legal profession and the more grim cases he heard about from fellow lawyers it became clear that such rehabilitation is only an academics dream.

Thus, we will add this hideous crime to the short list. We will not continue to warehouse these predators. We will not be maintaining expensive tracking systems on them. We will not waste years trying to figure out what if anything in their past may have caused them do such terrible things. The American public does not care! And this is a case of one (1) strike – or one more strike if they have a history of such activity – and they are out!

Therefore, going forward the individuals in this 'predator group' will know their life choices — either to permanently cease such activities or move to a country that allows such deviant behavior (and sadly there are those). For the very next time they are caught – they are finished! No exceptions and no plea-bargaining. One-by-one they will be eliminated.

And our children will again be safe.

- **Other pre-meditated crimes** – involving financial assault will be added to the list of DP-level offenses as American society slowly turns the screws down on free-will crime in America. The first types of financially oriented offenses to be considered for inclusion are:

  - Identify theft of individual credit accounts

- Identify theft involving person's Social Security Number
- Deliberately Swindling of people out of their savings and/or property
- Cyber-crimes of invasion against corporate or government facilities
- Cyber-crimes involving the distribution of destructive computer viruses

This will be the deliberate and unfortunately very necessary National *process of elimination* of those that would choose of their own freewill to perpetrate physical or financial assault.

They will be warned well in advance and then they <u>will</u> <u>decide</u> <u>their</u> <u>own</u> <u>fate</u>.

o   o   o   o

<u>*Please Try to Appreciate*</u>

In the odd case you are thinking these types of problem resolutions are easy to consider, develop, and write about — think again! These are the very hard, complex, and often painful public issues involving the lives of millions of our fellow citizens that are being boiled down to a precious few sentences — and there are more of them to come.

I am an average citizen. I am herein attempting of <u>my</u> <u>own</u> <u>freewill</u> — as a Systems Analyst and problem solver — to serve the country that I love so very much. I have cried many tears over these words and topics, and will shed more of them before I may <u>finally</u> write "The End" on CS2.

This is not an academic exercise – this is personal.

Across the scope of the public issues in An American Agenda there are very "human statistics" representing various grades of real human pain and suffering. And I think about them as I struggle with how to offer corrections to the conditions within our National System that <u>allow</u> such suffering to exist and continue.

We can imagine and see the counts — the thousands and thousands that have been murdered, raped, and the children that have been assaulted over the years and how many have suffered this very year-to-date. What we will be blessed to *never know* are the names of those in the future that will be spared such grief if We the People do what needs to be done and put an end to such *avoidable* chaos.

Consider, that today in real life, <u>you</u> or someone you love may be one of the many thousands of people that are only alive *now* because of the laws that Mothers Against Drunk Driving (MADD) were successful putting in place. Because one person, a mother, stood up and said enough! And then acted!

We know that thousands and thousands have been saved — we just have no idea which ones they are.

Appreciate that the Changes to laws and to the National System that you are now reviewing will save so many more. *We the People* need to stand together on many of these issues and say enough!

I needed to write that down.

o   o   o   o

National Laws and Local Agreement

In dealing with serious issues such as the use of the death penalty and realistic reform of National Drug Policy, both federal and state lawmakers need to get in lockstep with each other, to say nothing about the Supreme Court.

While States Rights need to be protected, the national environment needs to have certain laws and penalties that are standardized to provide predictable and consistent law enforcement across the nation so that citizens, non-citizens, and IOs will know the rules. Ant that the rules will be enforced!

Further, in order to assist local prosecutors in enforcing the law there need to be Common Agreements at the national level that are coordinated, publicly accepted, and <u>evenly</u> applied in all states and DC. In cases like these one size needs to fit all.

Drug Reform and the DEA

With the coming <u>full</u> legalization and decriminalization of marijuana by 2009, the ongoing struggle between many of the states trying to legalize it for at least medicinal purposes and the DEA/Justice Department will mercifully come to a practical end. For some years now, even after the voters of a given state have approved legislation for medical use of marijuana in public clinics to help those undergoing cancer treatments and with Aids, with no appetite — the DEA that is just doing their job could and does randomly charge-in, slam the facility, and lockup the mostly volunteers working there.

The decades old, failed Prohibition on Cannabis will finally end and our people with illnesses will be helped by a low cost, naturally growing, non-chemically treated, and God-given weed!

And the Pharmaceutical Industry will hate it! Amen...

Witness Intimidation

It appears that the courts in some cities are experiencing a growing number of instances where witnesses to various crimes are being threatened with physical harm to themselves and/or their family to the point where they will not testify against "obviously guilty defendants."

This known fault in the dysfunctional JLC needs to be legislatively addressed at the national level to provide public safety relief at the local level. To keep the bad guys from winning!

This legal problem would be addressed using a special Grand Jury to review the given case situation and if it is determined that Witness Intimidation Law (to be written) had been violated, it will be assumed that the defendant is guilty of the charges in question and the penalty for said crime(s) will be automatically assigned by the court. Yes, we can do that. Remember, we make the rules...

Such viable public policy is not rocket science, just *more common sense* (incidentally that was the original title of this book). Going forward society will greet harsh criminal activity, with thoughtful, fair, deliberate, and prevention oriented penalties.

o   o   o   o

Again, some people would say these do sound like a reasonable laws to establish, but how could we do that.

We must begin to realize and act as though it is our country. We can and must determine the rules of our society that will shape our nation's destiny, and that destiny starts in 2008 if We determine to make it happen.

We need only assert our Common Will upon the political system and make it crystal clear the politicians that we elect that they are to take care of our Common Good. The re-establishment of our Common Power must be felt by candidates for all offices from your local candidates to those desiring

White House, leading up to Election Day 2008!

Obvious Guilt

Here is raised the issue of reconciling a person's Civil Right within the American Criminal Justice System to a "fair trail" in determining their innocence or quilt <u>versus</u> society's reasonable expectation of a "somewhat" cost-effective Judicial System. To that end, let us review the publicly prudent, legal concept and definition of *"Obvious Guilt"*.

Victims Rights groups are going absolutely love this, and most law-abiding people (and tax-payers) will, as well. There are countless situations where a person is absolutely, undeniably, and with all certainty GUILTY as charged. And in spite of that, their trial turns into a multiple appeal, multi-year if not multiple decade ordeal. The Public Good is <u>not</u> being served and the victims and/or their loved ones are made to suffer as it is re-played over and over again.

However, the self-perpetuating JLC keeps rolling right along, worshiping 'The Law' and writing its own meal ticket with little regard for public safety. That wasn't written too sarcastically was it? How is your coffee doing?

o o o o

One PARTICULAR case convinced me to confront issue — the all too common and absurd legal recycling of cases within our "alleged" Criminal Justice System. As stated, the courts have made the letter of the almighty "Law" their chief concern, as opposed to the Common Good of American society and safety in our neighborhoods — which the laws are supposed to insure. What a concept!

I would label any related legislative changes, **The Sniper Laws**. Anyone living in the mid-Atlantic region knows what you mean when you ask about "the Snipers" and the endless multi-county and multi-state trials and retrials of two (2) obviously guilty criminals — who of their own freewill randomly selected and executed by ambush, thirteen (13) innocent human beings.

The **American Criminal Justice System** will be changed to allow "a" fair but expedient trial and prosecution of such criminals <u>and nothing more</u>, in such cases! Again, an open Grand Jury process could also be fairly utilized to conclude such litigation.

<u>Consider</u> that the primary "reason" that we have so much crime in this

country, is that our Criminal Justice System – the self-perpetuating Judicial Legal Complex allows it!

If the freewill taking of another person's life is not punishable by swift and terminal punishment then <u>what</u> <u>crime</u> <u>is</u>? Society then <u>has</u> <u>no</u> <u>rules</u> – anything goes – chaos will follow. We the People will end this madness starting in 2009, or, sit and watch as our society descends into a bad movie.

o   o   o   o

Twelve Angry People – One Too Many

And finally, the current Criminal Justice System procedurally requires 12 out of 12, or 10 out of 10 jurors to agree on the guilt of a person will be altered to be 11 out of 12, or 9 out of 10 to reach the same conclusion.

Our Judicial System was created by the Founders to insure that the Common citizen received a <u>fair</u> <u>trial</u> by a jury of their peers, in fair determination of their <u>guilt</u> <u>or</u> <u>innocence</u> — <u>period</u>. As simply stated to the King in the *Declaration of Independence,*

For depriving us in many cases, of the benefits of Trial by Jury:

It was not designed with the intent of allowing guilty individuals to walk free due to some technicality of the "Law" or through the <u>sick</u> <u>science</u> of jury selection by defense attorneys, where dollars too often equals freedom from the law.

**If, We the People,
are determined to have Law and Order
there must be swift Justice with predictable Penalty
assigned to those that of their own freewill choose to violate it.**

o   o   o   o

11   The Family Support Administration (FSA)

Issue/Problem

This National program area will be restructuring of the way public services are provided to help Americans in various areas that require federal, state, county, city, etc., tax-based funding.

The FSA proposal would streamline the functions of unemployment, welfare, housing, and any other subsidies that are currently administered in a somewhat uncoordinated manner. Again, we are already paying for the administration of these services.

This function will approach citizen needs for any publicly funded support as a "family unit" whether determining how to help one or x-number of persons.

The People's Sense

America was originally peopled by brave souls seeking a better life for their family and/or religious freedom. The *family unit* whether it is comprised of one or more people is the fundamental element of any society.

When it comes to protecting the quality-of-life of American families, especially those in need we will adjust our social service support network of programs as needed to efficiently focus on improving their overall situations. In turn, we will expect their full commitment to the same goal if they want any tax-payer funded support. Not too much to ask.

The FSA entity will work in conjunction with the functions of the aforementioned Re-Employment System to assist people and families, but only so long as they are willing to work towards bettering their personal and/or their family situation with regard to employment, education, and civil responsibility.

The FSA may very well come to be known among the American public as, *The Last Deal.*

We Americans as united people and as a nation born with a forgiving Christian character — will absolutely work to help those that want to help themselves progress. However, going forward we will show no tolerance for anyone that expects publicly funded support of any kind without the personal willingness to actively work on improving their educational level and/or vocational capabilities, as needed. They must also be prepared to work full or part-time while any publicly funded help is being provided to them and/or their family, as appropriate to their particular situation.

And for those that in their past were involved in crime, gangs, etc., we will diligently work to bring them into mainstream society with a "written understanding" signed of their own freewill that the nation will demonstrate zero tolerance for any future involvement in such activity. It very well could be their *Last Deal*, but we will offer it to them. This group will help to replace the IOs that will be repatriated!

The FSA program philosophy is for publicly funded services to provide a civil framework designed to help our citizens and their families progress toward a better life.

The intended focus of the Family Administration concept is to deliver a civilly responsible approach to "whole person" and "whole family" services. And to insure the most productive and efficient use of our tax dollars, as well. As stated before, it will be citizens first, Other Legal Occupants (OLOs) second, and there is no third.

We will absolutely help American citizens and their families when they need help and desire to build a better life.

At the same time, it will be made crystal clear that American society has the right, obligation, and responsibility to the Common Good to kick those that do not choose of their own freewill to be civilly responsible. And we will need to kick some of them very hard in the beginning! There will be no more pity parties and no more free rides.

The implementation of the FSA philosophy in the administration of publicly funded services working in conjunction with the U.S. Re-Employment System methodology will assuredly improve the quality of life within American society. It will do it one person and one family at a time.

There is not a lot more that really needs to be said about this proposal at this time since I believe you know, understand, and most likely approve of the common sense message above.

o   o   o   o

12   Family Basic Asset Protection

Issue/Problem

This oddly titled National proposal raises an important issue that American society needs to publicly debate, prudently consider, and reach Common Agreement upon. It seeks to help us resolve the definition of the *American Dream* and how it will be cared and accounted for within the National System.

Specifically, the issue is whether or not <u>every</u> American family has the right to have a long-term home or residence in which to live their life and to call their own.

This is a tough one because it involves the personal ownership of property – you know, what most wars are fought over!

We're not talking multiple homes, but a family residence that will be theirs over the years. We <u>know</u> this one will cause some banging and crashing! Dealing practically with the home ownership issue will challenge our national commitment to <u>American</u> <u>families</u> and their Right to the *American Dream*.

The People's Sense

<u>The American Family's Baseline</u>

As far as America is to be defined on this issue — every hard working American will be entitled (a sometimes ugly word) to a residence of their <u>own</u>. To possess a real piece of America and a fixed address — whether it is a single family home, a mansion, a townhouse, a mobile home, a condo, a houseboat, a duplex or whatever — is to most people the base upon which the American dream is built.

I believe most Americans will agree with that and the reality that due to various internal and external factors that Dream in recent years is becoming an American Fantasy for many of our citizens. It is particularly true for the youngest Americans trying to enter an over-priced housing market, but it is a reality for many of the Generational Groups within our society. Not only obtaining a home, keeping it as well.

<u>Let's Take a Look</u>

For starters, we <u>are</u> <u>not</u> talking about a residence that is given to someone by the government. Not going to happen. One way or another people will *work and earn* their piece of America even if they have to work and pay on it over their entire lifetime.

We <u>are</u> talking about family (one or more persons) housing that under special long-term financing programs will allow even the poorest American citizens a place to call their own.

Those long-term financing programs set-up and managed by the American Banking System. We will not be asking the Banking Industry to set them up — We will tell them the interest rates and the terms to be provided and they will put in place. This is a glimpse at a key part of the Re-Structuring of the Banking Industry to be presented later. Remember what I said about wars being fought over such things – it will get hot!

A few thoughts on how this complicated but very "family-value" issue will play-out:

• As life in our National System and the overall economy may uncontrollably erode a family's finances, they should not have to live in fear of losing their home. Or never even being able to afford one in the first place.

• The housing market went through a tremendous home valuation growth and general greed phase roughly from 2003 into 2006.

  That bubble was driven by a period of Bank supplied, very low interest rates, too many investors (many that are not American citizens) buying and selling homes, the banks continually lowering their qualifying standards in order to keep making loans, and the overall <u>un-controlled</u> status of the Banking and Investment Industry. The well-lobbied Congress letting the Banks do what they please.

• The Banks have contributed greatly to the housing bubble and will now be <u>directed</u> to help families, far more than investors, live through the hard downward adjustment in home prices that has already started (2nd quarter 2007).

• Banks will be **required** to refinance person's primary residence (only) and at a "decent" interest rate, say a <u>fixed</u> rate of no more than 3 to 4%. And that regardless of the property's appraisal having fallen below the amount that needs to be refinanced.

• Further, loan terms of 35, 40, and more years will be provided to assist homeowners in balancing their mortgage payment to their income.

- A one-time national adjustment will be "negotiated" with the Banking Industry and the public will come out on top! The Banks just like many other businesses and whole industries will not <u>even</u> try to do something positive for society unless it is <u>mandated</u>. They do not consider it their responsibility!

This is another case where We must be assertive and act as the true owners of our country. We make the rules for those that want to continue to play in our sandbox.

And remember, We are taking care of American families.

<u>From another angle</u>, the Public Housing projects in existence all over the country will be deliberately converted over to "owned" condos for which the current or future residents will assume the personal responsibility of a mortgage loan in order to possess or they will need another option.

<u>For Those Not Interested</u>

At the same time, it must be acknowledged that there are some numbers of people that do not want to own or be responsible for residence of their own – and that would be their choice. People will not be helped to own a home that they are not going to live in and properly maintain.

However, they <u>could</u> practically utilize the option of a guaranteed, long-term residence to benefit of their overall stability.

The option could practically be arranged through a formal, national Family Housing program where owners of properties register rental(s) for long-term, if not lifetime lease, by individuals seeking such a life arrangement.

However, this option does involve the traditionally unreliable and too often irresponsible maintenance of a given property by an owner — the dreaded Slum Lord scenario.

Going forward Slum Lords of any kind will not be tolerated if they desire to enjoy the tax benefits from such properties and/or being allowed to retain ownership thereof. Violators will lose their properties – in short order!

<u>On the Other Hand</u>

There is a bit of the flip side to the Slum Lord problems, and the Banks will be <u>required</u> to help resolve it. Banks in a practical effort to guard against risky loans generally do not like to make too many loans to investors. At the same time investors in rental properties often complain that they have limited resources to put into upkeep of said properties. Maybe they should not be permitted to have them in the first place then?

In <u>every</u> town and city in the country there are rental properties in which families are living in conditions that most of us would not care to even walk through, or to be offered a drink of water there. I know – I have seen a few of them and would not take a drink of water. That's the facts!

Banks will be mandated to make "Rental Home Improvement Loans" on a per property basis. <u>All</u> of the funds loaned will be designated for the <u>sole</u> <u>purpose</u> of bringing a specific property up to a publicly acceptable living standard — and keeping them there!

This single program will generate an "enormous" amount of home improvement work in every part of the country. And that means jobs!

The re-financing will be at reasonable rates and year-terms so that the resulting new mortgage will not (be allowed to) cause the rent for that property to be raised to a level that the existing tenant could not afford. The accountability of bank and borrower will be strictly monitored and penalties will be significant and swift, including the loss of property's ownership! And, owners will not use these loans to fix up and then flip the property.

Tenants will have long-term (decades) leases on properties set-up under this national program.

Various details will need to be worked out on this legislation, but the intent and family-oriented spirit of it is quite clear. Give it some thought.

"A home for every American family and a family in every home"

13   American Owned Business Preference Policy

Issue/Problem

This National program would very publicly formalize what should be a given within the American National System and business community. Going forward we will consider severely limiting, but not totally eliminating the opportunity for non-citizens to start and/or buy businesses small and large in America.

This proposal concept will be very difficult to implement considering how much property and how many businesses in America are foreign-owned. However, we must start somewhere, especially when considering that such controls and restrictions are a commonplace practice around the world (China for example).

Our current national legislation and policies on foreign ownership must be publicly presented, if not exposed for public critique. The issue demands a hard and practical public debate as We the People are shaping our nation's future.

The business ownership issue also ties a bit into the overall immigration control issue. We need Americans to own and operate businesses in this country. The Small Business Administration (SBA) for example will have its charter reviewed and modified as needed to reflect this clarified national priority. SBA loans to promote business creation by citizens will become the rule.

Again, America an Americans first!

The People's Sense

Frankly, America does not fully benefit when those with wealth from other countries come here to buy-up and/or start businesses with old world wealth. This decreases the opportunities for our own people to start, own, and operate businesses within their own communities.

Non-American ownership of businesses within our borders will not be totally suspended, but the "Everything in America Is on Sale to the Highest Better" cycle needs to be brought abruptly under control.

And more Americans must learn how to own and successfully operate businesses – which frankly not just anyone can do.

We will also regulate to a reasonable extent the future sale of businesses owned by non-citizens giving Americans preferential access to those purchases. Thus gradually increasing the percentage of citizen owned businesses in America. Consider it a side-issue in our national house-keeping exercise.

This proposal will understandably come under tremendous pressure from many sides, but the spirit of it could be summarized in looking at recent flap over the management of some of our seaport operations being sold to Middle-Eastern companies instead of to an American entity (and there is backdoor legislation in the works to get around the successful blocking of that deal).

While there were definitely political and foreign policy considerations to such deals — sales like this mainly represent the desire to sell to the highest bidder regardless of the fact that an American entity could make the deal at the same or a somewhat lower price, but would keep the ownership and jobs in country.

A hard issue to be addressed for sure, but we must take a long-term perspective on overselling our assets and in some cases, even placing our national security in question.

It is a situation that must be responsibly confronted for the Common Good.

o   o   o   o

3. Local Community Programs

*"It is time for We the People to start taking
certain critical matters into our Own Hands.
Then our leaders will follow us."*

o   o   o   o

14   Local Pride and Accountability

Issue/Problem – An Opportunity

This proposal is a small, but important piece in a book of over 140,000 words about, as I have described CS2 to folks – "What is wrong with America and how to fix it."

The proposal on Local Pride and Accountability is more a conversation about the opportunity for each of us to participate in the Change process being proposed in CS2. In working to "fix" America the Changes cannot happen in Washington, DC or your state's capital city. Again, the phrase on the cover of CS2 sums it up very well,

*"Society's most complex problems are made and solved
at the unit level – one person at a time"*

Meaning that each of We the People are the key to Change, <u>not</u> our government, and it has always been that way. It is for each of Us to decide whether or not to accept, promote, and personally participate in the national Change process. To determine whether or not to be <u>active</u> players in our nation's Second American Revolution, because that is what We are talking about in CS2. And nothing less than that level of popular support for the somewhat radical, but fully practical Changes presented herein is required for Us to confront many of our long-standing national problems – and declare victory!

It is now 2008 and realistically We cannot turn back the clock to better time in America, and We certainly cannot afford to let things remain headed in their current direction. Therefore, Change must happen and it falls to us to make those hard things happen now.

It has been estimated that less than 10% of the American colonists actively participated in the Revolutionary War. And of a 1776 colonial population estimated at less than three (3) million — under 300,000 brave people carried the fight for everyone's freedom. For our freedom! It was a glorious moment in history when the Few faithfully served the Many and in the end some 25,000 of them died in the process of winning the War of Independence for their neighbors.

Today, 10% of the American citizen population equates to thirty (30) million of us. Divided by 51 for all 50 states and DC that is over 588,000 people and 5% would still be some 294,000 of us. We could work wonders with that level of inspired, involved, and active citizen participation. We only need that patriotic core of citizens to rise up and to get the ball rolling, and I believe that the Masses, the Silent Majority will stand up and together to initiate our intense, yet peaceful Second revolution starting in 2008. The required leadership resides in every own communities.

And once We start this ball rolling, no Special Interest entity will be able to block the real progress that it will be demonstrating to an encouraged American public – the electorate.

The People's Sense

The Mechanics of Change

Beyond each of our homes the neighborhood, community, town, and the county or major city that make up our day-to-day world. The majority of our population rarely goes outside our home county or city except maybe to commute to work and then come right back — a daily pattern that is normal the world over.

Regarding the concept of "Local Pride and Accountability" – it is based on the idea the most of us can identify with our home county or the major city in which we live. The majority of us do not keep track of which one of the 435 Congressional districts we live in, but most of us feel some sense of a community bond with those living in our home county or city.

After the initial release of CS2, I will of course be promoting the overall message of the book and in particular the American Agenda you are now reading. To help facilitate the spread of this message and provide a general framework for those Americans that are moved to actively get involved I am forming a grassroots public activist group, the *Common Interest – Civil Responsibilities Union* or CICRU (sigh-crew). The CICRU will be the ultimate in a public and political action group, because You the People will need to bring it to life!

I am challenging my fellow American men and women of their own free will to find other people within their home county or city that are similarly motivated and to form a Local Chapter of CICRU (LCC). Work the Internet, run an ad in your local paper and just plain talk with people and see if they are interested. I talk with total strangers all the time about these issues and people are hungry for hope and positive Change. Spread the word and see who willingly responds. I expect that colleges, universities, and those in their twenties are great source for people that desire to see America on the right track, simply because they certainly have the most to lose if We do not get it right! And right now!

<u>Our Youth First</u>

My sense is that many of these public-driven Chapters could find their initial organizational purpose and be drawn together by their common interest in the next two (2) proposals that will be direct benefit to millions of our children and many adults, as well. They both target serious problems that can be rather easily addressed by implementing the programs they recommend into our public school systems. The concerned parents of struggling children in grades K thru 12 and in college will find real solutions and lives will be changed.

The initial charter of each LCC will be to *peacefully* review the contents of An American Agenda and determine how to best promote its message and proposals within your Local area. The critical operating characteristics of the LCC's:

- Without any apology, to be an American citizen-based and promoting group. The issues We are confronting must be resolved by open-minded and common sense driven communication and understanding. This must be between our citizens, any others may watch quietly from the sidelines and nothing more!
- To promote the proposals offered in An American Agenda within your area.
- To challenge any every candidate running for Congress or the White House for their personal position of each proposal in An American Agenda.

- To be if anything an Independent political group with aggressive moderate tendencies!
- NO party politics. No hard right or hard left rhetoric.
- To be for the Common Good for our citizens.
- To be for Civil Responsibility in people, business, and politics.

Each of initial meetings would review and discuss a few of the agenda proposals.

You get the idea.

And, again most importantly in 2008 — to bring the proposals of An American Agenda to every politician running for President and Congress in 2008 – and make them clearly state their position of the issues raised in CS2.

The driving concept that I had when starting work on this book on July 1, 2005 was that We the American people and our society in general did not have a common game plan. We do not have a common National Vision. We did not have a Common Agenda or Plan as to where our nation is or at least should be trying to go.

The concepts and proposals presented in *The Second Coming of Common Sense* are my sincere attempt to put such a National Vision for the Common Good down on paper for my fellow Americans to review, refine, and then agree to. And only time and the actions of others will determine how successful this effort will become. I am, but one citizen working and writing to and for 300 million others. There will be more on this in Part 5.

o   o   o   o

The CICRU has a basic, but well done website developed by a volunteer. It will be further developed as I begin to build my own LCC in Yorktown, Virginia and find other volunteers with the technical expertise to enhance and populate the site. It is called CICRU.org.

It contains basic information on the organization and ideas on how to set-up a Local CICRU Chapter in your area. With public involvement, in time some larger and more populated counties and cities could have multiple LCCs. That will be wonderful. Colleges and universities could easily establish and run their own LCC.

It also offers a free download of my 2004 National Drug Reform (NDR) Proposal (about 140 pages) previously overviewed in Proposal 8. The issue of first controlling and then removing hard drugs of our nation's streets is what started me on the 25 year path to this book and An American Agenda.

The site also facilitates the acceptance of donations to the group, and all contributions will be put to good use in building the CICRU and the LCC network across the country.

In time my goal is that CICRU.org will prove to be a Plain Truth information site that the public will rely upon for the facts on key issues and meaningful statistics. It will track and periodically report a standard set of informative public and what I call "human statistics" at the county/city level, as well as state and national levels. Basic, easy to interpret numbers showing the best to the worst. The intent is to track key statistics and show the public how the benefits of the programs presented herein are being realized within our National System and their local area.

Eventually, it could also generate a little bit of friendly competition between those county/city entities within each state, and between with the states. The goal of promoting Local Pride and Accountability, and actually improving day-to-day life in America in our neighborhoods — will be realized. And the process of Change begins in 2008 with your help.

That's all, my fellow Americans! This is a rather small proposal, but one with great potential for growing community spirit and local pride that will drive positive national Changes. America and Americans first!

o   o   o   o

15   Education – The "Final Answer" for Many Students and Adults

"Why Kids Can't Learn and How to Fix It"

Issue/Problem

The purpose of this proposal is to introduce a "corrective" learning system!

This could be described as a blatant commercial for a particular educational software package, and that is exactly what it is! But that's OK since I have personally seen what this outstanding software program can do for children <u>and</u> adults. I mean for the entire nation to finally be informed about its awesome capabilities. By the way, this is a non-paid endorsement!

My personal goal with this proposal is to see this system operating in every public school, adult learning facility, and long-term prison or jail in the nation. It would also used by the military services as needed to enhance the learning skills of their personnel, e.g., in the attainment of a GED for those that entered the military before obtaining their High School diploma.

Since at <u>least</u> 40% of Americans struggle with the learning problems that this software actually <u>corrects,</u> I am more than glad to take this opportunity to present the **Essential Learning System® (ELS®)** for your review. The benefits will be priceless to tens of millions of our people and for the nation as a whole.

As an unexpected side benefit, I would declare that ELS is most likely the closest thing we will ever find to a final answer for the floundering and not fully funded, No Child Left Behind program. It addresses the learning issues that cause so many children to be <u>left</u> <u>behind</u>! And the issues do not go away as they grow into adults.

<u>Why Kids Can't Learn</u>

An All Too Common Scenario

Try to imagine a student in the fifth grade that is assigned to a special program entitled "Gifted and Talented/ Learning Disabled" or GT/LD. To most of us those two terms would sound a little contradictory. Let me explain how a given student comes to be placed in such a program.

Typically, the child performs very well in kindergarten and into the fourth grade. Then they hit a learning wall and performance in certain coursework areas drops, often drastically. This scenario will sound too familiar for many parents, and while the child in this case has a high IQ, the same thing can and does happen with <u>any</u> student.

The problem has to do with what is going on behind the student's eyes and/or ears.

Visual Memory

The underlying problem in many cases is a Visual Memory Deficit (VMD) — the inability to retain information that is typically read from a book, or a computer screen, or off the board in a classroom. The reason for the drastic change in performance is that somewhere in the fourth or fifth grade the typical school curriculum changes to comprehension-based learning. This requires the analysis of learned information and the output of that analyzed data via speech and/or writing. Up until that point the curriculums only require students to retain facts or pieces of information, it does not demand the ability to read or hear, then recall, analyze, and output their thoughts in written or spoken form.

With VMD the student's <u>natural</u>, visual memory processing is not strong enough to properly store the visual input for their later recall and use. This is most often a condition <u>inherited</u> from the Mother and/or Father and again is <u>very</u> common. I would call 40 to 60% of the population "common".

Hear This! We are <u>not</u> talking about a learning disability – it is an information processing weakness within the brain that can be strengthened <u>permanently</u>.

This memory weakness easily explains why some students do not bring their homework assignments home. They physically cannot retain information long enough to read it on the board and then write it down in a notebook. This may sound like a trivial exercise, but when it happens to a young child week after week, month after month the student subconsciously grows tired of trying. Again this is far more common than you might think.

You may be interested to know long-term memory is the ability to retain information longer than 10 to 15 seconds <u>and</u> be able to recall it!

Auditory Memory

A second scenario applies to Auditory Memory Deficit (AMD). This is when someone cannot retain information or instructions that have been spoken or has been heard — examples being in a classroom, at a movie or from a training video.

While as with VMD it could be a natural, <u>inherited</u> condition, it often has another primary cause. Should a new born baby experience <u>multiple</u> and serious ear infections during the first 12 to 18 months of life, there is an increased and real potential for AMD learning problems to develop.

From the first days of life every child is instinctively learning the approximately 40 basic phonetic sounds of our language, by listening to their parents and other people talking. If the ear is repeatedly infected over that critical learning period, the basic sound patterns are <u>stored</u> in the brain <u>improperly</u>. They are hearing critical sound patterns virtually through liquid or a 'fuzzy' barrier, and are storing that garbled sound pattern for later use instead of the clear and proper imprint. That is simply the way it works in you, me, and everyone else!

As they grow and hear those same sound patterns in day-to-day life the brain naturally attempts to match those against the improperly stored sound patterns, but cannot and they have no idea it is even happening. The internal frustration this creates often manifests as learning and/or behavioral problems, just as it can with VMD.

> Imagine a child burdened with Attention Deficit Disorder (ADD) or Attention Deficit Hyperactive Disorder (ADHD) that is <u>also</u> struggling with such memory issues. Both conditions have negative impact upon the child <u>and</u> both tend to make the other condition worse. ELS helps the child effectively deal with one, thus making it easier to deal with the other.

AMD problems often manifest themselves well before a child enters school. For example, a child is told by a parent to do several tasks, but does not do all of them. When asked why they did not, the child acts as though they never heard them in the first place. They may have actually heard them, but truly do not remember them all.

o   o   o   o

As stated, visual memory and to a lesser extent auditory memory weaknesses are often in place from birth and are lifelong challenges. The cumulative effects of VMD and/or AMD on a child often lead to behavioral issues at home before they begin school, can grow worse when they are in school, and will persist throughout their life.

Hopefully this background offers many frustrated students, parents, and adults some explanation for their struggles.

> I know personally of these issues, since my personal struggle was with AMD caused by multiple serious ear infections in my youth. It was helpful and somewhat comforting to learn about all this even though I was in my early forties at the time.

Critical Public Awareness – VMD and AMD are <u>not</u> signs of learning <u>disability</u>, although the schools often treat them as such because they do not know what they are really dealing with! Rather they are correctable memory <u>weaknesses</u> that most often can be strengthened with dramatic and lasting results.

Further, VMD and AMD conditions have <u>absolutely nothing</u> to do with a person's underlying intelligence, but it hinders children and adults from fully utilizing and enjoying their natural intelligence. Thankfully, in most cases the condition(s) can be permanently improved.

o   o   o   o

Perspectives and Human Statistics

This may seem an odd presentation, but I have first-hand experience with AMD <u>and</u> helping some students and adults with such learning weaknesses. Again, this is something I have desired to see presented to the American public for many years and this is my opportunity. It truly does help explain why so many people struggle with learning throughout their life.

For a couple of years in the early 1990's in addition to my full-time job in the IT industry, as a part-time endeavor I worked with the Creative Education Institute® (CEI®) a company located in Waco, Texas. They offered a PC-based product called the Essential Learning System (ELS). A science teacher trying to help his own son that had multiple learning issues created the system. It took him over 15 years to develop and refine the ELS program. He was very successful and his son along with over 3 million others have <u>already</u> benefited from his loving and diligent efforts. In spite of those numbers and great success most of the country remains totally unaware of the ELS program's existence. Go figure.

I took training in Waco in the Memory Evaluation process, and the installation and administration of the PC-based program. I advertised in my local northern Virginia area and worked with children and some adults monitoring their progress in the home-based study program. It was wonderful to see the improvements this program made in people's learning abilities, attitude, and self-esteem — and to see their happy parents.

How It Works

The *Essential Learning System* is designed to 'permanently' strengthen or increase a person's Auditory and Visual Memory function. It is not a learning band-aid or another work-around methodology.

All of this background to say that the ELS program effectively addresses the learning struggle for both students and adults. Also, that the program is most efficiently administered by a third party (non-relative) in a school learning lab setting rather than in the home.

The ELS system is a series of multi-sensory PC-based and manual exercises that are very similar in function to a simple set of physical strengthening exercises to build muscle.

The simple exercises performed by the student in each lesson involve reading, verbally responding to prompts, visual recognition, writing, and other basic operations that cause the mind to recognize information, store it, and retrieve it. These are mental calisthenics for the brain. The ELS process actually helps strengthen and create the flow of information from short-term to intermediate to long-term memory – and back again. It actually builds the minds memory processing capability.

Each lesson takes the average student less than 45 minutes to complete and the lessons only need to be accomplished four times a week. The program begins to produce actual benefits within a few months and depending upon the severity of a given person's VMD and/or AMD condition(s) the program would be used for 6 to 12 months, sometimes longer.

At the start of the program's use in the public schools of Texas, the good news of its effectiveness was spread by word-of-mouth from parent to parent praising the results for their children. There is no better reference. Parents went to their schools and all but demanded that the program be brought in.

It is also used in after school programs to help adults. These types of learning issues do not go away with age, people just learn to deal with them or not!

The program also helps people recover certain brain functions after having suffered severe head trauma injuries. Some of the cases are truly incredible stories of personal recovery. It may very well help brain injured war veterans.

o   o   o   o

About Creative Education Institute (CEI)

Since is began operation in the summer of 1987, over 3,000,000 students in 5,000 educational organizations — including public and private schools, in libraries for adult education, and in correctional institutions — have used the CEI programs to encourage the learning process and yield improvement in both learning skills and test results.

Besides the ELS learning system, their *CODEBREAKER*™ reading program and the *Mathematical Learning Systems (MLS)* provide learning solutions that are keys to making a real difference and most importantly differences that can be measured by demonstrated results.

CEI has an excellent web site at www.ceilearning.com. The site contains many parent testimonials for public review. Check it out.

The People's Sense

Implementation Considerations

The cost of implementing this program in the public schools could be born by the Department of Education in conjunction with the states and local governments. The cost of the ELS implementation and operation will in time be paid for many times over, by the savings in other programs that it will frankly decrease the need for.

HOWEVER, another very practical funding approach (and the one that could make it happen NOW, rather than years from now!) was used in some Texas communities and involved private individuals (such as parents, grandparents, and alumni) and local companies that donated the necessary funds to sponsor the ELS program's installation for their local school(s). Some schools named the labs in the sponsor's honor. This type of community support will absolutely be encouraged to promote and to expedite the program's public school implementation. It would be a most worthy fund-raising project.

Like I said this could be considered a blatant commercial and that is fine with me, because these programs actually change lives. So let's look at the numbers.

Essential Learning System – School Pricing

Traditional Pricing

With this pricing, the school will own the software.

Initial Room License:	$21,500
Includes 4 Station licenses	
Additional Station License Fee:	$1,000
Annual Service Agreement Fee:	$3,500

Subscription Pricing

With this pricing, the school must renew License annually.

Initial Room License:	$8,500
Includes 10 Station Licenses	
Additional Station License Fee:	$350
Annual Service & License Renewal Agreement	$4,500

Both Pricing Structures Includes the following:

PC Compatible or Mac CD-ROM Software .
Single-user and Network Licenses

Assigned CEI Solutions Analyst
Training for 1 Facilitator for Every 5 Stations

User's Guide
Assessment Materials for Lab Students
Online Representation of Statistical Data
Toll-free Technical Support
Toll-free Customer Service Support

24/7 Web-based Support

24/7 Web-based Activity Center

Management System

Letter Recognition System

CEI *SHARE* Magazine

One Customized In-service Faculty Presentation

One Interactive Parents/Community Awareness Session

Achievement Certificates for Program Completion

Student and Teacher Recognition Awards

The very human bottom line is that the implementation of the ELS program is something for concerned parents to review with their local school's parent organization, school boards, and county governments.

This is where grassroots public action has **real meaning and direct human (child) benefit** — making it easier for our children to learn. Be part of a small concerned group of parents that decide to bring this learning system possibility to your child's parent/teacher group for consideration <u>and</u> action.

The positive results of the ELS program will be the cause for many future tears that <u>would</u> have been shed in sadness and frustration, to be shed in joy and happiness. What could be better?

Many of life's most complex problems are caused and can only be solved
at the unit level,
*one person – **one child at a time.***

o   o   o   o

16 Physical Fitness for Our Children

Issue/Problem

The title of this proposal says it all.

In the sixties, President John F. Kennedy initiated and promoted a somewhat revolutionary physical fitness movement in America. Regrettably over the years that program has become a non-issue in many of our public school systems and with the public in general.

Due to various reasons the physical fitness movement and concern for it has lost its priority in public school programs of America. Please know that I am not a fitness nut, but I know of my own disappointment as I observed the decline physical education programs in our public schools over the years, primarily due to budget cuts and the fear of frivolous lawsuits.

Consequently as study after study documents, and unfortunately our own eyes observe daily too many Americans are over-weight and out-of-shape. Therefore, more of us are putting our health in jeopardy and as a natural by-product are driving up our nation's current and future health care costs.

The Plain Truth is that we Americans need to be in better shape in order to enjoy a healthier, longer life — we need refresh President Kennedy's fitness movement across our nation.

Seriously consider that with the coming of National Health Care Insurance we will all be contributing to <u>and</u> helping to pay for the nation's health care bill! Therefore, we will naturally and prudently become more interested and informed about our own health and how to better maintain our bodies through better (not perfect) eating habits and some simple, regular exercise.

The People's Sense

Physical Fitness – Pre-K thru 12

This proposal addresses the physical fitness of America's youth in particular and addresses the excess weight that many of them are carrying and their general lack of physical conditioning. I will not bother you with any of the statistics we hear constantly. It is simply fair to say we all recognize the short and long-term negative impacts on the health of our children (e.g., diabetes) and the avoidable healthcare costs generated, as well.

Several years ago, one of my own doctors brought this issue to my attention. It is one of his personal concerns about the public's and especially children's health. He suggested that I add the issue to my list of things to research and write about. So I did.

Some time later, I was channel surfing one evening and watched a portion of an infomercial for Mari Winsor's well-known Winsor Pilate® personal exercise program. I observed that it could be strenuous and very productive, but was a low-impact exercise program that a person performs lying on the floor, preferably on a mat with no active, aerobic movement involved. The program includes basic to advanced workout routines, and the advertised cost of the full package was under $100 at that time.

Pilate is often talked about and are routinely used by actors, actresses, athletes, super models and other highly visible people that are concerned with maintaining their appearance and physical conditioning. Therefore, kids (and adults) could be very encouraged by that group recommending its use.

Of course some regular exercise is a great concept for all of us regardless of age, but taking the time and having the discipline to do it on a regular basis is difficult. It occurred to me that the Pilate program could <u>easily</u> and <u>inexpensively</u> be placed in every public school, K-12 in the country, even colleges. A few parents school could donate the money to buy the set(s) of program videos for their children's school. The most equipment required would be simple floor mats. It would be "pennies" per student to implement – the low cost to high benefit ratio would be outrageous!

The standard workout is 20 or 30 minutes in duration and needs to be accomplished three or four times a week. This would be a natural addition to the public school physical education program. <u>All</u> students would participate. The kids are there, the exercises are simple, each student would progress at their own rate, and over the initial weeks and months all children would slowly build up their fitness and experience the <u>personal</u> results.

Local fitness trainers in every community in the country could volunteer to help get the program implemented properly in the schools. This program will yield tremendous results for the U.S. Sport and Fitness industry as our children and their parents begin to see the benefits of basic exercise and more physical activity.

This fitness approach is practically a no-brainer, and every parent that I have shared the concept with liked it. I believe this program to be a real winner for our society in many ways. It would help renew President Kennedy's national physical fitness movement. Many of us grew up with that program and still benefit today from the leadership and personal challenge that JFK gave us.

A Nutritional Side Benefit

Any <u>viable</u> diet program, recommends regular physical exercise along with the given eating regimen to increase the short and long-term benefits to be realized. In this scenario, it will be exercise that will indirectly lead many students to learn about and use better eating habits.

The benefits for the young are that they will:

- will learn the basics on physical conditioning.
- over a period of weeks and months they will see and feel the physical results of routine exercise on their own bodies.
- will become familiar with physical fitness as a normal part of life.
- will learn about better eating habits.
- will have more energy to help them in school, at home, and life in general.

Again, the Pilate program will be low-cost implement, easy to use, and offers tremendous paybacks for the individual and society as a whole. It will <u>without</u> <u>any</u> <u>doubt</u> result in decreasing the number people that will suffer with diabetes and other excess weight related, *preventable* diseases. Therefore, it will absolutely reduce our nation's short and long-term healthcare costs, as well.

Parents Could Make it Start this School Year

The implementation of this beneficial fitness program in our public schools could begin as soon as the parents in each school decide to make it happen. Parents and school administrators could meet during <u>this</u> school year to plan how and how soon to begin incorporating the Pilate exercise program into their school's regular physical education program.

A very practical answer for our kids, and us too!

17   Community Service Training

Issue/Problem

This proposal relates somewhat back to Proposal 14 – Local Pride and Accountability in that it also promotes a "sense of community" among the people in your town, county or city. In this case, at a minimum We will be seeking to raise the bar of Civil Responsibility and various forms of Community Service (CS) participation.

For the Youngest Generation

In its simplest form students in elementary, middle, and high school will learn about the Civil Responsibility of Community Service and what they can do within their own neighborhoods with a just little of their time to make their locality a better place to live – things as simple as not throwing trash out the car window. Some may think these simple things, but it is where the seeds of civil accountability (or not) are planted. Again simply by utilizing the national school system as a public communication vehicle We will introduce the concepts and first experiences of CS to the youngest generation.

This is a simple expansion of the types of public service awareness that is learned in the Cub and Boy Scouts, and in the Brownies and Girl Scouts which have long promoted such awareness and involvement in the youngest generation.

Of course elementary school age children would not be out doing CS projects around their local area, but as they get older could be called upon to help in their local community when needed.

o   o   o   o

In many cases such common public communication programs would increase the general population's awareness of Local community service and public support groups. And as a natural result of such communication some people will be motivated to active involvement in those groups – not to be a leader, but to be another set of helping hands which is the most needed resource in the first place.

This improved awareness will help people to begin to develop an actual "community connection" with neighbors in good times so that in the event of local disasters like severe storms and/or flooding it would be easier for people to connect and be supportive of each other, and better organized to react more effectively. We know all too well how important community support coordination is after watching the Katrina disaster and the slow response from the government at <u>all</u> levels. Neighbors need to be willing and able to help each other, and not be shy or afraid to seek help when they need it — to know that other people nearby care about them.

Serving a More Complex Consideration

Again, looking back to Proposal 14 – Local Pride and Accountability the requirement to be overviewed below is an extension of the Local Account-ability concept, as well as tying <u>directly</u> into Proposal 7 – the U.S. Re-Employment System. It is a more complex Community Service 'consider-ation' within the National System that relates to Local people supporting the part and full time employment needs of businesses, both small and large within their geographic area.

I will keep this proposal fairly brief. My intent here is mainly to present several points and examples of how this practical extension of the Commu-nity Service concept would help to address other "local issues" — nation-wide.

- Businesses in many communities across the nation experience prob-lems finding part-time, full time, and seasonal employees when in re-ality there are people quite capable of filling those jobs that are avail-able, but not working. They are not working due to lack of motivation (laziness), not sure where the jobs are, don't really need the money, selling drugs covers their needs, etc.

- And currently some employers are giving the jobs to lower wage Ille-gal Occupants (IOs). This latter reason will become far less of a prob-lem as We begin the repatriation of IOs back to their home countries. As that happens, non-working Americans of all ages will be needed to fill any type of job they can in order to support local businesses. This will confront the notion that Americans do not want to do certain types of jobs — it is the dull rhetoric used as an "excuse" to let IOs to con-tinue to exist in our communities.

- There are various jobs in communities all over the country that could be easily be staffed by high school students in grades 9 to 12, college students, and adults twenty-something to senior citizens that are tech-nically available for part-time, possibly even full time work. Positions staffed to help local businesses to serve their Local community — help-ing businesses to survive and to grow providing more jobs.

High schools across the nation could implement programs that make 12th and 11th grade students available to support part-time and seasonal job requirements of local businesses. In areas hardest hit for workers, students could be all but required to support local businesses part-time, giving them work experience, some income, and doing their part to help their own community and local economy. This is not forced labor, it is supporting the community for everyone's benefit.

Consider, that with the High School drop-out rate reaching a staggering and ridiculous 25% — all those idle hands must be guided toward 'good' work. Since they are not currently communities are suffering and will continue to suffer the consequences. Read the local paper for all the examples of that you want.

- There needs to be an organized, standardized facility that the local businesses can utilize to obtain such staffing for their business – from that local 'citizen' labor pool. The U.S. Re-Employment System will help facilitate this requirement and will work with county/city/town employment services to identify part and full time, as well as seasonal job openings to be filled.

- Further, with the coming of Health Care Insurance for ALL Americans, it will in many cases be tied to employment. We will not be allowing Americans to sit on their 'butts' if they are physically capable of working and at least partially supporting themselves. Unemployment benefits, including Health Care coverage will be underlined directly dependent upon a person's active and consistent involvement in re-training and 'filling' any part-time to full time positions they are capable of performing while seeking viable full time employment – to the greatest extent possible. No more free rides on the tax-payers!

- IF, things are moving properly with the implementation of other proposals in An American Agenda, We will begin to see a decline in the illegal Drug Trade starting in 2009, as well as reduced Gang activity.

City and County governments will need to be guiding Americans that have been "recycled" through the Re-Employment System into public works programs that will be funded to start rebuilding America's crumbling infrastructure such as bridges and roads. Also to help demolish old buildings and clean-up the inner cities creating open areas and refurbishing homes. People will be working to improve living conditions in their own communities and putting money back into the local economy.

That last point will be a key component in transforming the National System from our current and failing Eternal Growth-based model toward the Maintenance-based Economic model discussed earlier.

o   o   o   o

The overall point being made here is that local businesses need to be better supported by the community they are trying to serve. Under the headings of Civil Responsibility and Community Service local citizens with some time on their hands need to consider making themselves available on an as needed basis to fill necessary job requirements.

There is a group of people in every locality that could step up and allow them selves to be on-call to fill such positions. This overall concept needs to be developed and used to put Americans young and old to work at whatever their community needs them to do. Think about it.

o   o   o   o

4. American Industry Restructuring (AIR)

Introduction

The AIR proposals address very complex, tedious and volatile national issues that all need to be approached based upon how the end results will
best insure the Common Good of the nation, the American family, the
worker, and in some urgent cases — *the environment*.

Critical components of the National System in our or any other country are
the domestic-based businesses and industries. Simply put, small (80%)
and large (20%) businesses provide Americans with employment opportunities. For better and for worse we have long since stopped being a nation
where the economy is supported by family farms and agriculture.

The relationship between **business** (management) and the American
workforce (labor) has always been a very difficult balancing act. Over the
years both sides have abused the other as the nation has matured and the
supporting economy has gone through its growing pains. However, business has had the best of the workforce most often – just as it does today.
And while holding someone's continued employment (their income) in their
hands does give the employer certain rights and liberties with regard to
treatment of staff, there is a point where an *unacceptable* level of *conduct*
can be reached and cannot be tolerated by a civil society. It is government's
job to protect the workforce from abusive business practices.

At the same time however, it must cut both ways. While the government
must always act whenever required to protect the American worker from
abuse by employers, it must also allow employers to terminate *worthless*
employees without the fear of baseless lawsuits. The U.S. Re-Employment proposal that facilitates the job counseling, re-training and/or placement of workers will provide the facility for "troublesome" employees to
be literally recycled into another job opportunity – thus providing the employee with the opportunity to make a fresh and more productive start.
Good employers deserve good employees, and none of us like to work
around dead weight!

It is a responsibility of **government** to promote and respond to the needs of
the American business community and to support them in creating and
maintaining domestic-based jobs for the American worker. The virtual
epidemic of out-sourcing of jobs and businesses must be brought to a controlled end. The companies that continue to do it will be made to pay a
higher price than any savings they would realize in seeking out cheap labor

and products. And, American companies need to employ American workers. Is that clear enough?

o o o o

Businesses Hurting Other Businesses

Government must not as it is currently doing, to continue to allow any given business or industry to hurt or impede the operation, the growth, or even the creation of other businesses and industries — entities that may represent them with viable competition or even their elimination! This flatly means that American business and industry must be protected from the negative, self-serving actions of other such entities, e.g., the medical insurance and petroleum industries to name a couple prime examples.

The relatively small set of AIR related proposals addresses some hard and negative realities within our National System. They offer purely functional problem solutions that must be openly debated during the 2008 political campaign and well beyond it. Proposed solutions to be openly presented to the American electorate for their review of the practical benefits they provide to the economy, our society, and the quality of life in our communities.

The electorate must stand up and challenge the candidates for every elected office, from President to town council, to state their position on the various proposals in An American Agenda.

It is my firm belief that the vast majority of the American public, after some time for private consideration will see the practical necessity of these seemingly radical Changes that are being proposed *against* the Status Quo of the National System — for the Common Good of our citizens and the nation.

At the same time, We the People will all acknowledge from the start that certain businesses and entire industries will fiercely oppose their deliberate restructuring that such publicly practical (and non-negotiable) Changes will bring to bear upon them. But the pendulum has been allowed to swing too far to one side and in the name of the Common Good it is now time to pull it back. Their irresponsible reign over the lives of our people and the nation is over. They and others not mentioned herein have "had their way with" the National System for far too long and have not demonstrated Civil Responsibility toward nor practical Concern for American society and the American people.

These solution-oriented proposals represent nothing less than a prudent and altogether practical, *extreme makeover* of key parts of the National System. Such publicly oriented Changes will surely not be welcomed by some of the Few that have benefited for many years from the avoidable pain that has been placed upon Many. A rate of public Pain that has only increased since 2001...

o   o   o   o

Concept and Adequate Detail for Now

Some people will be a little disappointed by the general nature of these key proposals, meaning a detailed implementation plan is not laid for each. Be assured however, that there will be **no doubt** as to the approach being proposed and purposes to be served the American public, our society, and the future of our economy. Thomas Paine did not lay out a detailed plan for the Revolutionary War — he just made the logical case for it! And as I keep repeating much of this is simply not rocket science – the required details of implementation will not be that complicated or difficult to work out. We are talking in months, not years.

As a frame of reference, it would be prudent to point out that Thomas Paine did present the entire case for the American Revolution, as well as the *Origin and Design of Representative Government* in 46 paperback size pages. If the concepts presented herein are in sync with the Common Will and mutual desires of the American public (which I believe they certainly are), we will only need to work out the details as we go forward.

Please understand that these concepts and proposals, as well as the others in An American Agenda are intended to initiate a great and defining public debate over the form and future of the American society, and the building of a *viable and maintainable* economic system to support it. Not an economic system from the Golden Age of American Capitalism that ran from the end of World War II — the mid-1940s into the 1960s. Or that of the late 1990s economic bubble that was referred to as the ".com Boom and Bust," but that in reality was more caused by the Year 2000 Date Conversion Crisis! News flash!

The AIR proposals challenge the U.S. Congress to act and begin to implement some of the proposed Changes over the course of the 2008 Presidential and Congressional campaign — to legislate as though a campaign was not even occurring! What a fantasy!

We the People are daring them with one last chance, to finally become

"<u>our</u>" leaders — to take the control of domestic and foreign policy away from the Special Interests and over <u>any</u> veto from the very lame duck and truly dysfunctional (to the Common Good) current occupant of the White House. To begin implementing the National System improvements which are of benefit to *the People* and our society as a whole. Changes that could collectively be of equal or greater benefit than the New Deal.

o　o　o　o

As has been mentioned before, we are talking about the prudent and deliberate Changes to the Status Quo of America's National System — the way America really works on a day-to-day basis. Such Changes have and will always create winners and losers – taking the form of individual businesses and American workers at <u>all</u> income levels. However, "if" the Changes are objectively determined to be in the best interest of American society and the American worker over the long-term, which they are designed to be — then said Changes will not be allowed to be diluted, delayed, or flatly killed in order to maintain a less than desirable and publicly dysfunctional Status Quo.

Therefore, let the legislative battle lines be drawn and the required intense national debates begin. These are the types of **real issues** that must shape and define the national discussion leading up to the 2008 Presidential Election – and well beyond it. Several of these proposals could (and should) be **confronted, decided, and the implementation begun prior** to that historic election. And the We the Voters will be watching very intently.

National Leadership is not wanted or wished for at this time. It is now required and will be demanded!

o　o　o　o

America's Economic Journey 1945 to 2008

"From Economic Agony to Ecstasy to Economic..."

In the post World War II era of the 1940's and 1950's in America, quite frankly a dog with a note could have made money – could have started and grown a good business! And I like cats and dogs!

Although most of us never consider the fact, the economic force called the Great American Middle Class as we know and refer to it, in fact simply did not exist before 1945! That's right. It was the Golden Age of American Capitalism — a very good thing. It was a wonderful economic time in America that seemed it would go on forever. We, and our Canadian cousins, were the only 'developed' countries in the world that had not been blown-up in the war!

Our tremendous manufacturing capacity that had been created out of WWII necessity was quickly "re-structured" from a war machine to support a booming peace time model — although, certain "Cold War" interests kept the Defense Industry going at a good rate. We were only show in town, and in those days when you said the word "inflation" Americans only thought about how much air pressure was in their tires! They were far simpler times.

The Last Great Leveling

The last time the Politically and Financially powerful Special Interests, with no practical regard for the Common Good truly drove the American economy into a Wall, was at the tail-end of the *"Roaring Twenties"*. It is called, *"The Crash"* — and it was not even caused by a war!

The last great Special Interest produced, "Economic Imbalance" in our National System "hit" the U.S. Economy and or entire National System with a vengeance over a few days starting Thursday October 24, 1929 and culminated four days later on Tuesday October 28th — known as *Black Tuesday*.

The Crash — led the way into *The Great Depression* which the nation struggled with through the 1930's, into the 1940's and the economy would have kept right struggling, but a little thing called World War II (WWII) came along and Changed *everything!*

Democratic President Franklin D. Roosevelt and the Congress reacted, developing and implementing the radical and historic **New Deal** programs intended to help millions of Americans and the devastated economy to recover. And while these programs were slowly beginning to help the National System to recover, the Plain Truth is that it really took WWII caused by tyrants in Europe and the Pacific, to resurrect our economy. Those are the historical facts!

Although it was not the primary reason for America to go into WWII, actual war efforts or — large government defense spending in relative peacetime — are unfortunately viewed by some as good thing! Especially those in that draw their paychecks and/or stock dividends from the Defense Establishment! We will talk about those characters more in Proposal 27 on the Defense (Military Industrial Complex) Industry. While the 'economic war boost' was valid in the unique case of WWII in bringing us out of the *Depression*, it did not have the same, desired economic effects with the optional Viet Nam War, Reagan's optional Cold War ending build-up, and now with Bush IIs optional Iraq War.

Again, in our country there are those that believe the wars and war time economies are good for the nation. While that belief and the growing Cold War mentality had something to do with our involvement in the Korean War, but it had plenty to do with actually starting the Viet Nam War, Reagan's military build-up in the 1980's, and now the Bush II/Cheney optional Iraq War. It is a strange mindset in America that manifests itself 'mainly' in the Republican Party, logically supported by Special Interests in the Defense Industry.

> The Plain Truth is that throughout world history people of any given country have either *allowed* themselves to be or more often have been *forced* into being taxed – both in money and/or some of their lives – in the name of National Defense. Consider that fact for a few moments.

The dysfunctional and self-serving mindset that has grown along with the Military Industrial Complex since the 1950's is all too willing to raise taxes for war. However, both Reagan and Bush II deliberately cut taxes and then turned right around and borrowed Billions of dollars that increased the National Debt to pay for it – just to be able to say to "their base" that they did not raise taxes. And those same "characters" scream at the mention of spending money on Domestic programs.

The National Debt that Reagan really helped to boost was still at $5.7 Trillion dollars in 2000. Bush II has willfully pushed it to $9-plus Trillion in 2007 and he isn't finished yet! But then everyone he knows or cares about is doing well.

o   o   o   o

Before getting into the AIR Program Re-Structuring proposals let's review a few pieces for common perspective and understanding, which are:

- An Economic and Presidential Review – since World War II
- Our Consumer-Based Economy Circa 2008
- Mastering Our Economic Crisis

I hope you find them of interest, <u>especially</u> the third one.

An Economic and Presidential Review

"Some Notes on the Last 63 Years"

We Begin with The War

World War II Victory in Europe – "V-E Day" May 8, 1945.

World War II Victory in the Pacific – "V-J Day" August 15, 1945; Surrender signed September 2, 1945

1945 to 1959

President #32 – Franklin Delano Roosevelt, Democrat, from 1933 to 1945

President #33 – Harry Truman, Democrat, from 1945 to 1952

The military manufacturing machine that got its start during WWII did not want to stop, and the start of the Cold War continued to justify the Defense budgets.

The Post WWII Baby boom began in 1947 and the annual birth rate in America jumped to around 4 million a year and has stayed very close to that number ever since. It was not a bubble, it was a tsunami!

Family Income – throughout the later 1940's, 50's, and into the early 60's families could live one income. In the 1950's more people than ever could get whatever they liked. Our consumer-based economy was born.

1950 to 1953 — The Korean War (yes, it was a **War** — not a 'conflict' as the politicians of the day wanted to call it) was the first contest of the Cold War. It helped to justify a Defense budget that practically should have been more reduced after WWII ended and helped promote the national mindset about the Cold War.

> Being true to my word, I believe this is an appropriate place to insert a direct comment from an older veteran I met in mid-2007 at the Home Depot in Newport News, VA where I am a kitchen designer (you must pay the bills while working on these personal projects). He *emphatically* made me promise to put his comment in this book and wrote it down, "The end of common sense began with America accepting mediocrity as a norm". He believes that shift occurred in the mid-1960's. I cannot recall for certain, but I believe he was old enough to have served in WWII and for certain

to have served in Korea. He name is Michael F. Kuzma of Princeton, New Jersey. And there it is.

o   o   o   o

President #34 – Dwight David Eisenhower, Republican, from 1953 to 1961

President Eisenhower in his historic farewell address to the nation the night before President John F. Kennedy's inauguration, the much respected general and two-term president warned the country about the potential build-up of the Military Industrial Complex (a title he actually created). As I offer many times in CS2 because it is so urgent, watch the DVD, *Why We Fight* – it explains so much. President Eisenhower's fears have been fully realized with the initiation of Bush IIs optional Iraq War.

1959 to 1975 – Technically the range of time of the U.S. involvement in the optional Viet Nam War.

1960s

President #35 – John F Kennedy, Democrat, from 1961 to November 22, 1963

President #36 – Lyndon Baines Johnson, Democrat, from November 22, 1963 to 1969

The false concept that a war would help the (entire) economy was part of the reasoning for creating the "optional" Vietnam War. The OPEC group did try to squeeze us with oil prices around 1967, but it did not work that time. They tried again far more successfully a few years later.

1972

President #37 – Richard M. Nixon, Republican, from 1969 to August 9, 1974

When the Viet Nam War finally ended on April 30, 1975 — it led to a post war economic recession. The economic dip painfully coincided with the 1970's Mid-East Oil crisis caused intentionally by OPEC cutting back on the flow of oil. Our friends! Again, see *Why We Fight* – the MIC and Oil are joined at the hip.

President #38 – Gerald R. Ford, Republican, August 9, 1974 to 1977

The Later 1970s

That Oil crisis passed and the Oil Industry spent the last 35 years covertly and overtly suppressing alternative fuel development and implementation. And not purposefully not building anymore domestic refineries.

President #39 – Jimmy Carter, Democrat, from 1977 to 1981

President Carter was the most decent person to hold that office in my lifetime (I will be 60 this year), as his post-presidential activities have clearly demonstrated. He had more problems thrown at him in one term than anyone could possibly handle — most of which could not easily be corrected and he took a beating in the Press. In spite of that Ronald Reagan only defeated him by less than 5% margin in popular vote at the state level.

Family Income – and in the 1970's two-income families became more of normal occurrence and national credit card debt was climbing.

1980

President #40 – Ronald Reagan, Republican, from 1981 to 1989

Then along came President Ronald Reagan and the last great military build-up of the Cold War, and while he must be given credit for pushing the Soviet Union into final collapse, it has been said that we won the Cold War mainly because the Soviets ran out of money before we did!

Reagan came into office and:

- cut taxes on the rich and corporate America,
- created a huge Defense budget (in relative peacetime, in that we were not under attack),
- the Savings and Loan regulations were relaxed and led to their collapse in the latter 80s,
- during his term there was a real estate boom and then bust,
- there was that Iran-Contra thing,
- the Stock Market suffered a severe Crash on October 19, 1987 — known as Black Monday,
- he took the National Debt from $1.0 Trillion to $2.8 Trillion, and by the time Bush I left office it was $4.1 Trillion.

Do you see the parallels with that record and what has transpired during Bush IIs nearly eight (8) years in office? Of course Bush II actually created the Iraq War to justify his Defense Budget buildup.

In his two terms in office Reagan did little in the way of helping with Domestic programs, although he did like talking about them. One of his less famous statements was that no one was hungry in America. He had to eat those words shortly thereafter.

And just why (?) in 2008 does the Republican base dream of Ronald Reagan and wish another one like him was running this year? Go figure.

1988 – The Hand-Off

President #41 – George H. W. Bush, Republican, from 1989 to 1993

And then it was time for Bush I, and the Berlin Wall that President Reagan had begun pushing over finally fell. Reagan practically <u>handed</u> the presidency to Bush I, his Vice President. It was somewhat fitting that a Republican president had to suffer the initial economic Recession consequences from the Reagan Defense build-up.

Bush I, conducted the first Gulf War in reaction to Iraq's invasion of its neighbor Kuwait and the threat to their Oil fields. After the abbreviated, one hundred (100) hour Gulf War I — Bush I of course had a high public approval rating. Winning even an abbreviated war makes leaders popular.

Therefore, when I told my then co-workers that Bush had just lost the next election they thought I was joking, which I was <u>not</u>. I said that for one thing, he did not take out the Iraqi dictator and many of the American public had their own sense that the dictator could cause more problems down the road. As was later found out, the decision <u>not</u> to take him out was a <u>pre-war agreement</u> between Bush I and leaders in the Middle East region. It was clearly understood <u>even then</u>, by Bush I <u>and</u> Secretary of Defense <u>Cheney</u> that removing him would more than likely de-stabilize the region.

And secondly, I noted to my disbelieving co-workers that Bush I did not have a clue (or maybe just had little interest) when it came to Domestic economic policy. Being a Republican he did not want to raise taxes to help with Domestic programs, and besides Reagan had already run up the National Debt paying for his war.

Finally I told them that unless the Democrats put up a real loser in 1992, they could stop Bush Is re-election. So, the domestic economy struggled along into the early nineties, dragging a still growing, post-Cold War National Debt.

1990's

Family Income – by the 1990's two-income families were all but required and national credit card debt continued to climb.

1992 – And Along Came Bill

President #42 – William J. Clinton, Democrat, from 1993 to 2001

The Democratic Party succeeded in putting up Bill Clinton and Bush I was gone. The Republicans and their Special Interest lobbyists were so enraged that they caused Clinton endless problems and mourned the unexpected loss of Power for 8 years.

The Democratic administration then began working on Domestic economic policy which of course is their traditional role — their thing! And for some reason Oil prices stayed pretty well in line during the Clinton years?

Then, as Clinton was wrapping up his easy re-election victory in 1996 — the Democrats, the economy, and national debt received an unexpected boost due solely to a historic and gargantuan case of business management procrastination.

You know what helped to drive the late 90's economic boom and that eventually led to the mid-2000 economic bust? It was one of the greatest business management failures in 80 years, also known as,

The Year 2000 Software Date Conversion Crisis!

o   o   o   o

My Perspective on the Late 90's Boom and the 2000 Bust

I am inserting this write-up to provide you with some insight into my Information technology (IT) career experience and my viewpoint on the economic Boom the National System experienced as the 20th Century drew to a close. And the economic Bust that immediately followed. I originally wrote this piece in 2003.

1996 to 12-31-1999

During 1996 in the professional part of my life in the Information Technology (IT) business, I became involved in that lovely project called the Year

2000 Date Conversion or Y2K software crisis!

I had worked a multitude of IT projects over my 34 year career. In practically every project there was someone within the user or operational organization that was sponsoring, if not championing the improvements or the new system being implemented. Most of the time the IT people side of the project enjoyed their role in supporting the particular user group improve their company's operation. And after all, supporting if not driving Change and process improvement are the basic functions of IT within business. IT for decades now has been responsible for the wheels of business turning in a faster and far more efficiently. As I have often said, IT professionals are literally the blacksmiths of the Information Age.

However, the Y2K project was unique. No one – the user management and staff, or IT management and staff liked the Y2K project. User management <u>had</u> to invest huge, unplanned dollars to upgrade their operational systems just to remain in business when the clock struck midnight at the end of 1999. They were required to spend Big dollars on something "just" to keep the wheels of their operation turning, <u>rather</u> than on improving their systems, their operations, and marketing.

Further, the IT professionals across the nation had to perform the very tedious, yet fairly mindless software changes required to expand the 2-digit to 4-digit year field in <u>every</u> system the company owned, as well as perform the largest, most expensive testing and certification process that the IT Industry had or will ever see. Nobody, except the IT consulting firms truly liked this project.

I inserted this bit of IT trivia for the purpose of making the following points:

- The Y2K Date Conversion project that struck American business and government agencies in the last half of a late 1990s was totally avoidable, but it could have been less dramatic and costly. There were IT managers that raised the flag earlier in the decade, requesting funds to start the date conversions. Most of the time these requests were rejected because of other company priorities and/or the time and sizeable dollar estimates that accompanied them. IT Department's rarely control what projects are to be worked, rather they control the projects that are selected.

  It is important to remind that anything that had a calendar or software in it had to be verified, if not upgraded or replaced before the clock struck midnight on 12-31-1999. This included manufacturing hardware and software of all kinds.

- This gargantuan case procrastination on the part of American corporate and government management resulted in the decade ending Y2K crisis. The amount of IT software changes and testing that had to be accomplished in a narrowing window of time with the *ultimate* hard deadline was gigantic. And the limited amount of IT resources – the software people – was limited causing the costs to skyrocket. It was classic Supply and Demand. IT consulting firms and independent consultants made a fortune.

- This last-minute management panic resulted in higher salaries and huge overtime payments for their internal IT resources. It also created the huge demand for high dollar IT software consulting groups and individuals. For example, the consulting company I worked for billed the client I supported the last few years of the decade, $190/hour for my project management services.

The Y2K requirements also required individuals (you and me), corporations, and all government agencies including the military to purchase upgrades to application software (e.g., accounting, manufacturing). Further, individuals, companies, government agencies had to purchase new Y2K compliant hardware and communication equipment of all kinds, not just PCs, and the compliant operating software to make it work.

As a result of this activity, software and hardware vendor manufacturing and sales of all types went through the roof, as did their profits and stock prices – simple cause and effect! The stock markets worldwide began to ramp up in late 1996, went on throughout 1999, and into the first quarter of 2000. As a result average people became involved with investing in and playing with the stock market.

- Therefore during the last four (4) years of the 1990s, the American economy had individuals – regular wage earning people with more money in their pockets to $pend from working the Y2K software changes; software service companies making record profits; software vendors with record profits; and software and hardware vendors also making record sales.

- These factors created the boom in the NYSE, American, and the NASDAQ stock markets. People were spending money like crazy in the retail economy and playing the booming stock market.

- It was a perfect example of what our two-thirds (2/3) consumer-based economy can do when it is running in high gear! It was a taste of the 1950's was like.

And, once again business mistakenly thought it would not end.

o o o o

And Then the Clock Struck Twelve

Happy New Year 01-01-00!

2000 – And the Party was Over

I personal do not agree with those that refer to what happened next as the "**.com Bust**". Certainly businesses of all sizes invested in the Internet, partly over the hope/hype that it would be an overnight success, cut costs, and generate sales. Some did it only because they knew their competition was building a website. However, the expected benefits that were so hyped did not materialize right away and took several more years for Internet use and buying to work its way into the National System.

The Congress <u>did</u> take the time to enact legislation that exempted Internet businesses from charging sales tax! It was said that it would help the "struggling" new industry to get off the ground. Well that might be alright for a while, but it would not help replace the sales tax revenue lost to us from regular retail buying!
As we all know, Internet sales volume has grown steadily each year and the industry is no doing just fine. So guess what? Late in 2007, the Congress <u>quietly</u> renewed the tax-exemption for Internet businesses. It is easy to see who they are working for, and it is not us.

Anyway, while I agree and personally saw that businesses were pumping real dollars into the new Internet technology, it was relative pennies compared to what they were <u>forced</u> to spend on Y2K. I actually feel that much of the hype over the ".com Bust" was just corporate propaganda for their stockholders intended to cover the huge dollars associated with the Y2K projects and the poor management planning that caused it to be so costly.

The bust in the stock market that really began to manifest itself toward the end of the first quarter of 2000 was helped along by totally "unrealistic" year 2000 budget projections by the majority of those same corporations, and by Wall Street analysts that also had on their rose-tinted glasses. Too many mangers in high places had blinders on, thinking or dreaming it would just keep going. They somehow expected people and organizations to keep on purchasing hardware and software, and software services in 2000 just as they had in 1998 and 1999. Wrong!!

The traditional annual corporate budget planning process never had to confront such a phenomenon, but more companies should have seen it coming. The smart manager preparing his or her budget in the last half of 1999 for the 2000 fiscal year should have shown a **significant and expected drop** in sales, revenue, and profits for the year. This would indicate that their regular markets were all but saturated by the sales bubble in 1998/99, thus justifying a dramatic drop-off in demand for products and services in 2000. Wrong, again!

My belief is that some realistic (and corporately brave) managers actually did raise the flag, but were told to go back and do a better job with their budget projections and to make the numbers work! Their concerns were just ignored and/or buried.

One Other Thing

Let me offer one more item for common perspective. The Y2K bust and the lack of realism in confronting the natural drop in sales for the 2000 fiscal year and beyond, combined to accelerate — *outsourcing!*

Outsourcing of course was already ramping up in the mid-90's as some companies were already struggling and trying to remain profitable in the global market by cutting overhead (product quality, benefits, and people costs) rather than selling more! Then along came Y2K and many companies used software services vendors to convert and test their Y2K changes. With the clients knowledge those vendors used "off-shore" software companies many of them in India and the Philippines to process the software changes and send them back (and I will add often with less than desirable results). This awakened corporate America to the potential of using outsourcing to cut their costs for other business functions. The off-shore groups many from India and other countries had grown their U.S. contact network around theY2K project cost savings. Also, some American vendors had set-up "cheaper" subsidiary operations in other countries to get a piece of the growing out-sourcing business. And so, the ugly and economically damaging out-sourcing game was on!

That is why for example, when you call your Bank or Credit Card company (Proposal 26) with questions you are talking to someone in India or Bogota, Columbia. We need to start bringing those types of jobs back to the US and dropping then in cities and town where jobs are scarce and our people need employment. That is an example of what Proposal 21 — Take Back Industries (TBI) talks about. If your call can be routed to India it could just as well be sent to Omaha, Nebraska. That's all on that.

o   o   o   o

The rest is history, as the stock markets in the U.S. and around the world declined back toward more 'normal' levels. That is my take on the air coming out of the late 90's economic boom and some of its side effects.

When people and companies spend/consume our economy does well, that is not a secret. That is why people and businesses are experiencing growing economic struggles **since 2002** — our people have less and less money to spend.

Over that time and at an <u>accelerated</u> rate, disposable and now required income is being taken by increased medical costs, prescription costs, gasoline and heating energy costs, mortgage rates (not just sub-prime), and food costs. When our "non-essential" spending slows down — our economy does as well. It is always easier to expand than to contract.

Now back to politics.

November, 2000 – A Questionable Election Result

President #43 – George W. Bush, Republican, 2001 to 2009

There are certainly mixed feelings about the "final" election result and I will not debate that dead issue here. The infamous "Hanging chads of Florida" were a mind numbing experience for the entire nation to endure. What most people do not know is that Florida has a consistent history of Election Day *problems* that they have never seemed to want to clean up. I would offer that it that appears to be underlying intent to make hard for some segments of their population to vote!

But, on the other hand if Al Gore had <u>only</u> won his own state of Tennessee — Florida would have been a non-issue, and Gore would have won not only the popular vote, but the Electoral, as well! As much as I do like and appreciate what Gore does especially about the environment, he ran an absolutely miserable campaign for president.

Further, consider that if Bush II had not been elected, we still would have gone into Afghanistan looking for PCM! Think about that one a while, you will get it. However, Bush IIs optional invasion of Iraq would have been <u>far</u> less likely to have happened under Gore.

September 11, 2001 – And We Are Attacked

The initial post-911 invasion and war in Afghanistan was absolutely reasonable follow-up after We were attacked. America was going after those that attacked us. That much was honorable and it was right to go after those that orchestrated the attack on our nation, killed and wounded our people.

However, the Iraq invasion was not necessary, was totally optional, and deliberate on the part of the Bush II and Cheney.

It has been publicly documented that Bush II, Cheney, and 'their people' were discussing an invasion of Iraq in <u>January</u> of 200<u>1</u>. And some in that group had been considering it since the early nineties. Put that in your peace pipe and smoke it!

Bush IIs, optional Iraq War is making some Industries and various people a lot of money, and they <u>knew</u> it <u>would</u> <u>before</u> going in. It has been a boom for the Oil and Defense (Military Industrial Complex) Industries, while Bush II has borrowed us into an even larger National Debt, and supported corporations and the rich with tax cut<u>s</u> that of course favor them. In doing so, Bush II had somewhat replicated what Reagan had done in the early eighties – when he optionally cranked up the Defense Budget, cut taxes, and ran up the National Debt all in the name of Defense. Again, both of these situations were <u>optional</u>, as in <u>not</u> <u>required</u>. Of course Reagan did it without putting our troops in harm's way. And at least Reagan had enough *common sense* and concern for our troops to *"cut and run"* out of Lebanon after our troops were blown up by the local zealots. Bush II obviously does not and/or has had other priorities that he does not choose to share with the public – the peasants.

Further, Bush II used a politically, *gutless* backdoor maneuver to send our National Guard overseas to avoid the public outrage over a real Draft to properly staff the Iraq War that he and his sidekick were determined to start. Therefore, the Iraq War is very similar in conduct to Viet Nam War. Both were optional wars started under false pretenses, and both were not given enough on the ground military resources to even have "a chance" to get the job done. Bush IIs "surge" is a paper tiger, as time will show.

And not that Bush II ever intended to leave Iraq during his term of office, but rather he has the military building long-term bases to keep us there indefinitely.

<u>Please Be Aware</u> — Bush IIs recent rhetoric about making an agreement to commit us to stay in Iraq (you notice he is not pushing one to stay in Afghanistan – no oil) after he leaves office is just more Bush II propaganda. Under the U.S. Constitution that he obviously does not believe applies to his presidency, he **cannot make** such an agreement without the vote **and** approval of Congress. **Period!** It is another case of distracting, politically motivated Domestic Propaganda that We must ignore.

o   o   o   o

The 2004 Election – Public Fear and the Manipulation of the Holy

One last scenario before we review a possible way out of our economic mess.

Bush IIs creative, political handlers starting working in 2003 to head off what they knew could be a re-lection loss in 2004. Like Bush I, Bush II had a struggling domestic economy, plus the cost of gasoline and many other basics of life had been going right up since he came to office, and then there was that Iraq War thing that was started under false pretenses. So what to do? Got it! Let's try stirring up the Christians, scare the public, and criticize a Viet Nam war veteran.

So for over a year they worked with church groups and beat the drums saying that same sex marriage would ruin the country and about the sin of stem cell research (regardless of where you stand on those issues, consider the intent and methodology used). The Bush Administration in the last few months leading up to the 2004 election released the steady flow of *terror alerts* and inferred that things were just too volatile to change presidents at such a dangerous time. And as we all know the terror alerts *ended* the week after the election. A Republican dirty trick is a nice way to put it!

o   o   o   o

And finally, the Republican attack dogs had a small and politically motivated veterans group criticize the Democratic presidential candidate John Kerry's Viet Nam War record. That takes unbelievable _____! No one is allowed to so criticize someone that has served this nation under fire — and on top of that, someone that could have easily avoided that military service altogether. But, they were all to willing to do did it in order to retain political power for "four more years." And ironically, to keep someone in office that did avoid the Draft!

> In the Fall of 2007, I heard a familiar 1970's war protest song and just laughed out loud. More than anyone else since that time the words applied to George W. Bush. "Some folks are born, made to wave the flag. Oh, they're Red, White, and Blue. But when band plays *'Hail to the Chief'* – oh, they're pointing the cannon at you".

> ***"Fortunate Son"***
> Written by Dan Fogerty
> Performed by CCR!

Nailed it!

o   o   o   o

The Republicans and their Special Interest handlers got their desired result. Even though the number of voters was higher than normal because worried and agitated people tend to come out and vote (as they are doing in the 2008 primaries), the scared and the church vote brought out more for the Republicans and Bush II was re-elected. Thus Bush IIs war continued, more of our troops and Iraqi citizens died, the Defense budget grew, the National Debt grew, energy costs went up, and the Special Corporate Interests continued to have a free for all with the National System.

It was early 2005 – the real estate boom still had life in it, but would soon turn down. The stage was being set for the Sub-Prime Crisis.

o   o   o   o

And, if that isn't enough. The expected post-Iraq War Recession could have been a minor reason why Bush II would not have wanted to ramp the war down on his watch (not that he ever wanted to). However, the trouble is Bush IIs Iraq Recession began ahead of time — in December 2007...

Happy New Year to us! And in 2009 the Democrats will not only get to take-over Bush II's Iraq War, but his Recession already in full swing! That is some serious food for thought for anyone thinking about voting for a Republican for president in 2008.

By now many are thinking that I am Bush II, Cheney, and Republican Party bashing – and they are absolutely correct. I certainly <u>am</u> because they <u>in particular</u> along with the both Parties in Congress have gained the America public's overwhelming Disapproval the old fashioned way – they have earned it!

I write for the Silent Majority — that can longer afford to be quiet!

o   o   o   o

<u>Our Consumer-Based Economy Circa 2008</u>

The U.S. economy was built upon and is only sustained by consumer spending. According to the experts, consumer spending comprises some two-thirds (2/3) of our economy. That means you, me, and everyone else we see everyday needs to be buying good and services. When we cannot buy things in the retail and wholesale market place, the economy begins to "stall" which is a nice way to put it.

The nation's Annual Economic Growth Rate moves up and down during any given year, hopefully at a 3.0% to 4.5% rate anyway. Generally the higher the rate, which is calculated each month and then averaged for the year, the better the economy is performing.

Personally, I do not worry about that rate any more than the average American, but again CS2 is in part intended to share perspective on issues that most of us do not usually think or hear about, for common understanding. Remember this is general information. Economics at the national level is very sophisticated (I will talk about that word in Proposal 26 on Banking) and there are more different schools of *thinking* on economic planning than you would care to believe.

No one complains when it is high, but when it goes down and stays down for too many months it is called a *recession*. This is when the government, partially in the form of the Federal Reserve Board (the Fed) plays with the Banking Industry lending rates and usually lowers one or more of them in an attempt to "stimulate" the economy. Sort of like economic speed!

Another way the government attempts to stimulate the economy is by cutting taxes to business and the people.

o   o   o   o

The Republicans like, no love to cut the taxes, especially to business and to the rich, more than to middle and lower income Americans. They work in favor of the *Few*.

President Reagan called his tax cuts "trickle down" — while some people called it "voodoo economics" — when he forced his tax reduction through Congress in the early 1980's. He also, intentionally ran up Defense spending and borrowed the country into a huge National Debt. That debt was left for Bush I to inherit and led to his one-term presidency. Bush I demonstrated 'little interest' in the realities of the domestic (the people's) economy, and Bush II has demonstrated even less over two (2) terms. Bush II, cut taxes like Reagan, and, he and MIC-Cheney created the optional Iraq War. He also has borrowed billions and billions from overseas to pay for the war, rather than raising taxes to help offset some of the costs.

In 2000, the National debt was about $5.7 Trillion dollars with a $261 million dollars *surplus*. Not exactly a small debt.

In 2007, the National debt was about $9-plus Trillion dollars with a $250 million dollars *deficit*. And, grimly Bush IIs Iraq War together with his Republican Congress' record (anti-traditional Republican) government spending — still has another year to make it worse.

The Democrats generally support tax cuts to business, but favor programs that target helping middle and lower income Americans. When they are in power, meaning the White House they promote government spending into domestic programs I would describe them as believing in a "bubble up" economic approach. It is getting federal dollars into the middle and bottom of the economy – *to the people*. Traditionally, they work in favor of the *Many*. However, in the last decade they have been voting far more like Republicans!

o   o   o   o

While both approaches have good points, in a consumer-based economy which everyone agrees that America has, which approach would *common sense* indicate that National Domestic Economic Policy should tend to favor. Hello!

I will remind the reader that I am writing to you from the viewpoint of a 34-year, career Systems Analyst, system designer, and business problem solver. It cannot help but sound at times like I am favoring one Party more than the other, but that is not the case. True objectivity and common sense applied to the problem solving process usually filters through the nonsense and distractions to yield logical conclusions.

And again my client in this project is the Common Good of 300 million American citizens. And their requirement is to identify the basic economic and societal Changes required to put our National System on a realistic and practical path to short and long term success!

With regard to Party politics, overall both parties in the last few decades have failed We the People. And in the last 7 going on 8 years in particular, the Republican controlled White House and dominated Congress have *loosed* the Special Interests upon the National System for fun, profit, and bonus checks – with little or no regard for the negative impacts on the overall economy or the general public. But, why be concerned about the peasants. They are not the ones paying for their re-election campaigns!

To continue

The overall solution requires a little bit of both philosophies, properly balanced and *"rationally adjusted"* over the years as required, to yield an economic model that We should then be able maintain. What gets in the way of such rational economic planning is the fact that the two Parties do not know how to or even want to work together — especially on things to improve the Common Good. That is why We need to vote 468 of 535 of them out-of-office on 11-4-2008.

For the last few decades, every time the White House changes parties it is like they are playing 'King of the Hill' and the new Party tries to jam their philosophy through Congress and into National System. Increasingly over the last twenty (20) years as the U.S. economy has been steadily contracting and Special Interests have taken greater and greater control over Congress, the Republican Party's philosophy has dominated National Economic Policy. Eight (8) years of Democratic policy with Bill Clinton was front-ended by twelve (12) years of Reagan and Bush I, and back-ended by eight (8) years of Bush II (and Cheney). That is 20 out of the last 28 years. Consider the following piece.

Their Traditionally Vicious Cycle

Some years ago the following perspective on national politics was offered to me and I found it interesting. How does it sound to you?

Historically, the Republicans have come into office, the White House in particular and after some years in power have succeeded in "screwing up" the economy! The American public finally loses patience and so hands the national leadership over to the Democrats. The Democrats take over, confront the mess, and somehow start to get things turned around. The People – us – with an all too short political memory see that business is going well and say hey, We should put the Republicans in charge because they are very pro-business and it will only make things better. The Republicans are then placed back in power and once again mess things up — and the cycle continues.

Sarcastic — somewhat, but in reality far closer to true than false.

o   o   o o o

In January of 2009, the Democratic Party — unless they shoot themselves in both feet (you never know!) or the Electorate loses its mind (that's us) — should once again assume control of the White House, as well as capturing a clear majority in both houses of Congress. Not that the public is not irritated with the Democratic Party as well, but their overall disgust with Bush II and the Republican dominated Congress must be punished. And We the People can punish politicians at the polls, and this November's Election Day will be a history making.

Therefore, it is most likely that the Democrats will inherit the historic mess that Bush II/Cheney and their Special Interest handlers have deliberately and irresponsibly created — and profited from.

And this time the Democrats will be challenged to clean-up not only another Republican generated mess, but this time on both the domestic and foreign fronts. And this beyond any question is the biggest one yet – equal in economic complexity to the *Great Depression*, and this time with a war on the side...

o   o   o   o
So where does the National System and
***We the People* go from here?**
o   o   o   o

Mastering Our Economic Crisis

"Structuring and Securing Our National Economic Future"

I will unashamedly resort once again to Thomas Paine to frame the content of what We are about to review. Thomas Paine framed changing the status quo and confronting the obvious flaws of colonial America in the first paragraph of *Common Sense*,

> "PERHAPS the sentiments contained in the following pages, are not yet sufficiently fashionable to procure them general favor; a long habit of not thinking a thing *wrong*, gives it the superficial appearance of being *right*, and raises at first the formidable outcry in the defense of custom. But the tumult soon subsides. *Time makes more converts than reason.*"

And with regard to the serious issues at hand – We are running out of time…

o   o   o   o

What follows may indeed at first seem strange, foreign, illogical, and to some possibly illegal (which it is not)! However, We the People must now do what our leadership has proven them selves incapable of doing. *The Second Coming of Common Sense* as you have read so far is all about confronting problems and applying publicly, practical Changes to directly benefit the Common Good of our citizens and improve the National System in which We all must live.

We now turn our attention to National Economic Policy matters. Standing together at the start of 2008, We all know how difficult things are becoming in our contracting economy for individuals, families, and for most businesses. Therefore, I will get to the recommended approaches to help place our National System on the bumpy, but viable path to our short and long term economic recovery.

There will undoubtedly be those that scream about these offerings, saying that they cannot work or that We cannot possibly do this or that. However, they will work and We can do whatever needs to be done because it is our country – no one else's. To any such source of opposition, I will challenge them right up front with the same comment I wrote in the National Drug Reform (NDR) Proposal to any potential critics – if they can present another approach that is of equal or greater merit to resolve the issue at hand, let them offer it now, but do not stand just there and defend the status quo.

BECAUSE, otherwise they are only representatives of failed policies and inaction – neither of which We the People have any inertest in or the time for.

Therefore, if anyone has better plan or rationale, I do hereby challenge them – *to bring it on!*

o   o   o   o

Transitioning to the American Maintenance-Based Economy

Confronting the Fallacy of an Eternal Growth Economy

The unrealistic view that in the increasingly Global Market Place, that the American economy could continue to grow as it did in the late 1940's and 1950's or even as it did for brief period in the late 1990's is a fool's perspective. That is an economy where companies can make 10% to 15% or more *real* profit annually by actually selling more goods and services. The modern fallacy of that eternal growth U.S. economy, where profits just keep rolling in and increase each year based upon actual growth in real sales of products and/or services – is just that, fallacy. The economic balance of the world has changed and cannot be turned back – and it cannot be ignored either.

Therefore, We must get smart and deliberately and boldly re-structure our National System to bring back lost jobs and industries, as well as create new ones — and the sooner We get started the better!

o   o   o   o

Over the last 63 years We have filled up the country from the East to the West coast and cannot practically accommodate or tolerate *illegal* growth in population. Yes, that issue comes up again. There are those that say no to that – that the more there are better, and they are the ones that have overtly and covertly facilitated the Illegal Occupant (IO) invasion. The time of uncontrolled borders must abruptly end and politicians must get that message in 2008.

Both Parties have perpetuated this blatant, national invasion. The Democrats forgetting that they are sworn in to serve American Citizens, not those that of their own free will violate our borders and then expect for sympathy, services, and citizenship. We did that in 1986 under Reagan and will not do that again. The Republicans talk a good game, but have done nothing to stop the flow. And Bush II is at least honest about his position, with his Open Southern Door Policy with Mexico. We need the IOs out so that We may determine how care for our own population. Some nation's must be forced to take care of their own population or to start practicing Planned Parenthood!

Moreover, today We struggle to take care of our own people's basic needs like food and shelter, which is a national embarrassment and disgrace. We continue to have crumbling infrastructure, like tens of thousands of bridges and our children's public schools in need of repair. And due to that "long habit of not thinking a thing *wrong*, gives it the superficial appearance of being *right*" mentality — We continue to allow certain industries and some too politically powerful groups to not only <u>influence</u>, but to <u>dictate</u> how the National System will be run — so that it serves their profits, needs, and short-sighted desires.

<u>So Enough is Enough</u>

The industrial and political power structures that were born in that Golden Age of Capitalism, circa 1946 into the 1960s and are now (still) bullying the National Agenda must and will now be realistically confronted. For the Common Good of our society and economy, some critical Industries will necessarily be *involuntarily Re-structured* and reorganized into entities "newly chartered" to support individuals, families, and other businesses, as well.

Further, corporate and individual tax policy that continues to favor corporations and the rich, even when the obviously contracting economy is choking the majority of businesses and our people — will be prudently restructured to correct such imbalances. Since We will no longer allow free rides and pity parties for the traditional seekers thereof, those at the other end of the economic food chain will be <u>cut</u> <u>loose</u> from their gravy train of handouts, as well.

We the People are now challenged to agree upon and implement an economic *Last Deal*.
All will contribute their fair portion.
All will work to support and strengthen our National System.
All will work to control and reduce avoidable costs to society, and,
<u>All</u> will share in the benefits that "American citizens" can expect by Right and keep by the Civilly Responsible Conduct.

o   o   o   o

American Industry Re-Structuring (AIR) Program

American-based corporations and in particular those that are public, stock held entities will be required to seriously consider modifying their traditional approach to making their profits that are totally unrealistic given today's global economic environment. And in this case, "seriously consider" is not just a suggestion!

Too many of them for too long have been cutting people, benefits, and the real quality and reliability of their products and/or services to satisfy their shareholders and number serving, non-productive stock market analysts. And far too many are contributing to the epidemic of out-sourcing of American employment and businesses, only to satisfy spreadsheets and causing our fellow Americans to suffer so that someone else can earn slave-type wages.

And while all this has been done under our 60 year old, Capitalist business model and 'technically' in good faith — in the sharply contracting economic reality of the last decade, it has done the National System and the Common Good of our fellow Americans far more harm than good! And in some cases it has been done with the full knowledge of the real damage it will cause our people, society, other businesses, the environment, and in a few hard cases even our National Security. This preventable chaos will now come to an end, or, We may soon need to learn how to spell c-r-a-s-h! Not a joke.

That said, We the People will now direct the U.S. Congress to rapidly and involuntarily re-structure the operation of *an initial set* of critical Industries within the American National System. The purpose being to reorganize those industries into a far more practical and functional component within the National System that in turn will improve the way America works on a day-to-day basis – thus bringing them deliberately "in line" with Civilly Responsible business conduct with regard to the Common Good.

The AIR Existing Industries proposals focus on a group of industries that are in some unavoidable manner woven into our National System and impact the lives of virtually every American, each family, and other businesses on a monthly if not daily basis. Therefore, as previously stated this somewhat odd set of bed-fellows has been categorized as *National Infrastructure Industries* (NII).

The initial set of Existing Industries to be addressed under the AIR Program proposals are by number:

Proposal 22	Health Care Insurance for ALL Americans
Proposal 23	The Pharmaceutical Industry
Proposal 24	The Tobacco (Nailing the Most Deadly Drug) Industry
Proposal 25	The Oil Industry
Proposal 26	The Banking and Credit Card Industry
Proposal 27	The Defense (Military Industrial Complex) Industry

How well *We the People* stand together and come to a <u>final</u> reckoning with such industries will define the heart and soul of our Second American Revolution, and to a <u>very</u>, great extent — our National Destiny, as well.

There are *of course* some other industries that could be included, such as:

- Coal,
- Natural Gas,
- Plastics (now made from oil),
- the Automobile industry or what is left of it,
- the Wall Street Investment Houses,
- and the Commodities and Spot Markets where someone <u>intentionally</u> and <u>wrongfully</u> once put Oil.

Just to name a few that could easily be on our list — and that will be dealt with in due time, either voluntarily or involuntarily. For now those that <u>most</u> deserve to be at the head of the Irresponsible Industry list and therefore, demand our immediate and <u>aggressive</u> attention are accounted for.

The Involuntary Restructuring of these major industries will set the corporate example and increase the public's expectations and confidence in the future. It will also present a working model for the existing management of other corporations <u>and</u> <u>their</u> <u>shareholders</u> to seriously consider following during our National Economic Reformation — if they so choose. As necessary, legislation will be quickly enacted to permit publicly held corporations to utilize such voluntary profitability controls.

o   o   o   o

I do not need to go into the details of the AIR Program Re-structuring here since it detailed in the Existing Industries portion of CS2 soon to follow. If you read the piece on American Industry Restructuring in Part 1 under Background, Terms, and Common Understanding you already have a good idea what awaits the Industries in this initial group.

The Challenge of Shared Sacrifice in 2008 and Beyond

"Shared Sacrifice and Shared Benefit for the Common Good "

Realistic U.S. Economic Re-Structuring

Our economy has actually receded back toward a state of economic normalcy with the rest of the first world nations. The Golden Age of American Capitalism that ran from the late 1940's to well into the 1960's has past into history. We all need to acknowledge its passing and prudently determine how We will proceed from this point on, for the Common Good. And I do mean for the Common Good – with all of our citizens in the boat!

I must say that this subject matter has been the most tedious and difficult to consider and develop, as well as trying to determine how to present it to you in a fairly concise format. I may well be criticized for being a bit wordy and/or redundant in the writing of CS2. And that is fine — my feelings cannot be hurt so long as the words are clear enough and the messages are delivered well enough that the concepts and solutions offered may be fairly considered by you.

Now let us review our Economic Reform approach.

This is a rather direct public policy. It will be fair, but decisive when it comes to giving the National System the *good jolt* — it so disparately requires. Our Economic Reform approach is overviewed under the following three (3) headings:

1. Macro Economics – Top Down Industry Restructuring
2. Industry Revitalization and Creation
3. Micro-Economics – Supplementing the Consumer Economy

o   o   o   o

The Heart of Our Problems and the Solutions

Do you want to know what our underlying and core economic problem is my fellow Americans?

One theme runs through this overall reform program, being that the Cost of Living (COL) in America has become too high for more and more American individuals and families to have a decent standard of living as each month passes. Please consider that bone-marrow reality for a few moments because that is the bottom line.

How you are affected? How are those you personally care about affected? And finally how are those Americans you observe in person and/or through the media affected?

Not to have a luxurious life style, but the basics of food, housing, viable employment, health care, education, safety, energy — whether as gas for your vehicle or heating and air conditioning for their homes, and the peace of a reasonably comfortable life in old age. People in each of the Generational Groups referenced earlier struggle with those "necessity of life" issues everyday.

This is the "people side" of society's most complex problems to be solved.

At the same time, American businesses small and large also struggle against the COL. Forgetting about taxes that every business *must* be required to contribute in some portion, they too, struggle with energy costs, being able to offer health care benefits at all to their employees, rising rental/lease rates for their business, and consumers with less dollars to buy their good and services. Further and dependent of their line of business, brutal competition from foreign entities with comparatively slave-type labor rates and no government oversight of manufacturing quality or product content – and knowing that the playing field will never really be level.

And for stock-held corporations, the task is making annual stockholder dividends happen as if by magic, when our economy is contracting without doing damage to their own employees' livelihood and the National System by sending parts of the operation overseas.

This is the "business side" of society's most complex problems to be solved.

The Basic Requirement to be Served

Therefore, the underlying challenge is to develop and deliver fair and practical policy approaches that will both stabilize and reduce the costs of the necessities of life for our people and American businesses, as well as increasing the real buying ability of the American consumer. Not exactly what you could call a walk in the park.

As you consider the remainder of Part 3 with the ten (10) proposals it offers, and the overall content of CS2 please do keep the challenge in those

56 words clearly in mind. Again, our united ability to prudently and practically, confront, and satisfy that most complex requirement will determine the success or failure of this our Second and Final American Revolution and determine the future of the nation We the People love so very much.

No one said this was going to be easy, but We can accomplish anything when standing together.

o   o   o   o

1. Macro Economics – Top Down Industry Restructuring

This is where the AIR Program Restructuring of <u>Existing</u> Industries applies. As just reviewed this somewhat odd set of bed-fellows has been categorized as *National Infrastructure Industries* (NII).

The rationale for converting each of these critical nation industries into centralized, non-profit organizations that will be administered by newly developed, Industry Management Consortiums is detailed shortly in each of their respective CS2 Proposals. It will deliberately and radically Change corporate America for the Common Good.

I will only offer a few comments on each industry proposal with regard to their place in the overall Economic Reform program. What I will say about this entire group is that over the last few decades they have grown to be more politically powerful than our Democracy should have <u>ever</u> allowed. However, during the Bush II years and in a period when more and more Americans are struggling to make a living, this group above <u>all others</u> has functionally acted with predatory and extreme irresponsibility toward and against the people, other businesses, our society, and the National System as a whole. They have acted just the predatory people that after a major natural disaster come around selling thirsty people a gallon of water for 5 to 10 times its regular price. What do you call that?

Each of these industries hold the annual delivery profits and stock dividends in higher purpose than the Common Good of the general public and the nation overall. Their only defense being, as one Oil executive was actually bold enough to publicly state, 'making profits for the stockholders is his job, not looking out for the public.' The Plain Truth. Our response to that going forward is that <u>our</u> job is to insure the Common Good of the public and the overall National System, not looking out for the stockholders of predatory industries!

Therefore, We the People are now forced to act to remove these corporations from the burden of stockholders which is driving their publicly, irresponsible business practices and draining the economic life out of our National System. And in the process We will modify their function within the National System so that it practically serves individuals, families, and other businesses for the Common Good of All.

o   o   o   o

Existing Industry Re-Structuring

Proposal 22 Health Care Insurance for ALL Americans

The proposal contained therein is the <u>only</u> way We shall achieve providing Health Care <u>Insurance</u> to ALL Americans in the next <u>couple</u> of years — and ramping up in 2009 if We get busy and demanding. Consider that the Democratic presidential candidates Hillary Clinton and Barack Obama – are talking about how they will be tough in negotiating with the Medical Insurance Industry. That will be far easier after We replace the Industry's management and negotiators.

The Republicans keep talking about tax incentives and Health Savings Accounts like everyone can utilize them. The industry lobbyists that promote those approaches with Congress know full well that large segments of the population cannot afford such things. And believe me somebody is <u>making</u> money off of those Health Savings Accounts or they would not be offered. When We have National Health Care Insurance for ALL Americans people will not need tax incentives and Health Savings Accounts! They can do other things with the money – like consume!

In Massachusetts they have implemented the 'near' mandatory purchase of health insurance and they are fining people that do not sign up, with the fine increasing each year. And they are already beginning to issue waivers to those that can justify why they cannot afford it. Bad policy.

In the CNN program Broken Government, *Health Care — Critical Condition* that aired after the Super Bowl on February 3rd it was noted that some 100,000 American die preventable deaths each year because of our current Medical System not taking care of people. Our lives are cheap to some corporate executives. It is false profits over people, and it will end <u>soon</u>.

Proposal 23 The Pharmaceutical Industry

The major Pharmas on the same track as the Medical Insurance Industry and We will soon have prescription and over the counter drugs at more reasonable prices. The new Pharmaceutical Consortium will be negotiating with the new single entity in the Medical Insurance Consortium and working for the public good. This is not Fantasyland folks! This is the new reality that We will *vote into existence* at the polls this November.

Proposal 24 The Tobacco (Nailing the Most Deadly Drug) Industry

The Tobacco Industry — that in recent years was somewhat penalized when it was found out they had been intentionally spiking of cigarettes to keep their 'users' smoking and 'hook' new nicotine addicts — has <u>had</u> their day. The charter of the American Tobacco Consortium will require them to reduce the level of nicotine and other addictive ingredients in cigarettes in a "couple" of years by 75% or so. Thus, making it easier for more of our people to quit and harder for teenagers to get hooked. Any questions?

Proposal 25 The Oil Industry

It is the end of Big Oil in America. No more of that industry overtly and covertly suppressing all forms of alternative fuel development and use. We will work to stabilize our national consumption of Oil and Oil-based products, mainly plastics, and then replace them with other options. Electric cars and plastic made from domestically grown Hemp for starters!

All for the sake of our economy, the environment, and that little thing called National Security.

Proposal 26 The Banking and Credit Card Industry

The Banking and Credit Card Consortium will oversee the final consolidation of the major banks, as well as bringing the Credit Card vendors under centralized control. Banking will be transformed into a National System resource to help individuals, families, and businesses small and large to progress. The Credit Card function will become less predatory, and interest rates will be capped and slowly decreased. Further, they will modify their operational configuration with their merchants to the model that is used in Europe, where it makes Identify Theft <u>far</u> less an issue.

Proposal 27 The Defense (Military Industrial Complex) Industry

Whether it is before or after you read Proposal 27, please get the DVD *Why We Fight*. I mention that movie probably too many times in CS2, only because it is critical to the public's understanding of the out-of-control Defense Industry and why We were led into Iraq. And I am not at all peace-nik!

Without putting our National Defense at risk, We will cap Defense Department spending, reduce our Iraq configuration and objective, and once and for all assume command and control the Military Industrial Complex. See Proposal 27.

2. Industry Revitalization and Creation

This portion of our Economic Reformation program addresses the requirement to expand existing, as well as create new industries to provide domestic employment for our American workers. The four (4) New and Renewal Industry proposals will be presented next. There a few comments on their role in our Economic Reformation.

New and Renewal Industry Re-Structuring

Proposal 18 Re-Cycling as a Major Domestic Industry

Each of the 435 U.S. Congressional Districts (USD) contains at least 600,000 Americans. Each will work with the major Waste and Recycling Management corporations to build recycling facilities. All Americans and businesses will begin to recycle plastic, metal, paper, etc. Consider that about half of your daily trash can be re-cycled rather than going to the landfill. This will create real jobs in every USD and decrease the draw on natural resources. And instead of shipping some of our trash to China where they process it and make products they tin turn sell back to us – We will figure out how to start doing it here at home for fun and profit!

Remember every time someone throws a plastic bottle or container in the trash, they are putting re-useable **oil** back in the ground!

Proposal 19 Hemp Industry – The Truth for a Change

You cannot get-a-buzz from smoking or eating Hemp – cannabis' cousin plant! American farmers have wanted to grow it for decades. We can make rope, canvas, cloth, paper (the U.S. Constitution was written on it), plastics, home heating oil, diesel fuel, and other things from that wicked plant! So much for seventy (70) years of federally insured and well-lobbied domestic propaganda.

Proposal 20 Domestic Cannabis Industry

With the Pharmaceutical Industry, their biggest opponent on Capitol Hill neutralized, cannabis will be fully legalized and de-criminalized in the America – and it should take effect by mid-2009. Seventy (70) years of stupidity and abuse of our citizens to satisfy Special Interests will end. An $87-plus Billion dollar business will be run by the states, creating jobs, and decreasing crime. It will finally be easily available to the sick and without a prescription. It will ease their pain and help them to eat.

Proposal 21 Take Back Industries (TBIs) – Domestic Manufacturing

Using a small business creation model that I call an Income Generating Entity (IGE), We will begin to reclaim businesses and industries, such as clothing manufacturing that in recent years have been lost to China, India, Mexico, etc. Using long-term, sole source contracts, and low-interest start-up loans to create small business based (non-stock involved), manufacturing employment for our people.

Remember that Proposal 7 – The U.S. Re-Employment System will be educating and training our people all over the country to be ready and able for employment. People will no longer be sitting around and drawing checks. They will be available for part-time and full-time jobs within their county or city while being trained. Resources will be made available for existing and new businesses to utilize as needed.

Beyond That Starter Set

Once We have broken the ice and have finally begun our national re-tooling process, the public's confidence and the expectations will be raised. There are other opportunities waiting to be ceased upon by the American small and large business community. The American entrepreneurial spirit lives in small towns and big cities all across our nation and it will be fed.

With the restructuring of the Oil Industry, the Automobile Industry can be freed from their Oil's lobbying that has so suppressed alternative fuel technologies. In a very short time, there can be alternative fuel facilities networked across the country. There are about 170,000 gas stations across America and We will soon be able to do whatever needs to be done with them.

The use of Duel Fuel cars and trucks will become a national priority as We — FINALLY — get very serious and realistic about our National Energy Policy. We can and will dictate that those vehicles are made in America by new non-stockholder, involved subsidiaries of our Automobile Makers.

Also, with a new and improved "green friendly" National Energy Policy, many business and job opportunities will be created — businesses that can utilize the IGE business creation model.

The Electric Car will be dug up, will be built in this country, and driven by our people.

And there will be countless other opportunities once the ball gets rolling.

We can and We will do these hard things! And with each passing month things will get easier.

o   o   o   o

3. Micro-Economics – Supplementing Our Consumer Economy

The concept is simple, straight-forward, and I believe a very practical economic function to add to the day-to-day workings of our National System. It is the creation of the Supplemental Income Stream (SIS) Program for our citizens and certain long-term, legal occupants, only.

Our Problem "To be Addressed"

Yes, this goes back to the Cost-of-Living (COL) in America and hard fact that more Americans all the time are not making enough monthly income to live. That is reality, and as a Democratic society We can no longer let it continue.

Therefore, instead of acting like the on-going problem does not exist or throwing the occasional Band-Aid on it when the bleeding gets real bad, let's confront it and begin to alter national budgeting and tax policy to properly address the public's economic issue.

The absolutely, critical need to devise such a supplemental income flow within America's National System is an economic and societal requirement. It is a *key indicator* of our determination to develop a new Democratic Economic System that is truly designed to address the Common Good of all of our citizens.

Around the world, too many nations either give lip service or simply ignore the economic imbalances which naturally evolve in all countries. Today, We technically must consider America in the group! We certainly do have various public service and help programs, BUT they are not getting this problem resolved and each month more of our fellow Americans are struggling to have a "reasonable" life, if not to survive. That is not intended to be dramatic. The human statistics verify this degradation within our society.

And do not consider these the words of a Liberal that is rolling out another public give-away program. Not me and not this program!

WE can either determine how to fairly and practically resolve this totally natural, but always destructive economic imbalance or be guaranteed to continue paying a growing price for the negative consequences it puts on the National System – crime, negative health conditions, drug use, etc. It is a sure thing – simple cause and effect.

Just as 1776, Democracy in Government changed and forever interrupted

Tyrannies' reign over the world. We the People of 2008 have it within our Power to, as I write elsewhere in CS2, present Economic Democracy to the world.

Like it or not, many European nations and Canada under England's direction provide the best economic models to have been developed thus far. *To those that ridicule* them as having a *"socialized economic system"* I say get over it! They have for example, a "socialized" Medical Systems that frankly serves their people better than ours does. The glaring difference is that they serve ALL of their people and promote both preventative and good health programs. Not that they did it intentionally, but after World War II was finished, everything was destroyed, and the Depression continued there longer than it did in America.

Europe was forced to create public systems with limited dollars that needed to be shared and that dealt with the common misery of all their people. If We would have had to re-build from scratch as they did, our systems would look the same today. The Plain Truth.

Enough on that for now.

I fully acknowledge that this program is not perfectly worked out yet, but neither was Democracy when We started out either. This is not an easy program to consider or create, but in due time it will prove its public worth and become an accepted and natural part of our National System.

I absolutely believe this is a key part of the answer to our growing COL and struggling, consumer-based economy issues. It ties into the other parts of An American Agenda. The Changes overlap in purpose and public benefit. The Big Picture must be considered.

o   o   o   o

Purpose

Instead of a *"random"* Economic Stimulus package used to send some dollars into people's pockets this will become a *"routine"* flow, most likely on a monthly basis – when it can really be of use by the public.

The primary *factoid*, to keep in mind in this scenario is related to the side issue of the routine extension of unemployment benefits. It has been stated that for every $100 issued, the benefit produced is about $175 back into the economy. Those are the 'official' numbers thrown around, and even if it is only $150, that is still a positive return on investment on taxpayer dollars or dollars We would need to borrow for a given program.

Random Economic Stimulus Package (ESP) Approach

It is early February 2008 and The Congress and the White House are currently struggling over an ESP program in response to the start of the 2008 Recession. This is the second such ESP program offered by the Bush II Administration.

The "random" ESP approach is used to boost the economy in slow economic times. The White House and Congress are still working out the details of this overall package. The new thus far is that the package could include:

- direct checks being sent out to individuals and couples – with $600 to $800 dollars for individuals making under x-dollars say $80 to $100,000 and double those amounts for couples earning $160,000 to $200,000 a year.
- extending un-employment benefits for x-months.
- tax incentives for business to purchase operational equipment, such as computer hardware and software, machinery, etc.
- of course, the ever-popular more tax breaks for businesses.
- there could be other features, as well.

It will be interesting to see how this package takes shape and its final content. An overall cost of $150 Billion dollars has been mentioned, but what does that number really mean until the details are nailed down.

o   o   o   o

As you can recall, this would be the second time the Bush II administration has used this approach. The "talking heads" on the network and cable news programs are of course all over the pros and cons of the approach depending upon the economic and/or political position.

Some say that the tax breaks for business are just another Republican giveaway to business and at best will take some months to produce economic benefits. Some say the while that putting $600 to $800 dollars directly into the pockets of consumers will of course provide the economy some help, that it will have only short-term impact just as the previous program.

The rub is how much of it would people need to turn right around and spend on basics such as gasoline, utilities, basic food, prescriptions and medical bills, and mortgages – rather of putting it into the retail economy.

Overall and politically it is viewed as certainly better than doing nothing and many in the public could use the funds. However, borrowing Billions more dollars from overseas to do it is not the "best" thing to do, since it will only run the National Debt up further. Time will tell what the ESP it will finally take, the size of the checks to be sent out, and what the final Federal Budget costs will be.

o   o   o   o

The Supplemental Income Stream (SIS) Program

The SIS Program is not a replacement for a Random Economic Stimulus Package (ESP) that still could be required in some form, from time-to-time as only future economic events can determine.

The SIS program will <u>not</u> include the typical components of an ESP such as tax incentives for business, tax breaks for business, extending un-employment benefits for x-months or any other stimulus feature.
However, if implemented properly into the National System and prudently fined tuned to support our consumer-based economy, the SIS Program could very well decrease the occurrence of such troubling events.

Again, I am proposing a variation to the typical ESP package that has been used to send a lump sum amount of $600 to $800 Americans for the purpose of boosting the consumer economy. It will be smaller amount distributed on a permanent monthly basis.

Initial and Long-Term Funding for SIS

When it comes right down to it, the hardest part in establishing the SIS Program is Common Agreement on its funding sources, especially during the start-up months. So let us first look at the end game strategy of the SIS Program in the National System. Instead of avoiding talking about the dollars and how this program will be practically funded <u>without</u> necessarily borrowing Billions of additional dollars, let's look at it.

And We will <u>not</u> be discussing the potential funding amounts (dollars) required for the SIS Program. Be assured that *the dollars and the details* will be worked out and explained to the public's satisfaction before the Program will be implemented. This program, <u>just</u> <u>like</u> Social Security is a public necessity, and We will make it work. And when time permits We will permanently fix Social Security as well!

o   o   o   o

Our challenge to be overcome with regard to funding is to reach the point where the gross costs of the SIS monthly allotment expenditures more than offset and thus paid for by a new Federal Sales Tax. I thought that would get your attention, remain calm. That would not be the only funding source for the SIS Program. Some of the possible funding sources are reviewed next and others will be determined as the program is developed toward implementation.

We must approach this tedious issue with the common attitude that *We will identify* the funding sources for the SIS Program, and *not if We will*.

Critical to Keep in Mind

Remember that only our citizens and certain long-term, legal occupants will be eligible to receive SIS allotments. It will take a little time in the beginning while the distribution process is refined, especially within the IRS roles. Some non-citizen groups may protest this citizen focused arrangement, but frankly We do not Care. If it bothers them too much, they can always leave. It is America and Americans First! No apologies will be offered.

Again, while a host of other people in our country will by virtue of being here, contribute to one or more of these funding sources, they too will not be recipients of the SIS Program monthly allotments. That will include people visiting for pleasure or business; foreign born students; Green Card holders; and around 15 million Illegal Occupants, as well.

o   o   o   o

Federal Sales Tax

A new Federal Sales Tax probably in the range of one half (1/2%) to one percent (1%) on all goods that are normally taxed by the states. This is the 'probable' near and long-term primary funding source that I envision for the SIS Program. This may need to be collected through state sales tax systems until the Federal Tax System is set-up.

Re-Directed Defense Funding

The initial month or two (2) of the program may well be funds redirected from the Defense Budget. That will wake up a few people, especially those that have not read Proposal 27, yet.

The Defense Department and its bloated Bush II, Budget will be capped, and reduced over a few years to a level that protects the nation, but will not bankrupt us either.

Borrowed to Prime the Pump

Not my first choice, but it is far better to borrow money that will go directly into the public's pocket and have a potential return of $1.50 for every $1.00 borrowed, then dumping it in the Defense Industry.

Internet Sales Tax

The Industry obtained that exemption when it was new, claiming it needed the tax break as it was gearing up. That's fair, even though We have been losing retail sales tax revenue in the process. Internet sales have certainly geared up over the ensuing years with sales volume growing annually. In spite of that growth, their lobbyists in recent months 'convinced' Congress to find the time to renew that exemption. That's not fair unless they have come up with a new publicly, acceptable justification for the extension. Otherwise, the recently renewed exemption from taxes being charged on Internet-based sales will be repealed. Those taxes could be funneled all or in part into the SIS Program and distributed across the country and thus, back into retail and/or Internet sales. That's fair!

o   o   o   o

That gives you some ideas of the potential short and long-term funding sources for the SIS Program. I am certain many others will be found, especially once our citizens start getting those SIS Allotment checks each month, want them to be permanent, and increased if possible. The Electorate could get real interested and creative with this.

o   o   o   o

The SIS Program Monthly Allotment

This is again a variation to the traditional economic stimulus package approach that occasionally distributes a lump sum to our citizens. While the actual amounts will be determined the following describes the system's practical characteristics and intent.

For Seniors

Each person currently drawing Social Security Income (SSI) will begin receiving $35 to $50 on a monthly basis. This SIS Allotment will be sent in the form of a separate check and not added to their current monthly SSI-based disbursement. No sense in complicating the SSI system.

For those American citizens, only, over say sixty (60) years of age, who for whatever reason are not eligible for SSI, but are receiving some other form of Federal sourced income such as through Medicaid, they will also receive a SIS Allotment check.

For Other Eligible Recipients

Again that includes other U.S. citizens and certain long-term, legal occupants, only. The initial thought is that all will be included — regardless of annual income!

Each person currently filing IRS, Federal income taxes and at least twenty-one (21) years old will begin receiving $75 to $100 on a monthly basis.

o   o   o   o

Personally, I believe We should start with the $50/$100 ratio to make it instantly worthwhile.

Use of the SIS Allotment

In simple examples, for the person really struggling $50 or $100 net cash (non-taxed or reported) each month will be a real help with many things. For someone like "The Donald" they will probably break it into 2 fifties and use it for tips! Excellent.

So how does all that sound to you, my fellow American?

Now let's go look at some real, problem solution proposals!

The Ten AIR Proposals

The American Industry Restructuring proposals address legislation and policies having to do with the operation of certain businesses and industries within America's National System. This grouping is divided into two (2) sets of proposals designated as either New or Renewal Industries – or — those pertaining to Existing Industries.

The first set is designed to enhance and create. It will build upon and initiate new economic opportunities for American businesses <u>and</u> workers.

The second set is designed for absolute confrontation and binding reconciliation. Those are intended to resolve some long-standing and destructive imbalances of influence within the National System that have blatantly assaulted the Common Good of our people. They will most certainly produce the greatest stir. And we need them to do just that!

New or Renewal Industries

This set of proposals concerns the types industries that do exist or that could be developed in order to be of practical benefit to society if approached in a more progressive and <u>realistic</u> manner. These **domestic-based** industries will be developed to provide jobs, goods, and services for Americans right here on our own soil:

18   Re-Cycling as a Major Domestic Industry
19   Hemp Industry – The Truth for a Change
20   Domestic Cannabis Industry
21   Take Back Industries (TBIs) – Domestic Manufacturing

Existing Industries

The proposals presented under this heading are focused upon a core group of heavy-hitter industries that are critical to our economic system and the impact the lives of virtually every American good or bad on a regular basis. That's why this particular group has also been categorized as National Infrastructure Industries (NII).

There are *of course* some other industries that could be added, but for now the group presented for Public Review and National Reconciliation is:

22   Health Care Insurance for ALL Americans
23   The Pharmaceutical Industry
24   The Tobacco (Nailing the Most Deadly Drug) Industry

25   The Oil Industry
26   The Banking and Credit Card Industries
27   The Defense (Military Industrial Complex) Industry

How *We the People* determine to come to terms with such entities will define the heart and soul of our Second American Revolution, and to a very, great extent — our National Destiny, as well.

o   o   o   o

American Industry Restructuring (AIR)

New and Renewal Industries

"First, a few proposals on the Lighter Side of things"

This set of Industry related proposals concern the types of businesses that currently exist and could be restructured and expanded, as well as those that could be created in order to benefit to the American economy, when approached in a more publicly beneficial and sometimes realistic manner! These will be **domestic-based** industries to be owned and operated by American citizens as *First Right*. Such businesses will provide local jobs and benefits to employees, while providing goods and services for the nation, and the always needed tax revenues. This proposal set addresses:

18   Re-Cycling as a Major Domestic Industry
19   Hemp Industry – The Truth for a Change
20   Domestic Cannabis Industry
21   Take Back Industries (TBIs) – Domestic Manufacturing and IGEs

18   Re-Cycling as a Major Domestic Industry

Issue/Problem

Recycling is not a problem rather it is a grand commercial and environmental opportunity at the national level. To say that we as a nation are not recycling enough is a gross understatement!

News Flash — Recycling in America is a potential source of more domestic-based jobs and will absolutely help the environment – win/win! It needs to, it must become a national priority and each of us needs to warm up to the habit of recycling everything we possibly can. Just developing a civilly and environmentally good habit!

I will not bother with a lot of statistics, because American society knows we are only scratching the surface when it comes to the benefits that could be derived from the routine and consistent recycling of materials, especially soda and beer cans, glass, plastics, cardboard, and newspapers.

This is where you and I come in. Individuals, families, and businesses need to become aware of their responsibility to recycle whatever they can every day. It will only take us the few moments required to set aside products that we touch almost every day, to be recycled rather than being tossed in a trash can. Yes, we might need to dirty our hands once in a while!

Landfills all over the country are filling up much faster than they need to, thus forcing new ones to be created at a far greater rate than necessary. City and county governments could then be spending less time fighting with the public on where to build the next landfill, as well as collecting our tax dollars needed to construct and maintain them.

Companies like Waste Management, Inc., and the other major recycling companies of America would see their business volume skyrocket! Vast amounts of raw materials would be re-cycled back into the manufacturing food chain rather than being "lost" into the ground. More jobs (county and city areas) would be created in both the collection and processing of recyclables – all over the nation – right where the trash is made!

Every city in the nation has people in need of work. Each municipality would work with the Waste and Recycling companies to create such collection and sorting centers. These would not be government jobs and would create full and part-time positions for local people.

Consider that the average population of the 435 US Congressional

Districts (USD) exceeds 650,000 people! There are seven (7) states with just one (1) USD in Congress and the largest population among them is Montana with over 900,000. Wyoming, also with one seat has the smallest USD in Congress with around 500,000 people (about the number of people tobacco kills <u>each</u> year)..

Each of the 435 USDs could easily establish major collection and re-cycling operation centers providing jobs for local people, helping the environment, and other worthwhile benefits to society. Creating jobs instead of continuing to bury them in the ground! Interesting?

Then maybe we could quit sending some of our trash to China to be processed into products that they sell back to us! The economics of that need to be laid out for public review. There must be a better way.

And all that each of We the People need to do to make such a positive national endeavor a gargantuan success is to remember to **"think before you throw."**

The People's Sense

This is so simple, talk about a total no-brainer. Recycling needs to become a routine practice for all Americans — and as natural as buckling our seat belt when we get in the car. We put on our seat belts to protect our lives and our children's — so we can all learn to recycle to help protect the environment of today and for the future our children and their's will be living in.

We will encourage every family unit (one or more people) to have a simple recycling bag in the kitchen — just a plastic grocery bag (or sack) hung over a door knob to drop items instead of the trashcan. We can begin promoting this with our kids in grades K to 12 – there are about 48 million of them!

Imagine, the numbers to be generated by one (1) bottle or can per <u>day</u> times 48,000,000 children for only five (5) days a week, spread over a single year:

- 48,000,000 items per day
- 240,000,000 items per 5-day week
- 12,480,000,000 items per 52-week year

And that is only <u>one</u> item per day, Monday thru Friday – not counting the weekends!! Obviously, it is only a tiny, tiny fraction of what could be saved from landfills and reused!

The American Recycling Movement (ARM)

And since we like everything to have name or title we could call it the American Recycling Movement or ARM!

This is a fundamental Act of Civil Obedience! Interesting? We the People could us this simple exercise to let our local and federal governments know that we do really care and are deeply concerned about such things, and that we demand their action.

We can unite and work to <u>bury</u> to our municipalities and the Recycling Industry (they would love us for it) in collected material. The gargantuan volume would force the federal and state governments to require related American businesses to use recycled resources, particularly metal, paper <u>and</u> the plastic that comes from oil, rather than drawing so much upon natural resources and worse yet, being required to import such materials.

It would help preserve what natural resources we have for future use. Some new businesses would be started and will be jobs created in the process. These are all good things!

Generation Outlets and Collection Centers

Let's assume that the growing number of recyclables we generate at home and at work locations as a result of people getting into the spirit of the ARM program will be taken care of as natural expansion of the existing Waste and Recycling industry.

Most of the business community is not currently seriously committed to the effort as they need to be. Grimly I have even seen some that actually do collect bottles, cans, and paper for recycling, but the materials wind up going out the back door into the regular trash. Rude! Business can do better.

That said now let's think of the other places that generate large amounts of recyclable products but usually do nothing to collect anything, but <u>trash</u> that goes directly to landfills, such as:
- Convenience stores
- Gas station/food marts
- Fast food restaurants
- Baseball, football, soccer stadiums
- Basketball, ice hockey arenas

- Car and horse racing tracks

You get the idea. And there are also public schools and higher education sites! A huge amount of 'stuff' that mindlessly goes in the ground.

We can do better than that "under the ARM" program — even though it will take each of us a little time here and there.

We can learn to responsibly separate at least some of the recycling when throwing away trash at Wendy's, McDonald's or the other fast food houses across the country – think of those coffee cups and salad containers going into the ground. Those businesses can coordinate with trash removal companies to place recycling containers in their parking lots. It is their civic responsibility.

Companies such as Home Depot and Loews can get on the band-wagon. Shopping centers and malls in every town, along with sporting facility parking lots normally with excess parking lot space can install large recycling containers for public drop-off.

It's a matter everybody doing a little bit to yield tremendous results for the environment, related industries, and American jobs.

Recycling is a personal action that helps each person <u>directly</u> <u>contribute</u> to the re-use and preservation of our natural resources. It is a mindset that is already growing and could easily be expanded among the American public.

You get the idea — just **"think before you throw."**

o   o   o   o

That proposal was fun!   Now for one that will finally kill a seventy (70) year old myth…

19 The Hemp Industry – The Truth for a Change

"Debunking 70 years of 'federally-insured' domestic propaganda"
"You cannot get stoned by smoking or eating Hemp"

Issue/Problem

This proposal is intended to provide the American public with the Plain Truth on the Hemp plant. To describe its potential uses and to kill the domestic propaganda we have been fed "by the feds" since the 1930's.

For more detail on Hemp and the ridiculously long struggle to make it commercially legal in America, just go to *Goggle*, type "hemp legalization" and just press **Enter**! You will be amazed.

o   o   o   o

As opposed to a restructuring proposal this is public introduction to an ancient and very viable crop for American farmers and the domestic manufacturing opportunities it will present.

American farmers have been lobbying for decades to have the right to grow Hemp. However, they have been regularly stuffed by lobbyists from the lumber, plastics, cotton, and the petroleum industries for a few examples. Do you find that surprising? Keep reading.

The Hemp plant, along with its cousin the cannabis (AKA *marijuana*) plant, is not native to be Americas, actually originating in India and China.

It is a little known, but interesting piece of American history to learn that the original Hemp seeds were smuggled into the American colonies by that well-known colonial drug trafficker Thomas Jefferson! He and his drug-distributing buddy George Washington grew it in abundance and suggested that everyone else should as well. If We cannot *Trust in God*, Tom, and George — who can we trust?

o   o   o   o

And now for a few facts about the much maligned **Hemp** plant, which speaks volumes on the issue of domestic propaganda. The majority of people I have spoken with have lived under the assumption that hemp and cannabis were one in the same physical plant, which they are not. I was unaware of that fact when I began my research.

While it is absolutely true that the naturally growing Hemp plant does contain the 'active' substance Tetrahydrocannabois, aka, THC just as its cousin plant cannabis, the scientific fact is that Hemp does **not** have the same level chemical content and therefore does not provide the sensory effect as its popular 'cousin'. The natural THC content in Hemp is less than one-half of a percent. Meaning that a person could smoke (or eat) Hemp non-stop for an hour, and would not get *a buzz*, or whatever you would care to call the physical reaction normally received from a few inhalations of natural growing cannabis.

Big Brother

However, the substance THC is listed on the Drug Enforcement Administration (DEA) Control Substance **Schedule Number One** (containing the most damaging substances), along with heroin, LSD, morphine, and GHB the "date rape" drug. Now to even the casual observer, THC would appear to have been blatantly misfiled and is in some very hard company.

I am not going to belabor this issue since it is so straightforward. It is yet another sad example of how certain industries and some supportive politicians have placed their interests over that of the public. In this case it is the commercial and environmental benefits of the Hemp plant that the public and our economy are being deprived of.

By the way, let's hear it for Woody Harrelson that willingly got arrested in a personal protest some years ago for having a few Hemp plants. Woody was right!

Regarding this Harmless Plant

* Marijuana was made illegal in the 1930's as part of a Federal, domestic propaganda campaign. Hemp was just added to the package. That highly political program was initiated during the early years of the Great Depression when too many American citizens were looking for non-existent jobs.

  The legislation was designed to promote the removal of foreign workers, mainly Mexican nationals that were working in the Southwestern states. The end result of which was the country's first repatriation legislation. Yes, we have done it before.

  Objectively, the terrible unemployment situation the country was facing made the non-American workers an economic and political liability. Does any of that sound vaguely familiar? Refer back to Proposal

#8, National Drug Reform for the historical details.

- From now on the commercial viability and the environmental qualities of Hemp will be realistically presented. This will be a welcomed change for American farmers, manufacturers, and retail merchants. The commercial legalization of the Hemp plant is a real winner for American farmers that have been unsuccessfully lobbying for the right to grow it for years. The opposition lobbies have up until now carried more weight than the American farmer — a sad reality.

- Due to the chemical properties of the naturally growing, *God-given* Hemp plant it is possible to produce:

  - o Paper products – our U.S. Constitution was written on it
  - o Cloth that is stronger than cotton fabric. Cotton farmers could switch; it requires little or no fertilizer, less water, and grows like a weed. It could be too practical.
  - o Rope
  - o Canvas used for centuries to make ship sails
  - o The Petroleum Industry lobbies hard against it because it could be used to produce:
    - Plastics
    - Lamp oil
    - Home Heating Fuel
    - And has Diesel Fuel possibilities, too

Again, the truth will set us free.

- In the 1930s, another radical by the name of Henry Ford was experimenting with Hemp-based, "diesel" fuel powered cars **and** actually manufactured the entire outer shell of a car using a Hemp-based composite material. However, that exercise came to an abrupt end when Hemp along with marijuana was made illegal in that decade. Maybe today's Ford Motor Company could check into this in old Henry's memory.

- It could possibly reduce the amount of petroleum now used in the production of some plastic products. A very good thing that could reduce our foreign oil dependency.

- Diesel fuel for trucks and cars can be produced from the Hemp plant, in a process similar to what we already utilize on a limited (and suppressed) basis using the soybean plant. For example, diesel fuel from soybean is currently being used to power some public bus services.

Hemp-based diesel fuel does burn significantly cleaner, relative to greenhouse gases than petroleum-based diesel fuel.

To be fair I have not researched the numbers on this issue, such as one acre of Hemp will produce x-gallons of diesel grade fuel, at y-dollars per gallon.

However, we already know that <u>corn</u> at the very best is <u>only</u> a small part of the answer to our oil-replacement problem.

The full details on the commercial viability of Hemp will be aired in public as this proposal is debated.

The People's Sense

The Hemp plant will be made available for farming and commercial purposes in America. It could also find its way to Central and South America as an alternative crop!

Of particular interest will be its viability in producing home heating oil, making plastics and hemp-based diesel fuel to help decrease our dependence on foreign oil and having cleaner air to breath! Sounds good to me – what do you think?

o   o   o   o

Did you like that one? The next is guaranteed to generate a national buzz…

And it will begin to turn the Drug World upside-down. The screamers, certain industries, the bad guys, and some bad governments will not like it. However, it is time that their irresponsible reign was over!

20   The Domestic Cannabis Industry

"The Time has finally arrived – Dylan will be proud of Us"

"Those who laugh last — never quit!"

Issue/Problem

In this realistic proposal we will overview how the newly legalized Cannabis plant will be turned into a viable domestic farming and manufacturing industry.

As mentioned before, the target date for full legalization and decriminalization of marijuana by the U.S. Congress is July 1, 2009, but preferably sooner. I will not be reviewing those issues in this proposal as they were addressed earlier in Proposal #8, National Drug Reform. Hopefully you read the history of cannabis in that earlier piece, if not you may want to read it now. It provides a true reality check for many.

o   o   o   o

In the case of the naturally growing plant cannabis or marijuana (I refer to it herein as M) we are actually talking about the restructuring of the existing, illegal $87,000,000,000 (billion) dollar M Industry in America into a legal domestic industry with employment in farming, production, distribution, and sale. And it will generate tax revenue, too.

Although, our <u>alleged</u> drug fighting buddies in Mexico provide us with a considerable amount of M across our uncontrolled (and currently un-fenced) Southern border, it is also grown "privately" and illegally in all 50 states and the District of Columbia everyday!

And in case you have not heard, drug cartels have been growing M right in America's <u>national parks</u> — and other remote areas for fun and profit. That is not a joke and our park rangers are under physical attack! The bad guys did it to cut down on the hassles of bringing tons of it across our wide-open Southern border. However, if Bush II succeeds in allowing Mexicans to drive big trucks right across our border, the bad guys may go back to doing it the old fashion way – smuggling in big trucks along with the cocaine and crystal-met!

o   o   o   o

We are talking about a *God-given,* naturally growing plant (a weed) that is easier to grow than alcohol was to make during the Prohibition on Alcohol (that was in effect from 1919 to 1933).

And while the American farm industry has not been lobbying to grow cannabis as they have been with Hemp, it too will prove to be a viable crop to expand our small domestic farming industry. The issues of farm production, packaging, and distribution are overviewed here for common understanding on this somewhat controversial topic.

Under the NDR proposal M will become fully legalized in America (a change in policy that would be quickly followed by Canada and Britain) – to be easily available for medical and personal use and be fully decriminalized regarding possession and legalized for controlled sale.

I will only offer that over the last few decades, in researching and developing what became the NDR proposal, I have spoken with a few thousand people and was initially amazed at how little opposition there was to legalization of marijuana. That is regardless of age, race, religion, political party, social status or any other differentiator of people — even some very conservative church leaders acknowledged that they viewed it the same or less of a problem than alcohol for some in their congregations!

Remember that everything you're about to read has been reviewed and refined by the direct feedback of the American public – your neighbors.

The People's Sense

For someone reading this material for the first time the following could sound as though it was coming from Mars — that is unless you were an adult in America prior to 1933! Some of this will sound a bit funny, but it is extremely serious and in fact what millions of law abiding Americans have been waiting decades to see happen.

Below, we will overview the approach to be used to initially set-up the legal Cannabis business in America. In this presentation I will refer to the National Drug Reform (NDR) Proposal. I will also use the terms cannabis, marijuana, and M – all with the same meaning.

The Legal Domestic Cannabis Industry

"The Time has Arrived"

How We Will Produce the Product

Overall, the newly legalized Cannabis Industry will be a great opportunity for small businesses.

Under the NDR, marijuana would be grown for domestic sale, consumption, and a legal export using the following three (3) methods:

1. Grown for personal use, only.

2. Grown by state Certified Micro Growers (CMGs), under controlled policies and procedures mirroring those currently used for Micro Brewers of beer.

3. Grown by the Individual States – America can grow all the M needed within our own borders if we so choose. Any future **legal** imports will have tariffs on them just like any other commercial product and Mexico will not receive any special treatment.

Some of the details and perspectives on these three methods are presented for common "understanding".

Grown for Personal Use, only

U.S. citizens would be allowed to grow M for personal consumption. Some people will only use M that they have personally grown! However, most people would not want to be bothered or have the space to grow it, just as most people do not produce their own alcohol or grow tobacco.

However, people being people, some will inevitably grow enough to sell some to their friends and acquaintances. It would probably be a small number and it is not worth wasting taxpayer money looking for them. However, if someone does get carried away they would eventually come to the attention of the police and courts, which would properly deal with them – fines only. Again, this would follow the same course as those individuals caught with a little too much moonshine, and selling it for fun and profit!

As mentioned in the NDR proposal, the relevant Federal drug enforcement agency will be renamed to the Bureau of Alcohol, Tobacco, Firearms and Cannabis (the ATFC) and have their charter prudently amended and expanded. It does sound odd at first, but it is a practical change that will need to be made.

Grown by Certified Micro Growers (CMG)

This option may at first also sound strange, however in reality there will be quite a number (thousands) of individuals — entrepreneurs that will jump to take advantage of this newly legal business opportunity. There are small towns in America where this already goes on with little interruption (a wink) by local police since it provides needed income for local residents.

In some states the CMGs could actually be the only farming entities required, as they could become large farms. Each state will need to determine what works best for them, but it will be legalized in all states and DC – we will finally end this national stupidity and all the human harm it has done.

Grown by the Individual States and DC

I initially imagined that this would be the primary method used in most states for crop production and distribution to the American public. The states will authorize certain local farmers, not agricultural conglomerates, to grow the crop under the proper controls. Again, these could be local growers not necessarily state run farms since the CMG approach would mean less overhead for the states.

Today, as for many decades, M has been the nation's #1 cash crop. Finally, it will become fully legalized, controlled, and prudently taxed.

Prohibited by Law

This new industry must be kept in the realm of small business. The Pharmaceutical and Tobacco Industries will be prohibited by nationally enforced law from touching this grand opportunity for small business. Although, before too long the Pharmaceutical companies will be adding it to their products so that they work more effectively – go figure. And they will buy M from the states.

The M business would never be allowed to become a stock-holder involved enterprise. If anything the American public will be the perpetual stock-holders of the Cannabis Industry.

How We Will Manage the Cannabis Business

The retail availability of these products will closely follow the controlled procedures currently used in the production and distribution of alcohol in the U.S., specifically for hard liquor.

Administration

- As stated before, production, and distribution would be <u>controlled</u> by the individual <u>states</u>, with minor federal oversight. The overall process would follow a standard federal program that is jointly developed by the state and federal legislators. The states will direct the industry, <u>not</u> the federal government.

- One suggestion is for an entity such as the **American Farm Bureau** could be responsible for coordinating this entire enterprise. There is absolutely no need to create an entire new government agency.

  Be assured that this will not be rocket science and therefore will be quick (a few months) to develop and put in place. We are talking about growing a (controlled) crop, and the packaging and distribution of a product similar in nature to cigarettes and pipe tobacco. We of course already have vast experience in these areas due to our legal, tobacco-based, *nicotine-drug* business. Yes, that was sarcastic, and so true.

Distribution and Reality

- It will be sold under the same laws and regulations as currently written for hard liquor per locality i.e., town, city, county, state, as appropriate.

  HOWEVER, the <u>nationally imposed</u> age for use will be 18 years of age – post-high school graduation! This is not a joke – it is reality. Once again my fellow Americans, we are <u>leaving</u> Fantasyland. We can easily control this using driver's license coding to certify High School graduation has been accomplished. Otherwise the person will wait until they are 21 years old to legally purchase such products.

  Yes, of course that has holes in it, but no more than our existing laws on youth access to alcohol and cigarettes – and they kill 1,000-plus of our people every single day! M, on the other has never caused the death of a single person, even in the Netherlands where it has been fully legal since the mid-1970's.

  Further, the Canadian government came to this very legal-age conclusion after a multi-year national study. If our National Drug Office (that has for decades been controlled by industry lobbyists) would quit pushing Canada and the UK <u>not</u> to make possession a minor parking ticket level offense, it would have been done a few years ago.

- It would <u>not</u> be sold as beer and wine are sold unless the given locality allows hard liquor, beer, and wine to be distributed via the same outlets.

- Some states maintain separate distribution facilities for hard liquor as opposed to beer and wine, which allows for better control over who gets what. In usage, there are many more outlets for beer and wine than for hard liquor. That is how we sell alcohol products in Virginia. We have the state-operated Alcohol Bureau of Control (ABC) outlets for hard liquor. M would be sold in ABC stores in Virginia, at least.

- States that currently allow all three general types to be sold via the same outlets may decide to add M products to the inventory or separate them for control purposes. Then hard liquor and M would flow through the same outlets.

- There could eventually be consumer, retail outlets similar to those that exist today in the Netherlands. The states may determine it is more cost effective to use that approach rather than create more state jobs and incur the related overhead costs.

- Overall, this legalization will really help the restaurant industry!

<u>Production</u>

<u>They must hear this very clearly</u>: The American Tobacco companies <u>will not</u> <u>own</u>, <u>run</u>, <u>control</u> or <u>directly</u> <u>profit</u> from the new Cannabis Industry. Although they will do everything in their power to capture that business – absolutely not!

- Before very long the majority of the M consumed in America will be grown domestically. This will be a boost to the farming industry, providing a significant new crop with the related jobs, income, buying power, etc.

- M will be distributed in various forms, much the same as cigarettes and pipe tobacco. Primarily in a loose form like pipe tobacco and in a pre-made cigarette form, although probably smaller in unit size!

- Each state will probably produce their own crop, thus helping their own <u>independent</u> farmers. It will also create packaging and distribution jobs, although to cut overhead some states may determine to develop cooperative programs with neighboring states in preparation, packaging, and possibly distribution.

The Tobacco companies could provide as needed practical support during the <u>start-up period, only</u>. They could assist the states in establishing the packaging and distribution functions.

Traditional, tobacco growing states will make up their own minds regarding the tobacco companies. This could get some farmers free and clear of tobacco farming. Also, the introduction of Hemp agriculture could also move some farmers to a non-publicly harmful and viable new crop.

<u>Quality Control</u>

- The quality and purity of the M crops would be strictly controlled. Existing users of imported, illegal marijuana sometimes suffer the bad side-effects of whatever insecticides and/or miscellaneous debris is harvested along with the crop in other countries.

- It is well-known that some dealers like to lace M with trace amounts of cocaine or other substances in an attempt to hook their unsuspecting clients on stronger drugs. Think about that fact parents. That danger will be removed from our streets.

<u>Pricing and Taxes</u>

Perspective – An ounce of 'decent' marijuana circa 1976 could cost $35. In 2007 it can cost $400 to $600 per ounce and probably still costs about the same amount to grow. Do the math.

- The legal M industry companies will have a minimum or non-profit (but tax paying) structure. They will be organized as Income Generating Entities (IGEs). There will be more background on them in the next proposal. Adding corporate profit margins on top would unnecessarily increase overall costs, decreasing margin for tax revenue, increase the market price to the consumer, and decrease the net funds available for better public uses.

- It will be produced in various grades or strengths just as is beer and hard liquor. And it would be priced accordingly.

Note: Product pricing <u>must</u> be reasonable. It will <u>not</u> be overpriced in a covert attempt (by the screamers and various lobbies) to price it out of reach of the general public. Overpricing would only promote an under-market and crime, which are key parts of today's drug problem we are trying to resolve in the first place.

- Pricing would include normal considerations for cost of production (paying the growers), packaging and distribution, taxes, and profit for the retail seller, as applicable.

- Each state will control and benefit from their portion of the M business from the production, sale, and state taxes generated.

- State <u>and</u> Federal taxes generated could be designated for specific funding purposes, such as National Health Care Insurance for ALL Americans!

<u>Other Items</u>

- There will be <u>no</u> public advertising of M on television or radio, much like hard liquor with the exception of specialty magazines and of course the Internet that is used today to advertise everything. This approach will also help keep overhead costs down and satisfy some public concerns. Word of mouth and the Internet will be sufficient.

- M related products e.g., pipes, etc., would be manufactured in America, by private (small business) companies. They would be sold in retail outlets and by mail order — as they already are! Any imported paraphernalia will pay a tariff.

o   o   o   o

As I have stated before, we do not live in Fantasyland. Therefore, Americans will now cease to live with such foolish rules, and to have our citizens prosecuted under laws that were obviously made there in the past.

Peace, Love, Dove....

21 Take Back Industries (TBIs) – Domestic Manufacturing and IGEs

"A Concept to Help Reclaim American Manufacturing and Jobs"

Issue/Problem

This is a business organization concept to be considered and embraced by the American business community, as well as state to local governments. And if I did not wholeheartedly believe that it has highly viable and practical potential within our economic system, it would not be included for your review.

The clear business goal behind what is called Take Back Industries or **TBIs** is to seed and foster the re-development of much needed <u>domestic</u> <u>manufacturing</u> in America and the various types of jobs it would provide.

The initial product targets would be things such as clothing and the types of items that are used in <u>every</u> American household and possibly by the business community on a fairly regular basis, if not daily!

Addressing the Out-Sourcing Epidemic

Over the last decade or so, a tragic and ridiculous number of America's manufacturing, Information Technology (IT), and numerous other jobs, if not entire industries have been <u>and</u> are being lost to China, India, Mexico, the Philippines, etc. For the details on this check-out Lou Dobbs at CNN. He does the absolute best job reporting on Out-Sourcing and the IO (Illegal Occupant) issue, as well.

This push really got going in the late 1990's in particular when the Year 2000 Software Crisis/Boom sent large amounts of IT work off-shore mainly to India for cheaper development costs (often with poor results, too).

> Someone once commented to me that all the rhetoric about building the 'Global Economy' was really nothing more than the grand search for lower and lower wage workers. That sounds about right.

Our <u>first</u> <u>priority</u> must be to get creative and begin bringing those jobs back to America!

And what may surprise you to read — as a secondary push America along with the nations in North, Central, and South America must work together to bring jobs and industries into the Western Hemisphere and away from

China, India, and other Asian and Pacific Rim nations. When you think about it, that concept practically ties into the Population Management and Re-Employment Systems we reviewed earlier.

The people (IOs) America will be repatriating to other countries in this Hemisphere will need jobs. To that end, the little talked about and fairly useless Organization of American States (OAS) needs to suffer a re-birth and become an entity for commerce and to promote the Common Good of all peoples of the Western Hemisphere. This organized Hemispheric Economy concept has practical possibilities whose time may have come. And I do not mean any more NAFTA agreements, either.

For now we will focus on America's approach to the TBI effort. It will provide a working model that could be utilized elsewhere.

The TBI Concept

The businesses created and/or restructured to fit the TBI model will have the following characteristics:

- They will produce products that are routinely used and/or required by the average American family and/or business. And although it does sound funny at first the two examples I use to make the point are underwear and light bulbs! Two simple examples of products that people have and will continually need to purchase over their lifetime.

- This new business organization model will have them set-up as non-profit, non-stockholder entities – therefore they will not be burdened with the overhead problem of stockholders and their dividend expectations. TBIs will be focused on providing products and/or services at a reasonable price that covers the cost of production, as well as income and benefits for the owner(s) and employees.

- They will not be tax-exempt. Taxes will be paid.

- I also refer to them as **Income Generating Entities or IGEs** meaning that their purpose is to create jobs providing regular income and benefits for American workers and their families.

- These businesses will be initially funded as needed by long-term, low interest bank loans sponsored by federal, state, county, or city sources. Some could be started with grant money and/or donations. These will not be government entities and therefore will not involve civil service jobs.

- They will be private enterprise businesses, and their management should be experienced in running businesses, not total rookies – any 'new' owners will be required to have experienced managers from the start.

- These will be American <u>citizen</u> owned and operated businesses.

- Cost of goods and pricing will be key factors in making this new business practices work for the American consumer and the retail outlets where such products are sold. This runs somewhat against the normal concepts of cost, pricing, and profit, but it is practical for us to consider new methods. The economic world has changed, therefore the thinking and financial mechanics that drives American business must be restructured, as well.

o   o   o   o

In the case of *underwear* – such products are currently made outside the U.S. and produced **very** cheaply due to foreign labor rates. Today, reportedly some 96% of our clothing is imported. We must make the 4% share grow, and I mean like yesterday!

Those low foreign labor rates need to be offset to some extent by other factors. For example, such products must be shipped via boat or plane to the US and distributed to retail outlets for sale. Those import shipping expenses will be reduced or eliminated under the domestic TBI model.

That may all sound a bit naive to some, but we must start somewhere. Those with better ideas need to please bring them to the debate.

Also, in the case of cotton or blended products, the material resources used to make such products overseas are "obviously" not grown in the U.S. (and that better be the case), thus decreasing opportunities for our farmers. This will not be the case under the TBI model – Hemp clothing, anyone!

So as you can see there will need to be trade-offs in the cost of production of such products for retail sale within the American retail economy.

The Potential Clincher

And one last hook that could potentially seal some deals. These new IGE business entities will be given multi-year sole-source contracts with American consumer outlets. And we are talking 10-year contract minimums, and probably permanent in some cases. Therefore, the financial models used to establish these enterprises would have that guaranteed market to bank on. Bingo!

So let the U.S. Congress work with state and county governments, the American business, and the pro-American financial communities on that concept for a while.

We are forced to compete in the world market with countries and economies that are not tied to stockholders, the constant annual demand for stockholder dividends or the burdensome cost of "for-profit" medical insurance! Therefore, we must consider approaches such as this in order to reclaim jobs and industries to employ our people. It is called being creative!

o   o   o   o

Another thing to consider is where these new businesses would be located. It could be interesting to see how counties, cities, and towns approach the possibility of setting up such businesses in their localities.

There are other positive aspects of the TBI model to be considered, but this should be adequate to get the movement started.

The TBI and IGE concepts present viable options for the American business community to apply.

We can do this...

o   o   o   o

This is the end of the four (4) New and Renewal Industry Proposals. As stated, they are the Lighter Side of the American Industry Restructuring Proposals. What comes next is quite the opposite scenario.

o   o   o   o

American Industry Restructuring (AIR)

Existing Industries

*"We the People — do not owe any company, corporation or industry
a profit or even its continued existence,
if it would come at the expense of our People and our Society"*

"Therefore, let the domestic battle lines be drawn"

o   o   o   o

Introduction

Those lines simply state where We the People find ourselves today relative to certain business entities and their self-serving perpetuators. Certain grave situations will either now be resolved to the Common Good of our citizens and American society, or our economy and indeed the Democratic way of life that we older Americans have known and that we desire for other children that are adults today, will cease to exist. And none of us will want to live in the society that will remain.

All of the other changes written about in An American Agenda and this entire book could be accepted and implemented, but if these and similarly avoidable dysfunctional components of America's National System are not realistically "dealt with" – then, We will watch as the Great American Experiment fails around us.

And it will fail because We the People – the adult American citizens of 2008 (me included) were not worthy of the Challenge. Any questions?

o   o   o   o

That was not intended to be dramatic, since it fairly describes our reality. If you thought what we have reviewed already was aggressive or intense at times, this my fellow Americans is where the discussions really begin and the heavy lifting starts! And I mean that with all due sincerity and my great love for our country.

I am sitting here on Tuesday morning, November 6, 2007 and it is 6:36am. The draft of what remains of Part 3 – this lengthy Introduction, the six (6) crucial Industry proposals, and the Closing of An American Agenda, a 50-

odd page draft Word document sits here. Yesterday I received the first 264 pages of CS2 back from the publisher to be proofed and it was absolutely wonderful to see. It contained Parts 1, 2, and more than half of Part 3. I have already forwarded Part 4 and 90% of Part 5, including the Closing of this book to the publisher and it is being prepped. Therefore, I have already written the end of CS2! The remaining piece of Part 5 on the 2006 and 2008 Elections, the last data research that will be needed, and the final proofing of the manuscript will be somewhat tedious to work through. However, it will be encouraging because it will mean the end is drawing near — time is so very, very critical.

And now I <u>and</u> We come to this. *It is all together fitting* that these proposals are near the heart of CS2.

o   o   o   o

The Challenges

My challenge in presenting this Introduction, the six (6) Industry proposals and the admittedly radical, yet publicly, practical concepts upon which they are based, is to be writing as Thomas Paine would put down his common sense reasoning — with his radical, yet logical determination. That is my solemn challenge.

> Paine's primary attack in *Common Sense* was on the roots of the Old World Order that the colonists suffered under. He wrote, "we shall find them to be in the remains of two ancient tyrannies." The first being, "the remains of monarchial tyranny in the person of the king" and secondly, "the remains of aristocratical tyranny in the persons of the peers."

> He was speaking against the ancient hereditary power of Kings and Queens, and those around them with wealth and absolute power over the people, the peasants — that was deliberately passed down from one generation to the next. Power passed down, and cruelly if needed in order to insure the status quo of the Few retaining that absolute power over the fate of the Many and control over their quality of Life.

> The American colonists were required to use a bloody war to correct that power imbalance, while not that many years later the French peasants used the guillotine to adjust theirs!

In these next pages that are undoubtedly the hardest to develop and write, this common sense literary attack (by the pen) will be against the similar and growing heredity of Power and Influence over the fate of the We the Many and the very quality of our Life. The Power and Influence of an un-elected group of industries, individuals, and enterprises — that with each decade since the 1950's have worked to increase its dominance in all facets of American business and government. These are "un-elected entities" that are continuously seeking Authority over the National System, without acknowledging or accepting Responsibility for the Common Good of our people, our society, and our economy — to say nothing about the threat-ened environment.

I determined that this group of critical industries would serve quite well to focus our nation's critical problem-solving energies. The publicly, rational restructuring of these industries could have productive side-effects through-out the National System. It could well cause an economic chain-reaction as the concepts applied to this high-visibility industries are applied in other businesses and industries – by voluntary action of their existing manage-ment and/or by stockholder dictate at future shareholder meetings. That is another goal of the AIR Program, to have American businesses freely adopt some of proposed operational Changes into their enterprise and promote its benefits within their community. It would be an economic revolution in America.

o   o   o   o

Your challenge, my fellow American citizen in reviewing these pages, is to *objectively* consider these sincerely prepared words and the common sense of these deliberate and admittedly radical Changes to these National Infra-structure Industries.

To guard against the normal human responses that say – that could never happen – or this guy must be dreaming or crazy – or there is no use in trying because they would never let us do that. Those are typical reactions that We common people have had throughout history. That is until they have had enough – and then Change happens and too often violence was the path taken to correct the abuses they had suffered under.

I observe that the American public, the Silent Majority now finds itself at, if not well beyond the point of total frustration. I know this from the reaction I receive from folks regarding the content of these 27 proposals.

In the early 1980's when I was first presenting the National Drug Reform

(NDR) proposal to people containing the full legalization of marijuana and the aggressive application of the Death Penalty against those that of their own free will decide to continue selling hard drugs — those are the typical human responses that came back to me. They were <u>not</u> necessarily against what they were hearing, but "they will never <u>allow</u> that to happen – or they will not <u>let</u> us do that" was a usual reaction.

However, as the 80's passed through the 90's, people's frustration with the failed National Drug Policy changed and their attitudes toward the need for real, national Change did as well. The general public's awareness that such a long-standing problem (in this case Drug Policy) could be fixed, but was deliberately not being fixed by our elected leadership due to Special Interest lobbying control over Congress, was overcoming their natural hesitance toward challenging the government. Over the years the typical person's perspective had evolved — to how <u>soon</u> we could implement something like the NDR Proposal.

At the end of 2007, the whole Congress had "earned" a public Approval rating scraping bottom at around 11% or as it should be presented – their Disapproval rating has climbed to 89%. Another session of the House and Senate have earned the combined title of a "do nothing" Congress. Which means they are doing little to nothing to secure the Common Good, but are working so diligently to Preserve, Protect, and Defend the status quo that the Few desire.

The result for the American public is that our society and the economy that most of us must live in, only continues to degrade and the status of the line items on the public's Grievance List grows worse and new issues are added.

o   o   o   o

Our challenge, therefore, is to prepare for the domestic battle of our lifetime. CS2 in general, and An American Agenda in particular are presented to help clarify where we really are today and what we can <u>really</u> begin do about it – and <u>now</u>!

The remaining content of Part 3 will first test our <u>individual</u> imagination and then our <u>collective</u> resolve in wrestling away and securing control over <u>our</u> national destiny — rather than remaining the mere pawns and peasants of the self-serving Few as they continue to orchestrate and decide it for us...

<u>Are Now Challenged</u>

CS2 is calling upon Americans to join in the final battle for control over America's National System. To confront the negative ways that our country *really works today* – and insure that *our Common Will dictates* the positive ways it shall *really work tomorrow!*

Our national ancestors stood and fought against a few thousand years of governmental tyranny and established a form of government intended and designed to serve the Common Good of the Masses instead of the pleasure of the Few.

As is mentioned a few times in CS2, the other side of the *Sword of Tyranny* still remains to be dulled.

We the People are now challenged to bring about a Democratic Economic System designed to benefit the Common Good of us all. A fair and balanced system that is designed under the Rights granted to us by our U.S. Constitution. It will be a binding, economic reconciliation and revolution that will directly confront the "natural evolution" of a Have/Have-Not society that is the cruel norm in too many countries, and is aggressively working to control all aspects of American society.

We cannot – We will not allow this to continue. It is nothing less than an Economic Reformation that is at the Democratic heart and soul of our Second and Final American Revolution. Yes, We the People are *now challenged* to confront the excessive power gained by the Kings and Queens of Industry, along with their campaign funded ministers now serving in the United States Congress, and the all too cooperative current inhabitant of the White House and his side-kick.

o   o   o   o

Many will initially question how We can demand such radical (though publicly practical) Changes to corporate entities, thinking what Power do We have to direct such Industry restructurings? Our short answer is because it is Our nation, it is not owned by the Few, the Oil Industry, the Defense Industry, or the Bankers for a few prime examples. We the People are to rule America, not be ruled as some certainly appear to believe!

The fed-up American colonists told the King what Changes they required via the *Declaration of Independence* and asserted the military Power required to make it happen — thus creating their nation, the *U.S. Constitution*, and the *U.S. Bill of Rights*.

Today, We the People are declaring that certain Irresponsible Entities will no longer be allowed to exert selfish influence over the Common Good. We too, will assert the necessary electoral muscle and submit the legislative Dictates designed to adjust the National System imbalances, and all under the legal umbrella of the U.S. Constitution that the Founders intentionally provided for us in order to deal with such wrong conditions. We will also reclaim the *U.S. Bill of Rights* as our own and restore its Honor from the damage done under Bush II.

Thanks to the U.S. Constitution that our national ancestors so thoughtfully provided for us, We the People of today will not be required to fire a single shot to successfully conduct our historical revolution!

And to be *crystal clear*, thus far several difficult public problems and their workable solutions have already been presented for your consideration in CS2. However, *none of them* are as volatile, or as required in order to secure the nation's future than those that will initiate and bring to a successful conclusion the binding reconciliation between:

- Business and Industry Interests
- The Un-elected Politically Powerful
- The Common Good

And the Common Good of our citizens and American society shall prevail!

o   o   o   o

The Big Picture

Why Implement the AIR Program

There are two (2) overriding and fully justifiable reasons — not excuses — why this initial set of six industries and others will be required to corporately suffer the mandatory AIR Program Reorganization process. Overall, the Plain Truth *reality* is that the entire U.S. economy – the engine that drives our National System — needs to be prudently over-hauled and soon – as in yesterday!

First, the necessary re-restructuring of key components of the economic mechanism that drives our National System *cannot be a voluntary exercise for business and Industry*. **Or it will never be accomplished!**

Second, We must confront and "put away" the foolish concept and the national fraud of the "eternal growth" economic model – the myth — that was born in the late 1940's and early 1950's. Then We must move the National System rapidly into a practical and realistic "eternal maintenance" economic model that will carry us ALL into a viable and controllable future.

I have been thinking about writing that down for a long time.

o   o   o   o

The Re-Structuring of Business and Industry Cannot be Voluntarily

"It is always easier to expand then contract"

That simple analogy realistically applies whether we are talking about the right-sizing the National System from unrealistic economic growth expectations – or, drawing-in our own waistlines! The required prudent adjustments in practical expectations and day-to-day routine must be made in order to avoid undesirable results.

In the first case the economy needs to be deliberately and with absolute, pre-meditated planning be prudently re-tooled, or it will be driven right of the cliff – it is already being pushed toward the breaking point into a clear Recession, if not into a Crash and Depression. That destructive, economic cycle is historically well-documented and "those that do not learn from the lessons of the history, are doomed to repeat them". It is time to deliberately recognize, acknowledge, and break the cycle — or it will be the end of us!

In the second case that many of us can directly relate to, it is to acknowledge that our somewhat lax, free-will habits of personal consumption (food, drink, smoking, etc.) having not been offset with a proper balance of exercise results in us carrying excess weight, causing stress on our overall physical condition. Often that imbalance manifests itself in various self-abuse illnesses, diabetes, lung cancer, emphysema, heart disease, or an ever-loving heart attack! And none of those ills happen to involve *illegal* drug use!

o   o   o   o

The first case of course is of collective importance and the necessity of the pre-meditated planning for the prudent re-tooling of our economy is what this Introduction and the six (6) proposals are all about.

The second case is of individual importance and is touched upon in Proposal 16 — Physical Fitness of Our Children. Increased concern about our personal health will be a natural by-product the implementing National Health Care Insurance for ALL Americans. Once we know we are all footing the bill for our individual and collective health, we will naturally begin to expect each other to take a bit better care of ourselves. Civil Responsibility as applied to personal health. What a concept!

That increased public awareness of our health, is not what the Medical Health Industry (in their private moments) wants us to be concerned with. Face it. The industry is structured to fix us when we break or are in the process of breaking down. They do not make their money on keeping us healthy.

o   o   o   o

In the first case – in extreme situations like where our National System finds itself today, the management that is driving it must be removed before they irresponsibly drive the economy (and the environment) head-on into a Wall! Rational people with an objective sense of the Big Picture must *step forward* and take charge to properly remedy the situation to avoid certain national disaster.

In the second case – although other people and society in general can challenge an individual to improve their health, each person decides what they will or won't do about their health.

Overall, individuals must have authority over and take responsibility for their personal destiny. However, self-serving individuals cannot be allowed to make decisions that have far reaching, potentially damaging, if not catastrophic consequences over the fate of other people, businesses, industries, the nation, or the global environment.

No one ever has, or ever will be granted that level of authority, at least not in our Democratic society!

o   o   o   o

"Our" Dysfunctional National Infrastructure Industries

The AIR proposals focus on a group of industries that are in some unavoidable manner woven into our economic system and impact the lives of virtually every American, each family, and other businesses on a monthly if not daily basis. Therefore, as previously stated this somewhat odd set of bed-fellows has been categorized as *National Infrastructure Industries* (NII).

There are of course other entities (e.g., Coal, Natural Gas, the Automobile industry or what is left of it, and the Commodities and Spot Markets where someone intentionally and wrongly once put Oil, to name a few) that could easily be added to this list and will be dealt with in time. But for now, those at the head of the Irresponsible Industry list, that most deserve to be there, and demand our immediate, aggressive attention are:

- The Medical Insurance Industry
- The Pharmaceutical Industry
- The Tobacco Industry
- The Oil/Petroleum Industry
- The Banking and Credit Card Industry
- The Defense Industry

Restructuring Existing Industries

The proposals presented under this heading are focused upon a core group of heavy-hitter industries that are critical to our economic system and the impact the lives of virtually every American good or bad on a regular basis. That's why this particular group has also been categorized as National Infrastructure Industries (NII).

There are *of course* some other industries that could be added, but for now the group presented for Public Review and National Reconciliation is:

22	Health Care Insurance for ALL Americans
23	The Pharmaceutical Industry
24	The Tobacco (Nailing the Most Deadly Drug) Industry
25	The Oil Industry
26	The Banking and Credit Card Industry
27	The Defense (Military Industrial Complex) Industry

How *We the People* determine to come to terms with such entities will define the heart and soul of our Second American Revolution, and to a very, great extent — our National Destiny, as well.

The De-Profitization of Infrastructure Industries

"De-Profitization" is a core concept of the American Industry Re-Structuring – AIR Program.

The concept of the "De-Profitization" of Infrastructure Industries firmly declares – that certain of our national industries and large individual businesses when found publicly appropriate, will prudently be restructured from their current operational charter and their for-profit, stock-held organizational status – some business entities running under a non-profit structure will also be converted. This will be an ethically correct, civilly responsible, and non-negotiable, national 'reckoning' of their currently excessive power and influence within day-to-day America.

o o o o

We must all acknowledge that real Change within any country's National System creates both winners and losers – it always has and it always will.

At the national level, Change has often been chaotic and violent as in our American Revolution, the French Revolution, and the Russian Revolution – when the Many have finally said, "enough". And countrymen fought and killed each other in turbulent, domestic reconciliations.

However, Change can be accomplished peacefully — as we will do it, in sharp contrast to the way it occurred in those domestically fought wars of bitter national reconciliation – between the Haves and the Have-Nots of their time — when the Few had exercised abusive power over the Many.

In our National Change scenario the Common Good of American citizens, workers, and families, as well as other domestic businesses will be the Winners. To be sure, Loss cannot mean destruction, because we are talking about our own people. However there will also be prudent limits to the considerations granted. Buying stock or investing in any corporation inherently involves *risk* — just ask the employees of Enron and some others.

In our peaceful, yet very tedious, domestic Revolution we will reasonably facilitate the transition of those *legislatively forced* to lose – the various businesses and especially the employees and existing stockholders – to the newly re-structured National System.

Remember, I warned at the start that these contents were to be taken as seriously as a heart attack and I was not being humorous! Therefore, everything is on the table. And the table is being set. We can get to there from here.

o o o o

The AIR Program – *Rules of Engagement*

The New Rules

Have no illusions regarding what is before us, my fellow Americans — this is where the rubber meets the road – and the bullet meets the bone!

For the Common Good of 300,000,000 American citizens and our Democratic society – to prevail over the naturally occurring evolution of Corporate Greed, the People shall now be required to debate and commonly agree as to how certain business and government entities will be *permitted* to operate within the American National System.

The entire essence of our current dysfunctional national condition and all that we must now determine to face together in order to Promote and Preserve our desired American way-of-life, is summarized that single paragraph.

o   o   o   o

Logically, we will acknowledge that certain 'essential components' of the National System have become operationally dysfunctional with regard to the Common Good of the people, and the economy we all must depend upon. The un-elected leadership of such business entities is continuously taking care of themselves without concern for the Common Good and all under the cover of "my job is making money for the stockholders." And unfortunately for us, our elected national leadership either willingly promotes the growing abuse or just stands around with a mystified look on his or her face.

That increasingly counter-productive (to the Common Good) national condition not only hits our families, but most businesses small and large as we find ourselves being forced to tolerate avoidable economic conditions (need I say Oil). Forced to tolerate such Economic Oppression by the unspoken, unwritten, and non-legislated "RIGHT" – that is silently being claimed by various commercial and bureaucratic entities.

This un-Democratic, subtle (at least until Bush II came to power), dictatorial Consolidation of Power will not be allowed to continue! *Reason* shall call this regressive economic oppression for what it is – the greed and self-serving domination of the Few at the literal expense in dollars and actual lives among the Many. Priceless American *lives are needlessly lost* every day due to a broken Medical system, the worthless National Drug Policy, and the fully optional and now failed Iraq war — to name just a few sources.

Someone *please* answer me this question. When in the last 50 years my fellow Americans did the *lives of our people become so cheap*? Worth so little that they are thrown away on such <u>preventable</u> problems. An undeclared Legislative Kill Factor (LKF) against We the People, that benefits certain self-serving, civilly irresponsible businesses, government agencies, and Special Interests has somehow been written into our national laws and policies. Think about that. It is the Plain Truth!

There is no common sense in any this — it is purely profits and control, over people and peace. "Beware ye, also of false profits".

This national Status Quo — that has increasingly been servicing the Special Interest — will be thoughtfully and deliberately confronted and restructured with the consent of the Many — in order to Preserve, Protect, and Defend the Common Good. Thomas Paine framed changing the status quo and confronting the obvious flaws of colonial America,

> "…, a long habit of not thinking a thing *wrong*, gives it the superficial appearance of being *right*, and raises at first the formidable outcry in the defense of custom. But the tumult soon subsides. *Time makes more converts than reason.*"

Certain business entities on the domestic front and those with increasing foreign entanglements (need I say Oil, again) have had their day and frankly their way with us! The People and the Common Good will now be served.

Key operational components of the National System that impact the successful operation of business large and small in America – will no longer be directed by faceless corporate executives and Boards of Directors, a politically powerful minority, and a nationally embarrassing and un-American foreign policy. The tail shall no longer be allowed to wag the dog!

This particular set of six industies will be involuntarily re-directed from their purely self-serving priorities and lobbying, to charters of operation that only promote the Common Good of our people, other businesses in the National System, and the society as a whole. The long held public perceptions of and the actual utilization of these Entities within our National System will be made-over to serve the Common Good of America's economy and society.

Again, these prudent and practical Changes to the American National System will <u>not</u> be <u>optional</u>, negotiable or voluntary!

Rules of Engagement — *Stockholders*

Being selected for implementation of the AIR program guidelines will result in the *mandatory restructuring* of certain publicly held (stockholder involved), as well as any "non-profit" corporations in the subject industry (e.g., medical insurance). Some basic points for consideration in the restructuring of such industries and particular corporations include:

- Any relevant stock/commodity trading will be strictly controlled and would be halted, as needed.
- The eventual removal from the stock/commodity markets in some cases.
- Freezing of share price (of publicly held corporations) on the stock markets at a publicly, reasonable point in time.
- Having the share price fixed for eventual buy-back.
- Existing stockholders would be bought out over a number of years to realistically spread the expense.
- Existing corporate assets could be sold off (to American buyers) to help expedite the buy-out process.
- Stock buy-back will make all that investment capital available for other purposes within the economy. A very good thing!

These publicly acceptable Changes will be kept plain and simple, very public, and will not be negotiable. No back-room deals will be permitted. New and publicly practical laws will be enacted, foolish laws and loopholes will be *rapidly* revised or eliminated, legislative corrections made where possible, and routine patterns of corporate greed will be permanently reconciled to the Common Good.

Changing a Bone Marrow Level Mindset

In the practical conversion of our National System from a *Growth*-based to a *Maintenance*-based economy, stockholders must be viewed in a new and initially disturbing light. In the beginning, they helped build what are today's large corporations and industries. The profits came easy through the 1960's and then started to get more difficult to obtain the old fashion way. Economic recessions, Market mini-crashes, things like the Savings and Loan debacle, and the out-sourcing of millions of American jobs and industries that began in the 1990's – are the manifestations of the growing global marketplace.

All the while, the on-going demand for annual profits and stockholder dividends in spite of a more competitive and shrinking marketplace does not stop!

It has caused stock-held corporation management to do whatever it takes to "create or take" profits, rather than getting them 'naturally' through increased sales. In the US, it is a fundamental reason for the out-of-control, Special Interest, Power struggle for control over Congressional and State legislators. The fight for control (in a Democratic society) over the legislation that would let business do whatever it wants to and direct tax-payer funding wherever business and industry desires in order to create or take — those "false" profits. Without any sense of Civil Responsibility for what their actions put upon the National System or the American people.

> Most recently this struggle for the retention or attainment of Political Control was clearly demonstrated in the final weeks of the 2006 Congressional Election – when the Republican Party knew they were at great risk of losing control of not only the House, but the Senate, as well. They dropped all rhetoric about issues, and challenged people to vote along Party lines to keep them in Power — which after all is all, that Congress and the lobbyists really care about. And as soon as the Democrats obtained the majority in both Houses of Congress, the lobbyists shifted the majority of the dollars their way.

The six (6) Existing Industries were selected for Re-structuring based on the fact their lobbying machines are now controlling and directing Congress, and some Federal agencies, and are happily, ringing money out of our individual and national pocketbooks – with obviously no concern for the economic, health, and environmental devastation it is creating and making worse.

That group and others are having an absolute field day with us, under the reign of the "whatever you desire" Bush II administration. My concern for a sometime is how much more damage that group and others will be permitted to put upon us before Bush II and his sidekick are out of office.

That is the Dark Side of the Big Picture. It is now time for *common sense* to be applied with a hammer!

Rules of Engagement — *Employees*

Along with the stockholders a given corporation's existing employees must be of concern during the restructuring process. Personally I feel that the fate of existing employees — the workers in these scenarios is more important.

The intent of AIR Program is not to eliminate businesses or the jobs that they provide. That would be the exact opposite of what America and our economy requires. In making some of these industries less redundant e.g., the Medical Insurance Industry — jobs will naturally be lost. I said Change makes winners and losers and this is where it hits home.

The initial purpose of the AIR Program and the absolute necessity for the sake of our economy is to overhaul certain industries that are draining our individual pockets and our federal and state tax revenue — and all in the name of stockholder dividends and excess executive compensation. Look at list again and you will see what I mean. The economically reforming those industries and some others such as the Automobile Industry along the way, some jobs will be lost – underline period. That is the way it has always worked.

We go back to Proposal 7, the U.S. Re-Employment System. The focus of that system will be the placement of American workers in jobs and assisting in their re-training and relocation if required around country. This goes directly to the hiring rules that state that American citizens will be employed first, and will have absolute preference before anyone non-citizen. They will have preference in attaining the better jobs that provide better pay and benefits. And to reiterate, that preference is absolute for all taxpayer funds jobs – federal, state, city, local, etc. Americans First!

A Gross Example of Redundant Overhead

While much of this "right-sizing" operation in the subject industries will not require mass lay-offs or will be a gradual reduction where workers can be assimilated into other parts of the job market, the Medical Insurance Industry (MII) will cause a stir. While there is redundant employment in the corporations that will be eliminated when those entities are merged, there are numerous State and/or County level jobs that will no longer be required. They only exist due to the gross inefficiency of the current Medical System. Each state regulates medical coverage that the greatest extent possible and it is a nightmare.

That is part of the reason why it has been difficult for the MII corporations to merge as they want to – to cross state boundaries. They have to adhere to coverage regulations in every state and sometimes at the city level as well, and it can take years to convert from old policy guidelines. The administrative redundancy is part of the reason why the original Blue Cross and Blue Shield nation-wide network had over sixty (60) separate non-profit corporate entities.

Under the new National Medical Insurance system that will cover ALL

Americans, there will be <u>very</u> few medical plans and medical coverage options will be standardized (and the stupidity and waste of annual re-en-rollment exercises will cease). The need for these regulatory jobs at all levels of government will be eliminated – and they will go away! So those civil servants will be available for transfer to other jobs or will enter the Private employment sector. That is what must and will happen.

o   o   o   o

This is all about positive economic Change – about Change that is deliber-ate and controlled to the greatest extent possible. Continuous and viable employment is critical to the quality of life of our people and the strength of our "consumer-based" economy. Let it be understood that the employ-ment of our people – of our citizens is the highest priority. This is not another management game aimed at eliminating or out-sourcing American jobs. Enough said.

At Their Beginning – *The Founding Entrepreneurs*

In years past, the Founding Entrepreneurs of today's large corporations, initially sought simply to build a business and provide income for their family and for their employees.

I have termed such basic forms of non-stock encumbered businesses, an Income Generating Entity or IGE. As discussed earlier in Proposal 19 — Take Back Industries, IGEs produce goods and/or services in the economy and provide local employment, income, and some level of benefits to the owner/operator and their employees. These are the types of businesses that built America and are absolutely required to sustain our economy.

Over the years many of those companies evolved into huge stock-held cor-porate entities. In time those founding men and women were succeeded by a series of corporate executives and Board of Directors that in recent de-cades are increasingly driven by spreadsheets and are primarily interested in stockholder dividends and their increasingly excessive compensation. Further, most of that management has a corporate field of vision that is no more than eighteen (18) months into the future, at best! That is the basic reason why it took the American Automobile Industry twenty (20) years to figure out they were getting their corporate butts kicked by foreign im-ports! And they are still dragging one foot.

> <u>Technically</u>, and the only justifiable rationale (*excuse*) for the civ-illy irresponsible actions of the un-elected management of these corporate entities is to acknowledge that — however their busi-

ness decisions may negatively impact the average American, another business or the overall economy — is simply <u>not</u> part of their job description. The Big Picture is <u>not</u> what they were hired to worry about! Some of them have even had the guts to acknowledge that publicly!

The Plain Truth is that a given executive's (freewill) ability to ignore of the Common Good of the people and of the nation, if necessary, in favor of the corporate bottom line and their own paychecks — is the very reason why *they <u>do</u> get paid the big bucks!*

If they would not do whatever needed to be done, they <u>would</u> <u>be</u> <u>fired</u>! The (not so) poor sole would be thrown off the plane in their golden parachute — and someone willing to do that job would replace them. It is all a big game my fellow Americans, and *We* are taking a beating.

Are there any questions?

<u>Rules of Engagement</u> — *Management*

Being selected for implementation of the AIR program guidelines will in most cases require the complete retirement of all existing Senior Management. That sentence probably woke up a few people, but as is known in the country, if you want to kill a snake, you must cut off its head! However, unlike the French, we will not be utilizing the guillotine! A few pertinent points for consideration include:

- Existing senior management will be retired probably within six (6) months. All golden parachutes would be honored, <u>but</u> all pay-outs will be reviewed for any last minute game playing.
- This includes full replacement of the existing Board of Directors.
- All future executive's stock option benefits and golden parachutes will be non-existent. And any "potential" bonuses will be based on new criteria.
- New management from the lower ranks will be installed whenever possible, rather than going outside. Those people run the day-to-day operation anyway.
- All executive salaries will have a ceiling of for the sake of discussion say, one to two million dollars a year – <u>no</u> <u>less</u>. I am very sorry, but running today's major corporations is just not rocket science and there is no shortage of very qualified people that could easily do those jobs.

To Seal the Deal – An Offer Some Cannot Refuse

And, one more item for our collective and hard consideration. There will be a <u>one-time</u> offer made to help some of the existing Management to exit shall we say, a bit more gracefully.

We will offer to hold them <u>and</u> their management <u>predecessors</u> (and <u>all</u> employees) "harmless" and free from any and <u>all</u> forms of law suits (including civil suits) due to any acts of omission and commission that occurred in their companies prior to the Restructuring start date.

I am not a conspiracy theorist and I am not a betting man, but, I do firmly believe that this "one-time stay out of court and maybe out of jail free offer" will find great appeal among some of those individuals! And considering the set of industries we are here focusing on – well just think about it for a while.

o   o   o   o

AIR Program – The Entity Re-Structuring Levels Overview

The AIR program will provide for **"levels of management, organizational and operational restructuring"** that will be applied to given industry or business strictly dependent upon what is required to achieve a functional reconciliation within the National System — one that is found to be acceptable with an informed American electorate – our citizens. The Restructuring Approach selected for a given industry and/or business will be tailored to best service to *our* nation's short and long-term economic health and the Common Good of Americans.

As a result of the overall AIR Program implementation, another "era of greed" in the American national voyage will be brought to an end — just as the Robber Barons, the Banks, the Savings and Loans, and the Wall Street scenarios of the past were eventually "dealt with" by legislation after recession or the occasional Crash! Now is the time for these Infrastructure Industries to be put in their proper place for the nation's sake – made to support the National System rather than irresponsibly controlling and pillaging it.

This time the National System and economy will have a controlled landing, not a horrific one followed by a reactionary clean-up exercise. At least as gentle a landing as possible considering the condition the Usual Suspects have placed us in. And We will do it right this time! Therefore, it will be the last *era of greed* that our country will be required to endure and to finally confront ever again. Period!

The Five Entity Restructuring Levels (ERL)

The following write-ups provide a basic overview of the changes to be considered in the Five (5) Entity Restructuring Levels (ERL) of the AIR Program, which are:

- ERL 1 – Operational Reorganization
- ERL 2 – Existing Management Retirement
- ERL 3 – New Management Structure and Charter
- ERL 4 – Stock Trading and Pricing Control
- ERL 5 – Conversion of IGE Model

This is an initial, but functionally, solid framework of Levels and Guidelines that will certainly be added to and refined as the AIR Program implementation progresses.

It is fair to point out that most of the industries in the initial set of six (6) industries will experience the <u>full</u> <u>force</u> of the AIR Program implementation. Most will be looking at a phased implementation against the levels and <u>may</u> not reach full ELR-Five implementation that involves the complete elimination, via buy-out, of all existing stockholders.

Other industries and businesses will logically be added to the AIR Program implementation, such as the Automobile and other Energy related entities — not all of them will not require a "complete" AIR Re-structuring exercise to come to proper terms with the National System and the American public.

I do believe that as the American business community becomes more familiar with the AIR Program Restructuring System, that some of them and/or their stockholders will seek to <u>voluntarily</u> utilize certain of the features it offers. It could facilitate practical Changes in their existing business model to be more in line with the *realities* of national and world economic conditions.

Bullet points are presented to indicate the type of Changes to be considered and/or applied depending upon the industry or company in question.

Now let's take a look at the Five (5) Entity Restructuring Levels (ERL) of the AIR Program.

Entity Re-Structuring Level 1 – Operational Reorganization

- When applicable, as in the example of the Medical Insurance Industry, redundant business entities will be operationally consolidated for both reduce administrative overhead and increase operational efficiency. This is the normal practice when similar business entities merge.

- The resulting operational structure could tolerate a prudent amount of redundant employment if deemed practical for the overall good of the public in given geographic areas, e.g., medical insurance claims offices, bank branches, etc.

- Any Out-sourcing activities of the domestic business operation and/or staffing would be ceased. Past outsourcing would be reviewed in light of the new business and financial model. When practical, staffing and operations that had previously been out-sourced would be reclaimed. We will reverse the flow.

The *Industry Management Consortium* — A Practical Management Hybrid

A *"consortium"* according to Mr. Webster is, "an agreement, combination, or group (as of companies) formed to undertake an enterprise beyond the resources of any one member."

To efficiently approach the AIR Program Re-Structuring of some industries a viable, new management entity would be utilized. There is a practical management facility to be created that lies *somewhere between* the purely privately-run and the often screamed about government-run models. It is the Industry Management Consortium (IMC).

The IMC function within the National System will vary from industry-to-industry and business-to-business depending on what practical form best accommodates the Common Good within our society. It will be designed to insure a viable future for the American people. And all this will be done with the "informed consent" of the American Electorate — our citizens — and no one else.

Among the initial six Existing Industry proposals, the IMC approach will be utilized to realistically restructure the Health Care Insurance and Petroleum (Big Oil) Industries, at least. That sentence will undoubtedly get some attention! The form and function of each IMC would vary by the industry, as would the scope of its authority, and the duration of its charter which in most cases will be permanent.

This will not be a re-structuring where the government would assume day-to-day control over these Entities. At the same time the existing structure driven by civilly irresponsible industry executives can no longer be afforded or tolerated, and *We* will not allow it to continue.

The United States Congress will not be negotiating the individual IMC configuration with existing management. We are no going to let that stupidity happen. We will no longer allow secret National Energy Policy meetings between the Administration and Energy Industry lobbyists. We will no longer allow Health Care Reform legislation to be written by the Medical and Pharmaceutical lobbyists.

Congress will only be responsible for writing and enacting the legislation required to implement the AIR Program driven Re-structuring of the targeted industries and businesses. They would simply use these CS2 proposals as their baseline blueprint – much of the work is already done for them. And We will be watching very closely.

A practical set of industry-by-industry IMCs will be created, as required to determine how to best apply the AIR Program — Entity Restructuring Levels (ELR) to the subject Industry or business. In affect, certain *American businesses* would be advising on how to best reorganize other *American industries and businesses*. The absolute intent will be to assist in making their operations more efficient and to benefit and protecting National System as a whole. Examples to include Health Care for ALL Americans and driving down the barrel price of Oil.

o   o   o   o

Entity Re-Structuring Level 2 – Existing Management Retirement

- There will be a mandatory retirement (exit) of all existing Senior Management and Board of Directors in the first year of the AIR Program implementation, if not within the first six (6) months. You cannot Change things if the Old Guard is still in place.

- The "Last of the Golden Parachutes" to be resolved with exit of the existing senior management. Those packages will be scrutinized for any last minute abuses.

- The official signing of the "Individual Non-Suit Liability Agreement" that will hold existing and previous management and employees *harmless and without criminal and financial liability* from any and all future legal actions against them for any acts of omission and/or commission – by any <u>and</u> all parties, <u>permanently</u>!

- The form and function of a new Board of Directors would be developed. Such a Board would be required to provide general oversight responsibilities for the proper functioning of the operation against the new Charter. They would not to run the operation, <u>or</u> be a meaningless entity and an avoidable expense to the bottom line.

Entity Re-Structuring Level 3 – New Management and Charter

- Development and <u>assignment</u> of a new public-interest focused Corporate Charter and Mission Statement.

  This prudent action will if many cases functionally *reverse* existing Special Interest lobbying objectives – which in turn will decrease the need for and therefore the expense to the bottom line for such activities. Yes. There is more than one way to attack to lobbying machine!

- New management would be put in place and if at all possible would be promoted from within. Often those people are the ones running the operation in the first place. Internal people also have the most to gain by keeping the operation running and so their jobs in place.

- Executive compensation would be capped in the one to two million dollar range or less with adequate perks befitting the position and job demands. Stock options would not be offered. Any annual bonus would be based upon results against the new Charter, and would <u>not</u> be excessive. No Golden Parachutes would be issued. There will be <u>no</u> shortage of qualified candidates for these positions, regardless of the industry.

Entity Re-Structuring Level 4 – Stock Trading and Pricing Control

Stock Trading Control

- For stock-held corporate entities the selling and therefore the buying of stock will be suspended until further notice – in some cases permanently.

- The stock price would also be frozen and would be assessed and possibly re-valued in light of the Re-organization.

- There would be full public disclosure regarding what entities and/or persons are major shareholders in the subject corporation(s). That could prove to be very interesting to the public.

- For non-profit entities, annual executive bonus compensation will be held and any pay-outs will be reviewed and approved before disbursements are issued. This would only be an issue in the year that re-organization occurs. Any bonus plans after that will be subject to guideline controls.

- All corporate assets will be frozen and therefore would not available for sale. Any sales executed in the months prior to the beginning of the Restructuring process will be scrutinized, any abuses will be severely dealt with and subject sales reversed if deemed appropriate.

- Annual profits would have a fixed ceiling placed on them for a number of years. An annual cap of five (5) percent or less (especially in the first few years) would be put in place, regardless of the on-going profitability of the operation. The profit cap would be evaluated based upon economic conditions.

- Stock dividends will be capped appropriately, regardless of the on-going profitability of the operation. Stockholders would retain their asset, but the return would be capped. Stockholders and Wall Street may not like that approach, but it is better than being Enron'd.

- Remaining profit revenue would be put back into the "domestic" operation and a portion set-aside for use in the stock buy-back process.

Pricing Control

- It is very simple — the dreaded practice of Price Controls will be utilized.

- For at least a few years, the pricing of goods and/or services in selected business entities will be controlled, probably be capped, and/or decreased for some prudent period of time,

- The simplest concept in business math is that the less demand there is for profit, then the pricing of goods and/or services offered by a business can be reduced, therefore making them are more competitive in the domestic (and global as applicable) market place. And helping to control (possibly decrease) the cost-of-living for the American public.

- The existing senior management will fight this feature out of custom, while their replacements will be far more open to the concept. Out with the Custom, and in with the practical Change.

Entity Re-Structuring Level 5 – Conversion of IGE Model

- Conversion to the Income Generating Entity (IGE) corporate model. Ultimately some industries, such as Health Care insurance will be completely divested of stockholders and revert back to the initial business model described above. Back to basics.

- An existing stockholder buy-back plan with options that could vary by industry would be determined and executed over a multi-year period.

- The new senior management and existing employees would again be working to provide quality goods and services for local to national customers. And the public would know this and would support domestically based enterprises.

- Foreign sales would be of secondary importance, if they mattered at all to a given business.

- Overall the decreased demand for annual stockholder dividends, decreased profit demands, and decreased expenses like Health Care Insurance will make these domestically based commercial enterprises more competitive in their pricing, which is intended to make their goods and services more desirable in the market place.

Why Write This Down

My primary hope is that what you are reading with regard to the AIR Program's industry restructuring actually sounds like what you have been waiting for *someone* to put forth for some time. I know this is what "I" had been waiting for our national leadership to present, be they Republican or Democrat, but they never have and probably never will.

So I decided to work on figuring it out for myself and write down so that we all could review it, improve on the processes offered herein, calmly resolve any issues, reach Common Agreement, and then together take deliberate and unstoppable action for the Common Good. And that advise, consent, and action scenario applies to all the proposals found in *The Second Coming of Common Sense.*

We Are Already in "Sudden Death" Overtime

The benefits to be realized by the AIR Program Re-structuring of these industries and others, as well as the other publicly, viable proposals in An American Agenda is too long overdue.

It will require – the publication of CS2 as early in 2008 possible, the attraction of the public and press to it, the general acceptance of its content, the national debate over its contents for the remainder of the 2008 Presidential and Congressional campaigns, and the historic declaration by the involved electorate that An American Agenda be implemented. That may seem like a tall order, but when the American public gets fired up We can do anything — and I believe this should do it.

During the national debate over the An American Agenda and other concepts CS2 presents, it should be made clear to the current Congress, the entire business community, and any Presidential hopeful that these proposals will have a Legislative Effective Date of January 1, 2009 (1-1-9) or sooner (if the current Congress decides to do something constructive before the November 2008 election).

Realistically my fellow Americans, the vast majority of the legislation required to implement the Agenda proposals will not even be touched until the new President and Congress are sworn into office in January 2009. The necessary legislation that would eventually enacted – much of it by July 1, 2009 — will have a retro-active Effective Date of 1-1-9! And the U.S. Supreme Court will need to get up to speed on certifying the retro-active legislation approach — without needless lawsuits. They too will be challenged to do their part!

That 1-1-9 Legislative Effective Date will be part of what the Electorate would be voting for in November 2008. This November Congress and the White House may really learn what getting a "mandate" means!

With particular regard to the Existing Industries, the subject businesses and corporations will know that their world could very well change as of 1-1-9, and they should therefore make alternate plans for physical year 2009. So get those Golden Parachutes ready – We the People are coming, and We are not in a negotiating frame of mind.

Our Example of Dramatic Public Driven Change

When the American colonists boldly took on England's King George III, his ministers, and the National System of the British Empire — they put it all on the line (and on the table). On July 4, 1776 when the *selected* representatives of the common people (all of whom the King viewed as peasants) stood together and made their *Declaration of Independence* — the war that had been simmering since 1774 truly began.

In that war, it was the brave *Few* that took up arms acting for the Many — went to war for themselves, their families, and their neighbors. In the end, approximately 25,000 of them or roughly one (1) percent of the colonial population lost their lives in that struggle. Against America's population today that would be about 3,000,000 of our people — some 900 lives lost from every county in our country or nearly 6,900 for each of the 435 U.S. Congressional Districts.

> By contrast the Afghanistan and Iraq wars have thus far cost the average county, in lost military lives, less than two (2) of our people and less than ten (10) for each U.S. Congressional District. Too many precious lives lost.

For a moment consider that level of human sacrifice that represented on the part of the colonial population. They were not professional soldiers — they were farmers, tradesman, merchants, and doctors one day – and some were dead in battle shortly thereafter. They represented the nation's first National Guard setting the standard for those that are bravely fighting for our country this very day.

Just as during the Revolution, these are citizen soldiers that have paid the ultimate price in battle or will carry the scars of war with them for the rest of their lives, and they come from communities in every state and DC. And it is truly, bad enough for our regular military to lose a single life or suffer such wounds. God bless all those that serve in our military.

o o o o

The Critical Battles of Our Second American Revolutionary War

We will constructively and solely for the sake of the Common Good of our citizens conduct binding arbitration with the six (6) *infrastructure* industries previously mentioned — five of which are currently pillaging our individual and collective pocketbooks.

And the sixth industry that is only killing around 500,000 of us every year – some 1,370 American lives taken every 24 hours – equaling a 9-11 every three days. Thus offering the absolute, ultimate example in *successful* Special Interest lobbying! Yes, that was sarcastic.

o   o   o   o

Having reviewed this Introduction you now have a better understanding where this is all headed. Therefore, you can see that no matter how radical or aggressive you may have viewed what was offered in some of the first 21 proposals, these six present the Front Lines in our Second American Revolution.

We the People of 2008 are presented with a choice strangely similar to the one that our National Ancestors of 1776 confronted. Our Decision is – to collectively take control of the forces of the Few that are now abusing the Many and create a Democratic environment for our selves and our neighbors – **or** – to individually be satisfied to be treated as and to live in the future as peasants.

THEY stood, physically fought a war, and won it, and then created our Democratic form of Government.

WE could now stand, legislatively fight our war, and win it, and create a Democratic Economic System to compliment that Democratic form of Government they gave us — thus We would finish the Design of People-driven Government and successfully completing the Great American Experiment.

We do have a choice.

o   o   o   o

As I know you can imagine after considering the six Industries that are such National System heavyweights, that they along with their entrenched Congressional lobbying machines will react as though the sky will fall when they hear what is coming at them. Talk about *screamers*!

In truth these Entities must be viewed as doing the American economy and our people far more harm than the practical good they could and should be providing. And all in the name of stockholder dividends, executive compensation, and maintaining their piece of the pie at any cost – to insure the status quo within our National System that benefits them!

Those six have all made their way to the head of this somewhat notorious list the old fashioned way – they have earned it! And now they will be made to pay the price for their abuses.

o   o   o   o

<u>We Must Have Initial Plans</u>

Next, we will next review the "Big 6" – the Existing Industry Re-Structuring proposals. They vary in the detail presented, and are as short and concise as I could make them. This Introduction has given you much insight into what is coming. My intent is to provide you with some pertinent details and a little background perspective on each, <u>but</u> that is all.

The proposals are somewhat briefer than I initially intended, but time is critical and this book must be completed in background content than I would prefer, simply because I am run out of time and funds. A family emergency that hit me the end of January that I had to attend to cost me several precious months – such writing takes time, peace, and solitude. It is already early November and for CS2 to have the best chance to be of public benefit and impact in the 2008 Presidential and Congressional campaigns it must find its way the general public as early in 2008, as possible.

The first of the six proposals is on Health Care Insurance for ALL Americans. It is the first industry issue that I developed and the AIR Program was built using it as a model. In that proposal you will see how the Five Entity Restructuring Levels model was formed. There is more background on "why" the AIR program is being applied to the Health Care Insurance Industry than in the other proposals. In those we will go right to restructuring approach to be used and varying degrees of background will be added.

Thankfully, each of us already know something about these Industries and more information is readily available on the Internet for those that desire to dig into it!

o   o   o   o

Each proposal lays out our initial Plan of Attack that will set us off in the Right direction. You could think of all 27 American Agenda proposals as Change battle plans, but it is <u>these</u> six (6) hard proposals that will comprise our *Normandy Plan*!

We will premeditatedly assault Irresponsible Power within the National System for the sake of the Common Good of our people and the nation. We will modify the initial plans as needed while this domestic, legislative war plays itself out over the next few years. And our eventual victory in each case is not in question — the only question is how soon we want it!

If, *We the People* do what is needed beginning in 2008 to deliberately and aggressively force these plans into action, the hard work will be done, the rock will be moved, and the rest will be far easier for us to control and contend with.

As We Join the Battle

It has been said that the, *'Love of money' is the <u>root</u> of all evil.*

I say to you that the, *"Lust for power and wealth"* — <u>and</u> <u>its</u> <u>retention</u> at any price — *is the <u>cause</u> of all evil.*

That lust now runs too freely through the halls of our Congress and far too much of corporate America. To be sure, We the People must now conduct and aggressively bring to satisfactory resolution a final reconciliation between our faltering National System and the Common Good of our fellow Americans citizens and society. Therefore, everything, and again I say <u>everything</u> is on the table.

o   o   o   o

Their American Revolution gave the world a living model of Democracy in Government Order designed for the Common Good of the Masses.

Our American Revolution will provide the world with a living model of Democracy in Economic Order also designed for the Common Good of the Masses.

We shall accomplish all of this for ourselves, for our children, and for theirs.

That is my Challenge...
That is your Challenge...
That is our Challenge...
We will confront the Common Challenge together...

And, We will not fail!

Existing Industries — Proposal 22

National Health Care Insurance for ALL Americans

"The End of the For-Profit Health Care Insurance Industry"

Issue/Problem

Simply stated, the absolute folly of "For-Profit" Health Care Insurance (HCI) in America can no longer be afforded by America's National System.

From the individual that needs HCI to the small and large corporations that struggle with the growing costs and shrinking benefits — we can no longer justify this avoidable and counter-productive strain upon America's social and economic systems.

Why is that? The most talked about issue is the pain and suffering of some 47-million 'citizens' without HCI coverage should be enough of a justification for the U.S. Congress to act in defense of the Common Good, but thus far it obviously has not. Next, the fact that those with HCI are paying more for less coverage <u>each year</u> thanks to the annual re-enrollment "ritual" put on the National System by the HCI corporations.

And finally there is the Plain Truth, that this critical and currently dysfunctional part of the National System is literally causing the *avoidable* <u>death</u> of some of our fellow Americans everyday. Any questions?

<u>Highly Recommended Viewing</u>

Even if you do not like the film maker Michael Moore, see *"Sicko"* the film is about the dynamic duo of the Medical and Pharmaceutical industries and their blatant control over <u>both</u> parties in Congress and so, our overall National Health Care Policy. It is excellent to the point that many Republicans even gave him credit for the film's content. They don't all have HCI, either!

In the film, it is noted that approximately 18,000 Americans die each year because they do not have HCI coverage. And even if that number is 50% over stated, it is still one (1) avoidable death of a real American <u>every</u> <u>hour</u> — do the math. This is a prime example of what I refer to as the acceptable Legislative Kill Factor (LKF) that has been lobbied into parts of our national, domestic policies.

Every American needs to see that film as soon as possible in 2008 — it is at Blockbuster on DVD.

A Origin of a Practical Economic Model

The AIR Program's Re-structuring and De-Profitization models were originally developed to address the nation's HCI Industry problem. The model was expanded upon and modified for use in practically addressing the nation's problems with the five (5) other industries in this set.

The HCI Industry easily falls under what was previously described as a *national infrastructure industry*. In keeping with the spirit of productive, people-oriented Changes to the National System the HCI Industry will be restructured — under the provisions of the AIR Program — to best serve the Common Good of all American citizens, as well as to help American business to be more competitive (instead of less so) in the world market. The American public needs to demand action on this proposal during the 2008 Presidential and Congressional campaign season and beyond, until it is accomplished to our satisfaction.

The issue of health insurance for ALL American citizens is a national problem and will require the restructuring of the entire HCI Industry. In the mid-1990's the Clintons and Hillary in particular, at least tried to do something to help the masses in President Clinton's first term and basically got cut off at the ankles by the entrenched Medical and Pharmaceutical industry lobbies (see *Sicko* for the details). More than 12 years later and we are still begging (like peasants) for Congress to grow some guts, correct this situation, and provide ALL Americans with reasonable cradle to grave HCI.

The on-going delay in finally doing what needs to be done continues mainly for the following reasons:

- The Medical and Pharmaceutical Industry lobbyists in Congress were too strong, both overtly and covertly.

- The Medical *Insurance* Industry (a subset of the overall Medical Industry) lobbyists in Congress were too strong, both overtly and covertly.

- The Baby Boomer generation was not yet old enough in the early nineties. We are now with leading edge turning "61" in 2008!

- Medical insurance premiums, co-payments, and the overall cost of health care had not yet reached their currently abusive levels.

- American business while already struggling with HCI costs and the negative effects on their competitive edge in the world market, had not yet reached the critical mass in employee health benefit costs they have faced increasingly since 2001.

- Federal and state budgets were not facing the magnitude of medical and other social service costs forced upon them the explosion of Illegal Occupants (IOs) that they are now facing. A situation made even worse since 2001 by the Bush II, Open Southern Door Immigration Policy.

- Budgets intended to help provide a safety net for our people are being taken by IOs.

- The number of Americans without health insurance had not reached the 47-plus million where it is now and only continues to increase. Almost one in six of the 300 million Americans without HCI.

And in recent years, those Americans with HCI are being hit annually with higher premiums, deductibles, co-pays, and too often for less coverage.

The Law of the Jungle in corporate America — profits over people, and avoidable deaths on top of that. These industries are collectively getting away with murder.

That is **until now**...

This Challenge is Hereby Issued to the U.S. Congress

On the behalf of my fellow American citizens, I do bluntly challenge the entire 535 members of the U.S. Congress to answer the following — Yes or No — question:

> Will the Congress once and for all, provide ALL American men, women, and children with basic cradle to grave health insurance – with the target date for said national coverage to take effect no later than 7-1-2009, if not retro-actively to 1-1-2009?
>
> A simple question requiring exactly 535, **Yes or No**, one (1) word answers.

It is time for Congress to come clean with the American public. And we will not accept a voice vote – it will be 535 individually cast and recorded responses (It will make it even easier to know why they will be fired in November of 2008 when we vote).

After all, working out this type of common public problem is exactly what the U.S. Congress was originally created and chartered to do. They are responsible to solve our common problems — issues that cannot be resolved at the local, county, city or state levels. It is their job....

And Their "Final" Answer Is

If their answer is **NO**, we can all simply quit wasting public resources perpetually studying and discussing it, and move on other issues. The growing number of unfortunate Americans without HCI can just accept living without it and **stop their constant whining and complaining!** (And so can those that are paying more for less HCI each year. I guess that pretty well 'covers' everybody doesn't it!).

Because obviously for some <u>decades</u> now the Congress of the United States of America and whoever the president happened to be, have been controlled by various Medical and Pharmaceutical Industry lobbyists and obviously **do not care** about *them*. The lobbyists have won the war! We the People have lost...

> Face it that **is** where we are today! The truth is <u>still</u> the truth even if it is being blatantly ignored. And that scenario applies in more than one public problem we will be reviewing.

However, if their answer is **YES**, and I could not imagine any other response **IF** the electorate <u>really</u> presses the issue in 2008 — than what possible forms could the new National HCI entity take?

o   o   o   o

Let's take a look!

o   o   o   o

The People's Sense – Part 1 of 2

What to Do About It?

The real question to be resolved is how we will go about insuring ALL American citizens with "reasonable" cradle-to-grave health insurance? And we are talking about medical, dental, vision, and long term care for the aged as the baseline to be addressed.

A secondary issue is how we provide medical services to **legal visitors** from other countries just as other "developed <u>and</u> lesser developed" countries have done for years. We have many operational models to choose from.

And finally, how will we strictly control any services to IOs – during the process of their repatriation of the vast majority of them over the next several years.

National Health Care Insurance (HCI)

Implementing the Inevitable

With the direct challenge made on behalf of 300 million Americans to the Congress, we will now overview the four (4) HCI options. The pure intent is to orchestrate the open debate of those options primarily between the American public and the American business community — and to a far lesser extent with the existing management of the HCI industry or any other business entity.

The absolute goal is the resolution of this medically dysfunctional, nationally embarrassing condition once and for all. Most Americans see this action as practical and inevitable, and the cost of finally doing it only increases every year. We will act to implement national HCI for ALL Americans. It is only a matter of which of four (4) options will be selected and how soon it is effective. The hard target date will be 7-1-2009, if not 1-1-2009.

Frankly, when the four are laid out side-by-side for review, the only prudent and publicly practical choice to be made is quite obvious. And right up front I am recommending that We the People go with Option 4.

Years ago, a government contracting officer shared with me the Contractors are brought in to do what they are assigned to do, while Consultants are brought in to help determine and recommend what needs to be done. In

CS2 I am serving as a Consultant and the Common Good of my 300 million Fellow Americans are the client being served.

As a side note, from 1998 until 12-12-2002 I worked first as a consultant and then as an employee of a major (non-profit) health care insurer in the Maryland and DC region, which does not make me an expert in the field, but does provide me with some first-hand perspective on the HCI Industry.

The Heart of the Matter

Until now HCI has been one of the un-holy grails within America's National System. Countless books, studies, and articles have been written on the failure of our government and the American Healthcare Industry to provide "ALL" American citizens with reasonable healthcare coverage.

A classic case of something being studied and restudied *to death* with no practical solution delivered. This is a negative, day-to-day example of how self-interested lobbies within the National System have worked and managed the Congress to prevent the implementation of such *common sense* programs that would protect the basic needs and welfare of our citizens. Those lobbyists have been doing their jobs very well. They will be among the first to go!

The proposals herein provide the basic set of options to be considered for the creation of a national HCI program to cover ALL Americans.

Insurance versus Providers

There are two basic functions that make-up the overall American Medical Industry in ours or any other country. One is the Health Care Insurance (HCI) function and the other is the Health Provider Network (HPN).

Health Care Insurance is a purely **administrative** function and has to do with enrollment, claims processing, control over coverage and cost of services, payment for products and services rendered, and identifying fraud. It is a *completely redundant* process currently being carried out by multiple companies performing the same routine procedures.

The Health Provider Network is comprised of doctors, nurses, hospitals, various laboratories, etc., those trained and charged with the **delivery** of health care services to the patient – you, hopefully.

The vast majority of people that I have spoken with on this issue believe that national HCI is a forgone conclusion. Their primary concerns are how much more or less will it cost me, what coverage would I have, what organizational form will it take, and when (how soon) will it <u>finally</u> happen? Not that a national HCI system is an exciting prospect to the public, but with insurance costs climbing every year and more people un-insured or less insured all the time, it is seen as a log overdue, practical necessity.

Do Health Care Insurance First

This proposal's approach is to address the HCI function first. The Provider function could be addressed at some later time after the practical improvements are made in administrative function and the resulting sharp reduction in overhead is being realized. It is certain that addressing the HCI function first is the logical approach. And it will certainly have publicly beneficial $ide effects on the Provider function as well. Follow the money!

The intent herein is to provide a very brief presentation on what are believed to be our only four (4) real options relative to national HCI. The four options are:

1. Continue the Status Quo
2. Government Managed Health Care Insurance
3. Total Privatization of Health Care Insurance
4. The U.S. Health Insurance Group

A brief overview each option is as follows:

Continue the Status Quo

The first option in <u>any</u> problem-solving exercise in your life, or in business, or in government is to determine to do absolutely **nothing** — to take no action!

This option would continue the Status Quo of the HCI system exactly as it is today. The 47-plus million Americans would continue being uninsured. Not counting the several decades prior, that has been the deliberate option taken by Congress for the last 12 plus years since the last real attempt (made by the Clinton Administration) and through six (6) Congressional elections. That may sound a bit sarcastic to some, but it is still the Plain Truth.

Of course this <u>is</u> the option favored by the Medical Industry and related Special Interest forces that have been controlling National Health Care Policy and the Congress. And until we determine to Change things that is exactly what will happen. We will continue to lose.

Government Managed Health Care Insurance

Granted this option does make many of us nervous whenever it is mentioned. It would have the Federal government takeover all insurance processing. In general this would require the government to assume the insurance processing now being performed by all for-profit (public stock) and non-profit insurance corporations.

Whether it is or is not a viable option remains to be seen. It may work very well since it does work in other countries despite on-going industry propaganda to the contrary. Of course they do currently manage Medicare, Medicaid, and Veterans Health Care Systems!

It will be interesting to see the real (non-doctored) numbers and review how this would be implemented. It may not be as bad as we generally fear, and that the lobbyist's predictable screams are always warning us about (domestic and corporate propaganda). It would be better than what we have now because everyone would be covered!

Total Privatization of Health Care Insurance

Under this option, all insurance processing would be turned over to (forced upon) the for-profit and non-profit insurance corporations, including functions that are now operated by the government!

The existing HCI Industry has been steadily merging into fewer and fewer corporate entities. Many of the remaining non-profit insurance corporations, such as those remaining from the original BlueCross BlueShield nationwide network, are either being absorbed into for-profit corporations or are working hard to convert to that status.

The biggest hole to point out in this approach, as well as a major obstacle to HCI for ALL Americans — is the Plain Truth that these are stock held corporations! It means that their management is expected to generate (one way or another) x% of stockholder dividends on an annual basis – desirably from 5 to 10% or more every year. After all these are stock-held corporations and senior management's real job is creating stock dividends. There is of course nothing wrong with that role in general, since that is the fundamental purpose of publicly held enterprises.

That said, the We the Masses must then frankly acknowledge that with regard today's Medical Insurance Industry their job is all about making profits and not about providing HCI for everyone. It never has been. Providing everyone with HCI would hurt their profitability and that is why they fight it.

Consider — if we were to project that requirement for stock dividends over the next 5, 10, 20 years and beyond, you can imagine what the cumulative affect (5 to 10% or more every year) it alone will have on increasing our insurance costs. And again that annual increase does not include the underlying and real cost increases of the Provider Network services — paying those that are actually performing the work of health care.

You can probably sense where this is going. Obviously, part of the reason our costs are high now is because they have been adding the HCI administrative overhead, profit percentage on for decades. Maybe not 5 or 10% a year, but added all the same. The entire Medical Industry's lobbyists can get away with this in a growing economy with "creative" lobbying to control congressional policymakers while more and more people have no or less coverage annually, but not when the economy is steadily contracting and the Baby Boomer generation — my generation — is reaching critical mass.

The Health Care Insurance Industry is the first of six industries in this set that, to the greatest extent their self-serving corporate lobbying could make possible, has blatantly demonstrated the Dark Side of Capitalism. Each has ignored the needs and well-being of the People and of the Nation to satisfy their annual desire for profits, stock dividends, and excessive executive compensation.

We, and every business in America absolutely can no longer afford this overtly redundant, HCI administrative function to continue it destructive, dictatorial, and on top of everything else its medically dysfunctional operation within the National System. Any questions?

So much for Option Number 3! Now let's fix it!

o   o   o   o

U.S. Health Insurance Group (HIG)

Finally, I offer the fourth option that will be something new in the HCI debate. And frankly, I believe to be our only viable, "final answer".

The basic concept is that the American business community will work together to assume control and management of the nation's HCI system. This approach would involve the following considerations:

- Creation of a fully, non-profit corporate entity administered by those selected from members of the American business community.

- The American business community would directly oversee the HCI system.

- The creation of this entity would be a joint venture between the federal government (We the taxpayers) and the American business community, including Wendy's, Ford, Starbucks, Sears, Home Depot, Hallmark — virtually every grocery store, every other small and large business in the country.

- The existing for-profit and non-profit HCI corporations would systematically and involuntarily be merged into this new entity.

- ALL Americans would be enrolled into the existing HCI entities during the transition process.

- The existing stockholders would be bought out over a period of years at a 'reasonable' stock price. Some corporate assets could be sold off (to American buyers) to expedite the buy-out.

- All existing government operated health insurance functions, would also be systematically merged into this entity.

- There would be operating units in every state, major city, etc., as required to support the enrollment, claims processing, and fraud prevention.

- The existing senior management and Board of Directors of these corporations would be involuntarily retired. No more Golden Parachutes will be issued, ever!

- The new management of these companies would be compensated with 'reasonable' high six-figure or so incomes, not the mega-million dollar compensation packages executives now receive. There will be no shortage of qualified people seeking those positions. I'm sorry, but running an HCI company in 2008 is not rocket science. Working to keep the Congress from doing the right thing for multiple decades has been management's mission, but no more.

- This new insurance entity's mission will be to provide the American public with a centralized and efficient HCI processing system.

- It would not be a government agency or a stock held corporation.

- Employment in this entity would follow a corporate rather than a civil service model.

I have reviewed this concept with numerous people of varying social backgrounds and political persuasion, and it has been very well received.

o   o   o   o

The People's Sense – Part 2 of 2

Those are the four (4) options that face the American public. I personally recommend that the only viable option for the short and long-term "health" of the American public — and to control the HCI costs to business, government and individuals — is the U.S. Health Insurance Group option.

The HCI Industry and their own entrenched Congressional lobbyists will be turned away from the halls of Congress.

Again, there is no easy way to make this point, but the existing structure of the HCI Industry and their successful lobbying against any form of National HCI causes the physical death of American citizens. Further, it often causes the financial destruction of families due to medical costs and bankruptcy every day. And under Bush II, the Bank Industry successfully pushed through legislation virtually killing a person's, a family's ability to file for bankruptcy. On April 20, 2005 Bush II signed the Bankruptcy Abuse Prevention and Consumer Protection Act — delivering the goods on that one to the Banking Industry – demonstrating the true "compassion" of his Conservatism.

American lives in this and other broken portions of the National System have somehow come to be considered cheap and throw away over the years! We the People will bring this legislative abuse to an end, and now. Enough is enough.

To be clear, our message to the U.S. Congress is that they will need to pass laws that will implement HCI coverage for all American citizens – with a hard effective date of 7-1-2009, if not sooner. Or they should not bother to run for re-election, because We will fire all 468 of them at the polls in November 2008.

This will be a most interesting struggle for the American electorate not only to observe, but to participate in, as well. The battle lines are thus drawn! And, We the People will surely win this war and see the desired results starting in 2009.

o   o   o   o

The AIR Program Re-Structuring

The Health Care Insurance (HCI) Industry

Overall Re-Structuring Approach

The American Health Care Insurance Industry will experience the full force of the AIR Program Re-Structuring process. Again, HCI is the industry for which the Air Program model was originally developed to practically confront — and finally deal with for the Common Good. And deal with it We will.

The U.S. Health Insurance Group (HIG) Implementation

All HCI corporate entities doing business in the U.S. will comply with this involuntary industry re-organization. This will not be a negotiation.

The remainder of this piece overviews the AIR Program's implementation and provides enough detail so that those involved in the HCI industry will know what is coming at them. We are coming. And the other details will be worked out in public during the 2008 campaign and early in 2009.

Initial List of Industry Entities

This is the initial and partial list of primary Health Care Insurance (HCI) corporations and companies to be included in the AIR Program Re-Structuring of the HCI Industry:

UnitedHealth Group
BlueCross BlueShield For-Profits
BlueCross BlueShield Non-Profits
Wellpoint
Aetna
Humana
Cigna
Health Net
Coventry Health Care
WellCare Health Plans
Amerigroup
Centene
Medical Mutual of Ohio
Molina Healthcare
Sierra Health Services

This initial, working list of corporate entities may very well be refined as 2008 progresses and the November 2008 National Election draws near.

By deliberate, united vote on that historic day, *We the People* can freely declare that such practical and prudent Change to the National System for the Common Good of us all — will be made.

AIR Program – The Entity Re-Structuring Levels (ERL) Overview

The Health Care Insurance (HCI) Industry

ERL 1 – Operational Reorganization

All existing HCI corporations both For-profit and Non-profit will become operating Divisions of the newly formed, Non-Profit Healthcare Insurance Group (HIG) – the Industry Management Consortium established for the restructured HCI Industry. A newly formed Board of Directors will comprise the first level of the new HIG Organization Chart.

Further any existing HCI corporation that is currently part of a larger (parent) non-HCI corporate entity will be transferred from that organization also to become an operating Division of the HIG. Such transfers under the AIR Program would not involve a purchase or a buy-out of stock as would be seen in a typical corporate merger, since this would not be a corporate merger in that the HCI business function is not the former parent organization's primary line of business. It would be a direct corporate transfer. In all, those Divisions will form the second level of the HIG Organization. Again, this corporate reorganization will not be optional.

Some will *scream* that this is nationalization of the HCI industry. They may call the AIR Program restructuring of the HCI Industry and the others to be presented whatever they care to. We do not care! In such situations, it will be interesting to hear how much revenue/profit those corporations announce they could lose in the transfer! I acknowledge that in some ways it is the 'hostile takeover' — of an industry that is making some people a lot of money, while in this case the nation suffers with a HCI System that is clearly dysfunctional to the Common Good. I call it bringing order to chaos.

Over the next few years the operational and administrative offices of the former corporations, now HIG Divisions would be systematically and efficiently consolidated into a network of regional HIG Operations facilities. This process always happens when companies merge, with an appropriate amount of operational consolidation, we have all seen it. However, as exists today there would be an on-going need for regional HCI facilities (in each state and major cities), so while some reduction in employment would occur, there will be an on-going requirement for nationwide service offices.

Note: Although the Consortiums are set-up as Non-Profit corporations, these HIG organizations will initially pay taxes. In the case of the medical insurance function, We may very well determine that the HIG paying taxes only increases their cost doing business and therefore our insurance costs, as well. Thus, they <u>could</u> be relieved of that obligation in the future.

o   o   o   o

There are non-profit HCI Corporations in the mix that of course do not have stockholders to pay, which will make them far easier and less costly to reorganize into the HIG. However, do not assume for a minute that they don't make profits! They pay-out those dollars within their organization instead – that is where the money goes — always to the Board and management, and sometimes to the employees. They will pay out based on 2008 year-end numbers. Calendar year 2009 will be the end of that money train at least at the executive level. Of course, many of those executives will be gone in 2009.

ERL 2 – Existing Management Retirement

<u>Existing Senior Management</u>

- Any member of senior management with a Golden Parachute will be retired by May 30, 2009. Any and all stock options in their exit package will be eliminated.
- No Golden Parachutes will be offered to future management, ever.
- Any remaining member of management with a base salary in excess of one (1) million dollars per year will have it cut to that amount as of July 1, 2009.
- All stock options for 2009 will be eliminated.
- All bonuses for 2009 will be reviewed by the HIG group and may be reduced.

And if a given person does not like those Changes – they know where the door is…

<u>Remember:</u> The one-time offer to hold current and prior management <u>and</u> employees harmless from lawsuit will be presented and I believe will be accepted. This offer will be made to the current and prior members of the Board of Directors, as well.

<u>Existing Boards of Directors (BOD)</u>

The existing BOD would be relieved of their positions by May 30, 2009. By law most, if not all corporations are required to have some form of BOD whether it is actually functional to the operation or simply ornamental! The future form and function of the new BOD established for the aforementioned HIG Consortium will be reviewed.

ERL 3 – New Management Structure and Charter

The *Industry Management Consortium* Requirement

Again, with the consolidation of the existing HCI For-profit and Non-profit corporate entities, we are merging a group of businesses that are pretty much doing the same thing – pure operational redundancy. Each of these entities will become operating Divisions in the HIG Non-Profit organizational structure.

Therefore, a single Board of Directors "entity" is all that will be needed and they will not be simply ornamental. The costs that were associated with all of the former Boards are eliminated and will go back into the operation.

The HIG's Board will be responsible to the American public for implementing, administering, strictly overseeing, and refining the new Charter of Operations. They will not manage the day-to-day operation within the Divisions. The management that remains after the existing senior people are retired will be given an opportunity to take charge of the day-to-day operation, but working under a new charter.

Some of the management and other employees from the Divisions will be transferred into first level HIG organization that will centralize certain key administrative functions such as insurance premium rates, coverage types, and the negotiation of pricing for goods and services from the Provider Network. With the number of qualified people in Divisions there will be little if any need to hire from outside staff for key positions – promotion from within will be the rule.

Recommended HIG Charter of Operations

The first level of the HIG will provide oversight and administrative control over the entire operation. While the majority of the HCI function will be performed in the Operating Divisions, the HIG Board of Directors and staff will facilitate and control HCI policy and act as the contact point for all vendors, other industries, state-level agencies, and the Congress. It will be a working Board of Directors.

Simply stated the HIG's Inaugural Operational Charter will include:

1. Oversight of the consolidation of all existing HCIs into the new HIG organizational structure.
2. Enrollment of the currently uninsured American citizens.
3. Facilitate and expedite the full implementation and simplification of cradle-to-grave Health Care Insurance for all American <u>citizens</u>. This will include medical coverage, prescriptions, hospital, vision, dental, long term care, etc.
4. Oversight of the conversion Health Services for the U.S. Congress into the HIG system!
5. Oversight of the HCI coverage for all <u>legal</u> <u>visitors</u>. They will be required to pay for such coverage as is done by Americans in other countries.
6. The HIG will be concerned with retaining and/or transferring current employees within Divisions as the restructuring takes progresses.
7. The HIG will end out-sourcing (off-shore) activities and work to reclaim positions previously lost in that manner.
8. The HIG will be the interface control point with the U.S. Congress in any issues regarding policy, dollars, and pricing. And will delegate as much day-to-day responsibilities to the Division level as they deem most efficient, but no policy decision authority outside of their day-to-day operation.
9. The HIG will be the interface control-point for the American Pharmaceutical Group (APG) the Industry Management Consortium being created to manage the restructured Pharmaceutical Industry.

<u>And the Big One</u>

Since the former individual HCI corporations are now Divisions within the new organization, the HIG will be <u>the</u> control point for with all other Medical Industry vendors seeking payment for their products and services.

This is where <u>We</u> will begin to publicly analyze and control the costs of medical products and services. The HIG will serve as Medical Industry's arbitration entity. It will insure that fair pricing policy is applied across the board and the games that "may have" been played in the past will come under prudent control.

o   o   o   o

This charter will be amended with full public disclosure as the AIR Program progresses.

We will also need to have a public dialogue regarding what to do with the Medicare and Medicaid Services, i.e., merging them into the HIG System or not?

And lastly the Veterans Administration Health Care function will be reviewed against the HIG structure and services. We will have an open debate on the most operationally and cost efficient way to cover our active military and veterans over the long haul, but will not diminish VA coverage. That is our responsibility to them.

Again, the only way to straighten everything out is to put "everything on the table."

ERL 4 – Stock, Profitability, and Pricing Controls

As is repeated in these six proposals — the following scenarios will begin taking effect as soon as possible in 2009 and will likely be applied retroactively when the required legislation is passed by the **new** U.S. Congress.

While We can always hope, there is probably little chance that the existing Congress and White House will move on this proposal before the November Election. These six Industry proposals need to be the **hottest topics** in the country during 2008. The electorate must bring these and the other American Agenda Proposals to the campaigns! We can do this.

Stock Control

Stock trading in the involved former HCI corporations (now Divisions of the HIG) will be suspended at some point in 2009. They will be moving to Non-profit status under the HIG. The initial list of the involved corporate entities was presented above and will probably be added to as the AIR Program develops.

The stock markets will be intensely watched (by the SEC and others) in the run-up during 2009 AIR Program Effective Date for any questionable stock trading or other game playing. Violators will be severely dealt with including fines and prison time in a State run facility. No Federal playpens for the rich and famous anymore.

Profitability Control

Going forward the Health Care Insurance function under the HIG's management will convert the former publicly held corporations to the pure IGE's or Income Generating Entity model previously reviewed. Minimum profitability will be required to cover reasonable operating expenses, including payroll, facilities, taxes, enrollment, claims processing, fraud prevention, etc.

The costs related to the annual Re-enrollment "ritual" will be all but eliminated, as will most of the lobbying budget and the lobbyists! The only remaining item is how to deal with over the first years of the HIG Operation being the buy-out of existing stockholders.

Profitability requirements under the IGE model will be based on those cost of doing business. The profits in excess of that in the first years will be put to practical uses such as:

- signing up and covering at least part of the costs of the currently uninsured
- internal operational spending
- operational consolidation expenses
- elimination of any out-sourcing activities
- "fixed' stock dividends pay-outs in future years until the buy-back process is complete
- set aside for the future stock buy-back process

Starting in 2009 the stock dividend pay-outs to former HCI corporate stockholders will be capped and frozen. The analysis of the annual stock dividends paid out since 1999 will be published. The dividend pay-out for 2009 and beyond until all stock is bought back will not be generous. People will moan, but another choice is to say that their stock is <u>worthless</u> and will <u>not</u> be bought back. They could all find themselves "Enron'd". Now that would be pure nationalization!

Not that We would want to do such a thing, but remember that investing in stocks is free will risk, is organized gambling, whether by individual or money market funds managers. A full buy-out of existing stockholders in a situation like We are addressing is optional, and everyone needs to approach it in that manner. These corporations have been sticking it to the National System for decades and killing people! It could all be righteously wiped clean, but that would hurt the people and the economy other ways. This is hard compromise and We need to resolve to do the best <u>possible</u> for all parties. *"We do these things, because they are hard."*

<u>Pricing Control</u>

In the best case scenario, all HCI premiums and coverage plan options for individuals and companies <u>will be frozen</u> at their 2008 plan schedules. The wasteful, annual ritual of **"plan re-enrollment"** will come to an abrupt end. The reduced demand for stockholder-profitability starting in 2009 as noted above will be accompanied with the dropping of the plan re-enrollment process and the associated (and now avoidable) expenses. The vast majority of the cost to the HCIs of the plan re-enrollment process will be eliminated, as well the loss of productivity the annual plan re-enrollment process forces on companies large and small across the nation.

> And think of the trees it will save! In an example of how things are connected, the lumber and especially the printing business will take a bit of a hit due to this change. The will need to adjust their 2009 budget projections accordingly.

In **Stage One** of the restructuring, people may continue with their current plans and coverage levels. Or they will be allowed to simply change their current plans and coverage levels. There would be a one percent (1%) premium, only rate increase for 2009 – with no reductions in coverage. All other deducible amounts, co-pays, etc., will be un-changed. That will suffice while the transition begins and the new HIG management is sorting things out in 2009 and planning for 2010.

The currently uninsured American citizens will be picked up by the existing HCIs within their geographic region. Thus, during the HCIs consolidation, all American citizens will be picked up by existing HCI corporations, thus finally attaining full national coverage.

It might be good to utilize the nationwide BlueCross BlueShield network of HCIs for this purpose. I believe they still cover all 50 states and DC, although many are now for-profit. That original nationwide network of HCIs could form the backbone of the new HIG structure. And it would only need a tune-up!

In **Stage Two** by the 2010 plan year the multitude of plans and options will be aggressively reduced to a very small and practical set. Simplicity will be applied across the board. Then, each of the insured people will have their existing plans and related coverage options converted to the new and much simplified plan and pricing structure.

How is all this sounding so far? Certainly not everything is worked out yet, but we will clearly be headed down the prudent and practical path. We can do this!

ERL 5 – Conversion of IGE Model

The AIR Re-structuring of the Health Care Insurance Industry offers the primary example and opportunity to transition a National Infrastructure

Industry into an Income Generating Entity (IGE).

Consolidation of existing HCI corporations into the non-profit Healthcare Insurance Group (HIG) will lead the way to their being converted to a pure IGE within the National System.

Over a period of years to be determined, the existing stockholders will be bought out. The stock amounts involved and how the stockholders will be compensated for their share value will be worked by the HIG as part of the AIR Program implementation.

And no, that is not avoiding discussing the hard dollars involved. The numbers are what the numbers are, and they will only continue to grow worse the longer We delay this Change of necessity to our National System. Therefore, I deliberately would not take the time extract and present that data on this or the others in this infamous group of six Existing Industries. Further, I predict those numbers will be one of the first things that the Special Interest lobbyists for that group throw out to scare the public.

The man said, "The only thing We have to fear, is fear itself."

But, We will not be afraid or deterred from our Common Goal – Health Care Insurance for ALL American citizens starting in 2009.

o   o   o   o

That is all.

Next the legal, hard drug pushers.

o   o   o   o

Existing Industries — Proposal 23

The Pharmaceutical Industry

"Controlling the Pharmas for Our Health and Our Pocketbooks"

Issue/Problem

The cost of prescription and non-prescription drugs is hurting the pocketbooks of the American public and business. This includes people with Prescription Drug Coverage (PDC) under their Health Care Insurance (HCI), as well as those without HCI coverage that are really at the mercy of the Pharmaceutical Industry practices and pricing. This industry is a major part of our problems with the overall American Medical System.

Note: The various Pharmaceutical Industry entities (corporations and companies) will often be referred to herein by their 'generic' name – Pharma(s).

American businesses small and large are struggling with the <u>annual</u> HCI cost increases and are often forced to pass more of those "monthly" costs on to their employees. The annual HCI rate increase can be larger than the annual increase in pay that individuals receive from their employer (if they get an increase). This cuts into the monthly household budget leaving less money for other things, whether for retail spending that drives the American economy or simply the bare necessities of life – like food! Ask those on Social Security.

During the annual HCI Re-Enrollment ritual, single people and those with families are all but forced to pay more for the same or less (but needed) coverage, even though they know it will hurt their budget someplace else. It is called selling to a captive audience.

In recent years some HCI plans have separated options for PDC plans where people must pick the coverage levels, deductibles, and co-pay amounts. The increases in PDC plan premiums are only a subset of the annual, anxiety producing and gargantuan, productivity-draining ritual of HCI re-enrollment suffered by people and business – an experience that will be coming to a merciful end as was laid out in the previous proposal on Health Care Insurance for ALL Americans. The rising cost PDC plans will be dealt with in the AIR Program restructuring of the Pharmas.

<u>Subsidizing Other Countries</u>

It is no secret that We are consistently paying more for prescription (and non-prescription) drugs than those in Canada, Mexico, and various European countries where they have those *dreaded national care health systems*! The reason they pay less is because when the Pharmas go to those countries they are forced by law to negotiate with that *dreaded single entity* — the Canadian government for example, when determining drug pricing. It is the *dreaded socialized medicine* approach that is structured to "actually" serve the needs of their public and reduce its expense to businesses large and small. What a concept!

And the other reason that those other countries get better drug pricing and that our Pharmas continue making big profits is that *We Americans are paying the difference — We Americans are paying the difference — We Americans are paying the difference!!!*

Therefore, it is fair to say that the American public under our existing HCI system has been partially *"subsidizing"* the lower prescription drug pricing in Canada and other countries, and have been doing it for decades! Aren't We nice people for doing that!

Add to that in the recent Medicare Reform Act, among other goodies for the Pharmas, the Congress wrote provisions into law that officially prohibits our government from negotiating as a 'single entity' with the Pharmas. Yes, it was written into the legislation for the Pharmas, by our U.S. Congress — your own members of the House and Senate. Now go and watch *Sicko*.

The implementation of national HCI in America will provide us with all the leverage required to reverse such dysfunctional legislation and to have practical control over the Pharmaceutical Industry. What will be happening to them is laid out on this proposal.

Required Viewing

Again, even if you do not like the film maker Michael Moore, see *"Sicko"* the film on the Medical and Pharmaceutical industries and their blatant control over both parties in Congress and so, our national health care policy. It is excellent to the point that many Republicans even gave him credit for the film's content. They don't all have HCI, either!

I Was Really Trying to be Civil

You know I was not going to lay into the prudence of taking the "major" drug companies off the stock dividend train – I was borderline on letting them go — feeling that they would get sufficiently 'nailed' by way of the Health Care Insurance Restructuring proposal. But, that was Wednesday January 11, 2007. On Friday January 12th and the front page of the Washington Post had an article titled, **"Drug Bill Demonstrates Lobby's Pull"** with the sub-title 'Democrats Feared Industry Would Stall Bigger Changes."

It was one of the finest, real life examples detailing the extent to which industry lobbying maintains absolute control over the U.S. Congress. All to the benefit of industry profits and the "re-election" campaign confers of both Parties – with no concern for, in this case the physical health of the American people.

I hope you share the same bone-marrow, level disgust that I do for such preventable public abuse! The following are points were taken from the article written by Washington Post Staff Writers — R. Jeffrey Smith and Jeffrey H. Birnbaum. For the complete text of this excellent article please access the Washington Post Archive facility on their Internet site.

Presented below are some key points I derived from the Jan 12, 2007 Washington Post article. As a point of reference remember that the Democrats had just won a 'numerical' majority in both the House and Senate in the November 2006 Congressional Election.

o   o   o   o

In the run-up to this legislation the Democrats deliberated proposing a government run prescription drug program that would deliver lower drug costs for seniors. They backed off submitting the legislation for fears that the Pharmaceutical lobby would hold it up in committee, and since Bush II said he would veto any Democratic proposal.

While drug industry money had favored the Republican majority, it already strong ties within the Democratic ranks, and with the election results began working to get closer to the new Democratic majority. In general, the industry has plenty of money to throw around. In January they industry spent over $1,000,000 dollars on a full page ads, promoting the existing Medicare program.

From 1998 and 2005, the Pharmaceutical industry out spent all other industries with a total of $900 million. Over that period, some $89.9 million was directed to federal candidates and party committees, with almost three-quarters given to Republicans.

The legislation that they are voting was initiated in 2003. The Republican backed legislation that lobbyists helped to develop restricts the government from negotiating with the Pharmaceutical industry to lower prices. No big surprise there! Over the 3 years period donated over $6 million dollars to Republican and Democratic campaigns, and had some '800' lobbyists working on members of Congress. Think of all the money the Pharmas spend on lobbying that will not need to be spent once We "fix" the industry. It will pay for a lot of health care insurance for those that currently do not have it.

Of course, the Bush II administration was absolutely opposed to having the government negotiate drug pricing for Medicare. Bush II received $1.17 million form the industry just for his 2004 re-election campaign.

And speaking of how lobbyists shape legislation to protect their profits, here are 3 provisions they saw to it were in the final legislation:

- a ban on the importation of cheaper drugs from Canada.
- A pro a provision that requires some 7 million Medicaid patients to buy drugs that do not have pricing limits
- And my favorite — a provisions requiring private health insurance companies to remain small and numerous, which of course decreases buying their leverage in negotiations with drug companies. That is a perfect example of why the Industry Consortium approach is made to order — in controlling Pharmaceutical Industry. They have had it their way for decade, and We will have our way with them for the Common Good.

The remainder the Post article goes on to say that the House leadership backed-off making any real change to the Republican legislation. It talks about the donations that some drug companies made to key members of Congress and how they began to shift more of their money to the new Democratic majority. It mentioned how some members of Congress traveled the country promoting the Pharmaceutical backed legislation to the public. Our tax dollars at work for them, not us!

And one last gem just for kicks. I will now quote directly from the Post article, "In an effort to bolster its image, Pharmaceutical Research and Manufacturers of America is also sponsoring a program that distributes low- and no-cost drugs to poor people, called the Partnership for Prescription Assistance. A few of the program's beneficiaries have been brought to

Washington and given media training so they can promote the program in local news outlets and in television ads."

Again, my personal thanks to Washington Post Staff Writers, Smith and Birnbaum for such a publicly, informative article.

o   o   o   o

Before We Can Continue

While I am far from being a prude, **Pardon Me**, but I must take a moment for all those shall we say "nice, nice" people (I won't mention any names because they know who they are) that in the 1990's severely criticized the television, movie, video, and music businesses for allowing child and family inappropriate subject matter to be distributed in the mass media. How is it that they now sit silently while the Pharmas were allowed to publicly air the following question,

"if you experience an er_____ lasting more than four hours you should call your doctor."

I believe it first aired during the Super Bowl a few years ago and without ceasing in various forms since that time. Is that question really *ready* for prime time? You know when Mom and/or Dad and the family are sitting around having a "Hallmark moment" watching the evening news, primetime television, and sports of all kinds – is it really relevant material that is enhancing the family viewing experience? Especially when the guy in the commercial looks to be as old as grandpa sitting there watching with them. Not! And how many times has little Johnny or Mary said, "Hey Mom (Dad, grand-__) what is an er_____?"

Where are the televangelists when you really need them? Or do they just have stock in those companies? Besides, We all know if any product is that good, it does not even need to be advertised — you know, like Hershey Bars! There are also multiple Pharmas "pushing" their version of the same drug. Not that you cannot find a similarly effective product in a much more natural (less chemicals) form at your local Health Food store or on their Internet site.

Of course, more recently there are other family favorites for kids to ask about, the one about the "potential for sexual side-effects" or "I did not know it would affect my ED".

And hey, that is not just me.

The People's Sense

There will be an AIR Program restructuring of the American Pharmaceutical Industry 'similar' to the one We will apply the Health Care Insurance (HCI) Industry.

The two industries are similar, but not identical because while the HCI Industry is a collection of purely, redundant administrative operations — the Pharmas actually make something. They perform real Research and Development (R&D) to produce new drugs which are intended (philosophically) to improve our lives by helping us get well when we are sick, injured, or make life easier if we have long term medical conditions. Therefore, the Pharmaceutical Industry requires some amount of R&D flexibility. Pure research must be funded.

At the same time, the Pharmas must be targeting medical conditions that need attention now and those that predictably will be growing problems as the Baby Boomer *tsunami* of a wave increasingly hits the American Medical System over the next twenty (20) years and then our children. With no offense intended, but bluntly put, our parents did not fix the Medical System problem! We cannot afford to make that same mistake. Have you got that my fellow Baby Boomers?

Further, small and start-up companies in the drug development arena, with real potential, need to be able to get "low cost" funding to support their work. There is that IGE business model, again.

With the coming AIR Program restructuring of the Pharmas the industry will experience the following changes:

* The implementation of the U.S. Health Insurance Group (HIG) will have a controlling affect on their pricing in a manner that will benefit both the American consumer and business. The U.S. will finally put in place the *dreaded single entity* to negotiate with Pharma pricing – one that will serve the Common Good of our People and the business community.
* They will continue to do R&D on life saving and quality of life improving drugs.
* They will no longer be overt and covertly lobbying against the availability of the cannabis plant for medical uses – or – its overall legalization in the U.S. and other countries. Those lobbying practices and some of their lobbyists will be the first to go!
* They will promote research to expand use of a natural form of THC found in the cannabis plant for use when applicable in their future prod-

ucts – using a God-given, natural substance in their 'mix' rather than pumping more chemicals into our bodies.

- They will halt further R&D on synthetically produced THC, as well as the production and distribution of those already marketed to the public. The synthetic was devised to replace naturally growing marijuana. By simple comparison the lab produced, synthetic THC on the market is functionally worthless and will no longer be required. At long last sick Americans with cancer, AIDS, and a host of other ailments will be able to get the Right Stuff to ease their pain, increase their appetite, and to keep their food and medicine down.

About Vitamins

And, the Pharmas will be stopped from slowly trying to take control of the "Vitamin" manufacturing and distribution Industry — for fun and profit. For decades they "talked against" consumers using vitamins or natural remedies saying they were not worth taking. Now since more and more Baby Boomers and our kids are realizing their real benefits, the Pharmas are attempting to control production, distribution, and of course pricing – and to crush the smaller, natural vitamin and health food supplement industry, as well. These practices will end starting in 2009.

Not much else to say really. That pretty well overviews the whole abusive, self-serving situation — don't you think?

American Industry Re-Structuring (AIR) Program

The Pharmaceutical Industry

Overall Re-Structuring Approach

The American Pharmaceutical Industry (API) will experience the full force of the AIR Programs – Entity Re-Structuring Level programs. The Industry Management Consortium created to manage the restructured Pharmaceutical Industry will be called the American Pharmaceutical Consortium or APC.

Reasonable Public Perspective

It would be appropriate to remind the reader that 5 out of 6 (excluding tobacco) of the industries in this group are National Infrastructure Industries (NII) – critical parts of the National System we really cannot live or live very well without in order to have a decent life. And all of these are industries have been abusing power for corporate gain regardless of the costs to the People and the society as a whole. And this group has had a particularly good time sticking it to the American public, under Bush II. It is now time for those in charge to pay the price for their deliberate, corporate irresponsibility toward society.

In all of these AIR Program Restructurings we will do our best to protect American society first, domestic jobs second, stockholders third, and there is no fourth! Society needs the products and/or services provided by five of these six industries, so it is of necessity that We put them on the right course to protect and insure our Common Good. While Americans need the jobs they now provide some will be surely be restructured away, that is to be expected, and we will take care to get those Americans re-employed as a priority. American citizens always first!

Stockholders will be reconciled in all these dealings *to the greatest extent possible*. Hear that. Remember that buying stock is a risk-based experience! For decades We have been on the receiving end of "we are doing it for the stockholders" and this set of Industries (and some others) have deliberately violated the Public Trust in favor of corporate profitability.

We will shed no tears for them now, as they did not shed any for us and the nation in the past. Each of these six is more costly in dollars to society than is practical and warranted. And each in their own way has needlessly cost some Americans their life.

In the earlier parts of CS2 we reviewed the public policy that *free will crimes of a physical and financial nature* against our people <u>will</u> <u>no</u> <u>longer</u> be tolerated, and that it applied not only to people, but businesses as well. These six industries are prime examples of such *abuses* among the business community. Look at each of them and think about that! Again, I will remind the reader that when I said these contents were to taken as seriously as a heart attack, I meant it! These six proposals in particular are true examples of "seriously". Actually <u>resolving</u> hard public issues requires and demands hard Changes to be effectively administered in order to accomplish the task.

The AIR Program for the Pharmas

All major American Pharmaceutical corporate entities, for-profit and non-profit, and all foreign based Pharmas currently doing business in the U.S. will comply with the guidelines of this involuntary AIR Program Industry re-organization. This will not be a negotiation.

The remainder of this proposal will highlight the AIR Program's application to the existing American Pharmaceutical Industry. As stated under Proposal 22, for some it will not include enough details, but to those involved in the industry it will be more than enough for them to know what is coming. Further, there will be volumes of detail disclosed as 2008 progresses and the political candidates and subject industries are forced to publicly discuss these proposals. At last, the various public interest groups that have fought so long for such changes and been fully suppressed by the Pharma lobbyists will have their open public forum. The tables will be turned <u>permanently</u> for the Common Good.

The Pharmaceutical Industry corporations and companies will be restructured from two (2) different perspectives — one being their Research and Development (R&D) function and the other being their Pricing and Lobbying Practices. The fact that the Pharmas actually do research, develop, manufacture, and distribute products that we all need makes this a bit more tedious of a restructuring procedure for us to manage over the next few years. But, We will get it done. It is not rocket science!

Research and Development (R&D)

Sufficient annual revenue will continue to be raised to adequately fund required R&D. It is a public health necessity. As stated above, the Industry Management Consortium created to manage the restructured Pharmaceutical Industry will be called the American Pharmaceutical Consortium or APC.

The APC management will have oversight responsibilities on the R&D projects, but will not impede the flow of research on life improving products. They will promote them — however, in due time we will not be seeing as many R&D efforts against the exact same product concept. When one R&D group successfully creates a new medical product most or all of the APC's Pharma Divisions could move to other projects. Some R&D redundancy is totally practical, especially on critical medical needs – the more brains and individual creativity applied to such tasks the better, because you never know who will get it figured out first!

On the other side of marketing, the Pharmas have reportedly been cranking out newer prescription-type versions of older products that are not always any better than what was already on the market — and that do not require a prescription to be written! However, their revenue pipeline requires x-number of products to hit the prescription drug market annually to make sales projections and keep Wall Street happy. I recall a news report in a few years ago where one of the Pharmas had a drug approval <u>rejected</u> by the Food and Drug Administration (FDA) that they were really counting on for revenue that year. To offset that revenue loss, that particular Pharma simply went into their piggy bank and put the necessary dollars in the stockholders fund for the year to keep them happy! Very interesting.

o   o   o   o

It has also been reported lately that the Pharmas are spending more on advertising than R&D. The Pharmas do seem to be one of, if not the primary advertiser on many of the network and cable television news programs. It is that obvious fact could be making it difficult for some corporate news organizations, "to objectively report and/or go after" the bad products, that the Pharmas are pushing out to the public. That is one of the few negative comments you will hear from me about the Press.

It also makes you wonder why there are more and more prescription drugs being re-called <u>and</u> found to have serious side-effects that you would think <u>should</u> <u>have</u> been caught on clinical testing with the FDA?

Pricing and Lobbying Practices

These necessary functions will be restructured and simplified in order to serve the Common Good and health of the American people. With the reform of the Health Care Insurance Industry and the creation of the HealthCare Insurance Group (HIG), there would only be one entity for the Pharmaceutical Industry to negotiate pricing with. We win. With the reform of the Pharmaceutical Industry and the creation of the American Pharmaceutical Consortium (APC), there would only be one entity for the HIG to negotiate pricing with. We really win!

And do not sit there and say this could never be accomplished or they will never let us do that. It will be accomplished and We will do just that. We only need to remember that this is our country and We make the rules for anyone that desires to keep doing business here!

Prime example — a huge shift in pricing will be made in AIDS related drugs. Right now it is a gravy train for the Pharmas and is draining our federal tax dollars. The future production and pricing (worldwide) will immediately be adjusted down to primarily serve the ill rather than the stockholders. You get the point, enough said.

The lobbying of Congress as it has been done for years will come to an abrupt end in 2009. There will always be the need for the industry to lobby Congress, but the publicly irresponsible, corporate greed switch will be turned off. Changes in lobbying objectives will target the health of our people and will not discourage and/or seek to suppress competition from smaller and start-up companies with good ideas.

And last but far from least, it has been stated that if every public school student took vitamins at the start of each school day it would be dramatically improved their health and other aspects of their day-to-day life. Of course that is just common sense and this is the type of public health program that will go forward.

The Initial List of Industries

This following identifies the universe of Pharmaceutical entities (corporations and companies) to be considered for inclusion in the AIR Program Re-Structuring of the Pharmaceutical Industry:

- Every Pharma that is currently paid for mediation by any agency of Federal, State, County, and City/town government's health plan.
- Every Pharma that is currently paid for mediation in any company based or individual plan.

That pretty well covers it, don't you think?

Compared to the number of HCI corporations there are far more Pharmas to be dealt with under the AIR Program. Thus, the Pharmas restructuring will involve far more moving parts than the HCIs did. It will be initiated with the largest Pharmas and over time work its way down to a practical level with smaller ones. Not all of the smaller companies will need to be included. We may find in the process that we really will not need all those that exist today and some will simply fold. Only time will tell. For now here is a **"starter list"** that identifies some of the major players in the Pharmaceutical Industry:

Johnson & Johnson
Pfizer
GlaxoSmithKline
Novartis
Merck
Abbott Laboratories
Wyeth
Bristol-Myers Squibb
Eli Lilly
Amgen
Schering-Plough

This initial, working list of corporate entities may very well be refined as 2008 progresses and the November 2008 National Election draws near.

By deliberate, united vote on that historic day, *We the People* can freely declare that such practical and prudent Change to the National System for the Common Good of us all — will be made.

The Entity Re-Structuring Levels (ERL) Overview

The Pharmaceutical Industry

ERL 1 – Operational Reorganization

A newly formed Board of Directors will comprise the first level of the APC Organization Chart.

Starting with the largest, the existing Pharma corporations both for-profit and non-profit will effectively become operating Divisions of the newly formed, Non-profit American Pharmaceutical Consortium (APC) – the Industry Management Consortium established for the restructured Pharmaceutical Industry.

Further, any existing Pharma corporations that are currently part of another corporation will be transferred from the existing corporate entity also to become an operating Division of the APC. They will not be purchased or bought out initially just because they are stock held corporation. Those Division entities will form the second level of the new APC Organization Chart. Again, this corporate reorganization will not be optional.

> There are of course situations where non-American based corporations are distributing prescription products in the U.S. Those will be required to deal with the APC, and their pricing will be adjusted accordingly or they may very well lose this business! Simple rules are easier to follow.

The operational and administrative offices of each of the existing Pharmas would be systematically and efficiently consolidated over a few years into a smaller network of APC Operations facilities. The R&D sites would not be consolidated until some of them proved to be no longer viable and/or redundant. Such operational and administrative consolidation always happens when companies merge, we have all seen it. Therefore some reduction in employment would eventually occur.

Note: Although the Consortiums are set-up as Non-Profit corporations, these organizations will pay taxes, at least in the initial years.

o   o   o   o

There may also be some non-profit Pharmas in the mix that of course do not have stockholders to pay, which will make them far easier and less costly to merge into the APC . However, do not assume for a minute that they don't <u>make</u> profits! They pay-out those dollars within their organization instead, that is where the money goes — always to the Board and management, and sometimes even to the employees. They bonus plans pay out based on year-end numbers.

Calendar year 2009 could well be the end of that money train at least at the executive level. Of course, many of those executives will be gone in 2009, if We do the right things at the polls in November 2008!

ERL 2 – Existing Management Retirement

<u>Existing Senior Management</u>

- Any member of senior management with Golden Parachute will be retired by May 30, 2009. Any and all stock options in their package will be eliminated.
- No more Golden Parachutes will be offered to future management, ever.
- Any remaining member of management with a base salary in excess of one (1) million dollars per year will have it cut to that amount as of July 1, 2009.
- All stock options for 2009 will be eliminated.
- All 2009 bonuses will be reviewed by the APC group and may be reduced.

And if a given person does not like those Changes – they know where the door is…

<u>Remember:</u> The <u>one-time</u> offer to hold current and prior management <u>and</u> employees harmless from all forms of lawsuit will be presented and I believe will be eagerly accepted. This offer will be made to the current and prior members of the Boards of Directors, as well.

<u>I personally believe</u> that there could well be some very, ugly skeletons in the closets of the Pharmaceutical companies. It will serve the nation to know what they are, so we may then act to correct what can be corrected. The freedom from all potential lawsuits, liability, and jail time will allow those that know such secrets to go public and clear their conscience. Time will tell. I am not a betting man, but I would even put 5-buck$ on that one!

<u>Existing Boards of Directors (BOD)</u>

The existing BOD would be relieved of their positions by May 30, 2009. By law most, if not all corporations are required to have some form of

BOD whether it is actually functional to the operation or just ornamental. The future form and function of the BOD of the new Non-profit American Pharmaceutical Consortium (APC) will be reviewed.

ERL 3 – New Management Structure and Charter

The *Industry Management Consortium* BOD Requirement

With the consolidation of the Pharma corporate entities, we are merging a group of businesses that like the HCI Industry are pretty much doing the same thing, but not the pure operational redundancy of the HCI corporations — as will be described more under ERL 4. Thus, only a single Boards of Directors "entity" is all that will be needed. The high costs that are now associated with all the existing corporate BODs is therefore no longer necessary and will go back into the operation — true trickle down! Those freed-up funds could pay a lot of health related insurance premiums for the currently uninsured.

The APC's Board will be responsible to the American public for implementing, strictly overseeing, and refining the new Charter of Operations. They will not manage the day-to-day operation.

Revised Charter of Operations

Simply stated the new APC's Inaugural Charter will be to:

1. Coordinate the consolidation of all existing American Pharmas into the new APC organizational structure.
2. Redefine and streamline the business relationship between Health Care Insurance and Pharmaceutical Industries.
3. Coordinate how the APC will impact the existing Medicare and Medicaid Systems. It should serve to bring down the costs.

This charter will be amended as the AIR Program progresses. The Veterans Administration Health Care function will be reviewed against the APC structure. We will not diminish VA prescription coverage, but we will have an open debate on the most operationally and cost efficient way to cover our active military and veterans over the long haul. Again, that is our responsibility to them.

ERL 4 – Stock, Profitability, and Pricing Controls

As is repeated in these six proposals — the following scenarios will begin taking effect as soon as possible in 2009 and will likely be applied retroactively when the required legislation is passed by the **new** U.S. Congress.

While We can always hope, there is probably little chance that the existing Congress and White House will move on this proposal before the November Election. These six Industry proposals need to be the **hottest topics** in the country during 2008. The electorate must bring these and the other American Agenda Proposals to the campaigns! We can do this.

Stock Trading Control

On a selective basis, meaning corporation by corporation, stock trading in the Pharmaceutical Sector of the stock markets will go into a state of virtual suspense. The buy-out share price will be initially set at its 1-1-2008 share price. Any negotiation and eventual buy-back activity will start at that price or lower and could possibly be adjusted by the individual stockholder's buy-in share price.

The Markets would be intensely watched (by the SEC and others) in the run-up to the 1-1-09 AIR Program Effective Date for any selling or other game playing. Violators will be severely dealt with including fines and/or prison time in a State run facility. No Federal playpens anymore.

Profitability Control

Annual profitability of the formerly publicly traded corporations, now Divisions of the non-profit APC will be capped effective 1-1-09 at no more than four percent (4%) for physical year 2009 and more importantly quarterly/annual stockholder dividend pay outs will be appropriately capped or fixed.

The profits in excess of that will be put to practical uses such as:

- covering the initial re-organization costs
- elimination of any out-sourcing activities
- internal operational spending
- used to decrease next year's rates
- help pay the premiums for those currently without HCI coverage
- set aside for stock dividends pay-outs in future years until the buy-back process is complete
- used for the stock buy-back process

Prescription Plan and Product Pricing Control

Prescription plan and product pricing that the Pharmas now coordinate with

HCI corporations will in the future be a discussion between two (2) Industry Management Consortiums and the management within their respective organizations — those being the HealthCare Insurance Group (HIG) and the American Pharmaceutical Group (APC). And, so there will be no misunderstandings, the HIG will be the Big Dog!

We really must keep our sense of humor as we go through these somewhat intense and tedious scenarios.

It would be wonderful if all this could be in place going into 2009, but that is too much to expect – even though it will be suggested! Therefore, both the HCIs and Pharmas will probably roll into 2009 with rate increases and the ritual of re-enrollment in HCI plans. It will be the last time.

Depending on how the legislation rolls along in 2009, and it will be unmercifully pushed through Congress, there would probably be excess revenue generated over the 2009 profits and stockholder pay-outs that will be retroactively capped for the 2009 physical year. Those dollars would be captured by the APC and put to good uses — some of which were noted above.

Looking ahead to 2010, Pharma prescription plans (to the extent they still exist) and product pricing would be capped at 4% or less while the system is sorting itself out.

This should be sounding pretty much like the HCI, AIR Program because it is. It is a restructuring assembly line. The first two have a lot in common and the other four will be very similar.

ERL 5 – Conversion of IGE Model

The AIR Re-structuring of the American Pharmaceutical Industry offers another opportunity to transition a National Infrastructure Industry into an Income Generating Entity (IGE).

Over a period of years, all existing stockholders will be bought out. The stock amounts involved and how the stockholders will be compensated for their share value will be worked as the AIR Program implementation of the Pharmas progresses. Again, that is not avoiding discussing the hard dollars involved. The numbers are what the numbers are, and they will only continue to grow worse the longer We delay these Changes of Necessity to our National System.

I deliberately would not take the time extract and present that data on this or the others in this infamous group of six Existing Industries. Further, I predict those numbers will be one of the first things that the Special Inter-est lobbyists for that group throw out to scare everyone with. But, that heated rhetoric will soon pass. We will not be afraid nor deterred from working for our Common Good. It is another big step in providing cost effective Health Care Insurance for ALL American citizens starting in 2009.

o   o   o   o

That is all.

Next, Dealing with the *Deadliest of Drug Pushers.*

o   o   o   o

Existing Industries
Proposal 24
The Tobacco Industry

"Finally 'Dealing' with the Deadliest Drug Industry"

Issue/Problem

It is only the *slow, often agonizing deaths* of approximately 500,000 Americans every year (fully 8 Vietnam Wars worth of kills each year). And then there are the millions of family members left behind.

The Plain Truth of this situation is that the U.S. government is allowing and sponsoring the manufacture and distribution of the nation's most additive and regularly used drug – *nicotine.* And all to "keep alive" an industry that has officially been known for over 40 years to be killing not only its active drug users, but innocent bystanders such as non-smoking family members by way of second-hand smoke and decreasing the general health of many others.

If it were only 450,000 per year (51 per hour!) since 1968, that is 18,000,000 dead Americans! Again the LKF – Legislative Kill Factor shows itself again. If you recall the birth year tables earlier in CS2, the average was about 4 million babies born each year. So that's 4 million births and more than 450, 000 deaths each year just due to cigarettes. Over that same 40-year period marijuana killed zero (0) Americans. And the government easily arrests over 500,000 Americans a year simply for possession. Two of the more outrageous examples of the negative public power the lobbyists exercise over Congress, *common sense*, and our lives.

o   o   o   o

And just why have "our" federal and state governments worked for decades to protect and perpetuate this assault on reason and public health?

First, caving into Tobacco state and industry lobbyists and gladly accepting their campaign donations. A close second is due to the huge amount of taxes that are raised from cigarette addicts regularly feeding their habit. Third is the predictable flow of customers into the Medical Industry – all those sick people equal profits and a steady income stream... Consider that the American Medical System is still structured to repair and manage illnesses — it does not work to prevent illnesses. Where would be the profit in that? The Dark Side of Capitalism.

And lastly, although the point was never really brought out in public until some years ago when one of the major tobacco companies was caught making a marketing pitch to a foreign country — trying to expand their international sales base. The tobacco company's report told that government that building up tobacco use and sales would generate revenue. It went on to say that tobacco use would also <u>decrease</u> the <u>life</u> <u>span</u> of those that smoked, and therefore would help to reduce that government's long term costs related to social and medical services! Needless to say the subject tobacco corporation took real heat when that gem went public. That really happened and you can put your own label on it!

This is the type of real life, public scenario I am talking about when I say that — sometimes it feels like We are living in a *grim fairy tale.*

Recommended Viewing

"Thank You for Not Smoking" is an interesting and well done film about the Tobacco Industry lobby. It takes a humorous approach to dealing with the issue of an industry that sells the "most used" addictive substance in the world.

o   o   o   o

Perspectives

The text of next two short pieces is courtesy of the folks at Wikapedia.com.

Yes, that *King James* – Authorized what we call the *King James Bible* in 1604; published 1611.

First Piece

As the use of tobacco became popular in Europe, some people became concerned about its possible ill effects on the health of its users. One of the first was King James I of Great Britain, he wrote *A Counterblaste to Tobacco* in which he asked his subjects,

> You have not reason then to be ashamed, and to forbeare this filthie noveltie, so basely grounded, so foolishly received and so grossly mistaken in the right use thereof? In your abuse thereof sinning against God, harming your selves both in persons and goods, and raking also thereby the marks and notes of vanitie upon you: by the custome thereof making your selves to be wondered at by all forraine civil Nations, and by all strangers that come among you,

to be scorned and contemned. A custom loathsome to the eye, hateful to the Nose, harmful to the brain, dangerous to the Lungs, and in the blacke stinking fume thereof, neerest resembling the horrible Stigian smoke of the pit that is bottomelesse.

Second Piece

In Summary

Tobacco smoking is the act of burning the dried or cured leaves of the tobacco plant and inhaling the smoke for pleasure, for ritualistic or social purposes, self-medication, or simply to satisfy physical dependence. Tobacco use by Native Americans throughout North and South America dates back to 2000 BC and there are depictions of ancient Mayans smoking a crude cigar. The practice was brought back to Europe by the crew of Christopher Columbus. Tobacco Smoking took hold in Spain and was introduced to the rest of the world, via trade.

Tobacco smoke contains nicotine, an addictive stimulant and Euphoriant. The effect of nicotine in first time or irregular users is an increase in alertness and memory, and mild euphoria. In chronic users, nicotine simply relieves the symptoms of nicotine withdrawal: confusion, restlessness, anxiety, insomnia, and dysphoria. Withdrawal symptoms in chronic users begin to appear approximately 30 minutes after every dose. Nicotine also disturbs metabolism and suppresses appetite. This is because nicotine, like many stimulants, increases blood sugar.

It has been determined that all forms of tobacco use are addictive.

Medical research has determined that chronic tobacco smoking can lead to many health problems, particularly lung cancer, emphysema, and cardiovascular disease.

My thanks again to those at Wikapedia.com.

About Addiction

In good old Mr. Webster's own words, *addiction* is defined as:

1. The quality or state of being addicted.
2. Compulsive need for and use of a habit-forming substance (as heroin, nicotine, or alcohol) characterized by tolerance and by well-defined physiological symptoms upon withdrawal; broadly : persistent compulsive use of a substance known by the user to be harmful.

A person I know, has battled alcohol and cigarette use over <u>many</u> years. She long ago conquered the drinking, but the fight against nicotine goes on. She attended countless AA meetings over the years and has knows many folks in that community. She very interestingly summed up the situation one time sharing that people with those problems want very much to get off and stay off alcohol, however they <u>do</u> <u>not</u> want to give up their cigarettes. They just like it that much. It is called addition.

Another person I heard about recently gets up every morning and has only one (1) cigarette! Then, just slaps on a 21-milligram Nicotine Patch to get through the rest of the day.

The typical Patch regimen to 'help' someone quit smoking is:

- Weeks 1 thru 6 – 21mg level; each box has 14 one-a-day patches.
- Weeks 7 thru 8 – 14mg level; each box has 14 one-a-day patches.
- Weeks 9 thru 10 – 7mg level; each box has 14 one-a-day patches.
- A total of five (5) boxes at an average price of $41. per box. Pharmacies keep these in locked cabinets that are <u>not</u> located behind the counter. If not locked up they are high theft items.
- There are no guarantees of success.

Aren't legalized drugs just wonderful?

o   o   o   o

The People's Sense

Let's face it folks, there simply is not a lot more to say here. If we could wave a magic wand, there would be no more cigarettes smoked in the United States of America or the cancers and other avoidable illnesses it produces. Sad to say, but our magic wand will never have that level of power — so what can We do?

Our "PLAN B"

To address this situation We have two (2) groups of people to consider – those that are currently smoking and addicted, as well as those that have not yet that started down that road.

For the Existing Smoking Population

The American Tobacco Producers will begin a mandatory process of decreasing the level of the addictive ingredients contained in their cigarettes.

Those ingredients were first added to make them "inhale-able" — that is why people do not inhale cigars; others to make the taste more appealing; and others, primarily nicotine to deliberately (and of their corporate *free will*) make it rapidly addictive to a person's body and <u>brain</u> – it is the "kick of the nic."

The logical main focus will be on cutting the level of nicotine and other addictive properties contained in cigarettes over only a few years — for example cutting nicotine down to possibly a quarter of what it is today. As the volatile 'discussion' ramps up over the reduction process, We will work out the details of reducing nicotine content, as well as any other addictive ingredients cigarettes now contain.

In the future access to Nicotine Patch 'could' require a doctor's prescription to obtain as part of an overall health recovery process under the new national HCI program. The nicotine drug content in Nicotine Patches (and similar products) will be reduced from the current of 21mg, 14mg, 7mg levels — the 21mg patch will be eliminated first and then the 14mg product as the program progresses.

And any foreign produced cigarettes wishing to <u>continue</u> selling their products in this country will reduce their content mix accordingly.

For the Potential Smoking Population – Our Youth

Since 18 years old is the age when a person is <u>supposed</u> to be able to make their own decisions and <u>is</u> <u>legally</u> <u>accountable</u> for their actions under the law — that will necessarily become the nationally acknowledged age of civil responsibility with *regard to smoking in public*! To increase the smoking age to 21 years of age would be flatly impractical and totally foolish.

Our national goals here are the exact opposite of what the Tobacco Industry strives for today. Our first goal is to minimize the number of our youth that try smoking in the first place. Secondly, for those that do try it, that they will be inhaling a far less addictive ingredient mix — thus reducing the number to that will get addicted to it in their first pack! Especially targeting those that are under 18 years old! Again, please see the movie, *Thank You for Not Smoking* – with your kid(s).

A few points to be made here:

- Going forward some of our youth under 18 years of age will still be exposed to cigarettes and some will always try it for various reasons just as they do with alcohol, marijuana, and other "adult" activities legal or not. That has always been life in America and We must begin living in reality!

- With the decrease in nicotine and other addictive ingredients, the *cancer sticks* will at least become "less" addictive for first time users – it is a good start.

- We will nationally prohibit public cigarette smoking by anyone under 18 years old. That will be a big one. This will not stop people from smoking, which We cannot do anymore than We have stopped some 20-plus million Americans from smoking pot regularly. However, it will work to decrease those that initially try the *coffin nails* in their early teens when the cigarette 'pushing' companies most want to hook them on nicotine.

- We must always remember that many of the people that get addicted to nicotine are unfortunately pre-disposed to being addicted to something in their life, simply by genetics – they factually inherited the trait. Alcohol, tobacco, prescription drugs, and food are just the easy points of satisfaction for them in our society. There is unfortunately a real chance that they will become addicted to something that could be physically damaging to their own health during their life and it usually starts in their teens and twenties.

- If it is not already the case everywhere, smoking will be prohibited on all public school grounds. Special smoking areas for students will not be allowed and it will not be allowed in high school parking lots very much longer, either!

- With the re-introduction of physical education in the public school system mentioned earlier, our youth will be taught what it takes to get and keep body in good condition to have better health. Such knowledge and the fact that they are in good physical condition will cause some of them to personally decide not to damage their health with tobacco. Bingo!

Overall, We will very quickly work to decrease the addictive properties of cigarettes. First it will help the existing cigarette addicts, even though it is acknowledged that many will not appreciate it. I know because I have bounced this proposal off numerous smokers – and had some very open and intense conversations at times to be sure. Their positions run from "I will dam well smoke cigarettes until the day I die if I want to" to acknowledging that it might help them to quit down the road.

Second, through public advertising We will aggressively attack the appeal — both social and chemical — of cigarettes to our under 18 year old youth population.

In early December of 2007, I asked one of my co-workers that is a long-time smoker (in his 50's) and knows about CS2, how he felt about me confronting the Tobacco Industry. His instant response was "Don't take my cigarettes away." A few weeks later I asked him how he felt about lowering the nicotine content of cigarettes to make them less addictive. He said that was OK — that he was trying to quit (again) because those things were killing him!

o   o   o   o

American Industry Re-Structuring (AIR) Program

The Tobacco Industry

Overall Re-Structuring Approach

The American Tobacco Industry will experience the full force of the AIR Program Re-Structuring program. Any questions?

Right up front it is acknowledged, that the production and distribution of tobacco products specifically cigarettes and chewing tobacco, cannot not be totally eliminated — at least not for many years to come. However, over the next few years, tobacco's addictive properties will be dramatically reduced. Further, the profitability to be made from their sale will be controlled and redirected to better purposes. All corporate entities wishing to continue doing business in the U.S. will comply with this involuntary Tobacco Industry re-organization. It will not be a negotiation.

There is no need to repeat the points that were made under the People's Sense section a few pages ago. Overall we will aggressively advertise to our youth under 18 years old not to start smoking cigarettes n the first place, as well as mandating the steady decrease in nicotine content and other addictive "ingredients" that are to be found in cigarettes as of 1-1-08. Again, not rocket science!

o   o   o   o

The remainder of this proposal shall simply overview the AIR Program's application to the existing American Tobacco Industry. If you read the previous two proposals this follows a similar pattern. And since the Tobacco Industry is a "totally redundant" operation from corporation-to-corporation, and the farming, production, and distribution are very straightforward — this will actually be the easiest of the six Existing Industry restructurings to facilitate. And the Plain Truth is that the majority of American society has grown more and more against their products and their physically, destructive properties.

The Initial List of Industry

This is the initial list of primary Tobacco corporations and companies to be included in the AIR Program Re-Structuring of the Tobacco (most deadly drug) Industry:

Altria Group
Reynolds American
Universal
Alliance One International
UST

Although the names are not what We might think about when it comes to the Tobacco Industry suffice it to say that all corporations that produce the cigarettes brands you see at the typical American retail outlet such as, grocery and convenience stores will find their onto this list.

This initial, working list of corporate entities may very well be refined as 2008 progresses and the November 2008 National Election draws near.

By deliberate, united vote on that historic day, *We the People* can freely declare that such practical and prudent Change to the National System for the Common Good of us all — will be made.

AIR Program – The Entity Re-Structuring Levels (ERL) Overview

The Tobacco Industry

ERL 1 – Operational Reorganization

A newly formed Board of Directors will comprise the first level of the ATC Organization Chart.

The existing American Tobacco Industry (ATI) corporations will effectively become operating Divisions of the newly formed, Non-Profit American Tobacco Consortium (ATC) – the Industry Management Consortium established for the restructured ATI.

Further any existing Tobacco corporations that are currently part of a larger corporation will be transferred from the existing corporate entity to become operating Divisions of the ATC. They will not be purchased or bought out initially just because they are a stock held corporation. Those Divisions will form the second level of the new ATC Organization Chart. This corporate reorganization will not be optional.

As with the previous industry reorganizations, the operational and administrative offices of each of the existing Tobacco corporations would be systematically and efficiently be consolidated over a few years. Such consolidation always happens when corporations merge, we have all seen it. In the case of the Tobacco corporations where their entire operations are extremely redundant, there will be more opportunity for administrative cost savings — with some a natural reduction in employment.

On a positive note, the coming commercial legalization of Hemp and cannabis will provide the opportunity for some other employment in those same geographic areas. Also, some current tobacco farmers will probably transition and become independent of the Tobacco companies.

The short and long term plan will be to deliberately reduce the number of teenage Americans that begin smoking in the first place. This will be accomplished by making cigarettes a less additive product and by enforcing the 18 year old age limit on cigarette purchase. The result will be a steady drop in annual unit sales of cigarettes over the next decade, as well as less smoking related illnesses and deaths in the future.

Note: Although the Consortiums are set-up as Non-Profit corporations, these organizations will pay taxes.

ERL 2 – Existing Management Retirement

Existing Senior Management

The same scenario as before.

- Any member of senior management with Golden Parachute will be retired by May 30, 2009. Any and all stock options in their package will be eliminated.
- No more Golden Parachutes will be offered to future management, ever.
- Any remaining member of management with a base salary in excess of one (1) million dollars per year will have it cut to that amount as of July 1, 2009.
- All stock options for 2009 will be eliminated.
- All 2009 bonuses will be reviewed by the ATC group and may be reduced.

And if a given person does not like those Changes – they know where the door is…

Remember: The one-time offer to hold current and prior management and employees harmless from lawsuit will be presented and I believe will be accepted. This offer will be made to the current and prior members of the Boards of Directors, as well.

Existing Boards of Directors (BOD)

The existing BOD would be relieved of their positions by May 30, 2009. By law most, if not all corporations are required to have some form of BOD whether it is actually functional to the operation or just ornamental. The future form and function of the BOD of the new Non-Profit American Tobacco Consortium (ATC) will be reviewed.

ERL 3 – New Management Structure and Charter

The *Industry Management Consortium* Requirement

With the consolidation of the existing Tobacco corporate entities We will be merging a group of businesses that have all but, pure operational redundancy. Each of these corporate entities will become operating Divisions in the ATC Non-Profit organizational structure.

Therefore, a single Board of Directors "entity" is all that will be needed and they will not be simply ornamental. The overhead costs that were associated with all of the former corporate Boards are thus eliminated and will go back into the operation.

The ATC's Board will be responsible to the American public for implementing, administering, strictly overseeing, and refining the new Charter of Operations. They will not manage the day-to-day operation within the Divisions. The management that remains after the existing senior people are retired will be given an opportunity to take charge of the day-to-day operation, but working under a new charter.

The AIR Program re-structuring of the Tobacco Industry will be unique in that We are not talking about maintaining a necessary industry, such as Health Care Insurance. Instead the ATC's long term goal will be to plan and manage the decades, long almost total shutdown of the American Tobacco Industry. That will be the hoped for end game strategy. No smoke and mirrors here – just the Plain Truth!

With the severe reduction in the addictive properties of cigarettes and chewing tobacco; with fewer new smokers as the rules on young teenage smokers are supported in communities; as some percentage of current smokers are able to free themselves from less additive cigarette content; as the American Medical System begins to practice preventive medicine and good health; and, unfortunately as many of the current smoking population die mostly from Tobacco related illnesses – the Tobacco business will in time, wind down to practically nothing.

That is our very achievable future. Believe it!

Some of the management and other employees from the Divisions will be transferred into first level ATC organization that will centralize certain key administrative functions such as pricing and public advertising. With the number of qualified people in Divisions there will be little if any need to hire from outside staff for key positions – promotion from within will be the rule. Some of the employees will be good candidates to work in Hemp agriculture!

Recommended ATC Charter of Operations

The first level of the ATC will provide oversight and administrative control over the entire operation. The majority of the Tobacco business of farming, production, and distribution of tobacco products will of course be performed in the Operating Divisions. The ATC Board of Directors and staff will administer the overall operation and act as the primary contact point for all state-level agencies, and the U.S. Congress. It will be a working Board of Directors.

Simply stated the ATC's Inaugural Operational Charter will include:

1. Oversight of the consolidation of all existing Tobacco corporations into the new ATC organizational structure.
2. Oversee the full public disclosure of the ingredients in cigarettes and chewing tobacco by brand.
3. Oversee the staged decrease in the addictive ingredients in cigarettes and chewing tobacco over the next few years, with full public disclosure.
4. Oversee the complete reversal of advertising into a campaign stressing that teenagers should not take their first poof and that cigarettes will no longer have the 'kick' they did before 2009!
5. To work with state and federal agencies regarding the eventual decrease in cigarette tax revenue. Their tax revenue stream will be partially if not totally replaced by cannabis taxes. Isn't life strange?

The initial Charter will be amended as the AIR Program progresses, and with full public disclosure.

ERL 4 – Stock, Profitability, and Pricing Controls

As is repeated in these six proposals — the following scenarios will begin taking effect as soon as possible in 2009 and will likely be applied retroactively when the required legislation is passed by the **new** U.S. Congress.

While We can always hope, there is probably little chance that the existing Congress and White House will move on this proposal before the November Election. These six Industry proposals need to be the **hottest topics** in the country during 2008. The electorate must bring these and the other American Agenda Proposals to the campaigns! We can do this.

Stock Trading Control

Stock trading in the Tobacco stocks will be in a state of virtual suspense. The stock will be initially frozen at its 1-1-2008 share price. Any negotiation and eventual buy-back activity will start at that price or lower possibly adjusted by the individual stock-holder's buy-in share price.

The Markets would be intensely watched (by the SEC and others) in the run-up to the 1-1-09 AIR Program Effective Date for any selling or other game playing. Violators will be severely dealt with including fines and/or prison time in a State run facility. Again, no Federal playpens anymore.

Profitability Control

Annual profitability of the formerly publicly traded corporations, now Divisions of the non-profit ATC will be capped effective 1-1-09 at no more than four percent (4%) for physical year 2009 and more importantly quarterly/annual stockholder dividend pay outs will be appropriately capped or fixed.

The profits in excess of that will be put to practical uses such as:

* covering the initial re-organization costs
* help pay the premiums for some of those currently without HCI coverage — An excellent development!
* set aside for stock dividends pay-outs in future years until the buy-back process is complete
* used for the stock buy-back process

Pricing Control

There could be a flat 2% to 3% product pricing increase for 2009 while the system is sorting itself out. Again, part of the excess revenues in the early years would be funneled directly to the ATC. We will see how this all develops.

ERL 5 – Conversion of IGE Model

The AIR Re-structuring of the Tobacco Industry also offers another opportunity to transition the American Tobacco Consortium (ATC) into an Income Generating Entity (IGE).

Consolidation of existing American Tobacco corporations into the non-profit ATC will lead the way to their becoming eventually being converted to a pure IGE within the National System. Over a period of years, all existing Tobacco stockholders will be bought out. The stock amounts involved and how the stockholders will be compensated for their share value will be worked as a AIR Program implementation of the ATC progresses.

Again, this is not avoiding discussing the hard dollars involved. The numbers are what the numbers are, and they will only continue to grow worse the longer We delay this Change of Necessity to our National System.

However, unlike the Special Interest lobbyists for the other five industries in question, I predict that the Tobacco Industry will know that their time has come and will quickly realize that the public will not be alarmed by their slowly fading in American history. The senior executives and existing Boards will collect their exit payments and go away quietly.

And a larger and larger part of their revenues will *righteously* go toward funding – Health Care Insurance for ALL American citizens starting in 2009. Those who have the last laugh, never quit!

o   o   o   o

That is all.

Next, a brief Intermission!

o   o   o   o

Intermission – **Before the Final Act**

I found it important and very useful over the years to maintain a sense of humor even when dealing with tedious situations. And We are in the middle of a tedious situation!

I am drafting this unplanned piece for you on Christmas morning 2007. A belated *Merry Christmas* to all!

For Our Common Perspective

We have completed 3 of the 6 Existing Industry Re-structuring proposals. If you read through the first three you are familiar with the similar pattern they each follow.

The first three on Medical Insurance, Pharmaceutical, and Tobacco industries are viewed as prudent and publicly necessary Changes for the sake of our individual and collective national Health. They are not little, but comparatively speaking they are the light-weights of these six proposals.

The last three on the Oil, Banking, and Defense industries are clearly the heavy-weights, yet are absolutely 'bone marrow level' required Changes to the National System. Such seemingly radical, yet fully practical Changes to these critical industries will need to be publicly mandated to insure their prompt implementation. Further, for us to realize the benefits such Change will bring to our economy and our National Security. They without a doubt are the heavy-weights of An American Agenda and represent the ultimate domestic battles in this, our Second American Revolution.

There are surely some that are wondering how We could actually do (be allowed to do) all that was laid out in the previous 24 American Agenda proposals. The final three will really have those citizens questioning the rationale of the writer! To those I say – consider that more than a few of the American colonists thought that Thomas Paine was 'a bit' irrational when he boldly wrote that the colonies needed to make a "declaration of independence" from England. And, as he wrote to the colonists on the hard issues of their day, in the opening words of *Common Sense,*

> Perhaps the sentiments contained in the following pages, are not YET sufficiently fashionable to procure them general favour; a long habit of not thinking a thing WRONG, gives it a superficial appearance of being RIGHT, and raises at first a formidable outcry in defense of custom. But the tumult soon subsides. Time makes more converts than reason.
>
> January 1776

It is now 7:03 am on New Years Day 2008, and I am refining this piece. It is the first day of the year that very well, will come to define our nation to ourselves and to the world. For it is the year of the most important <u>and</u> critical, Presidential and U.S. Congressional campaign of our lifetimes <u>and</u> in our nation's lifetime. That is a prime the Reason why I was driven to write this book. We must come to the defense of our country and our desired way of life!

o   o   o   o

The American colonists indeed did <u>not</u> have the Right to do what they collectively decided to do just six (6) months later. They deliberately claimed and took the Right to correct the obvious flaws in the National System of their day. To call to *justice* the Few that were in the *habit* of abusing the Masses for suit their selfish purposes or simply their mood.

My hope and intent is that by this point the reader has become somewhat comfortable with the Common Good based reasoning offered thus far in CS2, and the hard, prudence of the problem solving methodology used in the Medical Insurance, Pharmaceutical, and Tobacco proposals. That hoped for comfort level with this national Change process will be a true benefit as We now review the last three — most radical and absolutely necessary of the American Agenda proposals.

I would submit to you that We American Citizens have the Right and the Obligation to our selves, our families, and those that will follow us – to do <u>whatever</u> is deemed to be fair, appropriate, and necessary to Preserve the Common Good of the United States of America.

To passionately Protect it from any forces, foreign <u>and</u> domestic, that of their own free will would put at risk the Life, Liberty, and Pursuit of Happiness that the Founders declared, the blood of the American colonists secured, and that all those who so bravely served our country over those 232 years have faithfully guarded. That is our Common Challenge in 2008 and beyond — to our selves and to our Posterity.

> The Ends <u>Do</u> Justify the Means. Especially when it is used to reverse practices that were built using that philosophy – and that resulted in deliberate harm to people, other businesses, society, the economy, national security, and the environment. It is a reckoning!

o   o   o   o

In approaching the nationally, practical re-structuring of these essential national industries, We must seek to reconcile our shared perception of them. We must right now begin to look upon them as though We are their Common Owners and Leaders, rather than their Common Servants or Followers.

In Plain Truth, the Energy, Banking, and Defense functions in every country in the world are consciously structured to *serve and benefit either* – the Few that actually govern that National System and control the general population, or, the Many and to promote the Common Good. It is *a question of balance* of Power and Influence that every nation in the history of the world has and does struggle with.

Today in America, my fellow citizens the time is at hand for Us to rectify the growing, destructive imbalance to Protect and Insure the Common Good. This is our *unavoidable* moment in time.

These critical industry proposals may also seem somewhat brief, since they represent such large and somewhat complicated National System functions. However, We will address our relative issues with these industries and what I term the People's Sense regarding the desired resolutions to be realized. I write to the Silent Majority in the common interest of the Silent Majority.

As you review the final three American Agenda proposals, place yourself in the position of the caretaker and guardian of the Common Good of all 300 million of your fellow citizens – not a small subset thereof. Consider that We must now become the new stockholders and owners of these critical elements of our National System — and our Charge and Charter is to logically re-structure these currently dysfunctional, national necessities into a highly functioning Democratic Economic model. One that will first, stabilize the quality of all of our citizen's lives, and then will insure our American National System's viability for the future.

I assure you, my fellow Americans that We not only have the Right, but also have the Ability and absolute necessity to do *all these hard things*!

o   o   o   o

That is all.

Next, Payback Time for Big Oil.

o   o   o   o

Existing Industries — Proposal 25

The Oil Industry

"Introducing the Beginning of the End for Big Oil"

Issue/Problem

The American Energy industry, primarily oil, coal, natural gas, and nuclear easily falls under the "national infrastructure industry" concept previously described. The American Oil Industry (AOI) will be the first Energy Industry to be restructured, because it is by far causing the nation the most problems – and deliberately so! The others along with solar and other forms of under-utilized energy required to run our National System will be dealt with as we aggressively develop and rapidly implement a real National Energy Policy. A policy based upon people and the environment — rather than corporate profits. It will take months, not even a year to formulate and begin putting it effectively in place.

For now let's take care of our 'oil-based' problems for the sake of the economy and the environment!

This will be, in a hand full of years be the industry-wide restructuring of the American Oil Industry to address its obvious disregard for the needs of American consumers, other businesses, and again, the environment. That includes their decades of overt, covert, and *blatant* lobbying against any viable alternative fuels that would decrease our national dependence on foreign oil and decrease their profitability. And the entire Energy Industry will be moving in a similarly public serving direction.

For one thing, IF, Big Oil had not been lobbying so successfully for the last thirty-five (35) years, since the OPEC-driven oil crisis of the early 1970's things would be quite different now, and We might not even be in Iraq today. Yes, that is one of the two real reasons our troops find them selves in Iraq. The other is to indirectly justify to the American public, unnecessarily large Defense Department budget increases and the corresponding Defense Industry build-up, i.e., the Military Industrial Complex (MIC). I digress *just* a bit, but there will be more on the dynamic Oil/MIC industries duo and their primary sponsors that since 2001 have been in the White House, Bush II and Cheney, respectively.

This proposal will serve the Common Good of all American citizens, American business, and yes, that little thing called the environment – all of which as an Industry they obviously could not care less about.

And keep in mind that the Bush II administration 'invented' the term, *Climate Change* to be used in public communications, instead of the nasty words, *Global Warming*.

Recommended Viewing

There are so many, but for starters these should inform and move you.

1. A Crude Awakening: *The Oil Crash*

Directors Basil Gelpke, Ray McCormack; Co-Director Reto Caduff/2007

In the early Fall of 2007, I was channel surfing on cable and happened across this movie on the Sundance channel. A foreign produced film (www.lavatv.com), it was the hardest thing I have ever watched regarding an industry-wise perspective on the Oil "situation" the world is too fast approaching.

Hopefully, the Sundance, Science, Nature, or History channels will get a hold of that movie and play it frequently in 2008.

2. Syriana (Warner Bros/2005)

Many people have heard about this movie because it stars George Clooney, but many have not seen it since it is not a comedy or love story. It is about the 'dark side' of Big Oil's management, and Middle East power struggles.

3. Why We Fight

Writer/Director Eugene Parecki/2005

This is also referenced of course under Proposal 27 – The Defense (Military Industrial Complex) Industry.

If you have not seen it (most people have not even heard about it) please go to Blockbuster and get this movie and watch it. And parents with teenage children, make sure they watch it with you.

It starts with President Dwight David Eisenhower's farewell address to the nation the night before President John F. Kennedy's inauguration. In that historic speech the much respected president warned the country about the potential build-up of the Military Industrial Complex (a title he actually created). Then the movie goes on to show how it developed right up to the present day and Bush IIs optional Iraq War. President Eisenhower's fears have been fully realized. Senator John McCain speaks in the movie that to me added to its credibility. It is very *sobering*. Hopefully the History and/or Military Channels will be showing this for the public's convenience and information in 2008.

In case you are wondering why talk about the MIC when we are reviewing the Oil Industry – because just like the Medical and Pharmaceutical Industries, they are fully inner-twined – watch the movie.

o   o   o   o

The People's Sense

And, So What Are We Going to Do About It?

First thing that We all should do is open up a window or your front door and <u>scream</u> as loudly as possibly,

"I'm mad as hell and I'm not going to take it anymore."

The second thing we're going to do is put the American Oil corporations and the Energy Industry in general on short-term notice. We will deal with the issue of their loyal supporters in the US Congress, in Part 5 of CS2.

What follows is not fantasy or intended to be funny. And, We the People have the absolute Right and Power under the U.S. Constitution to insist that such Changes <u>will</u> happen for the sake of our economy and our national security starting in 2009. It will set the example for other oil dependent nations to follow.

The American Public's Basic Expectations

First and foremost, We will aggressively work and do what ever needs to be done — to <u>first</u> <u>control</u> and <u>reduce</u> the cost of gasoline at the pumps, along diesel fuel and home heating oil costs.

Next, We will simultaneously work to reduce our individual use oil imports particularly in passenger cars and trucks.

Since 2001, these costs have been steadily increasing and slowly taking away disposable <u>and</u> now essential income at the individual, family, and business levels. And it has only worsened since March of 2005 after Bush

II's re-election. The Oil corporations have taken the art of "profit-taking" to a whole new and nationally abusive level. Some would call it pillaging!

As I put it, Big Oil along with some other industries are getting everything they can get out of us — out of the National System before Bush II and the Republican Party are finally thrown out by the disgusted electorate in the 2008 election.

o   o   o   o

Next in 2008, our government will explain why We are shipping most if not all of our "precious" Alaskan oil to Japan? I know that surprised me to find out! We demand that all the details and dollars involved in this strange agreement to be spelled out to the public. Then the agreement will be re-written.

Starting in 2008, the Department of Energy will publish on a monthly basis the true and verifiable Oil Supply and Consumption Statistics, and among other publicly informative numbers to highlight:

- the barrel of oil production and export for every oil producing country.
- the barrel of oil importation for every oil consuming country.
- the American (U.S. territory, only) barrel production, specifying how much is used at home and how much is *exported* and to where, like Japan!
- the barrel break-outs of how the imported and domestically produced oil is being used, e.g., cars, commercial trucks, airplanes, and the Plastics Industry, etc.

All will be presented in easy find and understand statistics that the public and the watchdog groups can keep track of month-to-month.

Commodity and Spot Market Folly

Next, for the sake of the world economy the UN, the WTO, the World Bank, NATO or some collective group with an alleged brain — and supported by 90-plus percent of the world population — must act to remove Oil from the world Commodity and Spot Markets. And the world stood still...

Since 2001, the current international "set-up" has become nothing less than an oil speculator's and commodity manipulator, dream come true. And has allowed oil producing nations and Oil Corporations to arbitrarily and unnecessarily drive up the per barrel price of crude. They have reached a point where people do not even need to blow up pipelines to make it go up! Do they think We are that stupid? Yes!

Removal from those markets would help first stabilize and then begin reducing the barrel price and will help save some national economies – like ours!

At the same time or as a prelude to that, the Congress will act to secure our supply of oil for the next 10 to 20 years with "direct contracts" with the same oil producing countries that We have always bought our oil from, like Saudi Arabia, Venezuela, and Mexico. And our newest Oil-buddy Iraq — that is why We went there – to control and insure the supply. Any questions?

On the Home Front – Environmentally Speaking

I do not have a specific piece on the environment in CS2. This seems an appropriate place to insert a related and very practical program idea. Something that each of us can choose to do right away!

Beginning with a slow ramp-up in 2008, the current U.S. Congress and the legislatures of all 50 states and DC, will aggressively promote conservation of all things at the individual, home, and business level. Starting with simple cycling bins and/or large, truck-hauling, containers located at every Wendy's, McDonalds (all 14,000 of them – think of the paper, cardboard, and plastic), 7-11, Home Depot, mall parking lot, sports stadium, public school, and every other place of business in the country. And where you live!

Remember every time you see a public trash can over flowing with bottles and cans (We have all seen them) – or you — toss a *plastic* bottle or food container in the trash, you are putting **re-useable oil** right back in the ground. Funny how none of our 'leadership' never challenges the public about this?

> Consider, I was talking with a former U.S. Navy submarine man the other day. He told that on certain Classes of submarines they actually take some types of plastic containers and convert (recycle) them into useable lubricants for use while at sea. What can you say? It is a simple example of the types of reusable oil-based products that are buried in thousands of landfills all over our country and the world. To say nothing about metal cans.

The American public can kick start this National Re-Cycling Program any day We want to. The very same day you read this! In a deliberate and united act of Civil Responsibility each person and business can start putting out more re-cycling out every week than trash — you, me (I already do), and everyone else.

It would prove to be surprising that the first action that We the People collectively take in this Revolution — that will physically demonstrate to our irresponsible government and industries, that We have indeed had enough and We are coming to take care of business ourselves – is taking our recyclables to the curb!

And no one can stop us from doing it! We will bury our city and county governments and a very happy the American Re-Cycling Industry in re-useable natural resources.

With regard to creating domestic jobs — each of the 435 U.S. Congressional Districts have on average over 550,000 people living in them. Each District will work with the Re-Cycling Industry to build its own District Re-Cycling Centers, to handle plastics, metal, paper, cardboard, and personal computer parts.

And the Environmentalists screamed, YES!!!

o   o   o   o

Oh yes, and millions of television sets!

Yes, America, We are being forced into upgrading our television sets. This advancement in television technology is a growing boom for cable, satellite, and phone company service providers.

By February 2009, American television stations will cease broadcasting on analog channels, which will end service for millions of people using outdoor antennas and indoor rabbit ears. The conversion will leave many low and fixed income people without service or being required buy new hardware and/or televisions.

And the governmentally imposed deadline is October 2009.

Now, some of us will finally know how to spend that $600 refund Bush II sent us a few years ago that has just been lying around all this time waiting for some nationally urgent purpose to pop up!

o   o   o   o

To continue

Consider the national chain reaction this <u>will</u> start. We will become a bit more self-sufficient regarding the domestic supply of oil-based products, paper, cardboard, metal, etc. Less imports and less of a drain on our domestic natural resources. This will have to promote some forms of domestic manufacturing which could be built upon.

As mentioned before, the Plastics Industry will then be able to get some of its source product from the 435 District Re-Cycling Centers. They are also <u>seriously</u> advised to be checking into the viability of using Hemp as a partial replacement source material, as an alternative to Oil in the manufacture of all those plastic products! The Plastics Industry <u>will</u> <u>need</u> to be picking up where Henry Ford left off in the 1930's when he was using Hemp-based plastic materials to make the entire outer body of a car (and was powering the engine on Hemp-based diesel fuel).

> Did you happen to notice in the last half of 2007 that both the Plastics <u>and</u> Petroleum Industries were running public advertising on the television about all the things that are made with plastics and used to improve the quality of our day-to-day lives? This would be called a form of domestic (possibly subliminal) propaganda designed to make us fell better about all of the Oil that is currently being imported, without saying it out loud.

> Consider that one reason that things We buy at the grocery store are costing more is because so many things are now packaged in p-l-a-s-t-i-c! So the per product price goes up and/or the manufacturer puts less product in the package. That's called lose – lose!

We must start by demanding that the grocery stores put small plastic bags in the Produce area so We do not need to two potatoes in a bag 18 inches long! You know what I mean. And many products will need to go back to glass containers. It will be very interesting to hear how the Plastics Industry responds when such issues are raised.

<u>The Automobile Industry</u>

As a related program, our national leadership will begin forcibly re-structuring what is left of the American Automobile Industry with an eye toward bringing back U.S. manufacturing jobs! They were likely to be the seventh industry to be attended to by the AIR Program methodology and are a natural candidate for becoming an Income Generating Entity "Industry". It would relieve a lot of their problems by cutting some of their overhead and the public's costs of transportation at the same time. Win-win.

The most recent gross, joke of a National Energy Policy bill was happily signed by Bush II in December 2007. Again, he and Congress brought home the bacon for their masters in the Energy Industry. Among other things it "boldly" stated that automobiles will need to "achieve' a minimum of 35 miles per gallon in the **year 2020**! That is absolutely Beyond Sense (BS). At the same time, of course, the Bush II administration said that the state governors could not mandate their own more aggressive (and realistic) fuel efficiency standards – like "Arnold" in California. More BS!

We will make more aggressive demands of our national leadership, such as:

- By 2011, if not in 2010, no new car without at least duel fuel capability will be allowed as a business tax write-off – state and federal. Hello!
- The new DAF cars will be **Built in America! ALL OF THEM!!!** Manufacturing comes back with a vengeance…
- We will begin to convert millions of regular gas burning cars and trucks to Duel or Alternative Fuel (DAF) engines. I understand this can already be done in some vehicles, and We will get better at it. That will be far less costly, easier, and faster (by years) than waiting for everyone to replace all those vehicles. We will manufacture the required engine parts as well. More domestic employment and a lot of it in Michigan!
- We will make auto financing and tax programs for people that want to move to a new DAF car or truck. And some of the parts from the converted vehicles could find their way to the 435 District Re-Cycling Centers.
- Some of those Centers will be built to meltdown metals and prepare it for re-use!

You get the idea. "And let's just do it." We do not need to study this anymore. We will start by making the easy Changes and have success there – while working out the harder steps.

For example, We will find out where the electric car was buried and have it *resurrected!*

o   o   o   o

In all, Bush IIs first term was bad enough in Oil and Energy areas, but after he scared enough of the public (with things like false pre-election terror alerts) into getting him re-elected in 2004 the screws have really been turned down on us. Starting in about March of 2005, gas pump prices have steadily climbed and it is simply eating away the vital retail economy, nationwide. The Oil companies only had "four more years" of Bush II and had to jump on the profit <u>taking</u>.

> It has been pointed out that "unlike many other countries, two thirds (2/3) of the US economy is driven by consumer spending (we may soon need to find out how the other countries do it).

Individual, family, and business "disposable and necessary" income being poured into gas tanks and heating our homes. While at the same time Big Oil is racking up all-time record quarterly profits and *their* Congress no longer even bothers to hold hearings for public show anymore – does not even try to put an end to the abuse. Yet, more good reasons to fire the lot of them (468 of 535) in November 4, 2008. And retire the Big Oil executives in 2009!

As I believe I referenced once before, if you happened to grow up "in the country" like I did, you know that to really kill a snake you must cut its head off! That surgical maneuver is what We will figuratively do with the predatory American Oil Industry – remove their management.

That is really all that needs to be said on the nation's Oil problem. I will forego burying you in statistics at this time. We all know that the Energy Industry in general and Big Oil in particular have our National Energy Policy, the current White House, and the Congress completely under their control.

Consider – after We the People have demonstrated our wrath upon the Oil Industry, that the Natural Gas, and Coal Industries – their current management and stockholders – could very well have a whole new attitude and should begin dealing fairly <u>and honestly</u> with Us!

American Industry Re-Structuring (AIR) Program

The American Oil Industry

Overall Re-Structuring Approach

The economically destructive, national security threatening and self-serving American Oil Industry (AOI) will also feel the full force of the AIR Program Re-structuring process and our common disapproval of them.

If you have read the previous proposals on the AIR Program restructuring of the HCI, Pharmaceutical, Tobacco Industries then you already know 'the pattern' and I will dispense with some of the rhetoric in this and remaining two proposals.

Again, there is no need to repeat the points that were just made under the People's Sense section a few pages ago. That fairly well overviewed the framework of our nation's new approach to controlling Oil related policy, how We will work to control pricing, and begin to 'really' reduce our use of Oil related products from the pumps to Plastics.

It is a viable, initial plan and will start us down a *real* path toward alternatives to oil-based products and other energy forms, as opposed to the *mythical* path we have been led down for 35 years by our oil-based National Energy Policy. A fool's policy that was designed and paid for by the Energy Industry to insure their profits, that is influenced by self-serving foreign governments and that has put both our economy and national security at Risk.

o   o   o   o

Liar, Liar

You may remember a few years ago when gasoline first reached $3.00 a gallon and people went crazy, that Congress summoned executives of the six (6) Big Oil corporation to appear before at Congressional hearing to explain why. At the start of the session a minority Democratic member of the committee suggested that they should be sworn in (just like the Tobacco company executives did some years ago – and were later slammed for having flat out lied under oath). The majority Republican chair of the group immediately said that would not be necessary. The executives then they went right ahead and said whatever they wanted to the committee.

The American Oil Industry executives currently feels they are above having to deal honestly with the Congress, let alone the American public. That

Industry's abuse of the Public Trust will come to an end, and their executives will soon be retired!

o   o   o   o

The relatively few large American-based Petroleum corporations involved in foreign oil importation to be included in the AIR Program Re-Structuring of the AOI represent the upper tier and majority of the Oil related industry in America – they are Big Oil. The AIR Program will not initially and may never need to be concerned with the smaller, domestic-only operations.

As the AIR Program restructures Big Oil and the National Energy Policy revisions spread across the National System, prudent Changes will 'trickle down' as appropriate to the various entities within the industry – and all for the Common Good.

In fairly short order the Coal, Natural Gas, and Nuclear Industries will also be reviewed in the context of a real National Energy Policy (NEP) – one that is designed to:

- Actually decrease the use of Oil products <u>throughout</u> our economy.
- Severely reducing the use and burning of all fossil fuels into the air.
- Doing what can be done to repair and help clean-up the environment from the damage already done – in the U.S. and around the world.
- First stabilizing and then decreasing the cost of energy to the home and business consumer to the greatest extent possible.
- All but mandating conservation <u>and</u> recycling by individuals and business as a National Priority.

This will be the functional opposite of what is contained in the newest and still dysfunctional NEP that was designed and directed by Energy Industry lobbyists and focused on their own self-serving corporate priorities – profits, stockholder dividends, and excessive executive compensation – rather than the Common Good of us all.

o   o   o   o

The primary corporate entities in the AOI and others involved in doing business in the U.S. will comply with this involuntary industry re-organization. This will not be a negotiation.

This restructuring will likely impact relationships and existing agreements and various "deals" made with various foreign countries. As needed, in order to do what is best for the American public and our economy those will be re-written and/or eliminated. With the AOI restructuring, we are confronting the greed and self-serving policies of corporate America, as well as those of certain foreign governments.

Considering that our economy, national security, and the environment are on the line – Everything is on the table. The economies of too many countries and the global environment are at terrible risk and the Masses will now begin dealing aggressively with the Few.

Have no misunderstandings about what is at stake here my fellow Americans. The coming confrontation with management of Big Oil and the cast of other greedy characters around the world that are so deeply involved in this game of Profit, Power, and Control, will most certainly be a momentous event in world history. That realistic confrontation is what is <u>now</u> <u>required</u> to for us correct this destructive imbalance. It is the time for the Meek not to inherit the earth, but for the Masses to call the Mighty, but Few to accountability for their abuses against their own societies and the environment that All people require to sustain life on this Earth. It is to be a mandatory, binding arbitration and reconciliation between the Powerful and over 95% of the world's population.

That was not intended to be dramatic. It is the Plain Truth of our global situation and We all had better wake up to the Hard Reality the faces us.

The remainder of this proposal shall overview the AIR Program's application to the American Oil Industry. Some additional details beyond what was presented under the People's Sense are included herein, but far more will follow in 2008.

The Initial List of Industry Entities

The short list of the Big Oil Corporations (BOC) to be included in the AIR Program Re-Structuring of the American Oil Industry is:

Exxon
Chevron
ConocoPhillips
BP/Amoco
Shell
Valero Energy
Marathon Oil
Sunoco

This initial, working list of *major* Oil corporate entities may be refined as 2008 progresses and the November 2008 National Election draws near.

By deliberate, united vote on that historic day, *We the People* can freely declare that such practical and prudent Change to the National System for the Common Good of us all — will be made.

Again the smaller U.S. Oil companies are not directly involved in this initial phase of the AIR Program implementation. Time will tell how they could be affected by the Changes to Big Oil and the overall National Energy Policy.

Since there are so few corporate entities to deal with this AIR Program it will be easier to implement the required AIR Program changes, which will occur as soon as We demand that the Congress take the necessary actions that are overviewed in this proposal, and will be further developed as things progress in 2008 and 2009. There are certainly some details to be worked out (in public), but our desired path is clear and in 2008 We will get our collective wagons moving in that direction.

o   o   o   o

AIR Program – The Entity Re-Structuring Levels (ERL) Overview

The American Oil Industry

ERL 1 – Operational Reorganization

A newly formed Board of Directors will comprise the first level of the AOC Organization Chart.

The existing American Oil Industry corporations will effectively become operating Divisions of the newly formed, Non-Profit American Oil Consortium (AOC) – the Industry Management Consortium established to oversee the operations of the AIR Program restructured industry.

That means the American-based Big 5 Oil corporations (Big Oil) and others in America's top 10 to 15 Oil companies — will become Divisions within the AOC and form the second level of the Organization Chart. There could be some smaller Oil corporations added in the future, but they are not critical to this exercise and are not involved at this time.

The issue of a Big Oil corporation currently being part of a larger corporation and needing to be transferred from the existing corporate entity to become operating Divisions of the AOC should not apply to this situation. If so, as with the prior industry proposals they will not be purchased or bought out initially just because they are a stock held corporation. In any case, this corporate reorganization will not be optional.

The operational and administrative offices of each of the former Big Oil corporations would be systematically and efficiently consolidated over a few years. Such consolidation always happens when similar companies merge, we have all seen it. Since there is great redundancy in their operations, some reduction in employment would eventually occur.

Note: Although the Consortiums are set-up as Non-Profit corporations, these organizations will pay taxes.

ERL 2 – Existing Management Retirement

Existing Senior Management

The same scenario as before.

• Any member of senior management with Golden Parachute will be retired by May 30, 2009. Any and all stock options in their package will be eliminated.

- No more Golden Parachutes will be offered to future management, ever.
- Any remaining member of management with a base salary in excess of one (1) million dollars per year will have it cut to that amount as of July 1, 2009.
- All stock options for 2009 will be eliminated.
- All 2009 bonuses will be reviewed by the AOC group and may be reduced.

And if a given person does not like those Changes – they know where the door is…

Remember: The one-time offer to hold current and prior management and employees harmless from lawsuit will be presented and I believe will be accepted. This offer will be made to the current and prior members of the Boards of Directors, as well.

Existing Boards of Directors (BOD)

The existing BOD would be relieved of their positions by May1, 2009. By law most, if not all corporations are required to have some form of BOD whether it is actually functional to the operation or just ornamental. The future form and function of the previously mentioned Industry Management Consortium created for the Pharmas, the AOC, will be reviewed.

ERL 3 – New Management Structure and Charter

The *Industry Management Consortium* Requirement

With the consolidation of the existing American Oil Corporations, the nation is again merging a group of businesses that are pretty much doing the same things – for the most part it is complete operational redundancy. Each of the Big Oil corporations will become operating Divisions in the AOC Non-Profit organizational structure. Therefore, a single Boards of Directors "entity" is all that will be needed. The costs that are now associated with the existing Boards is therefore not necessary and will go back into the operation. Those freed-up funds will be put to good uses.

The AOC Board will be responsible to the American public for implementing, strictly overseeing, and refining the new Charter of Operations. They will not manage the day-to-day operation.

Recommended Charter of Operations

The first level of the AOC will provide oversight and administrative control over the entire operation.

The day-to-day operations of the AOC will of course continue to be managed and performed by the Divisions and the existing operational managers and staff – the people that do the work today. The AOC management their staff will administer the overall operation. The AOC management team will be comprised of industry-wise outsiders selected for these critical positions and a staff selected from the managers in the Divisions that remained after the senior Big Oil management was retired.

The AOC management team will serve as the primary contact point with the U.S. Congress, any state-level agencies, and will be the negotiating agent with all Oil producing countries. It have a working Board of Directors.

As you review this initial Charter, keep in mind the related points made under the People's Sense section a few pages ago. They will be blended into the AOC mandate.

Simply stated the AOC Inaugural Operational Charter will include:

- Oversight of the consolidation of the existing Big Oil corporations into the new AOC organizational structure.
- Elimination of the "whatever it takes" mentality and need to make profits for their stockholders at the expense of consumers and other businesses that are currently suffering with ever-increasing Oil pricing.
- The AOC and the Congress will aggressively promote a national awareness campaign that individuals and businesses reduce their use of Oil sourced products – conservation in daily use and seeking alternative energy sources will be the rule.
- The AOC will work in close coordination with the American automobile industry that will be producing duel and alternative fuel vehicles, and to facilitate the near term availability of alternative fuels at the 170,000 gas stations across the country. Something that Big Oil has blatantly fought for decades.
- The AOC will aggressively work to reduce the amount of oil imported to this country for use in automobiles, trucks, airlines, manufacturing, home heating oil, and in the making plastic products.
- We will cease stupidly asking the Oil and other Energy industry Components (e.g. Natural Gas and Coal) to support the development of alternative fuels — because that has never been their business!

<u>Only If We Act</u> — These and other nationally prudent Changes to be identified not only can happen – it must happen. And, We the People will demand that it starts happening in 2008!

Consider this Radically, Practical Scenario

First, the U.S. would begin negotiations to obtain direct contracts from our regular Oil supplier countries. These are the same countries we have been buying our oil from for decades, and of course we will now <u>add</u> Iraq to that list. Establishment of these contracts would remove us from the fluctuations and abuses of the Commodity and Spot Markets. That will in turn decrease in the per gallon price at the pump. And the American consumer, businesses, and retail industry can exhale.

It will sound strange at first, but it is win /win. The <u>suppliers</u> would have multi-year fixed-price per barrel agreements that will insure the sale of their oil exports <u>and</u> We the <u>buyers</u> would have a guaranteed source at a fixed price i.e., starting around $60 a barrel or less. Do not fall for any short-term, negative Oil Industry propaganda on this approach, the supplying countries <u>can</u> be attracted to this.

It is now 2008 and prior to November's National Election such negotiation <u>could</u> be done at any time by the Congress if they get their collective act together and put Bush II in his place. If the White House dares to try and block it, they should be told that impeachment will be back on the table for both GWB and RC. And as I understand, it could be accomplished in less than 90 days – some serious food for thought. Senator Joseph Biden and Rep Dennis Kucinich have both mentioned that action during the campaigns.

As a backup supplier and/or in addition we will pursue oil contracts with Russia that is now pumping almost the same amount of oil now as the Middle East and is still ramping up new oil fields.

The U.S. Congress (probably over the screaming objections from the oil-based White House) would aggressively work with other countries to remove Oil from the Commodities and Spot market as soon as possible – and that means before the end of 2008.

Otherwise, in early 2009 the new Congress and President will do the job.

The Creation of OPIC

I have wanted to write this one down for a while! I propose the formation of the Organization of Petroleum Importing Countries (OPIC). It will be the functional alter ego of OPEC, comprised mainly the Middle Eastern oil Exporting countries. The nations represented in the new worldwide OPIC organization would work together to share ideas and approaches on such common issues as:

- how to practically reduce their use of Oil and so their dependency on it
- how to practically reduce their use of Coal and the damage it is doing to the atmosphere and the air we all breath.
- aggressively increase use of solar and wind energy sources.
- aggressively increase electric power through all possible sources and the use of electris powered vehicles.
- aggressively work to repair the damage already done to the environment by Global Warming.

o   o   o   o

Now at the risk of sounding a bit crazy (not that some don't already have that opinion of me) I also had to write this down for common review and perspective. Some months I was watching a nature/science program and they were in an Antarctic-type setting with both ice and exposed land. They laid two (2) fabricated tiles about 2' by 2' on the ground in board daylight. One was black on top and the other was white. After a while they read the temperature on the surface of each. The black one had absorbed the sun's rays and held a high temperature, while the white tile had reflected the sun's heat and was still cold. Why couldn't we begin a deliberate covering of land area in the extreme Northern and Southern Hemispheres that have been exposed by the Global Warming meltdown? The Earth is not reflecting away the sun's heat as much as it needs to and that is major contributor to the warming of the atmosphere and the continued melt-off. It would be a huge project, but it could be done and potentially with gargantuan paybacks. In time it 'could' help re-grow the glaciers. I wonder what the Environmental scientists will say about that one. Think about that for a while folks!

o   o   o   o

To continue with OPIC

There is <u>no</u> <u>practical</u> <u>reason</u> for the life's blood of so many national economies to be at the day-to-day mercy of idiots with explosives, commodities traders, and greedy Oil suppliers – as it is today.

The Oil suppliers must be held absolutely accountable for insuring no disruptions in their operations. They need to be responsible for working to eliminate the people that would cause supply disruptions, instead of profiting for sudden spikes in per barrel prices when things go bang in the night.

This change will certainly require some Hard Ball negotiations with a few of the Oil supplying countries, but if we do not get the speculators and corporate junkies off the Oil train they are on — it is only a matter of time until per barrel price drives the world economy to a crisis (we are nearly there now) that would only yield horrible results.

The national security our and other nations cannot remain tied to the world Commodities and Spot Markets any longer. It is an accident waiting to happen, and it is completely avoidable.

Call your states' Congressional members and tell them to get busy on this or not to bother raising any more money for their re-election campaign.

ERL 4 – Stock, Profitability, and Pricing Controls

As is repeated in these six proposals — the following scenarios will begin taking effect as soon as possible in 2009 and will likely be applied retroactively when the required legislation is passed by the **new** U.S. Congress.

While We can always hope, there is probably little chance that the existing Congress and White House will move on this proposal before the November Election. These six Industry proposals need to be the **hottest topics** in the country during 2008. The electorate must bring these and the other American Agenda Proposals to the campaigns! We can do this.

Stock Trading Control

Stock trading in the former Big Oil corporations now Divisions of the AOCs will be in a state of virtual suspense. The stock will be initially frozen at its 1-1-2008 share price. Any negotiation and eventual buy-back activity will start at that price or lower possibly adjusted by the individual stock-holder's buy-in share price.

The markets would be intensely watched (by the SEC and others) in the run-up to the 1-1-09 AIR Program Effective Date for any selling or other game playing. Again, violators will be severely dealt with including fines and/or prison time in a State run facility. No Federal playpens for the rich and famous anymore.

Profitability Control

They have had a good ride during the Bush II years, but the party is over. Corporate profitability for publicly held (stock) corporations will be capped retro-actively to 1-1-09 at no more than **three** **percent (3%)** for physical year 2009 and stockholder pay out will be capped accordingly.

As a result there will of course be access (large) profits generated in 2009 as the AOC Management assumes control of eh American Oil Industry. The profits in excess of that will be put to practical uses such as:

- merger related expenses
- elimination of any out-sourcing activities
- internal operational spending
- set aside for future dividend payments to stockholders
- set aside for the future stock buy-back process

Pricing Control

Note: There could be a flat 1% to 3% premium increase for 2010 while the system is sorting itself out.

ERL 5 – Conversion of IGE Model

The AIR Re-structuring of the American Oil Corporations is another opportunity to transition a National Infrastructure Industry into an Income Generating Entity (IGE). Consolidation of existing Big Oil corporations into the non-profit American Oil Consortium (AOC) will lead the way to their eventually being converted to a pure IGE within the National System.

With an aggressive national movement toward reducing oil/petroleum use beginning to gear up in 2008, it just makes sense to consolidate their operations. Further, this approach to corporate consolidation avoids the time consuming merger negotiations, huge buy-out expenses, and legal hurdles they would face if they slowly merged on their own over the next decade or so.

Over a period of years, all existing stockholders will be bought out. The stock amounts involved and how the stockholders will be compensated for their share value will be worked as a AIR Program implementation of the AOC progresses. AS previously stated, that is not avoiding discussing the hard dollars involved. The numbers are what the numbers are, and they will only continue to grow worse the longer We delay this Change of Necessity to our National System.

Therefore, I deliberately would not take the time extract and present that data on this or the others in this infamous group of six Existing Industries because those numbers will be one of the first things that the Special Interest lobbyists for that group throw out to scare everyone with.

But, We will not be afraid or deterred from our Common Goals – to reduce the use of Oil and oil-based products such as Plastics, aggressively promote the use of alternatives to Oil in all facets of the National System, as well as help the environment.

o   o   o   o

That is all.

Next, the Money Lenders.

o   o   o   o

Existing Industries

Proposal 26

The Banking and Credit Card Industries

"The Ultimate Game of Smoke and Mirrors"

Issue/Problem

As a note, I had planned to address Banking and Investment House under this proposal however the Credit Card issue is more closely tied functionally to Banking. And the Investment House Industry is a separate piece of chaos to be sorted out and I had to draw lines. Therefore, herein the focus is upon the Banking and the subset Credit Card Industries (BCI) with regard to their function within the National System – with some very pointed comments about the Investment House Industry. It would not be difficult to add them to the BCI restructuring program!

o   o   o   o

With everything else in the world causing distractions under the two (2) terms of Bush II, the Banking and Credit Card Industries had been flying pretty well under the radar of the press and other watch groups — that is until the Sub-Prime mortgage debacle really hit in 2007.

A few points to be made here

- As previously noted, the Banks and Bush II administration through a severe Bankruptcy Reform Act and it was signed into law on April 20, 2005. It was written to make it difficult to impossible for people file for personal bankruptcy. That legislation was simply aimed at "insuring" bank and credit card corporations would have fewer losses — not helping the American public in a struggling economy.

  It must be said that while bankruptcy is not anything that people want to do, it is sometimes a person's or a families' only option in a financial crisis or when unexpected circumstances present them self (I know because I have been there).

- The Bank actuaries (financial forecasters) knew that since 2001 the under-lying economy was not really doing well; that bankruptcies were already on the rise; that Credit Card (CC) debt was climbing nation-

wide; that more and more Americans (at all income levels) were struggling as a result of the continuing trend toward the out-sourcing of
jobs, businesses, and industries; that emergency and major medical costs
were destroying family finances — all of that was putting more and
more people in stressed financial conditions and the potential for increases in the bankruptcy rate was an <u>absolute</u> certainty.

Besides rising national credit card debt problems that the Credit Card
Industry has helped create by their irresponsible marketing practices
over the years, the Banks knew that when the Prime started back up the
people that barely qualified for certain mortgage loans would be at
severe risk of defaulting. Trouble was on the way.

So the BCI wanted to reduce their anticipated future losses (the actuaries at work) as the economy contracted, so they wanted good old Bush
II and the Congress to bail them out – to help cut their losses ahead of
time. And although it took 4 years, Bush II, the lobbyists and their
Congress did the deal.

• Today, the hard fact is that the greatest number of personal bankruptcies is being caused due to medical expenses and catastrophic medical
emergencies. And consider that it is not just the people in the group of
47-plus million American citizens without HCI that are being destroyed.

Obviously, the campaign donations from Banks, CC Corporations, and Investment Houses to the members of Congress, both parties, and the White
House really paid off that time!

<u>Not Totally Happy with the Bush Man</u>

The Banks and their associates in the Investment House side of the overall
Financial Industry were rather disappointed when Bush failed to get the
<u>real prize</u> that they were "banking" on from their support of his presiden-
tial campaigns. That being the establishment of private Social Security
accounts.

This would have been a gargantuan moneymaker for the Investment House
Industry, but not even their well-connected lobbyists could force Congress
to walk that plank against the Common Good of the American public, and
especially against the bigger and obviously meaner Senior citizen lobbyists! And thank God for that.

o   o   o   o

During 2006 and into 2007 the disturbing chatter going around DC was that the World Banking System is running dangerously along the edge of a major "adjustment or correction." And they were talking about a 1929 style of the financial earthquake worldwide! It is driven by the Banks being up to their eyeballs in Derivative products and other 'sophisticated' games (like bundling and selling mortgages) that they are playing for fun and somewhat false profits. Such financial Crashes are not caused by the little people however We pay the hardest price when it all falls apart. The Masses typically only have a first floor window to jump from!

Hopefully it will not prove a viable rumor, or else 2008/2009 could get very, very ugly. That is unless We start taking prudent steps to avoid it. If such a crisis has a real potential of occurring, then hopefully American Agenda Proposal #26 and the discussions around it will bring a glaring Press spotlight and needed public scrutiny to some key industries that have been flying for too long under their radar.

Remember the only thing that brought the U.S. and the world out of the Great Depression was World War II.

Words of Life – A Set of Three

Every once in a while in my life someone has said something to me — just sentence, maybe a few of them, and they got stuck forever in my mind. One of the **first** was my Mother telling the teenage me that "you can get more done with a few well chosen words, than you can with a half of an hour of screaming." I have lived very well with that thought and it helped me many times. In the IT business when others were chaos and there was a panic about what to do with a given situation, I generally remained calm and focused on resolving the issue at hand. You may wonder where this fits into the current topic, but please read on.

For a **second** scenario — the best manager I ever worked for taught me many things about project planning and systems design methodology. One day I was going over a preliminary system design with him and made the mistake of saying there was something sophisticated about it. To which he countered, "Andy, what is the meaning of the word sophisticated?" I did not know exactly why, but knew I was had. So I put on my dunce hat and asked what it was. He answered, "Sophisticated is that which has been robbed of its natural simplicity." Wham!

Mr. Webster defines the word *sophisticated* as follows:

    1: not in a natural, pure, or original state: ADULTERATED, 2:

deprived of native or original simplicity.

His overall point to me being that sophisticated systems whether they are automated and/or procedural are harder to develop and implement, <u>and</u> are more difficult to use, change, and <u>maintain</u> over the long haul. Systems built around functional and operational simplicity are always the best.

When considering this proposal on the BCI, phrases like 'smoke and mirrors' and 'follow the money' came to my mind.

The **third** line was offered by a co-worker many years ago when we were talking about taxes and politics and he dryly offered that "the one's to watch out for are *the non-working rich*." That line came back to me many times as this book developed, when considering the primary forces that will naturally oppose Change to the status quo of the National System, and in particular this proposal. It could apply very well to the characters that will be directly and in-directly confronted by the types of public-oriented Change that will be initiated by this proposal.

o   o   o   o

I must acknowledge that of the six Existing Industries this is the one that is the most perplexing for me to address and write about because the Banking System (its Investment House cousin) and the Credit Card to a lesser extent have become far too "sophisticated" for their own good, and therefore, too sophisticated for our own good!

<u>Thus</u>, my purpose here is to initiate the BCI restructuring that is <u>now</u> demanded to in order to Protect and Defend the economic health of our National System. The AIR Program, operational consolidation of the major Banking and Credit Card corporations and the replacement of their self-serving senior management will set the stage for and <u>actually</u> <u>permit</u> a functionally prudent and practical National Financial Policy to be designed, and accepted by the public, and implemented. And it need only take months to bring to reality.

The Other *Bloody* Edge

As I previously noted, the first American Revolution brought Democracy in Government to deal with one side of the Universal Sword of Tyranny. Our Second American Revolution must now bring Democracy in Economic Reformation to deal with other side of that Sword – that being the Economic edge that can and too often does cut deep into any society — especially, if the Few of political and financial Power are left alone too long to play their games. Look around the world and observe all of the destructive national examples of such economic imbalance – and the great concentration of those current day examples being located in the Middle East Oil producing countries. But, let us not be distracted from or forget our domestic Power problems.

The People's Sense

Some Observations for Consideration

- The Bankruptcy Reform legislation needs to be revisited and adjusted to some mid-ground that on one hand protects the BCI corporations from those that abuse the bankruptcy option, but must also assist families (of one or more persons) that are in desperate situations. Period!

  It may need to take the form of an overall national plan to restructure most if not all individual debt in American society. Something that We could initiate if over 100,000,000 Americans are interested in doing it!

- Since Bush II came to Power and increasingly since his 2004 re-election, Energy costs mainly in the form of gasoline, diesel, home heating have eaten away disposable family income — if they even had any. Consumers were paying more for goods and services, as well as pouring more money into their gas tank in order to go and buy those goods in the first place. Add to that food costs and the previously addressed Health Care Insurance costs that are going up annually for less coverage, higher deductibles and co-pays?

- On Main Street the Cost-of-Living is being driven up by the cost of goods (groceries) and services that were forced upward due to the cost of Oil products rippling through the economy, meaning that businesses were passing more of the uncontrollable costs along to the consumer whether they wanted to or not.

  Consider – my fellow Americans — all of the products at your favorite grocery store that are packaged in p-l-a-s-t-i-c — which means they are wrapped in p-e-t-r-o-l-e-u-m! Product manufacturers are forced to eat the costs, increase the per product price, decrease the product content to offset their costs – or eventually 'D' all of the above! True "trickle down" on us in action… Hint – glass is made from s-a-n-d.

- Regarding, the monthly Cost-of-Living (COL) statistics, there is another novelty that was brought to us by the creative people in the Bush II administration. It is reporting the monthly COL statistics without including Energy costs. Then, as an aside mentioning Energy costs as if it was a separate issue and somehow unrelated to our COL! Is that supposed to make somebody feel better? But then they believe that most Americans do not have a brain and are dumb to their obvious games? That is the manner in which they often communicate to us.

As mentioned before, they also invented the term "Climate Change" to be used instead of the dirty words "Global Warming". It is still a duck.

And one more, thoughtful example — the Annual Inflation Statistics for 2007 were reported on January 16, 2008. The annual inflation rate was announced at 4%. BUT, it was explained "if you take out the costs of food and energy it was a more reasonable 2.4%." Talking down to the peasants!

- If the consumer had an adjustable-rate mortgage from the 2002 to 2005 Real Estate Boom, their monthly expenses slowly increased as 2005 rolled thru 2006, real estate went Bust, and the game playing Mortgage and related worldwide Investment Industry were exposed and corporate losses grew as 2007 progressed.

Not until the of Sub-Prime mortgage debacle really hit in 2007, when the home foreclosures went though the roof, and rippled through the sophisticated World Banking System — did anyone consider freezing some (yes, some) of the periodic increases on adjustable rate mortgages. What a concept! Oh, what do you mean we cannot get anymore money out of those peasants!

And do not forget that there also were 'non' Sub-prime mortgage holders were hitting the wall due to financial issues as well over this period. They just have not received the same amount of Press coverage.

- On a part-time basis in 2004 and 2005 I was a mortgage loan officer in Loudoun County in Northern Virginia – one of the hottest areas in the nation during the Real Estate boom, it is located about 45 miles West of the White House. When I began in 2004 if a borrower had a score let's say of 590 or less it was pretty difficult for them to qualify for most mortgage loans. Over the next 15-month period that changed drastically to the point where it seemed that some people with a strong pulse could get a loan with various lenders – not all of which were not Sub-Prime borrowers and lenders.

This was a deliberate change orchestrated by the Banks and the Investment Houses (Wall Street). There simply was (and still is today) a huge amount of investor money sitting out there looking for something to do. All Banks introduced Interest-only, No Documentation, and other mortgage loan "products" intended to get people qualified. And they made loans.

Not too long after the Year 2000 Boom crashed in mid-2000. In order to help stimulate the economy Federal Reserve Board (Fed) lowered the Prime Lending Rate over ten (10) times in the next few years — mortgage rates soon followed, and both went to record lows into 2005. This set the stage for and fueled the Real Estate Boom, as well as laying the groundwork for the future Sub-Prime problems when the *inevitable time would come* for the Fed to begin increasing the Prime rate in spite of the fact that the economy was still struggling!

The *Banks* — wanted to make mortgage loans every month because they *have to make loans* and earn the related fees from those transactions, or, they do not make their profits, paychecks, or bonuses.

The *Wall Street Investment Houses* — willingly supplied the money because they *have to make investments,* and earn the related fees from those transactions, or, they do not make their profits, paychecks, or bonuses. And one Investment House executive whose corporation took a major hit in 2007 received a "sweet" 60-plus million dollar bonus just before Christmas. Rewarding failure. Ho! Ho! Ho!

Everybody made money on the way down. However, on the way back up the Industry would suffer, the weak Banks and careless Investment Houses would suffer greatly and/or completely fail. The overall domestic retail economy would be hurt as more family income went to mortgage payments. And the People would suffer the most in their monthly finances, and loss or fear of loss of their home. In early 2008, the number of foreclosures would be over 2,000,000. And it is not just Sub-Prime mortgage loans that have been and are continuing to fail.

o   o   o   o

And remember that Americans – singles and families — desperately want to own their own home, their own piece of the pie.

Again, by 2002 the real estate market had reached the point where too many 'regular' people could not afford to buy a home. It was the damn peasants again. So the Fed continued lowering the Prime Rate and the Banks continued lowering the mortgage rates and qualifying guidelines, and made loans!

Over the years, the Banks and Investment Houses got into the habit of "bundling" and selling their loans thru the Investment Houses (worldwide) rather than holding their own "paper" over the life of the mortgage. You know when you have closed a home loan and the bank immediately informs that so-and-so financial entity will now be 'servicing' your loan. But that does not fully remove all their liability if the loan goes bad.

The Banks that continued to hold their own paper did not lower their guidelines as <u>much</u> as those who would were routinely passing the loans off to another entity. Thus, they made fewer potentially bad loans during the Real Estate Boom and therefore suffered less as 2007 progressed, compared to the other banks that collapsed and literally went out-of-business, 'bankrupt' in 2007! Irony.

The closely tied World Banking and Investment Industries took a hit and caused bank and investor losses around the globe. The Banking System and the Bush II administration surprisingly moved to freeze 'some' mortgage rate increases. An action that will hurt investors (here and abroad), but injure the Banks <u>less</u> than a foreclosures would. As I understand it freezing rates is about 50% less costly to the Banks as a foreclosure would be.

It took the Sub-Prime Mortgage debacle that really began manifesting itself in 2007, to slam the profits of both the Banking and Investment House Industries. Again, that recent development rippled through both the domestic and World Banking Systems, some of the sophistication I was writing about.

o o o o

<u>**News Flash**</u> – Today is January 23, 2008. It odd ways I now believe it has helped, that certain unavoidable things happened in early 2007 that then delayed the completion of CS2 for several months, until the first week in February of this critical year. One is seeing some of events happen or begin to happen such as the growing Bank problems around the world. It is not for the purpose of saying my political senses and/or observations are correct, but to point out that if an average American can logically, analyze readily available information on issues of the day – then why can't our elected leadership do the same. The Plain Truth is that they can and do, but deliberately <u>choose</u> <u>not</u> use that knowledge to shape constructive and preventative policies for the Common Good.

o   o   o   o

Eight Years of Corporate Greed

The American consumer and economy have been hurting <u>even</u> more since about March of 2005 when Oil prices really began getting *artificially* pushed up and making even more profits for Big Oil and their Oil producing country cohorts. They and a few other key National Infrastructure Industries have been making record profits and having a *wonderful life* literally at our expense since Bush II came to Power:

- Medical Industry
- Pharmaceutical Industry
- Oil and other Energy Industries
- Banking and Credit Card Industry
- Investment Houses
- Defense Contractors

That is precisely why most of those critical National System industries are proposed herein for the AIR Program Re-Structuring. And the management of the Investment Houses, the Energy industries other than Oil, <u>and</u> their stockholders should be paying very close attention. After We have taken care of the first lot, We will be back to reconcile a few more. The Automobile, Investment House, and Plastics Industries could also be addressed as 2009 progresses.

And none of this is revenge my fellow Americans – again, this is a National Reckoning!

o   o   o   o

Reeling Things In

I became aware of a few things as a by-product of my brief time in the mortgage loan business such as how many properties (houses) an individual investor could purchase through the Banking industry – fifteen (15) was the highest I saw, <u>not</u> counting what they could obtain through private investor financing.

And, besides citizens and Permanent Resident Aliens (PRA) being allowed to apply for mortgage loans – there are also those living here on a <u>temporary</u> basis, as well as <u>strict</u> investors <u>living outside</u> the country could purchase homes. If those in the two latter groups had a sizable down-payment there was not a problem. My sense is that those latter two groups, as well as the 'flipping' of houses by the investor community greatly contributed to the run-up (the artificial bubble) in housing costs and rental costs – driving the Real Estate Boom and directly contributing to the run-up and overpricing of real estate nationwide.

My sense is that while this investor "free for all" cannot be completely stopped it must rapidly be brought and kept under strict and deliberate public control. Therefore , on a monthly basis, the number of mortgage loans made and homes purchased by **type of buyer and seller** must be "plainly" reported on the Federal Reserve Board website (www.federalreserve.gov) and printed in the Wall Street Journal and local newspapers for public knowledge and oversight.

If left unchecked the real estate investor community will continue to buy and sell properties, and thus would price more Americans out of being able to own a <u>single</u> home of their own. America is headed toward a situation where our citizens and particularly younger Americans could be lifetime renters rather than home owners. This condition <u>cannot</u> <u>be</u> <u>allowed</u> in America.

<u>Prudent and Practical Adjustments Will be Made</u>

It has to be America and Americans First, and the Banks, Credit Card Services, and Investment Houses — like the Oil Industry — will now be made to start singing that tune. The current condition threatens the American Dream and the Civil Requirement of <u>American</u> <u>home</u> <u>ownership</u>!

By Common Agreement among the People — American home ownership — must be a National Priority, and We will insure that <u>all</u> <u>necessary</u> <u>adjustments</u> in tax and investment policy, mortgage lending rules, products, guidelines, rates, and terms <u>will</u> <u>be</u> <u>made</u> to that end. Period!

o   o   o   o

About the Credit Card (CC) Industry

This will be short and not very sweet. Instead of writing about all the predatory things the Credit Card Industry has been doing for decades and the wonderful time they are having while Bush II has been in office, here are a few things they will do differently under the coming AIR Program restructuring of their operations.

- Their continuous credit card offer mailings will be vastly decreased. Think of the trees it will save!

- They will quit targeting teenagers and senior citizens.
- They will quit sending seniors $5, $10, $20 checks with fine print that hooks them into various buying services. It is a predatory practice.
- The Banks and Credit Card entities will be modify the operational configuration (and data retention) between them and the merchants they serve to replicate the European model. That Change will severely reduce the incidents of identity theft. Europe does not have nearly the problem that America does and it can be fixed. The Industry has knowingly refused to alter their configuration despite merchant pleas, but have enjoyed building the 'identity theft insurance" product line and the fees it and other related theft-revenues are bringing in! Again, it is the Dark Side.
- All Credit Card (e.g., VISA, MasterCard, etc.) rates nationwide will be frozen and then steadily reduced to an appropriate rate structure that covers operational costs, reasonable investor return, and nothing more. The abuses will end.

You and they get the idea. The Banking and Credit Card Industries will become operations that support the American economy by providing various forms of short and long term financing to individuals and businesses. And the Investment House Industry had best be paying close attention. They would not be that difficult to add them to the first wave!

o   o   o   o

American Industry Re-Structuring (AIR) Program

The Banking and Credit Card Industries

Overall Re-Structuring Approach

The complex Banking and Credit Card Industries will also feel the full force of the AIR Program Re-structuring process. These National Infrastructure industries will be deliberately re-tooled into a people-friendly, public and business _serving_ rather than _taking_ component of the National System.

Please keep in mind the points that were made under the People's Sense section a few pages ago as you review the remainder of this proposal. This proposal overviews the AIR Program Changes to the BCI and provides an adequate amount of detail to jump start the national discussion over the fate of these critical functions within our National System. More of the grim financial details will surely continue to manifest themselves as 2008 progresses.

Tell Don't Ask

The bottom line in dealing with a business group or industry such as "The Bankers" is that you _do_ _not_ _ask_ them if they _would_ or if they _could_ Change their policies and procedures to be of greater service to individuals, businesses, and society as a whole – _you_ _tell_ _them_ what needs to be done and to go do it!

These publicly prudent and practical Changes cannot be and will not be a subject of negotiation! And if any of those remaining after the senior management is retired — resist the Change plan presented to them – they to will also be shown the door.

And that my fellow Americans, is where We are with the Banks and Credit Card Industries. We will now call those industries to Civil Responsibility in the name of the Common Good.

The AIR Program for the Banking and Credit Card Industry (BCI)

The primary corporate entities in the existing BCI and any related financial entities (e.g., the Investment House Industry) doing business in the U.S. will comply with the involuntary, re-organization of these industries. Again, this will not be a negotiation.

The BCI restructuring will certainly impact relationships and existing agreements with institutions in various foreign countries. As needed, in order to do what is best for the American public and our economy such agreements will be re-written and/or eliminated, as needed. This will take months not a year to accomplish. With the BCI restructuring, we are confronting the greed and self-serving policies of corporate America, as well as those of certain foreign governments. We will be fair, but We will not be fooled or foolish. Everything and everybody is on the table in this historic exercise. The economy of the U.S. and too many countries are at ever increasing risk and the Masses will now begin dealing with the Few.

This could also be observed as the moment in time when the Meek, Masses will come to final terms and reconciliation with the Powerful, Few. We Americans will now confront and deal with our economic imbalances, and it will then ripple around the world.

That is not intended to be dramatic. It is the Plain Truth of our situation and We had all better wake up to reality the faces us.

o   o   o   o

The Initial List of Industry Entities

This is the initial list of "major" Banks and Credit Card entities to be considered in the AIR Program Re-Structuring of that industry, includes:

Banking Entities

Citigroup
Bank of America Corp.
J.P. Morgan Chase & Co.
Wells Fargo
Wachovia Corp.
U.S. Bancorp
Capital One Financial
National City Corp.
SunTrust Banks
Bank of New York Co.

Credit Card Entities

Master Card Vendors
VISA Vendors

This initial, working list of corporate entities may very well be refined as 2008 progresses and the November 2008 National Election draws near.

By deliberate, united vote on that historic day, *We the People* can freely declare that such practical and prudent Change to the National System for the Common Good of us all — <u>will</u> <u>be</u> <u>made</u>.

o   o   o   o

AIR Program – The Entity Re-Structuring Levels (ERL) Overview

The Banking and Credit Card Industry

ERL 1 – Operational Reorganization

Corporate Re-Structuring Approach

A newly, formed Board of Directors will comprise the first level of the ABC Organization Chart.

The existing Banking and Credit Card Industry (BCI) corporations will effectively become operating Divisions of the newly formed, Non-Profit American Banking Consortium (ABC) – the Industry Management Consortium established to oversee the operations of these restructured industries.

This Industry Consortium will be different from those already presented since it will combine two (2) separate, but clearly related financial industries of the Banking and Credit Card.

Those corporations will combine to form the second level of the new ABC Consortium Organization Chart. There could very well be situations where an American Bank or Credit Card corporation is currently part of a larger corporation. If so, as with the prior industry proposals they will not be purchased or bought out initially just because they are a stock held corporation. In any case the corporate entities will be transferred to become operating Divisions of the ABC. This corporate reorganization will not be optional or negotiable.

As previously noted in other proposals, an appropriate amount of operational consolidation takes place when fairly redundant corporate entities merge, we have all seen it – therefore some reduction in employment would eventually occur. There is an absolute need to maintain many local bank branches to properly serve our communities.

Note: Although the Consortiums are set-up as Non-Profit corporations, these organizations will pay taxes.

ERL 2 – Existing Management Retirement

Existing Senior Management

- Any member of senior management with Golden Parachute will be retired by May 30, 2009. Any and all stock options in their package will be eliminated.
- No more Golden Parachutes will be offered to future management, ever.
- Any remaining member of management with a base salary in excess of one (1) million dollars per year will have it cut to that amount as of July 1, 2009.
- All stock options for 2009 will be eliminated.
- All bonuses will be reviewed by the ABC group and may be reduced.

And, as always, if a given person does not like those Changes – they know where the door is…

Remember: The one-time offer to hold current and prior management and employees harmless from lawsuit will be presented and I believe will be accepted. This offer will be made to the current and prior members of the Boards of Directors, as well.

Existing Boards of Directors (BOD)

The existing BOD would be relieved of their positions by May 1, 2009. By law most, if not all corporations are required to have some form of BOD whether it is actually functional to the operation or just ornamental. The future form and function of the previously mentioned Industry Management Consortium created for the Banking and Credit Card Industry, the ABC, will be reviewed next.

ERL 3 – New Management Structure and Charter

The *Industry Management Consortium* Requirement

With the consolidation of the existing BCI Corporations, the nation is again merging a group of businesses that are pretty much doing the same thing. As was described more under ERL 1, each of these entities will become operating Divisions in the ABC Non-Profit organizational structure. Therefore, a single Boards of Directors "entity" is all that will be needed. The costs that are now associated with all the existing Boards is therefore not necessary and will go back into the operation. Serious dollars!

The ABC's Board will be responsible to the American public for implementing, strictly overseeing, and refining the new Charter of Operations. They will not manage the day-to-day operation.

Revised Charter of Operations

Bank lending practices and/or certain national tax policies will be altered to help families that are <u>now</u> finding themselves in housing market where their home value and appraisal has fallen below the current amount of their mortgage. A one-time National Mortgage Adjustment program will be rapidly developed and implemented.

The first focus of this program would only apply to a family's <u>primary residence</u> and would involve a forced refinancing by the Banks where the appraisal is less than the amount to be refinanced. Again, keeping the American families in their homes must be a national priority.

- <u>On a permanent basis</u> — The Banking system and the federal government must be required to establish low, fixed-rate interest rate (i.e., about 3 or 4%) mortgage products for a families' primary residence, <u>only</u>. There must be a system established where Americans even in low income situations will have access to the funding required to obtain and enjoy a permanent family residence. Even if it means the mortgage term is spread for many decades in the future.

- Families looking for their first home must be given priority access to foreclosed properties and loan products to help them buy (and fix them up if needed) and move in.

- Finally, a national law must be enacted and aggressively forced at the city, county, and town levels that will target those persons that buy properties and turnaround and fill them with illegal occupants – the IOs again! Back to that nasty issue. Localities across the country are dealing with this issue and the federal government needs to take aggressive and clear action to reverse it.

  After a certain date, let's say September 1, 2009 — every city and town in the nation will have the legal ability to identify and seize these properties. The police already know where most of these houses are. Any IOs still living there will be deported and the house will be sold to Americans in need of a home.

  And if the owner is not a citizen, including being a Permanent Resident Alien they too could be subject to deportation and seizure of their property. We will take no prisoners.

Beyond those initial focus items, please refer to the points raised under the People's Sense above. The overall focus will be that Banking and Credit

Card functions within our National System will be re-structured to <u>prudently</u> support individuals, families, and businesses small and large to grow and to be productive within our societyl Their predatory practices will become a part of history.

o   o   o   o

ERL 4 – Stock, Profitability, and Pricing Controls

As is repeated in these six proposals — the following scenarios will begin taking effect as soon as possible in 2009 and will likely be applied retro-actively when the required legislation is passed by the **new** U.S. Congress.

While We can always hope, there is probably little chance that the existing Congress and White House will move on this proposal before the November Election. These six Industry proposals need to be the **hottest topics** in the country during 2008. The electorate must bring these and the other American Agenda Proposals to the campaigns! We can do this.

<u>Stock Trading Control</u>

Stock trading in the ABCs will be in a state of virtual suspense. The stocks will be initially frozen at the 1-1-200<u>8</u> share price. Any negotiation and eventual buy-back activity will start at that price or lower possibly adjusted by the individual stock-holder's buy-in share price.

The market would be intensely watched (by the SEC and others) in the run-up to the 1-1-09 AIR Program Effective Date for any selling or other game playing. Again, violators will be severely dealt with including fines and/or prison time in a State run facility. Again, there will be no more Federal playpens for the rich and famous.

<u>Profitability Control</u>

Corporate profitability for publicly held (stock) corporation will be capped effective 1-1-09 at <u>no</u> more than **four percent (4%)** for physical year 2009 and stockholder pay out will be capped accordingly. They too, have had a good ride during the Bush II years, but their party is over.

The profits in excess of that will be put to practical uses such as:

- elimination of any out-sourcing activities
- internal operational spending
- set aside for the future stock buy-back process

Pricing Control

Note: There could be a flat 2% to 3% annual product increase while the system is sorting itself out.

ERL 5 – Conversion of IGE Model

The ARM Re-structuring of the American Banking Industry Corporations is another practical opportunity to transition a National Infrastructure Industry into an Income Generating Entity (IGE). Consolidation of existing big Banks and Credit Card corporations into the non-profit American Banking Consortium (ABC) will lead the way to their becoming eventually being converted to a pure IGE within the National System.

With an aggressive national movement toward a National Banking an Credit Policy beginning to gear up by 2009, it just makes sense to consolidate their operations. Further, this approach to corporate consolidation avoids the time consuming merger negotiations, huge buy-out expenses, and legal hurdles they would face if they slowly merged on their own over the next decade or so. The economy cannot wait that long.

Over a period of years, all existing stockholders will be bought out. The stock amounts involved and how the stockholders will be compensated for their share value will be worked as a AIR Program implementation of the ABC progresses.

And no, that is not avoiding discussing the hard dollars involved. The numbers are what the numbers are, and they will only continue to grow worse the longer We delay this Change of Necessity to our National System. Therefore, I deliberately would not take the time extract and present that data on this or the others in this infamous group of six Existing Industries because those numbers will be one of the first things that the Special Interest lobbyists for that group throw out to scare everyone with.

Again, their false financial terror alerts will deter us from our Common Goals – We will take prudent and practical action and We shall prevail.

o   o   o   o

That is all.

Finally, Raging Against the War Machine.

o   o   o   o

Existing Industries — Proposal 27

The Defense Industry

"Coming to Final Terms with the Military Industrial Complex"

The challenge here far greater, yet somewhat similar to that We confronted with the Pharmaceutical Industry. Both are absolutely necessary National Infrastructure Industries and thus are required in some practical and functional form. However they cannot and will not be allowed to continue as they exist as of January 1, 2008.

o   o   o   o

IF, and I do mean IF,
We never intentionally start down the road to World Peace,
We are surely Doomed.

To deliberately travel that road to World Peace,
We must fully Reconcile with those that make their Living
by providing the Toys of War,
and Confront those that simply Love the War.

o   o   o   o

"Required" Viewing

Why We Fight

A must see movie mentioned before. If you have not seen it (most people have not even heard about it) please go to Blockbuster and get this movie. It starts with President Dwight David Eisenhower's farewell address to the nation the night before President John F. Kennedy's inauguration. In that historic speech the much respected president warned the country about the potential build-up of the Military Industrial Complex (a title Eisenhower actually created) and shows how it evolved to the present day. Senator John McCain speaks in the movie that to me gave it a bit more credibility. It is grim Reality.

Unfortunately for us with the creation and build-up of the Bush II/Cheney "optional" Iraq War, President Eisenhower's fears have now been fully realized.

In 2008, the Peace-loving and vast majority of American citizens must deliberately and aggressively confront the hard economic and foreign policy realities of the Military Industrial Complex because in the final analysis it has become far more of a threat to our National Security — rather than its Protector!

Lord of War – Distributed by Lions Gate Films

This film starring Nichols Cage provides insight into the arms merchants – those that facilitate the distribution of the Toys of War. It is hard, reality based movie that is educational and worth seeing.

o o o o

Issue/Problem

To be perfectly clear, the problem defined here is from the perspective of the Common Good. It is from the People's viewpoint, not that of the Defense Industry and the Department of Defense – those that profit from the recent build-up and super-sizing of the Military Industrial Complex, the MIC. Under the Bush II and Cheney tag team – the Big Oil and MIC lovers, respectively, the nation was fooled into Bush IIs optional Iraq War.

Again, and again, and again – to best understand the Big Picture on the overall Defense Industry please watch the movie *Why We Fight*. Consider it your patriotic duty to watch and consider it! Not to convince, but to inform. It will help you to better understand:

- why We are really in Iraq today.
- why We cannot stay in Iraq under the current arrangements with a fractured government.
- why We will of necessity remain in Iraq "long-term" only to insure and protect the oil supply, and its dependable flow. That is why Bush II took us there in the first place. Policing the oil supply will require a very, reduced force that will also be under far less daily threat. Thus, our troops will stop being a police force and national referee.
- why We will need to forcefully dictate the partitioning of Iraq into Shiite, Sunni, and Kurd provinces, and quickly conclude an equitable Oil-sharing arrangement between those parties and without our Big Oil companies complicating things.
- why We will put an end to the old mentality that "war is good for our economy." It will be very publicly be replaced with "peace and environmentally" oriented national policies – for fun and profit!
- why We will very soon control and reduce the profitability of the Ameri-

can MIC – the Defense Industry. An industry that has deliberately set itself up to provide employment in all 50 states, and DC of course.

And why We will do all those things for the Common Good of our nation and the world.

o   o   o   o

Perspectives on MIC Re-Structuring and Control

This particular proposal alone could be as thick again, as this entire book. And there are many things I would add to this piece, but again the time is running short bring CS2 to publication in early 2008 – today is December 14, 2007 and these six proposals and CS2 near completion.

As Keith Olberman/MSNBC said today, this is the 1,689[th] day since Bush II declared **"Mission Accomplished"**. You have got to love that kind of sarcasm. But, consider that in reality Bush II might have meant exactly what he said!

That climbing total is way beyond the 444 days that Iran held the American hostages and helped defeat President Carter's re-election. That *narrow* loss lead in turn to Ronald Reagan's election and the last major MIC build up (in relative peace time) that also left the nation with a huge National Debt. Bush II has exceeded that Debt and unfortunately for us and the domestic economy he is not done yet. Do not kid yourself the BC duo's intent going in was to keep us in Iraq for as long as possible, if not permanently.

For some perspective on the question of how long "they" want to keep us in Iraq, let's take a look at the approximate day count of a few major MIC events:

Germany	**2008 – 1945 = 63 years = 22,995 days**	
Japan	**2008 – 1945 = 63 years = 22,995 days**	
Korea	**2008 – 1950 = 58 years = 21,170 days**	
Afghanistan	**2008 – 2001 = 7 years =**	**2,555 days**
Iraq	**2008 – 2003 = 5 years =**	**1,825 days**

However, We did get out of Granada!

A Hard Reality Check

I suggest that in the real strategy of the dynamic Oil/MIC duo, of the Bush/ Cheney (BC), <u>actually</u> <u>had</u> been victorious! They got us and our military into Iraq! Their real *Mission* had indeed been *Accomplished*. Think about that.

o   o   o   o

Our military men and women had done their job very well and taken control of Iraq away from its dictator. Add to that, "C" more than "B" had <u>unnecessarily</u> blown-up water, sewage, and electric plants, bridges, and other civilian necessities and practically drove Iraq back into the Stone Ages — thus, greatly decreasing the post-dictatorship quality of life for the people of Iraq. Such deliberately planned, but avoidable destruction had little to do with winning a war – that they knew before going in that we would surely win — but everything to do with writing sole source re-construction contracts for certain American military contractors. The MIC at work! Consider that patriotic scenario for a while my fellow taxpayers.

And BC was not done yet. Shortly thereafter, they "decided" to formally discharge the Iraqi military rather than keeping it under Allied control and putting them to good use. <u>However</u>, to keep them under appropriate control during the predictably, tedious transition from dictatorship to some form of Democratic government it would require that they <u>got</u> <u>paid</u>! And that was not in BC's plan or budget that was designed for military contractors to support — so they *obviously* had to go. And besides, that would be too damn peaceful...

So they deliberately just sent over 500,000 well-armed and really, pissedoff Iraqi's home without a pay check. Smart MIC-thinking again, because since so many of them were Sunni, the Muslim minority in Iraq that had been used by the former dictator to keep the Shiite majority inline – often with a heavy hand – they were now open targets for that ever-popular, Middle Eastern, Old Testament game of "an-eye-for–an-eye" and the national blood bath was on!

Now some may think after reading those pieces, but how could that be or how could they know that would happen ahead of time. Because, for one thing the Pentagon's job is to analyze every possible scenario and they knew the failed history of such decisions. And <u>so</u> did the State Department. Going back to the early 1990's — Bush I and Cheney knew <u>and</u> publicly spoke about the clear dangers of taking out the Iraqi dictator in the first Gulf War. How it would create a power imbalance in that historically, volatile region, and that is why We did not do it. That was Bush Is pre-agreement made with the leaders of nations in the region before the Gulf War I was initiated, and why the ground war only lasted for three (3) days.

The Plain Truth is that BC of their own "free will" choose not to heed the knowledge and the lessons of history, and deliberately doomed us to endure this national embarrassment and the "avoidable" lost of so many precious American and Iraqi lives.

<u>Good and Bad Intent</u>

For those among us that for sincere or selfish reasons are actually satisfied with the present state of affairs relative to the MIC, they will not be swayed or informed at all by what I might write here, and frankly I am not writing to them! I am writing to the growing Majority of us that believe otherwise! I am not slamming those folks because they are entitled to their opinion, however do understand that people with their perspective, have over the years been deliberately used by self-serving Special Interests, and have helped to form Bush IIs *destructive*, National Defense policy and have helped create the chaos that our troops are sitting in today.

> In late 2007 I spoke with a women that was probably in her early thirties about watching "Why We Fight" and she volunteered that her uncle was a life long Marine and had served in wars, and in recent years was assigned at the Pentagon. She said he was frustrated and very disappointed with Iraq and what the military had become in general. And if a battle hardened United States Marine can come to that sobering conclusion, just what else is there to say.

The Purpose of a Nation's Military

In the movie "Why We Fight" that was released in 2006, it was pointed out that the U.S. military spending exceeds the "combined" spending of Russia, China, and the European nations (NATO).

Consider – The Russian, Chinese, and for the most part NATO do not have what I would term to be "foreign intended" militaries. For the sake of this piece I am focusing on Russia and China, since NATO has not <u>yet</u> been portrayed as being likely to attack us!

America has a foreign "intended military" <u>industry</u>! The initial MIC that President Eisenhower warned the adults of 1960 about was created out of necessity when the nation entered World War II, since the Great Depression had dismantled our WWI military.

The MIC has been kept alive and well since the end of WWII by Special Interest lobbying combined with the Korean War, the Cold War, the Vietnam War, and Reagan's *optional* military build-up against the Soviet Union that did promote end the Cold War, but only because they ran out of money before we did and left us with a huge national debt. But wait, now we have the grand prize — the ultimate "MIC-strategy" in the form of the Bush/Cheney optional Iraq War and their intended *never-ending* military occupation thereof. Believe it!

If the MIC industry does not have an external threat, real or fabricated, it simply cannot begin to justify the continuous use of so many of our tax dollars. There is that Plain Truth, again.

The reason that Russia and China spend far less than We do is because they have not made a regular habit of attacking other countries. They factually use their military for domestic population control (nice way to put it) and public works projects. The Russian military did venture out one notable time and got their butts kicked in Afghanistan (what was that about learning from the lessons history).

And tell me, please! Who if anyone going to attack Russia and/or China? If not us, who? And We are not going to war with them unless it is over Oil or form of Environmental Catastrophe. There are no other justifiable reasons. China could take over Taiwan tomorrow and so what! We would simply drop-in and finally free Cuba and call it even. The Plain Truth.

And as We finally begin to plan and act properly now, Oil will quickly become a far less threatening factor for us and the world in general. The nation and environment will be the benefactor of an America fully engaged in protecting both of them, rather than protecting self-serving corporate profits and perpetuating a "foreign intended" military – the MIC.

Today our biggest threats come from small groups of zealots and those that pull their strings, as well as a World Financial System that is playing Russian Roulette with the global economy. Both of which can be effectively dealt with without pouring more good money after bad into a bloated MIC and by dealing firmly with the World Financial System.

We can do these things together. When 95% plus of the nation's and the world's population decide to do the Right things, the less 5% of the population does not stand a chance of continuing to do the Wrong things.

Dealing with Redundancy

The AIR Program approach to effectively "dealing" with the gargantuan American Defense Industry is somewhat like resolving what to do with the Pharmaceutical Industry. Parts of industry will be streamlined over the next few years to reduce the drain on our tax dollars that continues paying for the redundant administrative and operational overhead that exists across multiple contractors.

Other parts of the MIC are needed from a R&D perspective, but We do not need to keep paying taxpayer dollars for multiple contractors to be developing their version of the same product. Further, We do not **need** to keep developing upgrades to certain existing weapons. From hand held weaponry to laser guided missiles that are already in place and are far superior to anything that our troops will run into in battle — and do the killing job quite well. In too many cases the Defense Industry is acting like the Automobile Industry that feels it must making newer models that looks a bit different and has a few more goodies on it (but over the last 35 years has not worked to produce an engine that will yield 50 to 100 miles per gallon).

It must be acknowledged that We have enough ways to Shock, Awe, and Kill anything and everything — already in our Defense Industry tool kit. We do not need to keep creating new ways to do it.

Re-Directed Public Funding

This is one of the cornerstones of the Economic Reform examples sited throughout CS2. As We confront and resolve our public problems such less crime, ending the Drug War, controlled immigration, etc.,, we can practically quit spending so much of national and state budgets on them. And then those funds will be shifted to positive public programs. We can do this.

In the case of reducing MIC-spending, those freed-up budget dollars can be re-directed and put to use in promoting, creating, and supporting non-military purposed industries and within the same states and communities that are now getting Defense funding. This can be done. We can absolutely transition away from an economy *overly dependent* on Defense Industry tax dollars.

Enough said on that I believe.

o   o   o   o

Regarding the Draft

This issue was touched upon earlier in Proposal 9 – Re-Considering the Military Draft – Saving Our Youth, but it is very relevant to this conversation.

My basic purpose in recommending that We bring back the Draft is actually to help resolve some Domestic issues, rather than building an Army for foreign assignment. My intent is not for us to build-up troop count in Iraq – as We need to get the hell out of Bush II's optional war, ASAP!

The practical, domestic policy reasons why We should have never stopped the Draft in the first place is sited in Proposal 9. However, the prudent National Security reason is that if We are ever again in a situation where it was decided that the country really had to go into a country *in force* such as Bush II wrongly decided in 2002 (BC were actually discussing the invasion of Iraq in early 2001), We must be able to draw upon as many trained troops/citizens as needed to get the job done and done quickly!

In 2002,We did not have the regular (non-National Guard) trained troops required to do the job of nation control in a volatile country like Iraq. If the Draft were still in place, We could have called upon several hundred thousand militarily trained Americans (that had been through at least 2 years of Army training) at the start of the war and Bush II might have actually pulled it off. Of course that available military force was not at our disposal because of an equally short-sighted decision in the mid-1970's. Where does that leave us, besides deciding how soon to "re-structure" and severely downsize our assignment in Iraq? The temporary success of the 'Surge' or not, our troops are still someplace they should never have been in the first place, or at least without the truth as to why they were really going there — to secure oil flow and corporate profits.

Going forward, after the Iraq experience, *We the People* must declare to the Congress that there is no valid reason for us to go war unless, as stated earlier it is over Oil or Environmental Catastrophe. Iraq had the largest military in the region and it of course was no match for our military.

I would expect that We will maintain Oil Flow Control Forces in Iraq and probably indefinitely. Absolutely! Our people have paid to high a price to get us on top of that Oil Reserve and therefore We will not leave those reserves open to problems that would only require us to go back in. Maybe not our current leadership, but We the American citizens and Electorate — are not that stupid!

With Oil from Iraq in our future, along with that from the Saudi Arabia, Venezuela, and Mexico at least, with a REAL, National Energy Policy cranking up in 2009, and the AIR Program restructuring of Big Oil — We will not need to go to war over Oil, as long as We keep doing the right things. And all that will also help us to avoid some Environmental Catastrophe scenarios, as well.

Beyond the Middle East and its Oil supply, there is no other place on the globe that would require us to go to war. We will never make a land assault on Russia or China, nor would they ever attack us in that manner or otherwise. And we will never attack North Korea with troops, although certain parties like to talk about that to stir up the People's fears. North Korea has a standing army of around one (1) million and it would be worse than if We would have invaded Japan at the end of World War II. Besides why go there? If they really started to get out-of-hand the Chinese would step on them rather than have us come over there and do something about it. It is just common sense.

With all that said, We must consider and determine to restart the military Draft. If you skipped Proposal 9, you might want to go back and take a look. For one thing, having our men and women trained in working effectively as a team would absolutely come in very handy in the event of any actual major storm or Environmental Catastrophe in the future. Communities would react better and frankly more of us would survive.

As a frame of reference, the Selective Service Draft was shutdown in 1973 after the end of the Vietnam War. Eleven (11) years later the Congress passed the Comprehensive Criminal Reform Act of 1984. As a Probation Officer told me in the 1990's, it was a decision to start warehousing the raising number of criminals in the country with cocaine and other drug related crime was on the increase. It was the result of a full decade of too many young males graduating from high school or dropping out and having no where to go. The Draft was not there to take them in, give them structure, some vocational training, and some direction in life even if they only served the standard two (2) years — cause and effect. It has now been 35 years with no Draft and communities across the nation suffer with the negative results.

We must boldly correct the obvious policy and legislative errors of the past for the Common Good.

o   o   o   o

Why Go To War

It has been obvious for sometime that BC had no intention or even the desire to begin downsizing our troop count in Iraq. AS mentioned before, in 2005 I heard former President Carter (a reliable source) interviewed and he commented that the Bush II Administration advised the leaders of the nations in that region 'before' the war was initiated that the intent was to keep bases in Iraq long-term (funny how something like that is not loudly reported on network or cable news shows – sorry Press).

You know We have got to sit on top of what is supposed to be the world's 2nd largest remaining Oil reserve! After all, that is one of the two 'reasons' why We went in there in the first place!

And you know, IF Bush II would have been up front with us about going into Iraq to secure us a new and longer lasting source of Oil, or, told us that immediately after his "Mission Accomplished Moment" on the aircraft carrier, it might have been easier to accept. It also would have altered our Iraq strategy from that day forward to serve that purpose. It could be that BC really believe that "we peasants" are just too stupid to understand all that at the time, but then they have had several years to come clean and finally make that point haven't they?

More over it is Bush II having Big Oil company profits foremost in his mind and Cheney cheer-leading for the MIC contractors, along with their inner-circle's "war is good for the economy" mentality – that makes the war drag on. And they still have not come clean on the long-term bases they are building and why they are there.

With the Democrats winning "alleged control" of both Houses of Congress in 2006 the public had some optimism that partial sanity might take control of the situation and We would begin an orderly re-grouping toward with-drawal of the majority of our troops. That is what the voters – the citizens told both parties in November of 2006. Unfortunately for the public's hopes and our troops' lives, BC continued to do whatever they wanted and in-vented the "Surge" to keep things going. Instead of there being fewer troops and fewer MIC dollars in 2007 it is just the opposite.

And why is that? I believe that after you put aside all of the rhetoric:

- Democrats not leading in Congress to restrict funding the war. The Congress has the literal power to do that if "enough" members of both parties determine to do it regardless of Bush IIs veto.
- Bush II threatening to veto any war funding legislation with a date to begin withdrawal election. Again, Congress can do it if they really wanted to.
- Each party being more concerned about how to play the 2008 Presi-

dential and Congressional campaigns. The Republicans already know they should lose the White House and probably more House and Senate seats, because the People are fed up with Bush II and their Party on both foreign <u>and</u> domestic issues. Over 25 congressional members have already announced they are "retiring" at the end of their current terms. The Democrats only need to keep from shooting themselves in both feet!

- If We do not fight them there, We will have to fight them here. Thankfully, We have not heard that gem for a while.
- If We leave Iraq it will become an extremist training base. They already had all the training sites they needed elsewhere before Bush II created the Iraq War and helped them with their recruiting efforts. This is just another case of domestic propaganda, you know like Terror Alerts that increased in frequency in the months leading up to the November 2004 Presidential election and then stopped the very next week.

The over-riding reason for the continuance of the Iraq War since the 2006 election is that the White House, the Senate, the House, both parties are too much in bed with the MIC contractors that help fund their re-election campaigns. It is a self-perpetuating old-boy and now old-girl, mutual admiration machine. Further, Bush II did not want the normal post-war recession to hit while he was still in office.

And as I write in CS2 more than once — more and more over the last 10 or 15 years the Democratic Party has acted and voted like the semi-Republican Party, in too many cases involving both Domestic and Foreign policy. And all of that my Fellow Americans unfortunately leaves We the People, our economy, and over 150,000 of our brave military men and women – below the bottom line.

So, it is January 18, 2008 and the Recession partially due to excessive war spending and some other causes already discussed has begun. Bush II, his advisors, and Congress are scrambling to stimulate the economy. The Bush II Reign of Chaos continues.

o o o o

<u>The Good, the Bad, and the Truly *Ugly*</u>

Consider the following scenario and some of the places in the world where it applies. Some people make their living, and in fact claim their <u>entire public identity</u>, by complaining about a given issue and/or deliberately helping to perpetuate the problem. They are as predictable as the rising and the setting of the sun.

Side Point: Let's all face the fact that if the turbulent small group Middle Eastern countries were not sitting on top of all that "dam oil" We would not care any more about them <u>or</u> about those suffering in Darfur in the Sudan — than all the other human catastrophes that are happening everyday across the African continent and other places. The Plain Truth — simple reality!

Again it is oil interests covertly utilizing the well-intentioned *Screamers for Darfur* to serve their corporate agenda. If We wind up sending troops into Darfur it will not be to save the people. It will be to move on Sudan's Oil resources and to interfere with China's growing influence with that nation's disgusting leadership.

Without apology, CS2 is about deciding to take care of our own before being too concerned about others. The simple reason that Darfur and so many other countries in the world are in a perpetual state of turmoil is because they have <u>too many people</u>, not enough employment, their have/have not imbalance is a crime, and the Few people with Power "<u>like</u> it and intend to <u>keep</u> it" that way. It is absolute power at its worst, the Few over the Many, just world history repeating itself over, and over, and over again… And it is not America's fault or mess to clean up!

Let me use the Middle East as the example. Whether you are talking Sunni, Shiite, Israeli, Kurd, Turk, Arab, Palestinian, religious extremist group, or any other blissful group in that four thousand year old *train wreck* called the Middle East it breaks down like this:

<u>The Good</u>

Without a shadow of a doubt some 90% of the populations (the common masses) in all of those countries **just want peace** (that includes Iraq's pre-war population of 22 million). They just want to live their lives with their families, do their jobs, and get along in peaceful, coexistence with their neighbors whether they are next-door or in the next country.

However, there's a smaller percentage that make their living off the wars and sometimes wonder what they would do if something strange like "peace" broke out. What would happen to their piece of the pie. But they are <u>not</u> the problem.

The next smaller group involves the actual "war" business interests both inside and outside a given country. They make their living off the act of war and supplying the tools of battle and death. If you have never considered that reality, it is time for you to expand your frame of reference and give it a few moments of thought! And watch the "Lord of War". Those special interests represent the MIC within a given country. They <u>are</u> <u>part</u> of the problem.

The Bad

Next, there are those in the Middle East that have their <u>entire</u> <u>public</u> <u>identity</u>, their power, their fame — purely based upon the ongoing hatred, battles, and the killing. The clerics make up a key part of this group although they do not like people to talk about them being directly involved and stay mainly behind the scenes. A recent exception to that in Iraq and a clear example of the clerics Power over the masses was when the Shiite Cleric Sadr ordered his army to stop killing Americans for six months! That is a main reason why the Surge is working.

And, while this Bad group is fully at the core of the on-going, day-to-day chaos and do shoulder <u>most</u> of the blame — We have finally reached **them**!

The Truly *Ugly*

The *worst* of the litter, the smallest percentage of the Few that exist on all sides – and I repeat on <u>all</u> sides of these perpetual, neighbor-on-neighbor, and country-on-country wars. They are those that <u>simply</u> <u>love</u> the **hatred** and the **killing!** They <u>live</u> for it. They aggressively encourage and often help to finance it working behind the scenes and are not necessarily even living in those countries.

They simply would not know what to do with them selves if the hatred and killing came to an end and the Masses had their dreams come true — and peace happened! This smallest group is responsible for promoting, producing, and perpetuating the greatest amount of the avoidable turmoil. And most often without even getting their hands dirty – let alone have them blown off!

o   o   o   o

If you personally do not accept that this last and most destructive little fraction of world inhumanity exists and exists on the side of the battle you support – **please ask the next person that you see to slap you!**

Middle East Peace could actually happen, BUT it will **only** happen if and when that sick, little minority is first dealt with. And frankly, many of them will probably need to die at the hands of their own people for that to ever happen. I said I was not going to sugarcoat this message. We get far too enough of that garbage all the time.

To be "crystal clear" my fellow Americans, We definitely do have those latter types in our own population, industry, and government. They comprise the ugly under-belly of the Military Industrial Complex that President Dwight David Eisenhower so validly warned the nation about in January of 1960.

o   o   o   o

In the movie "Why We Fight" there is scene at a Defense Industry contractors show (the 2003 AUSA Defense Show in Washington, DC). A representative from KBR (Kellogg, Brown, and Root) was talking to some military officers. His was doing some sort of a card trick and said,

"Now we have never met before, no collusion? Which is really odd because collusion is our business. Yes, collusion with the military!"

o   o   o   o

From My 2003 Presidential Website

Yes, I did have my very own "amateur, yet official" Independent presidential campaign in late 2003 and early 2004. I will share some background on that in Part 5.

The following is the exact text from my former website's Home Page. Consider that it was written in the late summer of 2003.

o   o   o   o

Resolving the Iraq Problem

For starters let me state that I am very much in favor of strong military for our country and always standing up for America's interests first.

I debated for some time whether or not to add these comments on the war in Iraq. However, this is an urgent national issue that any viable candidate will be questioned about by the press. Since I have discussed this scenario with many people in recent months and received positive response, I determined to include it here for public review. This campaign will not focus on domestic issues, only.

We must acknowledge that our troops are now involved in a guerilla war in Iraq. I spoke with a veteran the other day that served three and a half years in Vietnam. He stated that our troops are now facing the same grim situation that he and others faced years ago. They cannot tell the good guys from the bad guys, often until it's too late.

Parties from outside Iraq with various agendas have been moving into that country for months. Their intent is to disturb the peace process and cause physical harm to Coalition forces. Although the administration dances around the issue, our current policy will have our troops in Iraq for some number of years into the future. The intent of their presence is to produce day-to-day peace in that country, and so to provide a new Iraqi government with an orderly startup period. In a guerilla war, the first objective is all but impossible to achieve. History has repeatedly demonstrated that reality, especially when the native population is not directly involved in making the peace.

The administration is now trying to orchestrate a reduction in U.S. troop levels by mid-2004. Whether this is a strategically prudent thing to do, or is being done to facilitate the administration's run for re-election in 2004, or both, is strictly a matter of opinion.

Therefore, I offer this approach for your consideration. It is designed to force the arrival of day-to-day peace in Iraq within the next several months, or will at least remove our and other Coalition troops from harm's way. We will give the Iraqi people a very simple coice. That way they may freely determine their own future, but they must decide now!

In a war, peace is not asked or. It must be made.

Background

The U.S. lead Coalition succeeded in removing the Iraqi dictator, his military, and the Baathist Party for controlling and oppressing the lives of the 25 million Iraqi people. This action resulted in the citizens of Iraq experiencing freedom and more potential control over their lives than they have had in over 30 years. However, there are on-going problems:

- By recent news estimates there are about 5,000 outsiders now in Iraq to prevent the peace and to harm Coalition forces.
- Members of the former dictator's Baathist party are also causing trouble in the streets. It is believed by some that the former dictator is helping to orchestrate their actions.
- And obviously, the former Iraqi dictator is still very alive and kicking.

Apparently, the Iraqi people do not appreciate the newly found freedoms. Nor do they seem to care about the welfare of the Coalition troops that are simply trying to provide them with day-to-day peace. This situation cannot be allowed to continue for the basic welfare of the troops.

The Ultimatum

Our government will set a date 45 days after this announcement would be made. For example, if the announcement is made on December 15th the deadline would be January 31, 2004.

The announcement will be directed to the 25 million citizens of Iraq and their religious leaders, in particular.

The powerful Iraqi religious leadership, the clerics, that have the ability to direct and control the majority of the population will be required to bring peace to the country by the deadline stated. The various clerics influence the 60 percent of the Iraqi population that is Shiite Muslim, and the Sunni Muslim minority, as well.

The clerics and the native citizenry of Iraq, together, will need to seriously consider the following scenario:

By the date specified in the announcement, the religious and civil leadership Iraq will be required to bring about peace in the entire country. Simply meaning the 25 million Iraqi citizens will need to effectively "deal with" the outsiders and any other internal people that do not want peace and are there to cause harm to Coalition forces.

If a peaceful state of affairs in Iraq is not delivered by the date set, all Coalition forces will be withdrawn and all active support to rebuild Iraq will be suspended.

We decided to attempt to bring peace to their lives. They have decided that they could not appreciate it.

The possible withdrawal of the Coalition forces may make some groups and individuals feel a sense of victory. However, most will immediately realize that should the Coalition forces withdraw, it will set the stage for a probable bloody civil war for control over the country. The Shiite's and Sunni's, and the Baathists trying to bring back the former dictator would fight it out in the streets.

Now some might call this a barbaric proposal, but it is actually quite prudent. For the protection of our and other Coalition troops it could be the only logical response to the on-going situation. A true, self-preservation strategy driven by the complete lack of gratitude shown by the general population and the internal leadership Iraq, mainly the clerics.

They seem to have forgotten in just months, what their life was like for decades prior to the war. They are taking the situation and the Coalition for granted. We must not feel obligated to continue to support such thinking, especially at the cost of our troops. They have even let the United Nations and the Red Cross be attacked. Their continued national negligence is not worth the injury of one of our people and is currently taking far more than that.

If the internal leadership of Iraq and the native population, that is now well-armed, will not take it upon themselves to deal with those hostile forces, to facilitate a final peace in their own country, then the Coalition will cut their losses and withdraw. The world would watch how the 25 million people of Iraq deal with the real potential of the former dictator crawling out from under the rock he is hiding under and attempt to regain power over them once again.

These are very simple options for them to consider. And it should take them 45 days to "resolve" the matter internally, once they stare this reality in the face! They will have clear choices and they can determine their own national future.

The Coalition has no hope of ending or even controlling a guerilla war in Iraq. It is a mission impossible. It is not what we expected going in. We have been there before and have no rationale excuse for our troops to re-main under such conditions. I would rather see some stock prices fall, than one more person!

That is the approach that I seriously recommend we follow very soon. I hereby challenge the administration and the other candidates to respond to this suggestion. And hopefully with something more than, "This guy does not understand the whole situation." This is not rocket science.

It does not matter how someone feels about whether we should have gone to war in the first place or about the justifications offered beforehand. The bottom line is that our people are in there and it is a mess that the Iraqi's have full power to cleanup in short order. This is just another example of a self-interested minority causing avoidable pain for the majority, but that majority does not stand and protect its own interests.

I personally believe we must honor the casualties and the lives lost among our troops and those of other countries, by not allowing this random slaughter to continue — with no end in sight!

o   o   o   o

That is the end of the original campaign website text. It is now four more years later in Bush IIs optional war.

The People's Sense

People throughout history have allowed themselves to be taxed for Defense. They have accepted governmental taxation in dollars, as well as giving their lives in both voluntary and involuntary military service.

It is now January of 2008 and by this point in world history, Civilization has advanced to the place where war for avoidable causes should be just that. Avoidable!

o   o   o   o

We the People,

- Expect nothing less than a Strong Defense against any enemy foreign and domestic, especially considering the current magnitude of the Defense Department's annual budget and the Federal debt that Bush IIs optional war has created and is adding to daily.

  On the "Domestic (Homeland Security) Defense" front presented earlier, add the growing size and cost of the Judicial Legal Complex and all of the crime caused <u>daily</u> by Illegal Occupants that have entered the country over the last seven (7) more years – by airport, ship, and our Southern Border that remains wide-open.

- Expect that going forward the annual Defense budget to be presented and fully justified to the American public and specifically to the electorate. That would prove an interesting show.

- Expect the Defense budget, <u>including</u> any and all Defense "supplemental funding" expenditures to be capped at its FY2008 level — that runs from October 1, 2007 thru September 30, 2008 as the *Absolute Defense Budget Ceiling.*

- Expect that the FY2009 the Defense budget that starts October 1, 2008 will be less than that FY2008 *Absolute Defense Budget Ceiling.* That it will be reduced by five (5) percent at least across the board. And no adjustments for inflation will be considered, and no "supplemental war funding" will be allowed slipped in. FY2010 will also see a budget reduction as the overall Defense Industry is reeled in as our "foreign intended" Defense Policy is revised. In early 2008, Bush II is already preparing the FY2009 and the Defense Budget does not include all <u>known</u> war expenses.

- Expect that unlike in Gulf War I in 1991, our military will remove any and all useable military and non-military vehicles, machinery, weapons, and ammunition — and bring them back with them. Thus, the taxpayers will not need to pay <u>once again</u> to have them replaced! Some National Guard units could use some the excess 'stuff' ordered, but not used in the war. That would also save the states some money!

With Regard to Iraq – *We the People*

Expect the Iraq Strategy to be reformulated considering the types of perspectives as those presented above and those discussed under the Oil Industry proposal, as well. The American public and the Electorate in particular want our fighting forces to have a true "Exit Strategy" that is somewhere in this decade.

That does not mean all of our troops will be out of Iraq. Let's be realistic about the fact that some level of military presence will be required there for years – possibly decades – and I hate to think that, let alone write it down. Our strategy for 2009 must be built upon reality and Plain Truth, which will be the opposite of what we have received sine 2002. Some points to be reconciled in developing the Exit Strategy are:

- Our military men and women have been stretched to the breaking point. Multiple tours with little break in between.

- We cannot "win" a war as an occupying force when it is a combination of civil and ethnic neighbor-on-neighbor warfare – with a <u>little</u> guerilla on the side. The guerilla part is overly played to stir-up fears and scare some of the American public. We must realize that those guerillas <u>only</u> move about the country with the blessings and protection of one or more of the powerful Iraqi *clerics*. Otherwise they would be dead. Remember that the primary reason that our troop deaths went down is because one of the clerics told 'his army' to stop f killing Americans for six (6) months!

- We cannot afford this war any longer. Bush II and Cheney are breaking the Treasury with their war, and of course, just like Reagan will not be around as all of the bills come due. Although with the Recession inconveniently hitting early in 2008, Bush II will be forced to bear some of the bad press before he leaves town.

   Bush II following the classic Republican mantra of cutting taxes – even in wartime – simply continues each month to borrow Billions around the world to 'pay' for the war. This is nothing more than Bush II and the Republicans in Congress (with the help of some Democrats) writing a guaranteed tax increase that cannot not be put in effect until after his administration is long gone.

The National Debt still left over from Reagan's reign, was under $5.7 Trillion in 2000, with a budget surplus of $261 billion. By 2007 it had reached 9.2 Trillion, with a $250 billion deficit, and both are still growing.

We simply cannot afford to stay there! Doesn't the word Depression scare people anymore?

• And the alleged Iraqi government will not move to resolve the power struggle, so the only light at the end of the tunnel that anyone can see is an on-coming freight train!

There are of course others, but enough on that for now.

o   o   o   o

The Partitioning of Iraq Alternative

I have heard the pros and cons with regard to dividing Iraq up into religious/ethnic territories to help establish some form of order between the various *tribes* within the country. It is a form of authorized ethnic-cleansing, which in simple fact is what the tribes of Iraq have been doing rather violently since 2002. It is not what the world may want to see happen to the Iraqi people, but the world does not live in Iraq. And there are still too many people with a 15th Century, Middle Eastern view of the world – that unfortunately have day-to-day Control over the general population and have guns. There in lies the rub!

Therefore, for the sake of a workable Exit Strategy from Iraq, the following overview of a Partitioning Plan is presented for review. It will be built around the following basic requirements:

• The mandatory partitioning of Iraq into three distinct Provinces to be populated for the most part if not exclusively by Shiite (south), Sunni (middle), and Kurd (north) ethnic groups. And the peaceful Re-settlement of the ethnic population into the appropriate Provinces.

• The necessity for U.S. troops to remain in Iraq possibly "long-term" only to insure and protect the oil supply, and its dependable flow. That is why Bush II took us there in the first place. Some will remain on bases that are now being built for that reason. Policing the oil supply will require a very, reduced force that will also be under far less daily threat. Thus, our troops will stop serving as a domestic police force and national referee.

Part of the cost of the U.S. troops stationed in Iraq will be covered by Oil revenues.

• Each Province will be self-governing and maintain a police force with responsibility for maintaining civil order within the Province, only. No standing Army will be allowed or equipped until complete order has been maintained for a period of at least five (5) years.

• The Provinces will be responsible for purging any non-Iraqi from their territory by any means they choose. Cross border violence will not be allowed and perpetrators will receive immediate capital punishment.

• Travel for business and work reasons will be freely permitted between Provinces with proper identification and work permit.

• The mandatory and expedited conclusion of an equitable Oil-sharing arrangement between those three parties. One that "fairly" distributes the Oil revenues into four (4) Revenue Funds. The fourth fund will pay for the Administrative Central Government.

• Establishment of an Administrative Central Government (ACG) that will serve all 3 Provinces. It will not have political power over the Provinces, but it will have authority and responsibility to coordinate the Iraq Population Re-settlement and National Infra-structure Recon-struction across the Provinces. Reconstruction that will be performed by Iraqis with as few outside contractors as possible. They will work to re-build their own country.

The ACG will have authority to officially monitor the Oil production and exporting operations. It will be charged with distributing Oil rev-enues per the Oil Revenue Sharing Agreement. The entity will ini-tially be administered by the U.S. and Russia — with an equal number of seven (7) representatives from each Province. Eventually, the U.S. and Russia would step aside and the twenty-one would then takeover the Administrative Central Government responsibilities for the peace-ful nation of Iraq.

Those are the initial set of requirements that will begin an intense, but deliberately brief and very public 2009 negotiation between the new U.S.

Congress and the existing Iraqi leadership, as well as the American and Iraqi public.

o   o   o   o

Prudent Drawn Down and Controls

Starting in 2009, We will bring the National Guard back at home where they belong — they all are doing a great job. And We will also begin returning the majority of our full-time military back home after fighting the good fight for the nation.

I personally do not see how We and the Congress could allow BC to attack anybody else, i.e., Iran during the remainder of their term. After America removes the vast majority of our troops from Bush's optional Iraq war, the country will not tolerate another such exercise. I do not believe the Congress will allow BC to make a military assault on Iran. And don't worry over the scary domestic propaganda — we will <u>never</u> attack North Korea — with land forces anyway.

In 2008 Congress could still take the required legislative action to cut Iraq funding and/or removing Bush IIs war powers. The Congress can give it and the Congress can take it away. If they were brave enough.

Attacking Iran would be a disaster on many levels and Bush II does not want his administration to be considered a failure (although it is a bit late for that). Trying to send troops into Iran would signal the absolute end of his administration. I understand that a "fast-tracked" double impeachment (Cheney, too) could be accomplished in ninety (90) days.

o   o   o   o

We must all acknowledge that real Change within <u>any</u> country's National System can be a tumultuous experience and that it creates both winners and losers – always has and always will.

It is often chaotic and violent as we see so terribly displayed in Iraq. There, the warring entities – mainly comprised of the former dictator's Ba'ath Party and Sunni Muslim minority <u>versus</u> Shiite Muslim majority population along with the Kurds that were so harshly suppressed for many years — are now fighting it out of power and control — as the status quo with Iraq's National System is totally up for grabs.

And <u>everyone</u> wants to be in control and secure their piece of the pie (and

Oil rights and revenue) when it settles back down. That includes our soon to be restructured American Oil Industry.

And that pretty well sums things up.

American Industry Re-Structuring (AIR) Program

The Defense Industry

The Military Industrial Complex – *The MIC*

Overall Re-Structuring Approach

This is like swimming toward a school of barracuda and you just cut your toe on a pop-top!

The American Defense Industry will necessarily experience the full force of the AIR Programs – Entity Re-Structuring Level programs. The enormous and free-wheeling American Defense Establishment within the National System will be brought under prudent public <u>control</u>. All defense related corporate entities doing business and those desiring to continue doing business in the U.S. will comply, as applicable, with this <u>involuntary</u> American Defense Industry re-organization. This will not be a negotiation.

Due to the simple enormity of the MIC it will take some years to implement the AIR Program across the Defense Industry – right-sizing the MIC rather the letting it continue to be super-sized by Special Interests! However, significant Change will happen starting with the FY2009 budget that runs form 10-1-2008 thru 09-30-2009.

Realistically, the new President and the new Congress will need to sit down <u>together</u> in January 2009 and determine what Changes to make during the fiscal year, since it is hard to imagine Bush II and the old Congress would accomplish anything beneficial before they leave. Maybe they will surprise us in little, but productive ways?

The required Changes especially in how Defense cut-backs will economically impact all 50 states (and maybe even DC) is where the rubber meets the road. As mentioned before, a Recession of some size normally <u>follows</u> one of our wars. The end of a war, removes much the public justification for the increased spending the Military demands to support the fighting. Just as it did after the fall of the Soviet Union – remember the Base Closing Committees?

A Unique Crisis

In January of 2008, with the Bush II/Cheney duo pushing and funding an un-necessary Iraq War; with the Bush II/Republican controlled Congress spending money light the Democrats they still want to criticize for doing;

with the uncontrolled Oil Industry eating away at the vital consumer spending (2/3) part of our economy; with the other Existing Industries already presented taking everything that they possibly can get away with for fun and profit; and with other knotted strands that could be added to our tangled plate of spaghetti — the Plain Truth is that the post Iraq War Recession actually began in December of 2007.

I would call that a unique crisis! What do you think?

The nation is bleeding economically from the combined assault of all of those and other domestically generated problems. Demanding that our national leadership realistically alter our failing Foreign and Defense Policies, and therefore reducing the blood-sucking drain on the economy is an absolutely necessary accommodation to be made for the Common Good.

The dramatic and visible Changes in public attitude and expectations of our national leadership must start demonstrating themselves during the 2008 campaign. This is not just about reasonable Defense spending. We are talking about the Big Picture – America is on the line in this debate.

I will repeat some of this in Part 5. We have been in the habit of re-electing a set of U.S. Congress men and women and lately a president if 2004, that apparently only know how to perpetuate problems and promote failed policies on the Domestic and Foreign fronts. The luxury of allowing for such incompetence in high places has been and could be better tolerated in good economic times like the 50' and 60's. But that was then, and this definitely is now!

We are talking New Deal, if not "Last Deal" creativity and leadership to steer our nation's ship over the next several tough years. It can be done, but I personally do not believe the current membership of the U.S. Congress has the ability to do the job. And remember, solving the People's problems that cannot be properly resolved at the local and state levels – is their only job!

Policy, Budget, and Industry

Policy – the current "foreign intended" Defense policy in the Post-911 era will be revised and brought under practical control. First, refer to the comments under the People's Sense regarding a revised end-game strategy for Iraq. Second, We will need to objectively review our Afghanistan military and end-game strategy and determine what the rational path is for us to take.

Third, We will objectively review the War on Terror, define what it is, why it is, who is driving it, and who is allowing it to continue. We will then have high-level meetings with the <u>real</u> <u>leadership</u> of the countries involved whether they are bureaucratic, religious, tribal, or some combination thereof, We will them come to mutual and <u>final</u> understandings with them with regard to ending their participation in and/or support of all 'foreign intended' militant activities within their borders.

It will be a negotiation in the sense that <u>all</u> parties will have the opportunity the voice their positions and/or reasons for their participation in the ongoing violence. However, it will also take the form of absolute, binding arbitration. Everything will be on the table and everything will be resolved! At the end of those open and totally blunt exchanges an absolute agreement will be reached to reconcile and resolve all issues standing in the way of putting an end to any and all future military and/or terrorist activities.

This can be accomplished.

The true, leadership and Power within all nations (be they presidents, premiers, sheiks, clerics, tribal leaders, dictators, etc.) will be held <u>personally</u> <u>accountable</u> for any violence that extends beyond their borders to any other nation. That personal responsibility and accountability will not be negotiable. Nations and specific people therein will deliberately be made offers that they <u>cannot refuse</u>. That will start with the countries in the Middle East and North Africa and expand rapidly from there.

Consider that the first real level of success that must be orchestrated along the path to Peace, is to end the exportation of violence across national borders. Once that achievable goal is well on its way to being 'mission accomplished' on a global scale, the real work begins. It requires no less than a national reconciliation between the politically and financially Powerful Few and the Masses. For countries that are already is a normally, peaceful state of being like Iceland, there is little to be done if anything. For many others, it will be nothing less than a domestic Revolution, that is entered into with the entire world aware of what is being attempted and observing the progress or lack thereof — as judge and jury.

America government will now reluctantly begin our own version of this external foreign policy and internal domestic reconciliation.

Budget – Again, refer to the comments under the People's Sense regarding the FY2008 and FY2009, and FY 2010 Department of Defense budget controls. The *Absolute Defense Budget Ceiling* will be set at the FY2008 level and will be reduced annually until it is balanced against our revised and <u>prudent</u> National Security Policy. The enormous dollars formally spent on Defense will be partially re-directed to Domestic programs. We <u>will not</u> weaken our Defense capabilities, but We will not continue to spend excessively and needlessly for too much of it.

Industry – The remainder of this proposal will highlight the AIR Program's application to the existing American Defense Industry. As with the previous Existing Industry proposals, it will provide enough detail to practically overview the pending re-structuring of the major Defense Industry Contractors. Other details will be forthcoming during the 2008 campaign season.

Initial List of Industry Entities

This is the initial list of primary Defense contractors, or rather the MIC corporations and companies to be included in the AIR Program Re-Structuring of the Defense Industry:

Haliburton
KBR – Kellogg, Brown, and Root
McDonald Douglas
Lockheed Martin Corporation
Boeing Company
Northrop Grumman Corporation
Raytheon Company
General Dynamics Corporation
United Technologies Corporation
Science Applications International Corp.
TRW Inc.
Health Net, Inc.
L-3 Communications

This initial, working list of corporate entities may very well be refined as 2008 progresses and the November 2008 National Election draws near.

By deliberate, united vote on that historic day, *We the People* can freely declare that such practical and prudent Change to the National System for the Common Good of us all — <u>will</u> <u>be</u> <u>made</u>.

AIR Program – The Entity Re-Structuring Levels (ERL) Overview

The Defense Industry

ERL 1 – Operational Reorganization

This Defense Industry AIR Program proposal will follow the same track as the others, but will prove to be a bit more tedious. That is primarily due to the enormity of the Defense Establishment and the number of corporations involved in it.

The first phase of the Air Program will involve the major (prime) defense contractors, only. Many of the other companies below that top tier of Defense Industry contractors actually sub-contract through the prime contractors providing them with products and services. Therefore, AIR Program changes to the way that the prime contractors do business will automatically "trickle down" and begin to "ripple through" the network of supporting companies.

This initial phase will prove effective enough by bringing the Defense Establishment under reasonable financial control in 2009. With the practical Changes made at the top, additional restructuring at the lower level entities may not be required.

o   o   o   o

A newly formed Board of Directors will comprise the first level of the MIC Organization Chart.

The Defense Industry corporations will effectively become operating Divisions of the newly formed, Non-Profit Military Industrial Consortium (MIC) – the Industry Management Consortium established to oversee the operations of the restructured Defense related corporations.

What better way to label the management entity that will finally bring the out-of-control Defense Industry into a far more practical and logical order, than using the label that President Eisenhower placed upon the rapidly growing of the Defense Industry. Going forward "MIC" will be short for Military Industrial Complex and Military Industrial Consortium in the public's mind – just common sense.

Again, this means that starting with the largest Defense contractors We will begin a methodical merger of the major corporations that comprise today's American Defense Industry.

Those corporations will combine to form the second level of the new MIC Consortium Organization Chart. There could be issues where a given Defense corporation is currently part of a larger corporation. As with the other Existing Industry, the corporate entity will be transferred to become operating Divisions of the MIC. Again, these would not be purchased or bought out just because they are stock held entities – a simple transfer.

An appropriate amount of operational consolidation takes place when fairly redundant corporate entities merge, we have all seen it – therefore some reduction in employment would eventually occur.

This AIR Program restructuring will prove to be an unavoidable wake-up call to the Defense industry as a whole. As the restructuring implementation of the Defense Industry progresses other corporate entities not included in the top tier reorganization, may well decide — specifically their current Board of Directors and stockholders — to do some 'housekeeping' of their own!

Note: Although the Consortiums are set-up as Non-Profit corporations, these organizations will pay taxes.

ERL 2 – Existing Management Retirement

Existing Senior Management

- Any member of senior management with Golden Parachute will be retired by May 30, 2009. Memorial Day, how fitting. Any and all stock options in their package will be eliminated.
- No more Golden Parachutes will be offered to future management, ever.
- Any remaining member of management with a base salary in excess of one (1) million dollars per year will have it cut to that amount as of July 1, 2009.
- All stock options for 2009 will be eliminated.
- All bonuses will be reviewed by the MIC group and may be reduced.

And if a given person does not like those Changes – they know where the door is…

Remember: The one-time offer to hold current and prior management and employees harmless from lawsuit will be presented and I believe will be accepted. This offer will be made to the current and prior members of the Boards of Directors, as well.

Existing Boards of Directors (BOD)

The existing BOD would be relieved of their positions by May 1, 2009. By law most, if not all corporations are required to have some form of BOD whether it is actually functional to the operation or just ornamental. The future form and function of the previously mentioned Industry Management Consortium created for the Defense Industry, the MIC, will be reviewed.

ERL 3 – New Management Structure and Charter

The *Industry Management Consortium* Requirement

With the consolidation of the existing top-tier Defense Corporations, into the new Military Industrial Consortium (MIC) the nation is again merging a group of businesses that are pretty much doing the same thing. Of course, there are areas of specialty in the Defense Industry and specialized R&D that are peculiar to certain businesses. As with the Pharmaceutical Industry, targeted R&D must and will continue.

With the merger of the top-tier Contractors, only a single Boards of Directors "entity" will be needed. The costs that are now associated with all the existing Boards is therefore not necessary and will go back into the operation. Those freed-up funds will be put to good uses.

The MIC's Board will be responsible to the American public for implementing, strictly overseeing, and refining the new Charter of Operations. They will not manage the day-to-day operation.

Revised Charter of Operations

Simply stated the new MIC's Inaugural Charter will be to:

The first level of the MIC will provide oversight and administrative control over the entire operation.

The day-to-day operations of the MIC will of course continue to be managed and performed by the Divisions and the existing operational managers and staff – the people that actually do the work today. The MIC (consortium) management and their staff will administer the overall operation. The MIC management team and their staff will be comprised of industry-wise people – not loaded up with consultants – outsiders if needed, but mainly selected for these critical positions from the managers in the Divisions that remained after the senior management was retired.

The MIC management team will serve as the primary contact point with the U.S. Congress, as well as state, county, city and local agencies. It will have a working Board of Directors, with its staff at the first level of the Military Industrial Consortium.

As you review this initial Charter, again keep in mind the related points made under the People's Sense section and earlier parts of this proposal. They will not all be mentioned here but will be blended into the MIC operational mandate.

Simply stated the MIC Inaugural Operational Charter will include:

1. Oversight of the consolidation of the top-tier Defense Contractor corporations into the new MIC organizational structure.
2. To work with the Congress and Department of Defense to right-size the American Defense Establishment. This will be balanced against a revised external Defense Policy that will take form during 2008 andwill be refined in 2009.
3. To work with the states in determining how the definite coming decreases in Defense based funding from the Federal government can be "partially" and practically replaced with Domestic Infrastructure Improvement and Renewed Manufacturing Opportunity funding. Good titles!

Under the National Take Back Industries (TBI) program concept presented earlier and combined with the utilization of the Income Generating Entity (IGE) business model for creating *small businesses* – states and local governments will continue to receive some level of funding that was previously "ear-marked" for Defense-based businesses. The funding will continue to go directly to existing local contractors to help them transition to a right-sized Defense Industry, as well as helping some of themtransition to new non-defense lines of business.

State and local governments will aggressively promote the TBI/IGE program concepts to create jobs and industries that provide the goods and services required by the public and business on a regular basis especially, if those employment opportunities were pverviously sent overseas – outsourced — in the last decade.

Overall Intent

The focus on building such required domestic businesses is essential to moving the U.S. Economy toward an Eternal Maintenance Economic model. When products from light bulbs, underwear, Levis, automobiles, and tractors are truly made in the U.S.A., money is maintained, re-cycled if you will within our borders.

With the continued collapse of the Eternal Growth Economic model – the migration away from the archaic 1950's and 1960's style Capitalism American and now toward a self-sustaining, Eternal Maintenance Economic model is not only *common sense,* it represents our nation's economic survival.

ERL 4 – Stock, Profitability, and Pricing Controls

As is repeated in these six proposals — the following scenarios will begin taking effect as soon as possible in 2009 and will likely be applied retro-actively when the required legislation is passed by the **new** U.S. Congress.

While We can always hope, there is probably little chance that the existing Congress and White House will move on this proposal before the November Election. These six Industry proposals need to be the **hottest topics** in the country during 2008. The frustrated Electorate needs to bring these and the other American Agenda Proposals to the campaigns and challenge the candidates for all offices for their position on each! We can do this.

Stock Trading Control

Stock trading in certain Defense Industry corporations will be in a state of virtual suspense. The stock will be initially frozen at its 1-1-2008 share price. Any negotiation and eventual buy-back activity will start at that price or lower possibly adjusted by the individual stock-holder's buy-in share price.

The market would be intensely watched (by the SEC and others) in the run-up to the 1-1-09 AIR Program Effective Date for any selling or other game playing. Again, violators will be severely dealt with including fines and/or prison time in a State run facility. No Federal playpens anymore.

Profitability Control

Corporate profitability for publicly held (stock) corporation will be capped effective 1-1-09 at no more than <u>four</u> percent (4%) for physical year 2009 and stockholder pay out will be capped and adjusted retro-actively. The Defense Establishment has had their *last* good ride at the public's expense during the Bush II years, but their party is permanently over.

Remember, Reagan actually brought the Cold War to an end by driving the Soviet economy into bankruptcy trying to compete with his optional Defense buildup. They simply ran out of money before We did!

My fellow Americans — It is now 2008, and We cannot, We will not allow Bush II, Cheney, and their MIC supporters to drive our economy into a brick wall with excessive Defense budgets and continuing to borrow Billions to keep their optional Iraq war, and the <u>overly</u> <u>hyped</u> War on Terror going.

o   o   o   o

The 2009 and 2010 profits in excess of that will be put to practical uses such as:

- covering the initial re-organization costs
- elimination of any out-sourcing activities
- to develop and support a transition plan to return as many out-sourced jobs to American workers
- internal operational spending
- used to control/decrease future rates and pricing
- set aside for stock dividends pay-outs in future years until the buy-back process is complete

<u>Pricing Control</u>

This has more to do with defense contractor pricing for goods and services they provide to the Department of Defense. The AIR Program restructuring of the MIC corporations — combined with the capping and reduction in the overall Defense budget starting in FY2009 — will directly result in pricings controls across the entire Defense Establishment. In other words, no more $2,000 toilet seats.

ERL 5 – Conversion of IGE Model

The AIR Re-structuring of the American Defense Industry offers the *greatest opportunity* to transition of a National Infrastructure Industry into an Income Generating Entity (IGE). We will determine how to get the best bang for our Defense dollars and keep it that way.

Over a period of years, all existing stockholders will be bought out. The stock amounts involved and how the stockholders will be compensated for their share value will be worked as the AIR Program implementation of the Pharmas progresses. Again, that is not avoiding discussing the hard dollars involved. The numbers are what the numbers are, and they will only continue to grow worse the longer We delay these Changes of Necessity to our National System.

Again, I deliberately would not take the time extract and present that data on this or the others in this infamous group of six Existing Industries. Further, We know by now that those numbers will be one of the first things that the Defense Establishment lobbyists will throw out to scare everyone with. But, that expectedly heated rhetoric and domestic propaganda will soon pass.

We will not be made afraid nor will We be deterred from aggressively working for our Common Good. Ironically, this is to be the biggest battle in our Second American Revolution.

o   o   o   o

That really is all, folks.

And I truly hope that it is enough to get us started!

o   o   o   o

And with that, ladies and gentleman,
We have reached the end of this presentation of the
twenty-seven (27) proposals that comprise the initial version of,

An American Agenda for 2008 and Beyond

o   o   o   o

<u>Closing Thoughts on An American Agenda</u>

<u>National Problem Solving is Difficult – Not Mission Impossible</u>

<u>The Problem with Solving Big Problems</u>

This is the basic analogy I like to use to describe what is involved in solving complex business problems:

> It is like being challenged to untangle a plate of spaghetti and tomato sauce! Your mission, should you choose to accept it, is to untangle a full plate of warm spaghetti without snapping a <u>single</u> strand of pasta and always keeping the remaining pile on the plate.
>
> At first you might think, no problem, a nice plate of warm spaghetti with plenty of sauce, they will all slide right out. And maybe the first few strands you select do come out easily. However, as you keep pulling one strand will inevitably become entangled, knotted up with some others and won't come along quietly.
>
> You could just decide to keep pulling without first taking the time to carefully separate more of the strands, thus risking your mission with the breakage of a single strand of spaghetti.
>
> You have two basic options. The *first* is to ignore the complications presented by the other strands and run the real risk of not satisfactorily completing your mission.
>
> The *second* is to the take the time required to carefully dig into the tangle and separate more of the strands to loosen the knots so they are freed without snapping; and then patiently repeating the same tedious process as many times as it takes in order to successfully deal with all of the knots.
>
> Of course, if you *really* intend to ultimately be successful in your mission — you will select the latter option.

o   o   o   o

I tell you, my fellow Americans that any complex problem in the public or business sectors can be solved. It must be acknowledged from the start that while 90% of any problem-solving process will be relatively straightforward, it is that last 10% or less that will provide challenges to achieving success. In effectively "dealing with" that final fraction you must be tenacious, strong-minded, and sometimes fearless.

I read somewhere that, "Courage is the mastery of fear – not the absence of fear". In determining to once and for all address and resolve our Common National Problems, We will be joining together — to face and conquer the all so common human fear of Change itself. Therefore, be assured and also comforted that whatever We the People agree to and decide must be done — can and will be done.

o   o   o   o

<u>1776 versus 2008</u>

In *Common Sense*, Thomas Paine "only" had one problem and solution to present to the America colonists concerning how they could cure their collective ills — just by declaring war on their own country and the British Empire!

Some 230 years later, We find ourselves in a far more complex national situation, to say nothing of the added complications of the overall state of the world. Therefore, We have far more to consider <u>and</u> effectively confront in order to resolve our long-standing national problems. And while several of our hard issues found their way into An American Agenda and other parts of this book, we do have many more things yet to work out.

I have long believed that our people could come find to ways to terms with any <u>and</u> all of the long-standing national problems that plaque our National System, if only a Common National Vision worthy of our American Democracy could be presented for the People's review, open deliberation, and Common Agreement.

You have just read about how some of those hard, public issues could be effectively addressed by the implementation of the proposals in An American Agenda. My hope is that you have been provided with a better understanding on those issues and most importantly a greater sense of personal comfort that they indeed can be addressed for the Common Good of our people and our nation.

Further, I hope that what you have read thus far in CS2 is beginning to form an acceptable Vision of what America stands for and where We should be heading in the near and distant future.

Our Common Problem – A Lack of National Leadership

A publicly acceptable National Vision requires the presence of viable National Leadership to step forward that will lead us through the struggles required to bring those desirable Changes to reality in our and in the nation's daily life.

At the highest level America's problem-solving "problem" rests upon our elected and too party-minded, national leadership — that they are incapable of presenting us with a viable National Vision.

Today, We as a nation and as a now struggling world leader currently *do not know where we are going*! Please give that point some thought for a few moments! The nation is now some 230 years from the Declaration of Independence on our national voyage, with no particular destination in mind. We are presently on a national voyage to nowhere. And that is a dangerous state of national affairs.

As dreadfully obvious as it may sound, in order for us to ever develop a viable National Vision that will provide us a framework against which to solve our common problems, We must first acknowledge that there is no such Vision or Common Agreement. From that moment of national awareness – that shared national Epiphany — We will begin to build such a National Vision.

From that moment We will also begin to publicly and loudly declare that the problems that have plagued us for so long will not be allowed to continue unresolved. What a concept!

As mentioned early in CS2, fortunately or unfortunately most of those problems are easy enough to identify. You recall the Grievance List of public concerns:

- Automobile/Truck Theft
- Commodity Market Abuses
- Contaminated Food Supply
- Crimes of Physical Assault
- Crimes of Financial Assault
- Drug War in our Streets
- Employment/Income (viable and legal)
- Ending the Iraq War
- Gangs in Our Communities
- Global Warming
- Homelessness
- Housing Costs
- Hunger

- Illegal Immigration – ending it
- Interest Rates on Primary Family Residence
- Katrina Clean-up
- Judicial Legal Complex (JLC)
- Medical Insurance for all American citizens – cradle to grave
- Military Industrial Complex (MIC)
- Oil Industry Windfall Profits and Other Abuses
- Over-weight children, teenagers, and adults
- Poverty Among Our Citizens
- Public Education
- Pre-meditated Murder
- Pre-meditated Pedophile Crimes Against our Youth
- Pre-meditated Rape
- Prescription Medicine Costs
- Stem Cell Research
- Social Security Solvency
- War on Terror

It is fair to say that some of those problems were addressed in some practical manner in the American Agenda proposals. In order to solve our Common Problems, We must:

- Agree what our problems are
- Develop realistic approaches and solutions designed for the Common Good
- Agree on the proper solution to be implemented
- Enact the legislation required to implement the agreed Changes
- And finally to strictly and fairly enforce the Changes

As you can appreciate especially after reviewing the American Agenda proposals, actually confronting and practically resolving various problems in our National System requires determination, but it is possible.

In solving big problems there are always "other strands" that get involved and make the problem solving process more complicated. And the complications presented by those other strands must be addressed at some practical level, in order to arrive at a comprehensive and successful conclusion or result. Otherwise, those problems could very well continue, and cause your incomplete solution to be rejected or fail upon implementation.

That scenario accurately describes the primary difficulty in solving more complex public problems, which is dealing with those often nasty little **complications** — some that were totally unanticipated at first look. All too often these "knots" involve more tedious issues than the original problem itself! And in public problem solving those complications can be very disappointing.

Of course, if the solution development process were easy, We would have far fewer problems! The inter-connected problems I encountered while developing the NDR proposal taught me why more of our public problems are not yet solved. It is simply – difficult! However, I said they are **difficult** to solve, **not impossible** to solve! *As you well know*, our elected leaders are not working independently, creatively or aggressively enough to resolve any of our civil and economic problems.

Over my career I had the opportunity to work on and struggle through many complex business problems and situations, and was challenged by the absolute tedious nature of the process. The all so real complexity factor, especially in national problem-solving, offers small comfort and rationale for the lack of success on the part of our elected leadership in such areas as implementing National Health Care Insurance or ending the War on Drugs. I said **small** comfort, but no valid excuse or justification for their lack of success on the People's behalf — especially when such problems are causing death and misery among our people, every day.

o   o   o   o

On National Change

Our Struggle – the Common Good vs. Today's Status Quo

After all the tough things we living today and our national ancestors have already faced as a nation and conquered together over the last 230 years, we can do anything that we as a united people determine that should be done.

The Changes presented in CS2 represent what I consider to be a practical "ends just the means" mentality, and a prudent attack on bad, if not destructive public policy. That is precisely what the 1st American Revolution was all about — an attack against the powerful Few taking care of their priorities and their inner circle of players and hangers-on, with no practical regard for the Masses.

I will repeat the obvious — that the senseless preservation of today's status quo and where it is irresponsibly leading our nation – is not serving Common Good of the American people on many levels. Continuance is not worth the current hard costs and it will only grow worse with each passing day, month, year, and decade. We can no longer afford to support or allow this Special Interest status quo!

I could be talking any number of public issues, right? Iraq, the Middle East in general, illegal immigration, viable employment, health care insurance for all Americans Homeland Security, the Drug War, gangs, prescription drug prices, the environment, etc., to name just a few issues that makeup the Status Quo of 2008 in America. This ain't a pretty Big Picture is it? And *We* are allowing it to be painted!

Let's all look around people! Our younger generations in their thirties, twenties, and a growing percentage of older teens understand that the country is not doing well as they expected and the prospects do not look as good for their future as they could be and should be. And their worries about the future are wrapped around their real concerns about "viable" long-term employment and being able to afford a decent life for themselves and their family.

The Obstacles that Challenge Real Public Change at Any Level

What I learned over my analytical career about solving even complex problems is that with proper research and open dialogue, operationally practical solution options could be determined to resolve any problem. Management could then decide upon which option to implement that would best serve their operational requirements.

However, I also observed that obtaining the management commitment to first <u>implement</u> and then to <u>enforce</u> said improvements was often difficult to obtain (this is sounding too familiar). The corporate and governmental will (guts) to make real Change was often not provided. Therefore, the implementation of the approved changes could be slowed if not entirely stopped by those invested in maintaining the *status quo*. And so, the beneficial operational improvements were not fully implemented or were dropped all together. Such failures are far more common than any of us would care to imagine and most of us have observed this scenario on a smaller scale where we work.

> A glaring daily example of such failure at the Congressional level is their lack of enforcement of existing immigration laws, resulting in the "preventable" problems the Congress has <u>allowed</u> to continue to fall upon our people and American society.

Again, this "resistance to positive change" is true in corporations, as well as in local, state, and federal agencies, Congress, and the White House. Philosophically, government, business, and *even We the People* do want the progress that by definition demands Change in some form. However, all are not so receptive if Change could threaten their piece of the pie. This simple fact about human nature is as old as civilization, and it <u>still</u> applies to peasants, dictators, religious leaders, monarchs, kings, tens of millions of commuters, presidents, and the U.S. Congress, as well. Most if not all of us have felt that odd emotion at sometime in our lives.

<u>With No Pain, There is No Gain</u>

Again, <u>real</u> Change involves and demands individual sacrifice. It <u>cannot help</u> but create both winners and losers — it is a natural, unavoidable by-product of altering the status quo within any country's National System. Especially when We are talking about social and economic Change in a country of 300 million men, women, and children.

At many points in the coming struggle we will need to deal (reasonably) with those opposing a Change that will have some direct, negative impact on them personally.

We will no longer allow them to defeat Change for their narrow self-interest. In the end the Changes that will be made to the National System will be of practical benefit for the Common Good of the vast majority of our people and therefore, must be accomplished.

Our Responsibility — Dictate the 2008 Campaign Platform

As mentioned before and as will be discussed in greater detail in Part 5, We all <u>need</u> to embrace the fact that it is fully within our electoral Rights <u>every</u> two (2) years vote <u>out</u> of office all 435 members of the US House of Representatives, as well as 33/34 of 100 members of the US Senate.

Although, We did <u>not fully execute</u> our Democratic "option" on 11-7-06 — when part of the concerned and displeased electorate made a dramatic "trial run" — We certainly did get the attention of the members of Congress, both Parties, and their lobbyists! Therefore, Congress already knows that the next time more of them are very likely to be involuntarily retired. And in spite of that common knowledge, they are actually accomplishing even less in these *two more years* and We have had enough!

> *"The problem with doing nothing, is not knowing, when you're finished."*

Benjamin Franklin

In the critical months that remain, We do require and must demand an open, national, debate — and it must be very <u>loud</u> at times! It is to be a debate in which <u>only</u> American citizens will be included. All others (foreign and the domestic) must stand back, watch if they like, but just stay the hell out of the way! This will be a family feud and will be accompised with hard, binding reconciliation.

And the approximately 52 million youngest Americans, that will be ages 18 to 30 in 2008 *must be concerned and involved* for they have the most at stake – the most to lose if We do not act!

With the presentation of An American Agenda – We the People have a primary set of viable approaches to begin resolving several critical problems within our National System, as well as a true People's Platform that will be our checklist against which We will grade anyone running for the U.S. Congress and <u>any</u> person that considers themselves to be a qualified candidate for President of the United States for 2008.

o   o   o   o

Be Comforted

I would encouragingly state that We can be thankful that the answers and/ or solutions to <u>any</u> of our problems can be developed. But (there is always a but!), **only** after the Common Agreement by the People on a mandatory set of ground rules for a civilly responsible society and a Common National Vision.

And the baseline for those commonly accepted civil rules and a shared vision are what CS2 presents for your review and consideration.

We have in the course of this presentation reviewed the basic concepts of a common National Vision and what it will take to bring it to our daily reality. Ours will be a Vision that is independent of party politics and one that does not need to be altered every two, four or eight years to fit whatever party is attempting to maintain or obtain control the Congress, the White House, and our lives. Remember,

Where there are no rules, there is chaos...

I am herein addressing the 200 million-plus Americans of voting age regarding how We are to save our country from the future that We are not only headed for, but that We are currently living in. And <u>We</u> all know it! These conditions will <u>only</u> worsen unless We, as a <u>united</u> people, take deliberate, aggressive, and what some will certainly call radical actions to prudently adjust the social and economic structure of day-to-day life in America – the National System.

I have no doubt that We the People can and will do what is needed if the Vision presented in CS2 is found acceptable to you – and the rest of our fellow Americans. I believe that it will be, and I pray that it is.

o   o   o   o

In the remainder of the *Second Coming of Common Sense* we will review the critical actions of our predecessors, the recent political events that have brought us to this our moment in time, and what we can do and shall do to keep our Appointment with Destiny.

We the People,

- will Address the long ignored, difficult problems that once seemed unsolvable,
- will Confront the forces that have so jeopardized the Common Good of our fellow Americans,
- will Demand that the U.S. Congress serve the Common Good of our citizens above all others,

- will Prevail over adversaries of the Common Good to set ourselves on the proper national course,
- will Preserve, Protect, and Defend the Constitution of the United States of America,

and in so doing We will insure Life, Liberty, the Pursuit of Happiness for Ourselves and Our Posterity.

It is said the God saved America so that it could do great things for the struggling world. Our Predecessors over the years did what they <u>had</u> to do to preserve the nation – not what they <u>wanted</u> to do.

We must now stand together and do the things that <u>must</u> be done,

"not because they are Easy, but because they are Hard"

o   o   o   o

With Regard to *The Fourth Estate*
and some Significant Others

This little insert is one of those "items" that some suggested that I should not include in CS2 since it might bother some people. However, since my intent is not to bother, but to encourage some individuals and organizational entities to do good works for the nation – here it is anyway!

Courtesy of *Wikipedia, the free encyclopedia*

The term **Fourth Estate** refers to the press, both in its explicit capacity of advocacy and in its implicit ability to frame political issues. The term goes back at least to Thomas Carlyle in the first half of the 19th century.

Novelist Jeffrey Archer in his work *The Fourth Estate* made this observation: "In May 1789, Louis XVI summoned to Versailles a full meeting of the 'Estate General'. The First Estate consisted of three hundred clergy. The Second Estate, three hundred nobles. The Third Estate, six hundred commoners.

Some years later, after the French Revolution, Edmund Burke, looking up at the Press Gallery of the House of Commons, said, 'Yonder sits the Fourth Estate, and they are more important than them all.'"

My thanks to the people and contributors at *Wik.*

o   o   o   o

The Founders Appreciation

The Founding Fathers both praised and challenged the Free Press, and referenced them as *The Fourth Estate*. The Founders knew how critical open communication among the People was to the protection of the general welfare, as well as to the proper care and maintenance of the young and maturing Democracy.

In the chart below you will see an interesting mix of press/media people and news organizations, various political and entertainment celebrities, and a smaller group of organizations. I originally wanted to have about 50 to 75 names of media types – mainly newspaper, network and cable news – and a few public-oriented organizations that came to mind. However, the list kept growing as I determined to add his or her name or an organization – although I mostly wanted people. Those that reviewed the draft were interested by the variety of people on the List. They made some suggestions and everyone was added. I hope that the names and reference titles are correct, if not you have my sincere apology for any errors. AJ

I consider it to be a very good list to be on. And there are those names that I will wish I had thought to place on the list, after the cut-off date for publication has passed. For the most part, I observed these people and groups as trying in their own way to be a positive force in society, and it is obvious they are not all on the same side on the issues! I sincerely hope no one is offended "to be or not to be" on *the Fourth Estate* list.

My Challenge to Them

My intent is to publicly challenge this unique group of people and organizations, to please take a hard and critical look at the message and content of CS2, with particular attention paid to An American Agenda. And not only from a professional viewpoint as many in the media naturally will, but more importantly *in this case* as an American, a concerned citizen, and as a parent, even if it does not yet apply to you. Discuss things about CS2 that are positive, as well as those you may take exception to for whatever reason.

The American Press – written, heard, and viewed – is challenged to step away from growing culture of "corporate politically correct and tabloid media" that has been creeping into their world since the 1980's. I tried to put that as kindly as I could.

To me and I believe the vast majority of Americans, it is the American Press, above all others, that is supposed to "objectively challenge" if not harass the bad guys, bad business, and bad government. Just as Dan Rather regularly stood up in White House press conferences, asked the tough questions, and gave President Nixon hell! He was doing his job for the country and always represented his profession very well. What happened to him in recent times is, an example of how the "corporate media culture" has damaged the delivery of real news in favor of sensationalism — and the will gladly walk one of the best off a plank to protect themselves from the negative spotlight they deserve. Dan Rather remains one of the best reporters ever. And I am far from alone in that respect for him.

Called Upon to Raise the Debate

The celebrity names are included due to their past activity in the public's interest, such as Bill Cosby has done over the years and has sometimes been slammed for it. At least he has cared enough to try and do something along the way — and he was correct!

Overall, I am asking those on the List to assist me in getting the word out about CS2, and An American Agenda to the Masses of the American public — and the sooner the better. To promote it over and through the screams that Special Interest business may well throw at its message. I fully expect their criticism and I can handle it! As I tell people I was an IT consultant in DC for 30 years and I have been abused by professionals, or at least people that thought they were!

You and others like you that have a public voice – use it! Be critical, but fair about the proposals offered in the name of the Common Good of our fellow Americans. I have had thousands of conversations with ALL types of people over many years and I believe the nation yearns for such a message. Not everyone will like all of it — that is impossible — and not my mission in this personal problem-solving project for America.

So please give *The Second Coming of Common Sense*, a hard, but objective look and let's see how it plays on Main Street where it really counts.

Some will say this piece is just a marketing pitch to sell books. To that I say that selling books was a 'minor' positive consideration for adding the piece. If it really contributes to kicking-off the absolutely necessary national debate over the issues it raises and others — then fantastic!

My absolute and primary reason was to bring *critical public* attention to CS2 and An American Agenda. To do whatever possible to attract the public, the press, and book publishers! Consider that this is the type of non-fiction political book, which publishers won't touch until it is complete. And then it must seek the light of day and demonstrate some basic public appeal.

And if you think I would seriously consider doing something as blatant as sending one of my first copies of CS2, signed and with a dozen roses to Oprah – you would be absolutely correct!

Have nice day...

Individual/Entity	**Vocation/Public Identity**
Al Franken	Comedian/Activist
Al Gore	Former Vice President
Al Hunt	Bloomberg News
Al Sharpton	Civil Rights Activist
Alan Colmes	Hanity & Colmes
Ali Velshi	CNN Sr. Business Correspondent
Alison Stewart	NPR, The Bryant Park Project
Amanda Carpenter	TownHall.com
Amy Holmes	CNN Contributor
Amy Sullivan	Time Magazine
Anderson Cooper	CNN Host, Anderson Cooper 360
Andrea Koppel	CNN Correspondent
Andrea Mitchell	NBC News Correspondent
Andrew Sullivan	The Atlantic
Andy Rooney	60 Miniutes/National Institution
Anne Keisman	Reporter Loudoun Times-Mirror
Arianna Huffington	HuffingtonPost.com
Arnold Schwarzenegger	Governor of California, Former Actor
Barbara Streisand	Singer and Actress
Barbara Walters	The View, News Personality
Barry Scheck	Innocence Project
Benjamin Bradley	Retired Editor, The Wasington Post/Author
Bertha Coombs	CNBC, Financial Correspondent
Bill Bennett	Former Drug Czar, Secretary of Education
Bill Clinton	Former President #42
Bill Cosby	Comedian/Author/Activist
Bill Gates	Founder, Microsoft Corporation
Bill Hillsman	North Woods Advertising
Bill Kristol	Weekly Standard
Bill Maher	Real Time with Bill Maher
Bill Moyers	Bill Moyers Journal
Bill O'Reilly	The O'Reilly Factor, Political Talk Show
Bill Schneider	CNN Sr. Political Analyst
Bill Tucker	CNN, Lou Dobbs
Bob Dylan	The One and Only
Bob Garfield	Advertising Age
Bob Johnson	Founder of B.E.T.
Bob Shrum	Democratic Strategist
Bob Sullivan	Book, *Gotcha' Capitalism*
Bob Woodward	Author and The Watergate Duo
Brian Williams	NBC News Anchor
Brit Hume	Host, Speical Report with Brit Hume/FOX News
Bruce Fein	American Freedom Agenda
Calissa Lockhart	Actress/Activist
Candy Crowley	CNN Sr. Political Analyst
Carl Bernstein	Author and The Watergate Duo
Carson Daly	Host, Last Call with Carson Daly

Charles Gasparino	Book, *King of the Club*
Charles Gibson	ABC Evening News Anchor
Charles Grodin	Comedian; Book, *If I Only Knew Then*
Charles Krauthammar	Political Commentator
Charlie Cook	Cook Political Report
Chris Cillizza	Blog, The Fix; WashingtonPost.com
Chris Ferguson	Evening Talk Show
Chris Matthews	Hardball/MSNBC
Chris Rock	Comedian
Chris Wallace	Host, FOX News Sunday
Christine Amanpour	CNN Chief International Correspondent
Christine Romans	CNN, Lou Dobbs Correspondent
Chrystia Freeland	Financial Times
Chuck Todd	NBC News, Political Director
Cokie Roberts	Journalist/Author, NPR Contrib. Sr. News Analyst
Colin Powell	Former Secretary of State
Conan O'Brien	Late Night with Conan O'Brien
Craig Crawford	CQ Politics/MSNBC Analyst
Craig Ferguson	Late Late Show with Craig Ferguson
Cynthia Tucker	Political Commentator
D. L. Hughley	Comedian/Actor
Dan Popkey	The Idaho Statesman
Dan Rather	Political Commentator
Dan Savage	Columnist, *Savage Love*
Dan Tolivek	Reporter Leesburg Today
Dana Bash	CNN Correspondent
Dana Milbank	Washington Post
Daniel Shore	Columnist
David Becker	People for the American Way
David Brinkley	Political Commentator
David Brooks	New York Times
David Gergen	CNN Sr. Political Analyst
David Gregroy	NBC News Chief White House Correspondent
David Letterman	Late Show with David Letterman
David Shuster	MSNBC Hardball's Best Correspondent
David Yepsen	Des Moines Register
Dennis Kucinich	2008 Democratic Presidential Candidate
Denzel Washington	Actor
DeRoy Murdock	National Review Online
Diana Olick	CNBC, Realty Check
Diana West	Washington Times
Diane Rehm	Host, Diane Rehm Show, WAMU
Diane Sawyer	Good Morning America, ABC
Don Chedal	Actor/Activist
Donald Trump	Business Leader
Donna Brazil	Political Strategist
Doris Kearns Goodwin	Historian
Douglas Wilder	Former Virginia Governor

Dr. Charles Stanley	Pastor
E. J. Dionne	The Washington Post
Earl G. Graves	Founder Black Enterprise Magazine
Ed Rollins	Campaign Advisor
Ed Rosenthal	Cannabis Activist
Ed Schultz	The Ed Schultz Show
Eleanor Clift	Newsweek
Eleanor Smeal	An Original Feminist Activist
Ellen Degeneres	Host, The Ellen Degeneres Show
Erin Burnett	CNBC — Street Signs
Errol Lewis	New York Daily News
Ethan Nadelmann	The Drug Policy Alliance
Eugene Robinson	The Washington Post — Op/Ed
Fareed Zakaria	Editor Newsweek International
Franklin Graham	Minister and Billy Graham's Son
Fred Barnes	Political Commentator, FOX News
George Clooney	Actor, Activist
George Mitchell	Former U.S. Senator
George Stephanopolis	Host, This Week with George Stephanopolis
George W. Bush	Former President #41
Glenn Beck	Host, Glenn Beck Program
Gloria Borger	CNN Senior Political Analyst
Gloria Steinem	An Original Women's Rights Activist/Ms. Magazine
Gordon Peterson	Political Talk Show Host
Greta Van Susteren	Host, On the Record with Greta Van Susteren
Hank Sheinkopf	Democratic Strategist
Harold "Hype" Williams	Film Director
Harrison Ford	Actor
Hillary Rosen	Democratic Strategist
Holly Bailey	Newsweek
Howard Feinman	Newsweek, MSNBC, Sr. Political Analyst
Jack Germann	Baltimore, Political Commentator
Jack McCafferty	CNN Cable News
Jamal Simmons	Democratic Strategist
James Carvelle	Democratic Strategist
James Kilpatrick	New York Times
James LeCamp	Financial Radio Host
James Pindell	Boston Globe
Jason Jones	The Daily Show
Jay Carney	Times
Jay Leno	The Tonight Show
Jean Garafalo	Comedian/Activist
Jeffery Toobin	CNN Sr. Legal Analyst
Jeffrey H. Birnbaum	Staff Writer, The Washingotn Post
Jeremy Scahill	Taxpayers of Common Sense
Jesse Jackson	Civil Rights Activist
Jill Zuckman	Chicago Tribune

Jim Cramer	Host, Mad Money/CNBC, TheStreet.com
Jim Jeffers	Former Congressman, Vermont
Jim Lehrer	The NewsHour with Jim Lehrer
Jim Wallis	Book, *The Great Awakening*
Jim Warren	Chicago Tribune
Jimmy Carter	Former President #39, Activist
Joan Walsh	Salon.com
Joe Biden	U.S. Senator, Delaware, Democrat
Joe Johns	CNN Correspondent
Joe Klein	Journalist, Author of *Politics Lost*
Joe Scarbourough	Host, "Morning Joe" Political Talk Show
Joe Trippi	Campaign Advisor
Joe Watkins	MSNBC
John & Elizabeth Edwards	Former Senator and Wife
John Fund	Book, *Stealing Elections*
John Harris	Politico.com
John Harwood	Wall Street Journal
John Kerry	U.S. Senator, Massachusetts, Democrat
John King	CNN Chief National Correspondent
John MacLaughlin	Political Talk Show Host
John Nichols	Consitutional Law
John Roberts	CNN Political Analyst/Reporter
John Singleton	Film Maker
John Stewart	Political Talk Show
John Walsh	Child Protection and America's Most Wanted
John Zogby	Zogby International
Jon Soltz	VoteVets.org
Jonathan Alter	Newsweek, Political Analyst
Jonathan Capehart	The Washington Post
Jonathan Martin	Politico.com
Joyce Meyer	Joyce Meyer Ministries, Christian Women's Speaker
Juan Williams	Book, *Enough*
Judy Woodruff	PBS Correspondent
Karen Tumuly	Time Magazine
Kate Obeirne	National Review
Kathleen Crier	Author/Journalist
Kathleen Koch	CNN White House Correspondent
Katie Couric	CBS Evening News Anchor
Katrina Vanden Heuvel	The Nation
Katty Kay	BBC Political Commentator
Keith Olberman	Countdown with Keith Olberman
Keith Stroup	Founder of NORML in 1970
Kenneth & Gloria Copeland	Bible Minister and Wife
Kitty Pilgrim	CNN, Lou Dobbs Correspondent
Larry King	Host Larry King Live, CNN
Larry Kudlow	CNBC On-Air Editor
Latoya Foster	Host, "In the Know"
Laurence Fishburn	Actor, Director, Activist, UNICEF

Lawrence O'Donnell	MSNBC Political Analyst
Lester Holt	NBC News Correspondent
Lewis Black	Political Comedian
Linda Douglass	National Journal
Lorne Michael	The SNL Man
Lou Dobbs	CNN, Lou Dobbs Show
Lucas Guttenburg	ACLU
Lyndon LaRouche	Political Activist/Economist
Mara Liasson	NPR Commentator
Margaret Carlson	Bloomberg News
Marie Wood	Yellow Ribbon Fund
Mark Cuban	Entrepreneur
Mark Shields	Syndicated Columnists
Mark Taibbi	Contributing Editor, Rolling Stone
Markos Mouitas	Daily KOS Blog
Mary Matelin	Republican Strategist
Mary Snow	CNN Correspondent
Matt Cooper	Condena's Portfolio
Mel Gibson	Actor/Film Director
Melinda Henneberg	Book, *If They Only Listened to Us*
Michael Cooper	Center for Immigration Studies
Michael Eric Dyson	Book, *Know What I Mean*
Michael Goodwin	New York Daily News
Michael Moore	Political Film Maker
Micheal Baisden	Radio Show Host/Activist
Micheal Crowley	The New Republic
Michelle Bernard	Independent Women's Voice
Miguel Perez	Syndicated Columnist
Mike Barnicle	MSNBC Political Analyst
Mike Gravel	2008 Republican Presidential Candidate
Mike Murphy	Political Analyst
Mike Rogers	BlogActive.com
Miles O'Brien	CNN Cable News
Montel Williams	TV Celebrity
Mortimer B. Zuckerman	Editor-in-Chief, US News & World Report
Morton Kondracki	Political Commentator, FOX News
Mos Def	Artsit/Activist
Nancy Gibbs	Time, Editor-at-Large
Nina Totenberg	NPR Legal Affairs Correspondent
Nora Roberts	CNN News
Norah O'Donnell	MSNBC Chief Washington Correspondent
Oprah Winfrey	TV Celebrity/Public Activist
P. J. O'Rourke	Book, *On the Wealth of Nations*
Pat Buchanan	Political Analyst
Pat Robertson	PTL/Televangelist
Paul Begala	Political Commentator
Peggy Noonan	The Wall Street Journal/Author
Peter Fenn	Democratic Strategist
Pope Benedict XVI	Head of the Roman Catholic Church, The Vatican

R. Jeffrey Smith	Staff Writer, The Washingotn Post
Rachel Maddow	Air America Radio
Ralph Nader	Public Activist
Rehema Phillips	NBC News
Rich Warren	Pastor
Richard Goldstein	Political Strategist
Richard Viguerie	Conversative Activist
Richard Wolffe	Newsweek
Robert Reich	Political Commentator; 22nd U.S. Secretary of Labor
Robin Morgan	Women's Rights Activist
Roger Simon	The Politico
Ron Brownstein	L. A. Times
Rosie O'Donnell	Actress/Activist
Ross Perot	Business Community
Rush Limbaugh	Host, Rush Limbaugh Show
Russell Simmons	CEO/Celebrity Activist
Ryan Lizza	The New Yoker Magazine
Sam Donaldson	Political Commentator
Samuel L. Jackson	Actor
Sean Hannity	Hanity & Colmes
Soledad O'Brien	CNN News Anchor
Spike Lee	Film Maker
Stephanie Jones	The Drug Policy Alliance
Stephen A. Smith	ESPN Analyst
Stephen Hayes	The Weekly Standard
Steve Colbert	Political Evening C222Talk Show
Steve Harvey	Radio Show Host/Comedian
Steven Jobs	Founder Apple, Inc.
Susan Sarandon	Actress, Public Activist
Suzzane Malvo	CNN Correspondent
Tavis Smiley	Host, The Tavis Smiley Show/Activist
Ted Koppel	Journalist, ABC News
Terry Gross	NPR , Host of Fresh Air/Author
Thomas Friedman	Economist, *The World is Flat*
Tim Robbins	Actor, Activist
Tim Russert	Meet the Press Moderator
Tom Andrews	The Win Without War Group
Tom Beaumont	The Des Moines Register
Tom Hanks	Actor, Activist
Tom Joyner	Radio Jockey
Tony Blankley	Conservative Commentator
Tony Harris	CNN Daytime Host
Tony Snow	Former White House Press Secretary
Trace Atkins	Musician, Book, *Personal Stand*
Tucker Carlson	Host, "Tucker"
Walter Cronkite	Political Commentator
Warren Buffet	Business Community
Wolfe Blitzer	CNN Situation Room Anchor
Woody Harrelson	Actor and Hemp Activist

Zain Verjee	CNN,State Department Correspondent
All Things Considered	National Public Radio
BBC — London, England	Britsh Broadcasting Corporation
Canadian Broadcasting Corporation	Canada, Established 1936
FaceBook	Internet Social Site
History Channel	Cable TV Channel — Documentaries
MySpace.com	Internet Social Site
NPR — National Public Radio	A National Treasure
NRA, National Rifle Association	Gun Owner Rights Group
PBS Television	Public Broadcasting Service
Rolling Stone Magazine	Popular News Magazine
SLATE.com	Daily Online Magazine
TalkingPointsMemo.com	BLOG by Joshua Micah Marshall
The Colbert Nation	That Says it All
The National Press Club	Press Organization, Washington, DC
The National Review	National Political Magazine
The New Republic	National Political Magazine
Time Magazine	News Magazine
U.S. News & World Report	World Business and News Magazine
U-Tube	Internet Video Site
Wikapedia.com	*The Free Encyclopedia* Website
Arizona Republic	Phoenix Newspaper
Atlanta Journal Constitution	Atlanta Newspaper
Baltimore Sun	Baltimore Newspaper
Bismarck Tribune	Bismarck Newspaper
Boston Globe	Boston Globe
Chicago Tribune	Chicago Newspaper
Daily Press, Virginia	Newspaper, Newport News, VA
Dallas Morning News	Dallas Newspaper
Denver Post	Denver Newspaper
Detroit Free Press	Detroit Newspaper
Financial Times	Business Newspaper/London, England
Leesburg Today	Newspaper, Loudoun County, Virginia
Los Angeles Times	Los Angeles Newspaper
Loudound Times-Mirror	Newspaper, Loudoun County, Virginia
Miami Herald	Miami Newspaper
Journal Sentinel	Milwaukee Newspaper
New York Times	National Business/Financial Newspaper
Omaha World-Herald	Omaha Newspaper
Richmond Times-Dispatch	Richmond Newspaper
San Francisco Chronical	San Francisco Newspaper
Spokesman- Review	Spokane Newspaper
The Record-Argus	Newpaper Greenville, PA
USA Today	National/Regional Newspaper, Washington, DC
Virginia Pilot	Richmond Newspaper
Wall Street Journal	National Financial Newspaper, New York City
Washington Post	National Newspaper, Washingotn, DC
ACLU	American Civil Liberties Union

Bill & Melinda Gates Foundation	Philanthropy in Global Health & Learning
CORE - Congress of Racial Equality	Original Civil Rights Group
DPA - Drug Policy Alliance	Drug Legalization Group — Retired Police Officers
Green Peace	Environmental Activist Group
Harm Reduction Coalition	Drug Legalization Group
High Times Magazine	News Media
LEAP.com	Drug Legalization Group
Marijuana Policy Project	Drug Legalization Group
MinuteMan Project	A Citizens Vigilance Operartion
MoveOn.org	Anti-War Group
National Association for the Advancement of Colored People	NAACP/Original Civil Rights Group
NORML	National Organization for Reform of Marijuana Laws
Students for Sensible Drug Policy	Drug Legalization Group
TaxPayers for Common Sense	Public Tax Reform Group
VoterNewsNetwork.com	Voter Information Website

O   O   O   O

Part 4

Regarding Our Three Civil Wars

"Making the Founders Proud"

I offer for your consideration this perspective on the 230-plus years of the Great American Experiment and our nation's three (3) Civil Wars.

The Three American Civil Wars Analogy

Since the birth of our nation, America has been involved in many military conflicts and major wars. However, to me it is a precious few of those wars, only three that truly serve to define our society to our selves and to the world — those being the Civil Wars occurring upon our own soil.

Two of those Civil Wars our national ancestors engaged in and were successful in winning for the Common Good of the masses.

The third Civil War is the one that the *Second Coming of Common Sense* (CS2) was written to announce and declare.

It is a challenge to my fellow Americans to acknowledge that like it or not *We the People* are at the edge of a historic juncture in our nation's history, and to realize that We have the Power to determine its outcome for the Common Good.

Those three great American Civil Wars are the subject of this piece.

o   o   o   o

I absolutely desire to acknowledge with all due and proper respect, all of the other actions that our military men and women have so dutifully fought and that so many have died in — as well as the sacrifices of our people on the home front. Each of our nation's military actions is noted herein.

Our First American Civil War – *To Create*

The American Revolution 1776 to 1781

The American Revolutionary War was actually a "civil war" that England was fighting with a major colony. In fact the American colonists were fighting to secede from their colonial union with England and the British Empire. In order to accomplish that historic victory the "British" colonists were forced to take up arms against their own countrymen, thus it would properly be called the first American Civil War.

Actual fighting began in the Massachusetts colony with the historic battles at Lexington and Concord on April 19, 1775 where "the shot heard around the world" was discharged. That confrontation was followed on June 17th at Bunker Hill, where the order was given to the Minuteman militia not to fire "until you see the whites of their eyes."

The American Revolutionary War raged from 1776 until October 17, 1781, and the British surrender by Lord Cornwallis at Yorktown, Virginia. The War of Independence was won and our nation was created.

They Paid a High Price for Us

At the time of the Revolution, England had roughly 6.5 million people and the American colonial population was well under 3 million. Over 25,000 American colonists died fighting that war — approximately one (1) percent of the colonial population. Today that would be equivalent of 3,000,000 deaths! Those regular people endured a level of real suffering and sacrifice that we rarely, if ever even consider.

It was a Civil war that gave the colonists their freedom from a classic monarchical government of the Old World — and American Democracy took its first infant steps. The *Articles of Confederation* served as the initial governing document for the newly formed American government.

However, the *Articles* were not strong enough to adequately define and control this new governmental life form and serious problems soon arose. Responding to those "public issues" the Constitutional Congress struggled until 1787 to produce the original version of the *U.S. Constitution*. It included the first 10 amendments, commonly referred to as the *Bill of Rights*. It took until 1789 for it to be fully ratified by the states and go into full effect. With the successful, final ratification by the states of our historic *U.S. Constitution*, this new form of People-driven government had passed its first real test.

o   o   o   o

The Preamble of the U.S. Constitution

We, the people of the United States, in order to form a more perfect Union,

> establish justice,
> insure domestic tranquility,
> provide for the common defense,
> promote the general welfare,
> and secure the blessings of liberty to ourselves and our posterity,

Do Ordain and establish this Constitution for the United States of America.

o   o   o   o

With our Constitution in place American Democracy finally had a rulebook by which We the People were protected, that would oversee the government's conduct, and would allow the newly formed nation to grow and mature. We are still under the protection of our National Charter as long as we execute its provisions properly.

The American Revolution was a physical war followed by constructive legislation that clarified the governing principles of our land and a Common Agreement among the people and business interests regarding the Common Good.

It is now 2007, some 220 years since our National Charter was ratified. In all that time the Constitution has only been amended sixteen (16) more times as the profile of America and the needs of the People have changed — and not for trivial reasons.

o   o   o   o

Since the time of that historic Revolution, America has been called the "Great Experiment." A form of government designed and intended to be directed by the will __and__ popular vote of the People — not by the privileged Few. An experiment in Representative government that many people expected and that some wished would end in failure. However, the experiment has greatly succeeded. America had created the original Democracy, the living model of Liberty and Freedom – the standard that other nations have since followed, but that the people of too many others still only dream of.

Our Constitution is the greatest defining document of government ever developed. And it has stood strong over all these years. It is our source of Democratic strength and our guide as an evolving, open, and free society. It is the prudent and practical judge that has allowed our country to grow, change, mature, and to correct prior errors. And through some very difficult national struggles, it is the Constitution that held us together as a people and a nation.

I firmly believe my fellow Americans that it is time for our *U.S. Constitution* to come to the People's aid once again.

o   o   o   o

Nation Creating Documents

The three (3) documents referenced next were the keys to the American Revolution and the Creation of the Democracy that we are fortunate to live in today,

- *Common Sense*
- *The Declaration of Independence*
- *The Constitution of the United States of America*

These precious documents are rarely reviewed by most of us after we complete our early schooling. They are presented in CS2 as a refresher on the words, the feelings, and the spirit that moved our original national ancestors to take their bold stand, to create their nation, to begin the national voyage, and make our future a possibility!

Common Sense by Thomas Paine

The revolutionary writer and his radical paperback size pamphlet are referred to throughout CS2. The first edition of *Common Sense* was published on January 10, 1776 and contained 33-pages. Paine added some material, including a 'letter' to the Quakers for the second edition. The entire text of that classic edition of *Common Sense* as first published on February 14, 1776 is presented in Appendix A.

The Power of *Common Sense*

When Thomas Paine published Common Sense, the total colonial population was well under than three (3) million — the approximate current population of the state of Iowa. The first official count of the U.S. population did not occur until 14 years later in 1790 and set the total at 3,929,000.

Paine's little pamphlet sold as fast as they could be printed, selling an estimated 120,000 copies in the first three months. It is estimated that over 500,000 copies were sold before the end of 1776 alone, a truly phenomenal number considering the total population and the laborious printing technology of the era. The colonists desired to read Paine's exact words for their personal consideration, and so that they could better discuss the reasoning offered by Paine regarding a war for independence.

I have included the first challenging and inspiring pages of *Common Sense* here, starting with the content of the pamphlet's second edition cover page, as the colonist saw it in February 1776.

C O M M O N   S E N S E;

Addressed to the

Inhabitants

of

A M E R I C A,

on the following interefting

S U B J E C T S:

I.   Of the Origin and Defign of Government in general, with concife
      Remarks on the Englifh Conftitution.

II.   Of Monarchy and Hereditary Succeffion.

III. Thoughts on the prefent State of American Affairs.

IV.   Of the prefent ability of America, with fome mifcellaneous Re-
      flections.

A NEW EDITION, with feveral Additons in the Body of the Work. To
which is Added an APPENDIX: together with an Addrefs to the People
called QUAKERS.

Man knows no Mafter fave creating HEAVEN,
Or thofe whom choice and common Good ordain.
T H O M S O N

INTRODUCTION

Perhaps the sentiments contained in the following pages, are not YET sufficiently fashionable to procure them general favour; a long habit of not thinking a thing WRONG, gives it a superficial appearance of being RIGHT, and raises at first a formidable outcry in defense of custom. But the tumult soon subsides. Time makes more converts than reason.

As a long and violent abuse of power, is generally the Means of calling the right of it in question (and in Matters too which might never have been thought of, had not the Sufferers been aggravated into the inquiry) and as the King of England hath undertaken in his OWN RIGHT, to support the Parliament in what he calls THEIRS, and as the good people of this country are grievously oppressed by the combination, they have an undoubted privilege to inquire into the pretensions of both, and equally to reject the usurpation of either.

In the following sheets, the author hath studiously avoided every thing which is personal among ourselves. Compliments as well as censure to individuals make no part thereof. The wise, and the worthy, need not the triumph of a pamphlet; and those whose sentiments are injudicious, or unfriendly, will cease of themselves unless too much pains are bestowed upon their conversion.

The cause of America is in a great measure the cause of all mankind. Many circumstances hath, and will arise, which are not local, but universal, and through which the principles of all Lovers of Mankind are affected, and in the Event of which, their Affections are interested. The laying a Country desolate with Fire and Sword, declaring War against the natural rights of all Mankind, and extirpating the Defenders thereof from the Face of the Earth, is the Concern of every Man to whom Nature hath given the Power of feeling; of which Class, regardless of Party Censure, is the AUTHOR.

P.S. The Publication of this new Edition hath been delayed, with a View of taking notice (had it been necessary) of any Attempt to refute the Doctrine of Independance: As no Answer hath yet appeared, it is now presumed that none will, the Time needful for getting such a Performance ready for the Public being considerably past.

Who the Author of this Production is, is wholly unnecessary to the Public, as the Object for Attention is the DOCTRINE ITSELF, not the MAN. Yet it may not be unnecessary to say, That he is unconnected with any Party, and under no sort of Influence public or private, but the influence of reason and principle.

Philadelphia, February 14, 1776

COMMON SENSE

OF THE ORIGIN AND DESIGN OF GOVERNMENT IN GENERAL. WITH CONCISE REMARKS ON THE ENGLISH CONSTITUTION

Some writers have so confounded society with government, as to leave little or no distinction between them; whereas they are not only different, but have different origins. Society is produced by our wants, and government by our wickedness; the former promotes our POSITIVELY by uniting our affections, the latter NEGATIVELY by restraining our vices. The one encourages intercourse, the other creates distinctions. The first a patron, the last a punisher.

Society in every state is a blessing, but government even in its best state is but a necessary evil; in its worst state an intolerable one; for when we suffer, or are exposed to the same miseries BY A GOVERNMENT, which we might expect in a country WITHOUT GOVERNMENT, our calamity is heightened by reflecting that we furnish the means by which we suffer. Government, like dress, is the badge of lost innocence; the palaces of kings are built on the ruins of the bowers of paradise. For were the impulses of conscience clear, uniform, and irresistibly obeyed, man would need no other lawgiver; but that not being the case, he finds it necessary to surrender up a part of his property to furnish means for the protection of the rest; and this he is induced to do by the same prudence which in every other case advises him out of two evils to choose the least. WHEREFORE, security being the true design and end of government, it unanswerably follows, that whatever FORM thereof appears most likely to ensure it to us, with the least expense and greatest benefit, is preferable to all others.

In order to gain a clear and just idea of the design and end of government, let us suppose a small number of persons settled in some sequestered part of the earth, unconnected with the rest, they will then represent the first peopling of any country, or of the world. In this state of natural liberty, society will be their first thought. A thousand motives will excite them thereto, the strength of one man is so unequal to his wants, and his mind so unfitted for perpetual solitude, that he is soon obliged to seek assistance and relief of another, who in his turn requires the same. Four or five united would be able to raise a tolerable dwelling in the midst of a wilderness, but one man might labour out of the common period of life witho accomplishing any thing; when he had felled his timber he could not remove it, nor erect it after it was removed; hunger in the mean time would urge him from his work, and every different want call him a different way. Disease, nay even misfortune would be death, for though neither might be mortal, yet either would disable him from living, and reduce him to a state in which he might rather be said to perish than to die.

Thus necessity, like a gravitating power, would soon form our newly arrived emigrants into society, the reciprocal blessings of which, would supersede, and render the obligations of law and government unnecessary while they remained perfectly just to each other; but as nothing but heaven is impregnable to vice, it will unavoidably happen, that in proportion as they surmount the first difficulties of emigration, which bound them together in a common cause, they will begin to relax in their duty and attachment to each other; and this remissness will point out the necessity of establishing some form of government to supply the defect of moral virtue.

Some convenient tree will afford them a State-House, under the branches of which, the whole colony may assemble to deliberate on public matters. It is more than probable that their first laws will have the title only of REGULATIONS, and be enforced by no other penalty than public disesteem. In this first parliament every man, by natural right, will have a seat.

But as the colony increases, the public concerns will increase likewise, and the distance at which the members may be separated, will render it too inconvenient for all of them to meet on every occasion as at first, when their number was small, their habitations near, and the public concerns few and trifling. This will point out the convenience of their consenting to leave the legislative part to be managed by a select number chosen from the whole body, who are supposed to have the same concerns at stake which those who appointed them, and who will act in the same manner as the whole body would act, were they present. If the colony continues increasing, it will become necessary to augment the number of the representatives, and that the interest of every part of the colony may be attended to, it will be found best to divide the whole into convenient parts, each part sending its proper number; and that the ELECTED might never form to themselves an interest separate from the ELECTORS, prudence will point out the propriety of having elections often; because as the ELECTED might by that means return and mix again with the general body of the ELECTORS in a few months, their fidelity to the public will be secured by the prudent reflection of not making a rod for themselves. And as this frequent interchange will establish a common interest with every part of the community, they will mutually and naturally support each other, and on this (not on the unmeaning name of king) depends the STRENGTH OF GOVERNMENT,

AND THE HAPPINESS OF THE GOVERNED.

Here then is the origin and rise of government; namely, a mode rendered necessary by the inability of moral virtue to govern the world; here too is the design and end of government, viz. freedom and security. And however our eyes may be dazzled with show, or our ears deceived by sound; however prejudice may warp our wills, or interest darken our understanding, the simple voice of nature and of reason will say, it is right.

I draw my idea of the form of government from a principle in nature, which no art can overturn, viz. that the more simple any thing is, the less liable it is to be disordered; and the easier repaired when disordered; and with this maxim in view, I offer a few remarks on the so much boasted constitution of England. That it was noble for the dark and slavish times in which it was erected, is granted. When the world was overrun with tyranny the least remove therefrom was a glorious rescue. But that it is imperfect, subject to convulsions, and incapable of producing what it seems to promise, is easily demonstrated.

Absolute governments (tho' the disgrace of human nature) have this advantage with them, that they are simple; if the people suffer, they know the head from which their suffering springs, know likewise the remedy, and are not bewildered by a variety of causes and cures. But the constitution of England is so exceedingly complex, that the nation may suffer for years together without being able to discover in which part the fault lies; some will say in one and some in another, and every political physician will advise a different medicine.

I know it is difficult to get over local or long standing prejudices, yet if we will suffer ourselves to examine the component parts of the English constitution, we shall find them to be the base remains of two ancient tyrannies, compounded with some new republican materials.

FIRST - The remains of monarchial tyranny in the person of the king.
SECONDLY - The remains of aristocratical tyranny in the persons of the peers.
THIRDLY - The new republican materials in the persons of the commons, on whose virtue depends the freedom of England.

The two first, by being hereditary, are independent of the people; wherefore in a CONSTITUTIONAL SENSE they contribute nothing towards the freedom of the state.

To say that the constitution of England is a UNION of three powers reciprocally CHECKING each other, is farcical, either the words have no meaning, or they are flat contradictions.

To say that the commons is a check upon the king, presupposes two things:

FIRST - That the king is not to be trusted without being looked after, or in other words, that a thirst for absolute power is the natural disease of monarchy.

SECONDLY - That the commons, by being appointed for that purpose, are either wiser or more worthy of confidence than the crown.

But as the same constitution which gives the commons a power to check the king by withholding the supplies, gives afterwards the king a power to check the commons, by empowering him to reject their other bills; it again supposes that the king is wiser than those whom it has already supposed to be wiser than him. A mere absurdity!

There is something exceedingly ridiculous in the composition of monarchy; it first excludes a man from the means of information, yet empowers him to act in cases where the highest judgment is required. The state of a king shuts him from the world, yet the business of a king requires him to know it thoroughly; wherefore the different parts, by unnaturally opposing and destroying each other, prove the whole character to be absurd and useless.

Some writers have explained the English constitution thus: The king, say they, is one, the people another; the peers are a house in behalf of the king, the commons in behalf of the people; but this hath all the distinctions of a house divided against itself; and though the expressions be pleasantly arranged, yet when examined, they appear idle and ambiguous; and it will always happen, that the nicest construction that words are capable of, when applied to the description of some thing which either cannot exist, or is too incomprehensible to be within the compass of description, will be words of sound only, and though they may amuse the ear, they cannot inform the mind, for this explanation includes a previous question, viz. HOW CAME THE KING BY A POWER WHICH THE PEOPLE ARE AFRAID TO TRUST, AND ALWAYS OBLIGED TO CHECK? Such a power could not be the gift of a wise people, neither can any power, WHICH NEEDS CHECKING, be from God; yet the provision, which the constitution makes, supposes such a power to exist.

But the provision is unequal to the task; the means either cannot or will not accomplish the end, and the whole affair is a felo de se; for as the greater weight will always carry up the less, and as all the wheels of a machine are put in motion by one, it only remains to know which power in the constitution has the most weight, for that will govern; and though the others, or a part of them, may clog, or, as the phrase is, check the rapidity of its motion, yet so long as they cannot stop it, their endeavours will be ineffectual; the first moving power will at last have its way, and what it wants in speed, is supplied by time.

That the crown is this overbearing part in the English constitution, needs not be mentioned, and that it derives its whole consequence merely from being the giver of places and pensions, is self-evident, wherefore, though we have been wise enough to shut and lock a door against absolute monarchy, we at the same time have been foolish enough to put the crown in possession of the key.

The prejudice of Englishmen in favour of their own government by king, lords, and commons, arises as much or more from national pride than reason. Individuals are undoubtedly safer in England than in some other countries, but the WILL of the king is as much the LAW of the land in Britain as in France, with this difference, that instead of proceeding directly from his mouth, it is handed to the people under the more formidable shape of an act of parliament. For the fate of Charles the First hath only made kings more subtle - not more just.

Wherefore, laying aside all national pride and prejudice in favour of modes and forms, the plain truth is, that IT IS WHOLLY OWING TO THE CONSTITUTION OF THE PEOPLE, AND NOT TO THE CON-STITUTION OF THE GOVERNMENT, that the crown is not as oppres-sive in England as in Turkey.

An inquiry into the CONSTITUTIONAL ERRORS in the English form of government is at this time highly necessary; for as we are never in a proper condition of doing justice to others, while we continue under the influence of some leading partiality, so neither are we capable of doing it to ourselves while we remain fettered by any obstinate prejudice. And as a man. who is attached to a prostitute, is unfitted to choose or judge a wife, so any prepossession in favour of a rotten constitution of govern-ment will disable us from discerning a good one.

o   o   o   o

End of the excerpt from the first pages of *Common Sense*. Again, The

Appendix contains the entire text of Thomas Paine's classic. It is well worth reading again or for the first time.

o o o o

The Declaration of Independence, originally drafted by Thomas Jefferson

The Declaration of Independence

by Thomas Jefferson

THE DECLARATION OF INDEPENDENCE:
In Congress, July 4, 1776,

THE UNANIMOUS DECLARATION OF THE THIRTEEN UNITED STATES OF AMERICA

When in the Course of human events, it becomes necessary for one people to dissolve the political bands which have connected them with another, and to assume among the Powers of the earth, the separate and equal station to which the Laws of Nature and of Nature's God entitle them, a decent respect to the opinions of mankind requires that they should declare the causes which impel them to the separation.

We hold these truths to be self-evident, that all men are created equal, that they are endowed by their Creator with certain unalienable Rights, that among these are Life, Liberty, and the pursuit of Happiness.

That to secure these rights, Governments are instituted among Men, deriving their just powers from the consent of the governed.

That whenever any Form of Government becomes destructive of these ends, it is the Right of the People to alter or to abolish it, and to institute new Government, laying its foundation on such principles and organizing its powers in such form, as to them shall seem most likely to effect their Safety and Happiness. Prudence, indeed, will dictate that Governments long established should not be changed for light and transient causes; and accordingly all experience hath shown, that mankind are more disposed to suffer, while evils are sufferable, than to right themselves by abolishing the forms to which they are accustomed. But when a long train of abuses and usurpations, pursuing invariably the same Object, evinces a design to reduce them under absolute Despotism, it is their right, it is their duty, to throw off such Government, and to provide new Guards for their future security.

Such has been the patient sufferance of these Colonies; and such is now the necessity which constrains them to alter their former Systems of

Government. The history of the present King of Great Britain is a history of repeated injuries and usurpations, all having in direct object the establishment of an absolute Tyranny over these States. To prove this, let Facts be submitted to a candid world.

He has refused his Assent to Laws, the most wholesome and necessary for the public good.

He has forbidden his Governors to pass Laws of immediate and pressing importance, unless suspended in their operation till his Assent should be obtained; and when so suspended, he has utterly neglected to attend to them.

He has refused to pass other Laws for the accommodation of large districts of people, unless those people would relinquish the right of Representation in the Legislature, a right inestimable to them and formidable to tyrants only.

He has called together legislative bodies at places unusual, uncomfortable, and distant from the depository of their public Records, for the sole purpose of fatiguing them into compliance with his measures.

He has dissolved Representative Houses repeatedly, for opposing with manly firmness his invasions on the rights of the people.

He has refused for a long time, after such dissolutions, to cause others to be elected; whereby the Legislative powers, incapable of Annihilation, have returned to the People at large for their exercise; the State remaining in the mean time exposed to all the dangers of invasion from without, and convulsions within.

He has endeavoured to prevent the population of these States; for that purpose obstructing the Laws of Naturalization of Foreigners; refusing to pass others to encourage their migrations hither, and raising the conditions of new Appropriations of Lands.

He has obstructed the Administration of Justice, by refusing his Assent to Laws for establishing Judiciary powers.

He has made Judges dependent on his Will alone, for the tenure of their offices, and the amount and payment of their salaries.

He has erected a multitude of New Offices, and sent hither swarms of Officers to harass our People, and eat out their substance.

He has kept among us, in times of peace, Standing Armies without the Consent of our legislatures.

He has affected to render the Military independent of and superior to the Civil power.

He has combined with others to subject us to a jurisdiction foreign to our constitution, and unacknowledged by our laws; giving his Assent to their Acts of pretended Legislation:

For quartering large bodies of armed troops among us:

For protecting them, by a mock Trial, from Punishment for any Murders which they should commit on the Inhabitants of these States:

For cutting off our Trade with all parts of the world:

For imposing Taxes on us without our Consent:

For depriving us in many cases, of the benefits of Trial by Jury:

For transporting us beyond Seas to be tried for pretended offences:

For abolishing the free System of English Laws in a neighbouring Province, establishing therein an Arbitrary government, andenlarging its Boundaries so as to render it at once an example and fit instrument for introducing the same absolute rule into these Colonies:

For taking away our Charters, abolishing our most valuable Laws, and altering fundamentally the Forms of our Governments:

For suspending our own Legislatures, and declaring themselves invested with power to legislate for us in all cases whatsoever.

He has abdicated Government here, by declaring us out of his Protection and waging War against us.

He has plundered our seas, ravaged our Coasts, burnt our towns, and destroyed the Lives of our people.

He is at this time transporting large armies of foreign mercenaries to compleat the works of death, desolation and tyranny, already begun with circumstances of Cruelty & perfidy scarcely paralleled in the most barbarous ages, and totally unworthy the Head of a civilized nation.

He has constrained our fellow Citizens taken Captive on the high Seas to bear Arms against their Country, to become the executioners of their friends and Brethren, or to fall themselves by their Hands.

He has excited domestic insurrections amongst us, and has endeavoured to bring on the inhabitants of our frontiers, the merciless Indian Savages, whose known rule of warfare, is an undistinguished destruction of all ages, sexes and conditions.

In every stage of these Oppressions We have Petitioned for Redress in the most humble terms: Our repeated Petitions have been answered only by repeated injury. A Prince, whose character is thus marked by every act which may define a Tyrant, is unfit to be the ruler of a free people.

Nor have We been wanting in attention to our British brethren. We have warned them from time to time of attempts by their legislature to extend an unwarrantable jurisdiction over us. We have reminded them of the circumstances of our emigration and settlement here. We have appealed to their native justice and magnanimity, and we have conjured them by the ties of our common kindred to disavow these usurpations, which would inevitably interrupt our connections and correspondence. They too have been deaf to the voice of justice and of consanguinity. We must, therefore, acquiesce in the necessity, which denounces our Separation, and hold them, as we hold the rest of mankind, Enemies in War, in Peace Friends.

We, therefore, the Representatives of the united States of America, in General Congress, Assembled, appealing to the Supreme Judge of the world for the rectitude of our intentions, do, in the Name, and by Authority of the good People of these Colonies, solemnly publish and declare, That these United Colonies are, and of Right ought to be Free and Independent States; that they are Absolved from all Allegiance to the British Crown, and that all political connection between them and the State of Great Britain, is and ought to be totally dissolved; and that as Free and Independent States, they have full Power to levy War, conclude Peace, contract Alliances, establish Commerce, and to do all other Acts and Things which Independent States may of right do.

And for the support of this Declaration, with a firm reliance on the Protection of Divine Providence, we mutually pledge to each other our Lives, our Fortunes and our sacred Honor.

JOHN HANCOCK, President

Attested, CHARLES THOMSON, Secretary

New Hampshire
JOSIAH BARTLETT
WILLIAM WHIPPLE
MATTHEW THORNTON

Massachusetts-Bay
SAMUEL ADAMS
JOHN ADAMS
ROBERT TREAT PAINE
ELBRIDGE GERRY

Rhode Island
STEPHEN HOPKINS
WILLIAM ELLERY

Connecticut
ROGER SHERMAN
SAMUEL HUNTINGTON
WILLIAM WILLIAMS
OLIVER WOLCOTT

Georgia
BUTTON GWINNETT
LYMAN HALL
GEO. WALTON

Maryland
SAMUEL CHASE
WILLIAM PACA
THOMAS STONE
CHARLES CARROLL
OF CARROLLTON

Virginia
GEORGE WYTHE
RICHARD HENRY LEE
THOMAS JEFFERSON
BENJAMIN HARRISON
THOMAS NELSON, JR.
FRANCIS LIGHTFOOT
LEE
CARTER BRAXTON.

New York
WILLIAM FLOYD
PHILIP LIVINGSTON
FRANCIS LEWIS
LEWIS MORRIS

Pennsylvania
ROBERT MORRIS
BENJAMIN RUSH
BENJAMIN FRANKLIN
JOHN MORTON
GEORGE CLYMER
JAMES SMITH
GEORGE TAYLOR
JAMES WILSON
GEORGE ROSS

Delaware
CAESAR RODNEY
GEORGE READ
THOMAS M'KEAN

North Carolina
WILLIAM HOOPER
JOSEPH HEWES
JOHN PENN

South Carolina
EDWARD RUTLEDGE
THOMAS HEYWARD, JR.
THOMAS LYNCH, JR.
ARTHUR MIDDLETON

New Jersey
RICHARD STOCKTON
JOHN WITHERSPOON
FRANCIS HOPKINS
JOHN HART
ABRAHAM CLARK

The U.S. Constitution

by the Constitutional Congress

PREAMBLE

We, the people of the United States, in order to form a more perfect Union, establish justice, insure domestic tranquility, provide for the common defense, promote the general welfare, and secure the blessings of liberty to ourselves and our posterity, do ordain and establish this Constitution for the United States of America.

ARTICLE I

Section 1. Legislative powers; in whom vested
All legislative powers herein granted shall be vested in a Congress of the United States, which shall consist of a Senate and House of Representatives.

Section 2. House of Representatives, how and by whom chosen Qualifications of a Representative. Representatives and direct taxes, how apportioned. Enumeration. Vacancies to be filled. Power of choosing officers, and of impeachment.

1. The House of Representatives shall be composed of members chosen every second year by the people of the several States, and the elector in each State shall have the qualifications requisite for electors of the most numerous branch of the State Legislature.
2. No person shall be a Representative who shall not have attained the age of twenty-five years, and been seven years a citizen of the United States, and who shall not, when elected, be an inhabitant of that State in which he shall be chosen.

3. Representatives [and direct taxes] {Altered by 16th Amendment} shall be apportioned among the several States which may be included within this Union, according to their respective numbers, [which shall be determined by adding the whole number of free persons, including those bound to service for a term of years, and excluding Indians not taxed, three-fifths of all other persons.] {Altered by 14th Amendment} The actual enumeration shall be made within three years after the first meeting of the Congress of the United States, and within every subsequent term of ten years, in such manner as they shall by law direct. The number of Representatives shall not exceed one for every thirty thousand, but each State shall have at least one Representative; and until such

enumeration shall be made, the State of New Hampshire shall be entitled to choose three, Massachusetts eight, Rhode Island and Providence Plantations one, Connecticut five, New York six, New Jersey four, Pennsylvania eight, Delaware one, Maryland six, Virginia ten, North Carolina five, South Carolina five, and Georgia three.

4. When vacancies happen in the representation from any State, the Executive Authority thereof shall issue writs of election to fill such vacancies.

5. The House of Representatives shall choose their Speaker and other officers; and shall have the sole power of impeachment.

Section 3. Senators, how and by whom chosen. How classified. State Executive, when to make temporary appointments, in case, etc. Qualifications of a Senator. President of the Senate, his right to vote. President pro tem., and other officers of the Senate, how chosen. Power to try impeachments. When President is tried, Chief Justice to preside. Sentence.

1. The Senate of the United States shall be composed of two Senators from each State, [chosen by the Legislature thereof,] {Altered by 17th Amendment} for six years; and each Senator shall have one vote.

2. Immediately after they shall be assembled in consequence of the first election, they shall be divided as equally as may be into three classes. The seats of the Senators of the first class shall be vacated at the expiration of the second year, of the second class at the expiration of the fourth year, and of the third class at the expiration of the sixth year, so that one-third may be chosen every second year; [and if vacancies happen by resignation, or otherwise, during the recess of the Legislature of any State, the Executive thereof may make temporary appointments until the next meeting of the Legislature, which shall then fill such vacancies.] {Altered by 17th Amendment}

3. No person shall be a Senator who shall not have attained to the age of thirty years, and been nine years a citizen of the United States, and who shall not, when elected, be an inhabitant of that State for which he shall be chosen.

4. The Vice-President of the United States shall be President of the Senate, but shall have no vote, unless they be equally divided.

5. The Senate shall choose their other officers, and also a President pro tempore, in the absence of the Vice President, or when he shall exercise the office of the President of the United States.

6. The Senate shall have the sole power to try all impeachments. When sitting for that purpose, they shall be on oath or affirmation. When the President of the United States is tried, the Chief Justice shall preside: and no person shall be convicted without the concurrence of two-thirds of the members present.

7. Judgement in cases of impeachment shall not extend further than to removal from office, and disqualification to hold and enjoy any office of honor, trust, or profit under the United States: but the party convicted shall nevertheless be liable and subject to indictment, trial, judgement and punishment, according to law.

Section 4. Times, etc., of holding elections, how prescribed. One session in each year.

1. The times, places and manner of holding elections for Senators and Representatives, shall be prescribed in each State by the Legislature thereof; but the Congress may at any time by law make or alter such regulations, except as to the places of choosing Senators.

2. The Congress shall assemble at least once in every year, and such meeting shall be [on the first Monday in December,] {Altered by 20th Amendment} unless they by law appoint a different day.

Section 5. Membership, Quorum, Adjournments, Rules, Power to punish or expel. Journal. Time of adjournments, how limited, etc.

1. Each House shall be the judge of the elections, returns and qualifications of its own members, and a majority of each shall constitute a quorum to do business; but a smaller number may adjourn from day to day, and may be authorized to compel the attendance of absent members, in such manner, and under such penalties as each House may provide.

2. Each House may determine the rules of its proceedings, punish its members for disorderly behavior, and, with the concurrence of two-thirds, expel a member.

3. Each House shall keep a journal of its proceedings, and from time to time publish the same, excepting such parts as may in their judgement require secrecy; and the yeas and nays of the members of either House on any question shall, at the desire of one-fifth of those present, be entered on the journal.

4. Neither House, during the session of Congress, shall, without the consent of the other, adjourn for more than three days, nor to any other place than that in which the two Houses shall be sitting.

Section 6. Compensation, Privileges, Disqualification in certain cases.

1. The Senators and Representatives shall receive a compensation for their services, to be ascertained by law, and paid out of the Treasury of the United States. They shall in all cases, except treason, felony and breach of the peace, be privileged from arrest during their attendance at the session of their respective Houses, and in going to and returning from the same; and for any speech or debate in either House, they shall not be questioned in any other place.

2. No Senator or Representative shall, during the time for which he was elected, be appointed to any civil office under the authority of the United States, which shall have increased during such time; and no person holding any office under the United States, shall be a member of either House during his continuance in office.

Section 7. House to originate all revenue bills. Veto. Bill may be passed by two-thirds of each House, notwithstanding, etc. Bill, not returned in ten days to become a law. Provisions as to orders, concurrent resolutions, etc.

1. All bills for raising revenue shall originate in the House of Representatives; but the Senate may propose or concur with amendments as on other bills.

2. Every bill which shall have passed the House of Representatives and the Senate, shall, before it become a law, be presented to the president of the United States; if he approve, he shall sign it, but if not, he shall return it, with his objections, to that house in which it shall have originated, who shall enter the objections at large on their journal, and proceed to reconsider it. If after such reconsideration, two thirds of that house shall agree to pass the bill, it shall be sent, together with the objections, to the other house, by which it shall likewise be reconsidered, and if approved by two-thirds of that house, it shall become a law. But in all such cases the votes of both houses shall be determined by yeas and nays, and the names of the persons voting for and against the bill shall be entered on the journal of each house respectively. If any bill shall not be returned by the president within ten days (Sundays excepted) after it shall have been presented to him, the same shall be a law, in like manner as if he had signed it, unless the Congress by their adjournment prevent its return, in which case it shall not be a law.

3. Every order, resolution, or vote to which the concurrence of the Senate and House of Representatives may be necessary (except on a question of adjournment) shall be presented to the president of the United States; and

before the same shall take effect, shall be approved by him, or, being disapproved by him, shall be re-passed by two-thirds of the Senate and House of Representatives, according to the rules and limitations prescribed in the case of a bill.

Section 8. Powers of Congress

The Congress shall have the power 1. to lay and collect taxes, duties, imposts and excises, to pay the debts and provide for the common defence and general welfare of the United States; but all duties, imposts and excises shall be uniform throughout the United States:

2. To borrow money on the credit of the United States:

3. To regulate commerce with foreign nations, and among the several states, and with the Indian tribes:

4. To establish an uniform rule of naturalization, and uniform laws on the subject of bankruptcies throughout the United States:

5. To coin money, regulate the value thereof, and of foreign coin, and fix the standard of weights and measures:

6. To provide for the punishment of counterfeiting the securities and current coin of the United States:

7. To establish post-offices and post-roads:

8. To promote the progress of science and useful arts, by securing for limited times to authors and inventors the exclusive right to their respective writings and discoveries:

9. To constitute tribunals inferior to the supreme court:

10. To define and punish piracies and felonies committed on the high seas, and offences against the law of nations:

11. To declare war, grant letters of marque and reprisal, and make rules concerning captures on land and water:

12. To raise and support armies, but no appropriation of money to that use shall be for a longer term than two years:

13. To provide and maintain a navy:

14. To make rules for the government and regulation of the land and naval forces:

15. To provide for calling forth the militia to execute the laws of the union, suppress insurrections and repel invasions:

16. To provide for organizing, arming and disciplining the militia, and for governing such part of them as may be employed in the service of the United States, reserving to the states respectively, the appointment of the officers, and the authority of training the militia according to the discipline prescribed by Congress:

17. To exercise exclusive legislation in all cases whatsoever, over such district (not exceeding ten miles square) as may, by cession of particular states, and the acceptance of Congress, become the seat of the government of the United States, and to exercise like authority over all places purchased by the consent of the legislature of the state in which the same shall be, for the erection of forts, magazines, arsenals, dock-yards, and other needful buildings:

And, 18. To make all laws which shall be necessary and proper for carrying into execution the foregoing powers, and all other powers vested by this constitution in the government of the United States, or in any department or officer thereof.

Section 9. Provision as to migration or importation of certain persons. Habeas Corpus, Bills of attainder, etc. Taxes, how apportioned. No export duty. No commercial preference. Money, how drawn from Treasury, etc. No titular nobility. Officers not to receive presents, etc.

1. The migration or importation of such persons as any of the states now existing shall think proper to admit, shall not be prohibited by the Congress prior to the year 1808, but a tax or duty may be imposed on such importations, not exceeding 10 dollars for each person.

2. The privilege of the writ of habeas corpus shall not be suspended, unless when in cases of rebellion or invasion the public safety may require it.

3. No bill of attainder or ex post facto law shall be passed.

4. [No capitation, or other direct tax shall be laid unless in proportion to the census or enumeration herein before directed to be taken.] {Altered by 16th Amendment}

5. No tax or duty shall be laid on articles exported from any state.

6. No preference shall be given by any regulation of commerce or revenue to the ports of one state over those of another: nor shall vessels

bound to, or from one state, be obliged to enter, clear, or pay duties in another.

7. No money shall be drawn from the treasury but in consequence of appropriations made by law; and a regular statement and account of the receipts and expenditures of all public money shall be published from time to time.

8. No title of nobility shall be granted by the United States: And no person holding any office or profit or trust under them, shall, without the consent of the Congress, accept of any present, emolument, office, or title, of any kind whatever, from any king, prince, or foreign state.

Section 10. States prohibited from the exercise of certain powers.

1. No state shall enter into any treaty, alliance, or confederation; grant letters of marque and reprisal; coin money; emit bills of credit; make any thing but gold and silver coin a tender in payment of debts; pass any bill of attainder, ex post facto law, or law impairing the obligation of contracts, or grant any title of nobility.

2. No state shall, without the consent of the Congress, lay any imposts or duties on imports or exports, except what may be absolutely necessary for executing its inspection laws; and the net produce of all duties and imposts, laid by any state on imports or exports, shall be for the use of the treasury of the United States; and all such laws shall be subject to the revision and control of the Congress.

3. No state shall, without the consent of Congress, lay any duty of tonnage, keep troops, or ships of war in time of peace, enter into any agreement or compact with another state, or with a foreign power, or engage in a war, unless actually invaded, or in such imminent danger as will not admit of delay.

ARTICLE II

Section 1. President: his term of office. Electors of President; number and how appointed. Electors to vote on same day. Qualification of President. On whom his duties devolve in case of his removal, death, etc. President's compensation. His oath of office.

1. The Executive power shall be vested in a President of the United States of America. He shall hold office during the term of four years, and together with the Vice President, chosen for the same term, be elected as

follows

2. [Each State] {Altered by 23rd Amendment} shall appoint, in such manner as the Legislature may direct, a number of electors, equal to the whole number of Senators and Representatives to which the State may be entitled in the Congress: but no Senator or Representative, or person holding an office of trust or profit under the United States, shall be appointed an elector [The electors shall meet in their respective States, and vote by ballot for two persons, of whom one at least shall not be an inhabitant of the same State with themselves. And they shall make a list of all the persons voted for each; which list they shall sign and certify, and transmit sealed to the seat of Government of the United States, directed to the President of the Senate. The President of the Senate shall, in the presence of the Senate and House of Representatives, open all the certificates, and the votes shall then be counted. The person having the greatest number of votes shall be the President, if such number be a majority of the whole number of electors appointed; and if there be more than one who have such majority, and have an equal number of votes, then the House of Representatives shall immediately choose by ballot one of them for President; and if no person have a majority, then from the five highest on the list the said House shall in like manner choose the President. But in choosing the President, the votes shall be taken by States, the representation from each State having one vote; a quorum for this purpose shall consist of a member or members from two-thirds of the States, and a majority of all the States shall be necessary to a choice. In every case, after the choice of the President, the person having the greatest number of votes of the electors shall be the Vice President. But if there should remain two or more who have equal votes, the Senate shall choose from them by ballot the Vice President.] {Altered by 12th Amendment}

3. The Congress may determine the time of choosing the electors, and the day on which they shall give their votes; which day shall be the same throughout the United States.

4. No person except a natural born citizen, or a citizen of the United States, at the time of the adoption of this Constitution, shall be eligible to the office of President; neither shall any person be eligible to that office who shall not have attained to the age of thirty-five years, and been fourteen years a resident within the United States.

5. [In case of the removal of the President from office, or of his death, resignation, or inability to discharge the powers and duties of the said office, the same shall devolve on the Vice President, and the Congress

may by law provide for the case of removal, death, resignation, or inability, both of the President and Vice President, declaring what officer shall then act as President, and such officer shall act accordingly, until the disability be removed, or a President shall be elected.] {Altered by 25th Amendment}

6. The President shall, at stated times, receive for his services, a compensation, which shall neither be increased nor diminished during the period for which he shall have been elected, and he shall not receive within that period any other emolument from the United States, or any of them.

7. Before he enter on the execution of his office, he shall take the following oath or affirmation: "I do solemnly swear (or affirm) that I will faithfully execute the office of the President of the United States, and will to the best of my ability, preserve, protect and defend the Constitution of the United States."

Section 2. President to be Commander-in-Chief. He may require opinions of cabinet officers, etc., may pardon. Treaty-making power. Nomination of certain officers. When President may fill vacancies.

1. The President shall be Commander-in-Chief of the Army and Navy of the United States, and of the militia of the several States, when called into the actual service of the United States; he may require the opinion, in writing, of the principal officer in each of the executive departments, upon any subject relating to the duties of their respective offices, and he shall have power to grant reprieves and pardons for offenses against against the United States, except in cases of impeachment.

2. He shall have power, by and with the advice and consent of the Senate, to make treaties, provided two-thirds of the Senators present concur; and he shall nominate, and by and with the advice and consent of the Senate, shall appoint ambassadors, other public ministers and consuls, judges of the Supreme Court, and all other officers of the United States, whose appointments are not herein otherwise provided for, and which shall be established by law: but the Congress may by law vest the appointment of such inferior officers, as they think proper, in the President alone, in the courts of law, or in the heads of departments.

3. The President shall have the power to fill up all vacancies that may may happen during the recess of the Senate, by granting commissions, which shall expire at the end of their next session.

Section 3. President shall communicate to Congress. He may convene and adjourn Congress, in case of disagreement, etc. Shall receive ambassadors, execute laws, and commission officers.

He shall from time to time give to the Congress information of the state of the Union, and recommend to their consideration such measures as he shall judge necessary and expedient; he may, on extraordinary occasions, convene both Houses, or either of them, and in case of disagreement between them, with respect to the time of adjournment, he may adjourn them to such time as he shall think proper; he may receive ambassadors, and other public ministers; he shall take care that the laws be faithfully executed, and shall commission all the officers of the United States.

Section 4. All civil offices forfeited for certain crimes.
The President, Vice President, and all civil officers of the United States, shall be removed from office on impeachment for, and conviction of, treason, bribery, or other high crimes and misdemeanors.

ARTICLE III

Section 1. Judicial powers. Tenure. Compensation.
The judicial power of the United States, shall be vested in one supreme court, and in such inferior courts as the Congress may, from time to time, ordain and establish. The judges, both of the supreme and inferior courts, shall hold their offices during good behaviour, and shall, at stated times, receive for their services a compensation, which shall not be diminished during their continuance in office.

Section 2. Judicial power; to what cases it extends. Original jurisdiction of Supreme Court Appellate. Trial by Jury, etc. Trial, where

1. The judicial power shall extend to all cases, in law and equity, arising under this constitution, the laws of the United States, and treaties made, or which shall be made under their authority; to all cases affecting ambassadors, other public ministers and consuls; to all cases of admiralty and maritime jurisdiction; to controversies to which the United States shall be a party; [to controversies between two or more states, between a state and citizens of another state, between citizens of different states, between citizens of the same state, claiming lands under grants of different states, and between a state, or the citizens thereof, and foreign states, citizens or subjects.] {Altered by 11th Amendment}

2. In all cases affecting ambassadors, other public ministers and consuls, and those in which a state shall be a party, the supreme court shall have original jurisdiction. In all the other cases before-mentioned, the supreme court shall have appellate jurisdiction, both as to law and fact, with such exceptions, and under such regulations as the Congress shall make.

3. The trial of all crimes, except in cases of impeachment, shall be by jury; and such trial shall be held in the state where the said crimes shall have been committed; but when not committed within any state, the trial shall be at such place or places as the Congress may by law have directed.

Section 3. Treason defined. Proof of. Punishment

1. Treason against the United States shall consist only in levying war against them, or in adhering to their enemies, giving them aid and comfort. No person shall be convicted of treason unless on the testimony of two witnesses to the same overt act, or on confession in open court.

2. The Congress shall have power to declare the punishment of treason, but no attainder of treason shall work corruption of blood, or forfeiture, except during the life of the person attainted.

ARTICLE IV

Section 1. Each State to give credit to the public acts, etc. of every other State.
Full faith and credit shall be given in each state to the public acts, records and judicial proceedings of every other state. And the Congress may by general laws prescribe the manner in which such acts, records and proceedings shall be proved, and the effect thereof.

Section 2. Privileges of citizens of each State. Fugitives from Justice to be delivered up. Persons held to service having escaped, to be delivered up.

1. The citizens of each state shall be entitled to all privileges and immunities of citizens in the several states. {See the 14th Amendment}

2. A person charged in any state with treason, felony, or other crime, who shall flee justice, and be found in another state, shall, on demand of the executive authority of the state from which he fled, be delivered up, to be removed to the state having jurisdiction of the crime.

3. [No person held to service or labour in one state, under the laws thereof, escaping into another, shall, in consequence of any law or regulation therein, be discharged from such service or labour, but shall be delivered up on claim of the party to whom such service or labour may be due.] {Altered by 13th Amendment}

Section 3. Admission of new States. Power of Congress over territory

<u>and other property.</u>

1. New states may be admitted by the Congress into this union; but no new state shall be formed or erected within the jurisdiction of any other state, nor any state be formed by the junction of two or more states, without the consent of the legislatures of the states concerned, as well as of the Congress.

2. The Congress shall have power to dispose of and make all needful rules and regulations respecting the territory or other property belonging to the United States; and nothing in this constitution shall be so construed as to prejudice any claims of the United States, or of any particular state.

<u>Section 4. Republican form of government guaranteed. Each State to be protected.</u>
The United States shall guarantee to every state in this union, a republican form of government, and shall protect each of them against invasion; and on application of the legislature, or of the executive (when the legislature cannot be convened), against domestic violence.

ARTICLE V

Amendments

The Congress, whenever two-thirds of both houses shall deem it necessary, shall propose amendments to this constitution, or on the application of the legislatures of two-thirds of the several states, shall call a convention for proposing amendments, which, in either case, shall be valid to all intents and purposes, as part of this constitution, when ratified by the legislatures of three-fourths of the several states, or by conventions in three-fourths thereof, as the one or the other mode of ratification may be proposed by the Congress: Provided, that no amendment which may be made prior to the year 1808, shall in any manner affect the first and fourth clauses in the ninth section of the first article; and that no state, without its consent, shall be deprived of its equal suffrage in the Senate.

ARTICLE VI

1. All debts contracted and engagements entered into, before the adoption of this constitution, shall be as valid against the United States under this constitution, as under the confederation.

2. This constitution, and the laws of the United States which shall be made in pursuance thereof; and all treaties made, or which shall be made, under the authority of the United States shall be the supreme law of the

land; and the judges in every state shall be bound thereby, any thing in the constitution or laws of any state to the contrary notwithstanding.

3. The senators and representatives before-mentioned, and the members of the several state legislatures, and all executive and judicial officers, both of the United States and of the several states, shall be bound by oath or affirmation, to support this constitution; but no religious test shall ever be required as a qualification to any office or public trust under the United States.

ARTICLE VII

The ratification of the conventions of nine states, shall be sufficient for the establishment of this constitution between the states so ratifying the same.

The U.S. Bill of Rights

by the U.S. Congress

The Ten Original Amendments: *The Bill of Rights*

Passed by Congress September 25, 1789. Ratified December 15, 1791.

AMENDMENT I
Congress shall make no law respecting an establishment of religion, or prohibiting the free exercise thereof; or abridging the freedom of speech, or of the press; or the right of the people peaceably to assemble, and to petition the Government for a redress of grievances.

AMENDMENT II
A well-regulated militia, being necessary to the security of a free State, the right of the people to keep and bear arms, shall not be infringed.

AMENDMENT III
No soldier shall, in time of peace be quartered in any house, without the consent of the owner, nor in time of war, but in a manner to be prescribed by law.

AMENDMENT IV
The right of the people to be secure in their persons, houses, papers, and effects, against unreasonable searches and seizures, shall not be violated, and no warrants shall issue, but upon probable cause, supported by oath or affirmation, and particularly describing the place to be searched, and the persons or things to be seized.

AMENDMENT V
No person shall be held to answer for a capital, or otherwise infamous crime, unless on a presentment or indictment of a Grand Jury, except in cases arising in the land or naval forces, or in the militia, when in actual service in time of war or public danger; nor shall any person be subject for the same offense to be twice put in jeopardy of life or limb; nor shall be compelled in any criminal case to be a witness against himself, nor be deprived of life, liberty, or property, without due process of law; nor shall private property be taken for public use without just compensation.

AMENDMENT VI
In all criminal prosecutions, the accused shall enjoy the right to a speedy and public trial, by an impartial jury of the State and district wherein the

crime shall have been committed, which district shall have been previously ascertained by law, and to be informed of the nature and cause of the accusation; to be confronted with the witnesses against him; to have compulsory process for obtaining witnesses in his favor, and to have the assistance of counsel for his defense.

AMENDMENT VII
In suits at common law, where the value in controversy shall exceed twenty dollars, the right of trial by jury shall be preserved, and no fact tried by a jury shall be otherwise reexamined in any court of the United States, than according to the rules of the common law.

AMENDMENT VIII
Excessive bail shall not be required, nor excessive fines imposed, nor cruel and unusual punishments inflicted.

AMENDMENT IX
The enumeration in the Constitution, of certain rights, shall not be construed to deny or disparage others retained by the people.

AMENDMENT X
The powers not delegated to the United States by the Constitution, nor prohibited by it to the States, are reserved to the States respectively, or to the people.

The Additional Amendments 11 thru 26

AMENDMENT XI
Passed by Congress March 4, 1794. Ratified February 7, 1795.

The judicial power of the United States shall not be construed to extend to any suit in law or equity, commenced or prosecuted against one of the United States by citizens of another State, or by citizens or subjects of any foreign state.

AMENDMENT XII
Passed by Congress December 9, 1803. Ratified July 27, 1804.

The Electors shall meet in their respective States and vote by ballot for President and Vice-President, one of whom, at least, shall not be an inhabitant of the same State with themselves; they shall name in their ballots the person voted for as President, and in distinct ballots the person voted for as Vice-President, and of the number of votes for each, which lists they shall sign and certify, and transmit sealed to the seat of the Government of the United States, directed to the President of the Senate; the President of the Senate shall, in the presence of the Senate and House of Representatives, open all the certificates and the votes shall then be counted; - The person having the greatest number of votes for President, shall be the President, if such number be a majority of the whole number of Electors appointed; and if no person have such major-ity, then from the persons having the highest numbers not exceeding three on the list of those voted for as President, the House of Representa-tives shall choose immediately, by ballot, the President. But in choosing the President, the votes shall be taken by States, the representation from each State having one vote; a quorum for this purpose shall consist of a member or members from two-thirds of the States, and a majority of all the States shall be necessary to a choice. And if the House of Representa-tives shall not choose a President whenever the right of choice shall devolve upon them, [before the fourth day of March next following,] {Altered by 20th Amendment} then the Vice-President shall act as President, as in case of the death or other constitutional disability of the President. The person having the greatest number of votes as Vice-President, shall be the Vice-President, if such numbers be a majority of the whole number of electors appointed, and if no person have a major-ity, then from the two highest numbers on the list, the Senate shall choose the Vice-President; a quorum for the purpose shall consist of two-thirds of the whole number of Senators, and a majority of the whole number shall be necessary to a choice. But no person constitutionally ineligible to the office of President shall be eligible to that of Vice-President of the United States.

AMENDMENT XIII
Passed by Congress January 31, 1865. Ratified December 6, 1865.

Section 1.
Neither slavery nor involuntary servitude, except as a punishment for crime whereof the party shall have been duly convicted, shall exist within the United States, or any place subject to their jurisdiction.

Section 2.
Congress shall have power to enforce this article by appropriate legisla-tion.

AMENDMENT XIV
Passed by Congress June 13, 1866. Ratified July 9, 1868

Section 1.

All persons born or naturalized in the United States, and subject to the jurisdiction thereof, are citizens of the United States and of the State wherein they reside. No State shall make or enforce any law which shall abridge the privileges or immunities of citizens of the United States; nor shall any State deprive any person of life, liberty, or property, without due process of law; nor to deny to any person within its jurisdiction the equal protection of the laws.

Section 2.
Representatives shall be apportioned among the several States according to their respective numbers, counting the whole number of persons in each State, excluding Indians not taxed. But when the right to vote at any election f or the choice of Electors for President and Vice-President of the United States, Representatives in Congress, the executive and judicial officers of a State, or the members of the Legislature thereof, is denied to any of the male inhabitants of such State, being twenty-one years of age, and citizens of the United States, or in any way abridged, except for participation in rebellion, or other crime, the basis of representation therein shall be reduced in the proportion which the number of such male citizens shall bear to the whole number of male citizens twenty-one years of age in such State.

Section 3.
No person shall be a Senator or Representative in Congress, or Elector of President and Vice-President, or hold any office, civil or military, under the United States, or under any State, who, having previously taken an oath, as a member of Congress, or as an officer of the United States, or as a member of any State Legislature, or as an executive or judicial officer of any State, to support the Constitution of the United States, shall have engaged in insurrection or rebellion against the same, or given aid or comfort to the enemies thereof. But Congress may by a vote of two-thirds of each House, remove such disability.

Section 4.
The validity of the public debt of the United States, authorized by law, including debts incurred for payment of pensions and bounties for services in suppressing insurrection or rebellion, shall not be questioned. But neither the United States nor any State shall assume or pay any debt or obligation incurred in aid of insurrection or rebellion against the United States, or any claim for the loss or emancipation of any slave; but all such debts, obligations and claims shall be held illegal and void.

Section 5.
The Congress shall have the power to enforce, by appropriate legislation,

the provisions of this article.

AMENDMENT XV
Passed by Congress February 26, 1869. Ratified February 3, 1870.

Section 1.
The right of citizens of the United States to vote shall not be denied or abridged by the United States or by any State on account of race, color, or previous condition of servitude.

Section 2.
The Congress shall have the power to enforce this article by appropriate legislation.

AMENDMENT XVI
Passed by Congress July 2, 1909. Ratified February 3, 1913.

The Congress shall have power to lay and collect taxes on incomes, from whatever sources derived, without apportionment among the several States, and without regard to any census or enumeration.

AMENDMENT XVII
Passed by Congress May 13, 1912. Ratified April 8, 1913.

The Senate of the United States shall be composed of two Senators from each State, elected by the people thereof, for six years; and each Senator shall have one vote. The electors in each State shall have the qualifications requisite for electors of the most numerous branch of the State Legislatures. When vacancies happen in the representation of any State in the Senate, the executive authority of such State shall issue writs of election to fill such vacancies: Provided, That the Legislature of any State may empower the Executive thereof to make temporary appointments until the people fill the vacancies by election as the Legislature may direct. This amendment shall not be so construed as to affect the election or term of any Senator chosen before it becomes valid as part of the Constitution.

AMENDMENT XVIII
Passed by Congress December 18, 1917. Ratified January 16, 1919.{Altered by Amendment 21}

After one year from the ratification of this article the manufacture, sale, or transportation of intoxicating liquors within, the importation thereof into, or the exportation thereof from the United States and all territory subject to the jurisdiction thereof for beverage purposes is hereby prohibited. The Congress and the several States shall have concurrent power to enforce this article by appropriate legislation. This article shall be inoperative unless it shall have been ratified as an amendment to the Constitution by the Legislatures of the several States, as provided in the Constitution, within seven years from the date of the submission hereof to the States by the Congress.

AMENDMENT XIX
Passed by Congress June 4, 1919. Ratified August 18, 1920.

The right of citizens of the United States to vote shall not be denied or abridged by the United States or by any State on account of sex. Congress shall have power to enforce this article by appropriate legislation.

AMENDMENT XX

Section 1.
The terms of the President and the Vice-President shall end at noon on the 20th day of January, and the terms of Senators and Representatives at noon on the 3rd day of January, of the years in which such terms would have ended if this article had not been ratified; and the terms of their successors shall then begin.
Section 2.
The Congress shall assemble at least once in every year, and such meeting shall begin at noon on the 3rd day of January, unless they shall by law appoint a different day.

Section 3.
If, at the time fixed for the beginning of the term of the President, the President elect shall have died, the Vice-President elect shall become President. If a President shall not have been chosen before the time fixed for the beginning of his term, or if the President elect shall have failed to qualify, then the Vice-President elect shall act as President until a President shall have qualified; and the Congress may by law provide for the case wherein neither a President elect nor a Vice-President shall have qualified, declaring who shall then act as President, or the manner in which one who is to act shall be selected, and such person shall act accordingly until a President or Vice-President shall have qualified.

Section 4.
The Congress may by law provide for the case of the death of any of the persons from whom the House of representatives may choose a President whenever the right of choice shall have devolved upon them, and for the

case of the death of any of the persons from whom the Senate may choose a Vice-President whenever the right of choice shall have devolved upon them.

Section 5.
Sections 1 and 2 shall take effect on the 15th day of October following the ratification of this article (October 1933).

Section 6.
This article shall be inoperative unless it shall have been ratified as an amendment to the Constitution by the Legislatures of three-fourths of the several States within seven years from the date of its submission.

AMENDMENT XXI
Passed by Congress February 20, 1933. Ratified December 5, 1933.

Section 1.
The Eighteenth article of amendment to the Constitution of the United States is hereby repealed.

Section 2.
The transportation or importation into any State, Territory, or Possession of the United States for delivery or use therein of intoxicating liquors, in violation of the laws thereof, is hereby prohibited.

Section 3.
This article shall be inoperative unless it shall have been ratified as an amendment to the Constitution by conventions in the several States, as provided in the Constitution, within seven years from the date of the submission hereof to the States by the Congress.

AMENDMENT XXII
Passed by Congress March 21, 1947. Ratified February 27, 1951.

No person shall be elected to the office of the President more than twice, and no person who has held the office of President, or acted as President, for more that two years of a term to which some other person was elected President shall be elected to the office of President more that once. But this Article shall not apply to any person holding the office of President when this Article was proposed by Congress, and shall not prevent any person who may be holding the office of President, or acting as President, during the term within which this Article becomes operative from holding the office of President or acting as President during the remainder of such term. This article shall be inoperative unless it shall have been ratified as an amendment to the Constitution by the Legislatures of three-fourths of the several States within seven years from the date of its submission to the States by the Congress.

AMENDMENT XXIII
Passed by Congress June 16, 1960. Ratified March 29, 1961.

Section 1.
The District constituting the seat of Government of the United States shall appoint in such manner as Congress may direct: A number of electors of President and Vice President equal to the whole number of Senators and Representatives in Congress to which the District would be entitled if it were a State, but in no event more than the least populous State; they shall be in addition to those appointed by the States, but they shall be considered, for the purposes of the election of President and Vice President, to be electors appointed by a State; and they shall meet in the District and preform such duties as provided by the twelfth article of amendment.

Section 2.
The Congress shall have power to enforce this article by appropriate legislation.

AMENDMENT XXIV
Passed by Congress August 27, 1962. Ratified January 23, 1964.

Section 1.
The right of citizens of the United States to vote in any primary or other election for President or Vice President, for electors for President or Vice President, or for Senator or Representative in Congress, shall not be denied or abridged by the United States or any State by reason of failure to pay poll tax or any other tax.

Section 2.
Congress shall have power to enforce this article by appropriate legislation.

AMENDMENT XXV
Passed by Congress July 6, 1965. Ratified February 10, 1967.

Section 1.
In case of the removal of the President from office or of his death or resignation, the Vice President shall become President.

Section 2.

Whenever there is a vacancy in the office of the Vice President, the President shall nominate a Vice President who shall take the office upon confirmation by a majority vote of both houses of Congress.

Section 3.

Whenever the President transmits to the President Pro tempore of the Senate and the Speaker of the House of Representatives his written declaration that he is unable to discharge the powers and duties of his office, and until he transmits to them a written declaration to the contrary, such powers and duties shall be discharged by the Vice President as Acting President.

Section 4.

Whenever the Vice President and a majority of either the principal officers of the executive departments or of such other body as Congress may by law provide, transmits to the President Pro tempore of the Senate and the Speaker of the House of Representatives their written declaration that the President is unable to discharge the powers and duties of his office, the Vice President shall immediately assume the powers and duties of the office as Acting President. Thereafter, when the President transmits to the President Pro tempore of the Senate and the Speaker of the House of Representatives his written declaration that no inability exists, he shall resume the powers and duties of his office unless the Vice President and a majority of either the principal officers of the executive departments or of such other body as Congress may by law provide, transmits within four days to the President Pro tempore of the Senate and the Speaker of the House of Representatives their written declaration that the President is unable to discharge the powers and duties of his office. Thereupon Congress shall decide the issue, assembling within forty-eight hours for that purpose if not in session. If the Congress, within twenty-one days after receipt of the latter written declaration, or, if Congress is not in session within twenty-one days after Congress is required to assemble, determines by two-thirds vote of both houses that the President is unable to discharge the powers and duties of his office, the Vice President shall continue to discharge the same as Acting President; otherwise, the President shall resume the powers and duties of his office.

AMENDMENT XXVI
Passed by Congress March 23, 1971. Ratified June 30, 1971.

Section 1.

The right of citizens of the United States, who are 18 years of age or older, to vote shall not be denied or abridged by the United States or any state on account of age.

<u>Section 2.</u>
The Congress shall have power to enforce this article by appropriate legislation.

o   o   o   o

This is the end of the *U.S. Constitution* and all 26 Amendments.

Our Second American Civil War – *To Preserve*

The American Civil War – 1861 to 1865

The great American Civil War caused the populations of the North and South to struggle both on the battlefields and in their communities from 1861 to 1865. It was for the sake of this discussion America's 'second' Civil War. It was fought in order "to save the Union." It was a domestic war that was engaged to determine if the United States would be held together as a sovereign nation, or would be split in two. It was an economic and societal war in which the South desired separation in order to maintain a way of life and the region's economic system.

President Abraham Lincoln's first responsibility and goal was to preserve the Union. The issue of ending slavery was a secondary issue and was not even a major concern at the start of the conflict.

President Lincoln signed the *Emancipation Proclamation* on September 22, 1862 and it was enacted on January 1, 1863 toward the middle of the war. The document declared that the slaves,

"shall be then, thenceforward, and forever free"

o   o   o   o

When the Northern states prevailed over the Southern states, the nation remained united. Slavery in America was also ended. American-Blacks took their first big step toward equality at that point in time.
However, it would take another 100 years until the 1960s for them to take the final required step toward social and economic equality.

Again the Constitution had facilitated the correction of errors made in our nation's past — by way of legislative action that reflected changing public values and attitudes, and demonstrating the concern that Americans have for one another regardless of their differences. The nation was continuing to mature.

The conduct of the Civil War resulted in grim human numbers showing that the North suffered over 640,000 killed and wounded, while the South had over 335,000 killed and wounded on their side.

The Deadliest of American Days

In the first four days of July 1863 on the fields of Gettysburg, Pennsylvania over 50,000 Northern and Southern soldiers were killed. Close to the number lost in the entire Vietnam War (approx., 58,000) and even closer to those killed ion action during the Korean War (approx 54,000). And all in only four (4) deadly days! It has been said since that war that we Americans are better at killing each other than anyone else.

In November 1863, President Lincoln traveled to Gettysburg to dedicate the new national cemetery and there delivered his inspirational *Gettysburg ddress.*

This second American Civil War was also a physical and very bloody conflict followed by practical legislation designed to refine the National System for the Common Good of the people — and to *Preserve* the nation.

o   o   o   o

The complete texts of the President Abraham Lincoln's *Emancipation Proclamation* and *Gettysburg Address* are presented next.

The Emancipation Proclamation

Emancipation Proclamation as reprinted here was issued on January 1, 1863, under the heading, "By the President of the United States of America: A Proclamation."

Whereas, on the 22nd day of September, in the year of our Lord 1862, a proclamation was issued by the President of the United States, containing, among other things, the following, to wit:

That on the 1st day of January, in the year of our Lord 1863, all persons held as slaves within any state or designated part of a state, the people whereof shall then be in rebellion against the United States, **shall be then, thenceforward, and forever free;** and the executive government of the United States, including the military and naval authority thereof, will recognize and maintain the freedom of such persons and will do no act or acts to repress such persons, or any of them, in any efforts they may make for their actual freedom.

That the executive will, on the 1st day of January aforesaid, by proclamation, designate the states and parts of states, if any, in which the people thereof, respectively, shall then be in rebellion against the United States; and the fact that any state or the people thereof shall on that day be in good faith represented in the Congress of the United States by members chosen thereto at elections wherein a majority of the qualified voters of such states shall have participated shall, in the absence of strong countervailing testimony, be deemed conclusive evidence that such state and the people thereof are not then in rebellion against the United States.

Now, therefore, I, Abraham Lincoln, President of the United States, by virtue of the power in me vested as commander in chief of the Army and Navy of the United States, in time of actual armed rebellion against the authority and government of the United States, and as a fit and necessary war measure for suppressing said rebellion, do, on this 1st day of January, in the year of our Lord 1863, and in accordance with my purpose so to do, publicly proclaimed for the full period of 100 days from the day first above mentioned, order and designate as the states and parts of states wherein the people thereof, respectively, are this day in rebellion against the United States the following, to wit:

Arkansas, Texas, Louisiana (except the parishes of St. Bernard, Plaquemines, Jefferson, St. John, St. Charles, St. James, Ascension, Assumption, Terrebonne, Lafourche, St. Mary, St. Martin, and Orleans, including the city of New Orleans), Mississippi, Alabama, Florida, Georgia, South Carolina, North Carolina, and Virginia (except the forty-eight counties designated as West Virginia, and also the counties of Berkeley, Accomac, Northampton, Elizabeth City, York, Princess Anne, and Norfolk, including the cities of Norfolk and Portsmouth), and which excepted parts are for the present left precisely as if this proclamation were not issued.

And, by virtue of the power and for the purpose aforesaid, I do order and declare that all persons held as slaves within said designated states and parts of states are, and henceforward shall be, free; and that the executive government of the United States, including the military and naval authorities thereof, will recognize and maintain the freedom of said persons.

And I hereby enjoin upon the people so declared to be free to abstain from all violence, unless in necessary self-defense; and I recommend to them that, in all cases when allowed, they labor faithfully for reasonable wages.

And I further declare and make known that such persons of suitable condition will be received into the armed service of the United States to garrison forts, positions, stations, and other places, and to man vessels of all sorts in said service.

And upon this act, sincerely believed to be an act of justice, warranted by the Constitution upon military necessity, I invoke the considerate judgment of mankind and the gracious favor of Almighty God.

In witness whereof, I have hereunto set my hand and caused the seal of the United States to be affixed.

Done at the City of Washington, this first day of January, in the year of our Lord one thousand eight hundred and sixty three, and of the Independence of the United States of America the eighty-seventh.

By the President: Abraham Lincoln

William H. Seward, Secretary of State.

Abraham Lincoln's *Gettysburg Address*

Four score and seven years ago our fathers brought forth on this continent a new nation, conceived in liberty and dedicated to the proposition that all men are created equal.

Now we are engaged in a great civil war, testing whether that nation or any nation so conceived and so dedicated can long endure. We are met on a great battlefield of that war. We have come to dedicate a portion of that field as a final resting-place for those who here gave their lives that that nation might live.

It is altogether fitting and proper that we should do this. But in a larger sense, we cannot dedicate, we cannot consecrate, we cannot hallow this ground. The brave men, living and dead who struggled here have consecrated it far above our poor power to add or detract. The world will little note nor long remember what we say here, but it can never forget what they did here.

It is for us the living rather to be dedicated here to the unfinished work which they who fought here have thus far so nobly advanced.

It is rather for us to be here dedicated to the great task remaining before us—that from these honored dead we take increased devotion to that cause for which they gave the last full measure of devotion—that we here highly resolve that these dead shall not have died in vain, that this nation under God shall have a new birth of freedom, and that government of the people, by the people, for the people shall not perish from the earth.

Delivered on November 19, 1863
For the dedication of the National Cemetery at Gettysburg, Pennsylvania

o   o   o   o

Lincoln's address of just 267 words is considered one of the greatest political pieces ever written. Since then countless volumes have been written on the power of its message and the supreme humanity in its spirit.

Honoring Those that Paid the Ultimate Price

My intent from the beginning of CS2 was to minimize the various statistics presented. We hear, read, and are bombarded with so many numbers and my goal is to present solid, objectively developed concepts and to promote common understanding among our people – words rather than numbers.

However, then I began writing this piece on our Civil Wars and wanted to communicate some sense of the human loss, the level pain and suffering that our predecessors had endured for the good of the nation.

So I looked for the human numbers and located a very detailed statistical chart on the Internet. It was too much! It charted all the wars and conflicts that our military people have bravely fought since 1775, listing the harsh counts of all those Americans that had died and were wounded.

I felt they all had to be acknowledged in CS2. Those sacred numbers represent the men and women that bravely sacrificed themselves for us over the years, and those that unfortunately are doing so even today.

My hope and prayer are that each of us will quietly study those solemn numbers. That those *most human* statistics would provide each of us a real perspective on *true sacrifice* to consider as we individually ponder the potential for personal loss, if any, that you and I could realize from the implementation of the proposals in An American Agenda and others to come.

Most people will benefit more than they may lose, if they lose anything at all. However, some will absolutely experience personal loss and/or upsetting adjustments in their personal world in the order for the Common Good to be truly served. Such is the very nature of dramatic, public Changes in our or any nation's National System.

Such societal Changes are always happening in the world, but most are not of a positive nature.

The Human Cost of Our Wars

The first chart below presents key events in our nation's history and those of more recent times. I have provided the approximate counts for the Afghanistan and Iraq wars through September 11, 2007.

The War	Dates	Killed	Wounded
American Revolution	1775-1783	25,324	8445
War of 1812	1812-1815	2,260	4505
Texas War			
of Independence	1835-1836	704	138
Mexican War	1846-1848	13,283	32
Civil War – North	1861-1865	363,020	281,104
Civil War – South	1861-1865	199,110	137,102
Spanish-American War	1898	2893	1,637
World War I	1917-1918	116,708	204,002
World War II	1914-1945	408,306	670,846
Korean War – it was not			
a Conflict (Optional)	1950-1953	54,246	103,284
Vietnam War (Optional)	1957-1975	58,219	153,356
Granada	1983	19	100
Persian Gulf War (To keep			
the oil flowing)	1990-1991	363	357
Somalia – Bush I (Optional)	1991-1992	8	0

Operation Enduring Freedom
Afghanistan War

As of 02-04-2008	2001 to 20??	482+	1500+

Operation Iraqi Freedom
Iraq (Bush IIs Optional) War

As of 02-04-2008	2003 to 20??	3948+	28,770+

The Comprehensive Listing

The second chart is intended to be a comprehensive listing of all military events in our nation's history. These are the very *human statistics* from our nation's wars and military conflicts. Many of them you and I have never heard of before. My sincerest apology if anything is omitted.

Years	Location	Killed	Wounded
1775-1783 (1)	Revolutionary War	25324	8445
1789	Indian Wars	6125	2156
1798-1800	Franco-Amer Naval War	20	42
1801-1815	Barbary Wars	35	64
1812-1815	War of 1812	2260	4505
1814	Marquesas Islands	4	1
1822-1825	West Indies	3	5
1832	Sumatra	2	11
1835-1836	Texas War Of Independence	704	138
1846-1848	Mexican War	13283	32
1855	Fiji	1	2
1859-1860	Texas Border Cortina War	5	18
1861-1865 (2)	Civil War, North	363,020	281,104
1861-1865 (2)	Civil War, South	199110	137102
1853	Japan	5	6
1867	Formosa	1	0
1870	Mexico	1	4
1871	Korea	4	10
1898	Spanish American War	2893	1637
1899-1902	Philippines War	4273	2840
1899	Samoa	4	5
1900	China Boxer Rebellion	53	253
1902-1913	Moro Campaigns	130	300
1904	Dominican Republic	1	0
1911-1919	Mexico	19	69
1912	Nicaragua	5	16
1915-1920	Haiti	146	26
1916-1922	Dominican Republic	144	50
1917-1918	World War I	116708	204002
1918-1919	Russia North Expedition	246	307

Years	Location	Killed	Wounded
1918-1920	Russia Siberia Expedition	170	52
1921-1941	China Yangtze Service	5	80
1927-1932	Nicaragua	136	66
1941	North Atlantic Naval War	141	44
1941	Pearl Harbor	2388	—
1941-1945	World War II	408306	670846
1945-1947	Italy Trieste	6	14
1945-1947	China Civil War	12	42
1950	Inchon	670	—
1950-1953	Korean War	54246	103284
1954	Matsu and Quemoy	3	0
1957-1975	Vietnam War	58219 (4)	153356
1958-1984	Lebanon	268	169
1962	Cuba	9	0
1964	Panama Canal Riots	4	85
1965-1966	Dominican Republic	59	174
1966-1969	South Korea	89	131
1967	Israel Attack/USS Liberty	34	171
1968	Tet (Vietnam)	7040	0
1980	Iran	8	0
	Operation Desert One		
	1980-1991	Terrorism	28
0	1983	Grenada	19
100	1983	Beirut Lebanon	241
—	23-Oct		
1983-1991	El Salvador	20	0
1984-1989	Honduras	1	28
1986	Libya	2	0
1987 (3)	Persian Gulf	148	467
1989-1990	Panama	40	240
1990-1991	Persian Gulf, Op Desert Shield/Storm	363	357
1991-1992	Somalia, Op Restore Hope	8	—
1993, Feb 26	Terrorism, World Trade Center	6	1000+
1995	Terrorism Oklahoma City	168	400+

Years	Location	Killed	Wounded
1995, Nov 13	Terrorism	7	42
	Riyadh, Saudi Arabia		
1995-2000	Terrorism	77	—
1996, Jun 25	Terroism	19	500
	Khobar Towers, Saudi Arabia		
2000	Yemen, USS Cole	17	651
2001, Sept 11	Flight 93	44	-0-
2002	Operation Enduring Freedom, Filipines	12	—

The source of the expanded list along with the various references is located on the Internet at:

http://members.aol.com/usregistry/allwars.htm

For current information on <u>Operation Enduring Freedom</u> please reference:

http://www/icasualties.org/oef/

For current information on <u>Operation Iraqi Freedom</u> please reference:

http://www/icasualties.org/oif/

Also see, http://members.aol.com/veterans/warlib64.htm

I sincerely thank those organizations for developing and distributing such meaningful information on our military.

o   o   o   o

<u>The Real Bottom Line</u>

In reviewing those numbers, I was most personally struck when considering the *total* number of our people that have, and unfortunately to this very day are dying – for the welfare of the rest of us.

In reviewing the full chart of all military actions that America has been involved in since 1776 the number of military men and women that lost their lives exceeds some 1,262,000 — a very sobering number.

For perspective, I determined to calculate the cost in lives spread from 1776 to the end 2008, the next presidential election year – which totals 232 years and over 84,680 days. Continuing the grim math it first equates to 5,439 people lost per year.

And finally it calculates to some **14.9** of our military people lost each day from 01-01-1776 thru 12-31-2008!

A loss of **14.9** real people for each of our nation's **84,680** days.

Just think of all the tears!

o   o   o   o

And What of Today

And now our military is facing Bush IIs optional and "out of control" Iraq War. Through 2-4-08 it has taken 3,948 lives,

and is now averaging over two (2) lost each day since 3-19-2003.

Consider that in just the Iraq War to-date, all of the lives lost, bodies and minds wounded, and families forever damaged. It is far too much pain. And it is avoidable national pain. We can and we will do better than that in the future. And We must demand it!

o   o   o   o

It goes without saying that all of America's military actions contributed in defining and defending the nation, and in making our place on the world stage. However, those wars did not define us internally as did the Revolutionary (Civil) War of 1776, the Civil War of 1861, and the Civil War of 2008 and beyond which we are reluctantly approaching today.

This modern day, domestic-based, non-violent legislative war will do just as much and probably far more than the other two Civil Wars in clarifying and determining what we Americans stand for – and – in particular what We will not stand for!

o   o   o   o

As you consider any negative personal impacts resulting from the proposed Changes to the National System presented in An American Agenda, remember the sacrifice of the real people that are shown only as numbers on the charts above. Real Progress and Change in society is not free.

It is the Democratic Right of American society to call on each other for help, as well as for sacrifice **when it is justified** – in order to insure the Life, Liberty, and the Pursuit of Happiness of our fellow Americans.

And it is now so justified!

WHATEVER, any of us may need to give, pales in comparison to what they so bravely gave, so that we would continue to have the choice.

It would serve us all to remember President Lincoln's challenge,

> *"that we here highly resolve that these dead shall not have died in vain, that this nation under God shall have a new birth of freedom, and that government of the people, by the people, for the people shall not perish from the earth."*

When, We the People, join together to act compassionately and decisively for the Common Good of America – nothing and no one can keep us from achieving victory.

o   o   o   o

<u>Our Third and Final American Civil War – *To Control*</u>

<u>The Second American Revolution – 2008 to 2014 – Our Seven Year Civil War</u>

"How much does each of us really care about our fellow American citizens?"

What I have referred to as our Second American Revolution (SAR) is all about We the People demanding that our elected national leadership aggressively address the problems and issues we face today in our neighborhoods and as a nation – to fulfill their solemn responsibility to dutifully attend to the Common Good of our citizens. <u>To do their job</u>!

"Our" Civil War will reconcile the National Vision of where the nation expects to be tomorrow, and what prudent and practical changes will be required within our National System – the way America *really works* on a day-to-day basis — in order to begin making that Vision our daily reality – starting in 2008!

As we enter the year 2008, it is some 232 years since the start of the American Revolution and some 147 years since the start of the great American Civil War. The <u>unavoidable</u> time has come my fellow Americans for what we all must pray shall be our final internal battle to define what the United States of America stands for, what American Democracy means to every American citizen, and most importantly the specific path to be taken for our nation to realize that desired future.

As previously stated, this will not be a physical war although there will certainly be moments when it will be seem just as radical as our War of Independence and as intense as the brother-against-brother fighting in the war to save the Union.

The benefits of this our Final Civil War will be to *Preserve* the traditional fabric of American society, to insure the American Dream for our citizens, and to <u>save</u> American lives <u>everyday</u> that are now being *allowed* to be lost not only on the battlefield, but in our very neighborhoods. "Allowed" to be lost by a dysfunctional National System that is currently controlled an irresponsible and self-serving Few, and runs increasingly against the Common Good of the Many.

o   o   o   o

Should, the message of the *Second Coming of Common Sense (CS2)* gain public attention and popular acceptance, I believe the following years will properly come to be known as our Third American Civil War. "Our" Civil War will be fought in newspapers, on radio, network and cable television, on the Internet, and in literally tens of millions of discussions between two and more people as we as a nation determine who we are, what we stand for, what we expect of each other, what we expect of business, as well as what we <u>will</u> <u>tolerate</u> from other nations and their peoples, and **what we will not**!

It will be all those things, because that is what is needed at this our moment in time. This of necessity will be an absolute societal confrontation that will define the future Common Good of our fellow American citizens – you, me, and everyone else. It will be waged between the all too often Silent Majority of the American people and those Few that seek to and currently do exercise irresponsible control over the political and economic machinery that drives our National System.

It is a internal war that We the People can join in together **and win** for the Common Good of all Americans living today and those that will follow us in future generations.

Paine's *Common Sense* Analogy and Ours

<u>That was Then</u>

In *Common Sense*, Thomas Paine presented the not totally popular, yet practical and logical reasoning for the American colonists to do what seemed the impossible — to become a new nation independent from England. And why they needed to do it <u>now</u> and not put it off for some additional years down the road!

The analogy Paine used in his radical pamphlet was,

"Why should a Continent be ruled by an Island?"

It was a reasonable question for them to consider then.

<u>This is Now</u>

The social and economic problems we suffer with in today's America <u>can</u> be remedied if We the People decide to act upon viable solution-oriented proposals such as those presented in An American Agenda and others that will follow. Therefore, I ask you,

"Why should the fate of the Many be controlled by the Few?"

It is the reasonable question for us to consider now!

o   o   o   o

The disproportional balance of political power is the underlying and dominant reality in nations all around the world. This all too common power structure leaves too many opportunities for mischief and blatant abuse of power. Remember the classic warning regarding uncontrolled power, *"Absolute power corrupts, absolutely."*

However, We the People will not continue to be led down that old road, and We will not be made to bow to anyone or anything! We will not allow America to continue to digress to the political state that our national ancestors fought the Revolutionary War to rid themselves of. And that is where we are slowly being led now.

Consider This Perspective

In recent years the perpetual debate over *Creationism versus Evolution* has picked up some speed. And Creationism is now often referred to as "Intelligent Design" in the press, scientific, and academic communities.

I will not touch on that passionate debate herein other than to offer that at the very bottom line after having heard the strong arguments from both houses, it must be acknowledged that "both" are technically still theories. Reality strikes again.

For those that support Creationism or Intelligent Design, their viewpoint it is based upon faith in God and religious teaching — it cannot be proven even though some say the data points to that conclusion. *Webster* defines *faith* as, "firm belief in something for which there is no proof."

Evolutionists on the other hand, have not been able to provide the infamous 'missing link' between monkey and human – as much as they keep trying to "infer" it. Technically that missing link is wider than the Grand Canyon. Thus, neither has been proven and both remain theories. Period.

And pardon me, but frankly American society has far more important "issues" to spend our time and energy on. The constant and rather boring debate over what are personally based, private opinions will not do anything to resolve a single issue on the public Grievance List presented earlier. Not one.

During political campaigns and in between them — such issues serve only as distracting domestic propaganda. Belaboring such issues is a way for politicians that are supposed to be our national leadership to avoid discussing real public problems – let alone working to resolve any of them.

Far too much wasted time.

Not Theory – Historic Reality

I would offer that there has been a natural Evolution of government since the dawn of civilization. Unfortunately, from the beginning it has and today continues to follow the *law of the jungle* — survival of fittest. For all those centuries, indeed for thousands of years as civilization evolved it could only produce various dictatorial and oppressive forms of secular and religious governments where the Few ruled over the Many – and most often with a cruel, if not merciless hand.

Then along came *1776!* And the Common people drew a line in the sand of history, and **"intelligently designed"** and boldly implemented a radically new form of government under which the Many were to rule their own nation and control their own destiny. The democratic Right to *popular rule* was the Founders' absolute intention for We the People — for our national ancestors to be in charge of their national voyage.

Since that First American Civil War, America has experienced highs and lows along our national voyage and I will not mention any of those now. We the People have thus far accomplished some critical course adjustments over the course of our 232 year voyage. Although it is fair to say that it has often been achieved in reaction to or by recovering from crisis rather than avoiding it — and we can do better.

o   o   o   o

Today we find ourselves in critical need of domestic and foreign policy clarifications.

You have read the contents of An American Agenda, I hope. Those proposals aggressively confront hard issues, many of which if allowed to further digress will eventually force us to again react in crisis to correct. Or the worse case scenario — we do nothing, things deteriorate, and we just accept it! We become peasants, again.

That will surely happen if *We the People* will not decide to control our own destiny. It is our choice to make and we must decide now!

We can no longer stand around like peasants waiting for leadership that simply is not coming! Just as the American colonists of 1776 decided that enough was enough – the American citizens of 2008 – yes we must now decide that enough is enough. And as I like to say, when you finally reach the point where you want to scream that you have had enough, you have really had too much! How much have you wanted to scream in recent years?

Now at the Edge

We will make it known to all parties and beyond all doubt of our Common Intolerance for the dysfunctional status quo within our National System and that it will now be corrected for the Common Good. We will publicly declare and demonstrate that we are again assuming the Civil Responsibility to control *our* country and to insure *our* viable national destiny.

We are at the Revolutionary Edge of dramatic economic, social, and civil changes in our National System that could be equated to prudent and all too necessary adjustments to the Founders' original "intelligent design" for American society.

The types of logical policy changes that are required to set such an "intelligent re-design" of our National System in motion were presented in An American Agenda. And there will of course be others. We are considering significant and socially prudent refinements and corrections to the National System – and all under the proper control of the U.S. Constitution. This role is ultimately our Civil Responsibility in order to protect and defend the Common Good of our fellow American citizens and the Welfare of our nation!

Also consider that the issues that we are raising in An American Agenda and are encouraging for open public debate across our nation — will absolutely bring about similar outbreaks of conversation around the rest of the world. Such reaction could very well become an unintended side-effect of our Second American Revolution – America first and then the world.

That of course, is exactly what our First American Revolution caused to happen. The shock waves of that first Democratic "big bang" are still reverberating around the globe.

And it needs to happen again! And it needs to happen now!

They, the people of the American colonies were to strike the decisive blow against the oppressive Old World System. Theirs' was to be a historic and monumental stand against the Old World Order that had so tyrannically ruled all of the peoples, of all the countries in the world throughout human history.

Until the American Revolution and the coming of American Democracy

o   o   o   o

For just one moment my fellow Americans, consider that all those people, in all those countries, were really our common national ancestors. If each of us goes back far enough in our own family tree we will find that with very few exceptions, We the People — all of us — descended from humble beginnings. Go back far enough in your family's history and you will find the peasants — you will find the meek!

How many of our ancestors lived in circumstances where they could not have 'even imagined' such a way of life — to live in a free society that the American colonists found it within their power to create?

In the normal "course of human events" the leaders of the Old World were (and in too many cases still are) perpetually passing on power to their next generation of oppressors – whether family or political ally. And that self-serving cycle of political dominance would have continued along the same oppressive path if something like the American Revolution and Democracy had not gotten in the way. For after the living example of Freedom and Liberty for the Multitudes was out in the open for all to witness, the world would not let it go and the oppressors could not stop it.

The living example of "American Democracy" is a basic reason why the political and/or religious leadership of certain countries so dislikes America. It is because our mere existence demonstrates how failed their forms of government, their societies, and their oppressive domestic policies are. While still not perfect, our democratic form of government offers to our people far more than those governments are willing to provide their own people, even though it is totally within their power to give.

o   o   o   o

The bold actions taken by the Founders, supported by a relatively small number of brave colonists (and some timely help from the French!), succeeded in forever altering the "Old World Order." They established a new standard. They raised the bar of societal expectations and forever changed the entire direction of human and governmental history. They truly initiated the "New World Order" of their time and for all time!

The Leaders that the People fondly remember
and hold dearly in their collective hearts,
are the Leaders that were inspired to,
and by their bold actions,
led the People to a better life.

o   o   o   o

Part 5
We the People —
Will Decide Our Nation's Future

"It is Our National Decision –
Shall They Remain in Control
Or will,
We the People Take Control"

o   o   o   o

Deciding Not to Maintain the Dysfunctional Status Quo

We the People, under the sacred provisions of the *U.S. Constitution* are to be *In Control* of America. And as things stand today – We are <u>not</u>!

The *Constitution* is the Founders' gift to future generations and it is therefore our Duty and Responsibility to honor and maintain it as our nation's governing document. That is our solemn debt to all of those that preceded us in our national voyage – especially those that along the way paid the ultimate price to defend it. Therefore, We must determine to take action now. And to act decisively in order to wrestle the control of our National System and indeed our very government, from those Special Interest entities that are irresponsibly ignoring to the Common Good of the nation and our fellow American citizens.

As mentioned, those publicly irresponsible Special Interests include vital parts of the business community, as well as some of the politically influential whose narrow and self-serving agendas run contrary to the Common Good of the Masses. In all reality, this fight for ultimate control over the National System <u>is</u> happening right now in our America – a publicly damaging imbalance of power that already exists in <u>too</u> many countries around the world.

This particularly applies when the Few acting against the Common Good, threaten the day-to-day viability and peace of our domestic society and economic system, to say nothing of their putting our national security at risk.

To insure the protection of the average and <u>all</u> Americans is exactly what the Founders designed both the *U.S. Constitution* and the U.S. Congress to provide for and to oversee. And in the final analysis, the protection of the Masses from the selfish desires of the Few remains in fact the common problem in too many countries around the world. That protection of the Masses is a core defining principle that makes our Constitution the great document that it is — why it is the envy of people around the world, and why it is so feared by the various forms of dictatorial style governments that cause most of the world's problems today.

Practically speaking, the societal problems of the Many are not being re-solved because our elected leadership cannot or will not (be allowed to) present, let alone implement socially acceptable and prudent solutions to the public's problems. That is why that incomplete public Grievance List referenced several times herein exists and only continues to grow.

CS2 presents for public critique, viable solutions to several of our national issues and I sincerely hope has provided you with perspective on the com-plexity involved when developing such publicly acceptable proposals. With an understanding of the tediousness in developing the rationale and con-cepts required to explain the Change process at the national level.

At the start of my public problem solving journey some 25 years ago, I like most others had little insight into the difficulties in contending with the Special Interests and political zealots in that reconciliation process. How-ever, the smoke screen was slowly pushed away, and I did figure it out! It is a truly complex problem solving challenge when you are talking about reconciling the varying concerns and opinions of some 200 million voters. As I pointed out before, while these are complex public issues and prob-lems we are here confronting, do not allow yourself to continue to think for a single moment that they are impossible to solve. We can fix anything and everything. We only need to decide to do it.

o   o   o   o

Rudely and un-fortunately for us, the current 535 members of the U.S. Congress have not and sadly do not collectively possess the political lead-ership and "guts" to implement such nationally necessary Changes over the interference and selfish cries of the Few — those that quietly benefit from the growing dysfunctional nature of the status quo within our Na-tional System.

This is more than partially due to the fact that our political leadership has grown so openly influenced and controlled by certain industries, various interest groups and individuals with narrow, self-serving interests. Those with agendas aimed <u>only</u> at benefiting the Few, without <u>any</u> practical concern for negative impacts placed upon the Many – that Common Good thing, again!

While some of the ideas and approaches originated by the Few *could be* well-intentioned in their narrow view of the world, in hard reality they do not seek to address the concerns of the Masses. But, then that <u>is</u> <u>not</u> their job is it? And after all, why should the Special Interests care – even give a damn – about the Common Good when it interferes with whatever they want? You know – just ignore the little people, those millions of *peasants...*

After all, isn't that the way the world works most everywhere else? Yes it is! However, We cannot <u>and</u> will not allow it to be made that way under our American Democracy – and if not for our sake, then for our children and theirs.

<u>What Directs Our Leadership</u>

At the national level, it is technically our elected National representatives' job and responsibility to balance all of <u>our</u> needs and interests. It is <u>not</u> the care or responsibility of lobbyist's for Special Interests and the politically influential. In day-to-day reality — which is where the majority of us do find ourselves living, it is too easy to observe that those Special Interests are more and more getting the results "they want" simply because:

· They show up.
· They speak up.
· They get involved.
· They contribute money.
· They connect with the decision makers.
· And they will <u>crush</u> the opposition, as needed. Nothing personal, of course!

Any questions?

Therefore, since Congress is not being responsible to the Common Good, <u>they</u> get what they want far more often than the rest of us – you know the (Silent) Majority! Is that any big surprise? This irresponsible leadership has led, over the last few decades to a legislative process more focused to catering to the will of the Few in spite of the how it could negatively affect the Many. Again, that is why the Grievance List contains what it does, and it is far from complete!

The Special Interest lobbyist's driving motivation is to perpetuate the Status Quo for their portion of the National System, regardless of anything or anybody else. Or making their piece of the pie even sweeter! Forget about ethics, morals, and much abused concept of family values? Winning is all that counts – Period...

It has created a political environment in which elected officials, at all levels of government are not solving, let alone seriously addressing the really tough problems facing our society. To be fair local, county, and state governments are doing a better job than the U.S. Congress because they are closer to the day-to-day reality of life on Main Street in America – where the problems are felt. It is too easy for the Congress to ignore problems at home when their world is primarily inside the DC beltway. And the Congress' growing habit of inaction or wrong action in national legislation too often perpetuates and/or causes more problems for lower level governments, e.g., health care, the IO invasion, the No Child Left Behind program, and the failed (and domestically destructive) War on Drugs.

Their individual and collective dysfunctional performance, my fellow Americans, is not what our society requires of its elected leadership, and it is absolutely not what the Founders intended.

The Second Coming of Common Sense

I absolutely know that We, the until now Silent Majority do not desire nor do we intend to endure this sad state of national affairs any longer. The growing chaos must now be brought to proper order, and only We the People can actually force the required Changes to occur.

And the grim and undeniable, Plain Truth of that reality my fellow American men, women, and children — is the reason why I determined to write this book! And write it to you!

Because just as Thomas Paine attempted to do and did for his fellow colonists, one of us had to step forward and attempt to *rationally* write such a book for the rest of us to review and openly debate.

To present to my fellow Americans, objective perspectives on the key issues of our day, background on the forces that are selfishly attacking the Common Good, and the sometimes hard solutions to long-standing public problems that you have thus far read in CS2.

This is my sincere and patriotic effort to say what needs to be said – and to put it in writing for all to read and consider. To encourage the Masses as Paine did, that there is a way out of this growing national chaos. To challenge us all to action and action now starting in 2008 – not to wait some more years when things get even worse and are far more difficult to reconcile and repair.

This political writing is only what one of us had to do. And I what have attempted to humbly and boldly present. The plans for constructive Changes to the National System laid out in CS2 are not perfect, but it is very fair to say that they are the best plans we actually have or are likely to have any time soon — if ever!

Therefore, it is now upon us to join together and become active in what we could call, *Common Sense Politics* and boldly begin our Revolution. And as has been the case throughout history, you start into battle with a good initial plan and as things unfold and progress, you modify that plan as required to insure final success. That is what the Founders and the colonists did, and now it is We that must be about our nation's business.

Again, We the People must join together and take it upon ourselves to determine and direct how our society and our economy – the American National System – will be properly restructured over the next seven (7) years. And it will all be done it in order to insure our Common Good today – and that of the Generational Groups 5, 6, 7, and beyond.

Generational Group and Birth Year Range	Age in the Year 2008	Number of Years	Number of Males	Number of Females	Total Population
Group GG7					
1995 to 2008	0 to 13	14	27,433,805	26,152,136	53,585,941
Group GG6					
1979 to 1994	14 to 29	16	33,440,299	31,782,595	65,222,894
Group GG5					
1963 to 1978	30 to 45	16	32,534,722	31,974,819	64,509,541
Group GG4					
1947 to 1962	46 to 61	16	32,809,341	33,655,232	66,464,573
Group GG3					
1931 to 1946	62 to 77	16	17,418,133	19,207,656	36,625,789
Group GG2					
1915 to 1930	78 to 93	16	9,027,139	12,921,676	21,948,815
Group GG1					
188x to 1914	94 & over*	25+	982,124	2,527,269	3,509,393
Totals			**153,645,563**	**158,221,383**	**311,866,946**

Our Second American Revolution need not take seven years to accomplish. And it will not if WE act decisively, and do it NOW.

The Future of "Our" National System

You have been reading a 2007 critique of and literary assault upon the way some things are currently being done and run in our country.

To be crystal clear, the message of *The Second Coming of Common Sense* is written and presented with the same confrontational intent as Thomas Paine's writing in *Common Sense*. Only time and your response will tell if this equally sincere call to my fellow citizens rings as true today.

As noted earlier, our "national condition" could simply be framed as follows:

- Negative social and economic conditions in the National System have slowly grown to feel customary just because they have been <u>allowed</u> to exist for so long.

- Certain conditions appear normal or acceptable, even though they are a burden to society and/or are a functionally counter-productive, if not <u>destructive</u> part of the National System.

- There are day-to-day parts of the National System that the Masses are <u>forced</u> to tolerate — that the existence of which would be difficult to justify if they had to be explained to an outsider.

Not a very comfortable "national condition" is it?

As stated, the 'direction' of our National System increasingly over the last couple of decades has been determined by a minority of socially irresponsible, self-interested people, organizations, and corporations, as well as questionable business practices that are slowly destroying the fabric of our society and the future of America — one person, one family, one community, and one business at a time.

That pretty well sums it all up.

o   o   o   o

The Public Grievance List

The following is the public Grievance List initially presented in Part 1, identifying some of the public's areas of concern that the U.S. Congress and White House are not addressing:

- Automobile/Truck Theft
- Commodity Market Abuses
- Contaminated Food Supply
- Crimes of Physical Assault
- Crimes of Financial Assault
- Drug War in our Streets
- Employment/Income (viable and legal)
- Ending the Iraq War
- Gangs in Our Communities
- Global Warming
- Homelessness
- Housing Costs
- Hunger
- Illegal Immigration – ending it
- Interest Rates on Primary Family Residence
- Katrina Clean-up
- Judicial Legal Complex (JLC)
- Medical Insurance for all American citizens – cradle to grave
- Military Industrial Complex (MIC)
- Oil Industry Windfall Profits and Other Abuses
- Over-weight children, teenagers, and adults
- Poverty Among Our Citizens
- Public Education
- Pre-meditated Murder
- Pre-meditated Pedophile Crimes Against our Youth
- Pre-meditated Rape
- Prescription Medicine Costs
- Stem Cell Research
- Social Security Solvency
- War on Terror

Certainly not all, but many of our primary concerns will be positively addressed with the timely and appropriate implementation of the proposals presented in Part 3 — An American Agenda.

The Water is Getting Too Warm

There is a simple analogy I heard some years ago that applies to our situation – have you heard the one about the frog and the pot of water? Incidentally, my son and I absolutely enjoyed actually seeing it actually presented in animated form in Al Gore's worldwide, environmental wake-up call movie, *An Inconvenient Truth*? It is cute, but all too serious in both scenarios.

> If someone were to throw a poor frog into a pot of boiling water it will jump out immediately if it can, to save itself.

> However, if the frog is placed into a pot of *'cool'* water and the water is then slowly heated to boiling, the frog will not jump out, and it will cook! Please do not try that at home.

Now, my fellow Americans take one more, hard look at that list and consider how each item individually and collectively contribute to treating our society like a very large pot of water and you know who the 300 million frogs are. And not all of our national issues are even on that list.

That is where we realistically find life in America today. But things do not need to be that way anymore. The various preventable and correctable conditions listed above can no longer be ignored – for they are slowly eroding American society and the very economy required to support it. Viable changes must be made for the Common Good of the Masses, and in particular for the welfare of the younger generations of Americans that are observing this decline as their lives are just beginning.

It Will be Our Second Coming

Be encouraged! These are all correctable issues that are currently impacting the daily life of our families and that threaten their future peace and opportunity. In the final analysis, the current status quo of the National System <u>will</u> <u>not</u> be allowed to continue unchallenged, for it is threatening the very "Life, Liberty, and Pursuit of Happiness" deemed to be the Inalienable Rights of all American citizens.

The Power of the People, that Thomas Jefferson so boldly wrote about in the opening of the *Declaration of Independence,* will be brought to bear in the defense of our Common Good,

<blockquote>
"That to secure these Rights, Governments are instituted among Men,
deriving their just Powers from the Consent of the Governed,
that when ever any Form of Government
becomes destructive to these Ends,
it is the Right of the People to alter or to abolish it,
and to institute new Government,
laying its Foundation on such Principles,
and organizing its Powers in such Form,
as to them shall seem most likely
to affect their Safety and Happiness"
</blockquote>

o   o   o   o

The Origin and Design of Our Representative Government

If you review Thomas Paine's original vision on the design of representative government **"described"** in *Common Sense*, those elected to Congress are chartered,

> "to solve the problems that arise in society
> that are too large in scope for the "local" citizenry
> to work out or resolve amongst themselves."

That is the official job description of the U.S. Congress in 25-words, plain and simple.

o   o   o   o

Thomas Jefferson was of course the central author of the Declaration of Independence. After serious debate and several revisions, that document which gave birth to our nation was finalized and signed by the Founders in Philadelphia on July 4, 1776. Paine and Jefferson knew each other. They were revolutionary colleagues. If you take the time to review both documents you will find they share many themes and a common vision.

In *Common Sense,* Thomas Paine presented the American colonists with his vision of how an entirely new society could start and grow into a self-governing entity. He presented a *vision* to the colonists *of the origin and design of government*. It helped to clarify and lay the very foundation for our representative form of government.

This is very interesting reading. It provides a perspective on the times in which they lived and the actual rationale and concepts from which our American Democracy was born.

From the exact, original text of *Common Sense*:

> In order to gain a clear and just idea of the design and end of government, let us suppose a small number of persons settled on some sequestered part of earth, unconnected with the rest, they will then represent the first peopling of any country, or of the world. In this state of natural liberty, society will be their first thought. A thousand motives will excite then thereto the strength of one man is so unequal to his wants, and his mind unfitted for perpetual solitude, that he is soon obligated to seek assistance and relief of another who in his turn requires the same. Four of five united would be able to raise a tolerable dwelling in the midst of a wilderness, but

one man might labour out the common period of life without accomplishing anything; when he had felled his timber he could not remove it, nor erect it after it was removed; hunger in the mean time would urge him from his work, and every different want call him a deferent way. Disease, nay even misfortune would be death, for though neither might be mortal, yet either would disable him from living, and reduce him to a state in which he might rather be said to perish than to die.

Thus necessity, like a gravitating power, would soon form our newly arrived emigrants into society, the reciprocal blessing of which would supercede, and render the obligations of law and government unnecessary while they remained perfectly just to each other; but as nothing but heaven is impregnable to vice, it will unavoidable happen, that in proportion as they surmount the first difficulties of emigration, which bound them together in a common cause, they will begin to relax in their duty and attachment to each other; and this remissness, will point out the necessity, of establishing some form of government to supply the defect of mortal virtue.

Some convenient tree will afford them a State-House, under the branches of which, the whole colony may assemble to deliberate on public matters. It is more than probable that their first laws will have the title only of Regulations, and be enforced by no other penalty than public disesteem. In this first parliament every man, by natural right will have a seat.

But as the colony increases, the public concerns will increase likewise, and the distance at which the members may de separated, will render it too inconvenient for all of them to meet on every occasion as at first, when their number was small their habitations near, and the public concerns few and trifling. This will point out the convenience of their consenting to leave the legislative part to be managed by a select number chosen from the whole body, who are supposed to have the same concerns at stake which those have who appointed them, and who will act in the same manner as the whole body would act were they present. If the colony continue increasing, it will become necessary to augment the number of the representatives, and that the interest of every of the colony may be attended to, it will be found best to divided the whole into convenient parts, each part sending its proper number; and that the *elected* might never form to themselves an interest separate from the *electors,* prudence will point out the propriety of having elections often; because as the *elected* might by that means return and mix again with the general body of the *electors* in as few months, their fidelity to the public will be secured by the prudent reflexion of not making a rod for themselves. And as this frequent interchange will establish a common interest with every part of the community, they will mutually and naturally support each other, and on this (not on the unmeaning name of king) depends the *strength of government, and the happiness of the governed.*

Here then is the origin and rise of government; namely, a mode rendered necessary by the inability of moral virtue to govern the world; here too is the design and end of government, viz. freedom and security. And however our eyes may be dazzled with snow, or our ears deceived by sound; however prejudice may warp our wills, or interest of reason will say, it is right.

I draw my idea of the form of government from a principle in nature, which no art can overturn, viz. that the more simple any thing is, the less liable is it to be disordered, and the easier repaired when disordered; and with the maxim in view, I offer a few remarks on the so much boasted constitution of England. That it was noble for the dark and slavish times in which it was erected is granted. When the world was over-run with tyranny the least remove therefrom was a glorious rescue. But that it is imperfect, subject to convulsions, and incapable of producing what it seems to promise, is easily demonstrated.

Absolute governments (tho' the disgrace of human nature) have this advantage with them, that they are simple; if the people suffer, they know the head from which their suffering springs, know likewise the remedy, and are not bewildered by a variety of causes and cures. But the constitution of England is so exceedingly complex, that the nation may suffer for years together without being able to discover in which part the fault lies, some will say in one and some in another, and every political physician will advise a different mediecine.

– Thomas Paine

to continue

As you just read, Thomas Paine's vision of the primary function of Representative Government was that the peoples' *selected* representatives are responsible for solving the problems that become too large in scope for the local citizenry and their officials to resolve. I have repeated that baseline requirement <u>many</u> times herein. The representatives of government in a free society such as ours <u>are</u> chosen by the popular vote of the Masses to represent their interests.

The functions of government tend to expand as the population increases and societies' problems become more complex. The elected representatives are <u>expected</u> to identify, debate, and <u>resolve</u> issues and/or problems in order to protect the Common Good of the Masses. What a concept!

And when they don't — it is the People's Right and our solemn Responsibility to call them on it, and to then take prudent corrective actions to Insure, Protect, and Defend — the Common Good.

An American Agenda is a baseline framework with which to initiate those corrective actions. We will start with those requirements and build upon it to make our Vision for a better America a near-term reality.

We the People must do what needs to be done.

For if it is not us, then who?

If it is not to be done now, then when? If ever...

Our Dysfunctional U.S. Congress

Throughout all of human history up to this very day,
the Many have most often been oppressed by the Few.
Intentionally kept down within their own society,
rather than being led to higher ground.

Truly responsible political and public leaders will guide their society, the Masses where they desire to go, leading them on the often difficult path that needs to be traveled in order to progress.

o   o   o   o

From the second paragraph of *Common Sense*,

> *As a long and violent abuse of power, is generally the Means of calling the right of it in question (and in Matters too which might never have been thought of, had not the Sufferers been aggravated into the inquiry),*
>
> *and, as the King of England hath undertaken in his OWN RIGHT, to support the Parliament in what he calls THEIRS,*
>
> *and, as the good people of this country are grievously oppressed by the combination, they have an undoubted privilege to inquire into the pretensions of both, and **equally to reject the usurpation of either.***
>
> *– T. Paine*

Good old Mr. Webster defines *usurp* in the following ways:

1. to take possession of without legal claim.
2. to seize and hold (as office, place, or powers) in possession by force or without claim.
3. to seize or exercise authority or possession wrongfully

The bold and final rejection of the *usurpations* under which the colonists had been suffering became their American Revolution.

We must now reject the forms of *usurpation* under which our society is being made to suffer, thus rightfully engaging in our Second American Revolution.

o   o   o   o

Necessity of this Moment

The majority of the economic and social problem solution presented in An American Agenda will absolutely require legislative <u>action</u> by the U.S. Congress to be implemented (to say nothing about Presidential ownership). Unfortunately the grim fact is that the U.S. Congress and its consistently dysfunctional operation are currently the People's primary problem or road-block to those solutions being implemented. The *good news* is that it is within our electoral power to correct our elected leadership problem by *physically removing* that road-block! This agonizing situation must now be aggressively confronted and resolved as the first priority. And the absolute *necessity* for such a bold confrontation is as certain as the sun rising and setting.

The U.S. Congress is to serve as <u>our</u> national legislative body. It was established by the Founders in order to facilitate the <u>resolution</u> of the public's problems that could not be addressed at the local, county, and state levels. Simply, from the standpoint of the American public the Congress is <u>not</u> doing their job.

Not Been Getting What They Deserve

Consider this:

- In a poll taken in October 200<u>7</u> the Congress' overall public Approval rating had dropped to **11%**.
- Stated another way you would say Congress has an overall public **Dis**approval rate that has risen to **89%**.
- They have a higher Disapproval rating than Bush II, which is one race they should not allow themselves to be ahead in!

I ask you, how long would any of us keep our job with that type of performance rating? Toast!

Until the 2006 off-year election, when only a portion of the disgruntled electorate showed up at the polls and called the Congressional members of their respective states to task, the House and Senate incumbents "enjoyed" a comfortable **90+** percent re-election rate. Those aggravated voters did a great job and set the right example! Further, the Congressional races in many other states were far closer than the incumbents had ever seen.

Those state level votes were in affect our electoral "warning shot" to Congress — the virtual Bunker Hill of our Second American Revolution. It was the needed precursor to what could very well happen to the lot of them in 2008.

Let's face it folks — We the People do not have a lot of options here. In reality — *We* have always had a very viable option under the Constitution to exercise in order to exercise ultimate control the Congress. To vote all of them out! In November of 2008, the American electorate can vote 468 of the 535-Club out of office. Fire them!

I declare that it is time for us to seriously consider that prudent action and to finally deal with our dysfunctional U.S. Congress. I believe that you, I, and our fellow Americans know full well that our national Legislative Branch of government is broken and we must now act to resurrect it.

It is necessary to confront and bring an end to the *Political Party-based Heredity of Congressional Power* passed from one member of an "unauthorized political class" to the next. We will necessarily exercise the Civilly Responsible approach to Congressional Term Limits that has always been available to us.

By joining together and deliberately exercising our citizen's Constitutional Right on a single, momentous day in November of 2008 – We the People positively will transform the American political system for the sake of the Common Good of the Masses. To be clear, We have the Authority, indeed not the Civil Responsibility to replace the current members of Congress for not doing <u>our</u> work.

And in so doing *We* shall send a virtual tsunami of a political shock wave around the world.

The Heart of the Matter

"Politicians neither love nor hate.
Interest, not sentiment, directs them."

Lord Philip Dormer Stanhope Chesterfield,
1694-1774

An Anonymous Definition

How is this for a sarcastic, yet practical description of our two political parties?

> The Democrats like to throw money at problems.
> The Republicans just like to turn their backs and hope that the problems will just go away.

Does that sound about right to you?

Although under Bush II, the Republican Party has taken to throwing the money around so much that they make the Democrats look good!

About Our Two Political Parties

I did determine when initially drafting this book to speak sharply about Congress, business, industry, and any other domestic and foreign entity that is standing between we American citizens and the preservation of our Common Good.

Realistically speaking the actions of Congress and the current President and his side-kick, are solely and deliberately aimed at addressing the desires of those that they really care about serving! And bluntly put, that evidently does not include the vast majority of We the People, as well as and most small and large businesses in America either. They are equal opportunity abusers!

The Republican Party

Overall, the **Republican Party** is just taking care of business. That is big business and the politically powerful that are having a virtual field day under the Bush II and Cheney tag team. The dreadful combination of the Bush II *"oil-first"* mentality and Cheney's mantra of *"anything that is good for the Military Industrial Complex is just fine"* (especially an optional Iraq war) — has shaped our foreign and domestic policy with devastating results. Any question about that analysis?

And if left unchallenged much longer the Republicans and their unelected handlers will succeed in driving the National System and our American way of life directly into the ground along with what is left of the Middle Class.

The actual entities that drive the Republican Party are doing whatever they like utilizing the Law of the Jungle – "the survival of the fittest" – in exercising their blatant abuse of power and catering specifically to a precious few BIG business entities. Several of those industries and other Special Interest entities were reviewed in An American Agenda. Many of the items on the Grievance List clearly document their long term successes in maintaining that Special Interest driven status quo within the National System.

The only real question is how much _more damage_ they will "accomplish" on both the domestic and foreign stages before the 2008 election relieves us of their burden. Because the Democrats certainly do not look like they will resolve anything of importance prior to that date, do they? Next...

The Democratic Party

On the other hand there is the **Democratic Party** that continues marching on in functional disarray. The Democrats so desperately need a viable political agenda — a reasonable people-oriented, national agenda that will once again prove them to be the *"party of the people"* – of the regular American citizen. Our nation needs the Democrats to "actually function" as the other national party. It is critical to the proper functioning of our representative form of government. It is a baseline requirement of our Democracy and a question of practical political balance!

> To be more direct, the Democratic members of Congress and their party's leadership need to remember that they (and the Republicans) were sworn in to work for American citizens first and foremost. For fruitless political reasons they seem to have lost track of the very people, who's Common Good it is their responsibility to protect.

> A most glaring example of that is the IO — Illegal Occupant immigration issue. All else could very well succeed or fail based upon an issue that should be a political no-brainer for both parties.

> The Democratic leadership must step back and re-think the entire issue of the "pathway to citizenship" for millions of IOs from all

over the world that have invaded our country (since what was supposed to be the last and supposedly final Amnesty Act for IOs back in 1986). The American public demands an end to the immigration chaos. The Democrats need to grow some guts and serve 'us' – the American citizens. The newly elected batch of Democrats will have a clearer perspective on the issue!

If the Dems could decide to stand and do the hard work that needs to be done on that *bone-marrow* national issue, the voters might once again begin to consider the Democrats as the party of the regular American citizen – the Masses.

Overall, the Democratic Party can't seem to grasp what needs to be done to practically address the People's problems. They struggle to figure out how to explain to the American public the rational for the types of changes that are needed to Preserve the Common Good, let alone conceive of them in the first place.

Frankly, the entire Democratic Party needs to read this book. They need to study An American Agenda in particular and seriously consider embracing all of it as their own. Be assured that in so stating, I am not advocating the Democratic Party over the Republican Party. Both parties are currently failing us. Both need to read CS2 and start acting for the Common Good, instead of the Special Interest.

If we look at America as one huge business enterprise as Ross Perot once offered, the Republican Party and those that pull their puppet strings 'generally' represent Management. The Democratic Party and those that push their buttons, along with the party's historical concerns for the fate of the average person thus represent Labor.

> My personal opinion is that in too many cases over the last decade or so the nation has functionally had a Republican and semi-Republican Party! Consider that grim political reality for a few moments. It demonstrates the growing power of the Special Interests in driving both parties and the U.S. Congress.

o   o   o   o

The Abuse of Un-Challenged Power

Historically and to this very day, whenever power is left to its own devices and without a viable, public-driven, and functioning popular government — societies have always degenerated into a controlled chaos that continues to benefit fewer and fewer, with grinding conditions for the Multitudes. Consider these — the Few vs. the Many – Power vs. Powerless – Haves vs. Have-nots.

That is not a Liberal analysis, but it is that of a terribly concerned American citizen. And I know that I do not stand here alone.

o   o   o   o

Remember that growing out of the Great Depression the programs under the New Deal were only devised and enacted in unavoidable reaction to economic and social crisis. It was a politically critical moment in time when hard and publicly practical solutions to vital public problems (in the National System) **had** to be developed **and enacted rapidly.** It was effective, but reactionary national legislation and leadership on the serious issues of the day.

It is now some 70 years later and Congress still avoids pro-active legislation to address serious public problems (the Grievance List) and has a bad record in reactionary situations, i.e. Katrina.

Also, it was the Democratic Party that built those required New Deal public-oriented programs, such as the Social Security System that were enacted against the best efforts of the Republican Party and business to prevent it. Think of what it would be like if Social Security had not existed over the past several decades. Not a good thought.

Most thankfully, our *U.S. Constitution* gives *We the People* the Right and Authority to control both the Republican Party's under-lying, self-serving mentality that the Few know what is best for the Many – and the Democrat's foolish philosophy that people can just be given to without stipulating the level of responsibility and accountability expected in return. Again, there must be a practical balance and it evidently is our job to insure it.

Their Traditionally Vicious Cycle

As previously mentioned, some years ago the following perspective on national politics was offered to me and I found it interesting. How does it sound to you?

Historically, the Republicans have come into office, the White House in particular, and after some years in power have succeeded in "screwing up" the economy! The American public loses patience and so hands the national leadership over to the Democrats. The Democrats take over, confront the mess, and somehow get things turned around. The People – <u>us</u> – with an all too short political memory see that business is going well and say hey, we should put the Republicans in charge because they are very pro-business and will only make things better. The Republicans are then placed back in power and once again mess things up — and the cycle continues.

Sarcastic — absolutely, but far closer to true than false.

In 2008, the Democratic Party unless they shoot themselves in both feet will once again assume control of the White House and a capture clear majority in both houses of Congress. They will also inherit the historic mess that Bush/Cheney and their handlers have willingly and irresponsibly created — and profited from.

The Democrats will once again be challenged to clean-up a Republican generated mess on both the domestic and foreign fronts. And these very possibly are the biggest ones yet.

o   o   o   o

For a Viable Third Party – It is Too Late

My observation is that while a true Third political party in American politics may have once had a chance to develop and grow into a viable force — that time has passed and the door is closed forever.

Of course, if we simply get our floundering 2-Party system functioning properly and the nation embraces a Common National Vision, we do not need another party! Further, We just cannot afford to waste the many years it would reasonably take to build one. There is far too much time-critical work to <u>address</u> <u>now</u>.

And just <u>why</u> is it that a Third party is no longer viable? The primary reason is that the entrenched leadership and members of <u>both</u> parties have to the greatest extent possible 'rigged' things up for their easy reelection. They have configured the 435 U.S. Congressional Districts to discourage, if not blatantly prevent the intrusion of any Third-party candidates.

The self-serving, politically devious craftsmanship of the Congressional Re-Districting is one of the <u>only</u> things that both parties have collaborated and worked together on for the mutual preservation of their precious jobs!

Further, the 2-Parties and their handlers have successfully collaborated in shifting forward more and more of the Presidential primaries into a virtual log jam in January and February 2008. Why you ask? While in some cases it may be a given state scheming to obtain a bit more political clout in the Primary Season. Rather, it is because it makes it even harder for non-mainstream, alternative candidates – even those within their own parties to have much of a chance against the better financed and "party acceptable" candidates.

This intentional and loosely-coordinated early Primary Elections traffic jam could very well determine the nominees for president and vice-president of both parties before the end of March. And all efforts will be made for them to be Party-acceptable nominees, only. This is not a good development for Democracy, but it is seen as essential to the Few in preserving the status quo of political power within the National System.

<u>"Late Night" and Fast Legislators</u>

The mostly quiet Congressional Redistricting actions (we won't talk about Texas) point out that when the Congress is motivated to do something tedious and that requires real negotiation they can work together and get it done.

On the night of Sunday March 20, 2005 another and a most sad (if not pathetic) example of their legislative "abilities" occurred when, under the direction of a purely politically motivated White House and Republican Party, *some* the members of Congress flew back to DC to briefly debate, pass, and enact "late night" legislation.

As documented on a Congressional legislation website regarding Bill S686:

> This bill, which both the Senate and House passed in an emergency Palm Sunday session, gave federal courts jurisdiction in the matter and required a federal judge, upon the family's request, to launch a new inquiry into the legal and medical questions surrounding Terri Schiavo's condition, which was the result of a severe loss of oxygen to her brain when her heart temporarily stopped on February 25, 1990. The debate and final vote largely fell along the lines of the right-to-die and pro-life movements. The Senate version of the bill was passed on the afternoon of Sunday, March 20 (by voice vote — as a result, there is not an official record of this Senate action). The House followed suit just after midnight on Monday, March 21. The bill was immediately rushed to the White House, **where President Bush signed it at 1:11 a.m.**

The U.S. House of Representatives Vote

Party	Yes	No	Not Voting
Democratic	47	53	102
Independent	0	0	1
Republican	156	5	71
	203	**58**	**174**

This was a politically arrogant and gross interference in one (1) family's private struggle over the death of a loved one. And the *"decider"* dramatically flew in from Texas on Palm Sunday just to be there to sign "his" legislation into law.

A pathetically classic example of *Minority public* representation and leadership was delivered! The Bush II White House and some in Congress were quick to do what at least an 80% majority of the American public deemed inappropriate. It is really too bad they will not even consider performing a similarly aggressive action and intervene *to protect* two (2) wrongfully prosecuted and imprisoned Border Guards?

While that overt, after midnight operation did demonstrate beyond a shadow of a doubt how fast Congress can get something "different" done, it was far from their finest hour. It was blatant and *sinful*, political pandering to certain narrow-minded Special Interests and did not sit well with many of the Silent Majority. To their credit enough of the electorate reacted to that personally intrusive legislative action at the polls in November 2006 and it helped cost a few of those members re-election. Good going America!

o   o   o   o

To continue

Only Possible Opening

Today, in 2008 — the only practical **"Third Ticket"** option would be for a purely Independent President and Vice President political team to step forward and offer a Common Good based, aggressive Change platform (like an American agenda) and the strong political leadership that the nation now can only dream of being able to vote for.

Clearly such a political team must present themselves as providing only that brand of political leadership in order to be considered at all viable in 2008. Absolutely not as a Third party in the making for it would only muddy the water and make it easier for the 2-Parties to exploit and confuse the issue.

Realistically and sadly that is about all there is to say about our Third Party option. *We* must aggressively work the 2008 Presidential and Congressional campaigns across the country to take Control of the 2-Parties we now have and see to it that they know they must start working for us. Or else, we will decisively deal with them in November...

o   o   o   o

I will add that I do believe there could very well be an opening for such an Independent Presidential team in 2008. First, this could be the downside of the 2-Parties compressing the Primary Season and identifying their nominees so early in 2008. It will leave time for an alternative to step forward and catch on with the "disturbed" electorate.

Secondly, as most of the debates have clearly demonstrated, neither party has a platform! At least not one aimed at fixing the issues on the Grievance List and others that the public is concerned about. They only seem to talk about Iraq, Bush II, and their non-solutions to real problems like Health Care for all Americans, and Immigration Control.

The door could be opened. An American Agenda is waiting to be claimed...

o   o   o   o

Profiling the *Congressional System*

Yes, let us 'profile' the rarely discussed *"Congressional System"* – the American 2-Party Political Machine.

Has a non-All White Male Congress Mattered – Not Enough

Over the last 50 years, while the profile of the USC has changed, the results really have not. The intellectual promise was — that with the appearance of women and various minorities, that Congress would become more in sync with the needs of the People — more functionally in tune with the average working American. The expectation was that a 'blended' Congress would be more interested in fixing societies' problems and dealing with the issues faced by the Masses.

That much anticipated and hoped for positive impact of women and minorities in Congress since the 60's has not dramatically materialized —

just take another look at the Grievance List. How would you call it?

There have been a "few" signs of progress, with the Civil Rights Acts of the 60's and under President Clinton's much Republican-harassed two terms. However, considering our current state of national affairs I believe it is fair to conclude that the non-white, male members have more or less only gotten with the program and *"blended into"* the Congressional System rather than causing it to be re-tooled.

While many of them may have sincerely run for office and entered the Congress to make a difference and change the "way things work in Washington" — instead they all too quickly just became part of that Power-hungry closed community inside the DC beltway.

And objectively evaluating our Grievance List of long-standing problems which <u>still</u> plague much of our society, those Congressional members not in the American-White male group have simply learned how to get into the game, play the game, maintain their position in the game, and be happy multi-term members of the **535-Club** — for as long as possible. The free-will submission to the dictates of the Congressional System applies to every member of <u>both</u> parties, including your <u>and</u> my state's favorite sons and daughters! Ask not what they <u>have</u> done for you — ask what they have <u>not</u> done for all of us.

More than a **Color Blind** "Congressional System"

That "realistic" analysis points out the Plain Truth that the all-powerful "Congressional System" is truly color, gender, ethnic, and otherwise blind when it looks at the 535-Club members. To the Congressional System all members of the U.S. Congress look the same!

Consider that <u>your</u> Representative or Senator is one of 535 people chosen to be in charge of national legislation concerning the lives and livelihood of the other 299,999,465 citizens. Those are the numbers.
And they <u>each</u> have an average of 63 lobbyists running after them all the time offering goodies – like holding legal, campaign fundraisers for them! And get this. The first fundraisers that are held after a given election are held to help the winners raise money to pay-off any left-over campaign debts! Isn't it just wonderful?

Further, he or she is treated like near royalty by staff, and most of the public and the press! They are a *virtual rock star* in a suit or pants suit! Consider that when any person has all that for a couple years they easily can <u>and</u> <u>do</u> get real attached to the <u>position</u>! And just what does a person need to do to keep "their position" they ask? The response is – play the game exactly the way the senior members of the 535-Club tell you to play it. Maintain the status quo and do not rock the boat!

The American *Congressional System* is currently a well-funded, self-perpetuating 2-Party political machine running under the skillful mentoring of the dug-in senior membership of the 535-Club and its Special Interest handlers.

And that America is what is wrong with the National System. It is why the Congress does not fix or even seem to care about solving our long-standing problems. Their handlers do not want them to…

o o o o

Fortunately, my equally aggravated fellow Americans – as previously mentioned We can Change all that during the upcoming Presidential and Congressional campaigns. Together, we possess the full authority to reset-to-zero the terms of 468 of 535 of those Congressional members on Election Day 2008.

I strongly suggest that We need to declare Common Agreement on An American Agenda and at the same time need to put the absolute fear of an enraged electorate into the members of the U.S. Congress. To demand that they begin to initiate *Midnight Legislation* to take action with appropriate parts of the Agenda prior to the November 2008 Election Day. To somehow prove they are worth keeping their jobs, or else to expect to be replaced on our nation's historic voting day. I personally believe that no matter what they might try to do, they all need to be retired in 2008.

And remember that the U.S. Constitution is our fearless leader and guardian.

My Sense of the Public's Weariness

Over the last *30 years or so*, I have had the absolute pleasure of talking with literally thousands of other "regular" people about politics and various issues that we confront in our daily lives. In fact, talking with other people most of whom are total strangers about political and religious issues, I consider as my primary hobby! And since I will only discuss "politics and religion" with people, not argue about them, I have enjoyed many interesting conversations regarding their personal opinions, concerns, and dreams.

Over the last *15 years* I have observed that the average American has become more informed and conversational on political issues. I believe that demonstrates the fact that they are more concerned about the way things are going and what it means for their own future and that of their children and grandchildren.

And over these last *7-plus years* all of the negative conditions that continued to grow around us during the 1990s have accelerated with some reaching critical mass (and that does not include the Bush IIs optional and failed Iraq War).

Objectively this negative "national condition" must be credited to the combined 535-Club memberships of the U.S. House of Representatives and U.S. Senate — credited to both parties that are ignoring our common problems and their Constitutional responsibilities to address and fairly resolve them. Credited to our alleged national leadership that is acting more and more like spoiled children arguing over who will get their way and not accepting responsibility for their freewill, legislative actions and more so their consistent in-action.

It is all too easy to observe that the Masses of us have grown tired of Congressional inaction, and are disgusted with the current direction of America and with the growing dysfunctional nature of our National System. In both the domestic or foreign arenas our valid concerns have only grown more intense over these last years, as we have stood helpless and observed conditions truly worsen.

My sense is that the American citizen is more than ready for realistic, honest, and problem-solving oriented national leadership. I observe, that is where we stand as we approach the crucial 2008 national campaign and the pending Election Day.

A Tale of Two Georges

Let's face it. Even though we have now suffered through three (3) more "do little or nothing" Congresses, the truth is that things have been made far worse over those 6-plus years because of the current occupant of the White House and his very involved side-kick!

While I acknowledge that such comments about a sitting President do bother some Americans, frankly their number has steadily decreased year-by-year. As the old saying goes, "if the shoe fits wear it." And this ain't a glass slipper!

Bush II rode in proclaiming he was the "unite-r". However he has proven himself to be anything but that. His actual job performance has clearly proven him to be the ultimate "divide-r" and "ignore-r" — and his overall job failure applies in both the foreign and domestic arenas.

It could be viewed as a little ironic that as we approach our *Second American Revolution*, we find ourselves under a President *George* Bush II as opposed to a King *George* III. Today's George II is commonly known to have little interest in watching the news on television or reading newspapers (you know something close to reality) that only contributes to keeping him isolated, out of touch with the Masses, and safe in his own protected, self-serving, imaginary little world – just like King George III.

> For example, Bush II on his second or third trip to New Orleans after the Hurricane Katrina disaster was provided with a special DVD prepared by his staff that was comprised of news footage from network and cable news programs. This was done so he could have some idea as to what had happened there. Analyze that for yourself.

Sorry if you find this all a bit harsh, but there it is. Again, some consider criticizing the President in bad taste, but the truth is the truth, and this is one president that has truly earned it and has the public job performance disapproval rating to prove it!

I will share with you and it is disappointing for me to say, but Bush II is the first president in my lifetime that I am personally embarrassed to have as my president. Some had their problems with Nixon, Carter, Reagan, Bush I, and Clinton, but to me and many others Bush II easily claims that sad prize.

Clearly, Bush II took an absolutely grand opportunity to unite the world in a Common Cause after the tragedy of 9-11, but for the sake of Special Interest driven politics (oil), he single-handedly drove America's international standing (and federal budget) right into the ground. Of his own freewill he deliberately "decider-ed" to cater to the Few at the expense of the Many! Like I mentioned before in regard to party politics, Bush II is delivering the ultimate example of a Republican taking care of business – Big business. The thing that he may be grimly credited for in years to come is making things so bad – pushing the pendulum so far to the wrong side — that it caused American society to rebel and take the actions required to again Control their own government.

Grimly folks, there are many times we could close our eyes and sense what it was like to be a "peasant" in jolly old England! Of course, English Kings were expected to be *out of touch* with the peasants, while "real" American Presidents are supposed to be *in touch* with the concerns of American citizens — and to possess the personal and political determination to do something about the People's problems. Of course how could we expect compassion and concern for the average citizen, from a man that does not even offer his own wife his arm when they are walking down the stairs of Air Force One?

The privileged Few with financial and/or political power are currently having-their-way with the National System and demonstrating no practical regard for the negative "trickle down" consequences it places upon a growing percentage of American citizens. Further, they are not even demonstrating prudent regard for the Environment that their own families must rely upon in the future. Personal and corporate short-term gain is clearly more important than the public's universal, long-term, public pain – the Few over the Many.

o   o   o   o

To be clear, I am not for one moment saying that Bush II is solely responsible for the conditions we now face (except for Iraq) because he absolutely is not. However (comma!) his excessively Special Interest biased policies, his blatant political arrogance, his refusal to acknowledge his own policy blunders, and his practical disregard for the welfare of average citizens — combined with both parties in Congress more interested in fighting over everything rather than solving anything — have all combined to create the "national condition" that we Americans find ourselves struggling against today. In the last 6-plus years their combined efforts have worked to accelerate this decline. And the members of Congress expect to get re-elected?

If George Washington and the first Congress of the United States of America were to appear today and review the conduct and performance of our current president and Congress, they would be disgusted with them all! It is now October of 2007 and the job performance disapproval rating of the entire Congress is higher than that of Bush II. We the People are being subjected to a real time performance of *Worse and Worser!*"

o   o   o   o

Placing the Blame

In the final analysis, We must hold the 535 members of Congress far more accountable than our current and past presidents for our long-standing national problems. Referencing the reasoning of Thomas Paine in *Common Sense* as he first described the concept and workings of Representative government — it is the direct responsibility of the popularly elected members of Congress to solve the problems that cannot be practically addressed and resolved at the local and state levels — to dutifully represent the People that sent them there! As Paine wrote,

> *This will point out the convenience of their consenting to leave the legislative part to be managed by a select number chosen from the whole body, who are supposed to have the same concerns at stake which those have who appointed them, and who will act in the same manner as the <u>whole body</u> would act were they present.*

While our nation's presidents do come and go every four to eight years, the Senators and Representatives have come to build careers under that magnificent Capitol Dome. Career politicians are not what the Founders had in mind.

As previously stated, both parties to the greatest extent possible have redrawn the 435 U.S. Congressional Districts through blatant, partisan redistricting to all but assure their re-elections. As I heard one news commentator put it, "the congressmen are picking their voters rather than the voters picking their congressmen."

Incumbents increasingly run campaigns that are well-funded by key industry and other Special Interest dollars, aimed at *crushing* their opponent in the other party — and may well have done the same thing in a primary race against someone of their own party.

I clearly remember watching the evening news some decades ago, as a Congressmen stood up on the floor of the Congress and very <u>indignantly</u> stated that he and no one else he knew in Congress was swayed in their legislative decisions by lobbyists' influence! Today, how many would dare (could honestly) stand-up and make that statement?

The blatant and direct impact of big business and other self-interested lobbies is brutally obvious to us all now and it has been far worse during the Bush II years. Again, the ratio that is currently getting kicked around is that there are on average 63 lobbyists for each member of Congress that equates as 63 x 535 = 33,705! It would get pretty crowded under that lovely Dome, if the Congress was ever there! They only managed to have **97 days** in session in a recent Congressional year.

It is hard to realize how totally dysfunctional to the Common Good the Congress has factually become. For the Many of us to prudently confront those perpetuating the current and growing mess on both the domestic and foreign fronts, it will demand far *more common sense and collective commitment* than was required 230 years ago to birth our nation!

Therefore, We the People must now join together and let our alleged national leadership know of our Common Disgust with their counter-productive performance — that our electoral patience has been fully violated. That, *We the People*, are mad as hell and we are not going to take it anymore...

o   o   o   o

Calling Our Leadership to Task

Again and again and again — it is the responsibility of the members of the U.S. Congress to confront and resolve the problems of the American people that generally cannot be resolved at the local, county, and state levels. Unfortunately and obviously, and in too many areas of importance to the Common Good, the Congress is simply not getting the job done over the last few *decades*, and both of our political parties share equally in the blame.

It is more and more obvious to the American public (and to the world) that the Congress is far more concerned with serving the wants and desires of Special Interest entities and doing whatever it takes to hold unto their precious positions of public power — as opposed to fulfilling their proper responsibilities in addressing the needs of the American public and our Common Good.

It is for the U.S. Congress to oversee the Big Picture of American society and the National System for the People's benefit — not to the benefit of the Special Interested Few which is clearly their preference. And only to make things worse, as each election cycle passes the politicians are also becoming even more interested and focused upon their political party winning – rather than the average American.

And as I have shared with some of my fellow Baby Boomers, the conditions in of America today are simply not the way it was supposed to be when we grew up. The domestic chaos is almost unimaginable to the majority of us.

From a purely objective perspective the U.S. Congress has become more of a problem management and perpetuation entity, rather than the public problem-solving <u>force</u> it was conceived, designed, and so needs to be. This is not the way things are supposed to work in American Democracy!

o   o   o   o

At the bottom line, it is most important for We the Electorate to remember, that our elected officials – national to local — <u>only</u> continue to serve as a result of <u>our</u> votes cast to <u>re-elect</u> them.

We the People, do bear part of the responsibility for the on-going problems and it is time for us to claim our obligation to each other and take corrective action. Yes, We <u>are</u> partly to blame by letting them continue to have the opportunity to do a bad job!

Therefore, We must claim our Constitutional Right and the Obligation to each other to replace our elected politicians (at all levels of government) that of their <u>own</u> <u>free</u> <u>will</u> — choose <u>not</u> to attend to our Common Good.

And <u>that</u> my fellow Americans, is <u>our</u> job as laid down by the Founders!

Now is the time. This is our moment in time, for We the People to be about the nation's work, and to define <u>and</u> control our nation's future.

o   o   o   o

"Staging the Second American Revolution"

"Discharging the Full House and a Third of the Senate"

"Putting the Fear of the Electorate into the Current and Future Members of Congress"

o   o   o   o

All things considered, the U.S. Congress must be confronted in the most politically aggressive, yet fully appropriate manner that *We the People* possess under the provisions of our U.S. Constitution.

My absolute intent now is to present a direct challenge to my fellow Americans — a hard challenge to the American electorate that I have already not so casually alluded to several times in CS2.

Thomas Paine challenged his fellow colonists to reject the abusive control of the King and his ministers exercised over their lives and destiny.

I now, in the name of *Common Sense* do challenge my fellow Americans to reject the abusive control that U.S. Congress and our the Special Interest driven political parties are now exercising over our very lives and destiny.

I once and for all question the prudent rationale and functional practicality of <u>our</u> re-electing in 2008 and thus extending the public employment of 468 of the 535 members of Congress that are collectively performing our nation such a gross disservice.

The American colonists had to decide to take up arms and fight a bloody war to meet their challenge. We American citizens thanks to the Constitution that some of our national ancestors died to provide us, only need to decide to cast a solemn vote to meet our challenge.

o   o   o   o

The growing inability of our elected National leadership, regardless of party affiliation, to resolve or even to seriously attempt to address our very visible national issues and problems brings into absolute question why We the People, their employers should allow any of them to continue to do such an "inadequate" job for the nation. For us to allow our failed leadership to continue to walk the halls under the Great U.S. Capitol Dome, beyond their current term is without question lacking all practical logic and *common sense*.

Further, We the People <u>cannot</u> afford nor can we allow continued Congressional inaction. Especially, when the remaining months leading up to what will be a historic November day are wrapped around a presidential campaign. A period of time during which as history documents they accomplish even less — if that is even possible. We must aggressively disturb that traditional *legislative dead zone.*

Beginning in the early summer of 2006 I have been talking with people on the idea of the American electorate going to the polls and voting out every incumbent in the U.S. Congress regardless of party or platform. As stated before I talk with many people most of whom I have never met, and the response to the concept has been overwhelmingly positive. Needless to say it generated a little conversation at times, but at least 8 out of 10 would seriously consider such action. Not surprisingly more than a few were already planning to ride the anti-incumbent bandwagon and the near historic results of the November 2006 Off-year Congressional Election demonstrated the growing displeasure among the electorate — more on that encouraging event shortly.

The virtual pump of dramatic public change has been primed and is in readiness for November 2008.

Public Concerns Regarding an 87% Congressional Replacement

It goes without saying that such a voting action on our part would be a momentously radical, yet very controlled change in America's elected national level office-holders. <u>However</u>, it should <u>not</u> be viewed as a dangerous or reckless political action on our part. The peace and security in the nation would <u>not</u> be at risk. Although, the *chicken-little's* will be out in maximum force to announce and to declare that the sky will fall should we take such reckless action.

Just remember what the man said, *"The only thing we have to fear — is fear itself".*

To rephrase, consider for a moment that should this decisive Political Action exercise catch on with the voters during the remainder of the 2008 campaign, which after all is the absolute goal here, the suddenly *at risk* Congressional incumbents in the 535-Club will be crying that the sky will fall should they all be removed from their offices. Such rhetoric in poker terms is called, "bluffing." And We the People will be calling their bluff!

o   o   o   o

Here we will review some concerns and perspectives on Congressional Replacement from my conversations with some of our fellow Americans:

- First of all, be comforted that the losing incumbent's accumulated body of knowledge would <u>only</u> be one step removed from office, since the former Congressional members would still be available to the new members of Congress. Importantly, most of the Congressional Staff of former members with their own accumulated body of knowledge on how Congress functions would also be looking for work. And frankly, they do most of the real work on the Hill anyway. Many would not even bulk at changing parties if they were still serving their state <u>and</u> had a job!

  The newly "retired" incumbents would still be responsible to the residents of their respective states <u>and the nation</u> for the smooth and functional turnover to the new officeholders. As is standard procedure anytime a Congressional member leaves office, there is a formal transition and follow-up as needed. And the citizens of each state will <u>expect</u> nothing less.

- In one entertaining "public poll" (a few years ago) regarding Congressional job performance, people generally only had a 60% or so approval rating of <u>their</u> state's Senators and Representatives, but no more than 30% approval of everybody else's. You know — my state's people are OK but the other 49 are a problem! Not at all surprising.

  That false, yet common appraisal combined with the well-orchestrated Congressional Re-districting makes it more difficult all the time for a challenger to defeat any incumbent. "Lifers" in Congress is not what the Founders had in mind. And in objectively judging these long-term incumbents' dysfunctional job performance validates – it is absolutely not what the National System and our society needs either. Period!

- This highly dysfunctional situation must be seriously considered by <u>each</u> <u>voter</u> (yes, that means <u>you</u>) between now and what will be a nation defining 2008 Election Day. There are definitely those that will say that their Congress men and/or women take care of them and get their state funding and other types of goodies, and they will be very concerned about losing some of that leverage. A selfish, yet practical concern for certain.

  Frankly, this is one place where <u>each</u> of us will need to consider the Big Picture and think beyond our local and state boundaries. This goes directly to defining our national character and having a Common Vision as a Democratic society. Be encouraged that the newly elected members will be <u>very</u> interested in taking care of their state's concerns and people issues. Again, that is supposed to be their job.

> And just imagine how much more attentive to the Common Good of the <u>people</u> of their state, as well as the <u>nation</u>, the new members of Congress would be — IF — We the People execute what may well become known as the "November Surprise".

- Another "*hardball*" issue with people to be hit head-on is Party preference or allegiance. To be perfectly clear, we are talking about Democrats <u>voting out Democrats</u> and Republicans <u>voting out Republicans</u>. There are also a few Independent members to be dealt with as well.

This will be <u>extremely</u> difficult for some people to deal with and there will surely be those that will not be able to do it. And that is their absolute right as an American citizen. All that I can offer the discussion is the Plain Truth that while individually there are some good people in Congress (and you may <u>really</u> like your man or your woman in that office) the bone-marrow reality is that collectively they are <u>not</u> getting our job done.

Factually and grimly, there are real people in <u>every one</u> of the 435 Congressional Districts that are actually suffering from their failure to be effective national leaders.

Further, WE MUST ACKNOWLEDGE THE UNDENIABLE TRUTH — <u>scores</u> of our fellow Americans are literally dying needlessly <u>everyday</u> due to their collective legislative and public leadership incompetence. And I am not talking about our brave troops being lost in Afghanistan, Iraq, and elsewhere around the world.

And when is the last time we saw or heard of <u>any</u> member of Congress standing up and declaring that a given critical problem could be resolved with the proposal they were presenting. And would <u>not</u> sit down or be quiet until it became a national media event and finally saw to it that the required legislation was fully enacted. I am only talking about an issue of true importance to the Common Good of the American public. Don't strain yourself. It is always difficult to recall something that has never happened!

- More than one person in my conversations commented that they believed most members of Congress would pull whatever dirty trick necessary to get re-elected. And they did not always put it that nicely either!

- More and more in recent years Congressional elections (House and Senate — both parties) are pretty well <u>rigged</u> to reelect the incumbent. That is why Term Limits legislation never sees the light of day. We have the authority to reset 468 Congressional terms to *zero* on Election Day!

  The majority of the Congress (87%) would be replaced with an assorted group of people, most of whom never really expected to be elected — given the usual 90-plus percent incumbent reelection rate in Congressional races. The new members of Congress would be thrilled to have the position, the opportunity to serve, <u>and</u> would be anxious to please We the People that acted together to put them there!

  Party loyalty would suddenly take second place to People loyalty. It will be a new beginning.

- This new crop of truly 'elected' American men and women in Congress would absolutely have received a "mandate from the people." Not a false public mandate as sometimes claimed by the political parties after securing a resounding 51% of the vote with at best a 60% voter turnout. So let's see now — 51% of a 60 % voter turnout would seem to equal a 'mandate' from maybe 30% of the electorate. The other 70% of us needs to wake up!

- Consider that the new 435 House members will know to immediately be about the People's work — or else — in 24 more months (or 48 if the Amendment is passed) We the People will install yet another new batch of 435 Representatives in the House. Believe me they will us loud and clear!

  Further, the new House members will not need to focus on raising millions for their re-election race, because if they do a <u>good</u> job over the next 24 or 48 months We the People will reward them with easy re-election. However, if they do <u>not</u> get the message and do not aggressively attend to the People's issues, all the money they could raise will not keep them from the same electoral defeat as their predecessors in 2008.

  The new 435 members of the U.S. House of Representatives will technically be on 24 to 48 month job probation. Any questions?

- Consider also that the <u>next</u> batch of 34 of incumbent Senators up for re-election in 2010 may just as well plan on retiring should the American Electorate claim this Congressional housekeeping task as their own in 2008. Note that the Senate is structured such that one third of the 100 members are up for re-election every two (2) years (i.e., 33 in 2008, 34 in 2010, 33 in 2012, and so on.

They could go ahead and draft their 2010 farewell speech in 2008. And the remaining 33 can make similar plans for 2012. Three votes and they are all out! It will be a clean sweep!

- Another sticking factor in process is the single-issue voter. Prime examples are religion, the abortion issue, gun control, gay and lesbian rights to name a few of the hot button issues that too many politicians blatantly hype just for the sake of fundraising and getting reelected.

It must be said that every American voter has the right to personally and privately decide why he or she chooses to vote for or against a given candidate. My challenge to those Americans of deep conviction on a given issue is to please step back and look this one time beyond that single issue and consider the Common Good of the other 299,999,999 American citizens and our Common Interests.

Therefore, when you privately go into that voting booth and are casting your vote (firing your single shot in the Second American Revolution) with no one but yourself to answer to – consider the overall state of the nation and collective failure of our current national leadership. And then do what you believe is the right thing.

o   o   o   o

The bottom line of the current Congressional condition is that we have men and women in national leadership that provide lip service on major issues when they are fundraising and getting votes while running for office, but are doing nothing about them in between. This can only be described as irresponsible, manipulative, and *dysfunctional leadership* — which equates to *non-leadership* and in the end is literally *negative leadership*! They are functionally leading American society in the wrong direction!

The major reason that problems continue without resolution is simply because Congress can get reelected without addressing them. Frankly, we're mostly taken for granted on Election Day and then ignored.

Together, We have it within our United Voting Power to give social and economic change in the name of the Common Good a real opportunity! And the results will be astounding! It will be the Second Coming of American Democracy...

o   o   o   o

Consider This

What if we were talking about a business or an industry? To survive in the marketplace, a given business must be run in such a manner that it can provide the buying public with desirable goods and/or services or their business will fail being replaced by those that can.

Further, publicly held corporations must provide their stockholder's with dividends or the existing management will be replaced with those that can produce those returns. Otherwise the business will falter and/or be consumed by other business interests.

The subtitle of this book, *Our Second and Final American Revolution*, was not chosen to be cute or to be a catchy phrase. We not only have the Power, but we have a solemn Obligation to ourselves, our children, and theirs to call our elected leadership to task for the inadequate job they have done for us over these last few decades. We must determine to exercise practical corrective action. And We must do it now! We do not have 2, let alone 4 more years to waste.

Consider that our national ancestors, the American colonists of the 1770s had an absolute monarch controlling their daily life and destiny. It is now 2008 and we have a government of elected federal national politicians that we are currently under the control of, but that We have the Constitutional Right to have control over — but only if We act! And if We come together and agree to it, We can replace all of them with people that will be far more concerned about our Common Good.

As they say, like it or not it is our watch and we are responsible for straightening out and wrestling control over the National System from those that are so selfishly controlling it today! It is our decision and freewill choice to make. We can either permit this growing chaos to worsen or we will elect national leadership that will respond to our concerns and heed our direct suggestions for prudent, practical, and fair Change.

o   o   o   o

I do sincerely wish, as I am sure most Americans are, that this major change in our leadership and high percentage replacement of the U.S. Congress membership were not a practical necessity, but reality is reality. Once we have boldly,

- clarified our expectations,
- shown that We are their *managers* and not their *pawns*,
- clarified that they are civil servants not Kings and Queens,
- <u>declared</u> that the misuse political power of any business, industry, and the politically influential will not be tolerated —

our newly elected Congress will surely be about the People's business and be dedicated to preserving the Common Good.

o   o   o   o

With the accomplishment of such a historic, non-violent replacement of our national leadership, another and hopefully the last era of irresponsible political influence in American politics will be dealt with, and American Democracy will truly be born again!

When, We the People stand and lead, our leaders <u>will</u> <u>surely</u> <u>follow</u>.

America is for Americans

We Will Control Our National Destiny — Only If We Act!

With the chaotic combination of the nation being in another Republican Presidential cycle, the hard realities of the global economy, and the current version of the New World Order running amok — it seems America cannot really depend on the either Party or the collective resources of the U.S. Congress to figure out what to do to pull us out of the economic Recession We are in as 2008 begins.

And that is to say nothing about the serious issues on the public's Grievance List presented earlier. It is apparent to the public at least, that the growing negative economic and social conditions We are facing in 2008 and on into 2009 are going to take some strong medicine to remedy. Our alleged national leadership of both Parties in Congress waste far too much time doing functionally nothing with regard to our Common Good. That is why I have used the word dysfunctional so often when referring to them.

When starting this book on July 1, 2005 I already believed that neither Party had the vision or the political guts to effectively confront the Special Interest driven status Quo and resolve our Common Problems. It is now early February 2008 – and the events of the last 2 and a-half years, unfortunately have proven them even less capable or willing to confront those challenges.

It is just another reason why somebody had to write such a book as CS2 about really confronting and resolving some of those serious on-going problems – to call our People to action – and to propose our Second American Revolution.

In **1776,** it took *Common Sense* and our national ancestor's blood and determination to *create* America and our radical new Democratic form of government. They confronted the all too powerful Few within their own country, in the name of the Common Good of the Many and took control of their Destiny.

In **2008 and beyond,** it will take the *Second Coming of Common Sense* and the united actions of our fellow Americans to re-establish the People's control over the government and *preserve* our Democracy. We must confront the Few that are exercising far too much power over the Common Good and regain control over our national Destiny. That not being dramatic, because it is the Plain Truth.

We the People, must decide our nation's future. To confront our historic challenges of 2008 and decide whether or not to control our own destiny…

In particular I am challenging my fellow Baby Boomers for it is now our watch. We must show true leadership for the sake of our children's generation and for those that follow them.

And, like it or not, We will now <u>unavoidably</u> make that Common Decision — either by our deliberate action <u>or</u> our inaction.

As for me, I am <u>all</u> <u>in</u>, and I say We will stand together and fight!

o   o   o   o

We the People, can initiate our present day Revolution by performing one of the simplest and most precious of our Democratic Rights of American citizenship. By casting our historic Vote on 11-4-08!

That momentous November day would prove to be *our Declaration* signaling the start of our Second and Final American Revolution. We the People each get one shot! And if We boldly and deliberately launch this coordinated assault in the name of Democracy and for the Common Good of our people, *it will be heard around the world.*

We will challenge the Presidential and Congressional candidates during the 2008 campaign to address and respond to the concepts and proposals presented in An American Agenda.

We can challenge the Congress to take action on some of the proposals presented in that Agenda **prior to** the November 2008 election, even though based upon more than a decade of under-performance, there is little confidence that they would take such action.

Therefore, We will inform the incumbents of the House and Senate running for re-election that they have collectively and of their own free will decision failed in the sworn Responsibilities to the People. And for that failure they will not be re-elected. We will literally effectively clear the House and one third of the Senate on November 4, 2008.

We the People, can no longer tolerate or subsidize the Dysfunctional U.S. Congress and their Special Interest Puppeteers.

o   o   o   o

<u>Now About that Last Ten Percent</u>

You may recall that in the Introduction to Part 3, I mentioned that I had sent about 90% of Part 5 to the publisher. The next few, important pages represent that remaining 10%.

This is one of the spots in CS2 that this 175,000-plus word extended, personal letter to you from me, where the words get _very_ important and personal. And where the decisions We are reviewing could not be more critical. We are absolutely talking altering the future from its present course. Consider that for a moment. We hold the future in our hands if We choose to re-shape it.

In this piece I will briefly write about the encouraging results of the 2006 Congressional Election, complimenting the high voter turn-out, especially in those states that actually kicked-out some Congressional incumbents. That was just a taste of what could come this year.

We will then review the historic, Democratic action that the Electorate _should_ take in voting out 468 U.S. House and Senate incumbents this November. Although – We <u>might</u> consider giving the House rookies that won their first election in 2006 one more opportunity to show what they could do in a "refreshed, free, and independent" Congress. After all they would have An American Agenda as a guide.

And finally We will review the 2008 Presidential Election, its final players, and our options.

The potential benefit to the Common Good of the Electorate's general acceptance of An American Agenda, the deliberate firing of most of the Congress, the appearance of new Congress with an un-mistakably clear message and charter from the People, and a new President that knows exactly what the People expect them to do – would be as historic as the first days of the American Revolution.

We the People can direct all of those Good Things to occur by taking no more than a few hours of our individual time on a single day this November, to proudly execute our Right of Citizenship by voting as a united People to Declare our Second American Revolution.

We can now bring order to out national chaos. We must, each of us, accept that it is possible to correct the errors of the past and the present, and create the positive future We all desire to live in.

The 2006 and 2008 National Elections

The 2006 U.S. Congressional Election

"Our Opportunity Partially Claimed"

Again, my compliments on the high voter turn-out and to those states that succeeded in voting out-of-office some of their own state's Congressional incumbents. You have set the example for the rest of us to follow.

In the 2006 Congressional Election the Republican Party rightfully experienced their loss of the majority in both houses of Congress, although they retained the numbers to uphold the veto of any legislation that Bush II doesn't like, if they so choose.

I also want to acknowledge that in many other states in the 2006 vote like Virginia, the incumbents that won saw vote counts closer than they had ever seen. I consider the 2006 vote our Second Revolution's Battle of Bunker Hill of 1774 in that it occurred two years before the 1776 Declaration of Independence, just as We are building up *our declaration* in 2008.

The Republicans lost due to the fact that they and Bush II have allowed Special Interests to have their way with our economy and the National System. And that the Bush II White House landed us in a fully orchestrated and optional Iraq War and has been obstinately determined to keep our troops in harm's way. The momentum toward the probable Democratic takeover of the White House and a <u>working</u> majority in both houses of Congress in 2008 will only grows as the months go by.

What bothered me and so many other Americans about the Republicans the most in the <u>final</u> months before the 2006 election was their overriding concern about *losing control* of Congress — the fear of the loss of <u>Political Power</u>. At the end that was all that they talked about and tried to scare people with. It let us know where their true concerns are. The conversation never moved to the "radical idea" that they would want to keep control of Congress in order to do the Peoples work and actually resolve our common problems. That was and is never mentioned. It apparently is not their primary concern.

Some will be screaming that all this is Republican bashing and in fact it absolutely is! Be assured that if the Party roles were reversed over the last few decades I would be writing about the Democrats instead. However, it <u>is</u> the Republicans (and the Special Interest money that props them up) that deserves to be punished because of their dismal performance — *they have earned it!*

O   O   O   O

The 2008 U.S. "Congressional" Election

"Our Opportunity to be Seized"

Changing the Face of the 2008 National Election Campaign

The Republican Party through 2008 have been in control of the White House for 20 of the last 28 years, and going on the last 8 years they and their Special Interest operatives have displayed their *Truest Colors.* Our biggest concern must be how much more damage they will inflict during Bush IIs remaining year.

If We are truly bold enough to take deliberate *political action* at the polls on that momentous day this November it will undoubtedly prove to be the start of *our* Second and Final American Revolution — just as the *Declaration of Independence* started *theirs.* And this time it will upwards of sixty (60) million American citizens figuratively signing the document.

We the People, can calmly, deliberately, and without firing a shot retake Political Control of our government by calling the U.S. Congress and various business and industry "special interests" to Civil Responsibility in the Common Interest of the American people and the nation.

o   o   o   o

The patriotic intent is for We the People to have an agreed upon National Agenda that will serve us as a working blueprint as the tedious, yet fully necessary Changes are made working toward our common National Vision. And We are not only talking a long term Vision – it starts with a national awakening during the 2008 National campaign that carries us boldly into 2009.

We – America — can no longer tolerate the Parties trying to redefine themselves and our country every two or four or eight years. In 2008, We the People demand a National Vision of a future designed for our Common Good, and the bold and solution oriented National Leadership required to lead us there.

Our 2008 U.S. "Congressional" Decision

In the previous piece We reviewed the radical, yet common sense rational for the wholesale replacement of 435 members of the House of Representatives and the 33 Senators up for re-election this November, with the possible exception of the "new" House members elected in 2006. I will not recount any of that logic here.

The Bottom Line – At the End of the Day

The time has come for the U.S. Congress to reclaim their Rightful share of the Balance of Power in our Three Branches of government. For too many decades the members of Congress allowed more and more of their collective Power to be given or taken away. The have allowed their Responsibility for the direction of the country, as well as problem solution development — to reside within the Executive Branch and the occupant of the White House. Giving away Power and shifting Legislative Authority from 535 to 1. And that does not even sound good on paper!

Today, the current members of the U.S. Congress are apparently incapable or uninterested in reclaiming their Constitutional authority. Thus, they have of the collective free will, rejected their sworn Responsibility to Serve and Protect the People.

If We are bold enough **to consider taking** that deliberate political action at the polls, and **clearly let those 468 know it** – it will radically and positively change the face, conduct, and content of the 2008 Congressional campaign. It will give the challengers in those 468 races real hope that they could all accomplish what now seems to most of them an impossible dream — to *win* a seat in the U.S. Congress, representing their home state. Regardless of their Party affiliation they would begin to take *great interest* in the contents and purpose of An American Agenda, as the Electorate would be telling them to do.

If We are bold enough **to actually take** that deliberate political action at the polls, it will forever and positively change the face, conduct, and content of all future National Elections, as well. This November 4th election will be first of many more to come. A truly, new and inspired U.S. Congress will be sworn in this coming January and the American Press can finally have positive things to be reporting to us.

We the People, can do these things and so much more.

o o o o

The Historic 2008 U.S. Presidential Election

"We the People, in Order to Maintain a More Perfect Union"

There are some advantages to the multi-month delay I experienced in early 2007 that has caused me to be finishing this last piece of CS2 just after the Super Tuesday Primary Event of February 5th. For one thing it cleared the field of all but three (3) candidates – two (2) democrats and one (1) Republican. I was wondering if with so many primaries moved (jammed) into early February that possibly the final nominee of both Parties might be determined. Close, but not quite.

This campaign season that needlessly started many months too soon, has also demonstrated to the public that the candidates on both sides are still not talking about our underlying problems and real solutions to them! After you have read An American Agenda listening to their generalized rhetoric could become difficult. They keep talking about how someone voted years ago, about the war they have not attempted to end as We clearly told them (the Congress) to do in 2006, and about access to health care for ALL that they could have done six (6) or many more years ago.

And they each stand there and proudly declare that they are the Change candidate. It is a long time until November 4th and along the way they will need challenged by the Electorate to be talking more specifics on our real issues.

Setting the Stage — The Republicans Expect to Lose

Yes, the Party has expected to lose the 2008 Presidential election for at least a few years now, as well as more seats in both houses of Congress. It is something strangely similar to 1996 when President Clinton was up for re-election. The Republican Party knew that as much as they politically hated Clinton that he was doing a fine job from the general public's point-of-view and would get re-elected. So, they really did not have any rational expectation of winning and therefore did not put much into the election process. No offense or disrespect of any kind toward Bob Dole, a very fine American.

The Democratic Candidates

As of today February 8, 2008 the selection of the Democratic Presidential nominee is still up for grabs! I must say that it was unfortunate that John

Edwards did not have a more successful run. He was a sincere candidate, raised some hard issues, and I believe would have been a good president, but he ran into two competitors that each have the ability to make American political history. Unfortunately, it was the wrong political timing for him.

Hillary Clinton Could be the First Women President

Hillary Clinton (Clinton) is the first American-White woman to have a real opportunity to become President of the United States.

It has been my somewhat objective opinion, looking at the entire field of Democratic and Republican candidates that Hillary Rodham Clinton is functionally the "best of the bunch". That observation has not changed with the arrival of Barrack Obama.

Senator Clinton has the experience of 35-plus years, of a political career at the state level, in the U.S. Senate, and eight (8) years with President Bill Clinton, one of the best political minds since Lyndon Johnson walked the halls of Congress. And uniquely she has had the first-hand experience of being crushed by the Medical and Pharmaceutical Industries when more than twelve (12) years ago she had the nerve to try and get Health Care for us peasants.

So if Clinton becomes president, such Industries could have more than a little trouble dealing with her. Further, she has worked over her long political career to actually help those that need it.

From the Republicans viewpoint, as much as their "base" dislikes her for whatever reasons, they have known for a long time she would beat them at the polls. Because, if came down to a choice between her and any Republican, in the final analysis the women of America would put her in the White House.

Barrack Obama Could be the First American-Black President

Barrack Obama (Obama) is the first American-Black man to have a real opportunity to become President of the United States.

At First the Republicans Were Pleased

"Back" in 2007 when there were least ten (10) Democratic candidates running around and Obama first shot up the popularity charts prior to the Iowa

Caucus the Republicans were encouraged. Then the Republican Party would have loved it if he became the Democratic nominee for president rather the Hillary Clinton that they know they had little chance against.

Frankly, they figured they would have a better chance of beating him because of his overall inexperience in national politics and because he is an American-Black! I said this was a reality based book, with no sugar-coating added. I never write to be offensive, only truthful and realistic. And even though he was attracting many donations even my expectation was that he would probably fade when the actual voting began.

But, then Obama kept talking! And, he is without a doubt is the best, most patriot, public speaker to hit the American political landscape since Ronald Reagan. I will admit the I have been very pleased and surprised with the voter's acceptance of Obama the first American-Black to have a reasonable chance at winning the White House. When he won the Iowa Caucus in a state that is 95% American-White it was awesome. And he has done very well in other states with American-White voters. It speaks volumes on the progress our society has made over the last fifty (50) years – real progress that so many other countries with their own racial, ethnic, or religious differences have not begun to make.

It is something wonderful to be said about the Power of our Democratic form of government. Excellent!

To return to the Republicans and Obama, they are probably not feeling as good about running against him as they were prior to his showing in the primaries through Super Tuesday!

The Problem that They Both Have

It does look like they will be fighting it out for a while in the campaign and maybe clear through to the convention. Which ever one of them is the eventual Democratic nominee is not of concern to me in CS2, they could even wind up on the same ticket!

However, what is of concern and has all to do with traditional Party politics of the last few decades and their Party platform. As I once heard Clinton put it pretty well at one of the campaign stops shown on television, "what we need in the White House is a problem-solver".

If you read part or all of An American Agenda you have some idea what problem solving at the national level really requires. And for the most part neither Party offers a platform that really seeks to confront hard issues, as they are addressed in An American Agenda – proposals aimed at resolving our Common Problems.

For example, speaking of Immigration! This is a growing sore under the saddle of the majority of the American public, and not just from the well-publicized Central and South American countries – they come from everywhere in the world and all the time. If they are not walking causally across Bush IIs Open Southern border, they are landing at our airports and vanishing into the country.

Both Clinton and Obama are dancing around some form of amnesty with different labels on it. This is a bone-marrow issue with the Electorate and could actually hurt them in the National Election. It is the wrong policy and they need to start listening to the Majority of the People not their campaign donors. As I wrote before, the Democrats must all wake-up and remember they are sworn in to serve Americans and our society. Not any miscellaneous person or group that of their own freewill violated (as in trespassed) of our nation's borders and then screams for services and citizenship.

Their only hope on this issue is that McCain is also trying sell out to the Illegal Occupant, Special Interest lobbies.

o   o   o   o

My one wish would be that the Democratic Party would read An American Agenda, study it, and then embrace it as their own. It could very well prove to be the long lost Party Platform that they have been searching for.

They might also consider using me as a Domestic and possibly Foreign policy advisor, as well.

o   o   o   o

The Republican Party

Again, there is no logical, rational, common sense, or publicly justifiable reason why the Republican candidate for President should be elected this November. No matter whom it is — period end of statement! The Democrats would need to shot themselves in both feet to mess this one up.

And while they know that, it does not mean they will not do whatever it would take to sneak back in the White House if the Democrats give them an opening — that undeniable *lust* for political Power.

Considering what the Bush II White House, a Republican majority in the Congress for six (6) years and the continued Republican veto hold on Congress even after the 2006 mid-term election — has done to our nation since January 2001 – to give them the White House again in 2008 would be an epic tragedy for the nation, continue the wreckage of our struggling economy, and make the Electorate (us) look like absolute fool's to the rest of the world. And We already are looking pretty bad that way for having re-elected Bush II in 2004. Seriously, I was standing on the beach at Cape Hatteras, NC in 2006 and a lady from Germany asked me how we could have re-elected Bush II. What could I say?

It does not matter what issues are or are not discussed over the remaining long months of primaries; or what the general election campaign brings to the public; or if God forbid we have a terrorist attack; or what their totally probable nominee John McCain may talk about – their upset victory in November would result in 4 to 8 more years of the same old Special Interest lobbyist controlled Congress **and** White House. And most of you know as well as I do that We the People and the National System – cannot – take it anymore.

John McCain Gets His Opportunity

Unless something really unexpected occurs, John McCain will be the Republican Presidential candidate for 2008. He is good man, a patriotic American to say the least, was a great soldier, has been reasonable as Senators go, and he has tended to aggravate his own Party at times making him a bit independent minded.

"The Party Bosses" have never liked McCain. Bush II even trashed him in the 2000 primaries. He thinks for himself at times and does not follow the Party line as they like their Presidents to do. Strangely he only disagrees with them once on a while, but it is enough to have the "Republican Right" (right in their case does not mean correct) upset with him even as their probable candidate. So for the last few days since Super Tuesday he has been making nice with them at the Conservative Political Action Committee (CPAC) Convention, trying to get their support. These are the same people that so loved Bush II and some still do!

Mitt Romney that was running a distant second to McCain after Super Tuesday dropped out on Thursday making his announcement at the CPAC Convention.

And then there is Mike Huckabee. McCain is being pushed by some Conservatives to have Huckabee as his running mate. All I will say about that entire situation is at this point the Democrats are probably pulling for Huckabee to be on the ticket!

Not much else to say about McCain or the Republicans. For the good of the nation, let's just pray the Democrats don't start shooting their feet.

o   o   o   o

Go Where the Journey Leads You

These are the last few pages I will write in CS2. It is 11:35pm on Friday February 8th. The book will be completed in the morning. In a few weeks it will be on the Internet for Print-on-Demand sale and published! Amen...

My attention will now turn to finding a volume publisher and getting CS2 in the bookstores as soon as possible. It is a far easier sell when you have already published a book and have the new one finished, in hand, and already on sale.

I will start promoting the book and raising funds to get the grassroots group I mentioned in Proposal 14 – Local Pride and Accountability. It is called the Common Interest Civil Responsibilities Union or CICRU (sigh-crew). I will work to start the first CICRU Local Chapter (LCC) in the Yorktown, VA area where I have lived since March 2007.

It is somewhat fitting to start the Second American Revolution in the same town that the first one ended!

What is Likely to Will Happen Next

It has now been 32 months since I earnestly began this book project for my country. And it has been 62 months since I left my Information Technology career to finish my first book on our nation's viable and publicly acceptable solution to our decades old War on Drugs. In an email to several hundred of my co-workers at CareFirst BlueCross BlueShield in Washington, DC and Owings Mills, MD – I said that I was leaving to finish a book and "whatever projects" followed that effort.

This is my free will, now all-in project for America. And it has been far more than I could have ever expected. I have worked harder and pushed myself more than ever before. Those 34 years of IT project experience prepared me for these challenges. I have loved my project for America.

From this point the acceptance of CS2 and its appeal to the public and Press will tell if it has the hoped for impact on this years Presidential and Congressional campaigns. I pray that it will because that is the first intent of this book project.

CS2 could first impact the campaigns when people that read it take questions on the proposals to the candidates for national, state, and local offices. That will be tremendous.

There is of course very limited possibility that Clinton or Obama will pick it up and use it without heavy prompting from the public or maybe the Press. Miracles do happen and there is a real need for such content during the campaign. The serious and sad thing is that the public issues and problems addressed in CS2 are <u>not</u> going to go away. If nothing happens this year, CS2 will still apply in 2009. I believe that CS2 will find popularity with the public in due time – and the sooner the better for the good of the nation.

When the right publisher is connected with, a national book tour would be highly desirable. That will be the best way to get the word out on its contents, start building the network CICRU network, and get its message into the media. I believe the Press, as well as the public could use some optimistic news for a change.

Those are the logical follow-on scenarios to CS2's publication. And don't forget that Fourth Estate Plus List in Part 3, with those 350 entries! They are for good reasons.

Now for the Wishful Possibilities

You may have thought something like this was coming earlier, but I have intentionally hesitated to go there either to distract the reader from the message of CS2 or to be thought of as a dreamer or worse.

If I had my preference, I would be very interested in being an Independent Presidential candidate in 2008.

I expect that it is probably easier for the reader to consider that bold statement after having read CS2 than if I would have announced it in the Introduction to Part 1!

I will simply acknowledge the fact that I absolutely interested in being the next President, elected as an Independent candidate this November. I am not at all intimated by the office. I believe that I would bring valuable skills and abilities to the office and the country. There is no better place for a professional problem-solver, that is committed to the Common Good of our citizens and the nation to be in 2009.

If that granted remote prospect would not materialize or if I <u>did</u> run and the subsequent campaign was not successful, I would consider it to have been very successful. Even in such a loss the message, concepts, and proposals offered in CS2 would obtain national attention and <u>that</u> is the goal. For as many of the American public know about CS2 and its positive message them and the nation.

I honestly can tell you that when I sat down in July 2005 to begin this book, that was <u>not</u> the plan or a hidden objective — quite the opposite.

As previously mentioned, the driving concern I had when starting was that We as a nation and society did not and still do not have a Game Plan! We do not share a National Vision on where our nation should at least be trying to go. The concepts and proposals in *The Second Coming of Common Sense* are my objective attempt to present a National Vision designed for the Common Good of our citizens and nation. And believe me, there is a lot more ideas where those came from. CS2 is a presentation for my fellow Americans to critique, refine, and hopefully in due time declare their Common Agreement upon.

I would only become an official Independent candidate for that office if the general public responds to the writing in CS2 and begins the process within their respective state to put me on the ballot as an Independent — a possible side benefit of CICRU Chapters forming around the country.

For what I remember from my amateur, but fully official campaign for President in 2003 – the state of Texas has the earliest cut-off date in July, for filing someone as an Independent of president on the National ballot. Papers must be filled and a specific number of signatures must be properly collected and submitted. The same goes for most states, although for some it is only a simple filing fee.

Looking back I had not wanted to write another book right away, if at all. I had done my Independent campaign for president and had finished the book, *Common Interest* at the end of 2004. I was tired and burned out from the last 18-plus months of the intense campaign and book preparation activities. My campaign experience was extremely educational, but that was enough of that.

When I began this my second book it was due to my continued frustration that there was still no one in the country really trying to solve our hard problems, and the unfortunate start of Bush IIs second term. The Oil companies were having a field day, the retail industry was struggling, still no Health Care, and so on. The Status Quo not in our favor had won the election and We were in store for *four more years* of the dynamic Bush II and Cheney Show. We lost that time.

However, We are far from finished.

And in the End

This ends my personal observations on the State of Our Union. On the causes of our Common Problems, as well as what I and many people that I have shared these contents with over the years, believe to be practical approaches and publicly acceptable solutions to many of our long-standing national issues.

My only regret is to say to my fellow Americans as I write through these tears, that I could have said as much or even more in fewer words and pages. I am personally grateful to those of you that have read *The Second Coming of Common Sense* in its entirety. It has been my personal pleasure to prepare it for your review.

We the People deserve nothing, but to win and I believe that is now only a matter of time.

Thanks, A J

Reclaiming the National System and Our Nation

"What We do or don't do in 2008 will directly determine the quality of our national future"

The viable national future that we American citizens desire to build for our Common Good must begin to take form during the 2008 Presidential/Congressional campaign. And, it needs to be sealed with a historic exclamation mark to be driven into the ground on the November 2008, National Election Day!

If the Congress has moved the National Election Day to the first Saturday in November from the first Tuesday as proposed in An American Agenda, we will vote on Saturday 11-4-08. If and probably not, we will vote as usual on a Tuesday, that is 11-4-08.

However, it will be far from usual. Even if the National Election Day remains on a Tuesday for the critical 2008 vote — every potential voter is directly challenged to take it upon themselves to vote — even if they need to take part or the whole day off from their job. It is that important of an event for our nation and is a small price for any of us to pay considering what is at stake.

Why Vote

Actually, many Americas will (finally) need to register to vote before that date and be warned that the voter registration cut-off date varies by state. Inmost places it only involves a simple trip to your local Department of Motor Vehicles (motor-voter) to fill out a form and you are good-to-vote!

I challenge those that do not always vote, maybe have never registered or typically do not see the point of it considering the poor choices we normally have to pick from — and how little those elected actually accomplish for the average person. I have talked with many that fall somewhere within that group.

It is to them and the many others among us that are so understandably fed-up with the whole process, that I offer two (2) considerations.

First, to make the November 2008 Presidential/Congressional campaign and Election Day the historic national experience all that they need to be, We must show the Parties and politicians that we are involved. And short of showing up in greater numbers at 2008 campaign events that would generally demonstrate are increased involvement, a real "surge" in reported voter registration during 2008 across the whole country will provide a message they will not be able to ignore. It will create a political energy within the population. States could have an informal competition on how high a percentage of their illegible voters are registered by July 4th.

Secondly, and this is difficult to put in words so please bear with me. With the end of the military Draft in the 1970's and its replacement with an all voluntary military service system, the average American does not have to do anything except pay taxes as a price for living in this great country. And we all like to b_____ about paying taxes!

Therefore, the Civil Right and Responsibility that each American citizen has to vote, is the only way the Majority have to contribute in serving the country – to vote in or out those that are supposed to make public policy and protect our Common Good. It is an old line to draw on to say that those in our military are fighting in Afghanistan, Iraq, and other places around the world today – are protecting our Freedom and Rights, such as voting, but it is the Plain Truth.

I say the fact so many of us do not at least vote, is a primary reason that we have so many problems in our country and why we find our precious troops in such an avoidable mess as Iraq. In the 2006 election those that did vote were telling Congress in general and the Democrats in particular to get us out of Iraq. To take power away from George and Dick, and be our leaders! But not enough of us showed up. The message sent to our national leadership was not strong enough — We did not demonstrate our collective displeasure forcefully enough and so the Democrats (and Republicans) in Congress did not take the necessary actions. As a result our troops continue to die and the dynamic duo is building the case to expand their optional war into Iran. It must end.

Well shame on the Congress and shame on us! On a single day in early November 2008, We the People, have the opportunity and solemn obligation to those in Harm's Way, get off of our collective asses and start fixing this country.

And, We the People do it by taking a few hours out of one (1) day and marching to the polls. Understanding, that we will be firing our private single shot with every vote cast to throw out the incompetent, the dysfunctional, and the so-called leadership of the nation. We will finally be rid of Bush II and his sidekick thanks to the Constitution, but we must act to remove the rest of the failures – or at least 468 of the 535-Club.

Did I make my point?

o   o   o   o

Come Election Day 2008, every employer (they also happen to be voters) will be challenged to make it very easy for their people to have adequate time to vote. One suggestion is to allow employees with a last name starting with A thru M to arrive as late to work as necessary in order to go to the polls and vote — and to allow employees with a last name starting with N thru Z to leave work for the day in the early afternoon in order to go to the polls and vote. And to be paid for the time if possible! Either way – everyone just please do it!

Also, if Tuesday remains the Election Day for 2008, We could conduct a nationwide civil action that would make 11-4-08 a virtual national holiday. All across the nation people could take that day off as a non-violent civil action and vote! Parents could take their children with them for the experience.

o   o   o   o

Either way, We will let the politicians know that we all intend to get out and VOTE in November 2008 no matter if it is Tuesday or Saturday. That united and shared national mindset will begin the Changes required within our population and our national leadership's day-to-day agenda.

The November 2008 vote will be a magnificent and historic, revolutionary action by We the People. And not even a single shot will need to be fired. As a result, the door will be opened for certain national and local level policies to be realistically confronted for the Common Good, corrective action agreed to, and implemented without senseless delay.

The pure intent is that in the months leading up to Election Day, We the People will be openly discussing the slow decline in both the economic and social quality of daily life in America and the hard reasons for it – some of which have been presented for your consideration in CS2. We will challenge all candidates on our issues – such as those on the Grievance List during the campaign season – forcing them to respond with direct answers not the normal evasive and meaningless rhetoric. And then! We will physically demonstrate our Common Disgust with the Congress and both political parties with our historic national vote.

For a Shared Understanding

A primary objective of my writing to you in CS2 has been to communicate how absolutely crucial it is for We the People to acknowledge and increase our common awareness of the <u>real</u> functioning of the America's National System. The way America runs on a day-to-day basis and I mean the way it <u>really</u> works – which too often is in opposition to the practical concerns and the Common Good of our CITIZENS...

Various political, business, and industry Special Interests that are currently key components of the National System routinely oppose and/or discount the potential benefits of <u>any</u> proposed change to the way things currently work – guarding against any changes to <u>their</u> part of the status quo. They will continue in overt and covert ways to attempt to block and/or weaken corrective change. It is unfortunately the nature of the 'political' game and is what much of the congressional lobbying business is all about. Protecting the status quo no matter what or who it hurts or kills! And that is not over-stating the situation.

o   o   o   o

<u>Never</u> <u>forget</u> my fellow Americans that <u>we</u> <u>all</u> <u>came</u> <u>from</u> <u>peasants</u>. And if we do not desire to become peasants again or continue to be treated as such, we *must* actively work to <u>prevent</u> it from happening – otherwise *in the normal course of human events* – our society will be led to that natural, evolutionary end!

It is the control of the National System that we the American electorate must aggressively insert our united will and voting power into for our Common Good. Otherwise we must resign our selves <u>and</u> our descendents to living with a status quo that has been and will increasingly *be controlled* by those not concerned with the fate of the masses — We the People.

It is Basic Survival of the Fittest

Both corporate and public entities, their lobbyists, and the people that support them will not like to see "true Change" coming. It must objectively be acknowledged that some of their resistance as a natural, self-preservation reaction. It is often just a person's, an agency's, a corporation's, and an entire industry's survival instinct kicking in.

Many of us including yours truly, have known that odd feeling at some point in our working lives, when we thought our employment status could be or was in jeopardy for whatever reason, and we had no real control over the decision process. However, for corporate management it comes down to maintaining annual revenues, profits, earnings, and the sometimes "unholy" grail of stockholder dividends.

By this time we are all unfortunately aware of the potential <u>negative</u> outputs of questionable corporate management practices, that being the "false profits" and destroyed employees of corporations such as Enron, MCI, and too many others.

And we must not forget. We are living with oil and energy related costs that are higher than they have any practical reason to be or would be, IF, the oil companies (windfall profits), the U.S. Congress (in the pockets of Energy industry lobbyists), and the Bush I and II White Houses (old oil money) were working for people. But they <u>are not</u>! And such entities have collaborated for over three (3) decades to prevent <u>any</u> viable move toward alternative energy options.

"It" has been profits over people, other businesses, <u>and</u> country. "It" will be reversed!

o   o   o   o

At the same time, we must aggressively <u>support</u> responsible American businesses and industries, and the necessary employment that they bring to the table. This is absolutely in our national self-interest – Americans need viable jobs! We are no longer a society that can make our living off the land. And living in the greatest country in the world is not free, i.e., the cost of living! Existing jobs and businesses must be maintained and viable new ones created.

Therefore, as the Moody Blues once wrote it is "*a question of balance*". We must weigh the self-serving *screams* of <u>any</u> individual, business or an entire industry about the negative impacts of proposed changes, against the benefits to other businesses and most importantly to our society as a whole. The leadership of <u>all</u> nations weighs these situations, and too many including American leadership are ignoring some key and growing imbalances.

It is now brutally essential for us to debate, agree upon, and implement certain socially and economically radical, yet controlled adjustments within our National System. What do you think the first American Revolution was all about and accomplished!

Or, we will be satisfied being timid peasants and just to get used to being treated as such.

Isn't it nice to have such clear choices…

National Course Corrections are Required NOW

Today, in order to solve our major problems we must *boldly resolve* to make some critical course corrections on what I call America's national voyage – the one that began on July 4, 1776. It is time for us to put our nation on the right course toward a better future – and a desired future that starts to take real form in 2008.

We will set a course with a Common Vision that our fellow Americans can mutually agree to, as a united people and a Democratic nation. We will each be reconciled to make personal sacrifices and know that additional course corrections will need to be made along the way, as required. Overall, We will accept that there are no perfect solutions to our national problems and that not all individuals and groups could ever be totally pleased with the solutions and approaches finally selected By the People for implementation.

In social change, we must always be sensitive to the needs of individuals with special and/or possibly difficult situations, because they are some of us! And we must take care of our own citizens – all of us! However, and I do mean 'however' we must quit decreasing the quality of life of the Masses to address the less than reasonable desires of the Few.

It is the growing domestic economic and political power imbalances that make our Second American Revolution absolutely necessary.

o   o   o   o

Remember, just as Americans desire and need leaders and their leadership; the peoples of other countries need and desire good leadership and positive models as well. And if the American people do not to stand and lead the world toward a better place, who will?

We the People – Then and Now

On January 10, 1776, a regular American colonist, but one that was soon to become the great revolutionary writer Thomas Paine, *anonymously* published the 30-odd-page paperback size pamphlet simply entitled, *Common Sense*. Paine had only been in the American colonies for 18 months when the pamphlet was published. The determined 37-year old released a second edition *under his name* the very next month. It was 46 pages in length and is the one accepted as the classic revolutionary version. One of the true masterpieces ever written in the people's Common Interest.

Paine wrote to his fellow American colonists in the "common language of the day" and presented the politically radical, yet socially practical rationale as to why the colonists of the 13 American colonies of the great British Empire should join together to make what he called a *"declaration of independence"* from England. He challenged the colonies to become an independent nation with a new Representative form of government. He was asking the colonists, the regular people to declare a physical war upon the oppressive, tyrannical government of King George III.

Prior to Paine's publication, Sam Adams' personal evaluation of the colonial population "sentiments" toward such a break with England were evenly split with equal numbers for, against, and undecided. After reading the words of *Common Sense* the general public sentiment that had been unsettled regarding a major confrontation with England began to shift. The people could now sense that it was "possible" for them to control their own destiny. That those considered to be peasants could dare to defy the almighty King and his ministers and do what had seemed the impossible. That they could bring into daily reality what until "their moment in time" had only been a peasant's dream — to become free men and women, living in a nation of their own!

To do so, they would have to succeed in conquering a single enemy that was regrettably comprised of their fellow British subjects – for this was to be America's first Civil War. The colonists would be required to act as a united people in order to achieve what they could not possibly do as separate colonies. Theirs would prove to be one of the grandest accomplishments in all of human history – a victory that was achieved for the Common Good of the Masses.

Less than 6 months later, on July 4, 1776 in Philadelphia, the assembled Representatives to the Continental Congress of the thirteen American colonies signed the *Declaration of Independence*. Their war of independence from England that had been coming to a boil since the Battles of Lexington and Concord in April 1775 was officially declared!

o   o   o   o

The challenge of Paine's message to his fellow American colonists was for them to come together to unite to birth a nation – their nation, that is our nation today.

The American colonists — the common people – stood together, they fought, and some 25,000 – about one (1) percent of the population *died* in the fighting, and in the end they were victorious. Their independence was achieved by virtue of individual and united *public action* producing the world's first and still finest Democracy. The world was changed forever, and for the better. And our very future was made possible.

o   o   o   o

It is 230 Years into Our National Voyage

"Their decision was about Creating their Democracy.
Our decision is about the Civil Responsibility required
to Preserve that Democracy"

So it is the year 2008 and some 232 years since Thomas Paine boldly challenged our national ancestors to personal sacrifice and united action. And now another regular American has freely decided to prepare these confrontational contents for review by my fellow American citizens — to challenge you to personal action and We the People to united action.

In the end, the actions of Americans such as yourself and future events will be the ultimate judge of how effective a communication this has been. Only time will validate the public acceptability of this analysis of our "National System" – the way America really works on a day-to-day basis – for the good, the bad, and the ugly.

The essence of my message to *you*, my fellow American is for us to once again come together, to unite in Common Purpose to preserve our nation, our American Democracy, and so to insure the Life, Liberty, and the Pursuit of Happiness of all American citizens. And I cannot stress enough that the challenge is to insure nothing less than the Common Good of all American citizens.

The colonist's decision was about Creating American Democracy. Our ultimate decision is about Preserving American Democracy.

Today's challenge is for us to make a national *"declaration of responsibility"* at every level of American society. We will clarify once and for all our basic societal expectations and raise the bar of Civil Responsibility for each citizen, community, town, county, city, and state. And at the national level, we are talking directly to the current and future members of the U.S. Congress and the Supreme Court. Further, this Civil Responsibility challenge applies directly to all entities within business and industry, as well. Overall, We will expect more of each other and demand it from our elected officials and business leaders.

Herein, we have calmly reviewed the functional status of some key parts of our National System. Now, We will decide whether or not to confront the Plain Truth that the National System is increasingly controlled in critical areas by civilly irresponsible entities — comprised of people, groups, and entire industries that are functionally not supportive of, nor do they feel any human or national obligation to the Common Good of our citizens or even to our society. Not that "all" such entities are intending to be of negative impact on American society, but the net results of their collective efforts are <u>just</u> <u>that</u>!

Whether it is their willful intent to ignore or suppress the needs of the People – or – just the grinding, natural evolution of economic forces found in every country toward a have/have-not society, neither rationale will be considered acceptable. We will not stand for it!

o   o   o   o

Our Moment in Time

So guess what America? We are now the People, and it is "our moment in time". That is it will be if We determine by our united actions to make it so. It is our national free will decision.

We have the opportunity, if not the solemn responsibility to take this bold step as a nation. In doing so, we will begin to address the social and economic problems that ripple through the National System. It will be *awkward at first*, but the beneficial changes will soon become part of our improved National System, the "new and improved" way in which America really works.

o   o   o   o

As I first wrote the following short piece for your review early in Part 2 in order to offer some sense of pure, human emotion of Paine's words to the colonists. Now as my own sincere offering to you draws to an end and each of us quietly ponders our own thoughts on such dramatic national Changes, I repeat them and his words that are as near to perfection as may be written,

For some perspective on the words that helped the colonists to come to terms with Paine's overall challenge — that they should declare their war of independence from the British Empire, I have placed the closing words of *Common Sense* here for your review. It spoke to the colonists about finally facing and resolving their hard challenges – just as we will soon be coming to face ours.

> "These proceedings may at first appear strange and difficult; but, like all other steps which we have already passed over, will in a little time become familiar and agreeable; and, until an independance is declared, the Continent will feel itself like a man who continues putting off some unpleasant business from day to day, yet knows it must be done, hates to set about it, wishes it over, *and is continually haunted with the thoughts of its necessity.*"

– Thomas Paine, January 1776

Truly, the written word at it's very finest.

o   o   o   o

We, the American public have the intelligence and the Constitutional Power, should we choose to exercise it to resolve <u>any</u> of our national problems. In changing the National System to finally solve serious national problems winners and losers will be created, just as there has always been when any nation's system was dramatically altered.

We the People must unite our spirits and creativity just as the Founders did when they considered their options – focusing on the Common Good, to do what needs to be done to improve and maintain the Life, Liberty, and the Pursuit of Happiness for all Americans. To accomplish this, the Majority of us need to continue to act responsibly, and must rightfully <u>demand</u> that the Minority (all those that would rather not change) to do the same.

We the People must always be willing to help <u>our</u> people that are trying to better themselves. That pure humanitarian quality runs deep in our basic national character and was born in the Christian foundation of our country.

<u>However,</u> we must absolutely now be willing to get tough and be determined to back it up — to declare that from now on, those who will not be responsible for their negative freewill actions will surely know **the full fury of our disapproval**. This will be accomplished by raising the invisible Bar of Civil Responsibility and expecting that every American at least <u>try</u> to pull his or her own weight in our society. Their petty and lame excuses will no longer matter or be tolerated. The free rides will be over.

o   o   o   o

We will have a few very tough things to do to bring our national house to proper order. And although it is said that pain is relative, what we face pales in comparison to what those brave men and women that preceded us had to endure.

And now, our children and our national ancestors are watching us to see if We will have the vision and the courage — the individual and collective strength to face the challenge of our time and achieve victory for the sake of our fellow Americans today and our posterity tomorrow.

That is our challenge.

o   o   o   o

This Effort on Our Behalf

My objective in writing the *Second Coming of Common Sense* has not been to convince you to agree with <u>all</u> of the concepts and proposals presented herein.

First of all, considering the range of issues and the necessary aggressiveness of some of the proposed solutions, that expectation would be foolish on my part, as well as an insult to your individuality.

Secondly, and what may surprise you is that the problem solving measures contained in the proposals presented do <u>not</u> in all cases represent my personal values and opinions. That would violate the objective spirit of systems analysis! These are the findings of a Systems Analyst.

Let it stand that these contents are in fact the analytical findings of a career business systems analyst, with 30+ years of practical experience developing objective solution options for clients in both the corporate and federal government sectors. And in many cases, implementing those solutions!

Ultimately, I absolutely believe that after critical public review, with open public debate and the consideration by We the People that most if not <u>all</u> of what is presented herein will in prudent time, be mutually agreed upon by the Masses <u>and</u> implemented into our National System. For the words of CS2 are not my thoughts alone, they have been purposely refined based upon the personal feedback received in conversations with a few thousand of you.

Admittedly, We will not like the practical necessity of certain *required* actions anymore than our national ancestors desired to fight a physical war against mother England. However, with our common agreement, with a mutual understanding of where we truly are, with the acknowledgement that we cannot continue as we have been, and knowing what We have it within <u>our</u> <u>power</u> to do what is required to move forward into a desirable national future — We the People will truly be declaring and experiencing our Second American Revolution — and prayerfully the final one.

We will fulfill the challenge laid down by our national ancestors to preserve America – the Great Experiment in people-driven government that many said could not last without a monarchy.

"We chosen people" have it fully within our power and within our time to "complete" our American Democracy. We can realize the full potential of a government elected by and responsible only to We the People – We the

American Citizens, and <u>no one else</u>.

o o o o

Our National Challenges

As Thomas Paine wrote in the first page of *Common Sense*,

> "The cause of America is in great measure the cause of all mankind."

A very true statement then, and with regard to America's role to the world it is even more so today. Frankly, considering some of the deteriorating conditions in our nation and too many parts of the world today, whatever We the People determine to do (or not to do) over the next seven (7) years is just as critical as at the time of our nation's birth.

And considering that our destiny is <u>not</u> currently "in our hands" it is even more important...

For Them – Only One Challenge to Confront

It is not that it was simple. It was simply magnificent. The American colonists struggle against the oppressive and self-interested British Empire to claim their independence and to control their own future.

And it was not to be easy. However, they took the bold actions required to benefit their families, their neighbors, and their fellow colonists, and after years of actual warfare they became the first Americans. Those *chosen few* were the very first people in all of human history to feel the Freedom, the Liberty, and the absolute Blessings of being an American.

o   o   o   o

Today, We the People of all 50 states, and DC, are challenged to take bold action for the Common Good of all those that are now Americans. While we will not need to resort to physical warfare to resolve the national issues presented herein, it will prove to be an <u>absolute</u> <u>test</u> of our Peoples' common vision and united resolve.

It will be a domestic and foreign policy based — legislative war presided over by our U.S. Constitution. The contest will directly determine who will really be in control of America now and for "as long as we all shall live." We already live in the greatest nation the world has ever known. Our blunt challenge is to do whatever it takes to keep it that way!

We have our Democracy and our beloved U.S. Constitution that allows

America to mature and self-correct our society's course as we sail on our national voyage. It is time for us to come together, to unite in Common Purpose and to place steadier hands upon our ship's wheel, because we have surely drifted a bit off the People's desired course.

We only need to get back to some of the basic qualities, responsibilities, and principles that made America a great nation to start with and that have sustained this Great Experiment for 230 years. We the People need to clarify the basic set of Civil Responsibilities and Expectations of our citizens and our society. We must be absolutely firm in calling those to task that do not honor those Common Agreements, and in so doing, we will declare our resolve to make America's destiny one that will serve the Common Good of us all.

Should, after open public debate, the proposals presented herein be found to be acceptable to the People – and I do absolutely believe that the majority will be — We have it within our Power and our Rights to Demand that our elected officials implement them – and to do it now! Or we will aggressively keep replacing them until we find those individuals that will be true leaders.

It is our time to take action, to lead our leaders, and as a result reaffirm America Democracy as the model for the world of the ultimate system of government — a free and open society built upon the basic principle that every man, woman, and child **matters**. That we are all indeed created equal in the eyes of God and each other.

As 230 years of U.S. history demonstrate, once We the People come together to confront <u>any</u> situation that threatens our national well-being, and <u>agree</u> that the approach offered to resolve it is fair and prudent for the Common Good — We can do and accomplish anything.

o   o   o   o

For Us – Many Challenges to Confront

On the other hand, it is fair to say that our current national problems and the historic reconciliation we are now approaching are far more complicated than that faced by the American colonists.

We are now challenged, to take American Democracy to the next level of maturity.

We are now challenged, to fairly and forcefully address internal issues that will make America all it can be.

We are now challenged, to acknowledge the irresponsible and avoidable international foolishness that has caused the world to become a far worse place for its inhabitants over the last few decades — rather than the better place it should be at this moment in time. We will be admitting our direct role in some of it, but will also hold other nations and their leadership responsible, as well.

o   o   o   o

Now, it is Our Watch.

And while I am addressing all Americans in general, I am challenging my fellow Baby-Boomers in particular for we are now the lead Generation. It is now "40 years after" and the time has come for the second and final act in our generation's great two-act play to be performed. Not only because our children are watching us, but that some have grandchildren watching, as well.

We Americans must all stand together,
just as our National Ancestors did when they won their war and created our nation.

We all must now stand together
and take the actions that will Define and Insure our National Destiny.
To make us all proud to be Americans.

And most importantly,
to make our children proud of us.

o   o   o   o

WE THE PEOPLE, of the United States of America will now be about our Second American Revolution.

We will do these things for ourselves and for so many others around the world that dream of the things that we shall put in motion.

We will do these things because only We have the ability, the privilege, the solemn national Right to do what needs to be done – under our blessed U.S. Constitution.

It has been said that, "Those to whom much is has been given, much is expected."

It has also been said that, "We do these things not because they are Easy, we do them because they are Hard."

**And *We the People* can and will accomplish
all of these Hard things because**

We are Americans.

o   o   o   o

To You in Closing

I sincerely thank you for your time and attention in reviewing these contents,
that were dutifully prepared and offered for your personal consideration.

Only the actions of others and the passage time
will reveal what comes from this effort.

And so for now I simply pray that
God will bless you and your family,

And that God will continue to bless America.

A. J. Wildman

Appendix

Common Sense by Thomas Paine

That revolutionary writer and his 46-page paperback size pamphlet are referred to throughout this book. The entire text of the second edition of Common Sense published in February 1776 publication are presented in Appendix A. The first edition was published a month earlier and contained 33-pages. Paine added some material, including a 'letter' to the Quakers for the second and final version.

C O M M O N   S E N S E;

Addressed to the

Inhabitants

of

A M E R I C A,

on the following interefting

S U B J E CT S:

I.   Of the Origin and Defign of Government in general, with concife Remarks on the Englifh Conftitution.

II.   Of Monarchy and Hereditary Succeffion.

III.   Thoughts on the prefent State of American Affairs.

IV.   Of the prefent ability of America, with fome mifcellaneous Reflections.

A NEW EDITION, with feveral Additons in the Body of the Work. To which is Added an APPENDIX: together with an Addrefs to the People called QUAKERS.

Man knows no Mafter fave creating HEAVEN,
Or thofe whom choice and common Good ordain.
THOMSON

INTRODUCTION

Perhaps the sentiments contained in the following pages, are not YET sufficiently fashionable to procure them general favour; a long habit of not thinking a thing WRONG, gives it a superficial appearance of being RIGHT, and raises at first a formidable outcry in defense of custom. But the tumult soon subsides. Time makes more converts than reason.

As a long and violent abuse of power, is generally the Means of calling the right of it in question (and in Matters too which might never have been thought of, had not the Sufferers been aggravated into the inquiry) and as the King of England hath undertaken in his OWN RIGHT, to support the Parliament in what he calls THEIRS, and as the good people of this country are grievously oppressed by the combination, they have an undoubted privilege to inquire into the pretensions of both, and equally to reject the usurpation of either.

In the following sheets, the author hath studiously avoided every thing which is personal among ourselves. Compliments as well as censure to individuals make no part thereof. The wise, and the worthy, need not the triumph of a pamphlet; and those whose sentiments are injudicious, or unfriendly, will cease of themselves unless too much pains are bestowed upon their conversion.

The cause of America is in a great measure the cause of all mankind. Many circumstances hath, and will arise, which are not local, but universal, and through which the principles of all Lovers of Mankind are affected, and in the Event of which, their Affections are interested. The laying a Country desolate with Fire and Sword, declaring War against the natural rights of all Mankind, and extirpating the Defenders thereof from the Face of the Earth, is the Concern of every Man to whom Nature hath given the Power of feeling; of which Class, regardless of Party Censure, is the AUTHOR.

P.S. The Publication of this new Edition hath been delayed, with a View of taking notice (had it been necessary) of any Attempt to refute the Doctrine of Independance: As no Answer hath yet appeared, it is now presumed that none will, the Time needful for getting such a Performance ready for the Public being considerably past.

Who the Author of this Production is, is wholly unnecessary to the Public, as the Object for Attention is the DOCTRINE ITSELF, not the MAN. Yet it may not be unnecessary to say, That he is unconnected with any Party, and under no sort of Influence public or private, but the influence of reason and principle.

Philadelphia, February 14, 1776

OF THE ORIGIN AND DESIGN OF GOVERNMENT IN GENERAL. WITH CONCISE REMARKS ON THE ENGLISH CONSTITUTION

Some writers have so confounded society with government, as to leave little or no distinction between them; whereas they are not only different, but have different origins. Society is produced by our wants, and government by our wickedness; the former promotes our POSITIVELY by uniting our affections, the latter NEGATIVELY by restraining our vices. The one encourages intercourse, the other creates distinctions. The first a patron, the last a punisher.

Society in every state is a blessing, but government even in its best state is but a necessary evil; in its worst state an intolerable one; for when we suffer, or are exposed to the same miseries BY A GOVERNMENT, which we might expect in a country WITHOUT GOVERNMENT, our calamity is heightened by reflecting that we furnish the means by which we suffer. Government, like dress, is the badge of lost innocence; the palaces of kings are built on the ruins of the bowers of paradise. For were the impulses of conscience clear, uniform, and irresistibly obeyed, man would need no other lawgiver; but that not being the case, he finds it necessary to surrender up a part of his property to furnish means for the protection of the rest; and this he is induced to do by the same prudence which in every other case advises him out of two evils to choose the least. WHEREFORE, security being the true design and end of government, it unanswerably follows, that whatever FORM thereof appears most likely to ensure it to us, with the least expense and greatest benefit, is preferable to all others.

In order to gain a clear and just idea of the design and end of government, let us suppose a small number of persons settled in some sequestered part of the earth, unconnected with the rest, they will then represent the first peopling of any country, or of the world. In this state of natural liberty, society will be their first thought. A thousand motives will excite them thereto, the strength of one man is so unequal to his wants, and his mind so unfitted for perpetual solitude, that he is soon obliged to seek assistance and relief of another, who in his turn requires the same. Four or five united would be able to raise a tolerable dwelling in the midst of a wilderness, but one man might labour out of the common period of life without accomplishing any thing; when he had felled his timber he could not remove it, nor erect it after it was removed; hunger in the mean time would urge him from his work, and every different want call him a different way. Disease, nay even misfortune would be death, for though neither might be mortal, yet either would disable him from living, and reduce him to a state in which he might rather be said to perish than to die.

Thus necessity, like a gravitating power, would soon form our newly arrived emigrants into society, the reciprocal blessings of which, would supersede, and render the obligations of law and government unnecessary while they remained perfectly just to each other; but as nothing but heaven is impregnable to vice, it will unavoidably happen, that in proportion as they surmount the first difficulties of emigration, which bound them together in a common cause, they will begin to relax in their duty and attachment to each other; and this remissness will point out the necessity of establishing some form of government to supply the defect of moral virtue.

Some convenient tree will afford them a State-House, under the branches of which, the whole colony may assemble to deliberate on public matters. It is more than probable that their first laws will have the title only of REGU-LATIONS, and be enforced by no other penalty than public disesteem. In this first parliament every man, by natural right, will have a seat.

But as the colony increases, the public concerns will increase likewise, and the distance at which the members may be separated, will render it too inconvenient for all of them to meet on every occasion as at first, when their number was small, their habitations near, and the public concerns few and trifling. This will point out the convenience of their consenting to leave the legislative part to be managed by a select number chosen from the whole body, who are supposed to have the same concerns at stake which those who appointed them, and who will act in the same manner as the whole body would act, were they present. If the colony continues increasing, it will become necessary to augment the number of the representatives, and that the interest of every part of the colony may be attended to, it will be found best to divide the whole into convenient parts, each part sending its proper number; and that the ELECTED might never form to themselves an interest separate from the ELECTORS, prudence will point out the propriety of having elections often; because as the ELECTED might by that means return and mix again with the general body of the ELECTORS in a few months, their fidelity to the public will be secured by the prudent reflection of not making a rod for themselves. And as this frequent interchange will establish a common interest with every part of the community, they will mutually and naturally support each other, and on this (not on the unmeaning name of king) depends the STRENGTH OF GOVERNMENT, AND THE HAPPINESS OF THE GOVERNED.

Here then is the origin and rise of government; namely, a mode rendered necessary by the inability of moral virtue to govern the world; here too is the design and end of government, viz. freedom and security. And however our eyes may be dazzled with show, or our ears deceived by sound; however prejudice may warp our wills, or interest darken our understanding, the simple voice of nature and of reason will say, it is right.

I draw my idea of the form of government from a principle in nature, which no art can overturn, viz. that the more simple any thing is, the less liable it is to be disordered; and the easier repaired when disordered; and with this maxim in view, I offer a few remarks on the so much boasted constitution of England. That it was noble for the dark and slavish times in which it was erected, is granted. When the world was overrun with tyranny the least remove therefrom was a glorious rescue. But that it is imperfect, subject to convulsions, and incapable of producing what it seems to promise, is easily demonstrated.

Absolute governments (tho' the disgrace of human nature) have this advantage with them, that they are simple; if the people suffer, they know the head from which their suffering springs, know likewise the remedy, and are not bewildered by a variety of causes and cures. But the constitution of England is so exceedingly complex, that the nation may suffer for years together without being able to discover in which part the fault lies; some will say in one and some in another, and every political physician will advise a different medicine.

I know it is difficult to get over local or long standing prejudices, yet if we will suffer ourselves to examine the component parts of the English constitution, we shall find them to be the base remains of two ancient tyrannies, compounded with some new republican materials.

FIRST - The remains of monarchial tyranny in the person of the king.
SECONDLY - The remains of aristocratical tyranny in the persons of the peers.
THIRDLY - The new republican materials in the persons of the commons, on whose virtue depends the freedom of England.

The two first, by being hereditary, are independent of the people; wherefore in a CONSTITUTIONAL SENSE they contribute nothing towards the freedom of the state.

To say that the constitution of England is a UNION of three powers reciprocally CHECKING each other, is farcical, either the words have no meaning, or they are flat contradictions.

To say that the commons is a check upon the king, presupposes two things:

FIRST - That the king is not to be trusted without being looked after, or in other words, that a thirst for absolute power is the natural disease of monarchy.

SECONDLY - That the commons, by being appointed for that purpose, are either wiser or more worthy of confidence than the crown.

But as the same constitution which gives the commons a power to check the king by withholding the supplies, gives afterwards the king a power to check the commons, by empowering him to reject their other bills; it again supposes that the king is wiser than those whom it has already supposed to be wiser than him. A mere absurdity!

There is something exceedingly ridiculous in the composition of monarchy; it first excludes a man from the means of information, yet empowers him to act in cases where the highest judgment is required. The state of a king shuts him from the world, yet the business of a king requires him to know it thoroughly; wherefore the different parts, by unnaturally opposing and destroying each other, prove the whole character to be absurd and useless.

Some writers have explained the English constitution thus: The king, say they, is one, the people another; the peers are a house in behalf of the king, the commons in behalf of the people; but this hath all the distinctions of a house divided against itself; and though the expressions be pleasantly arranged, yet when examined, they appear idle and ambiguous; and it will always happen, that the nicest construction that words are capable of, when applied to the description of some thing which either cannot exist, or is too incomprehensible to be within the compass of description, will be words of sound only, and though they may amuse the ear, they cannot inform the mind, for this explanation includes a previous question, viz. HOW CAME THE KING BY A POWER WHICH THE PEOPLE ARE AFRAID TO TRUST, AND ALWAYS OBLIGED TO CHECK? Such a power could not be the gift of a wise people, neither can any power, WHICH NEEDS CHECKING, be from God; yet the provision, which the constitution makes, supposes such a power to exist.

But the provision is unequal to the task; the means either cannot or will not accomplish the end, and the whole affair is a felo de se; for as the greater weight will always carry up the less, and as all the wheels of a machine are put in motion by one, it only remains to know which power in the constitution has the most weight, for that will govern; and though the others, or a part of them, may clog, or, as the phrase is, check the rapidity of its motion, yet so long as they cannot stop it, their endeavours will be ineffectual; the first moving power will at last have its way, and what it wants in speed, is supplied by time.

That the crown is this overbearing part in the English constitution, needs not be mentioned, and that it derives its whole consequence merely from being the giver of places and pensions, is self-evident, wherefore, though we have been wise enough to shut and lock a door against absolute monarchy, we at the same time have been foolish enough to put the crown in possession of the key.

The prejudice of Englishmen in favour of their own government by king, lords, and commons, arises as much or more from national pride than reason. Individuals are undoubtedly safer in England than in some other countries, but the WILL of the king is as much the LAW of the land in Britain as in France, with this difference, that instead of proceeding directly from his mouth, it is handed to the people under the more formidable shape of an act of parliament. For the fate of Charles the First hath only made kings more subtle - not more just.

Wherefore, laying aside all national pride and prejudice in favour of modes and forms, the plain truth is, that IT IS WHOLLY OWING TO THE CONSTITUTION OF THE PEOPLE, AND NOT TO THE CONSTITUTION OF THE GOVERNMENT, that the crown is not as oppressive in England as in Turkey.

An inquiry into the CONSTITUTIONAL ERRORS in the English form of government is at this time highly necessary; for as we are never in a proper condition of doing justice to others, while we continue under the influence of some leading partiality, so neither are we capable of doing it to ourselves while we remain fettered by any obstinate prejudice. And as a man. who is attached to a prostitute, is unfitted to choose or judge a wife, so any prepossession in favour of a rotten constitution of government will disable us from discerning a good one.

OF MONARCHY AND HEREDITARY SUCCESSION

Mankind being originally equals in the order of creation, the equality could only be destroyed by some subsequent circumstance; the distinctions of rich, and poor, may in a great measure be accounted for, and that without having recourse to the harsh, ill-sounding names of oppression and avarice. Oppression is often the CONSEQUENCE, but seldom or never the MEANS of riches; and though avarice will preserve a man from being necessitously poor, it generally makes him too timorous to be wealthy.

But there is another and greater distinction, for which no truly natural or religious reason can be assigned, and that is, the distinction of men into KINGS and SUBJECTS. Male and female are the distinctions of nature, good and bad the distinctions of heaven; but how a race of men came into the world so exalted above the rest, and distinguished like some new species, is worth inquiring into, and whether they are the means of happiness or of misery to mankind.

In the early ages of the world, according to the scripture chronology, there were no kings; the consequence of which was, there were no wars; it is the pride of kings which throw mankind into confusion. Holland without a king hath enjoyed more peace for this last century than any of the monarchial governments in Europe. Antiquity favours the same remark; for the quiet and rural lives of the first patriarchs hath a happy something in them, which vanishes away when we come to the history of Jewish royalty.

Government by kings was first introduced into the world by the Heathens, from whom the children of Israel copied the custom. It was the most prosperous invention the Devil ever set on foot for the promotion of idolatry. The Heathens paid divine honours to their deceased kings, and the Christian world hath improved on the plan, by doing the same to their living ones. How impious is the title of sacred majesty applied to a worm, who in the midst of his splendor is crumbling into dust!

As the exalting one man so greatly above the rest cannot be justified on the equal rights of nature, so neither can it be defended on the authority of scripture; for the will of the Almighty, as declared by Gideon and the prophet Samuel, expressly disapproves of government by kings. All anti-monarchical parts of scripture have been very smoothly glossed over in monarchical governments, but they undoubtedly merit the attention of countries which have their governments yet to form. RENDER UNTO CAESAR THE THINGS WHICH ARE CAESAR'S is the scripture doctrine of courts, yet it is no support of monarchical government, for the Jews at that time were without a king, and in a state of vassalage to the Romans.

Now three thousand years passed away from the Mosaic account of the creation, till the Jews under a national delusion requested a king. Till then their form of government (except in extraordinary cases, where the Almighty interposed) was a kind of republic administered by a judge and the elders of the tribes. Kings they had none, and it was held sinful to acknowledge any being under that title but the Lord of Hosts. And when a man seriously reflects on the idolatrous homage which is paid to the persons of kings, he need not wonder that the Almighty, ever jealous of his honour, should disapprove of a form of government which so impiously invades the prerogative of heaven.

Monarchy is ranked in scripture as one of the sins of the Jews, for which a curse in reserve is denounced against them. The history of that transaction is worth attending to.

The children of Israel being oppressed by the Midianites, Gideon marched against them with a small army, and victory, through the divine interposition, decided in his favour. The Jews, elate with success, and attributing it to the generalship of Gideon, proposed making him a king, saying, RULE THOU OVER US, THOU AND THY SON AND THY SON'S SON. Here was temptation in its fullest extent; not a kingdom only, but an hereditary one, but Gideon in the piety of his soul replied, I WILL NOT RULE OVER YOU, NEITHER SHALL MY SON RULE OVER YOU _THE LORD SHALL RULE OVER YOU._ Words need not be more explicit; Gideon doth not decline the honour, but denieth their right to give it; neither doth he compliment them with invented declarations of his thanks, but in the positive style of a prophet charges them with disaffection to their proper Sovereign, the King of heaven.

About one hundred and thirty years after this, they fell again into the same error. The hankering which the Jews had for the idolatrous customs of the Heathens, is something exceedingly unaccountable; but so it was, that laying hold of the misconduct of Samuel's two sons, who were entrusted with some secular concerns, they came in an abrupt and clamorous manner to Samuel, saying, BEHOLD THOU ART OLD, AND THY SONS WALK NOT IN THY WAYS, NOW MAKE US A KING TO JUDGE US, LIKE ALL OTHER NATIONS. And here we cannot but observe that their motives were bad, viz. that they might be LIKE unto other nations, i.e. the Heathens, whereas their true glory laid in being as much UNLIKE them as possible. BUT THE THING DISPLEASED SAMUEL WHEN THEY SAID, GIVE US A KING TO JUDGE US; AND SAMUEL PRAYED UNTO THE LORD, AND THE LORD SAID UNTO SAMUEL, HEARKEN UNTO THE VOICE OF THE PEOPLE IN ALL THAT THEY SAY UNTO THEE, FOR THEY HAVE NOT REJECTED THEE, BUT THEY HAVE REJECTED ME, _THAT I SHOULD NOT REIGN OVER THEM._ ACCORDING TO ALL THE WORKS WHICH THEY HAVE SINCE THE DAY THAT I BROUGHT THEM UP OUT OF EGYPT, EVEN UNTO THIS DAY; WHEREWITH THEY HAVE FORSAKEN ME AND SERVED OTHER GODS; SO DO THEY ALSO UNTO THEE. NOW THEREFORE HEARKEN UNTO THEIR VOICE, HOWBEIT, PROTEST SOLEMNLY UNTO THEM AND SHEW THEM THE MANNER OF THE KING THAT SHALL REIGN OVER THEM, I.E. not of any particular king, but the general manner of the kings of the earth, whom Israel was so eagerly copying after. And notwithstanding the great distance of time and difference of manners, the character is still in fashion. AND SAMUEL TOLD ALL THE WORDS OF THE LORD UNTO THE PEOPLE, THAT ASKED OF HIM A KING. AND HE SAID, THIS SHALL BE THE MANNER OF THE KING THAT SHALL REIGN OVER YOU; HE WILL TAKE YOUR SONS AND APPOINT THEM FOR HIMSELF, FOR HIS CHARIOTS, AND TO BE HIS HORSEMAN, AND SOME SHALL RUN BEFORE HIS CHARI-OTS (this description agrees with the present mode of impressing men) AND HE WILL APPOINT HIM CAPTAINS OVER THOUSANDS AND CAPTAINS OVER FIFTIES, AND WILL SET THEM TO EAR HIS GROUND AND REAP HIS HARVEST, AND TO MAKE HIS INSTRU-MENTS OF WAR, AND INSTRUMENTS OF HIS CHARIOTS; AND HE WILL TAKE YOUR DAUGHTERS TO BE CONFECTIONARIES, AND TO BE COOKS AND TO BE BAKERS (this describes the expense and luxury as well as the oppression of kings) AND HE WILL TAKE YOUR FIELDS AND YOUR OLIVE YARDS, EVEN THE BEST OF THEM, AND GIVE THEM TO HIS SERVANTS; AND HE WILL TAKE THE TENTH OF YOUR SEED, AND OF YOUR VINEYARDS, AND GIVE THEM TO HIS OFFICERS AND TO HIS SERVANTS (by which we see that bribery, corruption, and favouritism are the standing vices of kings) AND HE WILL TAKE THE TENTH OF YOUR MEN SERVANTS, AND YOUR MAID SERVANTS, AND YOUR GOODLIEST YOUNG MEN AND YOUR ASSES, AND PUT THEM TO HIS WORK; AND HE WILL TAKE THE TENTH OF YOUR SHEEP, AND YE SHALL BE HIS SER-VANTS, AND YE SHALL CRY OUT IN THAT DAY BECAUSE OF YOUR KING WHICH YE SHALL HAVE CHOSEN, _AND THE LORD WILL NOT HEAR YOU IN THAT DAY._ This accounts for the continua-tion of monarchy; neither do the characters of the few good kings which have lived since, either sanctify the title, or blot out the sinfulness of the origin; the high encomium given of David takes no notice of him OFFI-CIALLY AS A KING, but only as a MAN after God's own heart. NEVER-THELESS THE PEOPLE REFUSED TO OBEY THE VOICE OF SAMUEL, AND THEY SAID, NAY, BUT WE WILL HAVE A KING OVER US, THAT WE MAY BE LIKE ALL THE NATIONS, AND THAT OUR KING MAY JUDGE US, AND GO OUT BEFORE US, AND FIGHT OUR BATTLES. Samuel continued to reason with them, but to no pur-pose; he set before them their ingratitude, but all would not avail; and see-ing them fully bent on their folly, he cried out, I WILL CALL UNTO THE LORD, AND HE SHALL SEND THUNDER AND RAIN (which then was a punishment, being in the time of wheat harvest) THAT YE MAY PER-CEIVE AND SEE THAT YOUR WICKEDNESS IS GREAT WHICH YE HAVE DONE IN THE SIGHT OF THE LORD, AND THE LORD SENT THUNDER AND RAIN THAT DAY, AND ALL THE PEOPLE GREATLY FEARED THE LORD AND SAMUEL. AND ALL THE PEOPLE SAID

UNTO SAMUEL, PRAY FOR THY SERVANTS UNTO THE LORD THY GOD THAT WE DIE NOT, FOR _WE HAVE ADDED UNTO OUR SINS THIS EVIL, TO ASK A KING._ These portions of scripture are direct and positive. They admit of no equivocal construction. That the Almighty hath here entered his protest against monarchical government, is true, or the scripture is false. And a man hath good reason to believe that there is as much of kingcraft, as priestcraft, in withholding the scripture from the public in Popish countries. For monarchy in every instance is the Popery of government.

To the evil of monarchy we have added that of hereditary succession; and as the first is a degradation and lessening of ourselves, so the second, claimed as a matter of right, is an insult and an imposition on posterity. For all men being originally equals, no ONE by BIRTH could have a right to set up his own family in perpetual preference to all others for ever, and though himself might deserve SOME decent degree of honours of his contemporaries, yet his descendants might be far too unworthy to inherit them. One of the strongest NATURAL proofs of the folly of hereditary right in kings, is, that nature disapproves it, otherwise she would not so frequently turn it into ridicule by giving mankind an ASS FOR A LION.

Secondly, as no man at first could possess any other public honours than were bestowed upon him, so the givers of those honours could have no power to give away the right of posterity. And though they might say, "We chooses you for OUR head," they could not, without manifest injustice to their children, say, "that your children and your children's children shall reign over OURS for ever." Because such an unwise, unjust, unnatural compact might (perhaps) in the next succession put them under the government of a rogue or a fool. Most wise men, in their private sentiments, have ever treated hereditary right with contempt; yet it is one of those evils, which when once established is not easily removed; many submit from fear, others from superstition, and the more powerful part shares with the king the plunder of the rest.

This is supposing the present race of kings in the world to have had an honourable origin; whereas it is more than probable, that could we take off the dark covering of antiquities, and trace them to their first rise, that we should find the first of them nothing better than the principal ruffian of some restless gang, whose savage manners or preeminence in subtlety obtained the title of chief among plunderers; and who by increasing in power, and extending his depredations, overawed the quiet and defenseless to purchase their safety by frequent contributions. Yet his electors could have no idea of giving hereditary right to his descendants, because such a perpetual exclusion of themselves was incompatible with the free and unrestrained principles they professed to live by. Wherefore, hereditary succession in the early ages of monarchy could not take place as a matter of claim, but as something casual or complemental; but as few or no records were extant in those days, and traditional history stuffed with fables, it was very easy, after the lapse of a few generations, to trump up some superstitious tale, conveniently timed, Mahomet like, to cram hereditary right down the throats of the vulgar. Perhaps the disorders which threatened, or seemed to threaten, on the decease of a leader and the choice of a new one (for elections among ruffians could not be very orderly) induced many at first to favour hereditary pretensions; by which means it happened, as it hath happened since, that what at first was submitted to as a convenience, was afterwards claimed as a right.

England, since the conquest, hath known some few good monarchs, but groaned beneath a much larger number of bad ones; yet no man in his senses can say that their claim under William the Conqueror is a very honourable one. A French bastard landing with an armed banditti, and establishing himself king of England against the consent of the natives, is in plain terms a very paltry rascally original. It certainly hath no divinity in it. However, it is needless to spend much time in exposing the folly of hereditary right; if there are any so weak as to believe it, let them promiscuously worship the ass and lion, and welcome. I shall neither copy their humility, nor disturb their devotion.

Yet I should be glad to ask how they suppose kings came at first? The question admits but of three answers, viz. either by lot, by election, or by usurpation. If the first king was taken by lot, it establishes a precedent for the next, which excludes hereditary succession. Saul was by lot, yet the succession was not hereditary, neither does it appear from that transaction there was any intention it ever should be. If the first king of any country was by election, that likewise establishes a precedent for the next; for to say, that the RIGHT of all future generations is taken away, by the act of the first electors, in their choice not only of a king, but of a family of kings for ever, hath no parallel in or out of scripture but the doctrine of original sin, which supposes the free will of all men lost in Adam; and from such comparison, and it will admit of no other, hereditary succession can derive no glory. For as in Adam all sinned, and as in the first electors all men obeyed; as in the one all mankind we re subjected to Satan, and in the other to Sovereignty; as our innocence was lost in the first, and our authority in the last; and as both disable us from reassuming some former state and privilege, it unanswerably follows that original sin and hereditary succession are parallels. Dishonourable rank! Inglorious connection! Yet the most subtle sophist cannot produce a juster simile.

As to usurpation, no man will be so hardy as to defend it; and that William the Conqueror was an usurper is a fact not to be contradicted. The plain truth is, that the antiquity of English monarchy will not bear looking into.

But it is not so much the absurdity as the evil of hereditary succession which concerns mankind. Did it ensure a race of good and wise men it would have the seal of divine authority, but as it opens a door to the FOOL-ISH, the WICKED, and the IMPROPER, it hath in it the nature of oppression. Men who look upon themselves born to reign, and others to obey, soon grow insolent; selected from the rest of mankind their minds are early poisoned by importance; and the world they act in differs so materially from the world at large, that they have but little opportunity of knowing its true interests, and when they succeed to the government are frequently the most ignorant and unfit of any throughout the dominions.

Another evil which attends hereditary succession is, that the throne is subject to be possessed by a minor at any age; all which time the regency, acting under the cover a king, have every opportunity and inducement to betray their trust. The same national misfortune happens, when a king, worn out with age and infirmity , enters the last stage of human weakness. In both these cases the public becomes a prey to every miscreant, who can tamper successfully with the follies either of age or infancy.

The most plausible plea, which hath ever been offered in favour of hereditary succession, is, that it preserves a nation from civil wars; and were this true, it would be weighty; whereas, it is the most barefaced falsity ever imposed upon mankind. The whole history of England disowns the fact. Thirty kings and two minors have reigned in that distracted kingdom since the conquest, in which time there have been (including the Revolution) no less than eight civil wars and nineteen rebellions. Wherefore instead of making for peace, it makes against it, and destroys the very foundation it seems to stand on.

The contest for monarchy and succession, between the houses of York and Lancaster, laid England in a scene of blood for many years. Twelve pitched battles, besides skirmishes and sieges, were fought between Henry and Edward. Twice was Henry prisoner to Edward, who in his turn was prisoner to Henry. And so uncertain is the fate of war and the temper of a nation, when nothing but personal matters are the ground of a quarrel, that Henry was taken in triumph from a prison to a palace, and Edward obliged to fly from a palace to a foreign land; yet, as sudden transitions of temper are seldom lasting, Henry in his turn was driven from the throne, and Edward recalled to succeed him. The parliament always following the strongest side.

This contest began in the reign of Henry the Sixth, and was not entirely extinguished till Henry the Seventh, in whom the families were united. Including a period of 67 years, viz. from 1422 to 1489.

In short, monarchy and succession have laid (not this or that kingdom only) but the world in blood and ashes. Tis a form of government which the word of God bears testimony against, and blood will attend it.

If we inquire into the business of a king, we shall find that in some countries they have none; and after sauntering away their lives without pleasure to themselves or advantage to the nation, withdraw from the scene, and leave their successors to tread the same idle ground. In absolute monarchies the whole weight of business, civil and military, lies on the king; the children of Israel in their request for a king, urged this plea "that he may judge us, and go out before us and fight our battles." But in countries where he is neither a judge nor a general, as in England, a man would be puzzled to know what IS his business.

The nearer any government approaches to a republic the less business there is for a king. It is somewhat difficult to find a proper name for the government of England. Sir William Meredith calls it a republic; but in its present state it is unworthy of the name, because the corrupt influence of the crown, by having all the places in its disposal, hath so effectually swallowed up the power, and eaten out the virtue of the house of commons (the republican part in the constitution) that the government of England is nearly as monarchical as that of France or Spain. Men fall out with names without understanding them. For it is the republican and not the monarchical part of the constitution of England which Englishmen glory in, viz. the liberty of choosing an house of commons from out of their own body - and it is easy to see that when republican virtue fails, slavery ensues. Why is the constitution of England sickly, but because monarchy hath poisoned the republic, the crown hath engrossed the commons?

In England a king hath little more to do than to make war and give away places; which in plain terms, is to impoverish the nation and set it together by the ears. A pretty business indeed for a man to be allowed eight hundred thousand sterling a year for, and worshipped into the bargain! Of more worth is one honest man to society and in the sight of God, than all the crowned ruffians that ever lived.

THOUGHTS ON THE PRESENT STATE OF AMERICAN AFFAIRS

In the following pages I offer nothing more than simple facts, plain arguments, and common sense; and have no other Preliminaries to settle with the reader, than that he will divest himself of prejudice and prepossession, and suffer his reason and his feelings to determine for themselves; that he will put ON, or rather that he will not put OFF the true character of a man, and generously enlarge his views beyond the present day.

Volumes have been written on the subject of the struggle between England and America. Men of all ranks have embarked in the controversy, from different motives, and with various designs; but all have been ineffectual, and the period of debate is closed. Arms, as the last resource, decide this contest; the appeal was the choice of the king, and the continent hath accepted the challenge.

It hath been reported of the late Mr. Pelham (who tho' an able minister was not without his faults) that on his being attacked in the house of commons, on the score, that his measures were only of a temporary kind, replied "THEY WILL LAST MY TIME." Should a thought so fatal and unmanly possess the colonies in the present contest, the name of ancestors will be remembered by future generations with detestation.

The sun never shined on a cause of greater worth. 'Tis not the affair of a city, a county, a province, or a kingdom, but of a continent - of at least one eighth part of the habitable globe. 'Tis not the concern of a day, a year, or an age; posterity are virtually involved in the contest, and will be more or less affected, even to the end of time, by the proceedings now. Now is the seed-time of continental union, faith and honour. The least fracture now will be like a name engraved with the point of a pin on the tender rind of a young oak; the wound will enlarge with the tree, and posterity read it in full grown characters.

By referring the matter from argument to arms, a new aera for politics is struck; a new method of thinking hath arisen. All plans, proposals, &c. prior to the nineteenth of April, i. e. to the commencement of hostilities, are like the almanacs of the last year; which, though proper then are superseded and useless now. Whatever was advanced by the advocates on either side of the question then, terminated in one and the same point. viz. a union with Great-Britain: the only difference between the parties was the method of effecting it; the one proposing force, the other friendship; but it hath so far happened that the first hath failed, and the second hath withdrawn her influence.

As much hath been said of the advantages of reconciliation which, like an agreeable dream, hath passed away and left us as we were, it is but right, that we should examine the contrary side of the argument, and inquire into some of the many material injuries which these colonies sustain, and always will sustain, by being connected with, and dependent on Great Britain: To examine that connection and dependence, on the principles of nature and common sense, to see what we have to trust to, if separated, and what we are to expect, if dependant.

I have heard it asserted by some, that as America hath flourished under her former connection with Great Britain that the same connection is necessary towards her future happiness, and will always have the same effect. Nothing can be more fallacious than this kind of argument. We may as well assert that because a child has thrived upon milk that it is never to have meat, or that the first twenty years of our lives is to become a precedent for the next twenty. But even this is admitting more than is true, for I answer roundly, that America would have flourished as much, and probably much more, had no European power had any thing to do with her. The commerce, by which she hath enriched herself, are the necessaries of life, and will always have a market while eating is the custom of Europe.

But she has protected us, say some. That she has engrossed us is true, and defended the continent at our expense as well as her own is admitted, and she would have defended Turkey from the same motive, viz. the sake of trade and dominion.

Alas, we have been long led away by ancient prejudices, and made large sacrifices to superstition. We have boasted the protection of Great Britain, without considering, that her motive was INTEREST not ATTACHMENT; that she did not protect us from OUR ENEMIES on OUR ACCOUNT, but from HER ENEMIES on HER OWN ACCOUNT, from those who had no quarrel with us on any OTHER ACCOUNT, and who will always be our enemies on the SAME ACCOUNT. Let Britain wave her pretensions to the continent, or the continent throw off the dependence, and we should be at peace with France and Spain were they at war with Britain. The miseries of Hanover last war ought to warn us against connections.

It has lately been asserted in parliament, that the colonies have no relation to each other but through the parent country, i. e. that Pennsylvania and the Jerseys, and so on for the rest, are sister colonies by the way of England; this is certainly a very round-about way of proving relationship, but it is the nearest and only true way of proving enemyship, if I may so call it. France and Spain never were. nor perhaps ever will be our enemies as AMERICANS, but as our being the subjects of GREAT BRITAIN.

But Britain is the parent country, say some. Then the more shame upon her conduct. Even brutes do not devour their young, nor savages make war upon their families; wherefore the assertion, if true, turns to her reproach;

but it happens not to be true, or only partly so and the phrase PARENT or MOTHER COUNTRY hath been jesuitically adopted by the king and his parasites, with a low papistical design of gaining an unfair bias on the credulous weakness of our minds. Europe, and not England, is the parent country of America. This new world hath been the asylum for the persecuted lovers of civil and religious liberty from EVERY PART of Europe. Hither have they fled, not from the tender embraces of the mother, but from the cruelty of the monster; and it is so far true of England, that the same tyranny which drove the first emigrants from home, pursues their descendants still.

In this extensive quarter of the globe, we forget the narrow limits of three hundred and sixty miles (the extent of England) and carry our friendship on a larger scale; we claim brotherhood with every European Christian, and triumph in the generosity of the sentiment.

It is pleasant to observe by what regular gradations we surmount the force of local prejudice, as we enlarge our acquaintance with the world. A man born in any town in England divided into parishes, will naturally associate most with his fellow-parishioners (because their interests in many cases will be common) and distinguish him by the name of NEIGHBOUR; if he meet him but a few miles from home, he drops the narrow idea of a street, and salutes him by the name of TOWNSMAN; if he travel out of the county, and meet him in any other, he forgets the minor divisions of street and town, and calls him COUNTRYMAN, i. e. COUNTRYMAN; but if in their foreign excursions they should associate in France or any other part of EUROPE, their local remembrance would be enlarged into that of EN-GLISHMEN. And by a just parity of reasoning, all Europeans meeting in America, or any other quarter of the globe, are COUNTRYMEN; for England, Holland, Germany, or Sweden, when compared with the whole, stand in the same places on the larger scale, which the divisions of street, town, and county do on the smaller ones; distinctions too limited for continental minds. Not one third of the inhabitants, even of this province, are of English descent. Wherefore I reprobate the phrase of parent or mother country applied to England only, as being false, selfish, narrow and ungenerous.

But admitting, that we were all of English descent, what does it amount to? Nothing. Britain, being now an open enemy, extinguishes every other name and title: And to say that reconciliation is our duty, is truly farcical. The first king of England, of the present line (William the Conqueror) was a Frenchman, and half the Peers of England are descendants from the same country; therefore, by the same method of reasoning, England ought to be governed by France.

Much hath been said of the united strength of Britain and the colonies, that in conjunction they might bid defiance to the world. But this is mere presumption; the fate of war is uncertain, neither do the expressions mean any thing; for this continent would never suffer itself to be drained of inhabitants, to support the British arms in either Asia, Africa, or Europe.

Besides what have we to do with setting the world at defiance? Our plan is commerce, and that, well attended to, will secure us the peace and friendship of all Europe; because, it is the interest of all Europe to have America a FREE PORT. Her trade will always be a protection, and her barrenness of gold and silver secure her from invaders.

I challenge the warmest advocate for reconciliation, to shew, a single advantage that this continent can reap, by being connected with Great Britain. I repeat the challenge, not a single advantage is derived. Our corn will fetch its price in any market in Europe, and our imported goods must be paid for, buy them where we will.

But the injuries and disadvantages we sustain by that connection, are without number; and our duty to mankind at large, as well as to ourselves, instruct us to renounce the alliance: Because, any submission to, or dependence on Great Britain, tends directly to involve this continent in European wars and quarrels; and sets us at variance with nations, who would otherwise seek our friendship, and against whom, we have neither anger nor complaint. As Europe is our market for trade, we ought to form no partial connection with any part of it. It is the true interest of America to steer clear of European contentions, which she never can do, while by her dependence on Britain, she is made the make-weight in the scale of British politics.

Europe is too thickly planted with kingdoms to be long at peace, and whenever a war breaks out between England and any foreign power, the trade of America goes to ruin, BECAUSE OF HER CONNECTION WITH ENGLAND. The next war may not turn out like the last, and should it not, the advocates for reconciliation now, will be wishing for separation then, because, neutrality in that case, would be a safer convoy than a man of war. Every thing that is right or natural pleads for separation. The blood of the slain, the weeping voice of nature cries, 'TIS TIME TO PART. Even the distance at which the Almighty hath placed England and America, is a strong and natural proof, that the authority of the one, over the other, was never the design of Heaven. The time likewise at which the continent was discovered, adds weight to the argument, and the manner in which it was peopled increases the force of it. The reformation was preceded by the discovery of America, as if the Almighty graciously meant to open a sanctuary to the Persecuted in future years, when home should afford neither friendship nor safety.

The authority of Great Britain over this continent, is a form of government, which sooner or later must have an end: And a serious mind can draw no true pleasure by looking forward under the painful and positive conviction, that what he calls "the present constitution" is merely temporary. As parents, we can have no joy, knowing that THIS GOVERNMENT is not sufficiently lasting to ensure any thing which we may bequeath to posterity: And by a plain method of argument, as we are running the next generation into debt, we ought to do the work of it, otherwise we use them meanly and pitifully. In order to discover the line of our duty rightly, we should take our children in our hand, and fix our station a few years farther into life; that eminence will present a prospect, which a few present fears and prejudices conceal from our sight.

Though I would carefully avoid giving unnecessary offense, yet I am inclined to believe, that all those who espouse the doctrine of reconciliation, may be included within the following descriptions. Interested men, who are not to be trusted; weak men, who CANNOT see; prejudiced men, who WILL NOT see; and a certain set of moderate men, who think better of the European world than it deserves; and this last class, by an ill-judged deliberation, will be the cause of more calamities to this continent, than all the other three.

It is the good fortune of many to live distant from the scene of sorrow; the evil is not sufficient brought to their doors to make THEM feel the precariousness with which all American property is possessed. But let our imaginations transport us far a few moments to Boston, that seat of wretchedness will teach us wisdom, and instruct us for ever to renounce a power in whom we can have no trust. The inhabitants of that unfortunate city, who but a few months ago were in ease and affluence, have now, no other alternative than to stay and starve, or turn and beg. Endangered by the fire of their friends if they continue within the city, and plundered by the soldiery if they leave it. In their present condition they are prisoners without the hope of redemption, and in a general attack for their relief, they would be exposed to the fury of both armies.

Men of passive tempers look somewhat lightly over the offenses of Britain, and, still hoping for the best, are apt to call out, "COME, COME, WE SHALL BE FRIENDS AGAIN, FOR ALL THIS." But examine the passions and feelings of mankind, Bring the doctrine of reconciliation to the touchstone of nature, and then tell me, whether you can hereafter love, honor, and faithfully serve the power that hath carried fire and sword into your land? If yon cannot do all these, then are you only deceiving yourselves, and by your delay bringing ruin upon posterity. Your future connection with Britain, whom you can neither love nor honor will be forced and unnatural, and being formed only on the plan of present convenience, will in a little time fall into a relapse more wretched than the first. But if you say, you can still pass the violations over, then I ask, Hath your house been burnt? Hath your property been destroyed before your face! Are your wife and children destitute of a bed to lie on, or bread to live on? Have you lost a parent or a child by their hands, and yourself the ruined and wretched survivor! If you have not, then are you not a judge of those who have. But if you have, and still can shake hands with the murderers, then are you unworthy the name of husband, father, friend, or lover, and whatever may be your rank or title in life, you have the heart of a coward, and the spirit of a sycophant.

This is not inflaming or exaggerating matters, but trying them by those feelings and affections which nature justifies, and without which, we should be incapable of discharging the social duties of life, or enjoying the felicities of it. I mean not to exhibit horror for the purpose of provoking revenge, but to awaken us from fatal and unmanly slumbers, that we may pursue determinately some fixed object. It is not in the power of Britain or of Europe to conquer America, if she do not conquer herself by DELAY and TIMIDITY. The present winter is worth an age if rightly employed, but if lost or neglected, the whole continent will partake of the misfortune; and there is no punishment which that man will not deserve, be he who, or what, or where he will, that may be the means of sacrificing a season so precious and useful.

It is repugnant to reason, to the universal order of things, to all examples from former ages, to suppose, that this continent can longer remain subject to any external power. The most sanguine in Britain does not think so. The utmost stretch of human wisdom cannot, at this time, compass a plan short of separation, which can promise the continent even a year's security. Reconciliation is NOW a fallacious dream. Nature hath deserted the connection, and Art cannot supply her place. For, as Milton wisely expresses, "never can true reconcilement grow, where wounds of deadly hate have pierced so deep."

Every quiet method for peace hath been ineffectual. Our prayers have been rejected with disdain; and only tended to convince us, that nothing Batters vanity, or confirms obstinacy in Kings more than repeated petitioning-and nothing hath contributed more than that very measure to make the Kings of Europe absolute: Witness Denmark and Sweden. Wherefore, since nothing but blows will do, for God's sake, let us come to a final separation, and not leave the next generation to be cutting throats, under the violated unmeaning names of parent and child.

To say, they will never attempt it again is idle and visionary, we thought so at the repeal of the stamp-act, yet a year or two undeceived us; as well may we suppose that nations, which have been once defeated, will never renew the quarrel.

As to government matters, it is not in the power of Britain to do this continent justice: The business of it will soon be too weighty, and intricate, to be managed with any tolerable degree of convenience, by a power so distant from us, and so very ignorant of us; for if they cannot conquer us, they cannot govern us. To be always running three or four thousand miles with a tale or a petition, waiting four or five months for an answer, which when obtained requires five or six more to explain it in, will in a few years be looked upon as folly and childishness—There was a time when it was proper, and there is a proper time for it to cease.

Small islands not capable of protecting themselves, are the proper objects for kingdoms to take under their care; but there is something very absurd, in supposing a continent to be perpetually governed by an island. In no instance hath nature made the satellite larger than its primary planet, and as England and America, with respect to each other, reverses the common order of nature, it is evident they belong to different systems; England to Europe, America to itself.

I am not induced by motives of pride, party, or resentment to espouse the doctrine of separation and independance; I am clearly, positively, and conscientiously persuaded that it is the true interest of this continent to be so; that every thing short of THAT is mere patchwork, that it can afford no lasting felicity, —that it is leaving the sword to our children, and shrinking back at a time, when, a little more, a little farther, would have rendered this continent the glory of the earth.

As Britain hath not manifested the least inclination towards a compromise, we may be assured that no terms can be obtained worthy the acceptance of the continent, or any ways equal to the expense of blood and treasure we have been already put to.

The object, contended for, ought always to bear some just proportion to the expense. The removal of North, or the whole detestable junto, is a matter unworthy the millions we have expended. A temporary stoppage of trade, was an inconvenience, which would have sufficiently balanced the repeal of all the acts complained of, had such repeals been obtained; hut if the whole continent must take up arms, if every man must be a soldier, it is scarcely worth our while to fight against a contemptible ministry only. Dearly, dearly, do we pay for the repeal of the acts, if that is all we fight for; for in a just estimation, it is as great a folly to pay a Bunker-hill price for law, as for land. As I have always considered the independancy of this continent, as an event, which sooner or later must arrive, so from the late rapid progress of the continent to maturity, the event could not be far off. Wherefore, on the breaking out of hostilities, it was not worth while to have disputed a matter, which time would have finally redressed, unless we meant to be in earnest; otherwise, it is like wasting an estate on a suit at law, to regulate the trespasses of a tenant, whose lease is just expiring. No man was a warmer wisher for reconciliation than myself, before the fatal nineteenth of April 1775, but the moment the event of that day was made known, I rejected the hardened, sullen tempered Pharaoh of England for ever; and disdain the wretch, that with the pretended title of FATHER OF HIS PEOPLE can unfeelingly hear of their slaughter, and composedly sleep with their blood upon his soul.

But admitting that matters were now made up, what would be the event? I answer, the ruin of the continent. And that for several reasons.

FIRST. The powers of governing still remaining in the hands of the king, he will have a negative over the whole legislation of this continent. And as he hath shewn himself such an inveterate enemy to liberty. and discovered such a thirst for arbitrary power; is he, or is he not, a proper man to say to these colonies, "YOU SHALL MAKE NO LAWS BUT WHAT I PLEASE.' And is there any inhabitant in America so ignorant as not to know, that according to what is called the PRESENT CONSTITUTION, that this con-tinent can make no laws but what the king gives leave to; and is there any man so unwise, as not to see, that (considering what has happened) he will suffer no law to be made here, but such as suit HIS purpose. We may be as effectually enslaved by the want of laws in America, as by submitting to laws made for us in England. After matters are made up (as it is called) can there be any doubt, but the whole power of the crown will be exerted, to keep this continent as low and humble as possible? Instead of going for-ward we shall go backward, or be perpetually quarrelling or ridiculously petitioning. —WE are already greater than the king wishes us to be, and will he not hereafter endeavour to make us less? To bring the matter to one point. Is the power who is jealous of our prosperity, a proper power to govern us? Whoever says No to this question, is an INDEPENDANT, for independancy means no more, than, whether we shall make our own laws, or whether the king, the greatest enemy this continent hath, or can have, shall tell us "THERE SHALL BE NO LAWS BUT SUCH AS I LIKE."

But the king you will say has a negative in England; the people there can make no laws without his consent. In point of right and good order, there is something very ridiculous, that a youth of twenty-one (which hath often happened) shall say to several millions of people, older and wiser than himself, I forbid this or that act of yours to be law. But in this place I decline this sort of reply, though I will never cease to expose the absurdity of it, and only answer, that England being the King's residence, and America not so, makes quite another case. The king's negative HERE is ten times more dangerous and fatal than it can be in England, for THERE he will scarcely refuse his consent to a bill for putting England into as strong a state of defense as possible, and in America he would never suffer such a bill to be passed.

America is only a secondary object in the system of British politics, England consults the good of THIS country, no farther than it answers her OWN purpose. Wherefore, her own interest leads her to suppress the growth of OURS in every case which doth not promote her advantage, or in the least interferes with it. A pretty state we should soon be in under such a secondhand government, considering what has happened! Men do not change from enemies to friends by the alteration of a name: And in order to shew that reconciliation now is a dangerous doctrine, I affirm, THAT IT WOULD BE POLICY IN THE KING AT THIS TIME, TO REPEAL THE ACTS FOR THE SAKE OF REINSTATING HIMSELF IN THE GOVERNMENT OF THE PROVINCES; in order, that HE MAY ACCOMPLISH BY CRAFT AND SUBTLETY, IN THE LONG RUN, WHAT HE CANNOT DO BY FORCE AND VIOLENCE IN THE SHORT ONE. Reconciliation and ruin are nearly related.

SECONDLY. That as even the best terms, which we can expect to obtain, can amount to no more than a temporary expedient, or a kind of government by guardianship, which can last no longer than till the colonies come of age, so the general face and state of things, in the interim, will be unsettled and unpromising. Emigrants of property will not choose to come to a country whose form of government hangs but by a thread, and who is every day tottering on the brink of commotion and disturbance; and numbers of the present inhabitants would lay hold of the interval, to dispense of their effects, and quit the continent.

But the most powerful of all arguments, is, that nothing but independence, i.e. a continental form of government, can keep the peace of the continent and preserve it inviolate from civil wars. I dread the event of a reconciliation with Britain now, as it is more than probable, that it will be followed by a revolt somewhere or other, the consequences of which may be far more fatal than all the malice of Britain.

Thousands are already ruined by British barbarity; (thousands more will probably suffer the same fate) Those men have other feelings than us who have nothing suffered. All they NOW possess is liberty, what they before enjoyed is sacrificed to its service, and having nothing more to lose, they disdain submission. Besides, the general temper of the colonies, towards a British government, will be like that of a youth, who is nearly out of his time; they will care very little about her. And a government which cannot preserve the peace, is no government at all, and in that case we pay our money for nothing; and pray what is it that Britain can do, whose power will be wholly on paper. should a civil tumult break out the very day after reconciliation! I have heard some men say, many of whom I believe spoke without thinking, that they dreaded an independence, fearing that it would produce civil wars. It is but seldom that our first thoughts are truly correct, and that is the case here; for there are ten times more to dread from a patched up connection than from independence. I make the sufferers case my own, and I protest, that were I driven from house and home, my property destroyed, and my circumstances ruined, that as man, sensible of injuries, I could never relish the doctrine of reconciliation, or consider myself bound thereby.

The colonies have manifested such a spirit of good order and obedience to continental government, as is sufficient to make every reasonable person easy and happy on that head. No man can assign the least pretence for his fears, on any other grounds, than such as are truly childish and ridiculous, viz. that one colony will be striving for superiority over another.

Where there are no distinctions there can be no superiority, perfect equality affords no temptation. The republics of Europe are all (and we may say always) in peace. Holland and Switzerland are without wars, foreign or domestic: Monarchical governments, it is true, are never long at rest; the crown itself is a temptation to enterprising ruffians at HOME; and that degree of pride and insolence ever attendant on regal authority, swells into a rupture with foreign powers, in instances, where a republican government, by being formed on more natural principles, would negotiate the mistake.

If there is any true cause of fear respecting independence, it is because no plan is yet laid down. Men do not see their way out— Wherefore, as an opening into that business, I offer the following hints; at the same time modestly affirming, that I have no other opinion of them myself, than that they may be the means of giving rise to something better. Could the straggling thoughts of individuals be collected, they would frequently form materials for wise and able men to improve into useful matter.

LET the assemblies be annual, with a President only. The representation more equal. Their business wholly domestic, and subject to the authority of a Continental Congress.

Let each colony be divided into six, eight, or ten, convenient districts, each district to send a proper number of delegates to Congress, so that each colony send at least thirty. The whole number in Congress will be at least 390. Each Congress to sit and to choose a president by the following method. When the delegates are met, let a colony be taken from the whole thirteen colonies by lot, after which, let the whole Congress choose (by ballot) a president from out of the delegates of that province. In the next Congress, let a colony be taken by lot from twelve only, omitting that colony from which the president was taken in the former Congress, and so proceeding on till the whole thirteen shall have had their proper rotation. And in order that nothing may pass into a law but what is satisfactorily just not less than three fifths of the Congress to be called a majority— He that will promote discord, under a government so equally formed as this, would have joined Lucifer in his revolt.

But as there is a peculiar delicacy, from whom, or in what manner, this business must first arise, and as it seems most agreeable and consistent, that it should come from some intermediate body between the governed and the governors, that is, between the Congress and the people. let a CONTINENTAL CONFERENCE be held, in the following manner, and for the following purpose.

A committee of twenty-six members of Congress, viz. two for each colony. Two Members from each House of Assembly, or Provincial Convention; and five representatives of the people at large, to be chosen in the capital city or town of each province, for and in behalf of the whole province, by as many qualified voters as shall think proper to attend from all parts of the province for that purpose; or, if more convenient, the representatives may be chosen in two or three of the most populous parts thereof. In this conference, thus assembled, will be united, the two grand principles of business KNOWLEDGE and POWER. The members of Congress, Assemblies, or Conventions, by having had experience in national concerns, will be able and useful counsellors, and the whole, being empowered by the people, will have a truly legal authority.

The conferring members being met, let their business be to frame a CONTINENTAL CHARTER, Or Charter of the United Colonies; (answering to what is called the Magna Carta of England) fixing the number and manner of choosing members of Congress, members of Assembly, with their date of sitting, and drawing the line of business and jurisdiction between them:

(Always remembering, that our strength is continental, not provincial:) Securing freedom and property to all men, and above all things, the free exercise of religion, according to the dictates of conscience; with such other matter as is necessary for a charter to contain. Immediately after which, the said Conference to dissolve, and the bodies which shall be chosen comformable to the said charter, to be the legislators and governors of this continent for the time being: Whose peace and happiness may God preserve, Amen.

Should any body of men be hereafter delegated for this or some similar purpose, I offer them the following extracts or that wise observer on governments DRAGONETTI. "The science" says he "of the politician consists in fixing the true point of happiness and freedom. Those men would deserve the gratitude of ages, who should discover a mode of government that contained the greatest sum of individual happiness, with the least national expense. [Dragonetti on virtue and rewards]

But where, says some, is the King of America? I'll tell you. Friend, he reigns above, and doth not make havoc of mankind like the Royal Brute of Britain. Yet that we may not appear to be defective even in earthly honors, let a day be solemnly set apart for proclaiming the charter; let it be brought forth placed on the divine law, the word of God; let a crown be placed thereon, by which the world may know, that so far we approve of monarchy, that in America THE LAW IS KING. For as in absolute governments the King is law, so in free countries the law OUGHT to be King; and there ought to be no other. But lest any ill use should afterwards arise, let the crown at the conclusion of the ceremony, be demolished, and scattered among the people whose right it is.

A government of our own is our natural right: And when a man seriously reacts on the precariousness of human affairs, he will become convinced, that it is infinitely wiser and safer, to form a constitution of our own in a cool deliberate manner, while we have it in our power, than to trust such an interesting event to time and chance. If we omit it now, some [Thomas Anello otherwise Massanello a fisherman of Naples, who after spiriting up his countrymen in the public marketplace, against the oppressions of the Spaniards, to whom the place was then subject prompted them to revolt, and in the space of a day became king.] Massanello may hereafter arise, who laying hold of popular disquietudes, may collect together the desperate and the discontented, and by assuming to themselves the powers of government, may sweep away the liberties of the continent like a deluge. Should the government of America return again into the hands of Britain, the tottering situation of things will be a temptation for some desperate adventurer to try his fortune; and in such a case, that relief can Britain give? Ere she could hear the news, the fatal business might be done; and ourselves suffering like the wretched Britons under the oppression of the Conqueror. Ye that oppose independence now, ye know not what ye do; ye are opening a door to eternal tyranny, by keeping vacant the seat of government. There are thousands, and tens of thousands, who would think it glorious to expel from the continent that barbarous and hellish power, which hath stirred up the Indians and Negroes to destroy us; the cruelty hath a double guilt, it is dealing brutally by us, and treacherously by them.

To talk of friendship with those in whom our reason forbids us to have faith, and our affections wounded through a thousand pores instruct us to detest, is madness and folly. Every day wears out the little remains of kindred between us and them, and can there be any reason to hope, that as the relationship expires, the affection will increase, or that we shall agree better, when we have ten times more and greater concerns to quarrel over than ever?

Ye that tell us of harmony and reconciliation, can ye restore to us the time that is past? Can ye give to prostitution its former innocence? Neither can ye reconcile Britain and America. The last cord now is broken, the people of England are presenting addresses against us. There are injuries which nature cannot forgive; she would cease to be nature if she did. As well can the lover forgive the ravisher of his mistress, as the continent forgive the murders of Britain. The Almighty hath implanted in us these unextinguishable feelings for good and wise purposes. They are the guardians of his image in our hearts. They distinguish us from the herd of common animals. The social compact would dissolve, and justice be extirpated the earth, or have only a casual existence were we callous to the touches of affection. The robber, and the murderer, would often escape unpunished, did not the injuries which our tempers sustain, provoke us into justice.

O ye that love mankind! Ye that dare oppose, not only the tyranny, but the tyrant, stand forth! Every spot of the old world is overrun with oppression. Freedom hath been hunted round the globe. Asia, and Africa, have long expelled her—Europe regards her like a stranger, and England hath given her warning to depart. O! receive the fugitive, and prepare in time an asylum for mankind.

OF THE PRESENT _ABILITY_ OF _AMERICA_, WITH SOME MISCELLANEOUS _REFLECTIONS_

I have never met with a man, either in England or America, who hath not confessed his opinion that a separation between the countries, would take place one time or other: And there is no instance, in which we have shewn less judgement, than in endeavouring to describe, what we call the ripeness or fitness of the Continent for independence.

As all men allow the measure, and vary only in their opinion of the time, let us, in order to remove mistakes, take a general survey of things, and endeavour, if possible, to find out the VERY time. But we need not go far, the inquiry ceases at once, for, the TIME HATH FOUND US. The general concurrence, the glorious union of all things prove the fact.

It is not in numbers, but in unity, that our great strength lies; yet our present numbers are sufficient to repel the force of all the world. The Continent hath, at this time, the largest body of armed and disciplined men of any power under Heaven; and is just arrived at that pitch of strength, in which no single colony is able to support itself, and the whole, when united, can accomplish the matter, and either more, or, less than this, might be fatal in its effects. Our land force is already sufficient, and as to naval affairs, we cannot be insensible, that Britain would never suffer an American man of war to be built, while the continent remained in her hands. Wherefore, we should be no forwarder an hundred years hence in that branch, than we are now; but the truth is, we should be less so, because the timber of the country is every day diminishing, and that, which will remain at last, will be far off and difficult to procure.

Were the continent crowded with inhabitants, her sufferings under the present circumstances would be intolerable. The more seaport towns we had, the more should we have both to defend and to lose. Our present numbers are so happily proportioned to our wants, that no man need be idle. The diminution of trade affords an army, and the necessities of an army create a new trade.

Debts we have none; and whatever we may contract on this account will serve as a glorious memento of our virtue. Can we but leave posterity with a settled form of government, an independent constitution of its own, the purchase at any price will be cheap. But to expend millions for the sake of getting a few vile acts repealed, and routing the present ministry only, is unworthy the charge, and is using posterity with the utmost cruelty; because it is leaving them the great work to do, and a debt upon their backs, from which they derive no advantage. Such a thought is unworthy of a man of honor, and is the true characteristic of a narrow heart and a peddling politician.

The debt we may contract doth not deserve our regard, if the work be but accomplished. No nation ought to be without a debt. A national debt is a national bond; and when it bears no interest, is in no case a grievance.

Britain is oppressed with a debt of upwards of one hundred and forty millions sterling, for which she pays upwards of four millions interest. And as a compensation for her debt, she has a large navy; America is without a debt, and without a navy; yet for the twentieth part of the English national debt, could have a navy as large again. The navy of England is not worth, at this time, more than three millions and an half sterling.

The first and second editions of this pamphlet were published without the following calculations, which are now given as a proof that the above estimation of the navy is just. [See Entic's naval history, intro. page 56.]

The charge of building a ship of each rate, and furnishing her with masts, yards, sails and rigging, together with a proportion of eight months boatswain's and carpenter's seastores, as calculated by Mr. Burchett, Secretary to the navy.

		[pounds Sterling]
For a ship of a 100 guns	–	35,553
90	–	29,886
80	–	23,638
70	–	17,795
60	–	14,197
50	–	10,606
40	–	7,558
30	–	5,846
20	–	3,710

And from hence it is easy to sum up the value, or cost rather, of the whole British navy, which in the year 1757, when it was at its greatest glory consisted of the following ships and guns:

Ships.	Guns.	Cost of one.	Cost of all
6	100	35,553	213,318
12	90	29,886	358,632
12	80	23,638	283,656
43	70	17,785	764,755
35	60	14,197	496,895
40	50	10,606	424,240
45	40	7,558	340,110
58	20	3,710	215,180

85 Sloops, bombs, and fireships, one with another, at		2,000	170,000

		Cost	3,266,786
Remains for guns,			233,214
		Total	3,500,000

No country on the globe is so happily situated, or so internally capable of raising a fleet as America. Tar, timber, iron, and cordage are her natural produce. We need go abroad for nothing. Whereas the Dutch, who make large profits by hiring out their ships of war to the Spaniards and Portuguese, are obliged to import most of their materials they use. We ought to view the building a fleet as an article of commerce, it being the natural manufactory of this country. It is the best money we can lay out. A navy when finished is worth more than it cost. And is that nice point in national policy, in which commerce and protection are united. Let us build; if we want them not, we can sell; and by that means replace our paper currency with ready gold and silver.

In point of manning a fleet, people in general run into great errors; it is not necessary that one fourth part should he sailors. The Terrible privateer, Captain Death, stood the hottest engagement of any ship last war, yet had not twenty sailors on board, though her complement of men was upwards of two hundred. A few able and social sailors will soon instruct a sufficient number of active landmen in the common work of a ship. Wherefore, we never can be more capable to begin on maritime matters than now, while our timber is standing, our fisheries blocked up, and our sailors and ship-wrights out of employ. Men of war of seventy and eighty guns were built forty years ago in New-England, and why not the same now? Ship-building is America's greatest pride, and in which she will in time excel the whole world. The great empires of the east are mostly inland, and consequently excluded from the possibility of rivalling her. Africa is in a state of barbarism; and no power in Europe hath either such an extent of coast, or such an internal supply of materials. Where nature hath given the one, she has withheld the other; to America only hath she been liberal of both. The vast empire of Russia is almost shut out from the sea: wherefore, her boundless forests, her tar, iron, and cordage are only articles of commerce.

In point of safety, ought we to be without a fleet? We are not the little people now, which we were sixty years ago; at that time we might have trusted our property in the streets, or fields rather; and slept securely without locks or bolts to our doors or windows. The case now is altered, and our methods of defense ought to improve with our increase of property. A common pirate, twelve months ago, might have come up the Delaware, and laid the city of Philadelphia under instant contribution, for what sum he pleased; and the same might have happened to other places. Nay, any daring fellow, in a brig of fourteen or sixteen guns might have robbed the whole continent, and carried off half a million of money. These are circumstances which demand our attention, and point out the necessity of naval protection.

Some, perhaps, will say, that after we have made it up Britain, she will protect us. Can we be so unwise as to mean, that she shall keep a navy in our harbours for that purpose? Common sense will tell us, that the power which hath endeavoured to subdue us, is of all others the most improper to defend us. Conquest may be effected under the pretence of friendship; and ourselves after a long and brave resistance, be at last cheated into slavery. And if her ships are not to be admitted into our harbours, I would ask, how is she to protect us? A navy three or four thousand miles off can be of little use, and on sudden emergencies, none at all. Wherefore, if we must hereafter protect ourselves, why not do it for ourselves?

The English list of ships of war, is long and formidable, but not a tenth part of them are at any one time fit for service, numbers of them not in being; yet their names are pompously continued in the list, f only a plank be left of the ship: and not a fifth part of such as are fit for service, can be spared on any one station at one time. The East and West Indies, Mediterranean, Africa, and other parts over which Britain extends her claim, make large demands upon her navy. From a mixture of prejudice and inattention, we have contracted a false notion respecting the navy of England, and have talked as if we should have the whole of it to encounter at once, and for that reason, supposed, that we must have one as large; which not being instantly practicable, have been made use of by a set of disguised Tories to discourage our beginning thereon. Nothing can be farther from truth than this; for if America had only a twentieth part of the naval force of Britain, she would be by far an overmatch for her; because, as we neither have, nor claim any foreign dominion, our whole force would be employed on our own coast, where we should, in the long run, have two to one the advantage of those who had three or four thousand miles to sail over, before they could attack us, and the same distance to return in order to refit and recruit. And although Britain, by her fleet, hath a check over our trade to Europe, we have as large a one over her trade to the West Indies, which, by laying in the neighbourhood of the continent, is entirely at its mercy.

Some method might be fallen on to keep up a naval force in time of peace, if we should not judge it necessary to support a constant navy. If premiums were to be given to merchants, to build and employ in their service ships mounted with twenty, thirty, forty or fifty guns, (the premiums to be in proportion to the loss of bulk to the merchants) fifty or sixty of those ships, with a few guardships on constant duty, would keep up a sufficient navy, and that without burdening ourselves with the evil so loudly complained of in England, of suffering their fleet, in time of peace to lie rotting in the docks. To unite the sinews of commerce and defense is sound policy; for when our strength and our riches play into each other's hand, we need fear no external enemy.

In almost every article of defense we abound. Hemp flourishes even to rankness, so that we need not want cordage. Our iron is superior to that of other countries. Our small arms equal to any in the world. Cannon we can cast at pleasure. Saltpetre and gunpowder we are every day producing. Our knowledge is hourly improving. Resolution is our inherent character, and courage hath never yet forsaken us. Wherefore, what is it that we want? Why is it that we hesitate? From Britain we can expect nothing but ruin. If she is once admitted to the government of America again, this Continent will not be worth living in. Jealousies will be always arising; insurrections will be constantly happening; and who will go forth to quell them? Who will venture his life to reduce his own countrymen to a foreign obedience? The difference between Pennsylvania and Connecticut, respecting some unlocated lands, shews the insignificance of a British government, and fully proves, that nothing but Continental authority can regulate Continental matters.

Another reason why the present time is preferable to all others, is, that the fewer our numbers are, the more land there is yet unoccupied, which instead of being lavished by the king on his worthless dependants, may be hereafter applied, not only to the discharge of the present debt, but to the constant support of government. No nation under heaven hath such an advantage at this.

The infant state of the Colonies, as it is called, so far from being against, is an argument in favour of independance. We are sufficiently numerous, and were we more so, we might be less united. It is a matter worthy of observation, that the mare a country is peopled, the smaller their armies are. In military numbers, the ancients far exceeded the modems: and the reason is evident. for trade being the consequence of population, men become too much absorbed thereby to attend to anything else. Commerce diminishes the spirit, both of patriotism and military defence. And history sufficiently informs us, that the bravest achievements were always accomplished in the non-age of a nation. With the increase of commerce, England hath lost its spirit. The city of London, notwithstanding its numbers, submits to continued insults with the patience of a coward. The more men have to lose, the less willing are they to venture. The rich are in general slaves to fear, and submit to courtly power with the trembling duplicity of a Spaniel.

Youth is the seed time of good habits, as well in nations as in individuals. It might be difficult, if not impossible, to form the Continent into one government half a century hence. The vast variety of interests, occasioned by an increase of trade and population, would create confusion. Colony would be against colony. Each being able might scorn each other's assistance: and while the proud and foolish gloried in their little distinctions, the wise would lament, that the union had not been formed before. Wherefore, the PRESENT TIME is the TRUE TIME for establishing it. The intimacy which is contracted in infancy, and the friendship which is formed in misfortune, are, of all others, the most lasting and unalterable. Our present union is marked with both these characters: we are young and we have been distressed; but our concord hath withstood our troubles, and fixes a memorable are for posterity to glory in.

The present time, likewise, is that peculiar time, which never happens to a nation but once, viz. the time of forming itself into a government. Most nations have let slip the opportunity, and by that means have been compelled to receive laws from their conquerors, instead of making laws for themselves. First, they had a king, and then a form of government; whereas, the articles or charter of government, should be formed first, and men delegated to execute them afterward but from the errors of other nations, let us learn wisdom, and lay hold of the present opportunity —TO BEGIN GOVERNMENT AT THE RIGHT END.

When William the Conqueror subdued England, he gave them law at the point of the sword; and until we consent, that the seat of government, in America, be legally and authoritatively occupied, we shall be in danger of having it filled by some fortunate ruffian, who may treat us in the same manner, and then, where will be our freedom? where our property? As to religion, I hold it to be the indispensable duty of all government, to protect all conscientious professors thereof, and I know of no other business which government hath to do therewith, Let a man throw aside that narrowness of soul, that selfishness of principle, which the niggards of all professions are willing to part with, and he will be at delivered of his fears on that head. Suspicion is the companion of mean souls, and the bane of all good society. For myself, I fully and conscientiously believe, that it is the will of the Almighty, that there should be diversity of religious opinions among us: It affords a larger field for our Christian kindness. Were we all of one way of thinking, our religious dispositions would want matter for probation; and on this liberal principle, I look on the various denominations among us, to be like children of the same family, differing only, in what is called, their Christian names.

In page forty, I threw out a few thoughts on the propriety of a Continental Charter, (for I only presume to offer hints, not plans) and in this place, I take the liberty of rementioning the subject, by observing, that a charter is to be understood as a bond of solemn obligation, which the whole enters into, to support the right of every separate part, whether of religion, personal freedom, or property. A firm bargain and a right reckoning make long friends.

In a former page I likewise mentioned the necessity of a large and equal representation; and there is no political matter which more deserves our attention. A small number of electors, or a small number of representatives, are equally dangerous. But if the number of the representatives be not only small, but unequal, the danger is increased. As an instance of this, I mention the following; when the Associators petition was before the House of Assembly of Pennsylvania; twenty-eight members only were present, all the Bucks county members, being eight, voted against it, and had seven of the Chester members done the same, this whole province had been governed by two counties only, and this danger it is always exposed to. The unwarrantable stretch likewise, which that house made in their last sitting, to gain an undue authority over the delegates of that province, ought to warn the people at large, how they trust power out of their own hands. A set of instructions for the Delegates were put together, which in point of sense and business would have dishonoured a schoolboy, and after being approved by a FEW, a VERY FEW without doors, were carried into the House, and there passed IN BEHALF OF THE WHOLE COLONY; whereas, did the whole colony know, with what ill-will that House hath entered on some necessary public measures, they would not hesitate a moment to think them unworthy of such a trust.

Immediate necessity makes many things convenient, which if continued would grow into oppressions. Expedience and right are different things. When the calamities of America required a consultation, there was no method so ready, or at that time so proper, as to appoint persons from the several Houses of Assembly for that purpose; and the wisdom with which they have proceeded hath preserved this continent from ruin. But as it is more than probable that we shall never be without a CONGRESS, every well wisher to good order, must own, that the mode for choosing members of that body, deserves consideration. And I put it as a question to those, who make a study of mankind, whether representation and election is not too great a power for one and the same body of men to possess? When we are planning for posterity, we ought to remember, that virtue is not hereditary.

It is from our enemies that we often gain excellent maxims, and are frequently surprised into reason by their mistakes, Mr. Cornwall (one of the Lords of the Treasury) treated the petition of the New-York Assembly with contempt, because THAT House, he said, consisted but of twenty-six members, which trifling number, he argued, could not with decency be put for the whole. We thank him for his involuntary honesty. [Those who would fully understand of what great consequence a large and equal representation is to a state, should read Burgh's political disquisitions.]

TO CONCLUDE, however strange it may appear to some, or however unwilling they may be to think so, matters not, but many strong and striking reasons may be given, to shew, that nothing can settle our affairs so expeditiously as an open and determined declaration for independance. Some of which are,

FIRST. — It is the custom of nations, when any two are at war, for some other powers, not engaged in the quarrel, to step in as mediators, and bring about the preliminaries of a peace: hut while America calls herself the Subject of Great Britain, no power, however well disposed she may be, can offer her mediation. Wherefore, in our present state we may quarrel on for ever.

SECONDLY. — It is unreasonable to suppose, that France or Spain will give us any kind of assistance, if we mean only, to make use of that assistance for the purpose of repairing the breach, and strengthening the connection between Britain and America; because, those powers would be sufferers by the consequences.

THIRDLY. — While we profess ourselves the subjects of Britain, we must, in the eye of foreign nations. be considered as rebels. The precedent is somewhat dangerous to THEIR PEACE, for men to be in arms under the name of subjects; we, on the spot, can solve the paradox: but to unite resistance and subjection, requires an idea much too refined for common understanding.

FOURTHLY. — Were a manifesto to be published, and despatched to foreign courts, setting forth the miseries we have endured, and the peaceable methods we have ineffectually used for redress; declaring, at the same time, that not being able, any longer, to live happily or safely under the cruel disposition of the British court, we had been driven to the necessity of breaking off all connections with her; at the same time, assuring all such courts of our peaceable disposition towards them, and of our desire of entering into trade with them: Such a memorial would produce more good effects to this Continent, than if a ship were freighted with petitions to Britain.

Under our present denomination of British subjects, we can neither be received nor heard abroad: The custom of all courts is against us, and will be so, until, by an independance, we take rank with other nations.

These proceedings may at first appear strange and difficult; but, like all other steps which we have already passed over, will in a little time become familiar and agreeable; and, until an independance is declared, the Continent will feel itself like a man who continues putting off some unpleasant business from day to day, yet knows it must be done, hates to set about it, wishes it over, and is continually haunted with the thoughts of its necessity.

o   o   o   o

Note: This is the end of the body text of Common Sense. Thomas Paine added the Appendix that follows to his February 1776 second edition. I do love the power and purity of that last paragraph. AJW

o   o   o   o

APPENDIX

Since the publication of the first edition of this pamphlet, or rather, on the same day on which it came out, the King's Speech made its appearance in this city. Had the spirit of prophecy directed the birth of this production, it could not have brought it forth, at a more seasonable juncture, or a more necessary time. The bloody mindedness of the one, shew the necessity of pursuing the doctrine of the other. Men read by way of revenge. And the Speech, instead of terrifying, prepared a way for the manly principles of Independance.

Ceremony, and even, silence, from whatever motive they may arise, have a hurtful tendency, when they give the least degree of countenance to base and wicked performances; wherefore, if this maxim be admitted, it naturally follows, that the King's Speech, as being a piece of finished villany, deserved, and still deserves, a general execration both by the Congress and the people. Yet, as the domestic tranquillity of a nation, depends greatly, on the CHASTITY of what may properly be called NATIONAL MANNERS, it is often better, to pass some things over in silent disdain, than to make use of such new methods of dislike, as might introduce the least innovation, on that guardian of our peace and safety. And, perhaps, it is chiefly owing to this prudent delicacy, that the King's Speech, hath not, before now, suffered a public execution. The Speech if it may be called one, is nothing better than a wilful audacious libel against the truth, the common good, and the existence of mankind; and is a formal and pompous method of offering up human sacrifices to the pride of tyrants. But this general massacre of mankind. is one of the privileges, and the certain consequence of Kings; for as nature knows them NOT, they know NOT HER, and although they are beings of our OWN creating, they know not US, and are become the gods of their creators. The Speech hath one good quality, which is, that it is not calculated to deceive, neither can we, even if we would, be deceived by it. Brutality and tyranny appear on the face of it. It leaves us at no loss: And every line convinces, even in the moment of reading, that He, who hunts the woods for prey, the naked and untutored Indian, is less a Savage than the King of Britain.

Sir John Dalrymple, the putative father of a whining jesuitical piece, fallaciously called, "THE ADDRESS OF THE PEOPLE OF _ENGLAND_ TO THE INHABITANTS OF _AMERICA_," hath, perhaps, from a vain supposition, that the people here were to be frightened at the pomp and description of a king, given, (though very unwisely on his part) the real character of the present one: "But" says this writer, "if you are inclined to pay compliments to an administration, which we do not complain of," (meaning the Marquis of Rockingham's at the repeal of the Stamp Act) "it is very unfair in you to withhold them from that prince by WHOSE _NOD ALONE_ THEY WERE PERMITTED TO DO ANY THING." This is toryism with a witness! Here is idolatry even without a mask: And he who can calmly hear, and digest such doctrine, hath forfeited his claim to rationality an apostate from the order of manhood; and ought to be considered as one, who hath not only given up the proper dignity of man, but sunk himself beneath the rank of animals, and contemptibly crawl through the world like a worm.

However, it matters very little now, what the king of England either says or does; he hath wickedly broken through every moral and human obligation, trampled nature and conscience beneath his feet; and by a steady and con-stitutional spirit of insolence and cruelty, procured for himself an universal hatred. It is NOW the interest of America to provide for herself. She hath already a large and young family, whom it is more her duty to take care of, than to be granting away her property, to support a power who is become a reproach to the names of men and christians—YE, whose office it is to watch over the morals of a nation, of whatsoever sect or denomination ye are of, as well as ye, who, are more immediately the guardians of the public liberty, if ye wish to preserve your native country uncontaminated by Eu-ropean corruption, ye must in secret wish a separation—But leaving the moral part to private reflection, I shall chiefly confine my farther remarks to the following heads.

First. That it is the interest of America to be separated from Britain.

Secondly. Which is the easiest and most practicable plan, RECONCILIA-TION OR INDEPENDANCE? With some occasional remarks.

In support of the first, I could, if I judged it proper, produce the opinion of some of the ablest and most experienced men on this continent; and whose sentiments, on that head, are not yet publicly known. It is in reality a self-evident position: For no nation in a state of foreign dependance, limited in its commerce, and cramped and fettered in its legislative powers, can ever arrive at any material eminence. America doth not yet know what opulence is; and although the progress which she hath made stands unparalleled in the history of other nations, it is but childhood, compared with what she would be capable of arriving at, had she, as she ought to have, the legisla-tive powers in her own hands. England is, at this time, proudly coveting what would do her no good, were she to accomplish it; and the Continent hesitating on a matter, which will be her final ruin if neglected. It is the commerce and not the conquest of America, by which England is to he benefited, and that would in a great measure continue, were the countries as independant of each other as France and Spain; because in many articles, neither can go to a better market. But it is the independance of this country on Britain or any other, which is now the main and only object worthy of contention, and which, like all other truths discovered by necessity, will appear clearer and stronger every day.

First. Because it will come to that one time or other.

Secondly. Because, the longer it is delayed the harder it will be to accomplish.

I have frequently amused myself both in public and private companies, with silently remarking, the specious errors of those who speak without reflecting. And among the many which I have heard, the following seems the most general, viz. that had this rupture happened forty or fifty years hence, instead of NOW, the Continent would have been more able to have shaken off the dependance. To which I reply, that our military ability, AT THIS TIME, arises from the experience gained in the last war, and which in forty or fifty years time, would have been totally extinct. The Continent, would not, by that time, have had a General, or even a military officer left; and we, or those who may succeed us, would have been as ignorant of martial matters as the ancient Indians: And this single position, closely attended to, will unanswerably prove, that the present time is preferable to all others. The argument turns thus—at the conclusion of the last war, we had experience, but wanted numbers; and forty or fifty years hence, we should have numbers, without experience; wherefore, the proper point of time, must be some particular point between the two extremes, in which a sufficiency of the former remains, and a proper increase of the latter is obtained: And that point of time is the present time.

The reader will pardon this digression, as it does not properly come under the head I first set out with, and to which I again return by the following position, viz.

Should affairs he patched up with Britain, and she to remain the governing and sovereign power of America, (which, as matters are now circumstanced, is giving up the point entirely) we shall deprive ourselves of the very means of sinking the debt we have, or may contract. The value of the back lands which some of the provinces are clandestinely deprived of, by the unjust extension of the limits of Canada, valued only at five pounds sterling per hundred acres, amount to upwards of twenty-five millions, Pennsylvania currency; and the quit-rents at one penny sterling per acre, to two millions yearly.

It is by the sale of those lands that the debt may be sunk, without burthen to any, and the quit-rent reserved thereon, will always lessen, and in time, will wholly support the yearly expence of government. It matters not how long the debt is in paying, so that the lands when sold be applied to the discharge of it, and for the execution of which, the Congress for the time being, will be the continental trustees. .

I proceed now to the second head, viz. Which is the easiest and most practicable plan, RECONCILIATION or INDEPENDANCE; With some occasional remarks.

He who takes nature for his guide is not easily beaten out of his argument, and on that ground, I answer GENERALLY—THAT _INDEPENDANCE_ BEING A _SINGLE SIMPLE LINE,_ CONTAINED WITHIN OURSELVES; AND RECONCILIATION, A MATTER EXCEEDINGLY PERPLEXED AND COMPLICATED, AND IN WHICH, A TREACHEROUS CAPRICIOUS COURT IS TO INTERFERE, GIVES THE ANSWER WITHOUT A DOUBT.

The present state of America is truly alarming to every man who is capable of reflexion. Without law, without government, without any other mode of power than what is founded on, and granted by courtesy. Held together by an unexampled concurrence of sentiment, which, is nevertheless subject to change, and which, every secret enemy is endeavouring to dissolve. Our present condition, is, Legislation without law; wisdom without a plan; a constitution without a name; and, what is strangely astonishing, perfect Independance contending for dependance. The instance is without a precedent; the case never existed before; and who can tell what may be the event? The property of no man is secure in the present unbraced system of things. The mind of the multitude is left at random, and seeing no fixed object before them, they pursue such as fancy or opinion starts. Nothing is criminal; there is no such thing as treason; wherefore, every one thinks himself at liberty to act as he pleases. The Tories dared not have assembled offensively, had they known that their lives, by that act, were forfeited to the laws of the state. A line of distinction should be drawn, between, English soldiers taken in battle, and inhabitants of America taken in arms. The first are prisoners, but the latter traitors. The one forfeits his liberty, the other his head.

Notwithstanding our wisdom, there is a visible feebleness in some of our proceedings which gives encouragement to dissensions. The Continental Belt is too loosely buckled. And if something is not done in time, it will be too late to do any thing, and we shall fall into a state, in which, neither RECONCILIATION nor INDEPENDANCE will be practicable. The king and his worthless adherents are got at their old game of dividing the Continent, and there are not wanting among us, Printers, who will be busy in spreading specious falsehoods. The artful and hypocritical letter which appeared a few months ago in two of the New York papers, and likewise in two others, is an evidence that there are men who want either judgment or honesty.

It is easy getting into holes and corners and talking of reconciliation: But do such men seriously consider, how difficult the task is, and how dangerous it may prove, should the Continent divide thereon. Do they take within their view, all the various orders of men whose situation and circumstances, as well as their own, are to be considered therein. Do they put themselves in the place of the sufferer whose ALL is ALREADY gone, and of the soldier, who hath quitted ALL for the defence of his country. If their ill judged moderation be suited to their own private situations only, regardless of others, the event will convince them, that "they are reckoning without their Host."

Put us, says some, on the footing we were on in sixty-three: To which I answer, the request is not now in the power of Britain to comply with, neither will she propose it; but if it were, and even should be granted, I ask, as a reasonable question, By what means is such a corrupt and faithless court to be kept to its engagements? Another parliament, nay, even the present, may hereafter repeal the obligation, on the pretense, of its being violently obtained, or unwisely granted; and in that case, Where is our redress?—No going to law with nations; cannon are the barristers of Crowns; and the sword, not of justice, but of war, decides the suit. To be on the footing of sixty-three, it is not sufficient, that the laws only be put on the same state, but, that our circumstances, likewise, be put on the same state; Our burnt and destroyed towns repaired or built up, our private losses made good, our public debts (contracted for defence) discharged; otherwise, we shall be millions worse than we were at that enviable period. Such a request, had it been complied with a year ago, would have won the heart and soul of the Continent - but now it is too late, "The Rubicon is passed."

Besides, the taking up arms, merely to enforce the repeal of a pecuniary law, seems as unwarrantable by the divine law, and as repugnant to human feelings, as the taking up arms to enforce obedience thereto. The object, on either side, doth not justify the means; for the lives of men are too valuable to be cast away on such trifles. It is the violence which is done and threatened to our persons; the destruction of our property by an armed force; the invasion of our country by fire and sword, which conscientiously qualifies the use of arms: And the instant, in which such a mode of defence became necessary, all subjection to Britain ought to have ceased; and the independancy of America, should have been considered, as dating its aera from, and published by, THE FIRST MUSKET THAT WAS FIRED AGAINST HER. This line is a line of consistency; neither drawn by caprice, nor extended by ambition; but produced by a chain of events, of which the colonies were not the authors.

I shall conclude these remarks with the following timely and well intended hints. We ought to reflect, that there are three different ways by which an independancy may hereafter be effected; and that ONE of those THREE, will one day or other, be the fate of America, viz. By the legal voice of the people in Congress; by a military power; or by a mob—It may not always happen that OUR soldiers are citizens, and the multitude a body of reasonable men; virtue, as I have already remarked, is not hereditary, neither is it perpetual. Should an independancy be brought about by the first of those means, we have every opportunity and every encouragement before us, to form the noblest purest constitution on the face of the earth. We have it in our power to begin the world over again. A situation, similar to the present, hath not happened since the days of Noah until now. The birthday of a new world is at hand, and a race of men, perhaps as numerous as all Europe contains, are to receive their portion of freedom from the event of a few months. The Reflexion is awful—and in this point of view, How trifling, how ridiculous, do the little, paltry cavillings, of a few weak or interested men appear, when weighed against the business of a world.

Should we neglect the present favourable and inviting period, and an Independance be hereafter effected by any other means, we must charge the consequence to ourselves, or to those rather, whose narrow and prejudiced souls, are habitually opposing the measure, without either inquiring or reflecting. There are reasons to be given in support of Independance, which men should rather privately think of, than be publicly told of. We ought not now to be debating whether we shall be independant or not, but, anxious to accomplish it on a firm, secure, and honorable basis, and uneasy rather that it is not yet began upon. Every day convinces us of its necessity. Even the Tories (if such beings yet remain among us) should, of all men, be the most solicitous to promote it; for, as the appointment of committees at first, protected them from popular rage, so, a wise and well established form of government, will be the only certain means of continuing it securely to them. WHEREFORE, if they have not virtue enough to be WHIGS, they ought to have prudence enough to wish for Independance.

In short, Independance is the only BOND that can tye and keep us together. We shall then see our object, and our ears will be legally shut against the schemes of an intriguing, as well, as a cruel enemy. We shall then too, be on a proper footing, to treat with Britain; for there is reason to conclude, that the pride of that court, will be less hurt by treating with the American states for terms of peace, than with those, whom she denominates, "rebellious subjects," for terms of accommodation. It is our delaying it that encourages her to hope for conquest, and our backwardness tends only to prolong the war. As we have, without any good effect therefrom, withheld our trade to obtain a redress of our grievances, let us now try the alternative, by independantly redressing them ourselves, and then offering to open the trade. The mercantile and reasonable part in England, will be still with us; because, peace with trade, is preferable to war without it. And if this offer be not accepted, other courts may be applied to.

On these grounds I rest the matter. And as no offer hath yet been made to refute the doctrine contained in the former editions of this pamphlet, it is a negative proof, that either the doctrine cannot be refuted, or, that the party in favour of it are too numerous to be opposed. WHEREFORE, instead of gazing at each other with suspicious or doubtful curiosity; let each of us, hold out to his neighbour the hearty hand of friendship, and unite in drawing a line, which, like an act of oblivion shall bury in forgetfulness every former dissension. Let the names of Whig and Tory be extinct; and let none other be heard among us, than those of A GOOD CITIZEN, AN OPEN AND RESOLUTE FRIEND, AND A VIRTUOUS SUPPORTER OF THE RIGHTS OF MANKIND AND OF THE _FREE AND INDEPENDANT STATES OF AMERICA_.

To the Representatives of the Religious Society of the People called Quakers, or to so many of them as were concerned in publishing the late piece, entitled "THE ANCIENT TESTIMONY and PRINCIPLES of the People called QUAKERS renewed, with Respect to the KING and GOVERNMENT, and touching the COMMOTIONS now prevailing in these and other parts of AMERICA addressed to the PEOPLE IN GENERAL."

The Writer of this, is one of those few, who never dishonours religion either by ridiculing, or cavilling at any denomination whatsoever. To God, and not to man, are all men accountable on the score of religion. Wherefore, this epistle is not so properly addressed to you as a religious, but as a political body, dabbling in matters, which the professed Quietude of your Principles instruct you not to meddle with. As you have, without a proper authority for so doing, put yourselves in the place of the whole body of the Quakers, so, the writer of this, in order to be on an equal rank with yourselves, is under the necessity, of putting himself in the place of all those, who, approve the very writings and principles, against which, your testimony is directed: And he hath chosen this singular situation, in order, that you might discover in him that presumption of character which you cannot see in yourselves. For neither he nor you can have any claim or title to POLITICAL REPRESENTATION.

When men have departed from the right way, it is no wonder that they stumble and fall. And it is evident from the manner in which ye have managed your testimony, that politics, (as a religious body of men) is not your proper Walk; for however well adapted it might appear to you, it is, nevertheless, a jumble of good and bad put unwisely together, and the conclusion drawn therefrom, both unnatural and unjust.

The two first pages, (and the whole doth not make four) we give you credit for, and expect the same civility from you, because the love and desire of peace is not confined to Quakerism, it is the natural, as well the religious wish of all denominations of men. And on this ground, as men labouring to establish an Independant Constitution of our own, do we exceed all others in our hope, end, and aim. OUR PLAN IS PEACE FOR EVER. We are tired of contention with Britain, and can see no real end to it but in a final separation. We act consistently, because for the sake of introducing an endless and uninterrupted peace, do we bear the evils and burthens of the present day. We are endeavoring, and will steadily continue to endeavour, to separate and dissolve a connexion which hath already filled our land with blood; and which, while the name of it remains, will he the fatal cause of future mischiefs to both countries.

We fight neither for revenge nor conquest; neither from pride nor passion; we are not insulting the world with our fleets and armies, nor ravaging the globe for plunder. Beneath the shade of our own vines are we attacked; in our own houses, and on our own lands, is the violence committed against us. We view our enemies in the character of Highwaymen and Housebreakers, and having no defence for ourselves in the civil law, are obliged to punish them by the military one, and apply the sword, in the very case, where you have before now, applied the halter— Perhaps we feel for the ruined and insulted sufferers in all and every part of the continent, with a degree of tenderness which hath not yet made its way into some of your bosoms. But be ye sure that ye mistake not the cause and ground of your Testimony. Call not coldness of soul, religion; nor put the BIGOT in the place of the CHRISTIAN.

O ye partial ministers of your own acknowledged principles. If the bearing arms be sinful, the first going to war must be more so, by all the difference between wilful attack, and unavoidable defence. Wherefore, if ye really preach from conscience, and mean not to make a political hobbyhorse of your religion convince the world thereof, by proclaiming your doctrine to our enemies, FOR THEY LIKEWISE BEAR _ARMS_. Give us proof of your sincerity by publishing it at St. James's, to the commanders in chief at Boston, to the Admirals and Captains who are piratically ravaging our coasts, and to all the murdering miscreants who are acting in authority under HIM whom ye profess to serve. Had ye the honest soul of BARCLAY ye would preach repentance to YOUR king; Ye would tell the Royal Wretch his sins, and warn him of eternal ruin. ["Thou hast tasted of prosperity and adversity; thou knowest what it is to be banished thy native country, to be over-ruled as well as to rule, and set upon the throne; and being oppressed thou hast reason to know how hateful the oppressor is both to God and man: If after all these warnings and advertisements, thou dost not turn unto the Lord with all thy heart, but forget him who remembered thee in thy distress, and give up thyself to fallow lust and vanity, surely great will be thy condemnation.— Against which snare, as well as the temptation of those who may or do feed thee, and prompt thee to evil, the most excellent and prevalent remedy will be, to apply thyself to that light of Christ which shineth in thy conscience, and which neither can, nor will flatter thee, nor suffer thee to be at ease in thy sins."—Barclay's address to Charles II.] Ye would not spend your partial invectives against the injured and the insulted only, but, like faithful ministers, would cry aloud and SPARE NONE. Say not that ye are persecuted, neither endeavour to make us the authors of that reproach, which, ye are bringing upon yourselves; for we testify unto all men, that we do not complain against you because ye are Quakers, but because ye pretend to be and are NOT Quakers.

Alas! it seems by the particular tendency of some part of your testimony, and other parts of your conduct, as if, all sin was reduced to, and comprehended in, THE ACT OF BEARING ARMS, and that by the people only. Ye appear to us, to have mistaken party for conscience; because, the general tenor of your actions wants uniformity—And it is exceedingly difficult to us to give credit to many of your pretended scruples; because, we see them made by the same men, who, in the very instant that they are exclaiming against the mammon of this world, are nevertheless, hunting after it with a step as steady as Time, and an appetite as keen as Death.

The quotation which ye have made from Proverbs, in the third page of your testimony, that, "when a man's ways please the Lord, he maketh even his enemies to be at peace with him"; is very unwisely chosen on your part; because, it amounts to a proof, that the king's ways (whom ye are desirous of supporting) do NOT please the Lord, otherwise, his reign would be in peace.

I now proceed to the latter part of your testimony, and that, for which all the foregoing seems only an introduction viz.

"It hath ever been our judgment and principle, since we were called to profess the light of Christ Jesus, manifested in our consciences unto this day, that the setting up and putting down kings and governments, is God's peculiar prerogative; for causes best known to himself: And that it is not our business to have any hand or contrivance therein; nor to be busy bodies above our station, much less to plot and contrive the ruin, or overturn of any of them, but to pray for the king, and safety of our nation. and good of all men - That we may live a peaceable and quiet life, in all godliness and honesty; UNDER THE GOVERNMENT WHICH GOD IS PLEASED TO SET OVER US" - If these are REALLY your principles why do ye not abide by them? Why do ye not leave that, which ye call God's Work, to be managed by himself? These very principles instruct you to wait with patience and humility, for the event of all public measures, and to receive that event as the divine will towards you. Wherefore, what occasion is there for your POLITICAL TESTIMONY if you fully believe what it contains? And the very publishing it proves, that either, ye do not believe what ye profess, or have not virtue enough to practise what ye believe.

The principles of Quakerism have a direct tendency to make a man the quiet and inoffensive subject of any, and every government WHICH IS SET OVER HIM. And if the setting up and putting down of kings and governments is God's peculiar prerogative, he most certainly will not be robbed thereof by us: wherefore, the principle itself leads you to approve of every thing, which ever happened, or may happen to kings as being his work. OLIVER CROMWELL thanks you. CHARLES, then, died not by the hands of man; and should the present Proud Imitator of him, come to the same untimely end, the writers and publishers of the Testimony, are bound, by the doctrine it contains, to applaud the fact. Kings are not taken away by miracles, neither are changes in governments brought about by any other means than such as are common and human; and such as we are now using. Even the dispersion of the Jews, though foretold by our Saviour, was effected by arms. Wherefore, as ye refuse to be the means on one side, ye ought not to be meddlers on the other; but to wait the issue in silence; and unless ye can produce divine authority, to prove, that the Almighty who hath created and placed this new world, at the greatest distance it could possibly stand, east and west, from every part of the old, doth, nevertheless, disapprove of its being independent of the corrupt and abandoned court of Britain, unless I say, ye can shew this, how can ye on the ground of your principles, justify the exciting and stirring up the people "firmly to unite in the abhorrence of all such writings, and measures, as evidence a desire and design to break off the happy connexion we have hitherto enjoyed, with the kingdom of Great-Britain, and our just and necessary subordination to the king, and those who are lawfully placed in authority under him." What a slap of the face is here! the men, who in the very paragraph before, have quietly and passively resigned up the ordering, altering, and disposal of kings and governments, into the hands of God, are now, recalling their principles, and putting in for a share of the business. Is it possible, that the conclusion, which is here justly quoted, can any ways follow from the doctrine laid down? The inconsistency is too glaring not to be seen; the absurdity too great not to be laughed at; and such as could only have been made by those, whose understandings were darkened by the narrow and crabby spirit of a despairing political party; for ye are not to be considered as the whole body of the Quakers but only as a factional and fractional part thereof.

Here ends the examination of your testimony; (which I call upon no man to abhor, as ye have done, but only to read and judge of fairly;) to which I subjoin the following remark; "That the setting up and putting down of kings," most certainly mean, the making him a king, who is yet not so, and the making him no king who is already one. And pray what hath this to do in the present case? We neither mean to set up nor to pull down, neither to make nor to unmake, but to have nothing to do with them. Wherefore, your testimony in whatever light it is viewed serves only to dishonor your judgement, and for many other reasons had better have been let alone than published.

First, Because it tends to the decrease and reproach of all religion whatever, and is of the utmost danger to society to make it a party in political disputes.

Secondly, Because it exhibits a body of men, numbers of whom disavow the publishing political testimonies, as being concerned therein and approvers thereof.

Thirdly, because it hath a tendency to undo that continental harmony and friendship which yourselves by your late liberal and charitable donations hath lent a hand to establish; and the preservation of which, is of the utmost consequence to us all.

And here without anger or resentment I bid you farewell. Sincerely wishing, that as men and christians, ye may always fully and uninterruptedly enjoy every civil and religious right; and be, in your turn, the means of securing it to others; but that the example which ye have unwisely set, of mingling religion with politics, MAY BE DISAVOWED AND REPROBATED BY EVERY INHABITANT OF _AMERICA._

F I N I S.

VOTE as if Our Nation's Destiny Depends on It.

o o o o

Because, it Really Does!